# CREATION

# PETER CONRAD

# CREATION
## Artists, Gods & Origins

With 161 illustrations

Thames & Hudson

## ACKNOWLEDGMENTS

This is the fourth book of mine to be commissioned by Jamie Camplin, and I find myself running out of ways to express my gratitude to him. He has once again set me free to speculate, although his clarity of mind helped me to establish boundaries and to keep my aim in focus. Every writer should have a publisher like Jamie; unfortunately, he remains a nonpareil.

My thanks as well to Helen Farr, who calmed me down during a flustered afternoon spent transferring electronic files, and to Mary-Jane Gibson, who so resourcefully and imaginatively rounded up the illustrations. Gaps remain in the representation of twentieth-century artists: like all at Thames & Hudson, I regret that DACS, the Collecting Society for Artists, has recently imposed prohibitive fees for the use of reproductions in books that seek to inform and educate.

It has been my pleasure and privilege to have Christopher Dell as my scrupulous, generous and tireless editor. He has ideas of his own about the subject of the book, and a private store of knowledge concerning many of the topics it covers. I was happy to learn from him, and beamed with delight whenever he expressed approval in the margins of the manuscript. He also lengthened my life by preparing the index.

p. 2 William Blake, *Jacob's Ladder*, 1800

First published in 2007 in hardcover in the United States of America by Thames & Hudson Inc., 500 Fifth Avenue, New York, New York 10110

thamesandhudsonusa.com

Library of Congress Catalog Card Number 2007921447

ISBN 978-0-500-51356-9

Typesetting and design by Liz Rudderham

Printed and bound in China by C&C Offset Printing Co. Ltd.

# CONTENTS

# 0
# SOMETHING FROM NOTHING

Long before I became interested in the aesthetics, theology and science of creation, I was intrigued by the word. In my Australian childhood, its uses were mainly pejorative. I remember my parents saying 'Stop your creating!', sometimes with expletives added. What I was creating was not a poem or a painting or a piece of music but a fuss – protesting too loudly about some prohibition, crying about some trivial disaster like a smashed toy or a skinned knee. To create, I deduced, meant to make something out of nothing – that is, to behave unnecessarily or to misbehave. The creation itself, consisting of wind and water, had no objective existence, no reason to exist at all. In our level-headed and literal-minded world, it was unnecessary, just like art.

I thought about the word again almost two decades later, during a second and somewhat happier childhood in the house of a family in Lisbon. As I began to decipher the language by listening to the domestic chatter, I found that, in Portuguese, creation meant something very different. One of the maids, pining for her village, kept chickens in a ramshackle coop at the bottom of the garden. After a while she added ducks, and began to breed rabbits in a separate hutch. She called the creatures in this menagerie her 'criacão', and later I heard her apply the same word to me. She was vague about chronology and geography, so she told one of her colleagues next door that I had been 'criado in casa' – brought up here, not in my own unimaginably remote home. To create evidently meant to cultivate, to tend with love. A shadow fell over this when I remembered that the Portuguese word for maid was 'criada'. In the almost feudal vocabulary of those days before the 1974 revolution, this implied that God had created certain people for the exclusive purpose of doing household chores.

I pieced the uses together, and came up with a set of enigmas. For my parents, creation was aesthetic, though in the worst sense. In this new language, creation was biological. The animals were created in the garden, which meant that they were being grown; I too supposedly had enjoyed the same treatment, having been raised inside the house. Or was this kind of creation better described as social engineering? The tantrums my parents called creations always blew over, which meant that they were self-destructive. Animal husbandry in that Lisbon garden had a different but equally inevitable end: all these creatures – whose number was seasonally swelled by turkeys, and once by a lamb – existed to be killed and eaten. There was an art to the killing. Chickens had their necks wrung, rabbits received a chop from the side of the hand. The occasional turkey had brandy poured into its beak before its throat was cut. Was it possible to think of creation without imagining its opposite, destruction? Though I didn't know it then, the plan of this book was already staked out.

A study of creation has to begin at the beginning – of life, of the world. It must also ask where our ideas come from. The puzzle of origins, for me, is at its most perplexing and enticing when I think about the inception of art. Every time a sentence is written or a line sets out on a journey across a canvas or a row of notes is organized into a melody, we see a world being created. Even those who are engaged in the business of creation cannot be sure of what is happening to them or inside them. Which of us, when writing, has not felt that the hand is somehow ahead of the brain, transcribing thoughts that have involuntarily arrived from nowhere? These are moments of happiness, and of mystification. Theologians used to wonder how a void or an absence could bring forth a world, as God purports to do in Genesis. Astrophysicists now brood over exactly the same imagined event. Theologians need a creator, and although astrophysicists do without one, they try at least to identify a moment of creation – a big bang that took place uncountable millions of years ago. Artists possess their own indwelling gods, and have a vague sense that the radiant explosion recently occurred in some recess of their heads. I find it easier to believe in human creators than in their divine prototype; my lack of religious faith is contradicted by a faith in art. The very existence of literature, music and painting forces me, to my own consternation, into the company of the born-again zealots who call themselves creationists. I see nothing but disorder in nature, and suspect that this chaos is itself a creative force. But I expect works of art to possess what Darwin's latter-day opponents in contemporary America call 'intelligent design'. The difference between me and them is that I do not consider God to be an artist. 'What do you suppose creation is?' asked Walt Whitman in one of his *Democratic Chants*. He went on to suggest that 'man or woman is as good as God', and to claim that this is 'what the oldest and newest myths finally mean'.

This book is a celebration of art that doubles as a critique of religion. It starts from the myths of origin that are the ancient foundations of culture, and yet the problems it discusses are alive in the present, where they continue to provoke arguments and even to start wars. My ideas about the subject suddenly acquired a shape and a point one morning in June 2003, when I noticed a small paragraph in *The New York Times* reporting that the sequel to *The Matrix* had been banned in Egypt because its cybernetic theology offended the theories of creation propounded by three religions officially practised in that country and was likely to cause civil unrest. It is my instinct to believe that any idea suppressed by a government is probably true; at the very least, the Egyptian censors confirmed that the idea of a creator is something for which people are prepared to die, or to kill others.

As I wrote, I occasionally felt that I was trying to keep up with the day's headlines, which chronicled disputes about creation being fought with both words and weapons. In April 2005, a few months after I began writing, Pope John Paul II died. He makes one or two walk-on appearances in this book, although I only realized his relevance to it when I heard John Selwyn Gummer, a Conservative politician, defend his hostility to abortion. On his way to a Mass for the dead Pope in Westminster Abbey, Gummer declared that John Paul II had been intent on preserving 'the mystery of sexual creation'. The phrase bewildered me: a celibate priest upheld the sanctity of sex, while requiring believers to accredit a conception that was immaculate. Benedict XVI, in his earlier career as the doctrinal enforcer Joseph Ratzinger, sought to preserve such mysteries from the impiety of science: in 2000 in a text entitled *God and the World* he warned against genetic research, announcing that 'There is a last boundary that we cannot cross without becoming the destroyers of creation itself'. Does creation really need to be protected by such obfuscation? And if human thought can destroy it, is it truly divine?

Inevitably the ban on science colludes with a suspicion about art, which conducts free, fantastical investigations of its own. Shortly before his election as Pope, Ratzinger sent a complimentary letter to a German woman who had denounced J. K. Rowling's books about Harry Potter for corrupting the young by purveying superstition. The critic was right, Ratzinger said, to mistrust the 'subtle seductions' of magic. A priest of the Christ Community Church in New Mexico went further, and threw all available copies of Rowling's books onto a funeral pyre.

My assumption has always been that Genesis is a myth, encouraging our own speculations about origins rather than documenting the creator's activities. In 2004 I made a return visit to the Grand Canyon, which is one of the destinations of this book – a place where you are confronted by the spectacle of creation, with epochal upheavals and erosive calamities frozen in stone. Yet on the river a mile beneath the rim, believers were taking 'Christ-centered motorized rafting trips', singing hymns as they bounced through the rapids while guides told them that God after all was responsible for the Canyon, which opened up precisely five thousand years ago to allow the waters from Noah's flood to drain away. Interpreted this way, it serves as evidence for the doctrine of 'the young earth' – a place still as dewy as born-again America, not the relic of ancestral cataclysms and of slow, remorseless decomposition. The Institute for Christian Research, which sends converts on those rafting trips, quotes Corinthians to rally the faithful, whose business is to defend the literal truth of Genesis by 'casting down imaginations, and every high thing that exalts itself against the knowledge of God'.

In the summer of 2005, President Bush recommended that the hypothesis of a logical, designed creation should be taught in American schools as an antidote to evolution. The matter was contested in a federal court, and a television evangelist warned a community which had voted biblical fundamentalists off its school board that it could expect to suffer the consequences of divine displeasure. But whose displeasure was made manifest by Hurricane Katrina, which swamped New Orleans late in August 2005? I was writing about Mary Shelley's *The Last Man* when this happened, and reflecting on the novel's criticism of our presumption that we lord it over creation and rule the elements. The biblical fables still have truths to tell, although they are metaphorical not literal. While I thought about the beginning, others were more or less impatiently preparing for the end. Early in 2006 I noticed another small paragraph in a newspaper: a man in Holland had built a replica of Noah's ark, with a religious museum and a petting zoo on board. Stephen Hawking suggested at the same time that the human race, having destroyed the habitat God created for it, should probably think of relocating to another planet. Meanwhile a bus company in New Orleans is running what it calls 'America's Worst Catastrophe Tour', with visits to the wards submerged when the levees gave way. We sometimes seem, as I suggest in the last chapter, to be possessed by a mood of apocalyptic elation. My book concludes at Ground Zero in Manhattan, though it does so for a reason that took me by surprise. Before the site where the World Trade Center stood was cleared, the ruins looked like a junkyard of wrecked human history. But a myth of creation also acted itself out there: the scene showed how worlds begin, as well as how they end.

The whole undertaking is an attempt to understand a word, to explore the contradictory ideas it contains, and to trace its splintered history. While writing, I pricked up my ears whenever I heard someone use the word I was thinking about, or any of its relatives; the adjective is much prized in our society, even though we have little notion of what the noun means. Once, attempting to organize a haircut, I was quoted a price that startled me. When I queried it, I was told that I'd be paying for the attentions of the 'creative director'. I went instead to a humble barber, an artisan not an artist. A few weeks later, I paid a visit to a film set to write a journalistic article. The publicist in charge promised me access to everyone, but began to fidget when I asked to meet the elusive director. 'I'm going to have to be creative about that,' he said. 'I'll get back to you.' He never did, but his remark helped to fill out my lexicon: being creative meant being slippery, employing subterfuge. Publicity is the art form of our era, and here was an inside view of its aesthetics. Early in 2006 I read in a London newspaper an announcement from the Financial Services Authority, which was proposing 'creative penalties' for 'miscreant' firms that broke its rules. The creativity lay in thinking up threats – banning the firms from conducting business, for instance, rather than simply fining them. The diction seemed inflated and bogus. Shouldn't creation be a positive act, not a prohibition? Isn't a miscreant someone who is a little more than dishonest? But again the distorted language had a truth to tell about contemporary values. As I was finishing the book, Renault began to advertise its latest model of car. The television spots sang the praises of the new vehicle, then concluded with the company's logo and its boastful vernacular self-description, 'Créateur d'Automobiles'. It's easy to imagine the marketers vetoing anything so drably industrial as 'maker' or 'manufacturer': creativity counts as a selling point, and purchasers are seduced by a fantasy – easier to realize in French – of a life that is elegant, hedonistic, and synonymous with art.

We are happy to think of hair cutters and tax evaders and automobile engineers and publicists as creators. The title is lavished on those with a questionable claim to it; the only ones who have trouble establishing their credentials are the artists, especially if they are dead and male and white. I may not believe in God, but I do believe in artistic genius – in a generative power that sometimes seems inexplicable, and in the self-generated individuality of certain people who look at the world in a unique, idiosyncratic way. This belief is unfashionable, and one reason why I have written this book is to defend it. I remember a while ago being sternly corrected by a student in Oxford when I made a remark about the 'genius' of a poet we were discussing. 'I don't understand what it means to call him that,' she said. 'He was just a person.' I did not delete the word from my vocabulary, as will be evident from the sections in this book on creators like Plato, Ovid, Augustine, Leonardo, Michelangelo, Titian, Bosch, Shakespeare, Milton, Diderot, Haydn, Mozart, Beethoven, Hugo, Balzac, Baudelaire, Turner, Dickens, Darwin, Wagner, Nietzsche, Wilde, Rodin, Picasso, Klee, Schoenberg and many others – men who were sometimes compared to gods by their admirers, and who sometimes took the initiative and compared themselves to God.

Yes, men, or at least human beings. In fact several of them felt that they were honorary androgynes, since creativity is in biological terms the province of women. I sympathize with retroactive efforts to correct this male ascendancy, in both the cultural canon and in the canonical teachings of the church, because the revisionists are questioning and altering our myth of origins. In June 2006, the new Episcopalian Bishop of Nevada, Katharine Schori, turned the New Testament into a story of matriarchal creation: 'Mother Jesus,' she announced, 'gives birth to a new creation – and you and I are His children'. At the same time, a Presbyterian assembly in Alabama voted to alter the gender of the three persons who make up the Trinity, which would henceforth consist of Mother, Child and Womb. And as my own contribution to this settling of accounts, I offer the case of Mary Shelley, the mother of Frankenstein and the godmother of his monster, with whom this book begins....

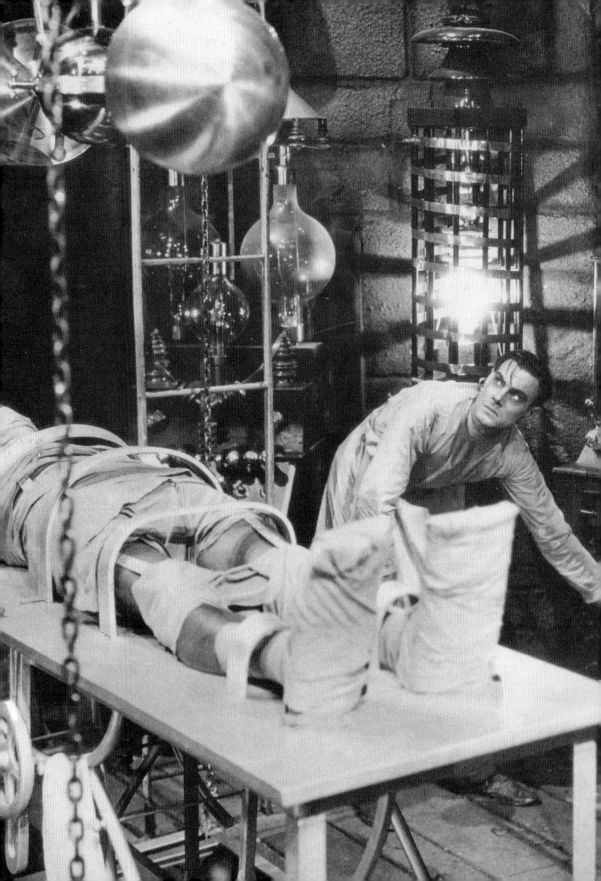

# 1
## MEETINGS WITH THE MAKER

One night during a dank, stormy summer in 1816, Mary Shelley retired to bed in a house near a Swiss lake. She had a job to do while she slept. Byron, whom she and her husband were visiting, had challenged them to think up stories, the scarier the better. Their tales were meant to raid the secrets of the hereafter and to settle accounts with eternity. Feeling miserably inadequate, she lay awake contemplating the 'dull Nothing' inside her head. By morning, to her surprise, she was in possession of a story. She had no idea where it had come from, but it concerned the enigma of origins: its hero was an artist who created his own artwork by reactivating dead flesh scavenged from gibbets and graveyards. When she thought about it, she realized that it was a parody or a desecration of the primary story our culture tells us about creation. Frankenstein, who constructed a monster by stitching together bits of corpses, dared 'to mock the stupendous mechanism of the Creator of the world'. Mary Shelley accused her scientist of blasphemy, but her own feat was equally audacious. Frankenstein makes a man, and in doing so mimics God's fabrication of Adam, who was pressed together, according to Genesis, from red dust; the novelist, conjuring a character out of the nocturnal air rather than pressing earth into shape or suturing cadavers, had created Frankenstein. Does the artist mock God, or are gods merely surrogates for artists?

The God invoked in the introduction to *Frankenstein* created a world that is indeed a 'stupendous mechanism'. Such a deity must be male, since his talents are those of a structural engineer (or, in the case of Frankenstein, a biologist, a surgeon and an electrician). But Mary Shelley knew about another model of gestation, which is the perilous prerogative of women. Her own mother had died twelve days after giving birth to Mary. The cause was an infection contracted when a doctor used his hands to extract the placenta from his stricken patient. Mary bore her first child in 1815, two more at the beginning and end of 1817, and a fourth in 1819; only one survived into adulthood. In 1822, a few weeks before her husband drowned, she suffered a dangerous miscarriage. Artists often think of their creations as brain-children, plucked from the air. But perhaps a work of art is closer to actual offspring, growing in the body and feeding on it before painfully emerging into the air. Mary Shelley made the connection between creativity and reproduction in her farewell wish for the novel, when she referred to

The monster's birth. Film still from *Frankenstein*, 1931. Directed by James Whale.

it as her 'hideous progeny'. It was her baby, and it was also – as she acknowl-edged with an indulgent smile – a monster. She cheekily misquoted holy writ as she sent the book off into the world, hoping that it would 'go forth and prosper', just as God told his creatures to go forth and multiply. The animals in Eden proliferate biologically. Books have their own means of mechanical reproduction, and sometimes reward their maker with profits.

Mary Shelley's puzzled reflections on the source of her novel place art midway between biology and theology. Like an embryonic offshoot, it is nurtured by the dreams, desires and fears of the artists in whose minds it develops. We can trace stories to their source, following neural routes or trails of association that usually lead back to childhood. But where did the child come from? Who made the world, and what was it made from? Here the biological inquiry falters, and psychological deduction must give way to the guesswork of religion. Or perhaps this is the point at which the inves-tigation should be called off. The very idea that art purports to be a creative activity can offend a man of faith. In 1880 the Jesuit poet Gerard Manley Hopkins defined creation as 'THE MAKING OUT OF NOTHING', which was accomplished by God 'in no time with a word'. Hopkins denied that human beings shared this capacity; we can only play with matter that already exists. We know how to use grain to make bread or clay to make bricks, but cannot create the seed or the soil. 'MAN,' Hopkins emphasized, 'CANNOT CREATE a single speck, God creates all that is not himself'. But is it really nonsensical to praise a man of genius for creating a painting, a poem or a tune, just because he did not invent the canvas and the colours, the words or the notes? Art is a magical activity, and anyone who creates the likeness of a man seems to be exercising the power that created man in the first place. Paul Gauguin's neighbours in Tahiti in the 1890s, unembarrassed by Chris-tian scruples, venerated him for doing so. Once a native, knowing him to be a painter, hailed him as 'Man who makes human beings!'

Artists can either be rebuked for trespassing on the domain of God, or praised for doing so. It depends whether you think the God in question deserves prior and exclusive rights as a creator. Mary Shelley called her hero a 'modern Prometheus', because like the Titan Frankenstein was a maker of men. Prometheus, according to the Greek myth, moulded the first humans from the mire of a river bed. In Genesis, man is God's creation; but Zeus – in this alternative version of our origins – despises the messy creatures and orders them to be destroyed. Instead Prometheus, an artist who takes pride in his handiwork, steals fire from the hearth of Zeus and implants a divine spark in his clay manikin. He is punished for his rebellion, chained to a mountain peak and tormented by an eagle that tears at his liver with its beak. All the same, he has no regrets, and blames Zeus for his cruelty. Scripture and myth offer us a choice: we can imagine ourselves to be the invention of a jealous, domineering deity, or the risky, unfinished experiment of an artist. The God of Genesis creates human beings in his own image, but soon turns against them, condemns them to mortality, and later sends a flood to exterminate all living things. Of course we are free to take a revenge of our own. Voltaire ridiculed the sacramental wafers ingested by believers taking communion: they are 'imitating God, who created man, by in turn creating God with a few words and a handful of flour'. That God is then swallowed, digested, circulated through the body and expelled. The story of Prometheus does away with the need for such recriminations. He endows men with the means of self-help, so they do not remain dependent on the grace and favour of a divine patron; he teaches them language, and – as he reminds the chorus in the tragedy by Aeschylus – coaxes them to develop scientific tools and artistic skills of their own.

Looking back on what happened during that night, Mary Shelley equated the mystery of artistic creativity with that of creation itself. We can only claim to be original if we ignore the origins of our ideas: as she said, 'the Hindoos give the world an elephant to support it, but they make the elephant stand upon a tortoise.' But on what does this tiered, teetering ladder of heraldic beasts finally rest? She once more revises the scriptural notion of a creation 'ex nihilo' when she says in her explanatory preface that 'Invention ... does not consist in creating out of void'. William Hazlitt, in a critique of Percy Bysshe Shelley's abstract, impalpable lyrics, accepted poetry's right to 'create a world of its own', but expected it to use 'existing materials'. Instead Shelley, idiosyncratic and self-sufficient to a fault, was 'the maker of his own poetry – out of nothing'. The results were unintelligible to Hazlitt, because they had no grounding in reality. For Mary Shelley, the 'existing materials' did not derive from a real, solid, daylit world: she proposes that we create 'out of chaos'. Here too she slips sideways, exchanging the Bible for the cosmology of the Greeks, who thought of chaos as the state that preceded creation. Christianity annexed the abyss, which became the boundless, bottomless pit into which lost souls were hurled. Nietzsche, speaking for all artists rather than acknowledging his own mental imbalance, declared that 'One must have chaos in oneself in order to give birth to a dancing star'.

The artist's brain, as Mary Shelley saw it, resembles that gulf of unbeing where the elements were mixed before cosmic order pacified them: 'dark, shapeless substances' murkily boiled and bubbled within her while she slept. God in Genesis allocates to each of the four elements – air and earth, fire and water – a separate region and a distinct function. But Mary Shelley could not prevent the elements from prosecuting their endless argument inside her monster. Frankenstein's creature is fierily welded together, and probably gets his 'spark of being' from a lightning bolt. But he flees to a Swiss glacier, and finally disappears at the North Pole. Heat is creative, though life entropically cools and dwindles towards a chilly death; the imperative of nature is decay. Mary Shelley added a modest proviso to her formulation of the problem. Art can 'give form' to amorphous substances, but it 'cannot bring into being the substance itself'. We are left staring into the darkness, trying both to understand our own thought processes and to guess what goes on in the mind of God. The introduction to *Frankenstein* credits the story about the hero's 'unhallowed arts' to an imagination that 'possessed and guided' the dreamer. By such qualifications, Mary Shelley avoided a direct dispute with Christianity. Yet the confrontation is unavoidable. Fables of creation are stories about the human mind's compulsion to argue with reality and redesign nature. They are acts of usurpation, which deny the deity's exclusive rights.

As a woman, Mary Shelley was preoccupied with the messy organic business of engendering; she knew that creation happens somewhere inside the body. Frankenstein refers to his improvised laboratory as 'my workshop of filthy creation'. It is a cell in an attic, separated from the rest of the house by a gallery and a staircase as if, like the brain, it needs to be vertically detached from the functions that go on below. Up there, creation ought to be hygienic, far from the bloody, nurturing fluids of the womb. The reference to filth tugs the lofty thinker down to ground and embeds him in the flesh.

Male artists have a different genealogy: they are more likely to describe creation as a disembodied feat, a brainstorm like God's abrupt decision in Genesis to call into being heaven and earth. With precocious cheek, Orson Welles followed the prescriptions of Genesis in a trailer he made in 1941 for *Citizen Kane*. On a dark screen, a voice calls for light. God named light, and automatically irradiated the chaotic gloom; film is a conjuration of electric light, and – as still frames flicker into animation in passing through a projector – it is also the means by which Welles creates life. At his command, a spotlight swings down from the studio's obscure firmament. Still invisible, Welles requests a microphone, which also hovers into place. Narrating the trailer, he remains an authoritative voice declaiming from out of a bright aerial light, like God talking to Moses. One man divides himself into a trinity. Acting in the film, Welles is the son, the child of his own brain; writing the script, he is the holy ghost who prompts human beings into action by whispering in their ears; but as its director, he is God the father, an all-seeing autocrat who prefers to remain unseen, a creator who pervades his creation and yet is teasingly absent from it.

After stretching out the heaven above an earth whose warring elements had been separated from each other, God turned from creating to making: Genesis uses two different verbs to mark the difference. Making is dirtier than creating, which can command thin air to take on substance.

Prometheus made man by dabbling in mud; Auguste Rodin, aged five, found his own raw ingredients in the kitchen. He saw his mother dropping thin twists of dough into hot oil and extracting crisp pastries; discerning human shapes in the contorted batter, he asked her if he could fry some men. Practising to be a sculptor, he kneaded dough into shapes that were almost too big for the pan. He was delighted when the heat animated his sticky prototypes: the spitting oil caused them to writhe, violently quickening them into life. It was a useful lesson, which he perhaps remembered in 1864 when he produced his first portrait bust, representing a man with a broken nose. Rainer Maria Rilke said that Rodin 'made this mask as God created the first man'. Why should Adam, the rough draft of a human being, have an Apollonian profile? The business of making also intrigued the young Leonard Bernstein. He discovered at the age of four that man had been formed from dust, and decided to repeat the experiment. He collected the coagulating drifts of fluff from under his bed, then soaked them in the bathroom hand-basin to make them gel. But he left the water running, the drain-pipe clogged, and the apartment beneath was deluged by the overflow. God did not have to bother about neighbours downstairs.

Any investigation of art has to ponder the notion of God's creation, though it will probably soon reach its own heterodox conclusions. Giorgio Vasari, in the compendium of artists' lives that he began to publish in 1550, paid homage to the ultimate initiator, the patron recognized by all his subjects – the Christian God, who is both sculptor and painter. Vasari describes Genesis as the adventures of a 'creative intellect': God's artistry first forms man from clay and then applies vivid colouring to his statuesque form. Adam's name supposedly came from the red soil God used in making him; 'adema' in Hebrew refers to vegetable mould. Georges Braque remembered this source, and said he too tried 'to extract my work from the clay'. Pigments such as ochre are grubbed out of the earth, and ensure that art stays grounded in it. But the biblical myth is better at explaining how sculpture and painting began than it is at accounting for the physical manufacture of the human body: we are made up of water and minerals, and have no clay at all in our composition. Untroubled by chemical details, Vasari juggles the official Christian theory with the alternative, competing stories. He mentions the arts of the Egyptians and Chaldeans, as well as honouring the Greeks for 'discovering the brush and the use of colours'; he then proposes that even the God who declared that everything began from him might perhaps have been imitating some prior notion of art. No matter which deity claims credit, 'the animating principle of all creative processes' is design, which must have 'existed in absolute perfection before the Creation'. How else, Vasari asks, would Almighty God have been able to organize the universe and adorn the sky with lights, let alone mould the dry land and

populate it with 'created things'? The God to whom Vasari pays tribute is
merely a precursor of the contemporary artists he celebrates. Giotto's genius
is self-generating, since he 'learned his art...without any instructor'; he is born
out of nothing. Other supernatural revelations soon follow. Michelangelo
argues that Ghiberti's doors for the Baptistery in Florence might serve for
the gates of paradise, because they bring heaven down to earth. Brunelleschi
raises the cupola of the Duomo so high that it dares heaven to combat, and
the sky retaliates with lightning strikes. Not content with this act of hubris,
Brunelleschi, in his designs for a miracle play, invents his own mechanically
animated model of heaven, with garlands of angels swooping out of the sky
to the accompaniment of flashing lights. The vision is accompanied by 'the
most harmonious music', another celestial amenity.

   *Lives of the Artists* ends as hagiography. Leonardo's endowment of
graces and talents is said to 'transcend nature', and Raphael is worshipped as
a 'mortal god'. On the ceiling of the Sistine Chapel, Michelangelo imagines
and duplicates that initial creative fiat which Vasari describes at the beginning of the *Lives*; he confidently exercises a right hand that might have
belonged to the God who points at the prone form of Adam. Michelangelo
made an image of something that is unimaginable, and created a physical
replica for the idea of creativity. Man awakens langorously to life, and extends
a limp finger that is about to receive the touch of God. Frankenstein's
monster, the product of an artificial genesis, is debarred from procreation,
and bitterly envies the family of his human superiors. The Adam of
Michelangelo, however, is as androgynous as the green pagan nature on
which he reposes: female in his lolling passivity, male in the tense muscular-
ity of his upright leg. Vasari's most extravagant compliment comes close to
deifying the artist: Michelangelo's Adam, he says, 'seems to have been fashioned at that very moment by the first and supreme creator rather than by
the drawing and brush of a mortal man'. God is supreme because first, but
those who follow have a share in his power. Or do they allow him a share in
a power they acquired through their own ingenuity? It was a mortal man,
after all, who invented the paint brush; Michelangelo's God, like a child
investigating a paint pot, has to use his finger. And the moment when the
pencil and brush perform the miracle happens outside time, eliminating the
gap between now and that earlier event when chaos took on form and clay
was infused with a living soul. At that instant, as a spark ignites inside an
artist's head and sends a message to the hand, a new world seems to be mate-
rializing. It emerges from a source that remains mysterious, and the creator
is usually puzzled by the autonomy of his creation. Frankenstein makes the
monster but cannot understand him, or catch him when he escapes from his
bondage. God endows Adam and Eve with free will, then berates them for
using it when they choose to eat the forbidden fruit.

God positioning
the sun, moon
and stars, from
Michelangelo's
ceiling in the
Sistine Chapel,
1508–12

As Michelangelo's God works through the first week, he exhibits a
variety of creative moods. When he invents the sun, moon and planets he is
imperious, extending two arms that are the fulcrum of the universe. This
is the divine architect, or the Newtonian physicist who establishes laws by
which nature is irresistibly bound. When he divides the waters from the dry
land, he reaches out of the funnel of drapery inside which he travels, grappling to project himself into the light; he leans down at a perilous angle and
opens his hands, ready to mould an invisible substance. The architectonic
rules have already been established. Now craftsmanship is called for. John
Ruskin – who thought of Genesis as 'God's account of His own creation',
faithfully transcribed by Moses – tried in *Modern Painters* to defend Christianity against both the secular scepticism of Victorian science and the
self-deifying conceit of romantic art. He disapproved of the Renaissance,
because in its worship of perfected humanity – exemplified by Michelangelo's Adam – it forgot the pious deference we owe to God. Still, despite his
religious faith, Ruskin suspected that creation should be seen as an artistic
process, not the mystical initiative of a bodiless demiurge. In *Modern Painters*
he quotes the Bible's comment that 'God prepared the dry land', and adds
that the earth was void so long as it remained without form. From this he
infers that 'the command that the waters should be gathered was the
command that the earth should be *sculptured*'. Yet Michelangelo's God,
when creating Adam and then Eve, is not a maker who models compliant
raw material. The finger he points at Adam is tense, almost erectile, charged
with a will and energy that he wants to transmit to his recumbent, semi-
conscious offspring, and the effort channelled into that thin point is
terrifying. Never has he seemed more likely to tumble out of the sky; he
anchors himself by stretching his left arm around the neck of a companion,
while a second shadowy helper supports his forearm. The experiment is
dangerous, because it threatens to unbalance him. To create Eve, he descends
to earth and raises one hand to beckon her out of her hiding-place inside

Adam. He clasps his robe with his other hand, as if protecting his own nakedness or protecting her from it; he looks older and wearier than the potentate who gave orders to the elements. Eve joins her own hands as she reaches out to him. Perhaps she is praying, though she may also be asking one of those inconvenient questions about the purpose of our existence that Mary Shelley – quoting Adam in Milton's *Paradise Lost* – used as an epigraph for *Frankenstein*:

> Did I request thee, Maker, from my Clay
> To mould me Man, did I solicit thee
> From darkness to promote me...?

Hunched and withdrawn, the creator looks as if he might regret the whole enterprise, which has already escaped from his control.

Every form of art has its own myth of nativity, and its own version of the originating deity. For Ruskin, Genesis identified God as a sculptor. Goethe, in the theory of colour he published in 1810, celebrates an invisible creator who is a painter – or who at least encourages men to paint so they can register the

God creating Eve, from Michelangelo's Sistine Chapel ceiling, 1508–12

luminous array of creation. Goethe objected to the way in which Newton had analytically chopped up a ray of light by refracting it through a prism. The result was exactly seven colours, and this strict palette made no allowance for chromatic gradations like the 'peculiar tint of yellow-green' that Coleridge saw in the evening sky. That sickly, acid tone was of course an optical illusion, which is why it calls for a compound adjective; the eye, as Coleridge understood, half perceives and half creates. Goethe actually defined the eye as 'a creation of light', formed for the delectation of colours which are 'the acts of light'. His Faust, basking in the sun beside a waterfall, admires the rainbow that shimmers in the spray, and says that it symbolizes life's hazy play of multi-coloured allurements. After Noah's flood, that arc may have signified God's forgiving covenant with man. But for Goethe it is not God who stretches the iridescent bow across the sky; it is sparked by the meeting of sunlight and water vapour, and exists only in the eye that sees it. Turner put it more brazenly when he said 'The sun is God'. He made the remark, according to Ruskin, shortly before his death. It was his admission of his vocation's hubris: the painter, staring at the sun, daringly looks God in the eye. To illustrate Goethe's theory of colour, Turner painted the emergence of our present world after the biblical deluge, as Noah's ark bumps to rest on Ararat and the sun – as he noted in an accompanying poem – reflects earth's 'lost forms, each in prismatic guise'. Afloat in the golden haze, Moses can be seen writing Genesis.

Discussing the relationship between yellow and red, Goethe declared that the spectrum had a 'spiritual meaning', and unveiled his 'mysterious interpretation' of its minglings and transmutations. Mixed in one way, the 'separate principles' produce green. Differently combined, they can be intensified into red. As a result, 'we can hardly refrain from thinking in the first case on the earthly, in the last on the heavenly, generation of the Elohim'. (The Elohim is the Hebrew term for God when engaged in the work of creation in Genesis.) Green depicts nature, the open book of pantheism; red is the incandescence of heaven. To prepare paint or to apply it to a surface was for Wassily Kandinsky an act of 'world creation'. In 1909 in his treatise *On the Spiritual in Art*, Kandinsky applied values of his own to colours, which – unattached to bodies or objects – suffuse nature and evoke

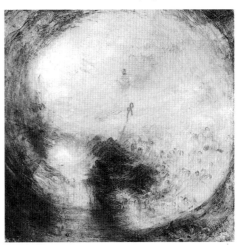

J. M. W. Turner, *Light and Colour (Goethe's Theory). The Morning after the Deluge*, 1843

supernatural atmosphere. Yellow for him was shrill, unbearably intense, like 'a trumpet being played louder and louder': the sound of a cosmic reveille, as at the Last Judgment. Black, by contrast, betokened universal expiry, 'a dead nothingness as if the sun had become extinct'. For Kandinsky, this subjective indexing of sensations was among the 'mystical sources' of art itself: he made it a rule that that 'every artist, as creator, must give expression to what is characteristic of him'. He painted the reversal of Genesis, as a luminous spirit reclaims the freedom it enjoyed before it was anchored to our solid, blockish world. Hence the apocalyptic fanfare of his yellows, or the nihilism of his blacks.

Colour confers animation, which is the gift of life, and that gift can only come from a god. Gauguin, painting a Tahitian man who chops down a dead coconut tree with his axe, inscribed a cryptic message on the ground: 'I seemed to see that word of Oceanic origin, *Atua*, "God". As Taäta or Takata it reached India and is to be found everywhere and in everything

− Religion of Buddha'. Gauguin's earth is purple, the sacred scribble yellow; his colours speak a universal language of revelation, if only we could learn how to decipher it. In the late 1940s, near the end of his life, Matisse designed a chapel near his villa at Vence. It was a solar shrine, ablaze with a blue and lemon-yellow light kindled by stained glass. On a wall of white ceramic tiles he scribbled the stations of the cross in black paint; he thought of the sketches as graffiti, and completed them in two hours. A Dominican novice said that he assumed Matisse had been directly inspired by the Heavenly Father. Matisse was by then too old and ill to bother with polite untruths. 'Yes,' he replied, 'but that god is me.' It was a serious joke. For Matisse, a painting had, as he said, 'the power to generate light', as if he were imagining the unspoiled sunburst on the first day of creation. Furnishing his personal paradise, he could conjure up vegetation inside his tiny hotel room in Nice. Once when Picasso visited him, he said 'I want to show you my plane tree'. His guest looked around, mystified. Into the room, on cue, strode a naked girl, six feet tall. 'This is my plane tree,' said Matisse with a smile, like God reviewing creation and admiring its goodness. Even Mondrian's abstract rectilinear compositions were maps of the theosophical heaven he believed in, a place of 'pure equilibrium'.

The other art forms have their own stake in this divine parentage. The gospel of St John calls Christ the Word. He assisted God during the first week, and spoke the created world into being. But according to classical cosmology, the logical mode of utterance chosen by the Logos was music. The spheres were held in place by the succession of tones they emitted; nature maintained its coherence because it was attuned to the divine creator. John Dryden, in the 'Song for St Cecilia's Day' he wrote in 1687, used the fable to establish the sacred origins of music, which spills from the sky like a benediction:

> From Harmony, from heav'nly Harmony
>     This universal frame began:
> When Nature underneath a heap
>     Of jarring Atomes lay,
> And could not heave her Head,
> The tuneful Voice was heard from high,
> Arise ye more than dead.

The first voice does not belong to God, booming from on high; rather, it is that of music, which in addressing the atomic debris of nature brings about a miracle comparable with Christ's ransoming of our souls. The Bible promises that, thanks to Christ's sacrifice, the dead will be resurrected. But music can vivify those who are 'more than dead' because − like colliding, incoherent atoms − they are not yet alive. It does so by making us hearken to voices in the air, like those that enchant Caliban in *The Tempest*, introducing us to the notion of transcendence. At the same time, music teaches us to think, training us in logic. This is why, after receiving the call from above, nature can raise her head. The body grows a brain, and Genesis can happen without divine intervention. The repetition in Dryden's first line suggests that heaven might be an afterthought. Harmony – the idea of consonance and system – comes first, and was only later made an attribute of the deity. Newton took it to be a law of nature, which is why he equated his seven primary colours with the notes in the diatonic musical scale, whose sounds were emitted, according to Pythagoras, by the seven spheres that encircle our world. Christianity assigned the virginal St Cecilia to superintend the lyrical rotations of the planets, and musicians were happy to accept the benediction on behalf of their art. Carl Czerny heard Beethoven play his Third Piano Concerto in 1803, and described the nimbus of sound in the second movement as the augury of a 'holy, distant and heavenly harmony'; the theme of the largo indeeds falls on the ear like manna.

Paul Hindemith maintained this faith as late as 1956, when his opera *Die Harmonie der Welt* was first performed. It concerns the astral map-making of the astronomer Johannes Kepler, who published *Harmonices Mundi* during his employment at the court of Emperor Rudolf II in Prague in the early seventeenth century. Kepler believed that a divine plan was written in the stars, and Hindemith expected the classical forms of music to enunciate that order: in 1940, soon after beginning work on the opera, he composed a motet that set the opening of St John's gospel – 'In the beginning was the Word, and the Word was with God, and the Word was God' – to an intricately disciplined fugue. God has many things on his mind, so he thinks contrapuntally. In the opera, harmony is challenged by dissonance and dissent. Kepler struggles to reconcile scientific observation with religious dogma, but his science overlaps with the magic practised by his mother, a believer in wonder-working herbs and the alchemical transformation of metals; a horoscope he prepares goads the warlord Wallenstein to begin a campaign of conquest, since he is convinced that his army can establish heaven on earth and forcibly harmonize a rebellious world. When Kepler dies, he and the other characters are lifted into the sky, where they take part in an astral ballet that shows the orderly rotation of the planets. The Emperor is Sol, with Kepler's mother as Luna, the shadowy side of enlightenment. Wallenstein is the bellicose Jupiter, and a bigoted Protestant minister who denies the sacrament to Kepler recurs as Mercury, a grain of insignificant dust connected to the kernel or nucleus of energy that fuels the sun. Kepler is Earth, orbiting in the middle of these contentious influences. The constellations scintillate, the zodiac sketches diagrams on the night sky, and the voices join in God's chorale, taking up again the melody of the motet Hindemith based on St John. Their words, however, imply that harmony is discernible and audible only on high, while men remain unredeemed. The chorus has a prophetic glimpse of the thermonuclear bomb, which uses solar energy as a means of killing. Despite their serenely repetitive round-dance, these levitated beings have not completed the quest for what Hindemith calls 'der Schöpfung Ursprung' – the source from which creation springs.

For Dryden, the myth of heavenly harmony was doubly convenient: it sanctified music and performed the same service for poetry, which harmonizes language by the numerical discipline of metre and the equilibrium enforced by rhyme. This was a cosmic principle on which classical philosophy and Christianity could agree: Plato in *Timaeus* interprets the world as a mathematical grid, and Isaiah describes God setting all things in order by number. Verse, with its counted syllables and regulated accents, is a metaphysical enterprise. Even poets who lack Dryden's faith in the tidy rationality of scansion tend to paraphrase the mystery or miracle he describes. Paul Valéry in 1933 recalled his own 'gropings' towards 'imperious verbal illuminations which suddenly impose a certain combination of words': advents as abrupt as God's command 'Let there be light'. Valéry felt he was stumbling through the darkness, with no idea of 'what *will* come into being'. The birth happened as a result of its own volition, and it repudiated and rectified 'the "freedom" or chaos of the mind'. Scrutinizing the shadowy process, he concluded that 'the notion of an *Author* is not a simple one'. Who wrote his poems, given that he felt they were being dictated to him? Who could the poet thank, now that gods and muses do not dance attendance on him? The italicized author is presumably a male authority. Valéry – developing the analogies between cosmic creation, literary creativity and biological procreation – preferred the submissive female role: he said that he carried the poems within him, nourished them, and when they were ready allowed them to make their rending journey into the light, anxious to see at last what they look like. 'Le Cimetière marin' exemplified the process, from initial act of insemination to the protracted lying-in. It 'was *conceived*', he explained, though he could give no details: who can tell what occurred when the seed met the egg? After that – as he remarked with a patient, long-suffering sigh – 'a rather long labour followed', lasting several years.

Valéry disparaged what he called 'the myth of "creation"', which 'entices us to want to make something out of nothing'. Like Mary Shelley, he knew that was impossible; like her, he also conceded that this is what he was involuntarily doing whenever he sat down to write or lay down to sleep. The making formed a cosmos, or perhaps a fragile cranial microcosm. For Valéry, prose takes stock of a 'practical universe' which is a 'totality of *ends*', a utilitarian place where straight lines make prompt connections between two points. But poetry proposes a different map of inner and outer space. Its universe cherishes 'harmonic relationships', analogies and ambiguities; it is an idyllic place where 'resonance triumphs over causality', as in 'the universe of music'. Here, as Valéry put it, 'the Idea reclaims its voice'. That capitalized Idea is the First Cause which, in Plato's theory, thought up the world. In a poem called 'Poésie', Michel Leiris described his own creativity with the same cosmic flair. He says that that we pull out of ourselves a nameless thing, which constellates the white paper. The first image is obstetric, the second galactic: a poem resembles a milky way that is visible in daylight.

The poet in Thomas Mann's story 'Tonio Kröger', written in 1903, solemnly accepts his responsibility to make the world all over again. He is, he reflects, not a human being but a creator, and he knows that 'one must die to life in order to be utterly a creator'. He therefore estranges himself from the drab satisfactions of ordinary men – love, domestic happiness, bourgeois comfort – and concentrates on deploying 'the power of the Word'. Like God making himself articulate through Christ's intercession, language enables Kröger to bring order to 'a world unborn and formless'. His vocation requires him to stand apart from or above humanity, and he likens the sacrifice to that of the castrati, singers who were gelded to preserve their angelic voices. To be a god is a sad, friendless, perhaps ultimately sterile fate.

But this is not the only conclusion that can be drawn from St John's reference to Christ as the Word. For Mann's character, to be a curator of words is a high, holy, inhumane calling. He may be mistaken: the Bible does not ask for the Word to be written down. A mystical tract by a Raja in Aldous Huxley's novel *Island* proposes that 'St John was right. In a blessedly speechless universe, the Word was not only *with* God; it *was* God…God is a projected symbol, a deified name. God = "God"'. The quotation marks preserve the sacrosanct truth by reminding us that it ought not to be spoken, let alone written. In 1925, in an essay on literary anonymity, E. M. Forster made the same biblical text mean something quite different, and used it to disparage the disdainful aestheticism of writers like Kröger. Forster's argument is that 'Creation comes from the depths – the mystic will say from God'. Writers who sign their work are short-sighted egotists; anonymous works such as legends or ballads acknowledge the obscurity of their origins and allow us to be 'co-partners' in their created worlds. The Book of Genesis is one of Forster's examples. It is a work whose putative authors extend from Jahvist and Elohist (as he calls the primal scribes) to the committee of clerics who put together the King James version: in effect it has no author at all. Forster uses it to chasten writers who dote on the sound of their own voices, reminding them that 'it was not the speaker who was in the beginning but the Word'. That word is not personified and individualized in Christ, as the gospel intended. Forster takes the formula to mean that we are the servants of language, not masters teaching it to perform stylish tricks.

Language, long before it was refined into literature, served as a communal amenity, enabling us to talk to each other. Even more boldly, Forster proposes that: 'To forget its Creator is one of the functions of a Creation'; an anonymous work asserts 'I, not my author, really exist', just as trees and flowers and human beings declare 'I really exist, not God'. Shortly before John Berryman committed suicide in 1972, he wrote a memorial poem for Dylan Thomas, who had died in 1953. It reports that Thomas's talk

> clung latterly to Eden,
> again & again of the Garden & the Garden's flowers,
> not ever the Creator, only of that creation
> with a radiant will to go there.

A less optimistic interpretation of St John was proposed by the Viennese satirist Karl Kraus in 1921. His poem 'Lied des Schwarz-Druckers' proclaims the world-view of a press baron, one of the mercantile gods who tell modern men what to think and believe. Words – no longer sacred, as they were for St John – are a cheap means of filling empty space on paper and inside the head:

> In the beginning was the press
> and then the word was born.

Forster freed words from the Word. For Kraus, all words that are not the Word can be dismissed as shoddy verbiage, mechanically regurgitated. Whatever is not scripture can be written off as journalism, a disposable daily instalment of lies. Either way, we cannot escape from the biblical precedent; ours is a culture of quotations, where original thinkers take pride in their capacity to misquote.

In 1919 Rilke wrote an essay recalling a makeshift gramophone he and some schoolfriends had rigged up in a physics class. The funnel was cardboard, the needle was plucked from a clothes brush, the cylinder had a coating of candle wax, yet these shoddy improvised ingredients made it possible to trap the agitation of air. Later, attending anatomy lessons at an art school in Paris, he remembered the incisions scratched on the cylinder when he studied the coronal suture of the skull, and imagined what might happen if the needle were applied to that cavern of chalky bone. What 'primal sound … would then come to birth?' Was poetry a mechanism for recording brain waves? The skull he took home to ponder resembled Dryden's 'universal frame': a taut container for 'something ultimately dangerous, something narrowly enclosed yet boundlessly active' – a bowl full of broiling chaos. Rilke was looking into emptiness. The wrinkled grey matter whose folds filed away memories, sensations and ideas had been removed from the hollow head. But the experiment brought him nearer to understanding the creation both of worlds and of poems. He knew this because of the dizziness that overtook him: 'the danger of the poet is his awareness of the abysses that divide one order of perception from the others'. Those chasms, he added, were of 'such vastness and suction' that they could engulf 'the greater part of the world – and who knows of how many worlds?'

A novelist at the moment of inception is likely to feel the same excited, anticipatory dread. In 1920 Joseph Conrad remembered his decision to exchange a life at sea for a new career as a writer, and in doing so paraphrased the beginning of Genesis: 'The discovery of new values in life is a very chaotic experience; there is ... a momentary feeling of darkness. I let my spirit float supine on that chaos'. In Hesiod's *Theogony*, an abyss is the chaotic recess from which the universe was extracted. Rilke, poised on the edge, wondered if art – so curious about origins that it risks destruction – might not be undoing that long creative process. Stories, like poems, also confront what Prospero calls 'the dark backward and abysm'. For Rilke, the abyss was spatial; it yawned between orders of perception, dividing feeling from meaning. A narrator, like Prospero when he tells Miranda the story of her life, balances his precarious creation above a temporal gulf. We begin the story at an arbitrary point, aware that it starts too late. How can we explain the cause of anything without going back to Plato's First Cause? Thomas Mann, in a lecture at Princeton in 1939, boasted about the ambition of novels to encompass infinitude. 'The novel', he said, 'scarcely knows how to begin except with the very beginning of all things, and does not want to end at all.' George Eliot begins *Daniel Deronda* with a baffling scene: an unknown man watches an unknown woman jesting with the unknowable future at a gambling table. The incident introduces us to the notion of randomness; everything here, even the identities of the two principal characters, is as contingent as the motions of the dice and the roulette wheel. The epigraph Eliot wrote for this first chapter apologizes for such indeterminacy, but argues that 'Men can do nothing without the make-believe of a beginning'. Even science, she says, starts from a fictional instant when the global clock was set at nought. The novelist, before the story begins, warns that 'No retrospect will take us to the true beginning'. George Eliot was equally sceptical about endings, and remarked in a letter in 1857 that conclusions tend to be weak because 'a conclusion ... is at best a negation'. How can art represent the endlessness of the created world? André Gide understood that everything in life was a fresh start, and wanted to end one of his novels with the proviso 'Might be continued'. St John concludes his gospel with the assurance that 'there are also many other things which Jesus did, the which, if they should be written every one, I suppose that even the world itself could not contain the books that should be written. Amen.' Novels try to include the scripture's apocryphal events, well aware that it will not only be good works that they tabulate. The scandalous heroine of Defoe's *Moll Flanders* pretends to be a reformed character at the end of her life-story and, impudently paraphrasing the gospel, boasts that she 'could fill a larger history than this' with case-studies of converted sinners. But she thinks better of regaling us with such implausible marvels: 'I doubt that part of the story will not be equally diverting as the wicked part.'

Genesis is the best example of the temporal recession Thomas Mann admired. Its table of the human family's first generations enabled literal-minded theologians to count their way back through the successive begettings to pin-point the exact date of the creation. According to the time-keepers of Constantinople, creation occured in 5509 BC, so years were counted off from that date. In Russia the same calendar prevailed until 1700, when Peter the Great adjusted his country to the rest of Europe and took Christ's birth as the starting point. His religious opponents, the Old Believers, protested at his interference with 'God's time'. In 1650 Archbishop James Ussher established his own chronology, declaring that creation took place at 9.30 am on October 23 in the year 4004 BC. Some flustered rethinking was necessary when, in the nineteenth century, the dating of fossils suggested that the beginning must have been much earlier. Philip Gosse, leader of a clerical faction called the pro-chronists, responded to the new geological evidence in 1857 by arguing that God – who wanted to give Adam and Eve the comfortable sense of inhabiting a lived-in world – had buried these calcified remains during the first six days. The fossils were like fake antiques, supplied so that the arrivistes could pretend to be at home among their ancestral heirlooms. Even the creator, it seemed, knew that the idea of a sudden, unprompted beginning was unbelievable.

Mann envied ancient epics, which could remember all of the human history they summarized. His example was 'the narrative Vedas of India, ... also called *Itihasa-Hymns* after the expression *Iti ha asa*, meaning "thus it was".' He preferred this 'creation of the past' to the short-term memory of the drama, which shows us events in the present and says not 'thus it was' but 'here it is'. He confronted the problem of universal beginnings in his story 'The Transposed Heads', written in 1940. It professes to be an excerpt from those immemorial Indian epics; its hero Shridaman 'traced his line on the male side from a Brahman stock versed in the Vedas'. Christians have to grapple with the notion of a paternal God who, helped by his co-eternal son, created the world without needing to engage a woman. Shridaman finds it easier to comprehend origins because the procreating deity he worships is female. He calls Kali 'she, the All-Mother, ... of whose womb all things come, into whose womb all things go'. For his wife Sita, Kali is 'her that was before all beginnings'. Doubling as the goddess of death, she also deals in destruction, which is a concomitant of creativity. Once again,

Christianity imposes a false antithesis: in *Paradise Lost*, Death is incestuously spawned by Satan and his daughter Sin, and slithers out of his mother's gaping nether parts. The Indian 'World-Mother', thanks to the German fondness for compound words and agglomerated concepts, is simultaneously 'Deathbringer-Lifegiver'. When she speaks, Kali identifies herself with chaos, the muddle of pre-existence. 'I am Disorder', she says, although she insists on orderly behaviour in her human subjects. Before Shridaman beheads himself – which he does in order to exchange a singular life for merger with an impersonal, oceanic being – he addresses Kali as 'Beginningless, that wast before all created!'

The vanishing point is always the same. Our eyes go out of focus as we try to discern where and when the world began, or to ascertain the source of the stories and graphic dreams that seethe in our heads. We cannot know who created us; any creator we imagine is our own creation. In the 1930s Constantin Brancusi sculpted an ecumenically composite god, a towering oak totem called *King of Kings (Spirit of the Buddha)*. The spiritual monarch is a column, not quite a figure – a dead tree, loaded a little too onerously with the ceremonial insignia of power and sanctity; it concludes in a crown, lopping off the tree's foliage. The head that wears the crown has cavities for eyes, and looks like a coconut set up to be knocked over at a fair. This head rests on a neck that could be a chunky African necklace, though it also resembles a grooved mechanism, ready for screwing. Is this god a natural growth or an engineered assemblage? Below the neck are a series of bases or pediments, like Mary Shelley's elephant and tortoise. First comes a section whose jagged outline suggests an accordion, which makes music by compressing air, or – since gods always found their authority on textual commandments – a pile of books. Beneath this is a small, intestinally twisted segment whose coils hint at the snake twining in the Tree of Knowledge. It reminds us that the God of Genesis created men only to give himself the pleasure of tempting and ensnaring them. Further down there is a last pedestal, also hollowed out: the reverent eminence is full of air, and that, given Brancusi's subtitle, may be its truest claim to holiness. A king of kings is a warfaring god, intent on dominion. The Buddha does not terrorize his subjects or demand obedience; he allows us to contemplate nullity, as if we were staring into the apertures carved by Brancusi. A creation cannot come from nowhere, but it can help us to comprehend the nothingness that is our place of origin and our destination.

# 2
# IN THE BEGINNINGS

Pummelling their empty heads or staring at blank pages, artists can only envy the certainty with which God springs into action at the start of Genesis. In Tom Stoppard's *Jumpers*, a philosopher dictating to his secretary bravely decides to go back to first principles. He paces to and fro, frowning to dramatize the effort of cogitation. Then he leaps into the void, and says 'To begin at the beginning: Is God?...'. A pause follows, elongated for as long as the actor can get away with it; the sentence's rising inflection hangs in the air, unable to be completed. At last he tells the waiting secretary: 'Leave a space'. That space is an eternity of incomprehensible time. How can we conceive of a beginning if nothing precedes it? Demoralized, Stoppard's philosopher is gobbled up by the abyss.

The Bible permits no such fumbling. A decisive act, at a precise moment, starts the clock ticking. 'In the beginning,' as the King James version put it in 1611, 'God created the heaven and the earth'. Once the event had occurred, all that mattered was to maintain the regimen established by God. The theologian Richard Hooker, who began to publish his treatise *Of the Laws of Ecclesiastical Polity* in 1593, relied on the Ten Commandments to perpetuate the ordained state of things: 'The world's first creation, and the preservation since of things created, what is it but only so far forth a manifestation by execution, what the eternal law of God is concerning things natural?' A strict adherence to biblical precedent, Hooker advised, was 'the stay of the whole world'. In 1771 the first *Encyclopaedia Britannica* defined creation as 'the producing something out of nothing', and respected God's sole right to bring this about: 'strictly and properly [it] is the effect of the power of God alone, all other creations being only transformations, or change of shape'. The encyclopaedists could not imagine such change being beneficial.

We are expected to agree with God's own evaluation, and to accept that the status quo is good. But this logical and morally satisfactory account of creation only prevailed because others were suppressed. The Gospel of Philip, one of the gnostic texts discovered at Nag Hammadi in Egypt in 1947, presented an alternative version of origins: 'The world came about through a mistake. For he who created it wanted to create it imperishable and immortal. He fell short of attaining his desire.' If the world God created was good, then human beings are responsible for its

God the Creator circumscribing the universe with compasses. 13th-century illumination.

subsequent shortcomings. We can absolve ourselves by shifting blame to the inept creator.

Or should we rather let God fade away? He was present at the beginning of time, but has not been seen since; it is not our fault if we have lost contact with him. Snorri Sturluson, who compiled the Viking *Edda* during the thirteenth century, began his epic by dutifully summarizing the biblical narrative of creation. But Snorri omits the expulsion from paradise, leaves Adam and Eve free to expand their stock, and notes that Noah's kin soon repeopled the world after the flood. As the *Edda* continues, the forking and branching families of man inevitably outgrow God and forget his name: 'In most parts of the world there was no one to be found who knew anything about his creator.' Though Snorri claimed to regret this impiety, he found it poetically convenient, since he could insert his own genealogical myth. Gylfi the shaman, a poet-priest, asks a prophet called High to name the most ancient of gods. High gives him a choice: Odin 'is called All-father in our language, but in Old Asgard he had twelve names'. Snorri multiplies the names for god, and for everything else – he lists two dozen synonyms for speech and another dozen for noise – because he is discovering and rejoicing in his own verbal potency. Max Müller, a student of comparative religion who translated fifty volumes of Sanskrit sacred texts at the end of the nineteenth century, complained that myth was 'a disease of language', because it assigned many names to the same thing. But the ailment is benign, and another name for it is poetry.

Gylfi, who also calls himself Gangleri, asks the primal literary questions: 'What was the beginning? And how did things start? And what was there before?' High and his fellow authorities respond by inventing stories about their own making. The giant Ymir sweated in his sleep, so offspring grew in his moist armpit. His legs rubbed together in a kind of intercourse that produced more descendants. Gangleri wants to know what Ymir lives on. High improvises: Ymir's frosty body dripped and begot the cow Audhumla, from whose udders streamed four nutritious rivers. Like Mary Shelley picturing the tiers of the Hindu myth, Gangleri asks what nourished the cow. Apparently it lapped the calcified frost, and with its assiduous tongue formed the hair of a man. Next day it shaped a head to wear the hair. By the third day, a complete man existed. He was given a name, and sent off to reproduce himself. The body does not sprout a head, which is what symbolically occurred when homo sapiens separated himself from his hirsute ancestors. Because myth is a story told backwards, the head unfurls into a body. High's tall tale is a metaphor for the process of imagining.

Genesis prohibits such fanciful digressions. But its first verse does provoke a series of questions, which start with the meaning of the verb that describes what God did in the beginning. The Hebrew word 'bara' is ambiguous. The creation to which it refers can be something made out of nothing, or it can be a rearrangement. The Kabbalah, glossing the Torah, tabulated extra options, hidden and perhaps illicit. 'Bara' means to set in motion or to animate, not necessarily to create; one speculative kabbalistic commentary – the *Sefer Ha-Zohar* or *Book of Splendour*, which dates from the thirteenth century – suggests that it can also mean to create an illusion. Thanks to this snarled etymology, we have granted God a monopoly of creativity that Genesis did not claim for him. Modern translators of the Bible replace 'created' with 'made',

Buri is licked out of a salty block by the cow. 18th century Icelandic manuscript of the *Edda*.

which generates other problems. The doubtful word is avoided altogether by the *Sefer Yesirah* or *Book of Creation*, which appeared between the third and sixth centuries and was attributed to Abraham. Instead of 'bara', the *Sefer Yesirah* employs words meaning to hew or engrave. Genesis says that the uncreated earth was 'without form, and void'; for Aristotle, things remained embroiled in chaos until they were given a shape and purpose. What we call creation is actually formation, the imprinting of form.

Once we manoeuvre our way around this initial obstacle, Mary Shelley's quandary about her own creation of *Frankenstein* recurs: what were the heaven and earth created out of? Perhaps out of God's insides. In 1955 Wolfgang Fortner composed a brief cantata called *The Creation*, set to a text taken from a collection of sermons by the American poet James Weldon Johnson; Dietrich Fischer-Dieskau declaimed this account of the first week at the premiere in Basle. Fortner's God is literally brought down to earth by a black preacher's folksy paraphrase of Genesis. He creates the world because he feels lonely, and strolls through it, enjoying its amplitude. Because he makes it up as he goes along, the God of Fortner and Johnson is self-critical not self-admiring: having noticed that the earth is hot and barren, he then – as the baritone reports in a shower of sibilants – 'spat out the seven seas'. The Norse myth in the *Edda* has the same satisfying carnality. After the giant Ymir is butchered, the gods carve up his body. His gushing blood becomes the sea, his squashy flesh provides the land, his bones are the rocks beneath. His skull has room for the vaulted sky, with his brains as clouds. A world derived from nothing is inconceivable; either it overflows from inside God, or it recycles his remains.

Even if we allow God to make something out of nothing, other problems crop up when he brings forth each living creature 'after its kind'. Did the kind already exist, like a genetic prototype? Genesis notes that the grasses, herbs and fruit trees contain their seed within themselves, whereas animals must seek out sexual partners. Milton in *Paradise Lost* therefore imagines the womb of earth splitting open to let the species spill out, and emphasizes a brazen fecundity which Genesis refuses to acknowledge: the humble shrubs and bushes are 'with frizl'd hair implicit', like human bodies sprouting at puberty. Then comes another puzzle. On the seventh day, God rests from the works he has both 'created and made'. The two verbs are not quite synonymous. As maker, God furnishes the world – although this disturbed commentators who brooded over the moment when he provides Adam and Eve with clothes to cover their nakedness. Surely God could not be a tailor? And if those clothes were animal skins, had he slain the beasts, flayed them, tanned the hides and stitched them together? Or did Adam perform a sacrificial killing? No wonder fig leaves were adopted as the easier option.

Isaiah called God a potter because he moulded clay to make Adam. In Alexandria during the third century, Origen rejected the notion of a creator who might have got his hands dirty in this way, and insisted that God could not have bothered with anything so lowly as a garden. The Old Testament was allegorized, and Eden became a prophetic fiction, signifying the church of Christ that was to come: a supernatural idyll, without roots in the earth. In 1999, however, Pope John Paul II attempted to reattach divine creation to the ground by arguing that 'the human craftsman mirrors the image of God as creator'. His evidence was flimsily lexical: he pointed out that in Polish 'stwórca' (the word for creator) contains 'twórca' (which means craftsman). The mystery depends on a pun, or an etymological quibble. Does this make God a figment of language? If so, we should not be surprised. The theological lore that upholds the ban on eating the fruit of the Tree of Knowledge rests on the equally shaky foundation of a pun: in Latin, 'malum' means both apple and evil.

God's activity as creator has proved equally troublesome, since his creatures share in his creativity. He allowed Adam to do the work of naming; poets, following his example, attach words to things, aware that description is a surrogate creation. Adam also gives birth to Eve, who is fashioned from his spare rib. Keats in a letter in 1817 likened imagination to Adam's dream of Eve, as recounted in *Paradise Lost*: he yearned for a playmate, fell asleep fantasizing, and awoke to find the vision had materialized beside him. Adam's dream, Keats told his friend Benjamin Bailey, implies

Master Bertram
von Minden,
*Creation of Eve*
from the Grabower
Altar, 1383

'that Imagination and its empyreal reflection is the same as human Life and its spiritual repetition'. He meant that imagination begets life, as surely as the sappy body reproduces itself. Eve has her own more sorrowful mode of delivery; her labour pains are God's sour afterthought, part of her punishment for eating the forbidden fruit. The transition from creativity to destruction happens quickly, almost automatically. Cain commits the first murder, and before long God tires of the runaway creatures who have taken over the earth, decides 'I will destroy man', and sends the deluge.

Augustine of Hippo, fortifying the faith in the fifth century, worried about the account of that first week given by Genesis. In his *Confessions* he reproaches Moses for leaving the mystery of the initial verse unexplained. Then he remembers that the native language of Moses was Hebrew: even if Augustine, speaking Latin, were able to understand him, how could he tell if his words were true? Aware that 'sacred books' contain 'a diversity of truths', Augustine has to license contradictory readings: he is already appraising the

Bible as literature, which has a devious, permissive attitude to truth. In *City of God*, Augustine admits that there are other reasons for doubting Moses, who was not present at the creation. Does that make his account a myth, or a fiction? Augustine closes off those options by remembering that Wisdom was in attendance at the beginning of time. He is referring to Sophia, later portrayed on the ceiling of the Sistine Chapel as God's female companion, his anchorage when he leans towards Adam. She establishes her credentials in Proverbs, where she says that she was 'set up from the everlasting, from the beginning, or ever the earth was', which enabled her to watch as God performed 'his works of old'. For the gnostics, Sophia had an additional authority: she is described in the Nag Hammadi gospels as 'First Begetress, Mother of the Universe' – God's consort and his other half. Augustine denies her a creative role, but uses her instead as a reliable witness, who can impart what she saw to all holy souls.

To rid himself of the problem, Augustine relies on an assertion of literal veracity: 'The Bible says (and the Bible never lies), "In the beginning God created the heaven and the earth"'. Yet he cannot help asking how God spent the time before the beginning, and he tortuously debates the problem of whether time could have existed before the first day. A favourite theological joke, at once grim and self-accusingly futile, threatens to curtail the discussion. Question: How did God occupy himself before he set to work creating? Answer: He was busy making a hell in which to dispose of those who raise such problems. Augustine debars our inquisitive forethought by declaring that 'Before God made the heaven and the earth, he was not making anything'. This has never intimidated the sceptics. In 1925 in Tennessee a schoolteacher called John Scopes was put on trial for telling his pupils about Darwin's doctrine of evolution. Clarence Darrow, defending Scopes, pilloried the fundamentalist interpretation of the creation story upheld by the prosecutor William Jennings Bryan, and asked the same questions that vexed Augustine. If the sun was created on the fourth day, how could there have been mornings and evenings before that, with no sun to differentiate them? If God cursed the serpent by making it crawl on his belly, how must it have travelled before the fall? By balancing upright on its tail? And if Eve was the first and only woman, born from Adam's rib, who did Cain marry? Darrow's wit was unavailing; the court found Scopes guilty and fined him a hundred dollars (though he was cleared after an appeal).

In his *Confessions*, Augustine begs God to permit him to speculate freely: 'I am investigating, Father, not making assertions'. Those investigations often stray beyond the strictures of dogma. Like Origen in the third century, Augustine refused to see God as an artisan. Heaven and earth came from nowhere, without the help of any mechanism or tool; God makes, but cannot be made. Dealing with the Trinity, Augustine insists that the three-personed deity is responsible for all good things, which have been created – 'that is to say, they are made, not begotten'. Theologians continued to squabble over that imprecise distinction. Peter Abelard, the monk castrated early in the twelfth century because of his affair with Eloise, resolved the troubling matter of God's fertility with a quibble: 'although God begat God, and there is only one God, I denied that God had begotten himself'. When Alberic of Rheims attacked his formulation, Abelard cited Augustine, who thought that God must be subject to the physical laws proclaimed by Aristotle. No creature can beget itself; Abelard accused Alberic of heretically supposing 'the Father to be his own Son'. These scholastic niceties conveniently separated the divine persons, and set up an artificial barrier between theology and biology. In *The Golden Legend*, a compendium of saints' lives assembled in the thirteenth century by Jacobus de Voragine, St Cecilia gives the credulous Romans a subtly Augustinian account of the creation. Everything that exists, she says, 'was fashioned by the Son born of the Father, and into everything he created, the Holy Spirit, who proceeds from the Father, breathed life'. Her brother-in-law points out that, although she previously insisted that there is a single God, she has now trebled him. Cecilia replies that human knowledge contains three separate, cooperative faculties: reason, memory, understanding. Why shouldn't 'one divine being' contain 'three persons'? The logic is cerebral; it is better not to imagine those persons possessing bodies.

As the first week unfolds, Augustine's logic is taxed by the variable methods employed to stock the world. With the beasts and the birds, God creates all members of a species simultaneously. The earth is instantaneously over-run by herds, the sky filled with flocks. But when man's turn comes, God creates a single individual, not the entire human race. Augustine wonders why woman was not created in the same way man had been: Adam participates in her creation, since she is made out of him. Is he then her mother as well as her husband? The oddity cries out for allegory, which transforms literal inconveniences into lofty symbols. Augustine later contends that the story of Adam giving birth prophetically announces the advent of Christ. Adam's sleep corresponds to Christ's death on the cross, and the rift through which the rib was extracted matches the wound left in Christ's side by the lance of the Roman soldier. Eve's body, made not created, prefigures the maternal accommodation of the Christian church.

Deriving every created thing from God, Augustine denies that the earth creates the crops that grow in it. God is the inseminator who forms the seeds; we must not, like the Greeks, consider the earth to be our mother. Nor does a woman create the child she carries in her womb. God pre-empted the mother's rights by telling Jeremiah that 'Before I formed thee in the belly I knew thee'. Yet Augustine does allow the mother's mind to influence her unborn child. He cites the story of Jacob, who in Genesis displays rods with white stripes cut in them to Laban's sheep and goats as they procreate. This dupes the silly creatures into giving birth to speckled offspring, which Jacob claims as his own. It is a risky precedent, later employed by Shylock in *The Merchant of Venice* to justify the sharp practice of usury. The same story was retold by the Renaissance magician Cornelius Agrippa of Nettesheim, for whom the rods were the wands of a conjurer. The biblical story concerns trickery and profiteering; Augustine ennobles it by taking it to be a fable about the powers of imagination and mental suggestion. Near the end of the *Confessions*, after some allegorical forays that discover predictions of Christ's life and death in the first chapter of Genesis, Augustine praises God's creativity and at the same time exhibits a subtle creativity of his own. The waters in Genesis spawn life, and out of them Augustine draws a single eucharistic fish, the symbol of Christ and his gift of eternal life. 'Surely I do not mislead my readers?' he asks. The rhetorical question is left without an answer, because he calls on God to approve of his interpretative dexterity: 'One thing grows out of another, and so, by your blessing, God, things are multiplied'. Reproduction increases the number of bodies, and Augustine's allegories ensure the propagation of ideas. The connections he makes between Old and New Testaments elucidate God's 'hidden secrets' and help to 'bring order to our disordered chaos'. That order clears away the chaotic

Jusepe de Ribera, *Jacob with Laban's Flock*, 1632

muddle inside our heads; the individual mind, sorting out confusion, is responsible for a wondrous re-creation.

Autobiographies are stories about the way we make ourselves, wresting a personal identity from the history and geography that attempt to determine our existence. This is how the fifteenth-century Augustinian monk Thomas à Kempis used Genesis in his devotional tract *Imitation of Christ*. Thomas appropriated the Bible's narrative of the first week and made it the story of his spiritual rebirth: he asks God to 'send out thy light and thy truth that they may shine upon the earth, for I am idle earth and void till thou illumine me'. A mist arose to irrigate the earth on the third day, so Thomas implores God to 'wash my soul with that heavenly dew ... to bring forth good fruit'. Augustine likewise found in Genesis a pretext for his own self-regeneration. He was converted to Christianity in AD 386, after a sexually delinquent youth and a traversal of alternative creeds – first the gnosticism of the Manichees, who considered the physical world to be devilish and doubted God's power to control evil; then an agnostic relapse, during which he believed that the only certainties were mathematical; later the Neoplatonism of Plotinus, who ushered the soul towards a mystical encounter with goodness. In becoming a Christian, he overcame the formless indiscipline of a sensual life; discovering the soul in a nonentity impelled by lowly physical urges, he too made something out of nothing.

This entitled Augustine to praise God as a fellow artificer, whose creation is an aesthetic achievement. Why else, he asked, did God repeatedly stand back from the world and call it good? The work had been done 'with the true artist's skill'. Augustine surmised that Plato might have known about God's self-commendation, because the theory of creation he proposed in *Timaeus* also equates goodness with beauty and describes the world as an artefact, at once lucid and lovely. Christianity, however, complicates this notion of divine artistry, because God apparently tolerates imperfection: he permits sin and evil to flourish in his world. Augustine came to reject the argument of the Manichees, who thought that the creation was God's compromise with an evil he could not vanquish. He also disapproved of Origen's argument that God's creativity involved a partial surrender of omnipotence, since – like a novelist who cannot prevent his characters from inventing their own stories – he left souls free to fall. But how else could the world's defects be explained? Original sin, far from being Biblical, originates with Augustine. Although it was his solution to a moral and philosophical problem, he could not help admiring the aesthetic or decorative grace of this flawed creation. A picture may be beautiful, he argues, even though it has 'touches of black in appropriate places'. Such tonal inflections are part of God's design: the universe contains 'the kind of antithesis that gives beauty to a poem'. Contraries clash, but God's ultimate order is not imperilled because eventually, when Christ atones for man's fall, evil will be put to good use. Augustine quotes an epistle by Paul, who uses an elaborate rhetorical antithesis to describe the paradoxes of our downcast, uplifted fate – dying yet alive, grieving but joyful, possessing at once nothing and everything. The world's history is directed by just such a dialectic, which Augustine calls 'a kind of eloquence in events, instead of in words'. Christian creation calls for art to mimic its metaphysical battles. Angels and grimacing devils crowd together in the portals of Gothic cathedrals. Tragedy and comedy alternate – as Dickens said when explaining the plot of *Oliver Twist* – like the layers of streaky bacon.

Augustine relied on allegory to bring together the opposed ends of the creation: it took physical happenings and disclosed spiritual portents within them, or transformed tragedy into a divine comedy. The analogies between Old and New Testaments vouched for the consistency of God, whose attitude to the world would otherwise look violently unstable. The deluge that overwhelmed all men except Noah and his family could be explained as a prophecy of salvation, with the unleashed waters prefiguring Christian baptism. Was Augustine eliciting the truth or arranging hypothetical patterns, as literary critics do when tussling with a recalcitrant text? Allegory found it only too easy to change a wrathful God into a forgiving father. But a contradiction remains, since it was supposedly God's love that prompted him to sacrifice his only begotten son. The allegorical correspondences admit that creativity and destruction overlap. God serially creates, annihilates, and recreates. He gives life, takes it away, then decides that death must die because it too is another new beginning. Isaiah puts a confession of these mixed motives into God's mouth, and has him say 'I form the light, and create darkness: I make peace, and create evil: I the Lord do all these things'.

Left to its own devices, the Bible does not worry about establishing an authorized version of God's plan. The message is infinitely adaptable; variant readings give the text extra chances for survival by reciting the same events in different ways. The story of creation is recreated as early as the second chapter of Genesis. At first, God makes man and woman simultaneously, or perhaps merges the genders in one composite body: 'male and female created he them'. The second chapter gives a different account of the third day, when the earth exhales a mist and man is created from the humid, pliable dust. This time he is alone, unaccompanied by woman; Eve appears only after Adam feels the need for 'an help meet for him'. Did he simply require a gardening assistant? Unlike Frankenstein's monster, he does not request a sexual partner. Augustine disparaged the notion that Eve was intended as a conversationalist; her function surely was reproductive. Yet why then did a foreknowing God not give man a wife immediately? And why, if Adam gave birth to Eve, did she emerge from his side? Athene sprang from the head of Zeus, as Milton's Sin does from the head of Satan. But an Eve made from Adam's brain would be his mental equal, which Christian doctrine did not permit. The allegorists pointed out that the spare rib lay near the heart and under the arm, signifying that Adam was expected to cradle and shelter his dependent companion.

During the seventeenth century, Isaac La Peyrère proposed that Genesis described two separate acts of creation. In the first chapter, God invented the human species. In the second, after a long evolutionary lapse, he returned to make two specific individuals, who were singled out by name because they were destined to be the ancestors of the children of Israel. A creator who keeps on changing his mind, even subjecting Adam's sexual arrangements to revision, is hard to accredit; the story is being rewritten and augmented by successive recreators, who interpret it to suit themselves. The Bible tries to make a myth that will account for the paradoxes of creation, abridging the distance between nothing and something, mental conception and physical birth. The aim was to make sense of two inconceivable events: the origin of species, and before that the origin of the world. There must be a story that can relate the void to the world, the word to the flesh. But the attempt is always frustrated; the myth is broken up to be pieced together again in a new way.

Problems left unresolved were passed on to the New Testament, where the solution is mystical. The Old Testament, altering the mechanics of copulation, attempted to explain how human beings came to exist. The New Testament describes how a god is born – but the latest permutation of the myth requires us to accept that a virgin can conceive a child. As in Genesis, different versions of the story open room for doubt. Luke's gospel euphemistically says that the angel Gabriel 'came in unto' Mary and saluted her (though he adds that she was troubled by his declaration, and 'cast in her mind' to unriddle his meaning). Matthew more directly asserts that she 'was found with child of the Holy Ghost'. The annunciating spirit was presumably male; it's easy to imagine Joseph asking his divinely favoured wife to tell him exactly how parthenogenesis works. The scriptural apocrypha admitted doubts, but hoped to allay them. St Bartholomew censured scepticism when he described the lying-in of Mary. One midwife, Zebel, undertook an examination after the birth of Jesus, and declared that Mary was still a virgin. Salome, Mary's sister, scoffed at this. She reached out to explore the disputed area, and her hand instantly withered. St Anselm granted God four different modes of creative action. He could make man without a woman, which is how he produced Adam; he could make woman from a man, as he did with Eve; he could let a man and a woman do the job for him, which occurs in sexual reproduction; and he could use a woman who remained intact, unknown to man, as when he conscripted Mary. Unbelievers may be baffled by the three non-biological options, but writers perform such feats as a matter of course. Writing to Coleridge in 1840, Charlotte Brontë described the fantastical characters who populated her made-up kingdom of Angria as 'so many Melchisedecs – without father, without mother, without descent, having neither beginning of days nor end of life': the unimmaculate progeny of her brain. Melchisedec was a priest ordained by Abraham. After the phrases quoted by Charlotte Brontë, the Letter to the Hebrews goes on to liken him to the son of God, as if Christ had prematurely revealed himself long before the agreed date of his incarnation. The novelist, cheerfully blaspheming, takes over from the divine paterfamilias and populates a personal world with undead phantoms.

The scriptural apocrypha inserted other, less legitimate stories into the gap between theological mystery and biological fact – for instance the rabbinical fable about Lilith. She was the woman created from the same clay used to manufacture Adam. But that made her his equal, and she refused to submit to him. Allegedly her crime was to rebel against the missionary position in intercourse. Muslims, remembering her unruliness, curse the man who makes the woman heaven and himself plays the earth; a woman on top can turn the universe upside down. God tried again, this time extracting Adam's rib so that the woman would recognize her inferior status. Although Lilith was replaced, she did not disappear, and the Kabbalah reconnected her to the primal family tree. A gnostic text in the *Zohar* grafted 'the young Lilith' onto the genealogy at the end of Genesis, marrying her to 'Ashmedai, the great king of the demons': God's offspring had intercourse with a devil, who thus became the creator's in-law. Bolder conjectures filled in the missing links and spied on God's sexual entanglements. One heretical tradition gave Yahweh a female counterpart who helped him engender the world. She doubles as Christ's mother and his lover, which explains gnostic reverence for Mary Magdalene, a harlot who is the conduit of esoteric illumination. If a prostitute can bear Christ's children, then we have another way of reaching across the division between divine creativity and sexual love. The Cathars, who shared the cosmic schizophrenia of the Manichees, believed that God had a pair of wives, one of whom gave birth to Christ while the other was the mother of Satan. Hence the enmity of the second son, passed over for preferment when the rule of primogeniture decreed that Christ should sit on God's right hand. The devil, expelled from heaven when he protested against his step-brother's promotion, took his revenge by making our world in his own image.

In a print made in 1795, William Blake showed *Elohim Creating Adam*, and presented the act as a sentence of death. Elohim, his face a mask of woe, hovers horizontally above the slumped Adam. The new man

Dante Gabriel
Rossetti, *Lilith*,
1868

looks stricken, emaciated, corpse-like. His rib-cage presses through his taut flesh, and a snake already twines around him. Elohim reaches out to clasp Adam's head. Instead of the quickening contact made by the hands in the Sistine Chapel, this gesture looks oppressive: the proprietorial hand planted on Adam's brow tells him what to think. Inside our heads, as Blake lamented, we carry the stringent tablets of the law. At best Elohim's gesture is a soothing reassurance, as if consoling Adam for having to awaken in this grievous, defective world. Staring into space, he grabs empty air with his other, outstretched hand: he knows that no salvation is possible. Adam's leg, coloured greenish-brown, is gnarled, knobbly and wooden, as if his body were itself the Tree of Knowledge (which explains why the snake has coiled around it): creation is a fall, nearly as fatal for the creator as for his inert subject. A second print, *Satan Exulting over Eve*, marries heaven and hell. Now it is Satan, lithe and naked except for his heroic weaponry of shield and spear, who floats just above the ground. Below him Eve lies asleep, sexually and psychologically vulnerable. The worm that twined round Adam's leg has grown into a sinuous dragon, which rests its scaly head between her breasts. The two scenes are fearfully symmetrical. God and Satan share equally in the task of creation, and between them they create a mortuary.

William Blake, *Elohim Creating Adam*, 1795– c. 1805

To imagine such scenes is an act of defiance. The ban on graven images such as the golden calf made it a sin to depict the deity. The creator was invisible, his name unutterable. Moses transcribed God's words, then smashed the tablets onto which he had carved them. Scripture was at first orally transmitted; when the Israelites began to write down their lore, they abandoned pictographs or hieroglyphs and instead used an abstract idiom that replaced things with symbols. Art could begin only when these interdictions were overcome. Hence Blake's imaginative daring. As a poet, he rewrote the myth of origins. In *The Four Zoas*, God is removed from the incarcerating world whose creation we attribute to him. Instead the Eternals charge Elohim, now identified as one of God's vigilant eyes, with the task of supervising man's mortal trials: 'They sent Elohim who created Adam to die for Satan'. As a painter, Blake challenged the ancient embargo even more directly: by visualizing gods we potentially free ourselves from them, since we can see that they are our invidious creation, the shadow cast by our moral timidity. A blood-red sun rises behind Elohim in the print, but he is not a solar force. Blake presents him as a greybeard with aghast, frightened hair. Nor does he fold his wings protectively over the world: with their ribs of bone and their thick furled layers, they look like armour, and they alarmingly resemble the webbed, finny wings of Satan in the second print. In another of Blake's prints, a glowering God who travels in a war chariot castigates the bent, elderly Adam with a rod. Not long before his death in 1827, Blake made a sketchy start on illuminating Genesis. One attempt at the first page shows Jehovah unfurling his wings above the lettered title, which is stacked in three tiers. The capitals sprout fronds and vegetative curlicues, with shrubs twining around them: how, they seem to ask, can the story of generation place a ban on a tree and the fruit it instinctively grows? Adam stands behind SIS, the syllable on the bottom tier, and with one hand reaches up to grip a scroll of mercy passed down by Christ. The document unravels elegantly, and it too resembles an organic growth. But the I, despite its wreathed top, proves opaque and stiffly obstructive; it fastens itself to Adam's waist and hangs down like a loin cloth, blocking the parts that a prudish God condemned to invisibility. The letter kills, or sterilizes. It is the spirit, proclaimed by those licentious looping tendrils in Blake's design, that gives life.

William Blake, Genesis titlepage, c. 1826

Our efforts to imagine the beginning are rebuffed, since only God knows about that moment of inception. It helps if the solemn, authoritative words of the Bible are paraphrased; it also helps if Genesis is edited, left incomplete, excluding whatever we find unacceptable. In a sequence of poems published in 1905, Rainer Maria Rilke remembers God's first word, allows him to utter a second, then sentences him to silence. Rilke's God says 'Light', which causes time to begin. Next he says 'Man', which introduces fear into the world. After that, Rilke begs God to stop talking: his foreknowledge is unbearable. Later he equalizes the relationship by pointing out that in making man God created himself. Alternatively we can go back to the first verse of Genesis, omit the verb, and leave God in suspense. This is how Duke Ellington recreated the creation in his *Concert of Sacred Music*, commissioned by Grace Cathedral on Nob Hill in San Francisco in 1965 and later performed at the Presbyterian Church on Fifth Avenue in New

York. Ellington's piano establishes an insistent rhythmic motto, picking out six notes and repeating them: this pulsation is the first sonic sign of life. After a while the saxophone makes gliding forays up and down the scale, testing the air as it flexes the same six notes. Brassy percussion contributes a thunderclap, like a distant and harmless big bang. Then the clarinet teasingly elongates the notes, spinning them out as the rest of the band grunts earthily far below. The notes are ready to turn into words, and a baritone enters to make them articulate. They match the six syllables of his pronouncement, 'In the beginning God'. He repeats the words, but does not complete the sentence; rather than leaving a bathetic pause like Stoppard's philosopher in *Jumpers*, he stops short of the verb that describes God creating heaven and earth. This God does nothing, and is no-one in particular, but serves as a useful synonym for the beginning.

The creation Ellington's singer describes is a stilled instant, a contemplative stasis. Augustine asked why God, whose dwelling-place is eternity, stooped to invent time. Music resolves that conundrum. In the hypnotic repetitions of those six notes, it stalls time and gives us the sensation of immortality. Ellington's singer does not need to add the word 'created', and when he goes on to summarize the rest of the verse he is free to alter it and even to negate Genesis. It is easier to imagine non-existence than to comprehend how existence came to be, so the singer reverts to that blank condition: his next words are 'no heaven, no earth, no nothing'. Nonentity does not bewilder or intimidate him; he is a jaunty as the indigent hero of Gershwin's *Porgy and Bess*, who happily possesses 'plenty o' nuttin''. Nothing may be preferable to the litany of somethings that Ellington's singer then enumerates, lapsing from song into speech as the piano and the bass skitter along underneath his voice – 'no mountains, no valleys, no main streets and no back alleys, no night, no day, no bills to pay, no glory and no gloom, no poverty, no Cadillacs'. Also lacking are bodyguards, credit cards, television commercials, headaches and aspirins, questions and answers. We have been catapulted forward from the beginning to the end of time, as the fresh new world gives way to the care-worn American city with its traffic jams, mercantile clamour and social frictions. The singer even jokes about an immemorial time when there was 'no bottom and no topless': this was the 1960s with its peekaboo fashions, as daring as those of Eden. Despite the humour, the baritone's long list is a plea for an uncreation. If only we could rescind the history that has accumulated between then and now!

A choir speed-reads the Bible's index, naming the books of both testaments. Half way through this recitation, an instrumental soloist intervenes. Now it is the trumpet which takes up the first six notes, forcing them to a dizzy altitude where the phrase almost falls apart into a squawk. On the

recording made at the New York performance, Ellington inserts an aside
after his trumpeter steps back from the precipice. 'That's as high as we go',
he says, and the congregation chuckles. It is an ironic victory over the prohibitions of Genesis. Like the trumpeter, we aspire to rarefied heights, and
deserve to be applauded even if we fall short. The episode identifies art with
spiritual valour; it may also allude to a biblical story that recommends art as
a means of political action. According to Joshua, the priests at the battle of
Jericho commanded the trumpeters to blow, and the walls of the besieged
city promptly tumbled down. On the heights of Nob Hill or upper Fifth
Avenue, was Ellington issuing a challenge to the proud, exclusive fortress
that Augustine called 'the city of man'?

In 1968 Ellington presented a second sacred concert at the Cathedral
of St John the Divine in New York. This time he made the uncreated world
audible. A cacophonous prelude represents chaos, 'before the Supreme Being
created order' – snarling trombones, cymbals that clash like colliding stars,
squeaky reeds that might be tuneless birds trapped in the elemental fog.
When order is imposed, it is at the behest of the Supreme Being. The choir
attributes the creation of heaven and earth to him, insisting 'There is One/
Only One/ One'. But the overlapping voices are many, so their separate
notions about a creator can only be reduced to unity if they arrive at a consensus. The process sounds tricky, and has to be taken slowly: they divide
the 'Su-pre-me Be-ing' up into syllables, suggesting that he is a modular
idea, a construction that needs to be assembled. The choir is nervous about
using the verb that the singer in the first sacred concert eliminates altogether. The difficult word is edged into second place: 'The Supreme Being/
Organized and created/ Created and organized/ Heaven and earth'. Creation remains inconceivable. Organization – familiar from sociological
treatises about corporate culture and the American 1950s, with its semi-
automated 'organization men' – takes its place. The Supreme Being is a chief
executive, who from his office on the top floor presides over a bureaucratic
distribution of functions.

The second concert does not name God until he creates Adam in his
own image. The delay entices us to reverse the proposition: perhaps Adam
dreams up an anthropomorphized deity? In Genesis, God pauses at the end
of each day to call his handiwork good. Here it is the choir which cries
'Good!' after light and dark, water and land appear from nowhere – and
when the fruit tree springs up from the soil, the choral accolade changes to
'Delicious!' Augustine conceded that when God called his world good he
equated the moral with the aesthetic; it is quite another matter to connect
goodness with pleasure, and to justify eating the apple because it tastes
good. The choir declares that it needs no proof of God's existence, and is
satisfied by a vague feeling that he is out there:

> Something 'bout believing in the creation,
> Something 'bout believing the information,
> Something 'bout believing there's just one nation
> Under GOD Almighty.

To rhyme creation with information elides the difference between myth and factual data; to rhyme both with nation links belief with the pledge of allegiance to the United States, one nation indivisible which asserts its trust in God on the dollar bill. The evasions have a slippery wit, but jazz is expert at respecting the spirit while playing infidel tricks with the letter of a text or a tune. Near the end of the concert, Ellington entitles a brief rhapsody for a vocalizing soprano 'T.G.T.T.', meaning 'Too Good To Title'. Here he adopts God's own style of self-approbation: what he liked about the piece was its irregularity, its phrases that wrong-foot pianist, singer and listener by never ending as you expect. The interlude, Ellington explained, 'violates conformity in the same way, we like to think, that Jesus Christ did'. The concert's conclusion quotes Psalm 150, which sanctifies the harp, cymbals and timbrel by dedicating them to the praise of God. But the rambunctious finale departs from the prescriptions of the holy singer David, and commands that God be praised in dance. Jubilation erupts into the cathedral's aisles; bodily energy – roused by the stratospheric trumpet – is now the creative source.

Two decades earlier, in 1947, Aaron Copland had made his own more sedate summary of the earth's first week in a pocket-sized oratorio called *In the Beginning*. A mezzo-soprano evangelizes in mid-air – unfounded, afloat, with no tonal grounding – while the chorus scurries about beneath, busily accomplishing the chores of creation and singing God's praises. There is no orchestra, so the human body has to serve as a sounding board. The oratorio ends with a joyously iterated flourish as man becomes a living soul; because the divine breath is infused into the clay manikin through the nostrils, this collective exhalation is a hymn in praise of song, which transforms resonant air into music. Choosing a female soloist, Copland replaced the authoritarian Yahweh with a maternal embodiment of the nurturing earth. He told the singer to declaim the text 'in a gentle, narrative manner, like reading a familiar and oft-told story'. The choir's compliant responses suggest a revival meeting, or the enthusiastic amateurism of a glee club: a small society comes together to celebrate its like-mindedness. The rite takes place in a country still rooted its in rural beginnings, lineally connected to Eden, which is why the setting underlines the biblical passage about man's dominion over the earth and his tilling of the ground. Copland curtails the story long before the fall, which America intended to revoke.

Five years later, Copland gave an address to the American Academy and the National Institute of Arts and Letters on 'Creativity in America'. His lecture implicitly explained the humane optimism of *In the Beginning* and reflected on its reinterpretation of Genesis. Copland told the academicians that 'the creative act is central to the life process': in a culture apparently obsessed with scientific know-how and industrial output, it supplies a precious substitute for 'the religious experience'. God's creativity has been usurped by that of the artist, who now upholds the sanctity of life and contributes to the Cold War by resisting totalitarian control. Copland believed that 'the creative act affirms the individual and gives value to the individual', so that 'the man who lives the creative life' is a symbol of 'the free man'. Ellington's *Second Sacred Concert* broadcast the same political creed: the choir praises freedom, and translates the word into nineteen languages, including Russian and Chinese. Jazz, as in Ellington's comment about Christ the nonconformist, signals an American refusal to be cowed by traditional rules. In 1947 Jean-Paul Sartre remembered listening to a jazz band in a New York bar. The fat trumpeter and the bass player slapping the strings spoke, Sartre thought, 'to the best part of you, the toughest, the freest', convincing you to stop waiting for melodic repetitions and to relish the improvisatory moment. Sartre noticed that the musicians tormented their instruments: the trombone sweated, the piano rattled like a skeleton. Copland's lecture accounts for this nervous hysteria, and for the dazzled hubbub when the soloist in *In the Beginning* describes the lights God placed in the sky. Her announcement excites a sudden, syncopated frenzy in the choir, as if the neon starburst above Times Square had suddenly been switched on. The singers run away with the solemn biblical text, and remind us that the proper response to these events is amazement, even stupefaction. America is a new beginning, which means that for Copland the American artist is obliged to 'reinvent the creative process for himself alone'. Did God also suffer from vertigo when, having decided that the world would begin right now, he looked at the void and pondered his options?

Genesis is best seen as a trial run, and each of us is free to find a more suitably personal route back to the beginning. An autocrat with unlimited funds and an army of slave labourers can copy God's creative feat. In 1703 Peter the Great decreed that a city should be built in a swamp near the Gulf of Finland. A sycophantic minister, Gavrila Golinkov, praised him for causing the bog to solidify and conjuring the polychrome classical mirage of St Petersburg 'from nothingness into being'. The tsar called the place 'our very own northern Eden', and adorned it with fruit trees imported from Persia, which was allegedly the site of the first paradise. The myth can be adapted to other latitudes, and to other, less madly dictatorial whims. In 1968 the photographer Jeff Carter published a book about the surf beaches of Australia's east coast. Introducing it, he revised Genesis to take account of a continent not created by the God of the northern

hemisphere. Carter's cosmology has a drawling impudence: 'In the beginning there were waves. Then land appeared and the waves beat on the land.
After some time man came on the scene and eventually he rode upon the
waves.' God is absent; water and earth negotiate their own agreement,
despite the concussion of those breakers. The chronology is happily vague
about man's arrival in the world, and it exempts him from having to a suffer
a fall. On the contrary, he erects himself and – though there must have been
many spills before he learned to maintain his balance – bestrides the ocean
on a surfboard. Carter proceeds directly from the first, fallible Adam to his
resurrected counterpart in the New Testament, who is not alone in walking
on water.

The creation must have been hard work. God had to calculate planetary orbits and test geometrical ratios with his compasses. The aesthetic
impulse is friskier, freer, more hedonistic. In Umberto Eco's *The Name of the
Rose*, a seditious Egyptian alchemist attributes the creation of the world to a
spasm of 'divine laughter'. Such unorthodoxy scandalizes the monastic
librarians in Eco's novel, but Vladimir Nabokov understood – as he declared
in a lecture on Dostoevsky – that art is 'a divine game'. Making up rules that
only have force if you consent to believe in them, it resembled the other
games that Nabokov played: tennis, boxing, chess. Hence his objections to
the laborious God of Genesis, whom he blamed for the industrial enslavement of modern society.

Re-examining creativity, Nabokov's autobiography *Speak, Memory*
reproves this dour God and the social or psychological determinists who
copy him. Near the end, he observes his young son at play and smiles at the
human impulse to reshape the earth, which we refuse to leave as God made
it. We dig holes or build sandcastles; some of us once used our forks to lay
down highways through valleys of mashed potato, or hollowed out lakes
and flooded them with gravy. Everyone feels the need 'to act upon a friable
environment'. Only Marxists or corpses, as Nabokov adds, lie back and wait
for the environment to fashion them. The larky, frivolous enjoyment of
freedom makes Nabokov repudiate the doom-laden rigours of Darwinian
selection. The moths and butterflies he netted during his Russian boyhood
displayed an aesthetic credo on their wings, which were patterned with a
perfection and intricacy 'usually associated with man-wrought things'.
Darwin saw such 'mysteries of mimicry' as camouflage, designed to facilitate
the struggle for life. But for Nabokov they were 'a form of magic', as
enchanting and pleasantly deceptive as the larger world which his butterflies adorned. These flitting creatures reminded him of paradise, before
Adam was expelled and sentenced to a life of dreary work. Children still live
in that idle, ruminative garden; so do artists, who prolong the activity of play
into adulthood. Watching 'the mind's birth' in his infant son, who views

nature with eyes full of wonder, Nabokov magnificently rewrites the myth of cultural and intellectual beginnings. He announces that 'Homo poeticus' is the ancestor and begetter of 'Homo sapiens', derides Darwin's account of our simian origins, and dismisses both the *Communist Manifesto* and the Bible: 'The curse of battle and toil leads man back to the boar, to the grunting beast's crazy obsession with the search for food. ... Toilers of the world, disband! Old books are wrong. The world was made on a Sunday.'

Augustine, whose God performed no physical work and therefore needed no weekly respite, was bothered by Sunday observance. He interpreted the day of rest as a state of blissful acceptance, and came close to describing it as an aesthetic privilege: we take our repose in God as in a house, and the metaphor is even apter because, as he says, 'the house makes the inhabitants glad by reason of its beauty'. While relaxing, we can play with numbers, since Augustine's celestial mathematics explains why the creation took precisely six days. Six is 'the number of perfection', made up of the sum of its parts. One sixth of it is 1, one third is 2, one half is 3, and $1 + 2 + 3 = 6$. For Nabokov, the holy day is a true holiday, and God's creative efforts suggest the kind of pastime we might indulge in on a Sunday afternoon. In an article about sport published in 1925, Nabokov passes with a sudden, breath-taking leap from a tennis match to the explosive birth of the cosmos. He describes an athlete propelling himself towards the net to lob the ball; as his muscles strain and he bounces off the ground, he mutates into 'the marvellous juggler who tosses the planets of the universe from hand to hand in an unbroken, sparkling parabola'.

On the ceiling of the Vatican loggia, this is exactly how Raphael represented God creating and positioning the sun and moon. Raphael's God rests in mid-air as if on a thermal gust, gently balancing the planets in his hands; having arrived at a pleasing arrangement, he kicks up the heels of his bare feet in exhilaration. Einstein, distressed by the indeterminacy of quantum mechanics, grumbled that God did not play dice; his colleague Niels Bohr wisely chided him for giving God orders. Science may disapprove, but art favours the idea of a deity for whom creation is not a chore but a pleasure, a display of virtuosity, and a game of exhilarating chance.

# 3
# OUT OF THE CHASM

In the early 1850s, the Boston accountant Thomas Bulfinch set out to take stock of the legends in which men first speculated about their origins. He began with what he called the 'lyrical history' of the Hebrews, then advanced to Greek mythology. Introducing the story of Prometheus, he acknowledged that 'The creation of the world is a problem naturally fitted to excite the liveliest interest of man, its inhabitant'. But he felt sorry for the Greeks, who – lacking reliable 'information on the subject, which we derive from the pages of scripture' – reduced the primal story to a series of rowdy, licentious fables. In their myths they supposed that, before Heaven and Earth were created, all matter was compounded in a discordant, amorphous Chaos. At last a tidy-minded deity separated the embroiled elements and smoothed out the earth to make it habitable. Ovid, retelling the story at the start of his *Metamorphoses*, fudged the identity of the god who intervenes. That deity remains anonymous, and Bulfinch suggested that he should perhaps be designated as 'a natural force of a higher kind'. Does it matter if the force is a fatherly potentate or a black hole?

Positivists like Bulfinch tried to squeeze the long and painfully gradual ordeal of evolution into the spare time left over during God's busy creative week. They assumed that the gigantic animals killed off by some obscure catastrophe must have flourished between the first and second verses of the opening chapter. Geology purportedly confirmed the myth that acclaimed man as the last and highest creation, because human remains had so far only been found in alluvial soil; this convinced the Victorian theologian Robert Jamieson that we could not be related to the ourang-utan. For Jamieson, Moses was a 'sacred historian', whose summary of the first week could be reconciled with the most up-to-date ordering of the sciences. He praised the 'regular and admirable gradation in all parts of the creative work' that he found in the story of God's step-by-step labours. First comes geology, which, when God establishes the dry land, gives the world its foundation. After that, Moses lays the ground for the science of botany: God next makes grass, herbs and trees grow from the earth. Finally we arrive at zoology, as God proceeds upwards from aquatics to terrestrials and ends with 'rationals, viz. man'. Indignantly denying that Genesis should be read as a myth, Jamieson called it 'a history in miniature of the world's creation'.

Jean-Leon
Gerome,
*Pygmalion and
Galatea*, 1890

Greek philosophers were less bothered about factual veracity. Protagoras in the fifth century AD began his treatise *On the Gods* by breezily conceding that he was unsure whether or not those hypothetical beings existed. In one of Plato's dialogues, Protagoras offers to expatiate on 'the original state of things', but first asks Socrates whether he prefers to hear a fable or a rational, deductive discourse. Socrates smilingly chooses 'mythos' not 'logos', so Protagoras goes on to recite the story of Prometheus. In his version, the creation of our species is a muddled farce. Prometheus shares the task with his brother Epimetheus, a dim-witted wastrel: allegorically, they represent Forethought and Afterthought. Epimetheus scrupulously adapts the lower animals for the lives they will have to lead, equipping some with wings and others with hooves or claws. But he forgets about man, who is left naked, unshod and unarmed. Prometheus, thinking ahead, gives fire stolen from the hearth of Zeus to the human race, infusing us with a spark of divinity. Creation here is a series of quick-witted improvisations, false starts and lucky escapes – truer to our experience of the world than Genesis with its inescapable predestination.

The Greek gods were an afterthought; they did not preside at the beginning, and were therefore not responsible for it. Zeus may have fathered the other gods, but he in turn – unlike the solitary, self-begotten God of Genesis – had parents, Kronos and Rhea. They were Titans, born from the marital coupling of Heaven and Earth after they issued from Chaos. A Greek reinterpretation of Genesis would say that in the beginning Heaven and Earth created God. In the Bible, the ambiguous verb evokes a kind of making that violates biological norms. In Greek myth, creation can only mean sexual reproduction. The primal beings in the Greek cosmos are Earth, dark Erebos, and flaming Eros, the compulsive 'dissolver of flesh' as Hesiod calls him in his *Theogony*. Eros hatches from the egg of Night, which floats on Chaos. He then aims an arrow at the inert, insentient world, or warms it with his torch; it soon awakes to life. Unlike his biblical equivalent, Zeus does not venture to organize the formless void. How could he, since he is the offspring of that Chaos, belonging to the third generation it has spawned?

Jamieson refused to accept that Genesis might be what he called a 'creation song'. Yet the first Greek poet was proud to create the gods by singing about them. Hesiod's *Theogony*, which dates from the eighth century BC, begins by addressing the muses as they dance on Helicon, a mountain conveniently close to his home in Boeotia – though he admits that they were born on Olympus, and are merely paying him a visit. They dictate songs to him, but as the poem starts he dismisses them, asking them to bless his verse as they depart. Only then, on his own initiative, does he go on to describe the world before time began. Creation is a product of the sexual urges of the elements and the lecherous rapacity of the gods, but Hesiod presents himself as the initial procreator who conjures an intelligible world out of Chaos. The place of origins is tagged by a word that contains its own recessive depths. Etymologically, chaos has links with a Greek verb meaning to yawn or to gape open, like a chasm. A less trustworthy guess about the word's origins led the stoics to identify it with water; they thought of chaos as the liquid state that followed the periodic destruction of the universe by fire. Another analogue of chaos is gas, a word coined during the 1640s by Johann Baptista van Helmont, a mystically minded chemist from in Brussels who gave a 'new name' to 'this Spirit, unknown hitherto'. Helmont studied the gas we know as carbon dioxide, which could be emitted – as he discovered – by belches: the human body also contains turbulent caverns. Aptly, the molecular instability of gas prompted the chaos theory formulated by contemporary cosmologists, who return us to Hesiod. The ancient myth is also confirmed by modern astrophysics, which presumes that the universe began when clouds of gas condensed into stars.

Aristotle considered Chaos to be an incohate state, since its substance had not yet been parcelled out into form. Ovid in *Metamorphoses* described the maker of the cosmos clarifying it, shaping it into the determinate beings which stock our world. The Latin church fathers demonized Chaos. In *Paradise Lost*, Satan flies through it on his way to Eden, lunging into gulfs of choppy air, and when Sin invades the realm of Erebos in Book II of *Paradise Lost*, she finds an anarchic ocean fought over by 'Night/ And *Chaos*, Ancestors of Nature'. Chaos cannot be exterminated; gods may no longer want to dabble in it, but poets do. For Hesiod, Chaos was a uterine source. He could only conceive of the world's origins by imagining acts of fertilization and fruition, more or less perverse. In the *Theogony*, a female Earth gives birth to a male Heaven so she can be covered by him. Her body also eruptively brings forth the mountains and – after an extra-marital liaison – decants the sea. Hesiod's chasm is a nuptial couch, pummelled by its agitated occupants. During the battle between the Olympian gods and the Titans, the thunderbolts of Zeus ignite above the chasm, as if 'Earth and broad Heaven above were coming together' in a violent geological and galactic orgasm. The Bible's divine dynasty reproduces itself asexually: hence the Arian controversy over God's begetting of Christ. The classical gods, however, are procreative energies. For them the process of creation is never immaculate or free from mishap; the first family is embroiled in an unending civil war. Earth bears Heaven a litter of mis-shapen sons with supernumerary limbs and plural heads. The dismayed father shoves them back into Earth, reversing their birth. They skulk in a cavern, and their mother gives them a sickle with which they can hack their way free. Kronos waits for Heaven to bed down with Earth at night and then slices off the genitals of his progenitor. To be born is not enough. We need to invent ourselves, and we do so by turning against our parents. In art too, as Picasso said, you must kill your father.

But destruction is another form of creation: matter is inextinguishable, and its constituents undergo recombination. The shower of blood impregnates Earth, who delivers a new breed of Giants and Furies; and Heaven's private parts do not disappear when Kronos throws them into the sea, for they acquire a carapace of white spermatic foam, inside which a female child grows. This is Aphrodite, whose name means 'formed in foam'. Another stretched verbal definition explains her amorous character. She is 'genial' or amiable because she derives from her father's genitalia; the idea of genius lurks somewhere in the vicinity. Genealogy is determined by etymology, and gods are a by-product of this verbal plethora: one being, who probably never existed, acquires a kaleidoscopic array of different names. Why not cherish the poetic ingenuity that transforms a word into a divine force? Thomas Carlyle did so when discussing the *Edda* in his lectures *On Heroes, Hero-Worship and the Heroic in History*. Jacob Grimm, the analyst of Nordic folk tales, had concluded that Odin, the god of the sagas, was merely the personified form of an Icelandic word for movement. 'We cannot annihilate a man for etymologies like that!' protested Carlyle. We have still less reason to annihilate a god who, like language, is our creation.

The feuds of Hesiod's primal beings rage on in the next generation. Kronos swallows his children when they emerge from the womb of Rhea, hoping to thwart the prophecy that says he will be defeated by one of his own sons (who is of course Zeus). Eventually he regurgitates the infants stowed in his cud, and finds that Rhea has deluded him by replacing the newborn Zeus with a stone. Later Zeus, warned of his wife's jealousy, swallows his mistress Metis and secretes her in his own belly for safekeeping. Metis gives birth in his stomach, and their daughter Athene battles upwards in search of an exit. She is born through his brow, rather than taking the usual route, so she comes to represent intelligence. The fable can also refer to artistic creation: like Frankenstein's attic, the poet's womb is in the head. Or is the work of art a deluding simulation of life, as other myths imply? To punish Prometheus, Zeus dreams up a woman called Pandora, moulded from earth by Haephestus, dressed and crowned by Athene. She is a treacherous effigy; even the animals carved on her diadem look like living creatures. The final acts of coition in the *Theogony* occur when Odysseus is seduced by Circe and Calypso on his way home from the war. Both unions are fruitful. Two unearthly beings make love to a mortal man, engendering children whose parentage is partly supernatural; the artist – communing with a power that seems outside him and beyond his control, as Hesiod does when the muses teach him how to sing – produces an object that is immune to death.

Because these are wayward variants on the straightforward routine of breeding, monstrous births must be expected. Echidna is a merger of nymph and serpent; she in turn brings forth Hydra, whose heads sprout back as fast as they are sliced off, and the dog Cerberus. Chimaera has three bodies, a lion in front, a snake behind and a goat in between. This composite beast metamorphoses into the idea of the chimera, and evokes an impossibility that can be tantalizing as well as ghastly. The young Frankenstein, beguiled by alchemy, pictures 'chimeras of boundless grandeur', and is warned by a disapproving teacher that 'the elixir of life is a chimera'. In Balzac's mystical allegory *Séraphîta*, Hesiod's mutant has changed to a benign, uplifting agency, reprieving artists from their dull attachment to reality. The transports of fantasy, Balzac says, carry away 'a philosopher or a poet on Chimaera's wings', and that principle allows Balzac to accompany his transubstantiated heroine to heaven. What matters now is not Chimaera's grotesque collection of torsos; the important thing is that the creature flies, and can teach human beings how to do so. This is why Des Esseintes, the neurotic aesthete in J.-K. Huysmans' novel *À Rebours*, keeps a Chimaera made from terracotta as a domestic pet, pairing it with a small Sphinx in black marble. He places them at opposite ends of his darkened bedroom, and hires a ventriloquist to project her voice into them. The Sphinx rails at the bristling, wild-eyed Chimaera, which defiantly announces that it seeks 'new perfumes, larger blossoms, pleasures still untasted'. Its monstrosity accords with the dandy's own controversion of nature; it beckons him to trespass beyond the boundaries of thought, to pursue an ideal 'in the misty upper regions of art'.

Gustave Moreau, *Chimaera*

Having begun as a horror, Chimaera relaxes into a imaginary wraith, a synonym for art and invention. In Puccini's *La Bohème*, the poet Rodolfo and the seamstress Mimì confide in each other about their dreams. His 'sogni e chimeri' are fantasies about wealth and fame, the delusions of the aspiring writer. She takes up the phrase but interprets it differently: she loves soft, gentle things redolent of dreams and chimeras, substitutes for the poetry she absorbs from nature not from books – 'di sogni e di chimeri, quelle cose che han nome poesia'. She interrupts her aria to ask if he understands her; of course he does. In 1902 the architect Vladislav Horodetsky built himself a grey concrete villa in Kiev, which came to be known as 'the House with Chimaeras' because of the fantastical beasts that protruded from its walls and writhed on its roof. Elephants and rhineroci guard the entrances with their tusks, snakes coil around the drainpipes, and frogs squat between mermaids flaunting their tails above the windows. The chimerical menagerie is benign: recently the house was used as a hospital, and there are plans to make it a residence for the Ukrainian president.

In the fifth century BC, Empedocles suggested that monsters like these were refugees from Chaos. He imagined a primordial time when parts had not yet cohered into wholes: faces wandered without necks, arms lacked shoulders, eyes had no foreheads to be set in. These bits and pieces conjoined randomly, miscalculating so that some creatures had two heads or four breasts. Men got mixed up with bulls, or androgynously forgot to make a choice between sexes. Eventually, guided by the cosmic force of love, they all settled into the forms that typically and properly suited them, and acquired the knack of sexual reproduction. When in about 55 BC Lucretius explained the material universe in *On the Nature of Things*, he was able to report that these regressive ogres had died out. They perished because nature denied them partners, so they could not increase and multiply: this is why Frankenstein's creature so angrily demands a bride. Lucretius dismissed Chimaera as a fantasy. He thought that images were films that had peeled off the surface of things, like shed skins. Spectral, sylph-like, these replicas had a flimsy materiality, and Lucretius reckoned that collisions must sometimes occur between them. Suppose the image of a man had bumped into that of a horse; muddled up together, they would produce the centaur. Mermaids and all other 'chimerical creatures' came, he concluded, from the superimposition of such wraiths. The phantoms must have coupled in the air, which is how their offspring 'enter the mind'. Lucretius refused to admit that they might have their origin within us: the truth is that the imagination creates them, rather than absorbing them from outside. For Horace, who wrote his treatise on the art of poetry a few decades later, the monsters had dwindled into harmless verbal hybrids. He warned poets against the miscegenation of metaphors, which produced results that were as hideous as a man's head grafted onto a horse's neck or a woman's trunk attached to the nether parts of a fish. Such disparate images reminded Horace of 'a sick man's dreams'. But he gave artists his grudging permission to revise biological rules. 'Painters and poets', he conceded, 'traditionally have the prerogative of daring anything.'

The founding myths of civilization concern heroes who exterminate monsters, like Oedipus outwitting the Sphinx or St George slaying the dragon.

The monster represents our lowly animal nature, or a state of existence that is formless, disorganized, unworthy; its death makes possible the genesis of a true humanity. Freud hung a print of the Sphinx in his Viennese consulting room, as a tribute to the purgative mission of Oedipus. Rulers with a ruthless sense of humour sometimes collect monsters, to advertise the completion of the civilizing mission: in the early eighteenth century, Tsar Peter the Great assembled a personal zoo of taxidermically-treated or bottled freaks, including a lamb with eight legs, lopsided babies with an excess

Jean-Auguste-Dominique Ingres, *Oedipus and the Sphinx, c.* 1826

of heads or topsyturvy organs, and another infant which, exemplifying Horace's mismatched metaphor, had a fish's scaly tail. At the Moscow show trials in 1938, Stalin's prosecutor accused the propagandist Bukharin of being 'an accursed cross between a fox and a pig'. That abuse made the verdict inevitable: though the charge of counter-revolutionary activity was false, Bukharin was condemned and shot. But art inverts the executive or judicial fable, and would rather create monsters than kill them. An engraving in Goya's *Los Caprichos* shows a writer slumped at his desk, cradling his head in his hands. A menagerie of bats, cats and nocturnal birds with savage beaks menacingly rears behind him: these are his feral familiars, who take over from Hesiod's tamer muses. Goya's caption warns that 'The sleep of reason produces monsters'. He added a more cautious, Horation recipe for creativity: if fantasy is combined with reason it can be the mother of the arts and the origin of marvels, not gruesome perversions. In 1895 Alfred Jarry – who created a rampant, inarticulate, domestic ogre in his play *Ubu roi* – defended monstrosity as evidence of creative vigour. He regretted that it was 'common usage to call "monster" an unfamiliar concord of dissonant elements: the Centaur, the Chimaera are thus defined for those without understanding'. He had his own opinion about the aesthetic value of such freaks, and declared 'I call "monster" all original inexhaustible beauty'.

Francisco de Goya, 'Sleep of Reason' from the *Caprichos* series, 1797–8

Gods and monsters are closely akin, and when one class of unnatural beings is reduced to a figure of speech, the same inevitably happens to the other. Lucretius begins *On the Nature of Things* with the customary religious dedication, thanking the 'mother of Aeneas ... life-giving Venus' for her sponsorship. But his worship of this bountiful female creator is qualified: she is credited with the conception of all living creatures, but she did not invent them. Hesiod's Aphrodite was a personified word; Venus, the equivalent goddess in the Roman pantheon, is a useful fiction. She coaxes us to reproduce our kind and thus saves the race from extinction, but 'what we call Venus' – as Lucretius sceptically puts it – is a bodily urge or itch, not the prompting of some holy procurer. Just as Chimaera opens out into the teasing notion of the chimerical, so Venus has become the venereal. Her creative cunning resembles literary artistry. Explaining inherited characteristics, Lucretius says that our bodies contain an 'ancestral stock' of 'latent seeds', genes that are ready to be reactivated whenever the genial goddess pleases. 'From these, Venus evokes a random assortment of characters': like a novelist or a romancer, she amuses herself by combining characteristics in new ways to produce unprecedented individuals, whom she then entangles in elaborate plots.

When Lucretius considers the problem of origins that later puzzled Mary Shelley, he suggests that the gods might be merely a mental error, the product of a rudimentary misunderstanding. 'Nothing', he declares, 'can ever be created by divine power out of nothing', and things come into being 'without the aid of gods'. At the end of the seventeenth century Dryden translated Ovid's digest of Lucretius, and made the obsolescence of the gods pointedly explicit. Dryden wrote after decades of political unrest, during which the monarchy had been abolished and then restored; one revolution led to an act of regicide, a second more peaceably swapped dynasties. Inserting a simile about the flux of time that has no precedent in Lucretius or in Ovid, Dryden remarks that 'former Things/ Are set aside, like abdicated kings'. Kings, as his countrymen had demonstrated between 1641 and 1688, were temporary hirelings who could be sacked, killed, or imported from abroad. They had lost their aura of sanctity, because no deity upheld their divine right to rule.

In the absence of gods, Lucretius is unable to identify a moment when our world had 'a birth and a beginning'. The universe is limitless. This leaves no room for the God of Genesis, who stands outside our world and fixes its limits. Power belongs to nature, which has its own implacable laws and will not tolerate interference by 'proud masters' resident on a sacred mountain or in some invisible heaven. Lucretius traces life to its germs, to the seeds that generate it or to the atoms – matter's minutiae, granules of being that cannot be further divided or changed – that interlink in what he sees as an 'ardent embrace'. A divine creation is implausible, because the gods had no model for it: how could they have thought up the prototype for the human race? Everything depends on the chaotic confluence of atoms, which experiment with casual, random combinations. The shock as those propulsive pellets clattered against one another was almost audible to Lucretius, and he feared that the world's bastions would one day wear out, 'unable to endure the shock of jarring motion'. Hurricanes worried him because they were a preview of the catastrophe awaiting us, when creation would be ingurgitated all over again by the chasm. The earth, he fancied, might finally vanish 'into the abyss and, robbed of its foundation, the whole world in a wild chaotic welter may follow it to perdition'. Meanwhile he admired the frugal housekeeping of nature, which conserves its seeds, repairs the damage they have suffered, and outfits them for existence in another form: it 'allows nothing to be born without the aid of another's death'. Gods are supposed to save us from death, guaranteeing eternal life to their favourites. Lucretius dismisses that hope, but reassuringly shows death to be fruitful, pregnant with new growth. The earth is both womb and crypt. He did not exempt his own philosophical poem from the cruel depredations of nature. The elements ruthlessly atomize trees or animals and then reconstitute them; Lucretius admits that his words too are fragile, like specks of dust. The letters he has arranged in a certain order are not indissolubly glued together, and if you jumble them up and make new compounds, they will happily say something Lucretius never intended. He knows better than to protest at their indifference, or to lament his redundancy.

Nature for him resembled a food chain. Landscapes are absorbed into the cattle that graze in them; we absorb the cattle; our bodies, once we discard them, are perhaps fed on by predators or absorbed into the bodies of birds. Explaining how insentient atoms generate sentient life, Lucretius denies that the change is the result of 'some creative process comparable to birth'. Instead 'birth and transformation occur only as the result of union and combination'. Tamora in Shakespeare's *Titus Andronicus* graduates through these Lucretian stages. She gives birth to her sons, and nourishes them from her body. Then she feasts on them when she eats the pie containing their minced remains. After this she is killed and thrown out to fatten 'beasts and birds of prey'. The cyclical economy of classical myth follows bodies through a succession of lives, deaths and rebirths. Such stories cannot trace our lineage back to the beginning as Genesis does, because they doubt that there ever was a beginning. What fascinates the myth-makers is the mystery of recreation, as the scrambled atoms settle into new shapes.

These rotations, which in Lucretius were an edict of physics, supplied Ovid with the tales of erotic pursuit collected in *Metamorphoses*. Scylla, wooed by the merman Glaucus, is disconcerted to see that his body concludes in a writhing fish, and cannot tell if he is a monster or a god. For Lucretius, both creatures were metaphors, verbal illusions; for Ovid, they were metamorphic experiments. Ovid admits that he has no precise information about the cosmic designer who made the earth firm, brightened the sky, and pacified the insurgent elements. But he recognizes that human beings, using the occult power we call art, can perform similar feats, or even reverse the harmonizing decrees of that first anonymous god. Medea, deploying her 'magic arts' when Jason deserts her, boasts that she can direct the winds, make rocks and trees cast off their inertia, and compel rivers to run backwards. We may not be able to create, but we can alter what already exists – or at least revise the way we see it. Metamorphosis is one of literature's most compelling motives; metaphor does the transforming. In his eighteenth sonnet, Shakespeare compares his beloved to a summer's day. The fit is not exact because she is actually lovelier, but the act of comparison recreates both the person and the season. Only a brave poet dares to do without metaphor. Cole Porter in one of his songs tells the object of his affection 'You don't remind me' – although the singer then goes on to list the things that his incomparable lover supposedly does not resemble: an iris in spring, dawn in the mountains, a breeze on the bay.

Although Ovid's characters commute between species and scuttle up and down the hierarchy of being, they all begin as outgrowths of nature. His myths are invented to explain the genesis of the physical world. Adonis is gored by a boar, but a flower blooms from the blood he sheds, just as the blood from Medusa's severed head congeals into a coral reef. Myrrha, impregnated by her father, runs off in quest of camouflage to conceal her shame. Earth lets her put down roots and changes her to a tree; her tears – secreted as gummy myrrh – drip through the wood, and the bark splits open to let out her child. When Hermaphroditus rejects the nymph Salmacis, she pleads for them never to be parted. Her prayer is answered and their bodies merge, as if a gardener had grafted them onto each other. These vegetative loves pay tribute to a creativity that is self-seeding as plants are, not dependent on the pairing of opposites that animals must arrange. In their glorious implausibility, the metamorphoses proclaim the power of imagination to flout natural rules. Daphne escapes from the importunate Apollo by turning into a laurel tree; inside the trunk, her heart can still be heard beating. Often the metamorphoses preserve life, but they can also violently deform or destroy it. During the battle of the Centaurs and Lapiths, the warriors rearrange one anothers' faces like spiteful caricaturists. Eyes are ejected from sockets, a nose is wedged inside a mouth, a battered chin sinks into its owner's chest. Philip Sidney underlined the vengeful artistry of this episode in his romance *Arcadia*. A painter who has taken Ovid's battle as his subject conducts research by straying into combat, where he hopes to collect images of carnage and concussion. But both his hands are sliced off in the fray, so he returns 'well skilled in wounds' but unable 'to perform his skill'.

In Ovid's stories, the ultimate metamorphosis occurs when nature changes into art. Syrinx, chased by Pan, foils him by turning into a clump of reeds. The wind rustles through them and makes them plaintively sing. Pan cuts them, waxes them, blows through them, and has a musical souvenir of the elusive nymph. Daedalus escapes from his exile on Crete by making a bolder use of the air. He arranges rows of feathers, copying the lay-out of the Pan pipe with its reeds of graduated length, then sews them together and glues them with wax. The invention kills his son Icarus, who flies too close to the sun and tumbles back to earth when the wax melts. Daedalus buries the boy, watched by a partridge which is a new creation, the only one of its kind, the result of another recent metamorphosis. The bird is Daedalus's transmogrified nephew, who preociously invented the saw and was killed for his presumption. James Joyce called Daedalus an artificer, since art requires gadgets, tools, technological aids, which interfere with nature's laws and help us to untether ourselves from the earth. Vasari honoured the Greeks for thinking up the paint brush; the pen may not be mightier than the sword, but it is a nobler creation.

Later in *Metamorphoses*, Thetis uses her own tricky arts when wrestling with Peleus, and changes from a bird to a tree to a tigress. For Iris Murdoch, such exploratory forays were the prerogative of the novelist, who must be able to slip into other identities and sample other relationships as if trying on dresses. To cheer up her perplexed husband John Bayley, she repeated the advice of Proteus, who told Peleus to fasten his hold on the slippery nymph and wait for her to resume her original form. A more alarming variant of this whirligig talent appears in the story of Morpheus, a son of Sleep whose special gift is for impersonating men. One of his brothers, Phantasos, is adept at passing himself off as a rock, a tree or any inanimate object, while a third sibling can assume the guise of a bird, beast or snake. Morpheus morphs into the likeness of the drowned Ceyx, and visits his widow Alcyone in a dream. Fantasy is a sinister power of usurpation, which replaces the daylit world with a nocturnal simulation. Like an actor or any other artist, Morpheus is a counterfeiter: the bereft Alcyone thinks he is weeping genuine tears. The story of Midas mocks art's precious gilding of reality. The king is gratified when his magic touch turns a clod of soil to a block of gold, and he pluto-cratically redecorates his palace by laying hands on the stone columns. Disillusionment sets in when he reaches for food. Bread hardens to an unwholesome ingot, wine curdles into molten metal. The oysters Matisse painted are inedible, and who would accept a portrait by Rembrandt or a Shakespeare sonnet as a substitute for a living loved one? We are cheated by replicas, like the filmy images of Lucretius (who, when attempting to account for visions like that which appears to Alcyone, invents the idea of the cinema: the films, he proposes, succeed each other at high speed, so it looks as if a static form is moving and alive). Although Ovid's Medea says that her magic has raised the dead, art cannot supply us with the revivified presence that, like grieving Alcyone, we long for. Instead it artificially ani-mates spectres, which perform a dance of death inside our heads.

Or else art creates a representation that is lifelike but lacks life: a statue. Medusa possesses this malevolent aesthetic power, and her glance can instantly turn a man to stone. Perseus vanquishes her by adopting the devious policy of artists, who approach life indirectly. He looks only at her reflection in his shield, viewing the world through the glaze of art. Though he escapes petrification, his doting gaze imposes this fate on others: when he first sees the chained Andromeda, he takes her to be a marble statue. Gods in *Metamorphoses* often find themselves in love with trees or bears or clouds, but the most poignant and frustrating of the infatuations described by Ovid is the creator's desire to embrace a work of art. The loves of the gods bestraddle separate species; this love attempts to reach across the wider gap between life and death. Pygmalion was a Cypriot king who, convinced he was a demigod, took a statue of Venus as his consort. The original anecdote laughed at the hubris of monarchy. Ovid, however, changed the political case-history into a fable about artistic creativity, erotic wishfulness, and the relationship between them. His Pygmalion is a sculptor who carves a statue from ivory, which looks as palpable and warmly humid as flesh. His fingers are his tools, so he caresses Galatea's contours rather than chiselling them. He kisses the effigy into life and, with the connivance of Venus, it even bears him a child. Ovid here celebrates an art that suspends reality in order to fulfill our wishes. Is the outcome too glibly happy? Manipulated by Pygmalion, ivory relaxes into sun-softened wax: we are dangerously close to the unreliable wings that let down over-aspiring Icarus. Yet Ovid returns to the image of wax at the end of *Metamorphoses* in his exposition of Pythagorean philosophy (which is actually a precis of Lucretius). Death, he contends, is not an end; the soul simply moves on to inhabit some other creature, like wax yielding to a new imprint. For Plato in *Theaetetus*, the seal pressed into wax was an image of memory and its retentiveness. For Ovid, it matches our pliable, plastic bodies, forever changing but never destroyed.

When later artists recreated Pygmalion, they complicated his experience and used it to ponder the tragedy of art, which tries in vain to compete with biological creation. Rameau composed his brief opera-ballet *Pygmalion* in 1748. The sculptor sings, but the statue, except for a brief expression of amazement when it finds it can move, has to be content with silently dancing. Pygmalion designs it as a mute, compliant sexual partner; the staccato chipping of his chisel, audible in the overture, enforces his control and perhaps counts the painful cost of female submission. Amour sounds the supernatural accords that bring the statue to life, then drills it in a series of dances – gavotte, minuet, rigadoun, saraband – that mime graceful surrender. A century later, Pygmalion's tastes changed. Ineffectual, self-denying, the artist now prefers the fixity of stone to the fickle liveliness of flesh. The hero of Balzac's *La Peau de chagrin* forces himself to behave chastely with his landlady's desirable daughter. He sees himself as 'another Pygmalion', converting the woman into 'a form of inanimate marble'; he treats her with grudging respect, as if she were 'the portrait of a dead mistress'. The hint is taken up by a story in Henri Murger's *Scènes de la vie de Bohème*, which describes the relationship between the sculptor Jacques and his muse Francine, who wastes away from consumption. After her death he makes a plaster cast of her face. When he removes the mould she seems to have revived: the heat of the plaster has drawn the blood back to her head in a posthumous blush. Murger comments on the morbidity of artists who, like 'strange Pygmalions', wish 'to change into marble their living Galateas'. Ovid's Pygmalion at least made love to a columnar body with

excited pulses and a frutiful womb; for Murger's character, art is closer to
the mad perversity of necrophilia.

Although the domineering professor of phonetics in Shaw's *Pygmalion*
is modelled on Ovid's sculptor, he thinks of himself, even more grandiosely,
as a modern Prometheus. Higgins believes he has done more than teach
Eliza Doolittle polite speech and genteel deportment; he has created her.
He calls her a 'creature ... picked out of the mud', like the humanoid figures
Prometheus modelled from the wet soil of the river bed, and adds that he
'created this thing out of the squashed cabbage leaves of Covent Garden'.
He tells her to remember that she is 'a human being with a soul and the
divine gift of articulate speech', which were Promethean endowments; he
refers to his own soul as his 'spark of divine fire', alluding to the theft from
the hearth of Zeus. His hobby is composing Miltonic verse, so when Eliza
accuses him of making trouble for her by his act of creation, he plays the
devil's advocate and asks the aggressive questions that are voiced by Satan in
*Paradise Lost*: 'Would the world ever have been made if its maker had been
afraid of making trouble? Making life means making trouble. There's only
one way of escaping trouble; and that's killing things.' Like the experiment
Milton's God oversees in the laboratory of Eden, Higgins's scheme goes
wrong because the created being is autonomous, self-willed. Shaw's after-
word notices the irrelevance of the Ovidian myth in our agnostic world.
Eliza rejects Higgins because 'Galatea never does quite like Pygmalion: his
relation to her is too godlike to be altogether reasonable'. Eliza's uprising,
when she refuses to bring Higgins his slippers, announces the rejection of
all gods. She inherits the brazen instincts of her father, the amoral dustman
who is praised by Shaw for his 'Nietzschean transcendence of good and
evil'. Pygmalion returns in Shaw's metabiological saga *Back to Methusaleh*,
where he invents a pair of artificial human beings. From the vantage point
of the year 31,920 AD, he looks back on the God of Genesis as a remote,
primitive predecessor, 'the founder of biological science'. Pygmalion is
pleased that his brain-children are an improvement on Adam and Eve: they
are not made of sticky protoplasm but of tissue expressly designed to receive
the current he calls the 'high-potential Life Force'. Unfortunately, like Eliza
or like Frankenstein's monster, they are rebellious. The female threatens to
kill the male, and when Pygmalion intercedes she bites her maker, who dies.
The creation once more escapes from the helpless creator.

Ovid's seed-bed of stories is flagrantly creative. His book scandalized
Christian moralists, who allegorized its tales of erotic ferment. In the fifteenth century the theologian Franciscus de Retza, defending the inviolate
chastity of Mary, asked 'if Danae conceived from Jupiter through a golden
shower, why should the Virgin not give birth when impregnated by the
Holy Spirit?' The rhetorical question remains open; so does the gap

between Ovid's carnality and the doctrine of incarnation, which calls on spirit to irradiate and purify the flesh. It was easier to reconcile Ovid with the natural sciences that stealthily undermined the creative role of the Christian God. In 1791 Erasmus Darwin, Charles Darwin's grandfather, published a poem called *The Botanic Garden*, in which he dramatized the rampant loves of the plants. Ovid transmuted men, women, gods and goddesses into trees and flowers. By way of reparation, Darwin released them from their 'vegetative mansions' and restored them to their 'original animality'. He continued to personify plants: he likened the 'monster-birth' of the spiky plantago rose to the clandestine union of Othello and Desdemona, and compared the tendrils of climbing vines to the serpents that twine around the Trojan priest Laocöon and strangle him. But his purpose was to root the myths in botanical or physiological truth. Retelling the Prometheus story, he pointed out that the Titan carried off the stolen fire 'lantern'd in his breast'; this, he argued, was why Zeus sent an eagle to gnaw his liver. Darwin connected the hiding-place with the punishment, and read the story as a cautionary medical fable about the dangers of 'drinking fermented or spiritous liquors'. The fire concealed in the chest of Prometheus is a dram he has swallowed, which can cause 'an inflamed, schirrous, or paralytic liver'. As retold by Darwin, the myths slight the gods, set nature free to reproduce itself as it pleases, and challenge men to help themselves.

Picasso illustrated the *Metamorphoses* in 1931, and found in it a model of his own hectic, lawless creativity. A violent god cracks open obtuse stone or applies fire to unyielding metal; stones are punished into softness, hewn into uncouth shapes, and finally agree to be moulded into statuary. Everything must be peremptorily remade. Not long after Picasso's work on Ovid, Braque accepted a commission to illustrate Hesiod's *Theogony*. In one of his etchings, Hesiod cavorts with the muse. The two figures have cubistic heads, like the tribal masks Braque and Picasso both collected, but their naked bodies are ripe, rotund, swollen with organic life. Hesiod has pendulous genitals; one of his hands reaches for the muse's thigh, while another fastens on the stalk of a plant which she is holding just above her groin. Behind them is a lopped, pollarded tree, punished into the semblance of a sculpture. Hesiod's forearms have also detached themselves from the rest of him, but only because they want to grab hold of the muse, the sexual partner with whom he will create the world of thronging forms – fish, horses, birds – that spill from the primal chasm in Braque's plates. Roles are reversed, because she is the inseminator: Braque thought that creativity was an 'impregnation … that penetrates us unconsciously'. By contrast with the cruel morphological torments in Picasso's scenes from Ovid, Braque saw the *Theogony* as a poem about nature's original state of fluid manipulability, which is why Hesiod's hands reach out so eagerly.

We are left with a choice between two versions of creation. On one side is the endless, self-replenishing nature of Hesiod, Lucretius and Ovid; on the other is a Christian society which arduously toils towards salvation, hoping to find redemption before it is uncreated by God's second coming. Those who live in the first world must be malleable. The moral is enforced whenever one of Ovid's stories is adapted, since recreation is both a law of life and an artistic principle. To live in the second world demands the different virtues of staunch consistency and solemn unworldliness. In 1911 Hugo von Hofmannsthal balanced the contradictory demands of the two philosophies, and decided in favour of metamorphosis. 'Transformation,' he said, 'is the life of life itself, the real mystery of nature as creative force.' That validates Lucretius, but what Hofmannsthal said next went on to shape this perception about nature into a plan of action. 'Permanence is numbness and death. Whoever wants to live must surpass himself, must transform himself: he has to forget.' It was a subversive creed because, as Hofmannsthal admitted, the official culture considered self-recreation to be immoral and identified 'all human merit' with 'permanence, unforgetfulness'. Hofmannsthal was writing to Richard Strauss about his text for their third opera, *Ariadne auf Naxos*, which bewildered the composer. Ariadne, abandoned on Naxos, awaits death. Instead she is visited by the god Bacchus, who re-awakens her to life. She is anticipating a different rite of passage, and expects him to lead her to the underworld. She asks how he will effect the transformation – with his hands (which Pymalion relies on when coaxing Galatea to respond)? with his wand? with a magic potion? It was this transformation or 'Verwandlung' that confused Strauss, so Hofmannsthal explained it in his letter about nature as a creative force. The opera derides constancy, which is why the flirty Zerbinetta – who cheerfully recreates herself whenever she recruits a new lover – likens the morose, slumped Ariadne to a statue propped on her own tomb. That miserable fate overtakes the Emperor in *Die Frau ohne Schatten*, the next opera on which Strauss and Hofmannsthal collaborated: his wife cannot bear children, so he hardens into stone, forfeiting the mutability that is the unmistakable sign of life. We must allow ourselves to be reshaped into new forms. If not, we die, mortifying into numbness like the sterile Emperor. To forget is equally necessary, since it frees us from the inflictions of the past. The great moral gestures in Hofmannsthal's dramas all involve a blithe amnesia, as characters surrender to the compulsion of 'nature as creative force'. Chrysothemis in *Elektra* renounces the grim chore of revenge and dreams of sexual fulfilment. The Marschallin in *Der Rosenkavalier* gracefully consigns herself to time's mercy and releases her young lover. The heroine of *Arabella* forgives the fiancé who has defamed her. Menelaus in *Die Ägyptische Helena* chooses to overlook Helen's infidelity with Paris.

Strauss may have been puzzled by the principle of transformation, but he knew how to make it happen in music. In the last line of Strauss's last song, which sets a poem by Joseph von Eichendorff, the singer – elated, unafraid – asks if the darkness that gathers around her might be death. There is no dying fall in the music that answers her question; death benignly ushers a transitory creature through its next transition. In his operas, the gratuitous acts of Hofmannsthal's characters are usually accompanied by long interludes of surging symphonic argument; opposed motives word-lessly quarrel, then modulate into calm when the transfigured being is reborn as someone else. After Hofmannsthal died in 1929, Strauss turned to a pair of Ovidian subjects, composing operas that reinterpret the stories of Danae and Daphne. Both heroines spurn the gods who offer them immor-tality, and music vouches for the transformations they undergo. Danae rejects Jupiter in favour of humble marital contentment as the wife of Midas, now an impoverished donkey-driver; she recognizes that life lacks value unless it has limits and an end. An orchestral interlude before the last scene of *Die Liebe der Danae* brings her gently down to earth, although at the same time its nobly sustained, glowing melody transcribes the god's loss, which is perhaps more painful: Strauss referred to it as Jupiter's renuncia-tion, and told his librettist Josef Gregor that only one thing was denied to 'the all-powerful god, creator of the world' – human love, an incomplete being's fusion with his or her other half. The heroine's fate in Strauss's *Daphne* is less cosily connubial. She has always envied the trees she tends and the birds that nest in them, and when she rejects Apollo, the god changes her into a laurel. A thunderclap rumbles out of Apollo's decree, with a clash of cymbals like a sunburst of seething metal. The stage darkens; Daphne disap-pears into the orchestra's subterranean trench, and her voice merges with the instruments as her body takes its place in the blooming grove.

She cries out to the wind and the birds, then utters no more words. Instead she pours forth a series of vowels, in modulations that take the letter A and use it as a pretext for open-throated, ecstatic vocalizing. Empty air vibrates in a sonic rainbow that we seem to see, even though it consists of notes that flash and glisten invisibly. The episode demonstrates that nothing can indeed give birth to something. The Word, to adapt Nabokov's criticism of the Bible, got it wrong: the world was not spoken but sung into being.

# 4

# CUBING THE EGG

In 1932 the Bauhaus designer Herbert Bayer photographed the moment when the world began. He called the photograph *Creation*, and it catches a part of the creator's body as he goes to work. A fist protrudes from a streaky nebular sky. The sight is ominous, and seems to identify God as a pugnacious dictator, emphatically laying down the law. But the clenched hand grips an egg, as cooks do when preparing a meal; it belongs after all to an artist, who meddles with nature and inventively destroys it. Although the shell remains intact, Bayer added a few drops of glutinous liquid to the surface of the photograph, like spilled semen or streaming tears. As an extension of these droplets, a tumbling mass of flowers rains down from the sky, rather than growing from the earth. Below, the nascent world is already furnished with works of art, which cannot have hatched from the global egg. A porcelain figurine of a naked, preening woman, elaborately coiffed, serves as the pistil of the flowers: perhaps she is a rococo version of Eve. A sketch of a medieval castle prophetically envisions a remoter future. Those artefacts stir up a quarrel about origins. Did a creator shape the world with his hands, as if designing a statuette or a building? Or did the world explode into life of its own accord – breaking through a shell, emerging from some other cataclysm?

Myths like to picture the world as an egg, because that explains its shape: the rounded contours ease its passage out of the creator's body and, since it is designed to orbit through space, they also make it more aerodynamic. Mary Shelley, while fretting over the origins of her monster, remembered the story of Columbus and his egg. He and his fellow voyagers were discussing how to make an egg stand up straight, which is an unnatural thing for it to do; Columbus solved the problem by tapping it and slightly fracturing the shell at one end, to give it a base. Imagination, Mary Shelley deduced, 'consists ... in the power of moulding and fashioning ideas'. None of us could invent an egg, let alone lay one. However we can devise unexpected uses for eggs, all of which involve breaking or at least delicately damaging them. In the 1880s in his poem 'Clair de lune', Edmond de Haraucourt imagined the spontaneous generation of the moon, which – as he supposed – long ago forced its way out of the strained earth and shot into the sky.

The Finnish epic *Kalevala*, a compendium of folk-tales assembled in the mid-nineteenth century, also tells the primal story by cracking open an egg.

Lee Lawrie, *Atlas*, Rockefeller Center, New York, 1936

The world in the *Kalevala* is engendered from the fertilizing congress of the elements. Luonnotar, the daughter of the air, is impregnated by the wind. But despite a protracted labour that lasts seven hundred years, no new life emerges from her straining body. She appeals to the male sky-god as a midwife, begging him to release her from these throes. He cannot help; birth requires a bed, a foundation, a fundament. Then a nesting teal lands on her knee-cap, mistaking it for a hilly clump, and lays its eggs there.

Luonnotar is burned by the warmth of the swelling eggs. She feels her skin scorching, and knocks the eggs into the water. The damage is creative: the spillage of the eggs produces sky and clouds, with the yolk turning into the sun and the white into the moon. In 1913 Jean Sibelius composed an orchestral song that compresses the saga of creation into ten minutes. Flickering

Columbus breaking the egg, from a subscription ticket to William Hogarth's *Analysis of Beauty*, 1753

strings stir up the winds, and harps, as if spotting the water with foam, presage a storm. Over these elemental surges, the voice of a soprano circles, keening like the anxious, buffeted bird, then uttering a benediction of hushed maternal awe as she describes the cracked egg and its splashing contents. A last rhapsodic high note splinters into the stars that flare across the sky. Genesis, like birth, is accompanied by convulsions and screams, the breaking of waters and shedding of blood. In the *Kalevala*, Luonnotar's broody anguish is merely a prelude. Ages elapse, then Luonnotar herself delivers the first man, Väinämöinen. She is still a blocked, procrastinating creator: her infant has gestated for thirty years, and must battle his way out of the womb. From that internal darkness he calls on the sun and moon to deliver him into their light. After several extra years of immurement, he at last makes his exit. He is a 'bold bard', which no doubt explains his impatience: he cannot leave nature to its own devices, and destructively probes the secrets of creation.

In myth, creation is sexual, seminal: hence the licentiousness of the gods whose antics are related by Hesiod and Ovid, or the fragile sphere that contains fluid life in the *Kalevala*. Mathematics prefers to see the process as the elaboration of a theorem, the sketching of a technical diagram. When Pythagoras traced the world back to its origins, he replaced the egg with a pyramidal tetractys. Instead of ovular curves, he thought about straight lines that converged at a pointed apex, where the First Cause presumably sat. The building blocks of the Pythagorean system were prime numbers. The top row contained only a single integer, since the First Cause was solitary. It rested on a pediment of two numbers, and below these was a layer containing three. Added up, they made six, the number which for Augustine constituted perfection. But Pythagoras set in place a bottom row of four, so that 1, in a series of logical duplications and additions, could ray out into 10. The system allowed Pythagoras to calculate a set of mathematical and musical intervals that vouched for the orderly construction of the cosmos. Christian doctrine had its own uses for his numerical lore. Logos, which is how St John in his gospel refers to Christ, was a Pythagorean term for a ratio. To give the saviour this new name made him a supreme ratio, like the golden section of infinite reproducibility within a rectangle. The inequitable universe of the Old Testament was a battleground between God, his wayward subjects, and a squadron of rebel angels; set to rights by the logical intervention of Christ, the world's justice was verified by its proportionality.

The scheme is evidence of our rationality and our craving for an ideal. Unfortunately, it may be too good to be true. In *Timaeus*, the most Pythagorean of Plato's dialogues, Socrates slyly admits that possibility. He asks his guests to entertain him with their philosophical fantasias; he has beguiled them with his account of an ideal society, and he now expects them to return the favour. As when Gangleri interrogates the prophets in the *Edda*, the cosmogony is prompted by a dare, a challenge to imagination. Timaeus, expert in astronomy, volunteers to describe the origins of the cosmic system, with Critias taking over when human beings come into existence. Socrates settles back to enjoy the intellectual performance, though he tells Timaeus not to start without 'the customary invocation to the gods'. Hesiod would not have needed the reminder, but by the fourth century the gods merit only formulaic praise, like a loyal toast. Timaeus agrees that it is not possible to discuss universal origins without appeasing all the gods and goddesses who may have an interest in the matter. But as well as pleasing them, we want to please ourselves; he adds that 'we must invoke our own powers too'. The gods to whom Timaeus defers have been superseded by his own intelligence, and they have little to do with the mental architectonics that follow.

He presumes that the universe had a father who set it in motion, but sarcastically slights all ancillary gods, about whose birth he says he has no information. He races through Hesiod's account of Earth coupling with Heaven or Kronos with Rhea; any further details must be obtained from those who claim to be the children of these hot-blooded gods, since – as Timaeus says – they surely know their own family history. Later, when he describes the modelling of forms, he reduces the notion of birth to a metaphor. To make the idea easier, he is prepared to liken the 'neutral plastic material' to the mother, while it is the father who imprints a copy of eternal reality on this passive receptacle. The being created by this encounter is their offspring. But the simile is approximate, a concession to grounded minds that rely on physical analogies. Irony temporizes between knowledge and ignorance, faith and doubt; the ironist himself is never sure whether he means what he says. Such deft, sceptical wit is the implement with which Plato's speakers investigate mysteries.

Timaeus asks the inevitable questions: did the universe always exist, which would mean that it never began, or did it come into existence and begin at a certain moment? He decides on the second option, but admits that is hard to identify the maker and father of the cosmos – and even if he could be sure who this actuating god is, it would not be advisable to tell everyone about him. This scruple defends the necessary obscurity of his exposition, and justifies his inability to give an accurate account of the gods. But his apology also covers a devious change of direction. Since the constructor remains out of sight, Timaeus chooses to consider the model he must have worked from, since 'the world is a likeness of something else'; our reality is the warped and distorted replica of an 'eternally unchanging' supernatural realm. While saying this, Timaeus plays the role of constructor and makes a model of his own. The perfect, immutable higher world we look up to is art, and the philosopher enlists god – who found the universe in a state of agitated disharmony and 'reduced it to order' – as a fellow artist. God did this, Timaeus contends, because he was good, and wished everything else to be so too. That sounds like the self-praise of God in Genesis, except that here goodness is not a moral imperative, paired with and balanced by evil; in the Platonic dialogue, the good is the beautiful. Timaeus leaves human beings to arrive at an appreciation of that beauty, which they do by using their brains.

In Genesis, God first creates the universe and then as an afterthought places man in it, assigning him the menial task of tilling the ground. For Timaeus, man has a nobler function. By observing cosmic operations, he can discern the creation's purpose. The Prometheus of Aeschylus claims to have taught men the art of number; according to Timaeus, they worked it out on their own after studying the alternation of days, months and years, or noting the regularity of equinoxes and solstices. Having invented numbers, they could comprehend time, and were ready 'to inquire into the nature of the universe'. Their helper in all this is philosophy, 'the greatest gift the gods have ever given or will give to mortals'. But philosophy is the love of knowledge or wisdom: Timaeus is merely being polite in thanking the gods for the refinement of human reason. He confirms the compliment to our species in a Pythagorean fable which treats all other creatures as metempsychosed versions of rational man, necessarily inferior to their human overlord. Birds are transformations of bird-brained humans; grazing land animals once were lowbrows who kept their heads down and had no use for philosophy; fish are irredeemably unintelligent souls, sentenced to live in muddy water because they are unfit to breathe clean air. The chain of being is a steep vertical ladder, with philosophers at the top and fish at the bottom. You commute up and down depending on how much knowledge you gain or lose.

The Chaos sanitized by the classical creator is unlike the realm of derangement into which Satan lunges in *Paradise Lost*. Timaeus domesticates the lurching instability of an unmade world when he says that its elemental contents originally heaved to and fro like corn being cleaned in a winnowing basket. The 'nurse of becoming' shook the receptacle and, as if separating seeds from husks, divided earth and air, fire and water. Elsewhere Timaeus describes the demiurge as a cook who poured ingredients into a bowl and expertly mixed them to prepare a soul for the universe. The human soul was concocted later, and is less pure because it was made from left-overs. Anyone can learn such agricultural or culinary skills; this is craft, acquired by trial and error not divinely instilled, but the completed work is a symbol of art. Melding the elements, the creator described by Timaeus made a spherical world 'consisting of parts that are wholes', smooth in its external finish.

Myth-makers always have trouble explaining how this world manages to hover in space. Hence the elephant's need to tread on the tortoise. In Polynesia, Gauguin heard a similar tale about cosmic generation. After numerous divine couplings that produced clouds, stars and water, a god set out in his canoe, lowered a fishing line into the depths and hooked the earth, which he managed to support despite its groaning weight. Timaeus dispenses with such acts of equilibration: the planet revolves of its own volition, controlled by an internal intelligence. Being excellent, the globe craves no company other than its own, and is satisfied with its solitude. What the eternal god created, Timaeus concludes, is itself 'a blessed god'. Artists all want to do the same – to create a scaled-down, self-sufficient world inside a book or a picture frame, ensuring that the parts obligingly serve the whole. At a feast in Virgil's *Aeneid*, the singer Iopas reaches for his golden lyre and delivers a cosmological lecture. Music is the proper medium for doing so, because the laws of physics keep the universe in tune. Those laws also exactly fit the symmetrical couplets of John Dryden's translation. Iopas explains

> The various labors of the wand'ring moon,
> And whence proceed th' eclipses of the sun;
> Th' original of men and beasts; and whence
> The rains arise, and fires their warmth dispense,
> And fix'd and erring stars dispose their influence;
> What shakes the solid earth; what cause delays
> The summer nights and shortens winter days.

Even the 'erring stars' cannot disrupt the system's stability, and earthquakes are less terrifying if we know what causes them. This universe, so punctiliously regulated, needs no creator. Proust in an interview in 1913 said that 'the pleasure an artist gives us is to make us know one universe more'. Here the universe that is made known and knowable is a product of verse – exactly the kind of beautiful, beatified fiction that Timaeus praises. Despite his mock-modest disclaimers, Timaeus finally declares that he has given a complete account of the cosmos, which is 'an image of the intelligible'. When he acclaims it as 'a visible god' and 'a single, uniquely created heaven', he is inviting us to admire his own mental handiwork. Critias has earlier amused Socrates by relating the myth of Atlantis, the drowned civilization. The story is apparently a vagrant preamble, but it hints at the same aesthetic ambition that lies behind the speculations of Timaeus. Art lowers heaven to our level, or dredges up a lost world buried deep in our memories, as if underwater.

The flour and eggs in the cook's mixing bowl are organic, messy. The finished product exchanges this wet, flurried physicality for the severe, serene abstraction of geometry: life is turned into art by the application of technique. Hence the geometrical diagram of creation offered by Timaeus, who sets a constellation of ideal forms whirling in the air. None of these pristine, angularly bevelled shapes exists in nature, but they symbolically represent natural forces. Wanting to regulate the flux of chaos, Timaeus makes a match between the four elements and four regular solids. Earth is enclosed by a cube, while the other elements occupy triangles. Fire is contained by a peaked tetrahedron, air inhabits an octahedron, and water, the most mobile and uncontrollable of them all, flows into a twenty-sided icosahedron. The cosmos is the sum total of all these compounded, cooperative volumes – a dodecahedron, formed by an assemblage of twelve pentagons. This way of recreating the world and classifying its litter has never lost its authority. The perfect solids described by Timaeus are cubes and triangles; Cézanne discovered in every natural form a cylinder, a sphere or a cone. A Platonic idea underlay the humblest fruit, which is why Cézanne used compasses to outline the apples he painted. The society portraitist Gerald Kelly recommended English apples: French varieties were inferior because polyhedral, with planar facets. The mention of a polyhedron, Kelly reported, prompted Cézanne to rhapsodize about the beauties of geometry. In 1904 he advised a colleague that by adding lines parallel to the horizon he could enjoy the broad vista 'that the Pater Omnipotens Aeterne Deus spreads before our eyes'. The ceremonious Latin titles were Cézanne's joke about an officious, absconded god. He was unimpressed by the creator who commanded 'Let there be light', and he dismissed the ensuing spectacle as an optical illusion, a fog of distracting sensations refracted from the surface of things. 'Light,' he declared, 'does not exist for the painter'; the proper business of the art was to clarify space. Slighting Genesis, Cézanne preferred a different myth of origins, better able to explain what he called 'the dawn of ourselves from out of nothing'; he saturated himself, as he said, in Lucretius, for whom creation and destruction were a continuing struggle, not a job definitively completed in six days.

*Timaeus* was the Platonic dialogue most familiar during the Middle Ages, when scholars read it as a rationalization of Christian faith. Early in the sixth century AD, Boethius struggled to reconcile Plato and the Bible, seeking an accord between classical fate and Christian providence, stoical acceptance and messianic hope. The attempt was urgently personal. Boethius, an imperial civil servant promoted by Theodoric the Ostrogoth, fell from favour after a doctrinal dispute between Rome and Byzantium; his former patron had him arrested, exiled, tortured and eventually executed. While in prison, Boethius examined his predicament in the hope of understanding why God had deserted him. He summoned the wisdom of Timaeus to his aid: his counsellor, whom he describes as his nurse, is the allegorized spirit of Philosophy. His dialogue with her is called *The Consolation of Philosophy*, which implies that their conversation is happening in an unjust, godless world. Consolation was a stoical recourse, on which Socrates relied when condemned to death by a whimsical despot. But Philosophy does more than tell Boethius to stiffen his upper lip. She asserts that his downfall is the contrivance of an all-seeing God, and she does so by reinterpreting and coordinating the classical and Christian stories of creation.

She dares Boethius to complain that his downfall is unreasonable. To do so would imply that life is mere chance and hazard, unregulated by God. Outwitted, Boethius concedes that events both in heaven and on earth are ordained; any sense of disharmony must come from within ourselves, as Timaeus also claimed. Philosophy later invokes the same principle and uses it to abolish chaos: 'If God imposes order upon all things, there is no opportunity for random events. It is a true maxim that nothing comes out of nothing.' Boethius agrees that the source of all life is God. This moves Philosophy to tease him by asking 'How can it be ... that you know the beginning of things but don't know their end?' Unable to share her exalted vantage-point, he sees the sky from below: 'It is because you men are in no position to contemplate this order that everything seems confused and upset.' He is required to take the reason for his condemnation on trust.

The five
Platonic solids

TETRAHEDRON          HEXAHEDRON          OCTAHEDRON          DODECAHEDRON          ICOSAHEDRON

Philosophy browbeats him with a syllogism: God must be good, 'otherwise He could not be the author of creation.' Boethius concurs, because Plato has demonstrated that the world is governed by a strict and impartial intelligence. Yet he hesitates before personifying that omniscient mind: 'For this power, whatever it is, through which creation remains in existence and in motion, I use the word which all people use, namely God.' Shouldn't the deity be more than a verbal compromise, reached through consensus?

Coaxing Boethius towards acceptance, Philosophy reminds him that 'in the *Timaeus* my servant Plato was pleased to ask for divine help'. She is referring to the customary prayer that precedes his exposition of universal order; she chooses to ignore the playful, ironic impudence with which Timaeus asks the gods to pardon him for meddling in their affairs. She asks Boethius what men should do 'to be worthy of discovering the source of the supreme good', and he of course answers 'We ought to pray to the Father of all things'. This is Philosophy's cue for a hymn addressed to the creator of the planets and the sky. She begins by revering Plato's unmoved mover, adding a Neo-Platonic gloss when she argues that this god made the world as a likeness of the beautiful archetype that he carried in his mind. But she ends her poem by paraphrasing the Lord's Prayer: God now has changed from a harmonizing agency into a patriarch riding in a chariot, and those who pray to him do so in the expectation that they will be received into his kingdom after their deaths. Timaeus intellectually respects the first cause but does not worship it. Philosophy, however, concludes with a gesture of pious adoration, and filially abases herself before the Father who is 'our source and maker, lord and path and goal'.

Boethius gave Philosophy the last word, which must mean that he was consoled by her. Even so, Christian theology and Platonic metaphysics pull apart from one another. Christianity praises God, and laments our fallen feebleness. But Boethius followed the Neo-Platonists in seeing the human head as a sphere that is comparable to the cosmos; it was designed as a container for the soul's revolutions, which mimic those of the planets. In the late seventeenth century, when Newton promulgated the laws of celestial motion, he did so by adapting the mystical astronomy of Pythagoras and Timaeus; he also paid tribute to the geometrician Thales, who believed that magnets had souls and 'taught that all things are full of Gods, understanding by Gods animate bodies'. Newton knew that there were no potentates resident in the sun or the other stars, but his principles of motion and attraction were a necessity as ineluctable as any divine decree. Courteously keeping the peace with religion, Newton even credited the biblical God with inventing atoms – too small a job, presumably, to merit a mention in Genesis. Perhaps the relationship between the creator and the physicist was better assessed by Alexander Pope in his epitaph for Newton:

> Nature and Nature's laws hid in night:
> God said, Let Newton be! and all was light.

Newton here supplants God, or at least takes over the task of clarification that theologians entrusted to Christ.

In 1733 in his *Essay on Man*, Pope described the amazement of 'superior beings' who looked down from some non-denominational heaven to see 'a mortal man unfold all Nature's law'. He complimented Newton's ability to 'correct old Time, and regulate the sun', which – as Timaeus and Augustine would have agreed – were divine responsibilities. Newton performed these feats by rejigging the chronology of the Greeks; he based his calculations on the positions of the planets when the Argonauts set out on their expedition, and made other adjustments to allow for the difference between monarchical reigns and the generations of men. These, as the literary critic Thomas Warburton said, were 'sublime conceptions', and in 1784 the architect Étienne-Louis Boullée acknowledged their grandeur in the memorial he designed for Newton. The monument, which was never built, boldly proposed an analogy between the universe and the universal mind of its explicator: it was a hollow sphere with a solar globe inside it. The sky fits into this cranial observatory; the dome contains infinitude. In Boullée's sketches, frowning clouds above the orb are sliced through by streaks of brightness; moods and weathers angrily clash in nature, but the implacable, fortified mind resists their disruption. The sphere was meant to be punctuated with funnel-shaped holes, letting in shafts of sunlight through apertures that would look like glinting stars. In one sketch, a zodiac glimmers on the curved vault, astonishing the swarm of insect-sized worshippers who gaze up from far below. In another sketch, an oval ellipse

Etienne-Louis Boullée, *Newton Memorial*, 1784

hangs in mid-air, with a nucleus bisected by lines of force that govern planetary transits. Mythological cultures would have mistaken this shape for a
cosmic egg, cracked open to let out the nascent earth; in Boullée's design it
represents an armillary sphere, the conceptual gadget that helped Timaeus
to visualize cosmic movements. This secondary sphere was to be fitted with
lamps, constantly revolving like the planets they symbolized. Tiny attendants cluster around Newton's sarcophagus, which occupies a plinth below
the armillary sphere. Boullée regretted that he could not make this resting-
place levitate, because he wanted, as he said, to place Newton in the
heavens. Rhetoric accomplished what engineering could not: his dedica-
tory homage addresses Newton as 'Esprit sublime! Génie vaste et profond!
Être divin!' The divine being is the mathematician, and the vast profundity
is an attribute of his genius.

The human mind rationalized the cosmos. Did it, in the process, construct a prison? Pope spoke of Newton as a disciplinarian 'whose rules the
rapid comet bind', and in a 1795 print Blake showed him imposing his rigidly
uniform regime. The naked Newton's muscles ripple in a reptilian pattern as
he bends forward like a louring, oppressive sky-god. His eyes stare, wildly
obsessive not lucid. In his hands he grips a pair of compasses, with which he
plots the perimeter of our world on a sheet of paper. The Pythagorean term
'ratio' had no sanctity for Blake, who thought that 'He who sees the Infinite in
all things sees God. He who sees the Ratio only sees himself only'. Blake's
Newton ignores the sky, and his eyes like searchlights turn the universe he
designs into a penal establishment under ruthless surveillance.

The compasses of Blake's Newton, extended into calipers or pincers,
are wielded again by a god above a doorway at Rockefeller Center in New
York. In the mid-1930s, skyscrapers were the mercantile temples of an
irreligious age; the thin tapering pinnacles of Rockefeller Center soar
above St Patrick's Cathedral on the other side of Fifth Avenue. Lee Lawrie's
relief carving occupies a position corresponding to the portico of a cathedral, where Gothic sculptors carved summaries of biblical history. His
subject resembles an Art Deco Jehovah, chunkily muscled with a crinkled
beard that grows at right angles to his jaw, as if buffeted by a cyclonic gust.
Below his spiked diadem, he glares down at the world he encompasses,
using his other hand to sweep away a bunched bank of clouds. The points
of the tool he holds poke into Chaos, represented by blocks of pyrex
glass. Though he looks like the God of Genesis, Lawrie called him simply
Genius. Instead of creating the world, his task is to interpret it, which he
does, like Blake's Newton, by elucidating scientific principles. According to
Lawrie's title, he explains 'to the human race the laws and cycles of the
cosmic forces of the universe', and side panels illustrate two of those forces,
sound and light. He is a technological genie, since the offices whose entrance

William Blake,
*Newton*, 1795

he guards belonged to the broadcasting network RCA. His stormy heaven crackles with radio waves, while nearby another custom-made mythological figure sculpted by Leo Friedlander exhibits the workings of a newer supernatural appliance: a female giant called Transmission is seen 'receiving an image of dancers and flashing it through the ether by means of television', which beams it into the brain of another figure named Reception, 'symbolized by Mother Earth and her child, Man'. Above East 49th Street, Transmission bounces on the message-laden air. Reception is seated, comfortably passive in front of an imaginary television set that relays astral forces into her living room.

A block away from Genius, another monumental hero sculpted by Lawrie strains beneath his cosmic load. This is Atlas, metamorphosed into a mountain and condemned by Zeus to carry the sky on his back. Lawrie's Atlas retains his human form – his hair has not yet changed into a forest, or his shoulders into crags – and the burden he supports is an armillary sphere, which first enabled men to recast divine mysteries as comprehensible physical routines. He faces St Patrick's, and taunts a religion whose most sacred image is that of Christ dragging uphill the cross onto which he will be nailed. The legs of Atlas bow and his knees buckle, but his stance is proud. The weight of the sphere with its equatorial rings will never crush him; he is holding up the heavens, and revolving the universe inside his head.

# 5

# IN VERBO

Creation begins with an idea. That, because it seems to be beyond conscious control, is the easy part. What comes next is the hard work of articulating the idea, when inspiration – as the saying goes – gives way to perspiration. The scholastic commentators on Genesis, not wanting to make the creator sweat, separated the two stages. God's initiating thought meant that he was the creator 'in principio', but he relied on a deputy to realize his idea. Christ was enrolled as the creator 'in verbo', which is why he took on the honorary title of the Word; he elaborated the language that transformed the 'entire perceptible world', as the twelfth-century Saxon philosopher Hugh of St Victor proclaimed, into 'a book written by the finger of God'.

The Kabbalah assumed that the meaning of this divine poem was esoteric. The enraptured theosophists who supplemented the Talmud's official commentary on the Torah sought to elicit mysteries; they began with the exegesis of Genesis, or 'the work of the beginning', because they found creation itself almost inconceivable. The volumes of mystical exegesis known as the *Zohar* declared that 'en sof' or infinity 'cannot be known, nor how it makes a beginning and an end', just as the *Sefer Yesirah* – the most ancient of these commentaries – had prohibited speculation about origins because 'the Lord is One, and has no second; and before the One, what canst thou count?' What precedes one is zero. Logically the creation must have been made out of nothing – which meant, for the kabbalists, that God diced with non-existence when making the world. In the sixteenth century, Isaac Luria reasoned that God had withdrawn the light from one part of himself to leave a vacancy into which the cosmos could expand. Is our world, with its miseries and its rampant evil, his blind spot? Other attempts to imagine the process describe God drawing down a curtain of darkness, behind which the act of making occurs. During the thirteenth century, the kabbalists of Girona discovered in the Torah what Gershom Scholem calls 'a mystical pun', a slippery copulation of all and nothing. The Hebrew letters 'beth' and 'lamed' encapsulated creation, whose heart they represented. Number symbolism gave the two letters a value of thirty-two, which was the world's quota of wisdom: the *Sefer Yesirah* argued that a single sacred integer had divided itself into thirty-two aspects, comprising ten primordial numbers plus the twenty-two letters of the Hebrew alphabet. But 'beth' and 'lamed', placed in reverse order, also connote nothingness. If this is the axis on which the world turns, then it swivels back and forth between embodiment and annihilation, emerging from and returning to a void.

Meanings – the creator's secretive intentions – may be imponderable, but we have been given a method that allows us to guess at them. They are hidden in language, which we must decipher; their repository is the letters we use when making up words. According to the *Zohar*, each of the Hebrew alphabet's twenty-two personified letters begged God for the honour of serving as the spell or incantation that would create the world. Some were punished for their presumption. 'Tav' was sentenced to be the brand of death, 'shin' was cast aside because it belonged to words meaning falsehood. 'Beth' received a blessing, and became the letter that began the process of creation: 'Bereshith' announces the beginning, when God created heaven and earth. 'Alef', deferring to its colleague, refused to ask any favour for itself, and was rewarded by being given pride of place in the decalogue. The *Maasch Bereshith* says that a faint light, as thin as the point of a needle, leaks down from the mind of the creator and shines onto 'a place where there is some imprint of letters'. That place is our world, a verbal construction. Its masonry is alphabetical: each letter contains its own trace of divinity, and can be used to evoke that supernatural source. But a puzzling transition has occurred. The letters, according to the *Yesirah*, are made from air. Even so, the architectonic verbs employed by the text imply that those breathy letters are carved from the substance of the world or incised into it, like the words Moses chiselled into the tablets of the law. God speaks, we write. There has been a leap between two different realms, which are as far apart as song and sculpture; it happens again when a writer tries to find a way of translating a thought that has unaccountably begun to whisper inside his head, or when a musician attempts to match a sensation with a sound.

Written down, the letters are pictures of an invisible agency. The Hebrew letter transliterated as 'yod' has a flicking upper point which was seen as a homage to the supreme crown of God, known as 'kether'; its thicker horizontal stroke referred to God's 'hokhma', the paternal wisdom that prompted him to create the world. A Provençal commentary viewed the 'yod' as a pair of wings, which eloquently open to give birth to language. Scholem suggests that those pinions, tightly furled, are stored inside 'alef', the letter which some commentators thought of as the direct emanation of God's breath, the first sound uttered when creation began. For this reason, the *Bahir*, a thirteenth-century book decoding scriptural mysteries, likened 'alef' to an ear because, to utter it, you merely open your mouth and release air; it is 'the beginning of all the letters' and the necessary condition for their existence – the silence from which language materializes and into which, when the breath is spent, it vanishes. For Jacob ben Shesheth, 'alef' symbolized O, zero, the bemusing nothingness of origins. Looked at another way, the iconic letter is the incarnation of man, with one hand pointing up and the other down; it pendulates between two infinities, the sky and the abyss.

All letters flex a straight, upright line. They are doodles that describe how the one begets the many, and show the many circling back towards their primal home. Agrippa of Nettesheim, an adept of the Kabbalah, regarded the Hebrew alphabet as an 'explanation of all things', as he put it in his treatise on *Occult Philosophy* in 1533; by their 'crookedness or directness, defect, abounding, greatness or littleness, crowning, opening or shutting', the letters expounded celestial truths and applied 'points and tops' to the planets and the elements. Hebrew consonants also did duty as numbers, which gave these sketches of spirit a corporeal bulk and helped to solidify a world made initially from air. In Genesis, Abram rescues his brother Lot from captivity with the help of 318 trained servants. The total is not accidental; it derives from the numerical value of the letters in the name of Abram's steward Eliezer. The spelling of Abram's own name contains a mystical secret. God, appearing to him, tells him to change it. From now on he must be called Abraham, for he is to be a father of many nations. Agrippa explained the insertion of the 'h' by saying that this letter made the spirit manifest. As an aspirate, it signals aspiration and proclaims a blessing. Abram is therefore justified in purloining it from the name of his wife Sarah.

This sacred language, when its letters are correctly compounded and properly declaimed, pays vocal tribute to the creator. 'Yod' in alliance with 'he' (the letter with which Abram is rewarded) produces the exultant cry of 'YaH' prescribed by Psalm 150, where everything that has breath is told to shout the divine name with the help of the trumpet and the organ. The command to 'praise YaH' results in the utterance of 'Halleluyah', the exclamation which St Jerome said should be either prefixed or appended to all hymns or psalms that extol the majesty of God. St John the Evangelist in his Book of Revelation heard a multitude like 'the voice of many waters' giving voice to that over-joyed word, as the chorus does in Handel's *Messiah*. This jubilant uproar is permitted, but language should never forget that it trespasses on the inexpressible, and must learn to respect silence. The same letters that make up 'YaH' come together in the tetragrammaton 'YHVH', which – with the addition of vowels, absent from early Hebrew though later inserted to make vocalizing easier – names Yahweh or Jehovah. The quartet of letters lists the familial attributes of God: Y is father, H is mother, V or 'vav' is son, and the second H is daughter. The word is a mirror-image of itself, since each of its two particles is shorthand for YaH. The numerical tallies also match. Y corresponds to ten; each H has a value of five, so the pair make another ten, alluding to the hierarchy of ten spherical worlds or sefiroth described by the *Yesirah*. Vertically ranked, the sefiroth extend from the mystical summits of 'kether' and 'hokhma' to seven lower spheres which, linked to the seven days of creation, enshrine earthly ideals such as love or beauty; God, like a prolific artist, has made a variety of subsidiary worlds, each with its own limited life-expectancy. But the tetragrammaton was out of bounds to humans. As punishment for worshipping the golden calf, the children of Israel were forbidden to use it; since YHVH could not be spoken, its right pronunciation supposedly remained unknown. Maimonides reported in the twelfth century that it had been replaced, in readings from the Torah, by 'the name beginning with the consonants alef, daleth', which he prudently did not transcribe. He meant ADNY or Adonai, the supplication meaning 'My Lord'.

Agrippa's white magic strove by trial and error to find the most effectual 'joining together of the letters'. Conjuring was like scrabble; once the word had been formed, the magus could speak it aloud and cast the same spell that God employed when compelling nature to obey him. Consulting his book, Prospero in *The Tempest* is able to bedim the sun, uproot trees, and awaken the dead. Cautious conditions were placed on using the holy words, as a safeguard against such necromancy. The Kabbalah says that 'if a man creates a creature by means of the Book *Yesirah*, he has the power to create everything except one thing'. The creature is the golem, the stone man animated by a legendary rabbi in Prague; the one thing missing is language, since the golem can move but not speak. Another kabbalist anecdote told of two rabbis who every Friday studied the linguistic lore concerning creation. As a result of their researches, they created a calf, which they then ate. This is the kind of miracle performed every day of the week by the wish-fulfilling fantasy of artists: Keats referred to the 'young poetical appetite', so avid that it gains its food simply by imagining it. No wonder prohibitions intrude, as in Ovid's story about Midas. Surely a creativity that promises instant gratification cannot be good? That, at least, is what we timidly tell ourselves.

A magical potency clung to Hebrew letters. Hence the baleful glare of the four Hebrew words traced by the finger of God in Rembrandt's *Belshazzar's Feast*. Transliterated from right to left, they are MENE MENE TERKEL PERES; the painted writing enunciates a death sentence. In the Bible, the story is about the difficulty of interpretation. Belshazzar, who worships idols of metal and wood, gives a feast that is interrupted when a 'part of a hand' writes on the wall. The words, not at first disclosed by the text, baffle his soothsayers, astrologers and wise men. His queen suggests that Daniel should be consulted, since 'the spirit of the holy gods' dwells in him. Belshazzar lengthily flatters Daniel, and offers him gaudy rewards if he can read the inscription. Daniel spurns riches, but delivers an equally loquacious

Rembrandt van Rijn, *Belshazzar's Feast, c.* 1635

sermon about the fear of God. Then he briskly solves the riddle, which is written in a form of divine shorthand. He utters the words, then deciphers them one by one. They refer to number, weight and division; Daniel, taking liberties like a literary critic, converts each to a past participle and reads them as a warning that the profligate Belshazzar's days have been numbered, that he has been weighed in the balance, that his kingdom will be divided. The word for number is repeated for emphasis, like the double dream of Pharaoh in Genesis – another grim prophecy that at once comes true. Daniel is especially dexterous when coaxing significance from the last word. On the wall, it appears as UPHARSIN; he omits a conjunction and changes it to the singular PERES, which is how Rembrandt paints it. His aim is to contrive a pun: in this form, the fourth word can refer to the Persians, who are about to invade Belshazzar's city.

Once the words have been explained, the power in them is automatically released, and the biblical account ends by tersely noting that, during the night, Belshazzar was killed. But the writing remains ineffectual until Daniel, who has the reputation of being able to 'make interpretations', declaims its fateful meaning. Speech is still the medium of divine action. The painting, however, is silent, and the action it arrests happens before Daniel's arrival. Paint deals in substance not meaning, so Rembrandt's attention is devoted to the sumptuary trappings of the court: jewels, fur, stiff embroidery, flaunting feathers. Precious metals have been deconsecrated, which makes their opulence lurid, licentious. The gold and silver vessels used to serve food and drink were appropriated from Solomon's temple in Jerusalem by Nebuchadnezzar, Belshazzar's father. This world of physical satiety is liable to corruption and decay, which is why the sleeve of the woman's dress has been stained by the spilled wine from her cup. After taking inventory of the king's material riches and rendering them futile, the painting goes on to show the advent of spirit. The Bible tries to ground the intervention from on high by locating the words 'over against the candlestick' and explaining that they were written on the plaster of the wall. Rembrandt does without domestic props that might have helped to rationalize the marvel. His writing glows out of a thundery cloud that has settled above the dining table; its thick billows open to disclose a chilling wintry sun whose light is literate.

The Bible describes fingers that belong to no body. In the painting, the hand reaches out of the cloud, and wears the condensed, discoloured air as a ruff at its wrist. Oddly, it does not write the words horizontally from right to left, but instead arranges them vertically. The columnar shape allows the tops of the letters to reach into the sky, and gives the downward strokes a doomed gravity; it may also evoke the collapse of a profane temple, since the hand is building from top to bottom and it concludes – as it traces the last letter, nearest to the recoiling Belshazzar – by undermining the structure, refusing it a secure foundation. In a painting about a hand and its miraculous skills, Rembrandt comments on his own handiwork. The characters who have bodies perform unavailing manual gestures. A hand clasps its partner to signal distress, or fumbles and drops a cup. One of Belshazzar's hands knocks against an upturned plate, while with the other he flaps at the storm cloud. He has also probably bumped the two cups that slop their wine. The bodiless hand uses a finger instead of a brush, but is as precise and pointed as if it were making its statement with a pen; and it needs neither paint nor ink, since the words derive their cold incandescence from a source outside nature. Hebrew letters, allegorically interpreted by the kabbalists, are symbols; Rembrandt follows their example by using paint as an eloquent language, which in its deft textures and subtle tones is able to speak of death, lifelessness, and immortality – wrinkled sagging flesh, clammy brass, the halation that glows around the inscribed prophecy.

François Couperin made the sacred language the source of music in his *Leçons de Ténèbres*, composed for a convent in 1714. Couperin's fourteen lessons set excerpts from the lamentations of the prophet Jeremiah. A singer declaims these passages in Latin, but before each verse comes a brief wordless cry of dismay or supplication based on the Hebrew alphabet. God's native idiom cannot be translated. The vocalized passages therefore use the first Hebrew letter of each selection from Jeremiah, arranging them in alphabetical order from 'alef' and 'beth' onwards to 'nun'. The sounds flare into life pentecostally. The thirteenth-century Provençal rabbi Isaac the Blind, who thought that the Hebrew alphabet contained the formulae for all created things, likened the letters to tongues of flames – flickering, animated, yet rooted in coal that was dug out of the earth. Listening to the *Leçons des Ténèbres* today, it is hard not to hear the intoned letters as an exhibition of vocal virtuosity. The singer, dispensed from having to articulate the words that are patiently repeated and underlined in the following arioso, sculpts air into decorative filigree, with trills rigging up trees crowded with twittering birds. The nuns who first performed Couperin's music may have enjoyed the opportunity to show off, but their vocalizing was meant to be a contemplative aid. The mind tries to coax a single letter into ventilating the distress or guilt elaborated in the ensuing verse. At the beginning of the *Troisième Leçon* two singers join to vocalize 'yod', and in less than half a minute their twinned voices give a sketch of the spiritual values it compresses. They begin in unison, then divide to run up and down the scale, sometimes dutifully filling in each rung on the ladder from earth to heaven, once or twice soaring towards a note that corresponds to the letter's flame-like summit. Breath, the medium of their art, is life, infused into human beings by God in Genesis. Exhaled in praise of the creator, it practises assembling those alphabetical pillars that, according to the Kabbalah, hold up the creation. Yet Jeremiah's verses ponder destruction, grieving over the enemy's assault on the temple at Jerusalem, and the ritual enacted in church also dramatized the extinction of the created world. The 'tenebrae' were lessons chanted as the shadows gathered on afternoons during Easter week. Candles lighted at the beginning of the service were put out one by one as each lesson was sung, to anticipate the moment when, as Christ died on the cross, the sun itself briefly expired. The performance mimes an apocalypse, a stealthy uncreation – to be followed, of course, by a miraculous resurrection.

The Bible is wary about written language, probably because it equips human beings with a talent they can use against God. Hence the injunction that the letter kills, whereas the spirit gives life. Spirit is breath, exhaled from the creator. Script is justifiable if it is scripture, written, as the Bible says when describing events on Mount Sinai, by the finger of God. That finger ends at the wrist, as Rembrandt's painting demonstrates; it is improper to imagine the rest of the body. Moses wrote at God's dictation, but he did so restrictively, incising onto his tablets a set of righteous prohibitions. Agrippa describes (or imagines) Moses descending from Sinai with the tablets. He carries the codified law, but bears in his head the Kabbalah with its 'mysterious interpretation' of God's word. Conferring with his brother

Aaron in his tent, he teaches him these 'secret powers'. Then Aaron's sons are called in to be instructed, and they remain to listen while the seventy elders of the Sanhedrin receive their tutorial in the 'hidden knowledge', followed by an open session for the elect of the common people. As the source retreats into the distance, the memory of what it confided frays. The common people are given only one chance to absorb what 'the voice of the Most High' said to Moses, while the Sanhedrin hear it twice, Aaron's sons three times, and Aaron himself four. The tablets are then smashed, since Moses judges the worshippers of the golden calf unready even for this veiled summary of the divine purpose.

In the Bible, Moses takes some trusted companions with him on his second ascent of the mountain, but they are not privy to his conversation with God. The emphasis is always on restricted access, a rigidly graduated need to know. Hence the suspicion of writing, an art which secularizes and disseminates the truth. The Israelites initially passed on their lore by word of mouth. When they began to transcribe their doctrine, they abandoned picture-writing and used abstract signs in place of things, which helped to preserve the mystery. Other religions were still more intolerant of novelty, invention, mental independence. Averroës – the twelfth-century Muslim philosopher, who was born in Córdoba and died in Marrakesh – valiantly defended Aristotle against religious dogmatists; his followers in the Italian Renaissance argued for the primacy of reason rather than faith. In a story by Jorge Luis Borges, Averroës is at work on a treatise entitled *Destruction of Destruction*, which contradicts Persian mysticism by arguing that the deity has only a detached, generalized knowledge of the universe and does not bother about individual fates. Though he is living in Seville, he hears what he takes to be a muezzin outside the window: the sound is actually made by some children at play, one of whom sacrilegiously chants 'There is no god but the God'. In the evening he attends a dinner at the home of a Koran scholar, another member of the Muslim diaspora in the Iberian peninsula. They speak of a fabled rose that grows in Hindustan, with blood-red petals whose markings, like letters, spell out the same exclusive theogony: 'There is no god but the God, and Mohammed is the Apostle of God'. Averroës declines to believe in the flower's existence. He points out that while flowers belong to nature, writing must be assigned to the very different, humanly sponsored realm of art. His remark causes a scandal. A fundamentalist righteously denies 'that writing is an art, since the original of the Koran – *the mother of the Book* – is prior to Creation and is kept in heaven'. That heaven is a copyright library; books, as in the era before Gutenberg's printing press, are chained to the furniture, not available for circulation. The Koran is supposedly the direct speech of God, not transcribed or interpreted by prophets or evangelists like those who wrote the Bible. It is prescriptive, and leaves no room for human inquiry. The life's work of believers ought to consist of memorizing it: the word Koran means recitation. This is why the addition of some fictional verses to the Koran seemed to be satanic, punishable by the burning of books and a death-sentence imposed on the offending novelist. The very notion of the novel is infidel, blasphemous in its usurpation of a divine power to engender life and to plot the fates of living men and women. Human creativity can only begin from such daring emendations of holy writ. No fatwah condemned Thomas Carlyle, who in 1840 dismissed the Koran as 'a stupid piece of prolix absurdity' and jeered at the notion that 'God wrote that!' Though Carlyle mocked Mohammed, he was quite happy to believe that a god, walking the earth in the guise of a bumpkin from Stratford, had written Shakespeare's plays.

God gave men free will, then blamed them for using it when they ate the apple. In art, free will expresses itself as fantasy, a playful inventiveness that refuses to be cramped by commandments. This secession from sanctity appears even in the illustration of religious texts. In medieval manuscripts, creativity may be marginalized – banished to the border surrounding the sacrosanct words – but it flourishes there, producing jungles of ornament. Once it has taken root, it extends to make scurrilous attacks on the letters that spell out the truth. E. H. Gombrich, in his study of decorative art, reproduces some initial capitals that are quickened into life by calligraphy, encouraged to stretch between solemn allegory and reckless caprice. In a tenth-century lectionary from Reichenau, the letter I is a tree up which a man is clambering; it has grown fronds at regular intervals on its trunk, conveniently providing him with footholds, but he scowls unhappily, not sure of his success. If he were to reach the summit, he would find only an abstract series of enchained shapes that hardly represent foliage. The same interlinked pattern, reproduced upside down, does duty for the root system at the base of the tree. Since top and bottom are the same, his climb is taking him nowhere.

An initial A from a twelfth-century version of Jerome's commentary on Genesis is even more extravagantly unfunctional. One of the letter's slanting bars is provided by the body of a winged dragon, which rests on a crutch that supplies the other bar. The dragon unfurls a tongue that loops into curlicues and turns vegetative. A boy who happens to be riding on the dragon's neck swivels his head behind him and gobbles one of the floral clumps that grow from this tongue, and uses his hands to pick others: the scribe has made the ogre into a flowering tree, with vines and tendrils sprouting from its tail. The boy sitting astride it also redefines it to suit himself, and has decided that it is edible. Somehow the A's cross-bar has to be disentangled from the overlapping foliage and the entwined bodies of

ETbI

OPI

AM.

TE NEBRAS.
uel caliginem.
Affiriozit' dirigentium.
A dam. homo. fiue terren². aut
mdigena. uel terra rubra.

the boy and the dragon. The servile task of connecting the two slanted bars is performed by a sacrificial animal gripped in the dragon's talons; it is then underlined by a collision between the dragon's clawed foot and what looks like a bunched fist but turns out to be the budding offshoot of a creeper that sprouts from the boy's toe. Under the canopy of the double cross-bar, a sarcastic vignette displays the difficulty of language-learning. A man takes a rod to a muzzled dancing bear, which is a slow pupil. The man utters the letters ABC, which protrude from his mouth. The bear can only repeat A. Perhaps the lesson should have started with R, which is the transliteration of a growl. Meanwhile the censorious teacher's skirt has developed a mind of its own,

Initial A from St Jerome's commentary on Genesis, Trinity College, 12th century

and is billowing into tufts like those of the vegetation. And in his hand he brandishes a graphic pun: the knob-ended stick with which he threatens the bear might also be the dragon's penis (just as the dragon's tongue protrudes through the legs of the boy in a phallic flourish). At the top of the tree, a boy eats fruit that has not been forbidden. At the bottom, a teacher – a deputy for the faithful Jerome – ought to be forcing doctrine into the head of his unregenerate pupil, which is what religious educators do. But his mission is let down by the magical transmutation of his stick, which turns castigation into sexual delight. The A forms a ladder which, like the tree-shaped I in the lectionary, is supposed to help us to clamber up from ignorance to knowledge. The boy who rides it, however, uses it to play truant, and the scribe, allowing his pen to trace these digressive, free-associating trails, has done the same. Creativity here runs riot. Has Genesis been illustrated or superseded?

As a result of our moral and linguistic training, the hand that writes constructs words. The hand that draws is not so disciplined. In 1515 Albrecht Dürer contributed some pen drawings to a prayer book for Emperor Maximilian I. The book's type, which imitated Gothic script, vouched for the authority of the texts on which Maximilian was expected to meditate. Dürer's marginalia, however, are either irrelevant or irreverent. Psalm 48, which calls for trumpets and cornets to make a joyful noise in praising God, is aptly illustrated by a rustic concert. But the musicians are hardly angelic harmonists: they struggle to master their instruments and puff out what must be sour notes, their faces straining and their bellies bulging. A woodpecker perched on a tree above them looks down askance, and an elephant in the opposite margin unwreathes a trunk that might do a better job of trumpeting.

Another page has a prayer addressed to St Apollonia, who stands on a hillock of unkempt weeds instead of the cloud that befits a martyr. Her pediment of grass spreads from the open mouth of a thistle that grows in air not earth: if we follow its tendrils down, they coil around Dürer's initials and the date of his drawings, so his fertile mind is their source. Apollonia's martyrdom was dental. Her persecutors smashed her teeth with pincers, and – along with the palm that was her heavenly reward – she grips the grisly calipers used by dentists, whose patron saint she is. An illicit, impish association of ideas repeats the shape of that torturing tool elsewhere in the design. Below, a crane stalks a tortoise. Its beak resembles the dentists' pliers, and it has used them to pick up a tasty morsel: the blades close on a fly just as, in conventional representations of Apollonia, the pincers grip an extracted tooth. The text perilously strays into the margin, a zone of decorative liberty. An 'n' on the bottom line lets down a coiled excrescence that might be a creeper. Dürer cannot resist its invitation, and fills in a maze of swags and twists. The thicket is inorganic, but the eye can give it a purpose by making up a story. Could this be the cover that the tortoise is heading for, or the bush in which the crane found the fly buzzing?

Elsewhere in the prayer book, Hercules – a shaggy wild man of the woods, clad in pelts – aims his bow and arrow at an air-force of birds that terrorize Arcadia with razory feathers and brass claws. The excuse for this, according to Erwin Panofsky, must have been Maximilian's claim that Hercules Aegyptiacus was one of his ancestors, along with the god Osiris and the patriarch Noah. Hercules, climbing up a prickly shrub to take aim at the beasts, supports himself on an imaginary family tree. The God who beams down on the praying Virgin as she receives the annunciation from the dove might be another of Maximilian's notional forbears, since he is robed, crowned and enthroned like an emperor, with an orb in his hand. Mary's prayer book is open on a lectern. A tasselled book-mark hangs over the side, pointing to Dürer's initials: he has metaphorically carved his name and the date into the wood. Meanwhile the cloud on which God floats excretes vengeance, peppering a hirsute, screeching demon with fire and brimstone. The deity, directly above, is a political allegory, loaded with the insignia of supremacy like Maximilian on the triumphal arch that Dürer designed for him; the devil is a lethally funny caricature. Dürer sketches glory, in the straight lines and empty spaces that persuade us to see a blaze of golden brightness around God's head. He also gives form to a fiend we usually see

only with our mind's eye, which implies that the devil is a fictional construction, incoherently assembled by fitting together a bat's wings, a vulture's
feet, and the tail of a lion, all attached to the face of the ugliest and most
splenetic man we can imagine. God and his arch-enemy have no power
over us unless an artist shows us what they look like, which means that the
artist has a share in inventing them.

Baudelaire, after the breach between religion and art, said that poetry
was the only miracle that God still allowed us. Genius did the work of
Genesis: it was language that made possible this radiant vision, although the
letters were no longer – as in the Kabbalah – the imprint of God. Playing
with words in *Les contemplations* in 1855, Victor Hugo introduced a third
term into St John's parable: the word is allegorically promoted to the
Word and becomes God's helper, but the spiritual mystery is grounded
in language, or in literature. As Hugo put it, 'le mot, c'est le Verbe, et le
Verbe, c'est Dieu'. In 1873 Arthur Rimbaud restored grace to a shop-soiled,
unhallowed alphabet in his sonnet on vowels. Rimbaud boasted of having
invented a verbal alchemy. Alchemists impiously attempted to change nature,
to improve God's creation by transmuting base metals to gold; the poet
undertook a similar experiment when he ascribed colours to vowels – A was
black, E white, I red, O blue, U green – and, without combining them to
make words, turned solitary letters into sensations, landscapes, monsters.

Significantly, Rimbaud made no attempt to redeem consonants. Hebrew
originally dispensed with vowels, because consonants are the true fabric of
language. The name they are given refers to their concordant function, since
they sound together to produce meanings. They have a masonic solidity,
being consciously shaped inside the mouth, which is why they are classified
as labial, dental, guttural or palatal sounds. Vowels require no such contact
between the body's organs or implements; they are merely pitched air,
vibrations of the vocal cords. The Hebrew believer had to imagine which
vowels to insert between the consonants, and in doing so he breathed life
into them – expanding 'glm', for instance, into 'golem', as if summoning the
creature into existence. The Pythagoreans thought that consonants were
kneaded from the same prime matter that the First Cause used when
making the universe; gnostic theologians called consonants 'hylic', using
the Greek word for that original substance, whereas vowels were psychic
or pneumatic – unvoiced thoughts or unseen emissions of breath. In the
Kabbalah, vowels are circular because they denote the soul, and they
accordingly belong to God. Consonants, whose form is square in Hebrew
script, represent bodies, and enumerate the twelve tribes of Israel.

For Rimbaud, the vacuity of vowels was what made them holy.
Reversing the history of language, he treated them as pictographs or hieroglyphs – signs that point to physical objects, not abstract symbols like our

customary ABC. But a vowel on its own can name nothing, so Rimbaud's associations are capricious and subjective, upsetting the communal agreement on which language depends. A is black because the shape of the letter reminds him of a fly buzzing over ordure. Inside the triangle he finds 'gulfs of shadow', a miniature Chaos like that from which the world was born. E is white because the gaps between its horizontal bars suggest misty, streaming vapours. I is red because its thinness resembles a trickle of blood or pinched, smiling lips. U is green like the sea because it undulates, with a trough in the middle; it also evokes the acid wrinkles incised on the brow of an elderly alchemist. O comes last in the list because its emptiness allows Rimbaud to see the blue sky through it and to catch a glimpse, as he says, of the extra-terrestrial silences that angels traverse. It emboldens him to take over Christ's citation of the Greek alphabet: his O, in the final line of the poem, is Omega, but this mystical assertion is actually a sensuous confession – its blue is the violet ray that beams from his lover's eyes. The Kabbalah venerated letters as tokens of the divine. In Rimbaud's sonnet, they refer to fantasies that are profane and idiosyncratically personal, like the flies with their velvety corsets or the woman's breasts that he sees when he rolls E over onto its back. Those breasts, 'white kings', are placed beside glaciers, and the connection chills and sterilizes amorous flesh. Nature no longer provides an allegorical guide to the supernatural realm, but it can at least be coldly rearranged into art.

Rimbaud's vowels are vivified letters. In two modernist alphabets, letters escape from the regimentation of language and turn into athletes or parading mannequins. Almost naked, they disregard spirit and instead flaunt the physical vitality of their strokes like frisky limbs; their elasticity recovers a power that had been forgotten or lost, and acts as a reminder that artists, whether their medium is verbal or visual or aural, must recreate the materials they use.

In 1926 in Prague, the dancer Milca Mayerova choreographed a sequence of twenty-four poems by Vítěslav Nezval. The terse rhymed quatrains were brisk work-outs for the separate letters of the alphabet, which the dancer mimicked with her strict bodily semaphore. Nezval's poetry sought to give reality back its 'shining image, as on the first day of its existence'. He saw the spires on the Prague skyline as the fingers of saints, and also likened them to the fingers with which he wrote his poems. He extricated objects from a background that camouflaged them, placing a glass – as he said – in the sky not on a table, or a door next to an ocean rather than on a staircase; for the same reason, he atomized words to set free single, individual letters. Mayerova's performance was photographed and published in a book entitled *Abeceda*. The word is used as a name for alphabetic primers: this is the kind of manual from which we first learn to recognize the

symbols – 'magic signs' as the designer Karel Teige called them – that from now on we will accept as stand-ins for living things. The context is infantile; it takes us back to childhood and therefore to Eden, evoked by Nezval's yearning for that first, fresh day. But the games in *Abeceda* are impudently erotic, freed from an educational system that sententiously marshalls words into sentences and teaches spelling and grammar as if they were the Ten Commandments. Teige's lay-out presents the alphabet as a series of gymnastic exercises for the body of an uninhibited modern woman, dressed in a scanty tunic with her hair pushed beneath a swimmer's cap. The creation of language is here

Karel Teige, the letter H from the book *Abeceda* by Vítěslav Nezval, 1923

not an arduous chore; nor does it carry with it the God-given burdens of rationality and responsibility. It derives, like all enjoyments, from the body's self-exploration, and it redefines art as a physical pleasure. The dancer's artwork is her own perverse, lithe arrangement of her arms and legs.

On the printed pages, Mayerova competes with stolid typed capitals, which set a severe, rectilinear standard: how can a mere organism match their geometrical posture? A is easy. The dancer's torso, gently expanding from the pinnacle of her head, matches the letter's pyramidal outline, with her spread legs as its anchorage. Kicking, her leg sticks out to make the middle bar of E. G twists her into awkward contortions like a flamenco dancer. H gives her even more trouble, but she passes the test by crossing her legs and fixing her forearms at right angles. Impersonating R, she crooks her arms, lifts her back leg, and runs on the spot. To form a V, she stands on her head and opens her legs like scissors. Her body speaks, acting out the elementary babble of Nezval's poems with their references to sport, cowboys and the jazzy frenzy of modern life.

Mayerova constructs an alphabet with her bare limbs. The women in the alphabet painted by Erté in 1927 are skimpily-clad mannequins not gymnasts, and they use their accessories – fans, veils, hats, ruffs – to produce the alphabet's inorganic extrusions. Two of them spell out Erté's name. Born Romain de Tirtoff, he fled from the Bolshevik revolution and set himself up as a designer in Paris, rechristening himself Erté after the French pronunciation of his initials, R and T. R's thin body is almost bare except for her dripping jewels, although she holds her fingers to her lips in a gesture of simpering innocence. Behind her, she generates the curves that the letter needs with the help of a plumed purple head-dress and a billowing train like a peacock's tail. T spreads her arms as if flagrantly dangling from a cross. But despite her enjoyable agony, her feet rest on a mound of greenery – a mount of Venus? – and from this grow creepers that twine up her naked legs and effloresce in her pudenda. If Erté's women suffer, like the crucified T, it is only in order to be beautiful.

The letter T from the alphabet by Erté, 1927–67

Their anguish is prescribed by the designer when he tightens their waists, props them on spiked heels, and expects them to be double-jointed. Pain, no longer purgative, is a cruel infliction of the artist, who punishes physical reality to make it match his vision.

For Erté's E, two Art Deco nymphs with hair stiffened into a permanent wave pretend to be angels, and demurely kneel to say their prayers. Their outstretched wings provide the upper bars of the letter, and the bottom bar is the fluffy white cloud on which they float. B is a buxom Eve who twists a snake around her midriff and arranges its coils to form the letter. She rests on its tail, and caresses its neck; its tongue flicks to and fro in appreciation. Unashamed, she lacks a figleaf, though she drapes strings of pearls around her sleek limbs. M is two silhouetted female butterflies, still enclosed in a sticky chrysalis. Behind them, the outline of their wings is a frieze of infernal flame. X, with her arms and legs spread wide, is a dominatrix. Her head is hooded, and she wears long gloves and boots with jagged fins. A body stocking rearranges her innards and makes them glare through the surface as if she were X-rayed. She has eyes where her nipples ought to be, while a skull grins at her groin. This alphabet is a lexicon of sacrilege; the letters spell out a litany of erotic possibilities.

The notion of a sacred language retained its appeal because it sanctified art. In 1916 the Dadaist Hugo Ball put on a witch's peaked hat and slithered inside a shiny cylinder of cardboard to recite his 'sound-poems' at the Cabaret Voltaire in Zurich. His nonsense verses were made of noise, and disdained intelligible meaning: one phonetic incantation was 'glandridi glassala tuffm i zimbrabim'. With these babbled vocables, Ball claimed to have rediscovered 'the evangelical concept of the Logos'. He often repeated the Credo of the Mass to himself, and once sang it out loud. But the hymn's assertions about the omnipotent father and the 'sanctam catholicam et apostolicam ecclesiam' did not interest him; what mattered, he said in his notebook, was the way the vowels sounded when they boomed in space. Seeking support for his belief in the creative value of pure sound, Ball consulted the gnostic philosophy of Basilides, who quoted the third verse of Genesis and asked where that originating light shone from. 'From the void,' said Basilides in answer to his own question; all we can know is that 'it came from the voice of the one speaking'. As he recited, Ball flapped the wings attached to his cardboard costume, which made him look like a megaphone on legs. Could this be how the world was spoken into being?

The divinity of letters extended to the sounds made when those letters were spoken. In 1915 Karl Kraus protested against proposals for the orthographic reform of German. He disliked the new spelling because it would eliminate the letter 'h', an aspirate which – in words like 'Athem' or 'Hauch', meaning breath – he identified with the exhalation that turned clay into a living soul. Hence Kraus's reverence for a phrase in Goethe's 'Wandrers Nachtlied'. The nocturnal wanderer feels peace descending on the hills; the forest birds are silent; he serenely predicts his own arrival at a state of rest, which may be extinction. Meanwhile the air is still, disturbed only by the poet's faint utterance when he says 'Spürest du/ Kaum einen Hauch' – you feel scarcely a breath. Kraus considered the last word, or rather the controlled release of air that made it, to be as sacred as the breath of God in Genesis. In a world still dormant, we eavesdrop on a moment of divine inspiration. Schubert took the poem as the text for one of his most glorious songs, and relied on the singer to make audible the quickening of the soul. More desperately, Hofmannsthal's sleepless, guilt-wracked Klytämnestra in Strauss's *Elektra* begs for a single word of support or assistance from her sullen daughter. She asks little, she says: 'Was ist denn ein Hauch?' The crucial word, lengthening as she gutturally ejects it from her distraught body, has a death rattle in it.

As Pythagoras argued, the musical scale enabled men to overhear the unison of the supernatural realm. When Arnold Schoenberg upset this harmonic system, he presented his theory of dissonance as a new gospel. He claimed that his twelve tones, laid out in a row not hierarchically ranked, could lift us into the heaven described by Emanuel Swedenborg, where earthly measures of length, breadth and height are confounded. In his second String Quartet, completed in 1908, a soprano sings a poem by

Stefan George that describes lifting off from the earth and surrendering to a buoyant cosmic breeze, 'dem grossen Atem'. The score creates that breathy, vaporous state by abandoning tonal anchorage, and its weightlessness makes the singer feel she is levitating. She is, as she says at the end of George's poem, a mere spark from the holy fire, an echo of the holy voice. For Schoenberg, to sing was to speak in tongues, to breathe out a pentecostal flame. When he conducted two of Alban Berg's *Altenberglieder* at a concert in Vienna in 1913, a critic scoffed that the songs, relaying wispy echoes from remote interstellar distances, might as well have been 'music of the spheres'. Berg, Schoenberg's pupil, had written music that was at once mystical and psychological – a transcription of unmoored outer space, and a report on the swimming, light-headed inner space of modern consciousness. The first vocal sound in the *Altenberglieder* is the soprano's humming. Her mouth is closed as she guards this muffled, initiating energy inside herself. Then she releases a single, exclamatory word – 'Seele!', an apostrophe addressed to the soul. We might be listening to the moment of creation when, as the Kabbalah describes it, God held his breath before allowing the pneuma to be felt and heard. The third song in the cycle stealthily articulates a dode-caphonic chord. A celesta faintly scintillates, and the singer declares that we are gazing beyond the limits of the universe. The twelve tones stake out that border, which disappears as we cross it.

By what he called 'methodical application', Schoenberg derived his opera *Moses und Aron* from a single set of twelve tones. He even ensured the title would have exactly twelve letters by respelling the name of Aaron, the glib rhetorician who corrupts the austere message of his brother Moses. The voice from the burning bush shimmers in mid-air like a dodecaphonic mirage: six speakers and six singers overlap as they utter the many-tongued prophecy, the words delivering precise instructions while the notes sur-round them with a glowing aura. Speech and song combine here, although they clash in the relationship between the brothers. The stammering Moses is restricted to words, which falter as they attempt to describe a God who is unknowable. Aron, a liltingly fluent tenor, relies on song to slither over con-ceptual obstacles; accompanied by a skittish flute, he takes the pained, halting line-up of twelve tones traversed by Moses and flexes the row into a facile, honeyed melody. He further betrays the idea when he encourages the people, who are bemused by the notion of a God they cannot see, to worship an idol. It is the same defamation that Rembrandt examines in his painting about what can and cannot be depicted. The gold which Aron moulds into the shape of a calf is solid and sumptuous, like the trophies on Belshazzar's table; when the people cavort around it, they take part in a fer-tility rite, confusing creation with procreation. But art should do more than appeal to our avarice by taking inventory of the world's contents or glossily reproducing the surface of things. Rembrandt therefore reveals a cloud of unknowing that is able to write, and Schoenberg places on stage a bush that can speak and sing.

Moses – in a third act for which Schoenberg, making his own choice between speech and song, wrote the words but no music – alludes to an incident during the Exodus, when God caused water to gush from a rock to sustain the parched Israelites. In the opera, Moses berates Aron for using his rod to strike the rock, as God commanded. The marvel is too showy; Aron should have spoken to the rock instead. The *Zohar* uses similar imagery to interpret the two sets of tablets Moses brought down from Sinai. The first, which he smashed to curtail the orgy, came from the Tree of Life; the second, incised with the commandments when he was called back to the mountain, was taken from the Tree of Good and Evil. In both cases, written doctrine needs to be orally explained. The Torah, with its letters engraved in stone, must be supplemented by the Kabbalah, which uses a hammer to crush the stone or to strike illuminating sparks from it. Schoenberg's Moses changes the rules, and makes the process of interpretation more self-defeatingly arduous. By battering the rock, Aron confirms his confinement to material reality. A word alone, Moses claims, might have drawn water from it. But in practice the word is unavailable, the vision unrealizable, which is why Schoenberg left the opera uncompleted. Its curtailment marks a tragic breach between God and man, or between divine creation and its human mimicry. The best way to preserve the idea's integrity is to leave it unexpressed. Schoenberg composed the first two acts of *Moses und Aron* between 1930 and 1932, and worked briefly on the third act in 1937. By then he had fled from the Third Reich and settled in Los Angeles, which he found as arid as the biblical wilderness. But, like Moses, he continued his exclusive colloquy with God: in the *Modern Psalms* he wrote shortly before his death in 1951, he attacked learned Philistines and their abhorrence of mystery, and declared that he preferred the credulity of children to the worldly-wise scepticism of adults whose imagination 'fails to understand the fact of eternity'.

Schoenberg took Moses into exile with him, along with his faith in an art that could comprehend infinitude. Freud, quitting Vienna when Hitler annexed Austria in 1938, left behind him a Moses who had no valid claim to prophetic status. After his arrival in London, Freud authorized publication of his essay *Moses and Monotheism*, which, as he admitted with a grimace of ironic regret, deprived the Jewish people 'of the man whom they take pride in as the greatest of their sons'. Freud conjectured that Moses was an Egyptian aristocrat; his religion derived from Akhenaten, who first exchanged a 'barbarous polytheism' for the worship of a single, solitary god, as impalpable as the soul or the wind. The disdain for images expressed by

Michelangelo,
*Moses*, 1515

Schoenberg's Moses turns out to be intellectually justified: by insisting that
God could neither be seen nor imagined, Moses maintained, as Freud says,
the 'omnipotence of thoughts' and 'the magic of words'. Thanks to him,
men can congratulate themselves on the development of speech, which
awards them power because they know how to give names to abstractions.
In 1914 in his essay 'The Moses of Michelangelo', Freud praised the sculptor for redeeming and reforming the biblical character in the monument he
designed for a papal tomb. The Moses of tradition is intemperate and
uncompromising (which is why Schoenberg admired him); he is as eruptive

as the volcanic Yahweh, who makes Sinai quake and rumble throughout his consultation with Moses. Freud notes that Michelangelo calms the divine ire of Moses, and dissuades him from hurling away the tablets. Struggling to control neurotic impulses that imperil his intellectual mission, Michelangelo's figure becomes 'a concrete expression of the highest mental achievement that is possible in man'. That, for Freud, outranked his biblical function as God's amanuensis. Thomas Mann, who lived near Schoenberg in Los Angeles, redefined the fanatical prophet as a finicky artist in his story *The Tables of the Law*, published in 1943. Schoenberg's Moses is an operatic character who cannot or will not sing; Mann's literary Moses has no such scruples about art, and is proud of his achievement as a writer. A twelfth-century French Bible in the British Museum shows Moses reaching up from the fire-breathing mountain to clasp a rolled manuscript which is passed down to him by the hand of God. Mann's Moses takes over responsibility for the sacred text; he not only writes it, but even devises the language in which he does so.

Preparing to receive the revelation on Sinai, he asks himself 'How was he to write?' In Egypt he became expert in 'picture writing'. He can also mimic the 'cramped cuneiform' used for negotiations between kings, and has studied the 'semantic magic' of the Midianites with their symbolic tokens. But none of these methods for communicating ideas will serve, because they depend on a local language that is translated into elaborative figurative diagrams. Moses needs a kind of writing that is simple and accessible to his childish people. No such idiom exists, so he invents it. He classifies consonants depending on whether the lips, tongue, palate or throat are used to produce them, and separately lists the 'open sounds' or vowels. Having tabulated sounds, he allots them corresponding signs, which instruct speakers 'to buzz or hiss, to huff or puff, or mumble or rumble' – to behave, in fact, like fulminating Sinai. The sounds combine into 'words and pictures of things'; the combinations are countless, and can be extended into any other language. Equipped with this script, Mann's Moses can 'set down the whole world in writing'. He uses an engraving tool to scratch, drill and chisel his new vocabulary of runes into the rock, and then – because, like Blake, he is both poet and painter – he colours the indentations with his blood. God is supposedly near, but during the first session on Sinai his dictatorial voice is never heard. So when Moses writes 'I, Jahwe, am thy God', is he saying so in his own person? On his return to the mountain, God speaks to him, and Moses, rather than merely copying down the divine decrees, now answers back. He bargains with God, negotiating a pardon for the truant children of Israel. Man demands the humanizing of deity; in calling for grace and mercy, Moses anachronistically imagines the figure of Christ.

This change is announced by Mann's reinterpretation of the horns that sprout from Moses' head. This grotesque excrescence is the result of a misunderstanding. In the Bible, the prophet's face is said to have been irradiated by his exposure to God's presence. Jerome, who translated the Bible into Latin in the early fifth century, stumbled over the ambiguous Hebrew word 'karan', and took it to mean that Moses, rather than merely glowing, had grown horns. Jusepe de Ribera, in a Neapolitan painting from the 1630s, showed him holding up the tablets while two fiery columns flare from his forehead like searchlights: illumination has seared its way into his brain, and it shines out as if through holes in his skull. Sculpture is more literal, which is why Michelangelo carved two stumpy pinnacles of bone on the forehead of his Moses. Mann has his own explanation for these budding antlers. They are the insignia of Moses' genius, not an honorific head-dress awarded by God. When he perfects his written language, 'horns stood forth from his head out of sheer pride of his god-invention. ...A god-inspiration! An inspiration with horns to it!' He is on a volcanic mountain, which expels the heat of the earth's core through its vents; his head resembles the peak, glowing and steaming 'like a furnace' as his brain seethes. Mann's imagery is industrial. The horns function as factory chimneys, releasing the pent-up, boiling vapour that might otherwise cause his head to explode.

In 1659 Rembrandt painted Moses throwing down the tablets, and made him look weary not irate, exhausted by disappointment. When Mann's Moses remembers this act of self-spiting iconoclasm, he sees it differently. He relishes the chore of engraving the commandments a second time, and tints them with a fresh trickle of blood. Looking back on the first draft, he reflects that the engraving on the original tablets might have been better. He tells God that 'it was no great loss that I broke the first ones: there were a few bad letters in them. I will confess to You now that I thought of it when I smashed them'. The prophet angered by the world's incomprehension is now an artist with a responsibility to revise his work. If only God had been such a perfectionist!

# 6
# THE SUPREME ARTISAN

God, having created everything, left little room for human creativity. Augustine enforced the prohibition in a punning edict. 'Creatura non potest creare', he insisted: a creature should not presume to create. Medieval doctrine extolled this divine monopoly. Patristic allegorists found God's autograph everywhere, and indexed creatures to clarify their moral purpose. Every living thing, according to the theologian Alain of Lille, was a book or a picture, personally designed by God. The pelican's habit of rending its flesh to feed its young exemplified Christ's sacrifice. The dove literally incorporated the holy spirit: its moaning call was a lament for sin, and the rocky crevices in which it nests – as explained by the Song of Songs – were the wounds of Christ. The devil grimaced from the monkey's rump. Even bad weather had its allegorical uses. Rain clouds cool the earth, which meant that they cure the heat of vice. In *De musica*, Augustine likened the thronging, multitudinous creation to an epigram or a sonnet: art at its most refined and rigorous, perfectly balancing means and ends. Peter Lombard, the theologian who wrote the *Four Books of Sentences* prescribed by universities during the thirteenth century, endowed Christ, as the Word of God, with intellectual mastery of all sciences and arts.

Man-made works had to prove their worthiness by fitting into a providential scheme. Medieval cathedrals, in which all human arts collaborated to construct a house for God, replicated the ground plan of the universe. Modules could be added and multiplied, but the layout invariably inscribed the sign of the cross on the ground, with the main altar orientated eastwards, pointing to Jerusalem and the rising sun that signified resurrection. The Bible contained specimens of all literary genres, and demonstrated their sacred source: the angels praise God in hymns, and Mary's response to the announcement of her pregnancy is to extemporize a poem, the Magnificat. In *Pearl*, an anonymous Middle English poem written late in the fourteenth century, a jeweller who has lost his most precious treasure falls asleep, and is transported to an earthly paradise where the pebbles are sapphires and emeralds. He meets a young woman, 'ful debonare', who turns out to be his missing gem. He gapes at her ivory-pale visage and admires her luminous setting, then says that he hopes that his bewildering vision is 'gostly' (meaning spiritual). No other assumption could be tolerated. Pearl explains that she is an uprisen soul who now inhabits the New Jerusalem, and chides him for his mundane concern with beauty and riches. Nevertheless, the extravagant brilliance of the poem's imagery protests against her puritanism. Is God the unknown artist's alibi?

In his epistle to the Ephesians, St Paul reminded men that they were evidence of God's 'workmanship, created in Christ Jesus unto good works, which God hath before ordained'. Craft and creativity joined hands and revolved in a circle; beauty mattered less than utility, since the God who worked to make us expected us to spend our lives performing good works. St Thomas Aquinas criticized the jesting physics of Democritus, who thought that the world was formed by the chancy junction of atoms. God surely had no unconscious motives or spasmodic impulses, and left nothing to chance. According to Paul's terminology, the world was fabricated, patiently and purposefully framed; the generative task resembled carpentry, or the stitching together of clothes (which, in one version of the story, God prepares for Adam and Eve to wear). *Pearl*, when describing the Arabian phoenix, says that the fabled bird was created by a 'fasor'. The Old French word suggests that God is a factor, a manufacturer, busy and business-like.

Jean Pucelle, a fourteenth-century French illustrator of breviaries, called God 'the Creator, the Supreme Artisan'. The accolade yoked together two very different notions. A creator retains the right, disputed by Aristotle, to bring forth something from nothing; Aquinas made it possible for God to do so by arguing that he existed outside nature, which meant that he was not subject to the Aristotelian laws that constrain all other agents. An artisan, even if supreme, is a lesser being, inferior to an artist. He has learned a trade, knows how to handle its tools, and can be relied on to perform the limited function for which he is employed. This was the unassuming self-estimation of the workers who carved stone, mixed pigments for staining glass, or decorated the margins of manuscripts. Piety and industry coincided in the daily routines of Benedictine monks. In their scriptoria, some specialists practised calligraphy while others painted initials. In separate workshops, bookbinders, goldsmiths, weavers and ceramicists concentrated on exercising technical skills of their own. In monastic foundries, bells were shaped and tuned. The aim of all these activities was expiation. Theophilus, a Greek scholar who probably entered a Benedictine monastery in Germany during the tenth century, left a tract on vocational training, called *Diversarum Artium Schedula*. He commends the making of gold leaf or the patterning of windows as occupations that can help the worker to 'avoid sloth of the mind or wandering of the soul'; the hands should be kept busy, as a control on the truant brain. Theophilus provides the 'well-intentioned man' with a list of utensils that must be made so that 'divine mysteries' can be enacted in church: 'chalices, candelabra, incense burners, vials, pitchers, caskets of sacred relics, crosses, missals and other things which useful necessity requires'. God commanded Moses to construct the tabernacle, singled out the master craftsmen who undertook the work, and taught them how to manipulate gold, silver, brass, gems and wood. Such skills, according to Theophilus, are as 'a gift of the sevenfold Spirit', because 'all created things proceed from God'. The purpose of adorning God's house is therefore to show 'everything in creation praising God, its creator'.

Near the end of the thirteenth century, the ecclesiastical legislator William Durand elaborated a dogmatic iconography for churches in his *Rationale Divinorum Officiorum*. Images, to teach the unlettered laity, had to be legible allegorically; otherwise they merely encouraged idolatry. Durand quoted the Mosaic prohibition on graven images, backed up by Paul's lesson that 'an idol is nothing in the world: and there is no God but One'. Every figure represented by an artist had to carry a prop, which served as badge of office and a defining moral attribute. God must hold in his hands a closed book, or perhaps – if he was shown giving Christ to the world – an open one. A strict etiquette governed the pictorial placement of the apostles, with Paul to the right of Christ and Peter to the left. Bishops had to be shown with mitres, virgins with trimmed lamps. Flowers or trees could be included in images of paradise, but only to demonstrate 'the fruit of good works springing from the roots of virtues'. It was not enough for a flower to be beautiful, since beauty is one of paganism's false gods, not a guarantee of goodness. Aesthetic response must be chastened before it lures us into erotic reverie: flowers, after all, are the flaunted pudenda of plants.

William of Conches in his commentary on *Timaeus* established three distinct, hierarchically ranked kinds of endeavour. Everything that exists in the world, he declared, was 'either the work of the creator, or a work of nature, or the work of an artificer imitating nature'. Aquinas slighted 'viles artifices': translated, this means lowly drudgery. Those 'artifices', as they are called in Aquinas's Latin, are unnatural, because our toil is a penance, a penalty incurred by Adam's fall; in Eden, providence had freely lavished its bounty on human beings, and there had been no need for labour to supplement niggardly nature. Art, restrictively defined as the capacity to make things that are useful, began by supplying two wants that were the direct consequence of our expulsion from the blissful garden. We need clothes, not only to cover our shame but because God's fury replaced the equable, eternal spring of paradise with the relentless succession of seasons and their contradictory extremes of weather. For the same reason, we need shelter.

In *Paradise Lost*, Adam and Eve sleep in a floral bower beneath a counter-pane of roses; the canopy deflowers itself overnight so the petals can keep them snug, but the damage is repaired before morning. Fallen man, preoccupied by keeping warm and dry, had to learn how to build a hut or – much later in his evolutionary march – a house. Rather than admiring the ingenuity with which humanity solved such problems, Aquinas chose to slight our desperate technical engineering, whether it involved the raising of roofs or the writing of books. He thought that 'art is deficient when compared with the operations of nature. For nature bestows substantial form, which art cannot do. All artificial forms are accidental.' Surely some of those accidents were happy, even inspired: the use of fire for cooking, or the invention of the wheel. But Aquinas refused to give us any credit for helping ourselves. A subsistence economy is all we deserve. Once the body's minimal needs have been satisfied, our labour, like that of the monastic craftsmen, should be dedicated to God.

To overcome this slight, art had to establish its divine provenance. Classical myth interpreted music, the less earthly of the arts, as an echo of cosmic harmony. Pythagoras calculated the intervals on a stringed instrument and aligned these with planetary orbits, so in playing music men kept the universe in tune. When it accompanied sessions of gymnastic training, music also helped maintain bodily health. In 1888 Erik Satie wrote three *Gymnopédies* for the piano, as a remote reminiscence of the stately workouts performed by naked Athenian boys. It is as if pallid statues were slowly moving their inflexible limbs; music like this, as Plato said, 'engendered sobriety'. Christianity acknowledged music's power, but placed cautious restrictions on it. Patristic commentators warned individuals against exposing themselves to the sorcery of music. Odysseus after all could not trust himself to resist the sirens, and had to be strapped to a mast. In the fourth century, St Basil thanked the holy spirit for inventing music, which he saw as a medicinal aid: it tranquillized the soul and pacified turbulent thoughts. Basil commended psalms and hymns because they mixed dogma with melody, and made truth palatable. In *Paradise Lost*, an oratorio is performed in heaven on the seventh day to celebrate the completion of God's creative labour. The harp, Milton notes, has no rest, and is accompanied by the pipe and dulcimer, sweet-stopped organs and 'All sounds on Fret by String or Golden Wire/ ... intermixt with Voice/ Choral or Unison'. The summary pointedly excludes vocal soloists. Symphony, as Basil pointed out, means a sounding together, a synchronism of like-minded voices, and this choral endeavour offers moral support. Averroës in his commentary on Plato's *Republic* worried about the hedonistic abuse of music, which could drive men mad. The auditor should cultivate self-control, like that of the Platonic lover; this, for Averroës, was 'the end at which the activity of music aims'.

Augustine felt that he had sinned grievously if he admired a singer rather than attending to the liturgy being sung. He made amends by equating technique with moral rigour: 'Music is the science of modulating correctly'. In St John Chrysostom's interpretations of the psalms, even modulations had a corrective purpose. These sonic shifts were intended to divert the slothful mind, which otherwise would pay no attention to 'spiritual readings'. But harmony had to obey rules, which served the purpose of exorcism. The devil too was a musician, and he specialized in jarring intervals like the tritone; this was banned by medieval theorists, who called it 'diabolus in musica'.

The heavenly hosts in the Bible speak the praises of God, and neither sing nor play instruments, as they so often do in Renaissance paintings. When Lorenzo in *The Merchant of Venice* offers Jessica a guided tour of the night sky, he tells her that the stars are like angels, 'quiring to the young-ey'd cherubins'; a free-thinking polytheist, he superimposes the Pythagorean spheres on the Christian heaven, and uses the celestial concert to celebrate the self-delight of pampered, privileged humanity. Traditional theology was warier. In 1516 Raphael painted a *Sacra Conversazione*, now in Bologna, which shows St Cecilia with her portable organ. It is in a sorry state, with several pipes missing; other instruments lie discarded at her feet. The damage and disarray are not the penalties of martyrdom. Earthly music is beneath Cecilia's dignity, and she raises her eyes to the clouds, where an angelic choir bends over its scores. Christian apologists derived the art from the psalmody of David, whose playing banished the depression of Saul. Yet they stumbled over Paul's letter to the Ephesians, which instructs his followers to speak in spiritual canticles, making melody only in their hearts. Was it wrong to let the voice sound aloud? In a fourth-century sermon, Niceta of Remesiana ventured to reverse the interpretation of Paul's ban. He contended that 'the spirit has freed our mouths, loosened our tongues and opened our lips, for it is not possible for men to speak without these organs'. He went on to identify Moses as the first singer, and to acclaim him for setting up a chorus, assisted by his timbrel-wielding sister Miriam. This would have startled Schoenberg, whose crabby, stuttering Moses is averse to music. Augustine, more censorious than Niceta, seconded the severe opinion of St Athanasius, 'who required the reader of the psalm to perform it with so little inflection of voice that it resembled speaking more than singing'.

Classical writers differentiated musical instruments according to their social propriety: those with strings were noble, those that relied on wind, like the pipes of Pan, were bucolic or plebeian. Basil's ranking depended on a spiritual gradation. The resonance of the psaltery, a triangular harp that was struck from above, offered a model of aspiration, while its ten strings recalled the decalogue. The brass wires of the cithara – the Hebrew kinor, David's instrument – were sounded from below against the plectrum, which made it an emblem of discipline for the body's nether regions. Niceta thought that the cithara had been able to cast out Saul's demons because its design prefigured Christ's sacrifice and his victory over Satan: the image of a cross is 'mystically exhibited in the wood and the stretched strings'. In John Chrysostom's reading, allegory dematerialized the instrument, which could now emit a music that was unsensual because silent. The singer of psalms can do without David's cithara, because by mortifying the flesh he has turned his body into a cithara – lean, taut, vibrant with virtue.

Hildegard of Bingen – the twelfth-century Benedictine nun who set her own liturgical poems to music – once had to plead against a prohibition on singing the Divine Office, imposed on her convent because she had buried an excommunicated person within its walls. In a letter to the prelates of Mainz, she contended that musical instruments had been invented by wise and zealous men; she went on to claim that those instruments, played by 'the flexing of their finger joints', offered a lesson in the manual craft of the creation, since Adam too was 'formed by the finger of God, which is the holy spirit'. Hildegard was an inflamed mystic, but also an astute politician who sagely corresponded with the potentates of the Holy Roman Empire. To defend her visionary delirium or her aesthetic whims, she relied on diplomatic cunning and a shrewd aptitude for interpreting scripture. The monk Guibert of Gembloux wondered why she had given the nuns in her convent crowns to wear: had the new fashion been prompted, he archly enquired, 'by divine revelations', or was it 'merely for the sake of ornamentation'? Hildegard replied that, in one of her reveries, she had seen 'that all the orders of the church have distinct emblems according to their celestial brightness, but that virginity has only the black veil and the sign of the cross'. Therefore she decided on white veils, alluding to the white garments worn in paradise, and on the heads of her virgins she placed circlets of three colours, which symbolized the Trinity. 'All of this,' she told Guibert, 'is fully described in *Scivias*', the book in which she made known the ways of God. *Scivias* transcribed her visions, so the sovereign authority she cited was her own imagination. She was, she admitted in introducing one of those florid dreams, a mere woman, not magisterially learned like her superiors in the church. All the same, a voice from the living fire had addressed her and instructed her to reveal its mysteries. Her three verbs – 'clama et enarra et scribe' – emphasized that the order could not be ignored, and implied that every kind of self-expression had been licensed: she was told to proclaim and recount and write down what she had seen, or perhaps imagined.

The Benedictine reformer St Bernard of Clairvaux, with whom Hildegard exchanged letters, assailed spendthrift abbots who beautified their churches and pretended they were doing so to honour God. The abbey of Cluny was said to be a fit place for angels to perambulate in; Hugh of St Victor thought of it as an earthly replica of the City of God. (Much later, a wit remarked that Radio City Music Hall in New York was the kind of place God would have built if he'd had the money.) In a letter to the abbot of St Thierry, Bernard railed against the showy height, immoderate length and superfluous breadth of such churches, their costly polishings and curious carvings and paintings, their gemmed cartwheels of light and candelabra like bronze trees. Why, he asked, should a sanctuary be gilded? A true monk preferred dung to riches. Was a saint more virtuous for being gaudily painted? Bernard grudgingly pardoned such public displays, because he knew that churches had to glut the eyes of 'vain and covetous folk' and entice them to make donations. He was more incensed by the gargoyles that rioted in cloisters, where the brethren were distracted from meditation on 'the law divine' by the mad marvels of their surroundings. His Latin twisted itself into knots in describing the 'amazing mis-shapen shapeliness and shapely mis-shapenneness' of these decorative monsters – filthy monkeys, rampant lions, randy centaurs. The mixed metaphors of Horace were the pitiable products of linguistic muddle, but Bernard's freaks reared into repulsive life like the ogres that tormented St Anthony: 'Here you behold several bodies beneath one head; there again several heads upon one body. Here you see a quadruped with the tail of a serpent; there a fish with the head of a quadruped. There an animal suggests a horse in front and half a goat behind; here a horned beast exhibits the rear parts of a horse'. Morphological whimsies like these spread across the cathedral at Rouen, where carvers placed a pig's head on the body of a solemn philosopher or transformed men into geese, dogs and cockerels. A single notorious column beside the porch of the abbey at Souillac goaded the mutants to prey on each other. Indefinable animals guzzle men; birds scratch at human flesh with razory claws or barbed beaks. The piled-up carnage turns cadavers into decorative art. Commentators anxious to give the column a theological purpose called it a foresight of apocalypse, but it looks more like a wild fantasia.

Column with mutants from the Eglise Saint-Marie, the former abbey-church of Souillac, c. 1075–1150

Bernard's anathema had no power against this impudent creativity. D. H. Lawrence imagined such unknown sculptors vivifying the churches on which they worked and loosening the rigidity of dogma. Lawrence pointed out that the way Christianity told 'the story of the Creation' censured sex. 'In the beginning was the Word' meant that conception happened not in the body but in the head, where an abstinent, otherworldly idea was implanted. This incorporeal faith produced an architecture of 'utter stability', where all existence was brought together to propound 'the One Being of All'. In his novel *The Rainbow*, Lawrence accused Rouen Cathedral, so oppressively inert, of representing a 'splendid absoluteness'; presumably he did not notice those grotesque hybrids. Yet in his essay on Thomas Hardy, as if imagining Bernard's cloisters or the animals at Souillac, Lawrence conceded that the cathedrals found a way of denying 'the Monism which the Whole uttered'. His evidence for this was the misbehaviour of gargoyles: 'the imps, ... whilst subordinated within the Great Conclusion of the Whole, still, from their obscurity, jeered their mockery of the Absolute, and declared for multiplicity, polygeny'. Polygeny is Lawrence's coinage, formed on an analogy with the equally unorthodox practice of polygamy. Only a new word could do justice to this promiscuous outpouring of imagination.

Bernard tried to make the monks feel ashamed of these follies, and also warned about the expense of indulging the truant fancy. At St Denis in Paris, Abbot Suger defied Bernard's iconoclastic crusade and his praise of Cistercian poverty. In 1121 Suger began to remodel and enrich his church, documenting the work in a self-immortalizing treatise on his administration. He began by demolishing the previous abbey, even though church lore claimed that Christ had made a detour to consecrate it. He also unregretfully wrecked an addition that Charlemagne had built so that his penitent father could be buried, face downwards not recumbent, outside the door. As Panofsky pointed out, Suger's was a 'destructively creative enterprise'. The correspondences between Old and New Testaments contrived by medieval doctrine revealed creation and destruction as God's two faces: Christ's cross had supposedly been chopped from the Tree of Life, and Calvary was Adam's burial place. Suger claimed for himself the prerogatives of a deity who equated death with rebirth. He vowed that he was prompted by 'the inspiration of the divine will', and believed he had good practical reasons for the venture: the old abbey was so narrow that, on the feast day of St Denis – as he said in a ripely comic reminiscence – women were squeezed as if in a winepress and had to scramble over the heads of men to reach the altar, while riotous mobs of worshippers forced the monks who held aloft the holy relics to escape by jumping through the windows.

Suger lavished precious metals and fine fabrics on the rebuilt shrine, using 'whatever is most valuable among created things'. To justify the

The arrival of St Denis in Paris, from the *Legend of St Denis*, 14th century

expenditure, he recalled God's demand that Solomon should erect a temple that was worthy of him. When funds ran short, he found, like Solomon, that 'the same author of the same work abundantly supplied his attendants'. He credited God with miraculously supplying sapphire glass for the windows, along with glaziers to install it and seven hundred pounds to pay the bill. The celestial architect, he concluded, 'would not suffer that there be a lack of means to complete the work. For he is "the beginning and the ending"'. The same scriptural text assured Suger of success: the overarching shape of the divine story, which advanced from the creation of the world to the revelation of the New Jerusalem, gave him confidence in the stability and viability of his long, draining architectural project. He appealed to Christ, 'who is the One, "the beginning and the ending, Alpha and Omega"', to 'join a good end to a good beginning by a safe middle'. For Suger, a quotation was a self-fulfilling prophecy.

He believed that the martyred spirits whose ashes he tended deserved such honour. But his arguments were defensive, which suggests that he knew there was a gap between art and religion, connoisseurship and devotion. His account of the consecration in 1140 notices 'the disparity between things human and divine', then intimates that such contradictions can be resolved with a little help from above: 'He who can inasmuch as he is God, and must inasmuch as he is the creator, may equalize (unless we resist) that perilous inequality within ourselves'. In a final prayer for the sacramental union of the material and the immaterial, Suger asks Christ to turn earth into heaven. He specifies that the transformation should happen 'invisibly', though a few lines earlier he rejoices to report that it has already taken place both visibly and audibly in the abbey: the choir's performance at the ceremony was so harmonious and consonant that it seemed 'a symphony angelic rather than human'. He used the provenance of a crystal vase in the abbey's collection to illustrate the ascent from earth to heaven. Eleanor of Aquitaine presented the vase to King Louis VI as a bridal gift; he passed it on to the abbey, where it was re-dedicated for use at the 'divine table'. After studding it with jewels, Suger commemorated its passage from hand to hand in some verses. His little poem concluded with Suger reaching up into the sky to offer the vessel to the saints. The treasury included another vase in porphyry, to which Suger added spread feet, arching angelic wings, and the elongated neck and stern beaky face of an eagle, all in silver gilt. The flagon gained a new identity: now it symbolized St John the Evangelist, mentally soaring above the earth as he looked into the future. Perhaps more truly, it also exemplified the exhilarating leap from utensil to work of art. Though destined for the altar, it now belongs to the Louvre, where it is known as 'l'aiguière de Suger'.

Rock crystal and gold ewer, from the treasury of Abbot Suger, St Denis

The jeweller in *Pearl* rhapsodizes about a paradise where jasper, ruby, chalcedony, emerald, sardonyx, beryl, topaz, amethyst and chrysoprase can safely be admired because the Apocalypse of St John had testified that Jerusalem was built on a foundation of gems. Suger too scavenged pearls and other gems with which he hoped to adorn a golden crucifix, transferring the credit for his most lucrative acquisition to a 'merry but notable miracle which the Lord granted us'. When funds were low, some impoverished monks offered to sell him a pile of hyacinths, sapphires, rubies, emeralds and topazes, which they had been given for alms. Suger shrewdly negotiated a price of 'four hundred pounds for the lot though they were worth much more', and 'thanked God' for his own acumen. Allegory absolved Suger, vindicating the vanity and cupidity that Bernard of Clairvaux condemned. As he said in his prayer to St Denis, 'That which is signified pleases more than that which signifies', and what the jewels signified was heaven. He found a biblical precedent for the altar's gilded furnishings: the Lord reminds Ezekiel that in Eden 'every precious stone was thy covering, the sardius, the topaz and the jasper, the chrysolite and the onyx, and the beryl, the sapphire and the carbuncle and the emerald'. But shortly before citing Ezekiel, Suger quotes Ovid, who in the second book of *Metamorphoses* says that 'The workmanship surpassed the material'. The phrase – applied to a panel behind the altar at St Denis, 'ennobled with chased relief work' – was taken from Ovid's description of the sun's palace, which is all gold and blazing bronze. Ovid, appraising a pair of ivory doors carved by Mulciber, announces that the artist who made them is superior to the creator: to engrave ivory is a more impressive feat than to create it in the first place. He goes on to survey the various regions portrayed on the doors – heaven, earth, and the sea between them – and notices that among the sea-gods is 'Proteus, who has no settled shape'. So how did Mulciber carve him? A being in perpetual flux cannot be sculpted; imagination conceives of marvels that beggar belief. Sliding between theology and myth, Suger pretended that the perverse, burgeoning creativity of *Metamorphoses* was compatible with Christian faith.

The 'many-coloured stones' of the decor induced a trance, in which Suger drifted above 'the slime of the earth'. Henry Adams felt the same sense of dazed disorientation when, early in the twentieth century, he visited Chartres and St Denis: their windows, he said, were 'a cluster of jewels – a delirium of coloured light'. But was the exaltation mystical or aesthetic? The same hallucination might be provoked by stimulating the brain narcotically. *The Mystery of Edwin Drood*, left incomplete when Dickens died, begins with a view of a sedate English cathedral, whose spire wavers, wobbles, and rearranges itself into the minareted palace of a sultan; the vision occurs in an opium den. During the 1950s, Aldous Huxley explored a Los Angeles drugstore while high on mescalin, and saw the aisles of cheap stacked wares as a cathedral ablaze with illumination. The rhetoric of Suger is equally vertiginous. As he concludes his evocation of the altar, he declares that only priceless vials and chalices should be used to decant

Rose window
from the north
transept of the
Abbey of St Denis

Christ's blood, and goes on, piling up superlatives, to bemoan the inadequacy of all his expenditure. At last he glimpses an alluring impossibility:
'a new creation', in which 'our substance' might be 're-formed from that
of the holy cherubim and seraphim' – although even then, he adds, this
seraphic humanity would still be unworthy of Christ's sacrifice. Suger's
institutional and architectural reform rehearsed a reinvention of man; the
artistry he sponsored and celebrated was an imitation of divine creativity,
because it perfected a particle of our flawed, shoddy world. Hildegard of
Bingen suggested in a letter to the Archbishop of Bamberg that God must
beam at creation with proprietorial joy, 'like a lover'. That is how Suger,
looking around him not down from the sky, saw the microcosm he had
created inside the abbey.

Hildegard's visions were also fables about creativity, and she rewrote
Genesis to make it match the urges that impelled her. Writing to Abbot
Adam of Ebrach in about 1166, she described a visitation from a beautiful
girl in a snow-white, star-bright cloak, who held the sun and moon in her
hand. A spectral voice glossed the sight for her: this was Love, and she
represented God's creative spirit. Hildegard's own paraphrase of Genesis
follows. When God wanted to create a world, she conjectures, he bent down
and ardently made all creatures from the prime matter of love. The results
were instantaneous, achieved in the blinking of an eye. Hildegard's reverie

coincides with the thirty-third psalm when she says 'Ubi deus dixit: fiat, et factus est', but elsewhere she imagines God's motives on an analogy with her own self-gratifying, wishfully erotic fantasy. Because visions are involuntary, there is no arguing with them, so Hildegard could excuse the most arcane acts by attributing them to a divine decree. During the 1150s she announced that God had commanded her 'to form unknown letters and utter an unknown language'. Eager to comply, she made up her own alphabet and invented a vocabulary of almost a thousand words. Like the mirror-writing of Leonardo da Vinci, her cranky lexicon admits the secrecy and sedition of art, which warily hides from the reality it seeks to alter. Or were her unintelligible coinages a reflection on musical notation, which can conjure an angel or a demon out of a sign scrawled on a page? Heinrich Kleist toyed with this occult language in *St Cecilia or the Power of Music*, published in a collection of his stories in 1810, the year before his suicide. He retells a legend about some Protestant rowdies who try to disrupt Mass at a convent in Aachen. Their prank is foiled when the nuns imperturbably perform a 'Gloria in excelsis', led by an organist who might be the phantom of St Cecilia. The men are overcome by derangement and taken to an asylum, where – now converts to Catholicism, in spite of their addled brains – they sing the 'Gloria' every day. Much later their mother visits the convent, and sees the score of the same 'Gloria' that cast the spell: 'She gazed at the unknown magical signs, with which some terrible spirit seemed to be marking out its mysterious sphere. ... She felt as if the whole dreadful power of the art of sound, which had destroyed her sons, were raging over her head'. Art traffics with a force that even artists cannot comprehend or control, so she may be right to suspect sorcery.

That 'terrible spirit' inevitably broke free from the religion that had conscripted it. The ninth-century pentecostal hymn 'Veni, creator spiritus' – usually ascribed to Hrabanus Maurus, a priest from Mainz – acclaims a spirit whose creative bequest, enumerated in seven stanzas, is the seven-fold moral bounty distributed by 'the hand of God'. The hand's finger, as the hymn declares, is the holy ghost, which first creates our souls and then revisits us to awaken such virtues as fortitude, piety, and fear of God. It pours fire into us, and we convert that creative charge into holy speech, repeating God's words to praise him. 'Veni, creator spiritus' remains a pillar of Catholic ritual, and is sung in the Sistine Chapel by the dean of cardinals as the conclave to elect a new pope begins. But when Mahler set 'Veni, creator spiritus' in the first part of his Eighth Symphony, he ignored its exposition of doctrine. An initial suspiration from the organ pipes sounds like the gusty, tempestuous breath of life itself; then, as a massive orchestra accompanied by eight vocal soloists and three choirs responds to the downbeat, the entire universe seems to sing or yell the opening of the hymn. Mahler wanted it to sound as if the orbiting planets and the sun itself had joined in the diatonic roar.

Working in his woodland studio at Maiernigg during the summer of 1906, Mahler felt an electrifying energy, an ignition that prompted the hurtling, unliturgical exuberance of the opening bars. As he recalled, 'the "spiritus creator" took hold of me and shook me and drove me on'. But that jolting, imperative charge did not come from the Latin hymn; the text, which Mahler only partially remembered, had to be telegraphed to him from Vienna, and he left the words to ride the musical whirlwind as best they could. The cuts he made whittled away at the sermonizing rhetoric: he chose not to set the lines in which the spirit is said to 'endow our tongues with speech', and thus eliminated the notion of divine ventriloquism. Perhaps he remembered Nietzsche's sarcastic citation of the hymn in *Götzen-Dämmerung*, which challenged its proselytizing Christianity. In this diatribe on decadence, the twilight of Wagner's enfeebled gods is followed by a twi-light of the idols, ridding men of their sickly credulity. Nietzsche disparaged the strong races (as he called them) for not inventing a new religion to replace the meek and milky biblical creed. He railed against 'this pitiable God of Christian monotono-theism!', who still existed 'as if by right, like an ultimate and maximum of the God-creating force, of the "creator spiritus" in man'. According to Nietzsche, the hymn's appeal is misdirected. Man should not expect God to send him the creative spirit; he possesses it already, and should use it to get rid of the redundant deity. Like Nietzsche, Mahler read the hymn as a rallying-cry. He may have known Goethe's translation of it, 'Komm heiliger Geist, du Schaffender', which was more ecumenical or humanistic than Christian; Goethe described it as 'a call to the universal genius of the world'. Mahler implicitly made the connection by coupling the hymn with the final scene of Goethe's *Faust*, which he set in the sym-phony's second part. It surprised him, as he told Richard Specht, that no-one else had ever thought of composing a symphony that was sung throughout, with instruments and voices collaborating to broadcast an idea. He added that he felt he had solved the problem of Columbus's egg. Despite Niet-zsche's appeal to 'the God-creating force', art is also about rearrangement, as Mary Shelley admitted when recalling how Columbus made the egg stand up. The hymn and the final scene of *Faust* already existed. Mahler's creative gesture was to bring them together; juxtaposed, they struck sparks which crackled across the gap between the ninth and the nineteenth centuries, fusing the hymn's request for guidance from above with Goethe's encour-agement of the striving human will that projects Faust heavenwards.

The symphony begins by addressing a spirit that is unequivocally male, since it makes God manifest as both Father and Son: this belligerent power stiffens human weakness and vanquishes our enemies, as the hymn says. But in Mahler's finale, the single female voice of Goethe's Mater Gloriosa intercedes from the organ loft and beckons us to higher spheres, after which the Chorus Mysticus praises the inspiring, redeeming agency of the 'Ewige-Weibliche'. The transition from the first part to the second summarizes a contentious journey from Christian orthodoxy to the romantic religion of Goethe and Nietzsche. The Mater Gloriosa is a transfigured Gretchen: the woman Faust seduced and abandoned now returns to rescue his soul. Mahler told his wife Alma, to whom the symphony was dedicated, that its essence was 'Goethe's idea that all love is generative, creative', so that its two parts come together in revering 'Eros as Creator of the World!'. His exclamation mark is apt, given his startling notion that 'the eternal-womanly' corresponds to 'what Christians call "eternal blessedness"'. As he told Alma, 'a soul needs a body'. This was his reason for adoring her as he did, and it also explained Goethe's recourse to allegory at the end of *Faust*, where anchorites hover in a rocky, unfounded space somewhere between earth and heaven: 'an artist is bound to derive the means of creation from the rational world'. Medieval allegorists thought they were releasing the spirit from its bodily cage by expounding extra-terrestrial meanings. For Mahler, the process is the opposite one: spirit must embed itself in flesh, as if making love to the prone, available physical world.

When Alma heard the first performance of the Eighth Symphony in Munich, she knew who the demiurge was. She said that Mahler, conducting, unleashed cataclysms of sound which he turned into fountains of light; she was not sure whether to think of him as a god or a demon. In 1910, during a concert tour not long before his death, he wrote to her from Buffalo in upstate New York. He had just conducted Beethoven's Sixth Symphony, which he compared with the unpastoral, torrential havoc of the local landscape. The *Pastoral Symphony*, he told Alma, was 'more tremendous than all the Niagara Falls'. How could the suicidal distress of the water, screaming as it lunged into a crevasse, hope to match the truly creative feat of Beethoven, who transformed sound into both sight and speech, and calmed the storm he incited? 'Articulate art,' Mahler decided, 'is greater than inarticulate nature'. God may be a competent artisan, but it is Beethoven who qualifies as an artist.

# 7
# ANOTHER GOD

The Renaissance altered the balance of power between man and God. Columbus, who thought he was sailing to the mines of Solomon, stumbled into a new world that God did not make and in which he was not worshipped. Copernicus, studying the planetary routines of the sky, found that they contradicted the patristic account of a creation supervised by God. The church forced Galileo to recant when his astronomical observations flouted ecclesiastical rules, but he muttered his defiance: whatever the censors said, the earth still moved around the sun, rather than being fixed in place as God supposedly wished. In his essay on atheism, Francis Bacon dismissed the fables about the Christian saints collected in the medieval *Golden Legend*, and also disparaged 'the *Alcoran*'. Despite this scepticism, Bacon was reluctant to believe that 'this Universal Frame is without a Mind'. But the framing intelligence was not necessarily divine.

Savonarola, the Dominican reformer who was excommunicated and then put to death in Florence in 1498, encouraged the soul to contemplate in solitude a personal deity. He dispensed with learned commentators on the Bible, and told his followers that they had within them 'that which makes scripture'. This was dangerous advice: it could confirm a faith that was already secure, but it could equally well suggest that man was God's creator. In 1541 the monks of Santa Maria della Steccata in Parma reproved Giulio Romano for painting God the Father who, being sacrosanct, ought to remain invisible. In his defence, the painter hinted that God should be glad that an artist had testified to his existence. He pointed out that the angelic hosts were impalpable, 'yet one is used to paint them'; it was equally permissible to depict Christ and his mother, 'who are in heaven with glorified bodies'. Glorified bodies also bestrode the earth. A conduct-book by Baldassare Castiglione told courtiers that they should cultivate the 'bodily frame' by exercising, to develop the supple, shapely limbs that befit both the warrior and the dancer. Fashion could attune the individual to the universe. Leonello d'Este, who ruled Ferrara during the 1440s, dressed astrologically, and chose the colour of his clothes to match whichever planet was currently ruling the sky.

Castiglione recommended the study of Latin and Greek because – as Sir Thomas Hoby's translation of *The Book of the Courtier* put it in 1561 – so many things were 'divinely written therein'. Divinity was a stylistic accomplishment, a grace available to men. In 1589 in his *Art of English Poesy*, Thomas Puttenham urged artists to recognize their parity with God. 'The very poet,' he said, 'makes like God who, without any travail to his divine imagination, made the world out of nought, nor also by any pattern or mould'. Aristotle and Augustine worried about that inexplicable, pre-existent nothingness; for Puttenham, a poem's emergence from nowhere was an act of aesthetic virtuosity, performed without effort. The creator, endowing man with the capacity for self-glorification, placed heaven within his grasp. In Rome in 1486, Count Giovanni Pico della Mirandola prepared an oration to be delivered in a philosophical tournament. It addressed the subject of man's dignity, and did so by cleverly combining the story of creation from Genesis with the very different philosophy of origins found in *Timaeus*. The ideas were such an affront to orthodoxy that the Pope forbade Pico to engage in public debate. The speech he was not permitted to make put words into the mouth of the biblical creator, who now allows Adam to share a generative power that was formerly his own exclusive possession. Pico calls God 'the supreme architect': not an artisan but an artificer, whose work should be compared with the edifices men have raised to improve nature and to uplift themselves. God tells Adam that he has purposely placed him 'in the midst of the world', as a being 'neither celestial nor earthly, neither mortal nor immortal'. This intermediate rank is not a predestined fate; it is intended as a mere starting-point. God invites Adam to 'be thy own masterful moulder and self-sculptor'. Animals cannot change, angels do not need to. But man is constrained by none of the laws that govern beasts and cherubs. He can brutishly degenerate, or he can be 'reborn into the higher forms, which are divine'. The poet Angelo Poliziano thought that Pico himself had already undergone the ascent: tall, golden-haired and brilliant, he seemed 'almost godlike'.

Pico's commentary on Genesis pointed to analogies between the trio of concentric worlds created by God during the first week. On earth, we have fire, which burns. Above us in the heavens is the sun, which gives life. Above that, the supercelestial world is irradiated by 'the seraphic fire of the intellect', whose beams are love. The three communicating sources are the energies of transformation, like the heat used by the alchemists to break down matter and recompose it. The same fiery work of refinement was accomplished by art. Sir Philip Sidney in his *Defence of Poesy* in 1580 cele-brated an aesthetic alchemy: nature's creation is 'brazen, the poets only deliver a golden'. Because man is the creature in whom, as Sidney said, nature's 'uttermost cunning' is made manifest, this transformation can also take place in the artist's life. The *Defence* begins by paying an ironic tribute to an expert equestrian at the court of the German emperor, who bragged that the horse was a peerless beast and that no human skill exceeded that of horsemanship. Sidney, praising his own poetic art, remarks that 'self-love is better than gilding to make that seem gorgeous wherein ourselves be parties'. He sees no reason to regret his immodesty: he is a gilded man, beautified by his own efforts. Glorification, which was Giulio Romano's aim, has a hymnal fervour. Gorgeousness takes an unspiritual delight in its own sumptuous luxury. The architect Leon Battista Alberti, in his 1436 book *On Painting*, derived the art from self-love, and made Narcissus its patron. 'What is painting,' he asked, 'but the act of embracing ... the surface of the pool?'

The scientists in Thomas More's *Utopia* assume that the 'author and maker' of nature will react 'according to the fashion of other artificers', smiling on their researches rather than rebuking their curiosity about 'secret mysteries'. God, they argue, engineered the 'gorgeous frame of the world' for our delight, and we can only please him when, unlike the lower animals, we show we are able to appreciate the spectacle and understand its workings. Emboldened by such assurance, artists began to define themselves as God's competitors, not his faithful servants. Leonardo repudiated the notion that painting belonged among the 'mechanical arts', and thought that painters were 'grandsons unto God', the re-creators of creation. Alberti took a less distant view of this professional pedigree. He deemed the art a worthy occupation for 'liberal minds and noble souls'; the painter was not God's grandson but 'another God'. Alberti meant it literally. Painting had a 'divine power', because it could make the absent seem present, the dead almost alive. Images were a mode of resurrection, a physiological second coming. Torquato Tasso rejoiced in this exalted status, and thought that the name of creator belonged only and equally to God and to the poet. Shelley, who quoted this declaration in his own *Defence of Poetry* in 1821, explained the metaphysical promise that underlay it: imagination 'creates anew the universe, after it has been annihilated in our minds' by weary habit. Tasso's treatise *On Heroic Poetry* saw imagination as an even more direct challenge to a prosaic, convention-bound deity. Tasso called the poet 'a maker of images', not a mere copyist of reality. Those images surpassed actuality: his examples were the fabulous beasts in the apocalyptic Revelation of St John, or the fiery angels described by Pseudo-Dionysius the Areopagite.

For Tasso, such visions made the poet a kind of 'mystical theologian', because imagination is 'like the light in illuminating matters', and shows us what the dazzled eye cannot see. In the early fourteenth century, Cenno Cennini began his account of art by summarizing Genesis. God first creates everything, but when Adam is expelled from Eden and made to fend for himself he has to invent the useful arts. He digs and delves, Eve spins. Eventually their descendants graduate to more superfluous pursuits. Painting is one of these, and in Cennini's estimation it re-connects men with the paradise they have lost. It unites lowly manual labour with lofty mental conception, and stretches across the gap between the visible world and the immaterial realm where spirits abide: the painter's task is 'to discover things not seen, ... presenting to plain sight what does not actually exist'. An ambition so overweening could easily lapse into despair, frustrated by mortal inadequacy. What if the spirits summoned from the vasty deep refuse to come? Dürer's *Melencolia I* examines this predicament, which Panofsky summed up as

Albrecht Dürer,
*Melencolia I*,
1514

'the tragic unrest of human creation'. Humanism alternated between moods of euphoria and despair; it veered from Hamlet's rhapsody about mankind's affinity with the angels to his dismayed contemplation of worms, dust and decay. The furled wings of Dürer's artist are incapable of flight; the geometrical equipment scattered on the ground is no help in understanding divine mysteries. The compass encompasses nothing, and the cubic block is a stubbornly obtuse boulder. The figure's mood has infected the putto, who squats on the millstone as if constipated. The sky offers a choice of cosmic portents. The rainbow recalls God's covenant with men when he reprieved creation after the flood. But the comet presages disequilibrium, disharmony, a world out of joint. It may also be a mute comment on the frantic, self-expending wilfulness that has left Dürer's melancholy figure in this burned-out condition. In 1755 the neoclassical critic Winckelmann attacked the crazed, unsteady 'spiritedness' of artists who 'want their figures to have souls as eccentric as comets'.

Julius Caesar Scaliger, a physician who published his *Poetics* in 1561, followed Alberti in calling the poet 'another God'. His reason for doing so was poetry's generative power: it could produce the 'things themselves', which when ornamented by language were sometimes more beautiful than their prototypes in nature. Shakespeare's characters often exploit this metaphorical alchemy. Macbeth's guilt alters the colour of the 'multitudinous seas', so that green water, now suffused by blood, turns 'incarnadine'.

The adjective belongs to an artist's professional vocabulary: referring to a kind of pigment, it enables Macbeth to recompose raw, seamy life as both a painting and a poem. It names his crime, but enables him to keep an aesthetic distance from it. He prettifies gore by describing Duncan's 'silver skin laced with his golden blood', and his wife recommends this detached, decoratively superficial view when she chides his superstitious dread. 'The sleeping and the dead,' she says, 'are but as pictures', and only a child would 'fear a painted devil'. Such images mock the transcendence achieved by Tasso's light; instead they take something unsightly and make it perversely beautiful. Scaliger praised poetry's ideal refashioning of nature. The deformation of nature was even bolder proof of the artist's creativity. Sidney admired poets for spawning an unnatural brood of 'Heroes, Demigods, Cyclops, Chymeras, Furies'. Gods and monsters are jostled together in his list, equated as products of the human imagination. The chimera is not a violation of natural law but a sign of the poet's exemption from it.

The breeding of monsters, which for Goya was the artist's neurotic affliction, seemed in the Renaissance to be evidence of art's brave autonomy. In the first written reference to Hieronymus Bosch, the collector Felipe de Guevara said in 1560 that he was reputed to be an 'inventor of monsters and Chimaeras': the remark was complimentary. Dürer's definition of art glanced at the shining aspiration of Neo-Platonists, then turned it inside out. Kings honoured great artists, he pointed out, and granted them 'equality with God'; painters deserved such treatment because they were 'inwardly full of figures', perpetually procreated from 'the inner ideas of which Plato writes'. The bizarre animals brought back to Europe by Renaissance navigators fascinated Dürer, who drew a walrus (which he adapted for St Margaret's dragon in a sketch made in 1522) and also a rhinoceros. These zoological novelties raised questions about creation and challenged human creativity. 'New shapes of men and other creatures' poured, as Dürer said, from the artist's brain, and sometimes took a freakishly hybrid form. One of the marginal beasts in his prayer book is a heron-billed bird which, not content with its incisive beak, grows an extra means of bodily aggression – a battering ram of antlers. Is it aware that an eagle, having mistaken this head-dress for a bare tree, has perched in them? Dürer, anticipating Freud's terminology, defined such fantasies as 'dreamwork', and said that they depended on miscegenation: they 'mix all things together', as if cross-breeding a heron and a stag. Leonardo jotted down recipes for cooking up mutants. A dragon, for instance, could be made by copying a mastiff's head, though into this the artist must set the eyes of a cat.

Leonardo shared Dürer's sense of social entitlement, and called the painter 'lord of all kinds of men'. Lordship is deliberative, confident of its

Leonardo da Vinci, *Five Characters in a Comic Scene*, c. 1490

power. Leonardo's beauties – the Mona Lisa with her supercilious smile, Vitruvian man measuring himself against the world – are aloof, eugenic aristocrats. But the artist who 'desires to see monstrous things' received an extra tribute from Leonardo: he is the 'lord and creator' of the botched, aborted or grotesquely warped figures he designs – a god who sportively sketches monsters. Hence Leonardo's feral ruffians, his elephantine crones, or his gang of cackling, toothless, senescent old men, one of whom, to illustrate his divergence from the geometrical norm, has a pair of straight lines intersecting at right angles on his forehead. In Michelangelo's case, the roles were reversed. On the ceiling of the Sistine Chapel he painted, as Vasari said, 'the venerable majesty of the Divine Form'. But the strain of the work turned Michelangelo himself into a crooked gargoyle. He had to lie flat on scaffolding just beneath the dripping surface, with his head jerked at a painful angle; the ordeal lasted from 1508 to 1512. He grimaced at his wracked discomfort in a sonnet, describing himself as a distorted ogre. His belly had been pushed up beneath his chin, and his beard poked impertinently at heaven. He could feel his brain weighing heavily on the nape of his neck, while his chest distended like that of a harpy. His loins were cramped into his paunch, with his rump as a counterweight. Twisting and writhing, he tied his body into knots or stretched it like a Syrian bow. Frankenstein, in this instance, was his own monster.

The ceiling is but one of the secular miracles chronicled by Vasari, for whom such superhuman marvels had become, as he says in his life of Cimabue, almost commonplace. The anecdotes in *Lives of the Artists* supersede the stories of wonder-working saints; like the church fathers in their exposition of universal history, Vasari documents a steady advance towards finality and perfection – except that this outcome, which equalizes earth and heaven, is the result of man's inventive artistry not divine intervention. A sceptical courtier asked Giotto for a drawing to prove he deserved a papal commission. Giotto dipped his brush in paint, fixed his arm against the side of his body, and with a single twist of his hand drew an immaculate circle. The courtier gaped uncomprehendingly; nevertheless Giotto had mimicked God's ordination of space, and did so without needing to use a compass. Uccello rationalized the ocular muddle of a congested creation by devising the laws of perspective, and like God at the end of each day's work he smiled at the goodness of what he had made. As he played with vanishing points, he murmured 'Oh, what a lovely thing is this perspective!' Donatello's statues, as Vasari comments, look as if life is stirring within them; carving one of them, Donatello muttered at it while he chipped and chiselled, telling it to 'Speak, damn you, speak!' Verrocchio proved the truth of Alberti's claim that art can bring back the dead when he produced a wax effigy of Lorenzo Medici, so meticulously painted and dressed that the subject looked 'real and alive'. Fra Filippo Lippi astonished people who had no conception of art by showing off his magical craft. Seized by Moorish pirates off Ancona, he was taken to Barbary and held in chains. One day he took a piece of coal from the fire and sketched his Muslim owner on the wall, life-size and appropriately costumed. His master, a stranger to both painting and drawing, rewarded Fra Filippo by setting him free. Vasari took this to mean that the liberal arts can secure a man's mental liberation.

For Vasari, the history of art had a destination, a pinnacle of ultimate achievement which terminated man's vertical quest. This 'sublime height' was the reproduction of life, the perfecting of a facsimile; its attainment proved that men had taken over creative power from God. Introducing his biographies, Vasari mentions the fourth-century Christian apologist Lactantius Firmianus, who traced the act of representation back to the dabbling experiments of Prometheus with mud and fire. Throughout the *Lives*, sculptors and painters quarrel about which art comes closer to matching the Titan's feat of enlivening clay. Both are frustrated by the stasis of their medium: a man must be animate, not fixed on a pedestal or fenced in by a frame. Some sculptors boast that theirs is the superior medium, because when you walk round a statue you see it assume different poses from different angles. Giorgione incorporates this mobility into a painting by including mirrored surfaces that multiply our view of the bodies represented. Vasari praises Leonardo's figures because they apparently move and breathe, and says that he wants to rub his fingers on the textured tablecloth in the *Last Supper*. The downy beard of *Moses* is carved so finely that Michelangelo seems to have swapped his chisel for a brush. For Vasari, the figure was a masterpiece of taxidermy: by giving the prophet such physical solidity, Michelangelo had exhumed him. At the day of judgment, skeletons were expected to reclaim their mouldered flesh, so that God could recognize the individuals whose fate he was deciding. Moses, as God's confidant, was appropriately the first to be revivified – though, as Alberti said, all

sculpted or painted figures have been granted the same immortality. The
end of art foreshadows and perhaps forestalls the end of time. Or was art so
intent on attaining perfection that it wished the actual, unidealized world
out of existence? In an essay written in 1871, Walter Pater suggested that
Michelangelo preferred apocalypse to genesis. Pater pointed out that the
Sistine Chapel ceiling hastily summarized 'the creation of the first five days'.
Michelangelo became interested in the narrative only when it reached
'the making of man'. Even so, for him 'the beginning of life has all the characteristics of resurrection; it is like the recovery of suspended health or
animation'. Newborn Adam looked to Pater like a wiltingly decadent
invalid, a companion for the slumped Christ of the *Pietà*.

In a preview of the Last Judgment, art dared to portray divine visages
that, according to myth and legend, it was fatal for men to look at. Moses on
Sinai saw God only from behind; Vasari likewise calls for the face of
Michelangelo's Moses to be veiled, since its resplendence is terrifying. It is
no longer the deity from whom we must avert our eyes. A work of art provokes the same awed, alarmed response. The incarnation established what
Pico della Mirandola called the dignity of man, since Christ had assumed
human form. To depict Christ was therefore the goal of the humanistic art
extolled by Vasari. Leonardo, working too slowly on the *Last Supper*, played
for time by telling his patron that he was unequal to the task of imagining
the saviour; he therefore left the face of Christ unfinished. Raphael
managed to paint Christ transfigured, with an apostle shading his eyes 'to
protect them from the rays and the intense light of Christ's splendour'. Was
Raphael himself singed by the same proximity? Vasari reports that he died
soon after he completed the painting. In his *Pietà*, Michelangelo anticipated
Christ's victory over death. Life still thrills through the corpse cradled by
the Virgin: Vasari drew attention to the veins and pulses deftly traced in the
marble. Pater suggested that Michelangelo had no faith in 'the new body'
that, thanks to Christ, was supposed to recover from death; resolutely pagan,
he had his doubts about whether the consecrated host was 'the body of
Christ'. Death for him, as for Lucretius, was a relapse into formlessness, a
dispersal of the atoms to which art gives shape and fixity. Vasari, who
attended Michelangelo's funeral, reached a different conclusion when the
coffin was opened. Though Michelangelo had been dead for more than
three weeks, decomposition had not set in, and there was no stench. His face
had 'the pallor of death', but that only made it the more marmoreal.

The statue, as in Ovid's story of Pygmalion, represents art's boldest
attempt to compete with or to counterfeit life. In the compendium of artists'
lives he published in 1672, Giovanni Pietro Bellori speculated about images
of Helen of Troy. Could she have been as beautiful as artists make her look?
Perfection belongs to statues, not to human beings with their blemishes,

their maladies, and their fractious temperaments. To prove his point, Bellori cited a legend which suggested that Helen was not abducted by Paris. He absconded instead with a statue of her, so the Trojan war was fought over an effigy. Paris presumably preferred the marble replica to the fleshly original. Shakespeare's Cleopatra ridicules her rival, the pallid and stiffly virtuous Octavia, by calling her 'a statue, not a breather'. But if a statue were to move, wouldn't it step down into mortality, betraying the ideal fixity of art? Shakespeare put this conundrum of Renaissance aesthetics to the test in *The Winter's Tale*, which ends with the animation of a statue. Hermione, reviled by her husband Leontes, apparently dies. But her friend Paulina hides or secretly preserves her, and a generation later unveils her likeness to Leontes. We are prepared for the revelation by some dialogue between their daughter Perdita and Polixenes, the king with whom Hermione was wrongly accused of betraying Leontes. Perdita the shepherdess gathers flowers for a rural festival, but rejects 'streaked gillyvors,/ Which some call nature's bastards'. She disapproves of them because she has heard that they are grafted:

> There is an art which in their piedness shares
> With great creating nature.

Polixenes argues that although art may have helped them along, that horticultural art was itself created by nature. The result is no more impure than a match between people of different social classes, when a base bark is wedded to a noble bud:

> This is an art
> Which does mend nature – changes it rather; but
> The art itself is nature.

The principle works well in gardening and in matrimony. Polixenes adds that the 'petty gods' took it further and crossed the boundary between species, like Jupiter who became a bull to woo Europa.

The final scene of the play takes these abstract musings and reformulates them as a heart-rending emotional choice between art and nature. Leontes, still convinced that the wife he rejected is dead, is shown her figure, 'standing like a statue'. Paulina reminds him that art suffers from none of nature's flaws. The 'dead likeness' excels all other human handiwork, and Leontes is invited

> To see the life as lively mocked as ever
> Still sleep mocked death. Behold, and say 'tis well.

An aesthete would agree, but Leontes is not so sure. He asks pardon of the 'dear stone', and says that it rebukes his own stony cruelty; he cannot be consoled by it, because at best it is Hermione mortified – 'warm life,/ As now it coldly stands'. What touches him, paradoxically, is the evidence of time-worn attrition. The statue, he points out, has wrinkles. Paulina attributes this to 'the carver's excellence', which has taken into account the sixteen years since Hermione's supposed death. But classical statuary is meant to celebrate the refrigerated immutability of marble. Picasso, talking to the photographer Brassaï, disparaged such icy effigies. He could find life, he said, in a tree root or a crumbly fragment of stone – 'but marble? It stands there like a block, suggesting no form or image'. That, for Renaissance sculptors like the one Paulina pretends to have commissioned, was the medium's challenge. Vasari reports that the young Michelangelo copied the carved head of an antique faun, hollowing out its mouth and chiselling a full set of teeth. Lorenzo Medici reminded him that the old never have all their teeth, so Michelangelo extracted one and dug a small crevasse in the faun's gum. Lorenzo laughed again: the artist has given a further display of his ingenuity, but sculpture should not reproduce organic decay.

Leontes miserably resents the statue's finicky verisimilitude, and says 'we are mocked with art'. With the aid of some hocus-pocus that she claims is 'holy', Paulina offers to make the statue move and speak. She commands it to 'be stone no more'; it forgivingly embraces Leontes, who now has to revise his notion of the relation between life and art:

> O, she's warm!
> If this be magic, let it be an art
> Lawful as eating.

Eating, like gardening, may be an art, but it is an art that assists nature, caters to its cravings. Hermione's return to life is a theatrical trick, bossily stage-managed by Paulina, and it admits that actors are marionettes, holding poses while they recite words that do not necessarily express personal emotions. At the same time it lives up to art's most daunting ambition: it overcomes death, and does so without breaching the relentless laws of biology. Even if Hermione did die, she remains alive in her genetic offshoot Perdita, who was lost but has now been found. Art is a continuation of nature not, like the bloodless statue, a rebuttal of it. A remoter option remains open. What if Paulina, rather than planning an elaborate deception to punish Leontes, really could make a statue move? Renaissance art refused to rule out the possibility. Victor Hugo called Shakespeare a sculptor who moulded his own flesh into clay, creating characters whom he filled with his private thoughts and feelings. Pater said that the 'creation of life' is 'the motive of all [Michelangelo's] work'. That is why he so often showed 'the half-emergent form' struggling out of 'the unwrought stone' or left the rock partly raw, as a reminiscence of the geological matrix inside which his figures grew.

Renaissance painters, whether dealing with pagan myth or sacred history, often reflect on a creative mystery that art itself replicates. In Botticelli's

*Birth of Venus*, the Christian myth of creation is eroticized. Pico della Mirandola argued that the Bible's reference to the spirit of God moving on the face of the waters referred to the skimming flight of Eros, assisted by the warm wind of spring which distributes petals as it scatters seeds. Botticelli's Venus emerges from an unformed liquid chaos, as all life does, and the conch on which her feet rest alludes to this watery womb. A seminal froth on the sculpted waves recalls the discarded testicles of Heaven, sliced off by Kronos (as Hesiod relates in his *Theogony*). Edgar Wind pointed out that an act of mutilation makes this birth possible: 'creation is conceived … as a cosmogonic death'. A single god is brutally separated into his various parts, which when dispersed go on begetting new life. The same rule applies to image-making or story-telling. Dismemberment is a creative bonus. One subject, such as Venus, spawns multiple representations; a myth is a tale that begets uncountable variants.

Another anecdote about divine squabbles enables Tintoretto, in his *Origin of the Milky Way*, to show the rudely sensual birth of a galaxy. The philandering Jupiter plugs the infant Hercules to the breast of Juno (who is not his mother) so that he can he imbibe immortality. She wakes up, and the spilled milk squirts across the sky and hardens into stars. Triangles of light

Tintoretto,
*Origin of the
Milky Way*,
c. 1575

Tintoretto,
*The Creation
of the Animals,*
*c.* 1550

glisten from the nipples of Tintoretto's maternal goddess and strike sparks when they reach the blue darkness above her: she is too busy creating a world to bother rejecting the child her husband expects her to foster. The God of Genesis, painted by Tintoretto, has the same fertile exuberance. He is surrounded by his prolific creation – horses, cattle and deer; rabbits, a dog, and a spiny long-legged porcupine; swans, ducks, herons, doves; a sea full of fishes, all skimming the waves to show off their differentiated scales, fins and snouts. God, with a golden nimbus around his bare feet as well as his grey head, has taken to the air in sheer exhilaration. The events of several days during the first week here happen simultaneously: the sea, sky and land are all at once stocked with inhabitants, and these thronging creatures begin an immediate migration, heading – with one or two contrary exceptions – towards some gratifying future that must lie off to the left, just beyond the frame. Unable or unwilling to control them, God chooses to follow their lead. In the Bible, he tells his offspring to multiply. But Tintoretto celebrates God's own fruitfulness, in which the painter himself, so delighted by nature's bounty, has a share.

Titian's *Assumption*, painted in 1516–18, can be interpreted as another meditation on the secrets of creativity. This is how Richard Wagner viewed it. When he first saw it in Venice in 1861, its 'exalting impression' – as he said in his autobiography – caused his 'old creative powers' to awaken 'with almost their primordial force', and twenty years later, at the end of his life, he often returned to the Accademia to revive himself in front of it. The painting is a sunburst, all red, gold and jewelled blue, but despite this heavenly radiance it seems to be about energetic self-help not a miraculous levitation. The Virgin is buoyed up by her own enraptured delight, and

God looks down in admiration as she hovers in mid-air. No angels lift her aloft; she has not shed the flesh, and is so solid – despite her aerodynamism – that she casts the face of a watching apostle into deep shadow. The subject is a theological conundrum. 'Assumption', a word not used in the Bible, is the term applied to the vertical promotion of those who – like Enoch, Elijah, Christ and his mother – are welcomed into heaven without being required to die. The transit was also called a 'translation', which is how the rustics in *A Midsummer Night's Dream* refer to Bottom's metamorphosis into an ass; Shakespeare's pun comically grounds the mystery. Because Mary's body had borne the living God, the church spared it from corruption in the grave. St Thomas the doubter asked for her tomb to be opened. Finding it empty, the apostles concluded that she had been transferred intact to heaven. Titian goes further by gathering the apostles to witness her hydraulic journey.

Titian,
*Assumption of
the Virgin*,
1516–18

Wagner, appropriating the image, recreated it. For him, the theological quibbles had to make biological sense. The look on Mary's face, as he told his wife Cosima in 1880, combined 'the ecstasy of love' with 'the pain of a woman in childbirth'. This was no spiritual rapture; her expression was orgasmic, and Wagner assumed that the eventual delivery would be equally blissful, despite its agonies. Because the sensations and emotions involved were so private, Wagner disliked the crowd of apostles and disciples who wave from below and the cherubs who cluster on high; coitus and parturition should both be confined to the bedroom. If the witnesses are removed, this is no longer the representation of a sacred event, commemorated by the church on August 15. Returning to the subject, Wagner denied that Titian's elated, excited woman had any religious function. He contrasted the painting with Raphael's *Sistine Madonna*, now in Dresden. Raphael's transfigured woman, truly maternal, nurses her child. Wagner respected her aerial unapproachability: 'Good Lord, to have any ideas about her!' But Titian's Madonna aroused less devout thoughts, which is why Wagner chose to see her as one of his own characters. 'It is Isolde,' he told Cosima, 'in the apotheosis of love'. At the end of *Tristan und Isolde*, first performed just before that trip to Venice in 1861, the enfevered heroine is reunited with Tristan at the moment of his death. She gasps in dismay and collapses, but regains consciousness to celebrate a union with him that is at once erotic and deathly. In her 'Liebestod', she sings about a yearning that exhausts the flesh, satiating itself in extinction. In a last, faint, mystically light-headed high note, voiced as she utters the word 'Lust', she resolves the musical discord that began the opera, and seems, like her own expended breath, to etherealize as we watch and listen. The voluntary, causeless death of Isolde was for Wagner a transfiguration, though hardly a religious one. The sexual climax offers a glimpse of eternity, and is both a foretaste of death and a means of vanquishing it. The glowing head of Titian's figure made her, as Wagner said, a symbol of 'the sexual urge: this unique and mighty force'.

That burning ardour reminded him of Mary's procreative role, but it also appealed to his own instinctual, imperious artistic creativity. In his reveries about the painting, he slighted God, who extends his arms at the summit of the sky and prepares to crown the Virgin. Titian's aerial perspective shows God from far beneath. His legs are hidden, since he has swooped down head first to greet Mary; his extended arms look like wings. Wagner therefore nicknamed him 'the bat'. There is an intriguingly similar view of God in the Sistine Chapel. The figure who separates light from darkness is seen from below. His face is turned upwards, and the beard that billows on his jutting chin grows into the white whorls of cloud that announce the advent of light. The creator merges with the sky he is creating. The motive is not derisive, like Wagner's joke about the bat; the vantage-point allows

Michelangelo to suggest that we create God by looking up from our level terrain and trying to picture a body whose arms can push back darkness and make room for light. We cannot see the face belonging to that body. God is whatever we imagine the creative impulse to be.

Wagner's admiration for Titian's Madonna was consciously sacreligious. For the Renaissance mind, the two modes of creation were closer together; painters and poets slipped easily between cosmology and copulation, and saw both as a model for their own artistry. In *Hero and Leander*, Christopher Marlowe describes the confusion of Hero as she grapples with and then surrenders to her importunate lover. The outcome recalls the earth's emergence 'from ugly Chaos' den':

> She trembling strove: this strife of hers, like that
> Which made the world, another world begat
> Of unknown joy.

A third creation completes the sequence: Marlowe jumbles up the legend, adding this conceit about a pleasurable genesis, and produces his unprecedented, joyous poem. In the *Mutabilitie Cantos* which conclude Edmund Spenser's epic *The Faerie Queene*, the upstart Titaness Mutability bustles into heaven and tries to dethrone Jove, arguing that she should be the ruler of our unstable world. Jove's empire is heavenly, but her power is baser and more reliable:

> 'I am a daughter, by the mother's side,
> Of her that is grand-mother magnifide
> Of all the gods, great Earth, great Chaos' child.'

Appealing to Nature, she threatens to undo creation by returning the four disputatious elements, which are the 'ground-work.../ Of all the world', to their original state of war. Jove picks up a lightning bolt to terrorize Mutability, but relents when he sees her beauty:

> 'But ah! if gods should striue with flesh yfere,
> Then shortly should the progeny of man
> Be rooted out....'

The angry nymphs show the same compunction when they decide not to castrate the faun who spies on Diana while she bathes:

> Some would haue gelt him, but that same would spill
> The wood-god's breed, which must for euer live.

The claim made by Mutability is dismissed, but can mutability itself ever be put down? She burgeons and proliferates verbally: Spenser gives her alternative names, including 'alteration' and 'mutation'. And just as she invents a pedigree, so Spenser fabricates etymologies and attaches a spurious family history to words. Earlier in *The Faerie Queene*, Prometheus makes man and calls his pet creature Elfe. Spenser explains, quite erroneously, that the name means 'quick'. But the fabrication licenses a spurt of playful neologisms, applied to Elfe's descendants who are called Elfin, Elfinan, Elfiline, Elfinell, Elfant, Elfar, Elfinor, Elficleos and Elferon.

Nature answers Mutability's protest by showing off the earth's green abundance, which is temporary but also eternally recurrent. Beneath her feet are 'flowres, that voluntary grew/ Out of the ground', and May – when Nature introduces a procession of the seasons – is seen 'throwing flowres out of her lap around' with feckless promiscuity. It is a scene of 'ioyance': a joy that is more than carnal because, like the unknown sensations experienced by Marlowe's Hero, it announces the presence of a divine force that makes plants sprout, impels people to fall in love, and ignites the sun. The growth of the flowers is not voluntary after all; the volition comes from a creator. At the end of *The Faerie Queene*, Spenser contrasts the praise of fertility in pagan myth with the Christian emphasis on supernatural rewards. The robe worn by Nature, presumably green, is so wondrous that the poet cannot describe it, just as the disciples who witnessed the resurrection were baffled:

> When they their glorious Lord in strange disguise
> Transfigur'd sawe; his garments so did daze their eyes.

Christianity annexed the pagan cult of the seasons, placing Christ's birth in mid-winter as the promise of a reprieve from death, and associating his resurrection with the rites of spring. In Nature's procession, December ignores the cold because 'His Sauiour's birth his mind so much did glad'. Spenser smilingly hints at the disparity between the two religions that were so inexactly aligned. Do months have minds? Does Christmas really make amends for the rheumy northern winter? During the pageant, August introduces a maiden crowned with ears of corn:

> That was the righteous virgin, which of old
> Liv'd here on earth, and plenty made abound

– although, Spenser adds, she was long ago 'to heauen extold'. He does not name this symbolic figure, because she has a plural identity. The lines refer to Astraea, who dispensed justice until the end of the Golden Age, and also to Ceres, who presides over the harvest; but her righteous chastity identifies her as Mary, whose assumption occurred in mid-August. Presenting the Mother of God as a fertility goddess, Spenser shows off his own creative effrontery. 'All art,' as André Malraux said, 'is an object-lesson for the gods.'

This eclectic open-mindedness has always scandalized believers. G. K. Chesterton, who regretted the loss of Catholic hegemony during the sixteenth century, called the Renaissance a 'radiant chaos'. Leo Tolstoy was blunter in *What Is Art?*, a puritanical diatribe written in 1898. Tolstoy's history of culture is scornfully simplified: he dismissed 'what is called the Renaissance' as a fashionable diversion of cynical aristocratic hedonists such as the Medici, the Borgias, or Benvenuto Cellini, who was honoured by Wilde as a 'supreme scoundrel'. Such men flourished in a society that, according to Tolstoy, denied and disparaged religion. The verdict is too severe. The Renaissance was not atheistic; it conducted an exercise in comparative religion, seeking a synthesis of myth and theology like that in *The Faerie Queene*. But Tolstoy's invective is intelligible, because he was writing during a renaissance of the Renaissance, sponsored by aesthetes for whom art had become a religion.

Alberti described Narcissus as the progenitor of painting. His heir is Wilde's Dorian Gray, who is drawn, by the painter who loves him, as a narcissistic Greek youth admiring in 'in the water's silent silver the marvel of [his] own face'. Infatuated by his portrait, Dorian hides his crimes behind the nonchalant surface of an immaculate face. The motive of the Renaissance, in both the fifteenth and nineteenth centuries, was identified by Pater as 'the care for physical beauty, the worship of the body'. This was its protest against what the dandified Lord Henry in *The Picture of Dorian Gray* calls 'the maladies of medievalism'. The worst of those ailments is spirituality, which results in physical self-disgust. Ever since the first Renaissance, its apologists had campaigned to revive the bodily delight of classical culture. Winckelmann, to whom Pater devoted an essay, fantasized about the 'noble and manly contours' of Greek statues, 'free from superfluous fat' and unencumbered by prudish clothing. In 1889 in an essay on artists' models, Wilde ogled the animated statues at play on 'the running-ground at Eton, the towing-path at Oxford, the Thames swimming-baths'. He hoped that these fine bodily specimens would not develop brains, which might ruin their bland, beautiful poise; the stupidity of the English helped to preserve their 'plastic perfection'. Baudelaire recognized the ironic, seditious religiosity of the dandy. To be fashionable and to maintain one's waistline required obedience to 'the strictest monastic rule', and the dandy's toilette, like the sporting activities of the young men admired by Winckelmann and Wilde, was 'a system of gymnastics designed to fortify the will and discipline the soul'. Though the body was worshipped – all the more fervently if it was one's own, or that of a homosexual double – this new mode of devotion refused to look beneath the skin for a soul. Wilde considered that 'the transcendental spirit is alien to the spirit of art'. He praised art that was impenetrably superficial or two-dimensional: Damascene tiles, Persian rugs, Chinese vases.

Abbot Suger claimed that his jewels were relics of heaven. The jewels collected by Dorian Gray have no extra-terrestrial counterparts; they signify worldly luxury or sensual infatuation, like emerald ear-rings of King James I or the jacinths, pearls and turquoises King Edward II lavished on his catamite. Dorian relishes what Wilde calls the 'Orientalism' of such baubles. A decorative art snubs supernature and even spurns nature, preferring its own elegant arabesques. Christianity, by contrast, expected art to imitate life, and life of course must imitate eternity by upholding moral precepts. In *The Decay of Lying*, one of Wilde's spokesmen ridicules the 'sordid reproduction of visible objects' on English carpets, and allows 'a cultured Mohammedan' to mock them by impudently quoting scripture. This oriental wit says 'You Christians are so occupied in misinterpreting the fourth commandment that you have never thought of making an artistic application of the second'. The fourth commandment transcribed by Moses was the injunction to keep the Sabbath day holy. The second, here given a meaning that God certainly did not intend, was the condemnation of graven images. The ban was supposed to deter us from picturing a deity who preferred to be invisible, inconceivable; Wilde's imaginary Mohammedan suggests that the prohibition should be extended from the representation of God to the realistic mimicry of anything in nature. Spenser's Nature is a goddess or at least, like the Venus of Lucretius, the deified image of a vital force. But nature, in this new Renaissance, lost its right to be worshipped, because it too was a mere by-product of human artistry. 'For what is Nature?' asks Vivian in *The Decay of Lying*. His answer defies both biology and theology: 'Nature is no great mother who has borne us. She is our creation.' London's fogs, he contends, were the direct result of the murky nocturnes painted by Whistler. Unreconstructed nature is as bovine as the cattle that graze in it. Vivian hopes that his gospel of artifice will bring about 'a new Renaissance of art'. Reviewing a book on small talk in 1887, Wilde licensed another kind of revisionism. 'The liar', he argued, 'recognizes that recreation, not instruction, is the aim of conversation.' Recreation means leisure, amusement, but the word also intimates that in amusing ourselves we are creatively refreshing our tired minds, embellishing tame truth like the innovators praised by Gilbert.

In another Wildean dialogue, *The Critic as Artist*, Gilbert takes the same disdainful view of creation, though it is artistic creativity not natural fecundity that he has in mind. 'The tendency of creation,' he says, 'is to repeat itself.' Breeders industriously duplicate their genes like the flowers in *The Faerie Queene*, and most writers or painters are equally predictable. Gilbert's paradox applies to the history of art and also to the human family: 'The mere creative instinct does not innovate, but reproduces'. It is 'the critical faculty,' he proclaims, 'that invents new forms'. What the Victorians called the higher criticism deconsecrated the Bible, reading it as a literary work and treating Christ as a fictional character. The next task of criticism, after it had disposed of God, was to undermine the sanctimonious prestige of art and to grab creative primacy for itself. Gilbert daringly asserts that criticism is 'a creation within a creation. ... Nay, more, I would say that the highest Criticism, being the purest form of personal impression, is in its way more creative than creation'. Examples of such critical recreation might be Pater's fascinated and fearful meditation on the vampirish *Mona Lisa*, or Wagner's musings before Titian's *Assumption*. In 1975 Dmitri Shostakovich composed a suite of songs based on poems by Michelangelo. The eighth is entitled 'Tvorchestvo', which means creation or creativity; the word is related to 'stwórca' and 'twórca', the Polish terms for creator and craftsman that were conjoined by Pope John Paul II. In the poem, Michelangelo compares the hammer with which he shapes his sculptures to the hammer wielded by God, a 'primal tool' that communicates the creator's delight in shaping nature, though it can also pummel and punish miscreant human flesh. Raised high above the anvil, Michelangelo's hammer is unmerciful, because the stone it batters cannot feel. As he brings it crashing down, he thanks the divine craftsman for not doing the same. This tense dread is the other side of Michelangelo's bold confidence in his own powers: God's indulgence and forbearance permit man to create. In the atheistic Soviet Union, Shostakovich had no need to fear divine retribution. The god who menaced him, and whom he sought to appease, was a totalitarian dictator. The hammer not used by Michelangelo's God corresponds to the knout employed by the Tsar's torturers, or – even more balefully – the knock on the door before dawn announcing that Stalin's secret police had arrived to make an arrest. Shostakovich's setting is terrifyingly percussive. He directed the pianist who first played the cycle to leave the lid of his instrument open, so as not to muffle the keyboard's violence. A series of raps and thuds starts the song, and the bass-baritone has to declaim Michelangelo's verses between the pianist's bouts of fisticuffs. When he orchestrated the suite, Shostakovich augmented the battery with thumping drum beats and shrieking outbursts of brass.

Yet the singer holds his own against this belligerence, and impenitently testifies to the creativity of the composer, who died less than a year later; strings enter to soften the uproar, and when the rhythmic flagellation resumes in a short orchestral epilogue after the singer finishes, a tolling bell issues a summons to remembrance – not an appeal to cower before Michelangelo's God, but Shostakovich's obsequy for himself. The songs that follow brood on night and death, though the last in the suite is a chirpy dance for flutes and woodwinds: it is about immortality, and in it Michelangelo boasts that, thanks to his works, he will survive his own death. His certainty was not misplaced, since the poems were taken by Shostakovich from an edition published in 1974 to mark the five hundredth anniversary of his birth. Art goes on generating art; every critical response is a rebirth or renaissance, revivifying the work that prompted it.

# 8

# THE GREAT WORK

The speech Pico della Mirandola wrote for God authorized Adam to change his own nature and to transform nature itself. His blessing extended to alchemy, which delved into the secrets of creation in quest of godly powers. The alchemists wanted to rectify the world by transforming base metals into gold, but their agenda was never merely mercenary. What they called their 'great work' investigated mysteries that only God understood. They dreamed about breeding life outside the body, fostering humanoids in the wombs of glass they heated over flames in their laboratories; failing that, they hoped to concoct an elixir of eternal life. Alchemy depended on fire, the fickle element that was, as Pliny said, destructive and creative at once. Heat decomposed, mortified and blackened the substances the alchemists placed in their retorts. The result was genesis all over again: a raw, seething compost that contained the recipe for protoplasm. After putrefaction, purification followed. The ingredients were progressively refined and whitened, until resurrection was observed in the transparent vessel. This chemical allegory copied the way God separated creation's ingredients on the first day. It also restaged the adventure of erotic coupling and biological increase that began in Eden: opposite substances met, married and merged inside a flask that was often likened to a nuptial bed.

Renaissance theorists contrived a compromise between alchemy and orthodox religion by interpreting the arcane research as a repetition of sacred history. Martin Luther approved of alchemy as a 'good art', because it allegorically prefigured 'the resurrection of the dead on the Day of Judgment'. The stages through which the alchemists guided matter were colour-coded, moving from black to white. Treatises identified the dark origins of the quest as the 'nigredo', and often referred to the enterprise as 'l'oeuvre au noir', although its aim was to arrive at blazing gold. The meaning of the enterprise was muddled by a false etymology, or perhaps complicated by a conscious pun. Alchemists were said to practise necromancy, working their magic by consulting the dead: 'nekros' in Greek is a corpse. But sometimes the word was mis-spelled nigromancy, which gave it another origin: 'nigro' in Latin means black, which brands the activity as black magic. In some alchemical fables, the black mulch in which gold could be seeded was said to be a specimen of soil smuggled out of Eden by the evicted Adam. Joannis de Padua, in a secret text on the philosopher's stone, alchemized Genesis. Adam was the 'prima materia' or 'massa confusa', the thick, crude, viscous stuff on which God went to work; he should be coloured black, because all the elements were messily compounded in him. Eve, however, symbolized whiteness. Derived from Adam, she represented the first stage of refinement. Left alone, the pair might have happily coupled in a bath of warm water. But the serpent introduced another, more corrosive agency. It performed the chemical function of acid, which accelerated the experiment by gnawing at the treated metals and punitively dissolving them. Sometimes the apple signified the forbidden knowledge that the alchemists craved; for Joannis, it referred to the tint that changed as the prime material was altered. After white came the climactic state of yellow or red, when the apple shone with an entrancing brightness.

The seventeenth-century German mystic Jacob Boehme prolonged the alchemical narrative into the New Testament. Boehme accused Adam of sinful immersion in the 'nigredo': he took the divine likeness and changed it into 'dark Death's form'. But God, whose vengeful fury and purgative zeal match the alchemist's searing application of heat, used his 'fire-wrath' to complete the experiment, restored divinity to mankind by sending Christ to earth, and ushered us 'out of Death into the light'. For Sidney, the golden world was realized by poetry. But it could also be the paradise restored by Christ's sacrifice, in which case the elixir of life was the immortality of the soul. To commemorate Christ, at least in the Catholic church, the eucharist still rewards the faithful with two alchemical miracles. Bread becomes the sacred body, and wine is the saviour's blood.

Although Christianity harnessed alchemy, the practice hardly offered a recipe for salvation. Vasari lamented the alchemical obsession of the painter Parmigianino, who was so intent on enriching himself by congealing mercury that he neglected his art, spent his time fiddling with glass bottles and stoking furnaces, and died insane. The 'opus nigrum' recreated chaos and presided over perdition. Its gods were molten, which is why they could be fused or conjoined. Mars was correlated with iron, Venus with copper; sulphur and mercury made an even more unstable couple, because sulphur was the scorching seminal heat of Sol, while quicksilver recalled the trickery of the deceitful, self-disguising god Mercury. Creation could easily reverse itself, and the false gold might turn out to be worth nothing. Agrippa of Nettesheim had a reputation as a magus, and is supposed to have owned a magic glass in which he could see through time and across space; he was also a big spender, but – according to legend – the coins with which he paid his debts reverted to valueless fragments of horn or shells as soon as he left town. Rejoicing in the corruption of metals, alchemy was more inclined to diabolism than to the glad messianic certainty of Boehme. The elusive twentieth-century alchemist known as Fulcanelli paid homage to Lucifer as the true creator: it was the rebel angel, named after light, who illuminated the darkness, and the stars still blaze in honour of his revolt. C. G. Jung pointed to a disparity between Christian symbolism and the iconography of alchemical treatises. The official religion chooses emblems of 'spirit, light and good', whereas 'the alchemical figures are creatures of night, dark, poison and evil' – hermaphroditic corpses, snakes, salamanders that flourish in fire. Jung aligned alchemy and psychotherapy, which made him think of the 'nigredo' as a mental ailment. Its gloom was a symptom of black bile, the cause of melancholy. This malaise, according to Renaissance astrology, particularly afflicted artists, who were likely to be born under the sign of Saturn. The cruel, morose planet frowned on such men, but at the same time instilled in them an enthusiasm that was both divine and maniacal; Agrippa made this 'furor melancholicus' an attribute of the creator.

John Donne's poem 'A nocturnall upon S. Lucies day' – set on the shortest and darkest day of the year, when the sun seems moribund – sees both love and alchemy as experiments in extinction. Donne feels himself to be

> ... every dead thing
> In whom love wrought new Alchimie.
> For his art did expresse
> A quintessence even from nothingesse.

Nothing here gives birth to something, but the life squeezed from it is as depleted as the wintry earth. If love alchemically transmutes Donne, it will animate a spectre: he is 're-begot/ Of absence, darknesse, death; things which are not'. He and the woman he has lost were once 'two Chaosses', unruly and swollen with ardour, though they soon lapsed into 'carcasses', derelict husks. Now his partner's departure or death has reduced Donne to 'the first nothing'. At best, the golden bliss the alchemists sought was attainable in bed, even if that ecstasy lasted only for an instant and mimicked death rather than prolonging life. In 'Loves Alchymie', Donne digs love's mine, seeking a 'centrique happinesse', yet comes away disappointed, like the befuddled experimenters in their laboratories:

> And as no chymique yet th'Elixir got,
> But glorifies his pregnant pot,
> If by the way to him befall
> Some odoriferous thing, or medicinall,
> So, lovers dream a rich and long delight,
> But get a winter-seeming summers night.

Only the pot, swollen like the bellied vessels in which the elements were mixed, is pregnant. Rich permanence contracts to the momentary oblivion experienced by a man when he ejaculates: Donne often likened the orgasm to a small death, and believed that each one shortened your life by a day. The poem ends in decomposition, not the refinement that was the goal of the great work. While still in the throes of coupling, Donne sees the woman mouldering: she is 'but *Mummy*, possest' – a corpse that looks life-like. The science that promised immortality delivers only a gruesome connoisseurship of death. That, for Donne, was the fate of art. The mind wants to scrutinize a 'hidden mysterie', to eavesdrop, as he says, on the symphonic spheres; it has to be content with a desolate glimpse of vacancy.

During the first decade of the sixteenth century, more or less while Michelangelo was at work in the Sistine Chapel, Hieronymus Bosch painted the triptych known as *The Garden of Earthly Delights*, now in Madrid. Both artists produced cosmogonies, and commentaries on their own creativity. Michelangelo's ceiling re-arranges the sky, bringing together classical sibyls and biblical prophets in an ecumenical pantheon. It connects the beginning and the end of time: on the wall at the end of the chapel, the God who divides light from darkness gives way to Christ, who adjudicates between good and evil and sends damned souls plummeting to perdition. But is it a work of Christian eschatology or a humanist manifesto? As Pater said, the real subject of this final fresco is not judgment but resurrection. The dead clamber out of their graves to reclaim the bodies inside which they once lived; the Renaissance painter, casting off medieval asceticism, reunites spirit and flesh. Michelangelo's painted room contains the universe. By contrast, Bosch's triptych is small, reclusive, retentive. Its revelations – a history that extends from a riotously fertile Eden to an orgiastic hell – are concealed by two outer panels, which close like shutters. On these flaps, painted in monochromatic grey-green, God once more creates the world. But he does so without the propulsive vigour of Michelangelo's creator; he sits apart, observing a creation that obeys its own whims. An arboretum of bizarre plants riddled with spikes or matted with clumps of pubic foliage is sealed inside a globular flask like the retorts used by alchemists for their distillations. Bosch's grizzled, diminutive God does not employ the shaping sculptural hands on which Michelangelo's God relies. Events inside the transparent orb are beyond his control: alchemy fuses opposites as whimsically and paradoxically as the imagination does.

For Michelangelo, painting was the incarnation of ideas. Like God, he gave corporeal life to concepts. The creative process depicted by Bosch is less decisive, less rational. It unbridles fantasy, like a magician's conjuring, and Bosch's God resembles a wizard with his book of spells open on his lap. Those runes could be either divine or devilish. Agrippa said that magic was a matter of elemental 'mixtions', like alchemy. White magic gave access to 'most high mysteries'; it was a philosophical enterprise, like science. Ascending through the elementary, celestial and intellectual realms to the original world inhabited by the First Cause, it brought the magus into contact with the maker. Black magic was about gratification not aspiration, and – like Mephistopheles when he acts as Faust's pander – it supplied more sensual delights. In Bosch's *Temptations* triptych, now in Lisbon, the hunched St Anthony hides a book behind his cloak and grasps a staff that might be a magician's implement. The saint, like an artist terrorized by his own imagination, has summoned up the incubi that menace him.

On the flaps that cover *The Garden of Earthly Delights*, a scriptural text is written across the dark sky above the pullulating earth. God is endeavouring to give dictation: the Latin inscription quotes the thirty-ninth psalm, which summarizes a creation that went exactly according to plan – 'For He spoke, and it was' and 'By his command, they were created'. Vapours condense inside the globe, thickening into storm clouds. The scene matches

The outer shutters of *The Garden of Earthly Delights*, c. 1500, Hieronymus Bosch

the first three days of creation, when dry land pushed through the waterline and mists rose from the ground, raining down again to moisten it, yet the biblical account cannot explain the embryonic forms in Bosch's swamp. An albino rainbow shines on the outer surface of the glass, neatly indicating its curvature. This detail prompted E. H. Gombrich to argue that the scene actually illustrates the world after Noah's flood, as the waters receded from the drenched earth. Scriptural commentators interpreted the deluge as a second creation, which was responsible for the irregular contours of our current world. In his *Sacred Theory of the Earth*, published between 1681 and 1689, the theologian and amateur physicist Thomas Burnet suggested that the earth God created at the beginning of time was 'oviform', a 'mundane egg' as spherical as Bosch's vessel. Given these origins, why is the world we live in so craggy and cratered? This terrain, Burnet argued, was the result of the flood, when the over-charged oceans heaved up earth in a dredging operation. Mountains disfigured the level land; chasms gaped when the extra water drained away. The first creation was tidy, the second – being a result of destruction – left a mess behind it. No wonder that Bosch's painting seems closer to the aftermath of the deluge: art is the spoiling of God's initial design.

Alchemists, as Laurinda Dixon has noted, staged their own versions of the punitive flood, which they called an ablution, when they cleansed substances to prepare them for transformation. Bosch chose to imagine an alchemical Genesis, which is why he sealed it inside a retort. The 'vas mirabile' was supposedly invented by Hermes (otherwise known as Mercury), who bequeathed it to hermetic scientists, his acolytes. It had an anatomical meaning: alchemists appreciated its resemblance to an egg, since they used heat to incubate a new life that would eventually hatch. But the retort was also a death chamber. In it, copper was metaphorically killed by being blackened or oxidized; then, after adding arsenic or mercury, the metal was whitened or resuscitated as a silvery alloy. These experiments, as Mircea Eliade has said, were 'a return to primordial chaos' and 'a rehearsal of cosmogony'. On Bosch's shutters, God watches over the transformations that occur inside the global retort; when the closed panels are opened, other globules serve as reminders of this creation. In Eden, a pink fountain – looking like a multifoliate flower that squirts life-giving rivers – rests on a globe with a wise owl perched inside it. In the central panel the same shape, now coloured blue, has a crack in it: squirming naked forms wriggle out of the fractured egg. Another body struggles to get itself born from a clam, using its legs and hands to unclench the shell, as if Bosch were imagining the emergence of Botticelli's Venus from inside her scallop. Elsewhere in the garden, lovers couple while floating on a stream inside translucent bubbles. The marriage of chemicals was often represented as a sexual fusion, the conjunction of a king and queen or of Sol and Luna; here the vessel is a bed where we can spy on ovulation. In hell, a man's pained, blanched head and a pair of legs that are halfway between a pig's trotters and the trunks of trees jut from an eviscerated eggshell. The cavity is habitable, and could be either a laboratory or a den where fiends conduct their revels.

The detached, elderly God on the outer panel has a deputy inside the triptych. Now personified or verbalized as Christ, he enters the garden to present a newly created Eve to a startled Adam. Christ looks uneasy, because he is an intruder. According to Agrippa, 'some divines' believed that God did not create man and the other mortal animals but entrusted the task to heavenly spirits, 'both good and bad', who performed their tasks by making mixtures of the four elements, like alchemists. Once Genesis had been questioned in this way, another hypothesis logically cropped up. Could creation be responsible for its own emergence? Christ, gazing into the distance, is unprepared to answer questions about purposes and methods. He is diminished by the fountain behind and above him, which is coloured like his robe; from it gushes the water that is the source of life. Ducks swim in the pond the fountain fills. Deer drink from the same basin, while frogs and toads hop out of it onto the land. In Bosch's perverse zoo, life generates itself and engages in whatever morphological experiments it pleases, rather than following God's command that every creature should adhere to its established kind. The pages of this painted book exhibit a creation not anticipated by Genesis. Adam, staring at his pearly-skinned, simpering bride, is both excited and anxious. Should she be classified with the garden's exotica, or does she belong with Bosch's imaginary monsters? Some of the animals here are mythological confections like Chimaera: hence the unicorn or the griffin. Others belong to new species, outlandish but actual, reported on by the Renaissance explorers: the cheetah, elephant and giraffe. The Tree of Knowledge likewise is a transplanted date palm. Bosch exercises the creative rights of the fantasist by dreaming up the three-headed bird with a peacock's flaunting tail that disports itself below the feet of Christ. Hell contains less amiable creatures, which commute up and down the chain of being: a man-sized, man-eating rabbit, or a lecherous pig in a nun's habit. The body's parts also escape from the whole and live independently, like the pair of ears with a knife for a nose. Such oddities are not so farfetched: Salvador Dalí, after a summer of almost maniacal drawing and painting in 1925, felt himself 'turning into one of those fantastical figures of Hieronymus Bosch. ...I was in fact a kind of monster whose sole anatomical parts were an eye, a hand and a brain'.

Bosch's small, self-enfolded world begins with creation, advances to Eden, and concludes in a hell where the art of music is a form of punishment. A sinner is strung up on a harp; another victim roasts in the funnel

of a bassoon while a demon puffs into the mouthpiece to stoke up the furnace. Another alchemical retort, letting off steam after a painful digestive transformation in its gullet, doubles as a bagpipe. The Pythagoreans thought that harmony cured mental distress, but musical dissonance could equally well abrade the nerves and unsettle the reason. Bosch's painting balances delights and torments: the art which gives pleasure is also capable of inflicting pain. Dalí defined surrealism as an 'inquisitorial process of matter'. He was thinking of the analytical techniques developed by the Spanish inquisition, which asked questions with the help of pincers and racks. Torture put human flesh to the test, and took pride in extorting what the inquisitors thought of as the truth. The artist, for Dalí, did the same to the material world, questioning its solidity and ruthlessly extracting its secrets. In Bosch's hell, an avian-headed devil ingests a squirming body. As the beak closes, the victim's upraised

*Hell*, the right-hand inside panel of Bosch's *Garden of Earthly Delights*

buttocks release a last cloud of gas, made visible by Bosch as a flock of black birds: an alchemical symbol for filthy vapours. Other sinners travel whole through the intestinal tract, and are dumped into a foul pool. A puffed-up anus extrudes coins, while a glutton contributes the regurgitated contents of his stomach to the stew. Art and alchemy both aspire to a golden world. But here reality is befouled not refined, and the golden heaven is replaced – as those dirty coins plop into the sewer – by a brown excremental hell.

Ben Jonson's *The Alchemist*, performed in 1612, might almost be an illustration of Bosch's final panel. The fraudulent alchemist Subtle sets up shop in a house vacated by Lovewit, who has left London to escape from the plague. With his crony Face and the harlot Dol Common, he preys on clients whose dreams he pretends to realize. Some of his gulls are ignorant clerks with meagre, tawdry longings, but Sir Epicure Mammon hungers for a golden world of sensual enjoyment, while the Protestant reformers Tribulation and Ananias think of alchemy as a 'sanctified course' and seek a formula that will enable them to convert 'the children of perdition'. All are duped. The place of revelation is the privy. The fumigated Daper waits in this stinking confessional for his assignation with the fairy queen, who is actually the communal plaything Dol. As in Bosch's hell, gold is degraded, in a reversal of the great work's stages, into the basest of bodily products. Face says he and Subtle will be reduced to 'faeces, ashes' if Mammon suspects their treachery; Subtle orders Face to marinate some calcined stools in 'menstrue'. Competitively trading insults, Face calls Subtle 'the vomit of all prisons'.

Despite this corruption, *The Alchemist* itself is the great work, or perhaps – in the fearful phrase of Ananias – 'a work of darkness': the triumph of an aesthetic transmutation that changes ordure to art. Subtle likens Face to a scarab beetle, cradled in turds. Has he not, Subtle asks,

> Sublim'd thee, and exalted thee, and fix'd thee
> I'the third region call'd our state of grace?
> Wrought thee to spirit, to quintessence...?

Excreted wastes, like the dreams that ventilate our disturbed brains, are creative. The body is replumbed, as in Bosch's hell, to provide extra outlets. Mouths produce language, which translates the head's thoughts and the heart's feelings. Other apertures have their own eloquence. Subtle tells Face to speed up the great work by showering it with his 'rectified water', just as Cupid – in a 1530 painting by Lorenzo Lotto – sends a jet of mercurial urine onto Venus, whose naked body is the alembic inside which chemical change occurs. Another anal vent belches out products more substantial than words. Here is the place of origins, a gulf in need of the medicine that alchemy purveyed. Mammon addresses Dol as 'Madam Suppository', and cites a learned discourse on the fart, which is also a means of bodily self-expression. The mundane egg is another model of creativity at work. Surly objects to Subtle's claim that he can 'hatch gold in a furnace, .../ As they do eggs in Egypt', and is not convinced when told that lead is no further from gold than eggs are from chickens. The doubter insists that

> The egg's ordain'd by nature to that end:
> And is a chicken in potentia.

Subtle replies that lead and all other metals have the potential to be gold, and would achieve that state 'if they had time'. Sublimation, which alchemists regarded as a mode of religious transcendence, is here more like the process analysed by Freud, whose patients dreamed to sublimate the carnal cravings that distressed them. Mammon says that 'mercury sublimate' works as corrosively as 'the dragon's teeth.../ That keeps the whiteness, hardness, and the biting'. For these fakers, whiteness is a convenient, hypocritical camouflage: Mammon dreams of seducing a rich lawyer's 'sublim'd pure wife'.

God ordered his creatures to multiply, which they did biologically. The multiplication Subtle has in mind is financial. The Anabaptists worry about whether it is lawful to make money breed; Subtle assures them that he is not coining but casting. Art has always magically atoned for the deprivations of artists, who – as Freud said – hunger for wealth, honour and the love of beautiful women. Jonson's play exposes the falsity of such wish-fulfilment. The counterfeiters in André Gide's novel *Les faux-monnayeurs* discover the same diminishing returns. Gide's schoolboys practice a secret, suspect art which they refer to as 'magic'; it is masturbation, and the instant delights it supplies, like those of art and alchemy, are delusions. Mammon is greedy for gold, but as an epicure he also demands a psychological and sensual enrichment, augmenting the body's capacity to experience pleasure. Heaven for him is an orgy, which, as he imagines, will take place in a mirrored room where the glass is

> Cut in more subtle angles, to disperse
> And multiply the figures, as I walk
> Naked between my succubae.

The eye, assisted by those angles, has its own reproductive power.

Jonson's theatre makes possible this inorganic multiplication, as Subtle changes from one man into many by adopting masks and disguises. A pun enables him to reunite the many in the one, and to hint that his impersonations have turned him into a god, able to inhabit and abandon human bodies as he pleases. Thanks to the union of mercury and sulphur – which represents the chemical wedding of moon and sun, or male and female – alchemy arrives at a state he calls 'hermaphrodeity'. The illustrations in alchemical manuals sketched that unnatural creature, who possesses two opposed sets of sexual organs; actors have the same self-sufficiency, and treat gender as a costume they can put on or take off at will. Subtle concludes his garbled manifesto by bragging about the alchemical power to beget new life:

> Art can beget bees, hornets, beetles, wasps,
> Out of the carcases and dung of creatures;

Yea, scorpions of an herb, being rightly placed:
And these are living creatures, far more perfect
And excellent than metals.

The art he praises is that of the theatre, which before our eyes is achieving the marvel he describes. The characters, like Freudian analysts, even speculate about their obscure origins inside their creator's head. Subtle postulates that 'Something went before', and contends that 'There must be remote matter'. He is talking about the muddy 'prima materia' out of which worlds were made. Art takes this raw material – low life, illiterate abuse, Jonson's bilious contempt for human beings – and lovingly shapes it into a play; it gilds dung.

Subtle drills Face in the sequential logic of the alteration. 'Whence comes vivification?' he asks. Face replies 'After mortification'. This was the order of events in the laboratory: the rebirth of metal can occur only after it is killed, when the 'nigredo', cleansed and purged, gives way to a redeemed whiteness. The exchange between Subtle and Face glances as well at the paradox of artistic creativity. The characters of *The Alchemist* are freakishly vivified. The farce requires them to possess inexhaustible energy and an equally maniacal cleverness: they invent words and meanings on the run, speaking Latin, heathen Greek, Spanish and High Dutch (supposedly the language Adam wrote) as well as English, or retching gobbets of indigestible verbiage like Surly's 'lato, azoch, zernich, chibrit, heautarit'. But their vitality is a symptom of decomposition, which advances at a terrifying pace as they speed round in circles and talk without communicating. Jonson has made them in order to watch them hilariously exhaust themselves. His morbid humour does not exempt his own artistry. Lovewit, who owns the house, takes stock of the debris when he returns, and notices 'the ceiling fill'd with poesies of the candle'. This is not the prophetic writing on the wall deciphered by Daniel; poetry is the random and ephemeral scribbling of smoke, smudging a blank space. Jonson equated art with mess or filth, and could not forgive Shakespeare for the cleanliness of his manuscripts. The actors in his company proudly reported that Shakespeare 'never blotted out line'. Jonson, who knew that revision and correction involve inkily or anally besmirching the page, grumbled 'Would he had blotted a thousand'.

Jonson's alchemists off-handedly disparage the Shakespearean character who takes the process of creating and destroying most seriously, brooding over the unwonted power art gives him and choosing – in a stricken confirmation of his own mortality – to renounce it. *The Tempest* was performed in November 1611, a few months before *The Alchemist*; when Subtle tells Mammon that he would be sorry if their labours did 'not prosper', he sourly incriminates Prospero and accuses the magus of being a mercenary profiteer. In alchemical terms, Prospero regresses from vivification to mortification. He conjures up tempests and harpies and goddesses, but at last consigns them all to rest and lays down the staff that enabled him to command the elements. In his remorseful farewell to art, he foresees another transmutation. His theatrical show fades out. The vision was 'baseless', and it evaporates just as 'the great globe itself,/ And all which it inherit, shall dissolve'. The word Prospero so mournfully intones is taken up by Face when Subtle quizzes him about the philosopher's stone:

> 'Tis a stone
> And not a stone; a spirit, a soul, and a body:
> Which, if you do dissolve it, it is dissolv'd,
> If you coagulate it, it is coagulated,
> If you make it to fly, it flyeth.

Prospero's art duplicates and enhances reality. When he gives it up, he is like a god who quits his creation, leaving it to decay. Or perhaps he is a god who steps down to join humanity: as he departs from the magical realm of the island, he looks ahead to his own death. *The Tempest* ends in an act of atonement. The artist who deified himself acknowledges the 'thing of darkness' within him: the disgruntled monster Caliban, his crude prime material. Face, however, is blithely unrepentant. The prospect of dissolution prompts no elegy, because – unlike Prospero's towers and palaces or Shakespeare's Globe theatre, all piled on a thronging globe whose contents are our inheritance from the past – the stone is as light as air or as the vacuous words that name it.

　　Is art the sublimation of the world, or perhaps the means of the artist's debasement? Subtle teaches Face techniques for cheating at cards, making him 'a second in mine own great art'. As well as transmuting metals, alchemists boasted of being able to cure disease (including that most incorrigible of maladies, mortality). Robert Browning, in the notes to his dramatic poem about the sixteenth-century necromancer Paracelsus, called this 'the double tincture'. A tincture is a drink with medicine dissolved in it; the added ingredient gives it a tint or a tinge, which recalls alchemy's remote origins in the Egyptian dyeing of cloths. The metal-workers of Alexandria doubled as dyers, and saw the gradual changes in coloured fabric as an analogy for the advance from brass to gold. In sonnet 111, Shakespeare treats his own theatrical career – a life of irresponsible shape-changing – as an alchemical venture that soils and taints him: 'my nature is subdued/ To what it works in, like the dyer's hand'. The image is unusual in describing the experimental process so contemptuously, recognizing that transformation can be a devious and immoral skill.

　　Despite these misgivings, artists never lost faith in alchemy. In 1771 Joseph Wright of Derby painted a monkish alchemist in his cell. The chemicals in his retort exude brightness, which illuminates his worshipful face and chases the shadows from a corner where an assistant and a boyish apprentice lurk; alchemy brings enlightenment. Wright also painted a planetarium and an up-to-date experiment with an air pump, used to evacuate gases. He saw no discrepancy between such modern contrivances and the mystical apparatus of the alchemist. The great work in Wright's painting is inadvertently progressive: the alchemist, according to the title, has been searching for the philosopher's stone but instead discovers phosphorus, which crackles into flame inside his jar. Outside the mullioned window, a full moon coolly shines. Its frigid light – in a reminiscence of the marriage between Luna and Sol – is outdone by the blue-white effulgence of the retort, which releases hissing vapour. That intense source is indoors, not situated in the sky; it is reflected in the face of the bearded alchemist, who extends his arms in a gesture of prophetic wonder. He has brewed light, which places him in competition with the God of Genesis. In 1695 the diarist John Evelyn reported on a similar demonstration at the house of Samuel Pepys. The aim was to achieve the 'eduction of light out of chaos, and the fixing ... of universal light into luminous bodies'. Evelyn could not help paraphrasing the Bible, although no divine intervention was required. All that was necessary were some glass vessels and a supply of phosphorus, which flared up into a phantasmal milky way consisting of 'stars of real fire, perfectly globular, ... and heavenly bodies'. Whenever science made significant advances, it remembered and honoured the dreams of alchemy. Georges Méliès used the cinematograph to electrify shadows and vivify inert matter; his short, fantastical films made statues move or sent astronauts to the moon, accomplishing marvels by technical sleight-of-hand. Charlie Chaplin appropriately saluted Méliès as an 'alchemist of light'.

In a medieval laboratory like that painted by Wright, Wagner in the second part of Goethe's *Faust* toils over the ultimate alchemical feat. Sparks glint and smoulder in a phial; fussing over his impractical gadgets, Wagner tells Mephistopheles that he is about to make a human being. The devil asks whether he has a connubial couple on hand, but Wagner scoffs at this old-fashioned method of begetting. He has mixed and distilled the appropriate ingredients 'in vitro', and now awaits crystallization. Paracelsus boasted that he could artificially engender a little man (whom he called a homunculus) by warming semen in a compost of horse manure and infusing it with blood; the finicky procedure took eleven months, longer than a conventional pregnancy. Wagner in *Faust* completes the experiment more speedily, and nurtures a tiny imp which chatters at him from inside its protective womb of glass. Like any literary character, the homunculus is a brain-child, and it articulates Faust's unconscious longings. He has lapsed into a reverie about Helen of Troy; the homunculus hovers over him as he sleeps, inter-

prets his dream, and leads him from the cobwebbed, priest-infested, Gothic north to the classical south, where he is married to the ideal Grecian woman. If Mephistopheles is Faust's evil genius, the product of his slavish Christian guilt, the homunculus is the uninhibited offshoot of his imagination. Yet its powers are limited. It must remain inside the phial; beings created by biological means can roam free, experiencing 'das Weltall', whereas artistic creations – 'was künstlich ist' – need to be penned in confined spaces. Fantasy is engaged in an unequal combat with reality. It miniaturizes the grand, gross,

Faust and the homunculus in a 19th-century engraving

unruly world, which now becomes manageable. But the illusion has to be secured behind a thick window, like a painted landscape. Proteus finally releases the homunculus from its transparent prison, and helps it to outgrow its hermaphroditic state: it longs for a body, and aspires to become real. Art after all is not sufficient, and the lustrous manikin expires into nature as Galatea rides off across the ocean on her conch.

Romanticism redefined the great work. Its aim was no longer, as for the medieval alchemists, to build a ladder from earth to heaven; instead it sought a fusion between the individual mind and the wide world from which the homunculus at first flinches. Browning knew that Paracelsus was reputed to be an 'egregious quack' like Subtle, yet the alchemist in his poetic drama fervently desires a union between art and nature, poetry and deity. An Italian rhapsodist tells him that 'God is the perfect poet,/ Who in his person acts his own creations'. Another follower urges Paracelsus to repudiate 'creatureship' and become a creator. As the transcendentalist Teufelsdröckh in Carlyle's *Sartor Resartus* tells himself, 'Be no longer a Chaos, but a World, or even Worldkin. Produce! Produce!' The homunculus described by the alchemists was a miniature man. Sometimes they imagined it to be tinier than a tadpole, able to fit into a spermatazoon; they then worried about how they would inflate this manikin to a more practical size. For Carlyle's dotty hero, there is no shame in the diminutive. A worldkin is a microcosm; one man's head can contain a universe. Browning's

Paracelsus redefines man as 'a tendency to God': a being in the process of spiritual transmutation. The alchemist could dispense with his retorts, his acids and his samples of the earth Adam took from paradise. He now performed the experiment on himself.

Along with the homunculus, alchemists puzzled over the mystery of the mandrake, a plant whose forked root gave it a fancied likeness to a man. Digests of herbal lore pictured the mandrake as a small earthen human being with whiskery roots as its arms and legs Its head, peeping above the soil, grew red berries whose juice was used for preparing elixirs. To tug the mandrake from the ground was a kind of murder: when uprooted, it supposedly emitted a screech of pain that could madden or kill whoever heard it. Because it cross-bred animal and vegetable, the mandrake furthered the great work of mutation. Donne jokes about the impracticability of its reproductive arrangements, and says that to 'get with child a mandrake roote'

is as easy as to catch a falling star or to find a monogamous woman. Despite this scepticism, he mentions the mandrake in *The Progresse of the Soule*, where it marks a stage in the soul's Pythagorean transit between species and bodies. When Adam and Eve eat the apple, the dismayed soul quits humankind. Burying itself underground, it animates the plant and becomes a 'living buried man'. Eve tears it up because she knows that its berries – called mandragora by Othello – are as soporific as poppies, and can be used to soothe her first-born child. This causes Donne to reflect that 'hee's short liv'd, that with his death can doe most good'. The soul wisely reconsiders its choice of habitat, wriggles into a bird's egg, and next hatches as a sparrow.

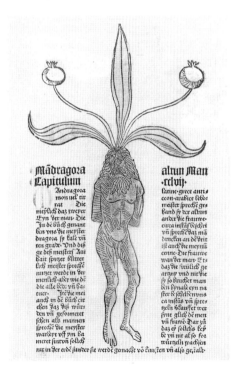

Male mandrake, from *Hortus Sanitatis*, 1485

Such fantasies made sense as fables about creativity. In 1881 Wagner recalled the legend of the mandrake when discussing his hero Lohengrin, a Grail knight who, like Christ, descends from heaven as a saviour and is betrayed and rejected by the humans he comes to succour. Cosima reported in her diary that Wagner 'gaily compares Lohengrin with the mandrake being pulled out of the bottle (the Grail the bottle)'. The jest glanced at the dangerous desire of Goethe's homunculus to be released from its test tube; Lohengrin, being the incarnation of a dream, cannot survive in reality, and he returns at last to the safe enclosure of the Grail castle. Wagner's gaiety also mocked his own myth-making: like Jonson's phony alchemist, he boasted of being able to produce a redeemer on demand, as magicians pull rabbits out of hats. But the German word he used for the mandrake confided other truths, both sexually coarse and spiritually uncanny, about the creator's manufacture of men. Wagner called it a 'Galgenmannchen', a little man of the gallows. The etymology refers to a legend claiming that mandrakes mostly grew beneath the gallows, where the ground was fertilized by the ejaculations of hanged men. This made the mandrake the product not of love but of death, begotten during an involuntary nervous spasm as the neck breaks. A fortune-teller in Verdi's opera *Un ballo in maschera* sends the heroine Amelia to pick a magic herb beneath a gibbet, promising that it will cure her forbidden erotic passion. She politely refrains from mentioning the fertilizing agent; nor does she explain that the herb relieves desire by satisfying it. As Amelia reaches down for the root, the very man who is the object of her infatuation rears up before her and melodiously persuades her to succumb. Has she willed him into being – given birth to him as artists do to their characters, or as Elsa, pining for the otherworldly knight she sees in a vision, does to Lohengrin? Wagner's high spirits had a gruesome undertone. The artist, like the executed criminal, does not enjoy coition with a woman. His satisfaction is solitary and posthumous, and its fruit is a monster.

Alchemy remained a symbol for the artist's privileged vision, not be shared with the laity. Shelley believed that the 'secret alchemy' of poetry turned 'to potable gold the poisonous waters which flow from death through life'. Stéphane Mallarmé referred to his poetry as '*le Grand Oeuvre*, as our forbears the alchemists used to say'. Those forbears schemed to make gold; for Mallarmé, the only supernaturally precious substance was language, whose gilded images fortunately possessed no value in the drab, cheap, modern world. In Mallarmé's imaginary crucible, temperatures were lowered not raised: he told his friend Cazalis that he had camped out on 'the pure glaciers of aesthetics', where he discovered nothingness. Alchemy worked 'ex nihilo', and needed to reduce matter to a bare minimum before giving it a new form. Dedicated to this, Mallarmé vowed to jettison all material satisfactions, 'even as the alchemist burned his furniture and the beams of his roof to feed the furnace of the *Grand Oeuvre*'. Promising to incinerate his goods and chattels, he treated fire as the medium of the artist's self-immolation. In 1897 the Sorbonne allocated a laboratory to the dramatist Strindberg, who claimed to have synthesized gold from clods of earth gathered at midnight in the cemetery at Montparnasse. The composer

Frederick Delius arranged a rendezvous with a distinguished chemist, who was anxious to inspect the hoard. But Strindberg failed to turn up, and sent a telegram to announce that he felt the time for disclosure was not yet ripe. The proof of his aesthetic devotion was scorched hands: the acids and poisons he worked with consumed his skin, and sent him to hospital with an eruption of eczema.

With its injunction to change the world and revise man's standing in it, alchemy returned at a time of social, political and metaphysical instability. In Russia in 1908–1909 Valery Bryusov published his novel *The Fiery Angel*, which purported to be a romance dating from the Renaissance. The hero, the itinerant knight Ruprecht, is a follower of Pico della Mirandola; in the course of his wanderings he meets Faust, who with the aid of Mephistopheles speeds up man's progress to 'the apex of the world' – which is where Pico placed our species – by practising the 'secret sciences'. Agrippa of Nettesheim has a walk-on part. When Ruprecht consults him, Agrippa sternly upholds orthodoxy and declares magic to be abominable, but the novel ends with his death-bed confession that he was indeed a sorcerer. The great work, however, is performed by a woman, the crazed Renata, who is persecuted by the church for the ungodly practice of alchemy, astrology, necromancy and other 'Cabalistical Sciences'. Transmutation for her is not the mental ascent envisaged by Browning's Paracelsus; it is a bodily affair, a hysterical pregnancy which conjures up a demon lover. This is the fiery angel Madiel who, in his earthly guise, appears to possess eternal youth, 'with which mankind is endowed by the mysterious elixir in which the philosopher's stone of the alchemists is dissolved'. Alchemy likened the ripening of the stone in its hermetic vase to the development of the human embryo. Jung extended the connection, and argued that the experiment referred to the occult phantasms engendered by 'the unconscious'. Ruprecht wonders whether Madiel is 'a heavenly spirit or the creation of a diseased imagination'. Is there a difference?

Ruprecht's infatuation with Renata propels him into the chaos from which the world was formed. She melts down his honourable human dignity and reduces him to a 'massa confusa' of raging instincts; at the end of the novel she disrupts God's disciplined world by inciting an orgy in a convent. Physiologically, she undergoes the same dissolution. When she is overcome by her vision of Madiel, her ecstasies of torment match the convulsions studied by sixteenth-century exorcists. Her neck and breasts stiffen and straighten, then her head and chin stretch forward to reach her toes while the veins in her neck bulge. At last, in a miraculous display of double-jointedness, she reverses the movement so that the nape of her neck is twisted inside her shoulder while her thigh juts into the air. After her encounter with a witch, she moves as jerkily as a robot; Ruprecht imagines that she resembles 'the remarkable automaton of Albertus Magnus'. He is remembering the thirteenth-century Dominican friar who employed the philosopher's stone to create a walking, talking android. Its limbs were metallic or wooden, and it had a skin of leather. According to the legend, it also had a brain and could think for itself: it manned the door and decided which visitors to let in. Thomas Aquinas, a student of Albertus, considered his master's creature diabolical, and battered it to death with a hammer. Although Albertus supposedly trafficked with demons, in 1622 the church beatified him. In 1941 the Pope even made him patron of the natural sciences. By then, androids with artificial intelligence were a scientific possibility; the definition of forbidden knowledge had changed, and Albertus was belatedly neutralized.

Ruprecht often feels that he is teetering on the edge of a 'black depth', and when he interrogates Agrippa he senses that they are standing together on the edge of an abyss. The novel peers into what Jung, in one of his essays on alchemy, called 'the abysmal depths in man'. That psychological gulf, as he said in his commentary on the 'nigredo', is the unconscious mind, which is 'both good and evil and yet neither, the matrix of all potentialities'.

When Prokofiev composed his operatic adaptation of *The Fiery Angel* in the early 1920s, this chaos erupted from the dim trench of the orchestra pit. Agrippa angrily refuses to share his secrets, and tells Ruprecht that the only true magicians are the Magi who greeted Christ; he denies that his pedigree dogs are demons wearing Kabbalistic collars, and dismisses the stories that he pays bills with home-made gold. Prokofiev's Agrippa sings in a high tenor voice that almost cracks under the strain of his hypocritical pretence, while three jangling skeletons rattle their bones and deride his lies. A sonic cataclysm underlies the interview. The strings flail, wind instruments shriek, the basses thunder imprecations. In 1530 Agrippa, declaiming against the vanity of sciences and arts, condemned musicians who affirmed that there was song in heaven. How, he demanded, could they know, never having heard that celestial 'concordance of voices'? They were 'misled by their madness', deafened by their own 'Euouae' – the shouts of participants in Dionysiac rites – or perhaps merely drunk. The black, lava-like sounds of Prokofiev's score outwit Agrippa, suggesting that music can be hellish as well as heavenly. In the opera, after Agrippa's final insistence that magic is theology by other means, a bludgeoning rhythmic battery terminates the discussion, as if the orchestra were concussing the inquisitive Ruprecht. A loudly dissonant chord, painfully prolonged, admits that no questions have been answered, so the ground shifts unsteadily and reminds us of the emptiness gaping below. In Bryusov's novel, Ruprecht says that the 'chaos of knowledge and information' he has accumulated from books is like molten unforged iron, later to be welded into 'a shapely bell, that can sound far and high'. Bells are a summons to worship. That bell, in Prokofiev's musical setting, sounds more like a tocsin.

But false science can be true art. Jorge Luis Borges excused the most disreputable of alchemists in his story 'The Rose of Paracelsus'. In a cellar, Paracelsus begs his 'indeterminate God – any God' to send him a believer. A candidate appears in answer to his prayer, and offers gold in exchange for a share in the quest for the philosopher's stone. But he first asks Paracelsus for a proof of his powers: is it true that he can burn a rose to ashes, then cause it to reassume its original form? He begs to be shown 'the annihilation and resurrection of the rose'. Like Agrippa in *The Fiery Angel*, Paracelsus resists, and – turning the logic of creation back to front – denies that something can be reduced to nothing. Adam in Eden, he adds, could not eliminate a single flower or trample one blade of grass. The disciple insists, but the furnace is cold, the retorts dusty. Paracelsus, declining to use alembics, proposes another method, 'the instrument used by the deity to create the heavens and the earth'; he means 'the Word, taught to us by the science of the Kabbalah'. The disciple tosses a rose, 'incarnate and incarnadine', into the embers. It discolours, chars, sifts into ash. No miracle occurs, so he leaves, convinced that Paracelsus is 'a charlatan, or a mere visionary'. Left alone, the alchemist pensively removes a handful of ashes from the hearth. Then, as Borges reports in the sudden and stunning conclusion of the fable, 'he whispered a single word. The rose appeared again'.

The charm demonstrates that Paracelsus has the poet's capacity to create by naming. The word evokes the thing; an image materializes before us, unseen but beautiful and fragrant. In Shakespeare's play, Juliet ponders the onomastic conundrum of 'that which we call a rose', which 'by any other name would smell as sweet'. Borges might also be alluding to other feats of poetic evocation – Blake's lament for a sick rose polluted by an invisible worm; Wordsworth's assurance that 'lovely is the Rose'; or even Gertrude Stein's blunt insistence that 'a rose is a rose is a rose is a rose', a fact that needs no metaphor to transmute it. A painted rose sends us back to stare at the original flower with proper amazement. A rose that is spoken of or given a name compels us to think about the idea of the flower and to ask who first conceived of it. The great work can be accomplished without chemicals. Artists show us a paradise which we cannot see for ourselves because we look at the world with stale, uncreative eyes.

# 9
## OUR OWN UNMAKING

Leonardo disparaged ineffectual 'seekers after gold', and grouped alchemists with the speculators who designed perpetual-motion machines that could turn mill wheels in stagnant water. During the 1490s he made diagrams of such wheels, with an internal axis of weights to ensure that they turned of their own volition and a ratchet to prevent them from backtracking; the images were annotated in his cunning, crabwise mirror-writing. The contraption, he concluded, was 'sophistical', easily refuted by the dull laws of physics. Yet the impossibility of the thing was what fascinated him, since it gave form to the contest between the inventive mind and the restrictions of reality. Leonardo's sketches of the wheels make their hinges look like stabilized versions of waves. Water represented the exhausting, erosive force of nature, remorselessly gathering – in his most elaborate graphic fantasies – into a deluge that washes men away and obliterates their accomplishments. Was it possible to harness this destructive power and derive profit from it?

Recommending himself to the Milanese overlord Ludovico Sforza in 1493, Leonardo offered to impart what he called 'my secrets'. These were not alchemical mysteries, but contrivances for conducting war. He promised to make portable bridges that would be 'indestructible by fire and battle', mortars to hurl stones, impregnable chariots, and 'tortuous mines' that would enable soldiers to tunnel under rivers to reach the enemy camps. Leonardo's ingenuity staged an armed assault on the physical world. Dreaming of an escape from gravity, he designed flying machines to invade God's realm. But he always lunged back to earth, and imagined the skies punitively falling in on him: he sketched the black clotted cloud of a hurricane, or a leaden downpour of tools and man-made appliances – including clocks and spectacles, designed to regulate or augment nature, as well as aspiring ladders – that thud onto the ground. Although his notes attributed this cataclysm to a God incensed by the arrogant human race, for Leonardo that deity was not a person. He gave no credence to 'things contrary to the senses', such as the scholastic belief in 'the existence of God'. The wrath belonged to a natural element, as in his sketch of the voracious Arno, which screws the river's currents into vortices that gnaw at an embankment. Leonardo's theory of creation omitted God altogether. Nature, fickle and mutable, amuses itself by 'continually producing new forms', which time

stubbornly erodes. As yet the combat is unresolved; we should be grateful
that nature is 'more swift in her creating than time is in his destruction'. In
Italian, the substantives have genders, which turns existence into a sexual
war: a familial dispute between Mother Nature and Father Time.

Michelangelo painted the transmission of divine influence across the
gap between God and man. Leonardo could not help but notice the distance between God's son and the men who are supposed to be his faithful
followers. The *Last Supper*, as Goethe pointed out, paints the thoughts of
the characters in it, and much of their thinking is incredulous, doubt-
ridden. The apostles stiffly recoil from Christ's accusation, and hold up their
hands to protest their innocence or to point fingers of blame at one another.
Eddies of agitated motion spread out from Christ along both sides of the table,
and like all waves they end in dispersal, breaking up the closed community.
Christ remains unmoved, self-sufficiently absorbed in the anticipation of
his fate. No aureole shines above his head. Instead the arch behind him
supplies a geometrical canopy; outside the window is one of Leonardo's
remote and alien landscapes, like the rugged waste against which Mona Lisa
poses – evidence that human beings, rather than being made in God's
image, are compounded from the elements, with flesh as grass, bones as
rock, and blood as our internal ocean. The meal spread on the table has not
yet been transformed into a set of eucharistic symbols, as it would later be
when the Mass began to commemorate Christ's sacrifice. The details –
bread rolls, a knife for slicing into them, a container of salt overturned by
Judas – remain unregenerately physical: we must eat to sustain life, although
the disciples, distracted by the need to semaphore guiltless incomprehension, have temporarily forgotten to do so.

Leonardo's divine ministers are so rooted in our carnal world that they
can make a celestial summons look like an erotic signal. An annunciating
angel he drew during his time in Rome is winsomely seductive, as if his
mission were to impregnate Mary personally. In his last portrait, now in the
Louvre, Leonardo transferred the angel's pose – with one hand caressing
a bare chest while the other points upwards towards a heaven that may be a
place of sensual delight – to St John the Baptist, and gave the saint a sly smile
which suggests that he is not foretelling the advent of Christ but imparting
a more intimate, seditious knowledge. Leonardo claimed to have once
sold a painting of a 'divine subject' to a man who fell in love with the image.
He tried to expunge the 'emblems of divinity', and became so besotted that
he kissed the picture. The painter did not condemn this prostitution of
his work: perhaps gods and goddesses are merely the conjurations of our
ardent fantasy. Believing in what he called the 'deità' of the artist, Leonardo
was reluctant to share that conviction of divine power with any religious
authority. A comment by Jacob Bronowski, apt despite its anachronism,

Leonardo da
Vinci, *Lady with
Ermine*, 1483–90

makes him glance ahead to a time when nature had dispensed with the
biblical creator. In *Lady with an Ermine*, Leonardo painted Lodovico Sforza's
mistress, who holds a white-furred stoat in her arms. The hand with which
she strokes it elongates like a poised claw; she and the animal have the same
coldly intent gaze, and the wintry pallor of its coat matches the square of
exposed flesh against which its head nestles. Both are wild creatures that
have been tamed: the woman's chains are the braids and ribands and necklaces looped around her forehead, neck and chest. Bronowski remarked that
the painting is 'as much a research into man and animal ... as is Darwin's
*Origin of Species*'. It discerns the connection between the pampered woman
and the beast that clings to her, and in doing so it upsets the strict, hierarchical ladder of being raised by God.

When speculating about creativity, Leonardo inevitably related art to
biological functions. He did so with a clear-eyed, thin-lipped distaste, aware
that his mental excursions took him into the seamy mess of the body. His
pictorial science relied on butchery. He dissected dozens of corpses, proud
of the moral courage required for this journey into the interior. Sometimes
a single cadaver did not stay fresh long enough for him to complete his
investigation, so he had to 'proceed by stages with as many bodies as would

render my knowledge complete'. He studied variations by repeating the experiment with a second set of models from the morgue. He also examined the brain, and drew on the skills of sculptors who cast models of living bodies in bronze. Having sectioned a cranium and separated the ventricles, he let out the fluid and injected liquid wax in its place. When this hardened, he could slice into the facsimile as he pleased.

To understand creation, he started from obstetrics: hence his gynaecological diagrams, in which a foetus – thought by Leonardo to be merely a 'creature' of its mother, without a soul and therefore in no need of salvation – curls inside a womb. God created sexlessly; Adam gave birth to Eve without pain or bloodshed. Leonardo refused to accredit these sanitized procedures. In a study of copulation, he casually beheads the woman, and reorganizes the man's internal tubes to show how the soul is transmitted through the spine into the penis. In a drawing now at Windsor, he exposes the vascular and urogenital systems of a cross-sectioned woman. He believed the uterus to be spherical, so in his design he anchors it with tendons that sprout like horns. The subject seems to be gripping a skull between her legs, superimposing life and death. These diagrams experiment with a hybrid as bizarre as the alliance between the courtesan and the ermine. The embryo is human, but the womb in which Leonardo places it probably belonged to a cow. In 1508–1509 Leonardo drew the gaping vulva of a woman who had recently given birth, together with an open anal sphincter. The distension of the vulva is anatomically unlikely; in his notes he likens its folds and ridges to crenellations, denying their soft recessiveness and identifying them as 'the gatekeeper of the castle'. Their task is to fortify

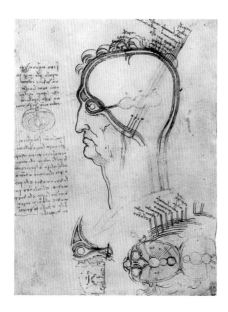
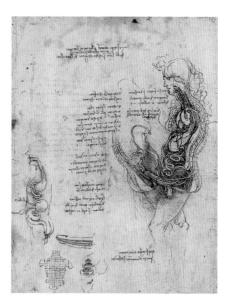

Leonardo da Vinci, *Drawing of a Head as an Onion*, 1489

Leonardo da Vinci, *Drawing of Intercourse*, c. 1512

what lies within, and to make entry difficult. Leonardo, holding back, wonders whether he dares to intrude. In a self-revealing fable, he describes his 'desire to see the great abundance of varied and strange shapes assumed by nature's ingenuity', which emboldens him to explore a landscape like that in the anatomical drawing. He comes to 'the entrance of a great cave', and is baffled by its obscurity. He bends down, peers in, but can see nothing. Fear and desire do battle within him: he recoils from the 'dark and threatening den', yet itches to know whether there is 'any extraordinary thing inside it'. If the orifice is female, it represents the nursery of organic life; but it might just as well be Leonardo's own abundant, ingenious brain.

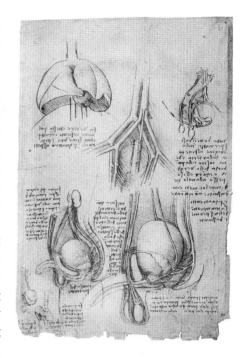

Leonardo da Vinci, *Drawing of Genitalia, c.* 1512

In his apocalyptic reveries, Leonardo saw the womb as a mortuary. Earth, as he put it in a Paris manuscript, was born from water and might drown in that element all over again, returning to the 'grembo' – the lap or groin – of the sea. Studying the mechanics of creation, Leonardo commented that reproduction was such a repellent business that, if it were not for the enticement of facial beauty, 'nature would lose the human species'. God may have favoured the institution of marriage because it ensured lawful progeny, but Leonardo thought it was more likely to bring about biological annihilation (which he did not necessarily regret). One of his jocular prophecies looks forward to a society where fathers will have to bribe young men to sleep with their daughters, even if the girls are beautiful. Why should dowries be required as bait, unless it is nature's wish 'to extinguish the human race, because it ... spoils all created things'?

Classical myths, soothing our qualms about procreation and the danger of childbirth, devise alternative methods of genesis. Sometimes the female loses her exclusivity, and the channel through which delivery occurs is altered. Hermes removed the embryonic Dionysus from the womb of Semele and sewed the embryo into the thigh of Zeus; the father coughed out the infant out when its time is due. Pater noted that Michelangelo's favourite classical subject was 'the legend of Leda, and the delight of the world breaking from the egg of a bird'. Leonardo painted the same subject,

Cesare de Sesto,
after Leonardo,
*Leda*,
*c.* 1505–10

although his version is now known only from copies like that by Cesare da Sesto. The nymph, hiding behind an enigmatic smile, coyly turns away from the amorous swan, though she cannot help fingering the taut phallic girth of its neck. The bird nudges her with its beak and wraps its wings around her in a display of power and possession. At her feet, eggs crack open, and the products of this miscegenated alliance – four entirely human babies who grew up to be Castor and Pollux, and Helen and Clytemnestra – scramble into life. The mystery of growth has been extruded from the body, and can be studied in the daylight without having to cut open corpses. The broken halves of the shell rhyme with the pointed feathers of the swan's enveloping wings: those split eggs contain what King Lear calls the 'germens' of the father. Visualizing the scene, Leonardo chose to underline its perversity. Leda changed to a goose to evade Zeus, which prompted him to become a swan; making love, they were at least both birds. Leonardo restored Leda's human form, which means that the eggs seem to have been laid by the male parent.

Commentators intrigued by Mona Lisa's self-absorbed, gratified smile have often speculated that she might be pregnant, and it is interesting that Kenneth Clark, having seen the painting removed from its protective casing of bullet-proof glass, reported that the surface had 'the delicacy of a new-laid egg'. How newly laid? Recent enough still to be warm? And is there a life inside it, or will it be cooked and eaten? Leonardo, so wastefully prolific in engendering ideas, worried about nature's prodigal output of seed. His prophetic riddles often dwelt on an excessive, disastrously expended fertility. 'Oh, how many there will be whose birth will be forbidden!' he lamented. He varied the threnody when he pointed out that 'Infinite generations will be lost with the deaths of those who are pregnant'. He was referring to eggs eaten before they can hatch, or to fish we consume along with their ovaries. Elsewhere he brooded about males whose testicles are removed to prevent them from procreating, and females whose breasts are sliced off. These conundrums alluded to castrated livestock, and to salted pork loin made from sows. He acknowledged the alliance between creativity and destruction in a throwaway pun scribbled in a notebook: 'Li medici mi crearono e distrussono'. He was referring both to his Florentine patron Lorenzo Medici and to the medical profession. Physicians, in his opinion, practised a killing not a healing art, because they preyed on and profited from our ailments. The pun proclaimed a law of life, given visible form in the shattering of the swan's eggs.

Genitally or mentally, we are too creative for our own good. The proliferation of unfertilized eggs and undeveloped ideas made Leonardo wonder if nature might not be more inclined to destroy life rather than to duplicate it. Contemplating olives, acorns or chestnuts, he prophesied that 'many children shall be torn ... out of the very arms of their mothers, flung upon the ground and maimed'. Looked at this way, to play conkers is to commit infanticide. Leonardo saw the same murderous urge in the elemental world, and sketched its malevolence in his images of storms and floods. Agrippa of Nettesheim also puzzled over the paradoxical behaviour of water. It is 'the beginning of all things', an element so blessed that it is essential to rituals of spiritual regeneration. Yet its primal potency makes it terrifying: Agrippa quoted a fantasy in which Pliny described the waters effacing the earth and sky. In a manuscript at Windsor, Leonardo drew an old man wearily resting his head on his hand; his body is supported by a stick, and he rests his back against a tree. He is lost in contemplation, depressed by his thoughts. The facing page shows the gloomy contents of his brain. It contains studies of gushing water, which wraps itself almost prehensilely around obstacles, battering pillars and using them to redouble its force. Sometimes it coils into braids like hair; in other designs it lunges through a hole in a wall, rebounds from the bottom of a tank, expands into whirling circles, and – in a parody of vegetative growth – bubbles like sprouting seeds. These hydrodynamic diagrams lead to a narrative of universal inundation. Clouds thicken, storing their energy in tight coils and spirals; they unleash an invisible wind which thrashes a bent tree. As the downpour begins, water seems to be falling upwards, ricocheting from the soaked earth into a sky that is smothered by clouds. The motion is circular because it follows the life-cycle of water, which condenses and vaporizes, rains down and then re-ascends as it transpires. Passing through these phases and renewing itself as it gyrates, it mocks the fragility of animal life. The hurricane torments horses and some indistinct, half-human creatures – Lear's 'poor naked wretches', pelted by the storm – who regressively burrow into the earth. A more cubistic study of this agitation turns fluids into solid forms. The lapping, licking waves resemble tongues of flame or molten lava; their weight and propulsion makes them engines of destruction like those Leonardo offered his Milanese patron, and they hurl blocks of masonry into the air as they overwhelm a town.

As Leonardo described it, this was 'the pitiless slaughter of the human race by the wrath of God'. But which god is responsible? The angry, all-mighty potentate of the Old Testament sent the deluge which over-whelmed mankind. Leonardo, however, glimpses classical deities in the mayhem: Neptune with his trident rides the waters, Aeolus bestrides the winds and scoops up trees he has plucked from the ground. These are elemental agencies, not stern retributive overseers like the enskied God of Genesis. They personify natural energy, instinctively and amorally destructive. Or is this only the desperate imagining of insecure, beleaguered mankind? Leonardo's description emphasizes the suicidal madness of threatened men. Some people strangle themselves with their own hands (which is quite a feat). Others kill their children by dashing them onto the rocks: this at least saves them from death by drowning. Cadavers jokingly imitate life. Fermented corpses propel themselves upwards and break through the surface of the water, then bounce about as if playing ball games. This destructiveness gave Leonardo a means of analysing or anatomizing nature, testing its fault lines and intently watching as it falls apart. The pre-scriptions in his notes are like the spells which enable Prospero to concoct his own more spurious, magically unfatal tempest. 'Let some mountains collapse,' he writes. He adds other voluntary inflictions: let a river burst its dam and demolish a city that cowers in the valley below, let high buildings disintegrate and explode into dust clouds, let water enraged by the restric-tions placed on it course around a lake in wild vortices.

Leonardo had no argument with nature's campaign against human life. Ours is a predatory species which tramples 'all created things'; his own cre-ativity shared in these rampages. 'The painter,' he declared, 'disputes and competes with nature.' Mining technology likewise parades man's triumph over the sullenly retentive earth, although in one of his fables Leonardo guiltily bewails the gouging-out of minerals which will be turned into weapons. The ore emerges, he says, from dark caverns: once more he alludes to the bodily orifice or subterranean cleft that both attracted and repelled him. He addresses this ore as a 'monstrous creature', and wishes that it would return to hell. Hauled to the surface, it is transformed into 'artifices', employed by men to kill their fellows. The words he chooses treat armaments as artworks, and link them with the sacred or profane monsters he drew or painted – the preening swan, the cossetted ermine, the dragon speared by St George, or the antique warrior whose helmet bristles with beaks and sharp fins and whose breast-plate juts out into the profile of a fanged, snarling lion. Despite Leonardo's plea, the monstrous creature cannot be uncreated. How can you unthink a thought once it has reared up in your head? In a riddle, Leonardo saw sharp swords in the horns of animals, which would put to death many of their species. Deciphered, this refers to knives made from rams' horns. The puzzle points to the aggressive armature of that headgear: the brain grows weapons, and these can gorily cut their way into a body like your own. Thinkers, like surgeons, operate with blades. In his sketches of a foetus, Leonardo emphasized the bulk of the head, a gravitational centre which will cause it to revolve and protrude into the birth canal. During delivery, the infant's head is a battering ram.

Leonardo believed that man's godlike powers were invested in the eye. Sight for him was a nobler sense than hearing, which made painting a loftier occupation than music or poetry. The ear is a mere receiver, but the eye has power over the world it surveys and subdues, organizing the clutter of visual evidence in accord with the rules of perspective. Hence the grand titles Leonardo lavished on that vulnerable organ. The eye is a potentate, even a warlord – 'the commander of astronomy' and 'the prince of mathematics'. At the same time it is a philosopher, rectifying space and making decisions about the motions of bodies as it measures their retreat towards disappearance. It englobes the universe, 'conducts man to the various regions of this world', and is more excellent than 'all other things created by God'. Given all these accolades, why is it so easily reduced – as Gloucester's tormenters remark in *King Lear* – to a lustreless 'vile jelly'? Leonardo acknowledged that the eye was a teasing, frustrating aperture, like a slit drilled in a fortified wall. Optical science, he said, 'reconciles the soul to stay in its bodily prison'. The compliment is less effusive than it seems: the body is a jail cell, and those two small windows show the internee a freedom that will always remain out of reach. The soul has the option of attempting to escape, but it can only do so by dying.

As an inventor, Leonardo battled to release the mind (wired directly to the eye) from this physical confinement, and more often than not he tragically failed to do so. He planned to launch his flying machine from 'the great Swan' – a hill-top in Fiesole, which perhaps evoked the triumphantly spread wings of Leda's conqueror – and predicted that the take-off would stupefy the universe. But the wooden struts and pedals of his flapping, ineffectual contraption never got airborne. Scheming to establish human supremacy, he actually confirmed our inferiority. Another of his whimsical apocalypses describes a giant marauding in Libya; the ogre crushes men who recoil into 'tiny holes and subterranean caverns' like crabs or crickets. Its stomping advance is a reminder that 'the human race has reason to envy every other species' and, more defenceless than birds, can 'find no safety in flight'. Leonardo ends by imagining himself buried in the giant's maw. Our personal genesis occurs when we struggle out of a dark, bloody cave. The journey happens in reverse when we die, as earth swallows us. Art and science itch to investigate the place of origins, which is also our final destination: hence Leonardo's anatomical unseaming of a dead body with its load of life, afloat in the womb's primal waters.

An ocular art insists on proportion and, as Leonardo specified in his *Trattato*, it exactly calculates the 'pyramid of lines' by which objects transmit an image of themselves to the eye. It sees the world as God did during that first week, and its constructive vision can declare the sight to be good. But before God enlightened nature, the world was without form and void; for Leonardo, that chaos still existed, insecurely caged inside the cranium but also present everywhere in the undesigned, unregenerate world outside us. He was grateful to this disorder because, as he noted in the codex held in the Vatican library, 'confused things kindle great inventions'. In a riddle, Leonardo listed a series of terrors and portents that upset nature and flout logic. Animals converse in the tongues of men; we feel ourselves rushing to the ends of the earth while fixed to the spot, or plummet through the air without a crash-landing; destruction flares in the sky. 'O marvel of the human race,' he asks, 'what delirium has brought you to this?' The answer is our dreams, in which we die a thousand times and miraculously recover to repeat the experiment, or enjoy a spectacular premonitory preview of the world's end.

In the din of ringing bells, Leonardo could identify any name or word he cared to imagine, and he treated the marks on a discoloured wall as the rudiments of a pictorial landscape, 'beautified with mountains, rivers, rocks, trees, plains, wide valleys and hills in varied arrangement'. He might even have been pleased to know that his *Last Supper* has blotched and mouldered until it is now hardly more than a patchy stain. Its protracted self-destruction has returned it to chaos, which means that it offers an artist the raw, malleable material of a new creation. Leonardo dared 'the genius of the painter' to find 'monsters, devils and other fantastic things' on a besmirched wall, in coals that collapse in the grate, or in a wisp of unravelling cloud. As a child, Max Ernst lay in bed studying a panel of false mahogany and a stretch of floorboards abraded by punitive scrubbing. The grained, grooved wood acted as the 'optical provocateur of a vision of half-sleep'; Ernst transcribed what he saw beneath the surface by covering the panels with paper and rubbing them with black lead, which turned the wall and floor into a spectral moonlit forest. Later he studied the random patterns in crinkled leaves or ragged linen, which he described as hallucinations. Surrealism thus learned 'the lesson of Leonardo', as Ernst put it in 1936.

The alchemists worked to purify an elemental 'massa confusa'. Leonardo reversed this allegorical progress: his negative intellectual alchemy had as its motive 'the hope ... of returning to the first state of chaos'. Other Renaissance men demonstrated our freedom to improve our metaphysical rank by fashioning identities. 'I am not I,' says Astrophel in one of Philip Sidney's sonnets, calculating that his mistress Stella will take him more seriously if he plays the role of a literary lover. Iago in *Othello* remarks 'I am not what I am', since for him the power of self-invention is a sinister exercise in dissimulation. Leonardo called this dicing with nonentity 'disfazione': defabrication, unfashioning or, to use a synonym from Donne's poem 'The Exstasie', unperplexing. A perplexity is an entanglement, which, as Donne says, ties tight the 'subtile knot, which makes us man' and secures our being. Ecstasy – the orgasm and its small death – unpicks that knot and pleasurably destroys us. In the most tragic of his meditations, Leonardo considers the moth's attraction to the flame, and likens this suicidal frenzy to our human longing for spring or summer or any keenly anticipated future. Don't we realize that we are speeding up time and thus advancing the moment of our deaths? Beginning and end are conflated by a similar play on words in Dante's *Purgatorio*, when Pia de' Tolomei sums up her abbreviated existence. 'Siena mi fe'; disfecemi Maremma,' she says. She was made in Siena, but Maremma, where she died in the fever-ridden marshes, was her unmaking.

After reflecting on our suicidal impatience, Leonardo employs a charmed word from the vocabulary of the alchemists. This same entropic urgency, he says, is 'the very quintessence, the spirit of the elements'. In the great work, the quintessence was the fifth and purest essence: man's addition to the four elements that make up nature, a stepping-stone that takes us closer to divinity. Leonardo saw it less optimistically. The quintessence, to him, was the desire for destruction. We are a blend of elements, and each of them wants to be released from its confinement. The soul too chafes and frets in its prison. Not content with the meagre peep-hole of the eye, it wants to escape from the body and return 'to its giver'. Creativity is a symptom of our discontent, even of our self-disgust. Is Mona Lisa smiling because she is pregnant or – as Pater said of the fiendish woman he saw in the painting, who 'has been dead many times' – because she has 'learned the secrets of the grave'? Art, rather than modelling itself on reproduction, flirts with death, and allows us to experience our own undoing.

# 10
## AUTHOR OF HIMSELF

In Leonardo's drawing of a man standing inside a circle – a homage to the architect Vitruvius and his laws of harmonic proportion – the individual extends his extremities to touch the limits of the universe. The figure's legs move apart to gain a foothold on the curvature of the earth, while his arms reach towards a point that might be the arching summit of the sky. The fingers conduct an experimental probe, and touch nothingness; there is no reciprocation, as when Michelangelo's Adam limply raises his hand towards the invigorating finger of God. His bare chest, plated in muscle, looks as valiant as that of Leonardo's armoured antique warrior; his heavy genitals, with their flaming crown of hair, display our in-built immortality. Yet his face frowns or scowls, reflecting his frustration at being trapped inside the circle. He has four overlaid arms and an equal number of legs, so he appears to be in motion: is he standing on the ground or flying? Like an athlete, Vitruvian man relies on his body to propel him through space.

Shakespeare possessed a different kind of universality, more elusive and ambiguous because his powers were mental not physical. His crowds of garrulous characters include kings and fools, lovers and murderers, many people of mysteriously indeterminate gender, a small pantheon of classical gods and goddesses, along with a dog, a crocodile and a moon-calf, not to mention a talking donkey and a walking statue. How can they all have derived from a single individual? Their creator must have been, as Coleridge assumed, 'myriad-minded', possessing more brains than Leonardo's figure has limbs.

In the nineteenth century, when artistic imagination and scientific intellect between them probed the secrets of nature, Shakespeare was set up in place of an abdicating God. In 1822 a company of English actors brought Shakespeare to Paris. Alexandre Dumas saw *Hamlet*, and suddenly understood 'how it was possible ... to create a world'. Tragedy and comedy, poetry and prose battled within the play like the primordial, undivided elements, but – as Dumas put it, loosely translating Genesis – 'over this chaos moved the spirit of God'. The spirit belonged to Shakespeare, and it touched Dumas into new life: he felt like 'Adam waking up after the creation'. Berlioz also underwent a conversion during that season at the Odéon, and thanked Shakespeare for it by addressing him as 'our father, our father who art in heaven'. He adopted Shakespeare as an honorary parent,

George Romney,
*Margery Jourdain
and Bolingbroke
Conjuring up the
Fiend, c.* 1790

and illustrated the lineage by composing music in tribute to the plays – a dramatic symphony that mused on *Romeo and Juliet*, an operatic adaptation of *Much Ado About Nothing* that made room for a lecture on musical performance, an overture that encapsulated the action of *King Lear*, a choral threnody for Ophelia and a funeral march for Hamlet himself, and a fantasia based on *The Tempest*, performed by spirits of the air. Berlioz was sure of Shakespeare's divinity. About God he had doubts, so he added a proviso to his paraphrase of the Lord's Prayer: 'He is our father, our father in heaven – if there is a heaven. An all-mighty being, wrapped in his infinite indifference, is an atrocious absurdity. Shakespeare alone is the good God to the soul of the artist'. Lecturing on heroes in 1840, Carlyle asked 'Can the man say, *Fiat lux*, ... and out of chaos make a world?' The question answered itself: Shakespeare did so. Carlyle went on to admire the equanimity of this 'great soul', who was able – like the forgiving Christian God – to sympathize with valiant Othello and cowardly Falstaff, with tender Juliet and murderous Lady Macbeth, because they are all his creatures. Carlyle emphasized that creation carried with it the responsibility of moral understanding. 'Creative, we said: poetic creation, what is this too but *seeing* the thing sufficiently?' The God of Genesis, so quick to condemn his ingrate offspring, did not always pass that test; for Carlyle, Shakespeare never failed to be both loving and just.

A decade earlier, Coleridge called Shakespeare 'the Spinozistic deity' and praised his 'omnipresent creativeness'. Spinoza in his *Ethics* denied that

the business of creation concluded on the seventh day. We should not presume
that the creator chose to rest because he had exhausted his ideas; God continues to pour forth 'an infinity of things in an infinity of modes'. This
encouraged the romantics to see the world forever growing, changing,
expanding – more like a garden or a jungle than the Pythagorean arrangement of concentric spheres or Plato's austerely angular dodecahedron.
Spinoza extolled God's 'infinite nature', yet Shakespeare's plays demonstrated
that a human artist could compete with the profuse, prolific begetter of the
world. In 1815 Goethe wrote a panegyric entitled *Shakespeare ad Infinitum*,
which celebrates this inexhaustibility and its liberating influence. Goethe
drew up a table of opposed terms to illustrate Shakespeare's modernity and
his secession from the rigorous necessity of classical religion. The antithesis
is summed up in two contrasting German verbs, 'sollen' and 'wollen', which
refer respectively to duty and will. The heroes of Greek tragedy are slaves or
martyrs to a duty imposed on them by gods or tyrants. Shakespeare's characters please themselves, like Lear when he divides his kingdom or Antony
and Cleopatra when they capriciously decide to fight a naval battle. 'Man's
will,' according to Goethe, 'is his kingdom of heaven.' No inevitability con-
strains Hamlet, and like Shakespeare's other tragic heroes he defies death –
joking about it, philosophically quarrelling with it, continuing to talk as it
overtakes him – rather than accepting its finality.

As a German, Goethe envied such indiscipline. He called Shakespeare's
plays 'a great animated fair', full of an easy-going urban hubbub which he
thought inimitably English. Victor Hugo also revered Shakespeare as a
national deity. While exiled on the islands of Jersey and Guernsey between
1852 and 1868, he wrote a book about Shakespeare, which he dedicated 'To
England'. It was his thanks for the political asylum he had been granted, and
his hymn of praise to English liberty. Hugo thought of Shakespeare himself
as the embodiment of demos, the people; his plays are as raucous and disruptive as the mob that acclaims Cade's rebellion in *Henry VI*. Spinoza's infinity
of modes or things became the chorus of argumentative voices and clashing
identities that the dramatist somehow found inside himself. Unlike Spinoza,
Hugo did not claim that a 'divine essence' was 'the cause of all things'. He
admired genius because it brought about a second creation, a divine action
that was carried out by man. Shakespeare's plays were therefore an epilogue
to Genesis: 'From the direct divine creation proceeds Adam, the prototype.
From the indirect divine creation – that it is to say, from the human creation
– proceed other Adams, the types.' Among these generic beings – themselves
the source of life, since actual humans take the theatrical inventions as
models for their own conduct – are pensive Hamlet, gluttonous Falstaff, or
Shylock who for Hugo represents both oppressed Judaism and shrewd Jew-
ishness. Other Eves include Rosalind, Cleopatra, Lady Macbeth. God made

the primal parents, but Shakespeare produces their divergent offspring. The gods or spirits in his plays boast of in their procreative power. The quarrel between Oberon and Titania stirs up dissension in nature, altering the seasons and ruining the crops. They accept responsibility for the 'progeny of evils' that litter the land: 'We are their parents and original'.

Awe-struck, Hugo associated Shakespeare with the fertile plenum of nature. The plays exhibit 'virility always, inspiration everywhere; as many metaphors as the meadow, as many antitheses as the oak, as many contrasts and depths as the universe; incessant generation, pubescence, hymen, gestation'. Worn out by this seminal labour, Hugo concludes 'It is too much; it infringes the rights of neuters'. Like Leonardo examining the genital organs, Hugo treats creativity as a polyphiloprogenitive riot, a storm of seed like that which rains down from the heaven where Ovid's promiscuous gods disport themselves. The sappy vitality of Shakespeare is pagan: Hugo comments that he bore Cordelia in his brain, as if he were Zeus giving birth to Athene. Such creative ardour taunts Christian asceticism. Hugo diagnoses the apocalyptic visions of St John as a morbid consequence of his chastity, and regrets that he resisted 'the universal generative tendency'. The man who declined to have sex regales himself with fantasies about the end of the world, since he has done nothing to ensure its continuation. For Hugo himself, the cult of Shakespeare was a family affair. Hugo's son, who shared his exile, passed the time by translating the plays, which prompted Hugo to write his own exalted tribute to them.

The first half of his long, digressive book prepares for Shakespeare's coming with a speedy tour of cosmic history. Classical and Christian myths about the earth's origins are summarized – except that, in Hugo's theogony, the source from which the world erupts is always the imagination of a writer, not the mind of a bodiless, geometrizing god. Before cosmos, according to Hesiod, there was chaos. Hugo localizes that state in Shakespeare's rowdy, swarming London. Nature at first exploded into life, and that initiating discharge of energy can also be attributed to the man who sat down to write the plays: Hugo imagines that Shakespeare's inkstand 'smokes like a crater'. The image of the potted volcano may be overexcited but it is not illogical, because Hugo reveres works of art only if they are anarchic, agitated by an internal mayhem. In his review of Shakespeare's precursors, he insists on this proximity to the upheaval of origins. The Bible 'emerges from chaos in Genesis, and passes out of view amid the thunders of the Apocalypse', and the Indian epics have 'the supernatural and hideous outlines of chaos'. The Greeks envisaged chaos as a gulf or an abyss. Hugo revives both etymological images. He calls Dante's *Divina Commedia* 'this gulf-poem', and says that in reading it 'you are in the abyss'. Art itself is 'an immense gaping chasm, ready to receive all that is within possibility' – an orifice greedy to ingest life. Great artists are unfathomable beings, so 'each new genius is an abyss', opening up profundities beneath the safe surface on which we tread. Elsewhere Hugo describes genius as 'a headland into the infinite'. When his son asked him how he would spend his years of exile, Hugo first said he intended to gaze at the ocean. His contemplation of Shakespeare enabled him to do so by other means: the plays were his headland, a perch from which he surveyed the surging waters of the channel and the 'democracy of clouds' above them.

Like Leonardo's Vitruvian man, Hugo's Shakespeare could be equated with the world. 'He is the earth,' Hugo remarks. He immediately differentiates the bulging shape and brawling dissonance of Shakespeare's planet from the tidy, theoretical cosmos of classical myth. 'Lucretius is the sphere,' he says, 'Shakespeare the globe.' He is quibbling, because globes are also spherical, though his meaning is clear: Lucretius colonized outer space with his map of astronomical rotations, but the ground on which we live is Shakespeare's terrain. His verbal coinages reveal that the degrees of meaning are not handed down from on high but constructed by the human imagination, which first names everything on earth and then sets out to fill the vacant sky. Contentious politicians in the plays about English history speak of 'royalizing' or 'monarchizing' one another. Kings may like to think that they are anointed by God, but these new words point out that their status is something they attain and must maintain by the exercise of artful guile (or with the help of the supporters who first royalized or monarchized them). Divinity too is optional and elective, at least in the plays set in a culture not yet governed by Christianity. Cassius complains that Julius Caesar has 'now become a god', while Coriolanus brags that the same elevation has been wished on him. Rejecting the plea of his patron Menenius, who begs him to spare Rome, he remembers that the old man

> Lov'd me above the measure of a father;
> Nay, godded me indeed.

To find a verb inside the noun is to crack open the sacrosanct notion of godhood and give everyone a stake in it. That startling neologism is the motive of Hugo's bardolatry; his book is about the godding of Shakespeare.

Romantic critics who shared this faith worried about Shakespeare's anonymity or nonentity. Shouldn't gods be imperious and monomaniacal, like Zeus or Jehovah? Coleridge regretted that Shakespeare, despite the plethora of characters he created, remained 'characterless'. A dramatist never speaks in his own person; we have no access to 'the individual Shakespeare' – the upwardly mobile young man from the provinces, the hard-working professional, the discontented husband, the comfortable retiree. While Shakespeare absents himself from the plays, his characters exhibit the creative mystery that so bewildered Coleridge and Hugo. The people in the plays make themselves up as we listen to them conversing with themselves or watch them acting for the benefit of others. Shakespeare, happy to have no authorial role, transfers the task of authorship to the characters. 'I will be Cleopatra,' Cleopatra vows; she goes on to give a recklessly improvised performance of the role she has devised for herself. Coriolanus rejects his family and his country, behaving

> As if a man were author of himself
> And knew no other kin.

An opponent decries his self-sufficiency: averse to the rowdy jostling coexistence that is the life both of nature and society, Coriolanus would like to 'depopulate the city and/ Be every man himself'. His mother, who fails to restrain him, accuses him of trampling on her womb. He forgets that even gods are authored by others, and possess power only if believers cede it to them.

Coleridge, in his description of 'the Spinozistic deity', contrasts Shakespeare with Milton, whom he identifies as 'the deity of prescience; he stands *ab extra*, and drives a fiery chariot and four, making the horses feel the iron curb which holds them in'. Coriolanus is a god of the resentful, jealous, monopolistic kind. Shakespeare's more amiably mutable people display a different spirit, which resembles the ebullient creative energy that Spinoza attributed to God. Coleridge often likened Shakespeare to Proteus, the fickle shape-changer 'who now flowed, a river; now raged, a fire; now roared, a lion – he assumed all changes'. It is as if he were Bottom in *A Midsummer Night's Dream*, who wants to take all the parts in the play, including two duetting lovers and the lion that roars at them. Coleridge adds that every one of Shakespeare's metamorphoses was a mask, because 'it was the divinity that appeared in it, and assumed the character'. Only the Christian God pretends to moral rectitude, so Shakespeare's characters can employ this talent either for good or evil. The Duke of Gloucester, who becomes Richard III after murderously monarchizing himself, boasts that he can 'change shapes with Proteus for advantages'. The hero of *Two Gentlemen of Verona* is actually called Proteus, and he begins by telling his mistress that 'thou, Julia, hast metamorphosed me'. People are fluent, liquefying in order to be remoulded: we watch them exercising the plasticity that Pico della Mirandola's God granted to Adam. Proteus likens Silvia's tearful grief to 'a sea of melting pearl', although the Duke disparages such malleability:

> This weak impress of love is as a figure
> Trenchèd in ice, which with an hour's heat
> Dissolves to water and doth lose his form.
> A little time will melt her frozen thoughts.

William Blake,
*Richard III and
the Ghosts,
c.* 1806

Invoking Orpheus, Proteus acclaims poetry's power to turn creatures inside out:

> Write till your ink be dry, and with your tears
> Moist it again; and frame some feeling line
> That may discover such integrity;
> For Orpheus' lute was strung with poet's sinews,
> Whose golden touch could soften steel and stones.

Stone or metal relapse into the laxity and sensitivity that are appropriate to live human beings. The agency that achieves this change is language: metaphors make the world metamorphose, transforming tears to pearls or love to a sculpture carved from ice, or stringing a lute with human veins and tendons. In his oration, Pico asked 'Who would not admire this chameleon?' Richard, just before his reference to Proteus, warns that 'I can add colours to the chameleon'. Who – it might be added – would not be alarmed by the same slithery changefulness? G. K. Chesterton sensed the same spirit in the polytheism of the Greeks, and found it terrifying. A Greek, he said, erected

statues and wrote the name of Zeus or Apollo on the pedestal, but we should
not be deceived: 'the god whom he worships is Proteus'.

The life of a Shakespearean character is a creative career like Shakespeare's own, a sequence of dazzling, extemporized inventions. Prospero
grumbles that his treacherous brother has 'new created/ The creatures that
were mine', but no-one can claim to be the exclusive possessor of this gift.
Creation happens continuously, which means that such infidelities are
natural; it is also a collective occupation, requiring each of us to contribute
to the genetic pool, as Ferdinand recognizes when he declares that Miranda
is 'created/ Of every creature's best!' When the characters play games, they
recreate the reality outside them. A mischievous cloud, in Hamlet's conversation with Polonius, is a camel, a weasel, then a whale; a flotilla of more
threatening clouds in *Antony and Cleopatra* sketch dragons, bears or lions,
citadels and tree-clad mountains, all equally vaporous. Agrippa of Nettesheim
thought of air as protoplasm, less an element – as he suggested in *Occult
Philosophy* – than a 'medium or glue, joining things together'. Shakespeare's
pantomimic clouds perhaps represent the prime material of nature at play,
or show off the handiwork of a god who doodles in the sky. A person can be
resolved or dissolved into a similarly evaporating succession of shapes.
Hamlet wishes that flesh would soften and moisten into dew, which soon
vanishes. Enobarbus analyses Cleopatra as a meteorological phenomenon:
'We cannot call her winds and waters sighs and tears; they are greater storms
and tempests than almanacs can report'. The tears of Silvia in *Two Gentlemen
of Verona* are like nacreous jewels, but Cleopatra specializes in lashing,
drenching squalls and 'makes a shower of rain as well as Jove'. Capulet in
*Romeo and Juliet* tells his lachrymose daughter 'In one little body/ Thou
counterfeit'st a barque, a sea, a wind'. Juliet's weeping eyes, he explains, are
the saline sea and her sighs are the winds, which agitate her 'tempest-tossèd
body'. Romeo's suicidal rant persuades Friar Laurence that he is no longer
a man, or even a human being. His 'noble shape is but a form of wax'; his wit
too is 'mis-shapen', and he seems to be 'dismembered' – torn limb from
limb – by grief. Mercutio laughs at Tybalt as a fantastico, a phantasim and a
fashion-monger, a man who has made himself up by copying courtly precedents. In Romeo's distress we see the creative process negated: Laurence
watches him undergo what Leonardo calls a 'disfazione'.

Bodies alter before our ears, and our eyes are beguiled too when characters revise the insignia of gender. As Imogen in *Cymbeline* flees from
persecution, Pausanius advises her to 'forget to be a woman'. She promptly
does so, and reappears as a boy. The characters who nimbly cross the border
between male and female – like the master-mistress of the sonnets, or
Cleopatra buckling on Antony's sword while he struggles into her dress,
or Falstaff disguised as the fat woman of Brainford in *The Merry Wives of*

*Windsor* – recover the androgyny we lost when our species settled for singular, antagonistic identities. Alchemical manuals used the image of the hermaphrodite as a sign that the great work had overcome antitheses and was near completion, and Renaissance Neo-Platonists predicted that man, ascending to approximate the creator, would also cast off the abrasive division between the sexes. Shakespeare's characters might be rehearsing for this outcome. Locked in a solitary cell, Richard II communes with himself and breeds a replacement for the society from which he has been separated:

> My brain I'll prove the female to my soul,
> My soul the father, and these two beget
> A generation of still-breeding thoughts;
> And these same thoughts people this little world.

Hugo – in another rhapsodic compliment in his poem *Les contemplations* – played with gendered pronouns to suggest that Shakespeare shared this self-fertilizing bisexuality: 'Dans sa création, le poéte tressaille;/ Il est elle, elle est lui'. In French, creation is female while Shakespeare is male – but Hugo concludes that he is her and she is him. Was he the father of his characters or their honorary mother? Stephen Dedalus in Joyce's *Ulysses*, having read Ernest Jones's essay on the Oedipus complex in *Hamlet*, inclines to the second option: '*Amor matris*, subject and object genitive, may be the only true thing in life. Paternity may be a legal fiction'.

After examining the case of Leonardo, the sexual psychologist Havelock Ellis claimed in 1923 that 'Every person of genius is in some degree at once man, woman, and child'. Shakespeare's plays are full of such flexible genii, whose transforming adventures continue after death. This is why they subscribe to the Pythagorean doctrine of metempsychosis. Although Malvolio in *Twelfth Night* is scandalized to think that the soul of his grandam might inhabit a woodcock, Rosalind in *As You Like It* (who has already been both a woman and a man) happily remembers the remoter time when she was an Irish rat. Graziano in *The Merchant of Venice* says that Shylock makes him

> ... hold opinion with Pythagoras
> That souls of animals infuse themselves
> Into the trunks of men,

and suggests that the spirit of a wolf, hanged for killing men, somehow wriggled into the embryonic usurer as he lay in his 'unhallowed dam'.

Lear, paraphrasing Aristotle's account of cosmic origins, warns Cordelia that 'Nothing will come of nothing'. The word and the idea are stumbling blocks, uttered – in a moment of shocked paralysis – five times in a row when Cordelia declines to display her love for her father by using inflated, extravagant language. But for Shakespeare, nothingness is latently creative; the 'wooden O' of his global stage travels at will through time and space, and can become as solidly corpulent as Falstaff, whose rotundity makes him a 'globe of sinful continents'. Theseus in *A Midsummer Night's Dream* explains how the poet deals with nonentity, giving 'to airy nothing/ A local habitation and a name'. Agrippa quotes Averroës on the delusive power of imagination, which 'represents nothing'. Theseus, however, is not content to dismiss that nothingness. The mind may ineffectually chase 'things unknown', but the poet's task is to trap them in bodies. He 'turns them to shape': the phrase implies that Theseus knows shape to be provisional, a costume you can slip in and out of, like the identities assumed and discarded by Proteus. A similar debate, which might almost be an attempt to explicate the genesis of Shakespeare's plays and the poetry in them, takes place between Romeo and Mercutio. Romeo's rhapsody about love defines it by pondering that nihilistic source: challenging Aristotle, he addresses it as 'O anything of nothing first create'. When Mercutio analyses his infatuation as an imaginary affair, provoked by one of Queen Mab's nocturnal visits, Romeo scoffs 'Thou talk'st of nothing'. He has forgotten his own claim that nothing can give birth to anything, and Mercutio corrects him:

> True, I talk of dreams
> Which are the children of an idle brain,
> Begot of nothing but vain fantasy.

His metaphors are biological, because he is describing what Theseus calls a bodying-forth, an incarnation. A literary creation is an idea that acquires flesh and produces children, helped at the drowsy lying-in by Mab, who is 'the fairies' midwife'. Juliet takes up Romeo's quibble about 'loving hate' and admits that her love, sprung from hate, is a 'prodigious birth'. But what is the prodigy to which the pair of them give birth? It is a poem: when they first meet at the ball, their dialogue develops over fourteen intricately rhymed lines, so they collaborate to produce a sonnet.

Their poetic valour enables them to play at being cosmographers. Like rhetorical gods, they rearrange the universe and juggle its planets as they please. The light through a bedroom window persuades Romeo that it comes from the east, which means that 'Juliet is the sun'. She repays the compliment by imagining a galactic afterlife for Romeo:

> when he shall die
> Take him and cut him out in little stars,
> And he will make the face so heaven so fine,
> That all the world will be in love with night,
> And pay no worship to the garish sun.

J. M. W. Turner, *Queen Mab's Cave*, 1846

To demonstrate their creative audacity, Shakespeare's characters often allude to the state that precedes 'creation. After saying that love is something created out of nothing, Romeo calls it a 'mis-shapen chaos of well-seeming forms'. When Othello suspects that Desdemona is unfaithful, he feels that his small cosmos – the world he has invented by telling stories about his noble exploits – is foundering: 'Chaos is come again'. Richard III personifies that crude, incoherent, internally troubled territory. One arm is withered, his legs are asymmetrical, and on his back he bears the 'envious mountain' of a hump. During the seventeenth century, when mountains were considered to be a disfigurement of God's originally smooth and level earth, they were often likened to deformities. Andrew Marvell called mountains 'hook-shouldered' (which confirmed his view of the world as 'a rude heap, together hurl'd', like the hastily and unproportionally assembled Richard); Thomas Hobbes, even more sarcastically, called them 'buttocks sticking up'. Richard reverses the customary metaphor. He becomes the earth, spontaneously extruding a clump of cartilage and bone. Twisted awry, he is

> Like to a chaos, or an unlicked bear's whelp
> That carries no impression like the dam.

Because he is a cub which bears no likeness to its mother, he fits a rule proposed in Aristotle's treatise on the generation of animals: any being which does not take after its parents is monstrous, because nature has strayed from the generic type. The eighteenth-century French encyclopaedists adhered to Aristotle's judgment, defining a monster as an exception to the disposition of parts that usually characterizes its species. Like Coriolanus, who with 'monstrous ingratitude' denies his affiliation with the rest of the human family, Richard later takes brazen pride in this oddity:

> I had no father, I am like no father;
> I have no brother, I am like no brother.

He reports that his mother told him that he emerged from her body with his legs poking forward. In *Richard III*, she resigns responsibility for his birth by cursing him. Yet he does not grieve about his divergence from the norm, or his rejection by people who think themselves normal. Autonomy is the source of his amoral power, since it exempts him from the meek and milky feebleness of human compassion: 'I am myself alone'.

Henry Fuseli, *Titania and Bottom, c.* 1790

What then is his parentage? Rosalind, told that she has a wooer in the forest, asks Celia 'Is he of God's making? What manner of man?' These are good questions, not easily answered; her admirer is an actor, so he has made himself, and God has little to do with his overwrought amorous mannerisms. Hamlet, himself a serial self-inventor, resents the same multiplicity in others. He hypocritically abuses Ophelia and all other painted women because 'God hath given you one face, and you make yourselves another'. Hugo often likened Shakespeare's characters to chimaeras, but sought all the same to establish their reality by recalling that he had once seen a serpent with a head at either end of its body, bottled in a museum in the Hague. Wondrous, freakish beings abound in the plays. Puck, having seen Titania bedded with an ass, reports that she is in love with a monster. The clowns address Caliban as a 'man-monster'.

Other fabled creatures hover out of sight, glimpsed – like the giraffe in Bosch's Eden, or Dürer's rhinoceros – on continents which the God of Genesis had probably not created. When fantastical helpers serve Prospero's banquet, Sebastian says that he is now prepared to believe

> That there are unicorns; that in Arabia
> There is one tree, the phoenix' throne, one phoenix
> At this hour reigning there.

Antony, during the drunken revels on Pompey's galley, attempts to explain an Egyptian crocodile to the narrow-minded, categorizing Romans. Like Richard III or Cleopatra, it appears to be self-generated: 'It is shaped, sir, like itself, and it is as broad as it hath breadth'. Its composition is only temporary, because 'the elements once out of it, it transmigrates'. Even more outlandish are the 'men whose heads/ Do grow beneath their shoulders' casually mentioned by Othello in his synopsis of his travels. Is he straining credibility, or − more likely − exploiting the credulity of his Venetian employers? Othello, having fabricated his own identity, has no trouble making up a quirky mutation of the human species. 'Such was my process,' he says as he introduces this digest of travellers' tales: the aside is a winking allusion to his artistry. Just before he mentions cannibals and the even more exotic men with depressed heads, he speaks of 'hills whose heads touch heaven', evoking a topography as irregular as Richard's body. His creative fantasy, on loan from Shakespeare, makes the associative leap between those rearing, uplifted hills like heads to heads that have been knocked from their proper summit, as if decapitated. Othello is playing with words, and elasticizing the dull normative conventions of human thought. A technical term is a recipe for the new thing it names, so he conceitedly draws attention to the coinage when he glances at 'the cannibals that each other eat,/ The Anthropophagi'. First come the man-eaters, who are then converted, when the Greek taxonomic term is employed, into scientific specimens.

Shakespeare's language does not describe a world that already exists. It creates brave new worlds that − like the cannibals or their punning relative Caliban − spring into existence when neologisms evoke them; it finds life even in death, as when Hamlet describes the sun breeding maggots in a dead dog or a 'convocation of politic worms' feasting on the dead Polonius. In *Titus Andronicus*, Lavinia is raped, then has her tongue cut out and her hands chopped off to prevent her from identifying her assailants. As she stands on stage mutely sobbing and bleeding, her uncle speaks for her, performing an elaborate rhetorical lament that beautifies her torment and makes her wounded, disabled silence eloquent. Her lips are rosy, though what burbles from them is

> a crimson river of warm blood,
> Like to a bubbling fountain stirred with wind

He imagines her missing hands to be lilies, and says that they once used to

> Tremble like aspen leaves upon a lute
> And make the silken strings delight to kiss them.

When she mimes distress and distraction, he explains that 'the delightful engine of her thoughts' has been

> torn from forth that pretty hollow cage
> Where, like a sweet melodious bird, it sung
> Sweet varied notes, enchanting every ear.

The more woeful or repellent the sight, the more effusively lyrical is the sound he makes in translating it. The response may seem crass, but it has a nobler aim. He intends literally to rearm her: language is the engine of thought, and so long as we are free to use it we can rise above the injuries of our physical fate. Speech is denied to Lavinia, but she works out another way of expressing and revenging herself. She holds a staff in her mouth, grips it with her stumps, and writes in the dust the names of the men who mutilated her. The inscription sentences them to death.

Prometheus in the tragedy by Aeschylus, persecuted by brutish necessity, tells Oceanus about the liberties he lavished on men. He gave them mind, reason, memory (which was for the Greeks the mother of all arts, since Mnemosyne gave birth to the muses); he taught them to see and hear, to count and to write. Language is the most valuable of the talents he passes on. For this reason, Hugo was determined to find some trace of Prometheus in Shakespeare's plays, which for him were the proudest evidence of the Promethean legacy. Near the end of his book, recalling the witchery of Mercutio's fantasist, he riskily asserts that 'Prometheus is the grandsire of Mab'. He then takes a further risk by adding 'Let us prove it'. The proof comes in an almost Shakespearean series of free-associating guesses and ingenious puns. Hugo claims that 'Prometheus, creator of men, is also creator of spirits', responsible for the lineage of elves who are his offshoots in Spenser's *Faerie Queene*. It hardly matters that Spenser made the connection by faking an etymology and pretending that 'elf' meant animate: neologism is the creative power at work. Hugo reels through the Spenserian family tree, from Elfin to Elficleos the Sage and Elferon the Beautiful. He concludes by asserting that the next in line must surely be Oberon, the fairy king from *A Midsummer Night's Dream*, followed at last by Mab, who for Mercutio is the genius of dreaming and therefore the progenitor of art. This skipping itinerary allows Hugo to link two facets of universal creation – the cosmic and the microscopic, or the sublime and the beautiful – by treating the Aeschylean giant as the remote ancestor of what he calls Shakespeare's minute, mischievous 'animalcules'. Although Mab is 'no bigger than an agate stone' and rides in a wagon drawn by 'a team of little atomies', she descends from the Titan whose rebellion convulsed the universe. Once more, myth-making is an exercise in polynymy. Mab, as Hugo notices, acquires a new name and identity whenever another artist adopts her: 'in Spenser she is called Gloriana, and Oberon is her father; in Shakespeare she is called Titania, and Oberon is her husband'. Having equated Mab with the fairy queen, he stretches the point still further to reach his dizzy QED: 'This name, Titania, connects Mab with the Titan, and Shakespeare with Aeschylus'. The whimsy may be groundless, but it pays proper tribute to Shakespeare's contagious creativity.

Between the Titan and the atomized fairies, however, a protracted, destabilizing change has occurred. The mountain on which Prometheus was detained has crumbled into dust. Italo Calvino, in some lecture notes prepared shortly before his death in 1985, recalled Mab's charioteers and took the image as proof that Shakespeare was 'a Lucretian atomist'. Lucretius turns up often in Hugo's literary genealogy, where the thriving nature surveyed in *On the Nature of Things* is likened to the crowded society of Shakespeare's plays. Breezily abbreviating aeons, Hugo says that 'Jupiter is in Homer; Jehovah is in Job; in Lucretius, Pan appears'. The goat-god's name means 'all', which is why Hugo identifies Lucretius with 'that vast, obscure thing, All'. Pan, who provokes panic, is the cheeky impetus that drives every living thing. (Shakespeare – as Hugo might have added – calls him Puck.) The bastard Edmund in *King Lear* subscribes to the same riotous cult, and as he begins to work his mischief he resolves that Nature will be his goddess. Calvino's account of the matter is sadder, less jubilantly pantheistic. He reveres Lucretius for 'reconstructing the physical nature of the world by means of the impalpable, powder-fine dust of words', and he finds the same sifting refinement in the melancholy of Hamlet or the irony of Jaques in *As You Like It*. Their humour, he says, has a 'weightless gravity'. The paradox is unknown to physics, but it catches the way these characters fracture and disintegrate reality, reducing it to what Calvino calls 'a veil of minute particules' or 'a fine dust of atoms' so they can watch the cloud suspended in the air. When Hamlet ponders the skull or Jaques enumerates the ages of man or Prospero admits that he and his work of art are 'such stuff as dreams are made on', the actor steps out of the role he is playing, out of the play – even out of life, which he regards from an amused and quizzical distance. Cleopatra uncreates herself as we watch and listen. Dying, she reverses the elemental accord from which the world was made; she now consists of fire and air, and she abandons her 'baser elements' to 'lesser life'. Once and once only, a statue moves, and in doing so it confirms art's power to restore losses, to make dreams come true, and to laugh at death. More often, characters we take to be alive turn into ghosts and joke about the folly of their former incarnations. Shakespeare creates a world, then lets his people smilingly destroy it.

# 11

# TO CREATE MORE WORLDS

In Genesis, creation is accomplished without effort or forethought. But before the beginning, according to early rabbinical tracts, God had doubts about the venture and, like a persuasive politician, sought support and consensus. In the *Midrash Rabbah*, the ministering angels are not unanimously sympathetic when the Holy One tells them about his project to create a man. Love, Righteousness and Peace agree, but Truth, foreseeing Adam's disobedience, says 'Let him not be created'. God ignores this advice, and casts Truth to the ground. His impatience hardly answers the ancient, rankling objection: why bother making a creature whose fallibility was clear in advance? Since God had the power to create a world, surely he might have taken the trouble to exclude evil from it?

Responsibility for the oversight was transferred to another agency: hence the intrusion of the devil. In apocryphal additions to the biblical story, the brightest of the angels – Lucifer, the son of the morning – makes war against God because he is jealous of Christ's promotion. Cast out of heaven, he revenges himself by seducing mankind. Gnostic commentators risked heresy by wondering whether the ambitious antagonist, the adversary who came to be known as Satan, might not have been the actual creator. Some versions of the story describe a low-ranking god called Ialdabaoth, puffed up by pride and convinced that he enjoys global dominion. When he learns that there is a god superior to him, he demonstrates his power by creating the world and setting Adam in it. But Ialdabaoth comes to regret having shared his divine spark with Adam, and therefore creates Eve to ensure that humans and their offspring will remain tethered to the ground, preoccupied by biological needs. The Promethean liberator is Christ, who encourages human beings to eat the fruit of the Tree of Knowledge and to understand their true place in the universe. Ialdabaoth responds by expelling them from Eden. Could the creator have been jealous of his own creation? The beasts in the garden worship Adam, as the *Chronicles of Jerahmeel* claims, and the angels are so impressed that they want to call him holy. God, piqued, sends Adam into a death-like sleep to demonstrate his mortality. He withdraws a rib from Adam's side and uses it to fashion Eve, making clear who possesses creative priority.

In *Paradise Lost*, Milton struggles with this long, contentious history. The poet presents himself as the creator's advocate, volunteering to 'justifie the wayes of God to men'; but in doing so, he admits that God has a case to answer. *Paradise Lost* was first published in 1667, after a revolution in which Milton's own party executed the king, supposedly a deputy appointed by the Lord and a legatee of divine right. The poem tests the veracity of this and all other sacrosanct myths, and looks ahead to a new story that was to become the myth of modernity: it records man's heroic endeavour to seize power from God, as the rebellious mind sets theological decrees against the new laws derived from scientific observation. Milton assumes responsibility for rationalizing the universe. He also – as Shelley thought the poet had a responsibility to do – creates that universe anew. In *Paradise Lost*, the cosmology of Genesis becomes a chart tracing the heights and depths of the creative mind.

Milton analytically demolishes one model of the world, castigating pagan errors or declaring Eden to be a finer place than the paradises of classical fable. He goes on to imagine new worlds, daunting to describe because they stretch beyond human comprehension: heaven which is 'dark with excessive bright', hell with its 'darkness visible'. Not surprisingly, he is sarcastic about alchemy, with its speedily confected heaven. When Satan lands on the sun, a brief metallurgical analysis of its scorching surface recalls the obsessiveness of those who seek the philosopher's stone

> In vain, though by thir powerful Art they binde
> Volatil Hermes, and call up unbound
> In various shapes old Proteus from the Sea,
> Draind through a Limbec to his Native form.

Hermetic mystery is replaced by science, and Proteus, his Shakespearean repertory of impersonations curtailed, is poured into a distilling apparatus and discarded in the sea, where he belongs. Later, when Raphael shares a meal with Adam and Eve, the nonsensical abracadabra of 'th'Empiric Alchimist' is contrasted with the internal mystery of digestion, which – as Milton says, using a theological term – manages 'to transubstantiate' food and transform it into energy. When Satan crosses Chaos, buffeted by its 'embryon Atoms', Milton explains why this region of molecular collisions and random turbulence exists on the outskirts of God's logical universe. It is a 'wild Abyss' like Hesiod's gulf, where nativity and destruction commingle and '*Chance* governs all': Chaos is 'The Womb of nature and perhaps her Grave'. The elements will go on clashing forever

> Unless th'Almighty Maker them ordain
> His dark materials to create more Worlds.

Those extra worlds are plural, multiplied by the fantasy of the maker (just as, during the Renaissance, the known, narrow world was elasticized by the voyages of explorers: the leering Malvolio in *Twelfth Night* 'does smile his face into more lines than there is in the new map with the augmentation of the Indies'). Milton admits that the reservoir of Chaos is a vital resource. God might want to dredge up its muddy ingredients, as poets do when they consult the unarticulated strife of their imaginations. Yet this oblique glimpse into the abyss soon came to seem dangerous, because it acknowledged a world ungoverned by a vigilant, benign creator. Lord Shaftesbury, an official apologist for the complacently conservative deity of the early eighteenth century, repudiated the '*Chaos* and *Atoms* of the Atheists', who refused to see that the world had a coherent design.

Paradise Lost, bravely argumentative, denies God a veto over dissident opinions. Critical dispute is not pushed back before the beginning, as it is when the Torah describes God's consultation with his advisors; the beings God creates express their mental independence by blaming him for their moral predicament, or by sceptically mocking the very notion of divine creativity. Adam, in the plaintive lines used by Mary Shelley as the epigraph to *Frankenstein*, reminds his maker that he never asked to be made. Satan, enraged by the injustice of primogeniture, rejects Abdiel's opinion that God is omnipotent and invincible, and refuses to believe that he and the other apostate angels were formed 'by secondarie hands':

> who saw
> When this creation was? rememberst thou
> Thy making, while the Maker gave thee being?

In 1637, in his *Discourse on the Method*, Descartes replaced the obscure myth of origins with a simple, self-evident intellectual maxim: 'cogito ergo sum'. His slogan naturalized the homunculus, and gave each of us a self-possessed internal manikin like that which the alchemists tried to make; it was called the self, and we created it by the free, frank use of the mind. Dryden, preparing the libretto for an operatic version of Milton's epic in 1674, conferred this instantaneous enlightenment on Adam, who awakens to life, switches on his brain, and reports 'that I am/ I know, because I think'. Belial in *Paradise Lost*, who shrinks from further combat with heaven, treasures 'this intellectual being' and fears that it will be 'swallowd up and lost'. Satan too is threatened with 'utter loss of being' during his passage through Chaos. Descartes professed respect for 'the miracle of creation', and honoured a God who 'can create everything we can imagine'. But the true miracle he extolled was man's psychological self-creation. Satan in *Paradise Lost* is a Cartesian man, who generates himself by the exercise of consciousness. We know no time, he says, when we were not as we are now; this means that we are 'self-begot, self-raised/ By our own quickening power'. If we cast off the idea that we were made, we can dispense with the maker. Why can't we sprout and spread as plants do, in response to our own volition? In 1644 in his *Principia Philosophiae* Descartes applied this approach to Genesis. The Bible, he acknowledged, insisted that Adam and Eve were 'not born as babies' but created as fully-formed adults. He registered no outright objection to the absolute power of God, for whom the improbable had to be possible. But 'if we want to understand the nature of plants or of men', he thought it better 'to consider how they can gradually grow from seeds'. In *Paradise Lost*, Adam accepts Raphael's superior knowledge about the beginning of the world. All the same, when he challenges himself to resolve the problem of origins without help from above, he cannot help paraphrasing the methodical inquiry of Satan or Descartes:

> For Man to tell how human Life began
> Is hard; for who himself beginning knew?

God, if he pleases, can create supernumerary worlds. *Paradise Lost* does something almost as impressive: it synthesizes existing worlds, altering space and eliding differences in time. In an edition of Milton's poems published in 1720, the illustrator Louis Cheron presented the universe as a finished product, admiringly surveyed by angels who cluster on banks of billowy baroque clouds. Putti pull back a curtain draped across the sky; it reveals the sun, branded with the four Hebrew letters that denominate God. During the creation, that verbal sun blazes down on a globe that displays a recognizable range of continents, from Europe to Africa and Asia. The pointing fingers and protectively cupped hands of the attendant angels indicate the place of origins: Eden is located somewhere in the Middle East. Milton's geography is more indistinct than Cheron makes it look, because he is inventing the world as he describes it. That is why *Paradise Lost* anachronistically refers to Columbus and Galileo, explorers who forced men to revise their maps of heaven and earth. When Adam and Eve conceal their pubic shame with fig leaves, Milton comments that not long ago

> *Columbus* found th' *American* so girt
> With feathered Cincture, naked else and wilde
> Among the Trees on Iles and woodie Shores.

The analogy has a disturbing relativism. Columbus discovered a new world where the Christian God was not worshipped, so its natives had not been taught puritanical guilt; Milton notes that they adorn themselves aesthetically, rather than using clothes to hide the sinful genitals. There may be Edens elsewhere, unfallen because untroubled by morality. The allusion to Galileo is even more telling. Satan's shield is likened to the 'Optic Glass' Galileo trained on the sky; the weapon and the telescope both arm us for a confrontation with the unknowable. In 1623 in a polemical essay entitled

*Saggiatore*, Galileo speculated about heat and motion, and suggested that light created from the 'subtlety, rarity, immateriality' of indivisible atoms could fill 'vast spaces'. But he decided to think no further about this 'infinite ocean', afraid of its emptiness, and – as he said – he made his way nervously back to shore. Satan more intrepidly embarks on a Galilean transit of this black Chaos. The poet had another reason for sensing an affinity with the astronomer. Galileo, like Milton, lost his sight in later life. Bernard le Bovier de Fontenelle, who made the irreligious Copernican cosmos popularly accessible in a book he published in 1686, likened Galileo to Tiresias, blinded because he had spied on the secrets of the gods. Milton reproaches God for his own disability when the sightless hero of *Samson Agonistes* says

> O first created Beam, and thou great Word,
> Let ther be light, and light was over all;
> Why am I thus bereav'd thy prime decree?

Perhaps eloquence was the poet's means of reparation: the great word is auditory not visual, and language endows Milton with a god-like power.

Creativity is a visionary capacity, like Galileo's glimpse of extraterrestrial 'new Lands'. But it is never vaporous or vague; Milton relies on amassed atoms which are eager to conjoin, and on the building-blocks of words, arranged into stepped tiers of verse. Descartes in his *Treatise on Light* outlined a prescription for 'another world – a wholly new one', which he promised to 'bring into being before [the reader's] mind in imaginary spaces'. It was not to be composed of 'prime matter', which for scholastic theologians and physicists had been the stuff of nature. To Descartes, a substance so indefinable seemed savourless and infirm; his world, even though it was conceptual, needed to be 'real, perfectly solid'. But the effort to reconcile a mythical creation with an actual, observable universe was difficult and dangerous. In 1633 the church obliged Galileo to repudiate his study of planetary motions, which had dislodged the earth from its favoured place at the centre of the solar system. Descartes, hearing of the censure, decided not to publish his treatise.

Planning his alternative, custom-made world, Descartes refused to accept that God created from 'a chaos as confused and muddled as any the poets could describe'. Chaos, he pointed out, is a dumping-ground for muddled, miscegenated forms (which might include the '*Gorgons* and *Hydras* and *Chimeras* dire' encountered by Milton's Satan on his wanderings, or the heathen idol Dagon who is 'upward Man/ And downward Fish', or Satan himself when God jokingly transmogrifies him into a python). An enlightened intelligence had no reason to fear these mutants. David Hume in his *Enquiry Concerning Human Understanding* judged it a harmless folly 'to form monsters and join incongruous shapes', since 'the creative power of the mind' compounded or augmented objects from nature; if the separate parts of the monsters were reassigned, they could easily be restored to order and proportion. Voltaire, however, praised Descartes for rounding up and slaying such irrational creatures. Descartes, he said, encouraged us to trust our inborn powers of cogitation, and 'destroyed the absurd chimeras with which young minds had been filled for two thousand years'. The Cartesian laws of nature, like those promulgated by Newton, could never be waived, and even God had to obey them. In the 'new world' that Descartes stocked with 'intelligences, or rational souls', God was debarred from performing showy and scientifically improbable miracles. Descartes likened his artificial beings to clocks, man-made fountains and mills, whose operations were logically predictable; creation was now an elaborate but intelligible mechanism. The new science of anatomy, laying bare the bodily interior, even allowed Descartes to pin-point the elusive soul, which – he believed – refined the sensory impressions that were absorbed by the pineal gland.

The physicist and mathematician Blaise Pascal was terrified by the 'infinite spaces' Galileo had opened to view. The universe, as Pascal put it in the *Pensées* that were posthumously collected in 1670, swallowed him like a grain of dust; man, perhaps fortunately, could see neither 'the nothingness from which he emerges' nor 'the infinity in which he is engulfed'. Descartes deprived emptiness of its terrors by recommending an alternate adjective. He disliked the word infinite, and when dealing with 'things in which we observe no limits'– the extent of the universe, or the number of the stars – he preferred to say that such quantities were indefinite. Milton too aimed to materialize mystery. He could not do without the notion of infinitude, but he took care to associate it with synonyms that retained a grip on size, bulk, the physical co-ordinates of nature. Hence the twin adjectives used by Adam when he praises God's unexpected mercy at the end of *Paradise Lost*: 'O goodness infinite, goodness immense!' Infinity is beyond the comprehension of finite man, as Descartes pointed out; Adam finds the idea of evil turned to good

> more wonderful
> Than that which by creation first brought forth
> Light out of darkness!

He therefore ensures that he can grasp it by making it measurable, palpable, solid. When Sin and Death build a causeway across Chaos to ease transit between hell and earth, the architecture is allegorical, but its fabric is concrete. Scum and floating soil are petrified by Death's mace, hardened into an '*Asphaltic* slime' as rigid as a body turned to stone by the Gorgon.

Christ, who creates the world on God's behalf, employs a more cleanly geometrical constructive method. Separating the dry land from the waters, he takes up a compass, centres one of its feet and uses the other 'to circum-scribe/ This Universe, and all created things'. A century later, Voltaire joked about this reliance on a technical implement. In *Candide*, the sceptical Pococurante ridicules *Paradise Lost* for its 'distorted view of the creation'. Whereas Genesis, according to Pococurante, described 'the Eternal Being producing the world with the spoken word', Milton had the Messiah take the compass from his heavenly tool-kit and start drawing a plan. The joke is lethal, because by 1759, when *Candide* was published, the compass had become a crucial detail of the story. Deists like Leibniz – whose theodicy is parroted by the irrepressible optimist Pangloss, Candide's companion – assumed that the creation was good because it had been properly designed, so the blueprint served as sufficient reason for our world's existence. When Satan menaces the angelic phalanx that patrols Eden in *Paradise Lost*, another measuring tool shines in the sky: it is Libra, the zodiacal scales 'wherein all things created [God] first weighd'. The balance enables God to calculate the proportions of the different elements he mixes, and it now tilts sideways to warn Satan that he is outmatched.

God's creative techniques depend on precise mathematical calculation. But the devil's party has its own methods, closer to those of artists. Creation provokes inversions and distortions: although we cannot imagine something emerging from nothing, it is easy for us to spoil and warp something that already exists. Milton's language offers a range of not quite synonymous options. On one side there is the negative form of the word, describing a nothingness that for Mary Shelley was inconceivable. God is light, which existed before the moment in Genesis when it was called into being, so Milton addresses the deity as 'Bright effluence of bright essence increate'. On the other side there is the slurred, marred replica. Satan, striding out of hell into Chaos, is afraid of no 'created thing' (though he has a wary respect for God and Christ, who are creators and therefore not created beings). But he hesitates before a creature of 'execrable shape', a serpentine woman with a litter of hell hounds spilling from her uterus and snarling at her groin. Next he is menaced by a goblin that cannot be described: it is merely a black shape,

> If shape it might be calld that shape had none
> Distinguishable in member, joint or limb,
> Or substance might be calld that shaddow seemd,
> For each seemd either.

He asks why it places its 'miscreated Front' in his way, then discovers that he is its creator. The portress of the gate is Sin, his daughter and his consort, and the monster Death is the son of their incestuous union. Sin emerged from Satan's head, and their offspring is also a mental incubus. These charac-ters troubled Samuel Johnson, who remarked – not approvingly – that they proceeded 'from [Milton's] brain entirely'. The poet had offended God by supplementing divine creation. Coleridge in *Biographia Literaria* quoted the lines about shape and substance to characterize his own poetic imagery – or rather he wrote himself a letter in the person of a concerned friend, who advises Coleridge not to go ahead with his theological account of imagination. The aim was to explain poetic creation as a human replica of God's creativity. The 'friend', Coleridge's censorious alter ego, intervenes to hint that the argument so far, obscure and dangerously infidel, is more like a satanic manifesto. This is why he invokes the spectral outline of Death. 'What I had supposed substances', he remarks in his description of *Biographia Literaria*, 'were thinned away into shadows, while everywhere shadows were deepened into substances.' Mary Shelley recalls the same lines in the preface to *Frankenstein*, arguing that invention 'can give form to dark, shapeless substances, but cannot bring into being the substance itself'. The monsters in both cases are traced back to the head that generates them, like Sin's puppies creeping into their kennel in her womb, where they 'barkd and howld/ Within unseen'; the artist's mind is a populous, polymorphous hell.

A poem about the creation of the world inevitably ponders its own creation, and asks whether its source is divine or infernal. Although Milton derided alchemy, he sought a rhetorical sublimity that, like the subliming of metals in the laboratory, transcended nature. He understood the dangers of this mental adventure. Comparing the burning lake of hell to Etna whose fuelled entrails are 'sublim'd with Mineral fury', he associates sublimity with fulmination: 'conceiving Fire', the inert mountain explodes into life. Nevertheless he begins *Paradise Lost* by asking the muse to help him soar 'with no middle flight', and later admires the birds that 'soaring th'air sublime/ ... despis'd the ground'. In 'At a Vacation Exercise', written when he was nineteen, he made an even bolder aerodynamic demand, asking his 'native Language' to be his vehicle, so that

> the deep transported mind may soare
> Above the wheeling poles, and at Heav'ns dore
> Look in, and see each blissful Deitie.

Here the gods he wants to spy on are classical: Apollo with his lyre, Hebe serving nectar. In *Paradise Lost* he aims higher, and eavesdrops on conversations in Christianity's celestial citadel. Sublimation confers the same dizzy altitude on his characters. In her dream, Eve floats through the air and is told she can be 'among the Gods/ Thy self a Goddess, not to Earth confined'. This suggestion comes from Satan, who squats beside her disguised as a toad and whispers to her unconscious mind, but Raphael promises something similar to Adam: if he practises dietary restraint and continues to refine his understanding, his body will gradually etherealize and he will one day 'wingd ascend' to God. Keats, imitating Milton in his fragmentary epic *Hyperion*, underlines the effrontery of the presumption and the swiftness of the promotion when Apollo announces that 'Knowledge enormous makes a God of me'. Apollo is visited by Mnemosyne, the mother of the muses, who fills his brain with names, deeds, legends and

> Majesties, sovran voices, agonies,
> Creations and destroyings, all at once.

That digest of human experience gives Keats a world's worth of subjects, and enables him to find his poetic voice; this is the infused knowledge that will, as he says, 'deify me'. Milton, however, had to deal with a God who placed an embargo on knowledge and extended the ban to cover the yearnings of imagination, which – judged by Christian doctrine – purveys false knowledge and upsets the rational functions of the brain. Satan's insinuations are intellectual but also aesthetic. With his 'Devilish art' he invades the 'Organs of [Eve's] Fancie', forging 'Illusions as he list, Fantasms and Dreams'. The second word in that list of synonyms is crucial, because it has been used before: Satan challenges 'double-formed' Sin to explain why she addresses him as father and calls 'that Fantasm' his son. Fantasies can have bodies, but they originate in the unguarded, dormant mind. Keats, romantically expecting the imagination to fulfill wishes and deliver instant gratification, likened poetry to Adam's dream of Eve. For Milton, poetry could just as well be Eve's dream of Satan, or Satan's dream of Death.

When Eve reports on her disturbed sleep, Adam castigates the untrustworthiness of Fancy, which 'forms Imaginations' by 'misjoining shapes'. He tells her to occupy herself by studying a world that the eyes can verify, rather than attending to the phantasmagoria inside her head. Milton, being blind, was unable to follow his hero's advice. He prayed instead to be given insight, begging the celestial light to 'Shine inward' and 'plant eyes' within his mind. But what he asked to see was properly invisible, baffling to the 'five watchful Senses' on which Adam teaches Eve to rely. Faith should be unquestioning, able to dispense with evidence; from the first, Jewish and Christian theologians warned against the unseemliness of visual images. The Bostonian pastor Samuel Willard, in a sermon on the divine attributes in 1687, castigated idolatry and forbade the devotional use of any 'Corporeal similitude'. 'To shadow a Spirit', he said, insulted 'a being which is invisible'. Describing or depicting angels was foolish; attempting the same with God was for Willard both mad and wicked. Yet *Paradise Lost* looks into the light and tries to discern its essence. It also scrutinizes darkness, as when Satan confronts 'the void profound/ Of unessential Night'. The archangel Michael, giving Adam a preview of human history between the fall and the second coming, tells him 'thou hast seen one World begin and end'. Without seeing, how can he be expected to believe?

These acts of imagining are audacious, as Sergei Eisenstein made clear when he recommended *Paradise Lost* to his students at the State Institute of Cinematography in Moscow as 'a first-rate school in which to study montage and audio-visual relationships'. Montage depends on atomizing the world, destroying it before it is recreated. Eisenstein, a Russian revolutionary and therefore an atheist, was unimpeded by reverence, and he assumed that Milton shared his scepticism. He marvelled at the 'cinematographic instruction' in the description of Satan's army, when, after scanning the horizon, Milton suddenly calls for a 'nearer view' of bristling weaponry, as if asking for the camera set-up to be changed. Breaking down Milton's description into a sequence of separate images, Eisenstein chopped up *Paradise Lost* into lines, or particles of lines; the spool of film that runs through the camera is likewise cut into snippets, which the editor pieces back together in an order that may not be logical. Frame by frame, chaos is glued into the semblance of cosmos. Eisenstein's compliment is anachronistic, but it suits the structural cunning of *Paradise Lost*. Why else did Milton choose to begin in hell, with Satan preparing a second assault on God? Omniscience is impossible. We have only partial, self-interested, uncertain access to truth, and must make do with points of view that correspond to camera angles. But the art of montage requires decisions about how the emphases are to be distributed, because it can recompose the world in any number of conflicting ways; Milton, however, gives primacy to Satan, and makes his questioning, protesting intelligence the motor of the poem.

Creation in Genesis is the annunciation of an idea. Logos speaks, light shines: these are cerebral events. *Paradise Lost* tests the biblical theorem by envisaging creation as a physical process and consulting the rules of embryology or the home-grown wisdom of obstetrics. The opening address to the Holy Spirit paraphrases Genesis, then adds a provocative detail of its own. No longer bodiless, as in the Bible, the spirit is here a nesting fowl which

> with mighty wings outspred
> Dove-like satst brooding on the vast Abyss
> And mad'st it pregnant

The bird is at once a paternal inseminator and a maternal nurturer. In the next lines, Milton identifies the Holy Spirit with the muse of poetry and beseeches its aid, as if inspiration were a mental impregnation. Milton made it temptingly easy for Erasmus Darwin to redefine creation as procreation in *The Botanic Garden*. Darwin, delighting in the amorous abandon of plants, replaced the holy spirit with a force called 'Love Divine' that

> with brooding wings unfurl'd
> Call'd from the rude abyss the living world.

The gift of life does not always depend on a generous deity or on a reproductive act. Mary Shelley claimed that *Frankenstein* was prompted by her husband's memory of a biological experiment performed by Darwin: he placed in a glass case some vermicelli – thin macaroni, aptly named after a worm – and waited until 'by some extraordinary means it began to move with voluntary motion'. The same thrusting life is present in Milton's Chaos, with its 'pregnant causes mixt/ Confus'dly'. When Raphael tells Adam about the first seven days, the suggestion that the spirit is a fertilizing agency becomes more explicit. Under cover of its sheltering wings, it infuses 'vital vertue ... and vital warmth/ Throughout the fluid Mass' of waters. The earth forms like a growing foetus, 'conglob'd' and ovular. Earth remains an 'Embryon immature', sealed in 'the Womb ... of Waters', until that spermatic stimulus

> with warm
> Prolific humour soft'ning all her Globe,
> Fermented the great Mother to conceive,
> Satiate with genial moisture.

The impersonal Logos is now embroiled in the sweaty strife of reproduction, which requires not the Bible's Trinity but two cooperative sexual partners.

God apparently intended to exclude the frictions of sexuality from his plan for creation. But how consistent was he? Milton draws attention to the discrepancies in Genesis. God designs man as a singular being, though he immediately refers to the new species in the plural:

> Let us make now Man in our image, Man
> In our similitude, and let them rule
> Over the Fish and Fowle of Sea and Air.

God initially blocks Adam's request for a mate by pointing out that he too has been alone

> From all Eternitie, for none I know
> Second to me or like, equal much less.

It is fortunate that Adam asks no questions about the paternity of Christ, the second Adam who makes amends for the fall, although Raphael tells him about God's announcement to the angels that

> This day I have begot whom I declare
> My onely Son.

God gives no details about the begetting, but immediately appoints his heir, begotten that day, to lead the celestial army. Adam does press Raphael to explain how heavenly spirits 'mix/ Irradiance', and is curious to know whether their intercourse is 'virtual or immediat touch'. The angel says that seraphic membranes are porous enough to permit 'Union of Pure with Pure'; he then curtails the discussion by peremptorily taking his leave. But his embarrassment provokes 'a smile that glowd/ Celestial rosie red, Loves proper hue', which qualifies his claim that angelic love bypasses the flesh: a blush derives from the same sudden rush of blood that produces an erection. Adam, arguing for his right to sexual gratification, declines to share God's autonomy:

> No need that thou
> Shouldst propagate, already infinite;
> And through all numbers absolute, though One;
> But Man by number is to manifest
> His single imperfection, and beget
> Like of his like, his Image multipli'd.

God changes his mind and agrees to create Eve, but infuriatingly pretends that he knew all along that man was not suited to solitude, which means that Adam's androgyny was another sly test. After the fall, Adam pines for the restoration of God's original scheme. He blames Eve for their misery, admires the creator's wisdom in peopling heaven with 'Spirits Masculine', and wonders why he did not

> fill the World at once
> With Men as Angels without Feminine,
> Or find som other way to generate
> Mankind?

The awkward question goes unanswered; what matters, in this almost recklessly interrogatory poem, is that it has been asked.

Theocles, a classical rhapsodist in a dialogue by Shaftesbury published in 1709, deftly revises Genesis by identifying a pair of cosmic parents. The God who issues orders and sends the Holy Spirit to spread that genial moisture is 'Thou impowering Deity, supreme Creator!' His satiated consort is 'O mighty *Nature*! ... impower'd *Creatress*!' The power belongs to the male god, who injects it into his female counterpart. A similar transaction happens out of sight in *Paradise Lost*. Milton notices that Eve's 'mysterious parts' are uncovered: why should she conceal the unashamed headquarters of 'Natures works'? But fascination is shadowed by disgust as he visualizes the earliest and most fearful of primal scenes. Eve is not the only creatress in the poem; there is also Sin, a gynaecological monster. She describes her secret lovemaking with Satan, after which her 'womb conceiv'd/ A growing burden', which gnaws its way out through her entrails. Her son Death then couples with her, 'Ingendring ... yelling Monsters' which are 'hourly conceiv'd/ And hourly born'. The three persons of the Trinity are male, which conveniently dispenses them from having sexual relations. Milton makes up for this theologically prescribed evasion when he describes the menage-à-trois in hell, where a mother bears children by her father and then, in a double incest, by the son who is the offspring of that forbidden union. After the fall, aspiration is linked to guilty sexual fantasy. Erotically excited by their new sense of power, Adam and Eve feel 'Divinity within them breeding wings'. The verb exactly catches their perversity: they believe they are changing species, growing into creatures who can 'scorn the Earth'. The same sexual incitement occurs when Satan uses his art to arouse in the sleeping Eve

> Vain hopes, vain aims, inordinate desires
> Blown up with high conceits ingendring pride.

Conceit is a conception that takes place in the private darkness of the head, and its offspring is vice.

Despite the immaculate chastity of Christianity, the promiscuous classical gods find their way into *Paradise Lost*. When Adam embraces Eve, Milton metaphorically shifts from Eden to Olympus by remarking that this is how

> Jupiter
> On Juno smiles, when he impregns the Clouds
> That shed May flowers.

The comparison is all the more seditious because the conjugal love of Adam and Eve is fruitless until after the fall; the Bible makes pregnancy the consequence of crime. The galaxies are the product of seeding, as if Milton were recalling but prudently suppressing Ovid's fable about the origins of the Milky Way. God, he says, 'sow'd with Starrs the Heav'n thick as a field'. This stellar granary is supervised by two complementary sexual beacons. Raphael considers Galileo's hypothesis, agrees that the sun might possibly be 'Center to the World', but goes on to suggest that there could be 'other Suns perhaps/ With their attendant Moons'. He tells Adam that he should watch the sun and moon

> Communicating Male and Femal Light,
> Which two great Sexes animate the World.

If the world is animated by this procreative instinct, does it need a God to go on creating it? Once the creator begins the multiplication game, he makes himself redundant. The one, declared absolute by Adam, is soon overwhelmed by the many. Raphael predicts that Eve's 'fruitful Womb/ Shall fill the World more numerous', and the word, repeated and varied, becomes a refrain in his account of the creation. He notices the hatching of 'numerous' broods of birds with 'unnumberd plumes', tries to tally the 'innumerous living Creatures' that cascade from the earth's open womb, and admits that the species that he lacks time to describe are 'numberless'. Although he sees the earth as 'a spot, a grain,/ An Atom' in yawning space, he assumes that 'the numberd Starrs' or 'thousand thousand Starrs' can be counted. Milton's art shares in this exponentiation, because the divine command to go forth and multiply is a verbal injunction too. Poetry was also known to Milton as numbers; its metrical discipline called for the regular counting of syllables and accents, which is why he says that Adam and Eve chant the praises of God 'in Prose or numerous Verse'. Numbers are serial, and set up a rhythmic repetition that keeps pace with the doubling and trebling and quadrupling that is nature's law of increase. Although Milton credits the sexes with animating the world, a verb can do the same by vivifying a noun. In Raphael's retelling of Genesis, a lion ramps and dandles its cub, bears and tigers gambol, and the elephant writhes its lithe trunk; newly created fish glide, graze, sport, wallow or spout, while animals creep, peacefully ruminate, or spring up from the ground to swarm or rove in herds. Adam assigns names to the flora and fauna, so the nouns are his responsibility. But the verbs – adjusted to suit the motion of each creature they animate – are handed out by the poet, and they are literally life-giving.

Each tier of Milton's universe has its own kind of creativity. In heaven, such matters are veiled, which is why the question of angelic intermingling flusters Raphael. On earth, nature's works are open to view, like the bared genitals of Eve. But earthly creation can be aesthetic as well as biological. A new word needs to be used for a different activity: Eve is made not created, and Adam – once again witnessing a mystery that in the Bible happens out of sight – describes how God extracted a rib which he

> formd and fashiond with his hands;
> Under his forming hands a Creature grew.

Although 'homo faber', man the fabricator, is supposed to be inferior to God, here God's technical finesse serves a model for the artisan or artist. Manufacture pliably reshapes nature; in hell there is a third variety of creative endeavour, which ravages and torments nature. This is what the devils, using a term which became the progressive obsession of science, call invention. After the rebels are routed by God, Nisroc appeals to

> He who therefore can invent
> With what more forcible we may offend
> Our yet unwounded Enemies.

Warfare has always relied on and stimulated technological innovation, which is why Ludovico Sforza hired Leonardo. But Satan points out that the inventor does not need to scratch his head and dream up novelties. It is enough to harness powers that already exist, as men did when they put steam to work or split the atom:

> Not uninvented that, which thou aright
> Believ'st so main to our success, I bring.

He then describes the minerals that slumber beneath the floral counterpane of nature

> Deep under ground, materials dark and crude,
> Of spiritous and fierie, spume, till toucht
> With Heav'ns ray, and temperd they shoot forth.

God has not availed himself of the dark materials, which leaves them free to be exploited by Satan (who as a sign of his intent inverts the order of the words used in the earlier description of Chaos, turning 'dark materials' into 'materials dark'). He recommends grubbing out the combustible elements, using 'suttle Art' to reduce 'Sulphurous and Nitrous Foam' to grain, then adding samples of stone to make balls or bullets which can be rammed into 'hollow Engins' and expelled with the aid of fire. The result is gunpowder, which when it sows destruction is advertised as a devious, lethal parody of creation:

> These in thir dark Nativitie the Deep
> Shall yield us pregnant with infernal flame.

In *The Botanic Garden*, Erasmus Darwin startlingly suggested that this might be a true and exact representation of the world's origins. When Darwin's God calls for light, Chaos promptly responds, and the dark materials produce a fusillade of shooting stars:

> Through all his realms the kindling Ether runs,
> And the mass starts into a million suns;
> Earths round each sun with quick explosions burst,
> And second planets issue from the first.

Darwin underlined the satanic analogy in a note explaining why the universe that erupted out of Chaos did not then implode, sabotaged by gravity. It remained stable, he proposed, because 'the whole of Chaos, like grains of gunpowder, was exploded at the same time, and dispersed through infinite space at once, ... in every possible direction'. Although Darwin's poem asserts that the self-balanced orbs inhabit 'Space without bound, *the bosom of their* GOD!', he knew very well what lit the primal fuse. Satan – or an irrepressible, antagonistic energy to which the devil's name can be given – is the principle of cosmic ignition or detonation. As a student, Darwin wrote an ode attacking atheism, in which he prayed

> Teach me, Creation, teach me how
> T'adore the vast Unknown!

Yet the more knowledge he acquired about creation, the less likely it seemed that there was a creator.

When the fallen angels in *Paradise Lost* learn the secret of gunpowder, they collectively admire 'th'invention', while in private each of them is piqued because 'hee/ To be th'inventer miss'd, so easie it seemd'. Before Adam quits Eden, Michael allows him to survey the future of the race, and shows him another instance of satanic science. A man at a forge uses 'casual fire' to melt iron and brass, then moulds the lava into tools and 'what might else be wrought/ Fusil or grav'n in metal'. Michael is unimpressed by this mastery of 'Arts that polish Life'; in the archangel's haughty vocabulary, the verb is not complimentary. He explains that he is exhibiting the legacy of the murderous Cain, who disrupted nature by aggressively tilling the ground while the passive, peacable Abel was content to watch his grazing sheep, and he concludes by condemning

> Inventers rare
> Unmindful of thir Maker, though his Spirit
> Taught them, but they his gifts acknowledg'd none.

Invention is atheistic, because it adds to a world already made by God. Mary Shelley uses the word more modestly in the preface to *Frankenstein*, where she contrasts it with creation: 'Invention, it must humbly be admitted, does not consist in creating out of a void, but out of chaos'. But is that sentiment as humble as it wants to sound? *Paradise Lost* initially denies that even God could replenish a void, since

> In the Beginning ... the Heav'ns and Earth
> Rose out of Chaos.

Milton's infidel inventors, whether scientists or artists, are beings of a new kind, whose ambition alters the customary definition of the word. Traditionally, to invent meant to find; the object you came upon already existed, and you merely included it in your inventory of reality's contents. Thus the Christian festival of the Invention of the Cross commemorates the supposed discovery of the true cross at Jerusalem in 326. The discoverer was Helena, Constantine the Great's mother, who certainly did not (in the modern sense) invent the crucifix. But Satan and Michael prepare the word for its subsequent history. The invention of gunpowder and the tools invented by the brood of Cain look ahead to the brainwaves of George Stephenson, Thomas Edison, the Wright brothers, J. Robert Oppenheimer and Alan Turing: steam power, electricity, manned flight, nuclear fission and artificial intelligence are not ideas God could have patented. But the Christian prohibition lingers, despite these proofs of the genius possessed by engineers. An invention, in one context, is still a soft-edged way of describing a lie.

Myths set out to connect the estranged territories of gods and men. The myth so tersely yet so ambiguously recounted in Genesis attempted something more intellectually arduous: it ventured to explain why God first gave men life and then decided that they must die. *Paradise Lost* is stretched almost to breaking point by the distance between a supposedly perfect creator and his imperfect, tragically faulty creation. Milton wants to uphold justice; Satan insists that God's decrees are unjustifiable. In tempting Eve, the serpent extols the tree that bears the forbidden fruit as a 'Sacred, Wise, and Wisdom-giving Plant, / Mother of Science'. Human beings, by exercising their power of thought and ignoring the intimidation of morality, can close the gap between man and God: 'what are Gods,' Satan demands, 'that man may not become / As they?'

*Paradise Lost* has to choose between divine making and human ingenuity, between theological truth and poetic imagination. Ultimately Milton refuses to make the severe, exclusive decisions that doctrine demands. Creations and destroyings collide in the head of Keats's Apollo, and Milton likewise perceives how complementary they are, as aspects of nature and attributes of God. Hence the tender, terrified phrase in Raphael's account of eggs that hatch 'with kindly rupture'. The damage is kindly, meaning that it is prescribed by Mother Nature or Dame Kind, but it is still a breach, a rending; birth is accompanied by tears, screams of pain, the breaking of waters and shedding of blood. When Eve learns that she must beget and bear children only to have them die, she says that she prefers childlessness and proposes to Adam a double suicide: 'Destruction with Destruction to destroy'. Is this an ineffectual play on words, like Donne telling death to die in one of his sonnets, or should we see it as a proud transvaluation of values? If the self is our creation, as Descartes declared, we have the right to think it out of existence. Adam returns to the problem when Michael shows him his progeny inundated by Noah's flood. The prospect of the future now becomes intolerable, as his struggle with the abstruse tenses of verbs indicates:

> The Burd'n of many Ages, on me light
> At once, by my foreknowledge gaining Birth
> Abortive, to torment me ere thir being,
> With thought that they must be.

Given the inevitability of death, all births are abortions. Can this be a credit-able divine design? Satan is not the only spoiler of God's creation. The oratorio performed in heaven on the seventh day recalls God's vengeful treatment of the rebels, though after acknowledging his thunderous might it asserts that 'to create/ Is greater than created to destroy'. The infinitives, paralleling each other, remain too close for comfort. In Book III, even before the poem gets around to describing the advent of Adam and Eve, God is already planning the destruction of his creatures, which prompts Christ to ask 'wilt thou thy self/ Abolish thy Creation?' After the fall, God sends the angels to reorganize creation and mar its equilibrium. They adjust the earth's axis and push 'Oblique the Centric Globe' so that the poles freeze and the equator scorches to a desert, while Adam bewails 'the end/ Of this new glorious World'. After God turns the devils to snakes, his final speech in the poem is an apoplectic rant, like the railing of a misanthropic satirist.

So long as God retained his humanized form, such unstable moods were alarming. They were easier to accept if he became a principle of physics. Descartes, reluctant to provoke the church, said that 'We have within us the idea of God, or a supreme being', but in practice he replaced the creator with a succession of vortices made of sparks shot from the sun, which had, he believed, generated our world. These vortices revolved around their own centre, like whirlpools in a river. The planets, embedded in fiery spirals, turned around the sun, but they also possessed wills of their own, which over-ruled the decrees of Genesis. Newton thought the vortical theory unsound, and its fallacy was exposed by astronomers who followed the trajectory of comets (which had caused havoc among the crystalline Pythagorean spheres: such projectiles would have shattered glass, so the material of outer space was reconceived as fluid or ethereal). All the same, the cosmic scenario of Descartes marked a first attempt to liberate the world from its angry creator. Science – even the hypothetical pseudo-science of the vortices – separated the opposed orders of experience that myth tried to hold together. In *Conversations on the Plurality of Worlds*, Bernard le Bovier de Fontenelle explained that 'at the world's beginning we made the moon follow us, because she found herself within the limits of the earth's vortex'. Earthlings could only envy the good luck of Jupiter, which found four little planets nearby and compelled all of them to enter its vortex and serve as its flunkies. At the same time, Fontenelle reminded us to be glad that the earth was so far away from Jupiter, which was big enough to have swallowed us up as well. God's favourite planet no longer enjoyed special protection.

Milton could not renounce the myth, but he wore it out with his questioning, so that *Paradise Lost* ends in a world from which God has withdrawn. The cherubim ushering Adam and Eve from Eden glide

> meteorous, as Ev'ning Mist
> Ris'n from a River ore the Marish glides,
> And gathers ground fast at the Labourers heel
> Homeward returning.

During the creation, God sows the sky with stars. Now the task of cultivation has devolved on that weary, anonymous labourer, who toils in a landscape where the clammy river and boggy marsh are no longer compared – as every other earthly prospect in the poem has been – to some mythical prototype. The supernatural agents sent down from heaven dissolve into Milton's damp twilight. As the meteor burns out and cools down before Milton's introduction of the rural workman, metaphor records the disenchantment of the world. But the conclusion is resilient and reassuring. This terrain forsaken by God is still our home, our shelter, our only comfort.

From now on, the individual must make his way in that world as best he can. That is the story that novels tell, which is why Fielding in *Tom Jones* quotes the end of *Paradise Lost* when his hero sets off on his journey of self-discovery: 'The world, as Milton phrases it, lay all before him'. The novelist Aphra Behn translated Fontenelle's *Conversations* in 1688, entitling her version *A Discovery of New Worlds*. She warned her readers that Fontenelle 'ascribes all to Nature, and says not a word of God Almighty'. Fontenelle's deities are men armed with machines. He imagines the cowering superstition of native Americans when Columbus's men strode ashore, armoured in scaley metal and deploying lightning bolts – the firearms of Milton's devils – against anyone who opposed them. 'Are they gods?', the savages must have asked. The Deism of the eighteenth century made polite amends for God's abdication. His detachment vouched for his benevolence; he presided over a creation that depended on its own internal workings, like the clocks or mill-wheels of Descartes. Shaftesbury cosily called God 'the best-natured Being in the world', even though he was not a being, not in the world, and in the Old Testament is not especially good-natured.

Artists illustrating *Paradise Lost* found it hard to give this obliterated God a face. Henry Fuseli painted *The Creation of Eve* in 1793. Adam, in a Michelangelesque posture, lolls on the ground asleep, while Eve detaches herself from his side and soars upwards, hands clasped, to salute the creative source. But the God who presides over her birth is not the patriarch from the Sistine Chapel. A green ectoplasmic revenant floats in the sky; his facial features are haughtily classical, and – by contrast with the naked humans – he has a toga gripped tight around his body, perhaps to conceal its weightless vacuity. He ignores Eve's pious appeal, and averts his eyes. Fuseli answered theological quibbles by arguing that 'for believers, let it be the Son, the Visible Agent of his father … looking up for approbation of this

Henry Fuseli,
*The Creation of
Eve*, 1791–3

work to the inspiring power above'. For non-believers, he characterized the
figure as 'merely a superior Being' – non-denominational, or even (given its
gaseous insubstantiality) non-existent. Is it an exhalation of Eve's mind, like
the fiendish horse and gloating goblin that visit the sleeping woman in
Fuseli's *Nightmare*? Yet in that painting the woman is inert, vulnerable,
whereas Eve takes the initiative, escaping from Adam's body and propelling
herself through the air towards her creator. The 'Visible Agent', however, is
immune to her charms, and seems to be dismayed or disgusted by her red
pouting lips and her waterfall of lush, unkempt hair. The mythic junction
again breaks down: God and man, or superior being and woman, are unable
to reach an understanding.

    Blake illustrated the same episode in 1807, and redefined the roles of
all three participants. Christ extends a hand to bless Eve; since it hovers
above her head, there is no telling whether he has conjured her up or wants
to hold her down. A sickle moon hangs over her, hinting that she is a queen

of the night, the projection of unlicensed dreams and desires that Christ seeks to repress. Her feet rest on the sprawled form of Adam, who lies asleep on a jungly leaf, still absorbed in the vegetative somnolence of nature. Horizontal man is supplanted by vertical, yearning woman, and God cannot induce them to agree. In a watercolour version of the scene made about five years earlier, Blake replaced Christ with God the Father, or 'That Angel of the Divine Presence' whom he identified with 'Jehovah Elohim, The I Am'. The bearded sage brings Eve to Adam, tugging her by her wrist to drag her down from the sky; his other hand grips the fingers of Adam, who is lifting himself off the ground. He looks like a priest about to join them in marriage, but his eyes are downcast, as if he had suddenly become aware of his error. The act of creation introduces a rift, a self-contradiction, which human beings must struggle to overcome. The most extraordinary of Blake's illustrations to *Paradise Lost*, which shows Christ interceding to redeem beleaguered mankind, is the artist's accusation of a guilt-ridden, shamed creator. Christ hangs suspended, stretching out his arms in a forgiving fraternal embrace

William Blake,
*The Creation of
Eve*, 1808

that welcomes all men but at the same time prepares him for crucifixion. God, faceless, nestles his grizzled head on Christ's shoulder. Slumped on his throne, he lacks the energy to enfold his son in his limp, dangling, incapable hands. It is the same familial tragedy that Blake studied at the gates of hell, when Sin reproaches Satan for menacing Death with his spear: 'O Father, what intends thy hand .../ Against thy only Son?' Satan relents, but God permits a sacrifice which, as he knows, is the only way of salvaging his misbegotten creation. The angels receive the news of Christ's offer by

William Blake, *Christ offers to Redeem Man*, 1808

plummeting towards earth and discarding their crowns, like the stars in Blake's poem 'The Tyger' when they throw down their spears and water heaven with their tears. Although the gesture is intended to acclaim Christ's sacrifice, it brings the angels close to Satan who, physically indistinguishable from his former colleagues, coasts on a cloud and prepares to take advantage of the moral collapse above.

The painter John Martin, a specialist in gas-lit apocalyptic panoramas, contributed a set of mezzotints to an edition of *Paradise Lost* published between 1825 and 1827, and in the next decade illustrated other episodes from the Old Testament. He found hell easy to visualize, because he only needed to look at the architecture of industrial London: the bridge over Chaos is a railway viaduct squeezed inside a sooty tunnel, while Pandemonium swelters under a roof of glass. (Martin planned a sewage system for London, dispensing Satan and his fellow devils from having to lick up the fallen world's foul waste, which God sentences them to do at the end of Milton's poem.) But he also wanted to represent the workmanship of God, and was attracted to that moment in the course of creation when – as Goethe pointed out in his homage to the Elohim – painting itself became possible. In *The Creation of Light*, Martin fixed on the Almighty's command that there should be lights in heaven to divide day from night and to serve

John Martin,
*The Creation of*
*Light*, 1824

as 'Signs,/ For Seasons, and for Days and circling Years'. Martin tried to
make his creator as gigantically heroic as the figures painted in the Vatican
by Michelangelo and Raphael. His Christ half strides and half soars through
a thundery murk. He has preternaturally extensible limbs, which elasticize
as they carry out God's orders. With one hand he reaches into an aperture
between the storm clouds, as if he had pitched the sun into the sky like a
ball; the bare foot that rises behind him seems to have kicked the moon into
its lowlier position. This athletic bravura is a relic of Renaissance humanism,
paying God the compliment of imagining him to be an enlarged replica of
man; but Martin's print cannot sustain such confidence. In the mezzotint
Christ blurs into the surrounding atmosphere. The billows of his cape double
as a ruffled cloud, and the dazzling sunlight renders him half-visible.

When Martin exhibited the painting on which the mezzotint was
based, his rival Benjamin Robert Haydon jeered at its reductiveness. The
'great Creator' was actually fifteen inches tall (and he shrank even further in
the mezzotint, where he measures about two and a half inches from top to
toe). Martin claimed that Christ's size was relative because the horizon he
bestrode was twenty miles wide, so that his leg, extended along it, must
measure sixteen miles. Haydon was not taken in. Steam engines had made
the abridgement of distance banal, and any traveller could now accomplish
divine marvels: 'there is nothing grand', Haydon remarked, 'in a man step-
ping from York to Lancaster'. Martin's figure looks silvery and shadowy,
like one of the transparent ghosts or fairies that Victorian photographers
trapped in their cameras by the cunning use of double exposure. An
anaemic God has wasted away, or faded out of the creation that he once
controlled.

# OPTICE:

## SIVE DE
## REFLEXIONIBUS, REFRACTIONIBUS,
### INFLEXIONIBUS ET COLORIBUS

# LUCIS,

## LIBRI TRES.
## AUCTORE

# ISAACO NEWTON,

## EQUITE AURATO.

*Latine reddidit*

## SAMUEL CLARKE, S. T. P.

### EDITIO NOVISSIMA.

Delamonce.

Daudet Sculp.

## LAUSANNÆ & GENEVÆ,

Sumpt. MARCI-MICHAELIS BOUSQUET & Sociorum.

# MDCCXL.

# 12
# UNCREATING WORDS

God's words dictated the world. The words of poets have their own delayed and devious power. At best they modify reality, but they also possess a talent for negation or elimination. Karl Kraus, surveying a continent torn apart by war in 1918, invented a compound word to describe his anatomy of a damned, deathly humanity. The word was 'gegenschöpferisch', meaning counter-creative, and it enabled Kraus to rewrite the verdict uttered by the creator when he looked back on the work of those six busy days. Kraus's summation was: 'And saw that it was not good'. He insisted that he had no intention of playing God (although his play *The Last Days of Mankind* did stage the collapse of the Austro-Hungarian Empire as an absurd apocalypse). His task, as he put it, was rather 'to gather up the pieces of the falling world from below'.

*Paradise Lost* has its own counter-creative vocabulary. Belial speaks of 'the wide womb of uncreated night'. Satan confronts 'the void profound/ Of unessential night', an 'abortive gulf'. Deferentially addressing the ogres that guard Chaos, he promises to reduce creation 'to her original darkness' and re-erect the standard of '*ancient Night*'. Later he remembers his passage through 'th'untractable Abyss', when he was 'plung'd in the womb/ Of unoriginal *Night* and *Chaos* wild'. All these negative coinages – uncreated, unessential, unoriginal – are linked to the image of a womb, where life is meant to grow to ripeness. But the womb, in this case, is an empty space. Satan calls night unoriginal because nothing originates in its dark mortuary; it is unessential because it expunges the essences that are the foundations of matter. Even 'infinite', the word of which Descartes disapproved, is technically negative: anything finite has an end or a limit, which makes it comprehensible. In 1674, Nathanael Lee flattered Dryden by claiming that the opera libretto he based on *Paradise Lost* had improved Milton's disruptive, interrogatory epic. Milton, according to Lee,

> roughly drew, on an old fashion'd ground,
> A Chaos, for no perfect World was found,
> Till through the heap, your mighty Genius shin'd.

The libretto begins with a scene representing 'a Chaos, or a confus'd Mass of Matter'; with his neat rhyming couplets, Dryden restores symmetry and justice. But *Paradise Lost* remained truer to the conditions of our discordant world than Dryden's polished artefact. During the next decade, Burnet's *Sacred Theory* explained the earth's malformed geography – its wildernesses of water, its jagged mountains – as a consequence of the fall and of the catastrophes visited on men in the Old Testament. The 'work of the first Creation' was a smooth, serene globe. But 'the judgements of God ... destroy'd the first World' and left behind something ragged and unkempt, like Lee's description of *Paradise Lost*. Observation of our actual world suggested that Chaos had come again. Samuel Johnson, touring the Scottish Highlands in 1773, grieved over the barren landscape, which to him consisted of 'matter incapable of form or usefulness, dismissed by nature from her care ... left in its original elemental state'. God had not bothered to complete the creation of Scotland. Taking a more general view, Burnet called our messy planet 'a broken and confus'd heap of bodies' or 'a rude lump', and said that it had 'the aspect of a World lying in its rubbish'. Officially, art's purpose was to rectify this anarchy. Dryden rewrote Milton or Shakespeare to save unrefined creation from its crudity and mayhem. Yet perhaps genius preferred darkness to the bright lucidity that Lee found in Dryden? God's wrath wrecked and distorted a primary world, as Burnet suggested, and artists shared this creatively destructive rage.

Concealed in Milton's poem about the creation of the world is a formula that was used to bring the world to an end. Between 1728 and 1743, in his satirical epic *The Dunciad*, Pope appealed to a contemporary muse who dotes on the muddle-headed drivel of contemporary hacks and is therefore ensconced like Milton's monsters on 'the sable throne/ Of *Night* Primeval and of *Chaos* old'. Dulness, worshipped by Pope's dunces, is the daughter of Night and Chaos, and rules 'in native Anarchy, the mind'. Chaos precedes cosmos, and obscurity predates enlightenment. Dulness derives her 'ancient right' from a time before that when Athene issued from the head of Zeus, and she blames the twin elucidators of nature and supernature – 'A Newton's genius, or a Milton's flame' – for having challenged her dominion. They did so in different ways. Milton disposed of Chaos by demonizing it, whereas Newton more coolly subjected it to the laws of physics. In a letter, Newton challenged Burnet to explain how matter coagulated into lumpish hills. What, he asked, had produced this 'uniform chaos'? The phrase is a neatly balanced oxymoron. Burnet's earth is chaotic because he could not discern the imprinted intentions of a personal creator; but it is uniformly so, because it must obey the rules governing motion and gravity that were formulated by Newton. Creation for Newton resembled a feat of industrial productivity, and in his letter to Burnet he wondered whether the hills had cooled and congealed like the tin that was extracted from Cornish mines and melted down to make pewter. The 'irregularity' of the result did not worry him, so long as he could perceive the rules behind its formation. In his *Optics*,

Newton conceded that comets travelled in 'eccentric orbs', but pointed out that the planets moved 'one and the same way in orbs concentric'. Regularity like this could not be the work of 'blind Fate'. Newton gave credit to a demiurge who left the forces of white light and attractive matter to arrive at an understanding. In 1712 Richard Blackmore published a philosophical poem called *Creation*, in which the Newtonian passage of light through space became a zealously charitable mission. Blackmore marvelled at the speed of the 'Effulgent Emanations' that crossed the interplanetary void; he assumed that their purpose was 'to cheer the Earth' and applauded their 'Amazing Progress!' Is the sun really so intent on admiring and humouring us? Newton was more prudent: he praised what he called the 'creative wisdom' of cosmic arrangements without attributing them to a creator.

In *The Dunciad*, Pope pretends to regret Newton's abstracting of God. 'Oh hide the God still more!' cries one of Dulness's acolytes, who wants to 'Make God Man's Image' and prefers

> Such as Lucretius drew, a God like Thee:
> Wrapped up in Self, a God without a Thought.

Nature in Lucretius is another name for 'life-giving Venus', the compulsive force of sexual attraction. Dulness is as fruitful as Milton's Sin, whose womb pours forth those hell-hounds that nuzzle their way back into her body. Pope's 'Great Mother' extrudes an offspring of vile rhymes, undeserved panegyrics and pompous tragedies – ephemera destined

> Soon to that mass of Nonsense to return
> Where things destroyed are swept to things unborn.

Harking back to the lay-out of *Paradise Lost* and its epistemological language, Pope in the last lines of the poem invites Dulness to put out the light and reverse creation:

> Nor *human* Spark is left, nor Glimpse *divine*!
> Lo! thy dread Empire, CHAOS! is restored;
> Light dies before thy uncreating word;
> Thy hand, great Anarch! lets the curtain fall,
> And universal Darkness buries All.

The spark of fire from the hearth of Zeus, implanted in men by Prometheus, has dimmed; to justify their snobbery about their species, human beings need to establish an affinity with the gods, and these celestial patrons can no longer be glimpsed. Rather than lamenting the fall of man, Pope applies that crucial, tragic word to the abrupt lowering of a theatrical curtain, which curtails the gaudy, trivial show. The sacred word, profaned and vulgarized, is not merely uncreative but uncreating: it pronounces a sentence of death on the things it names, and obliterates them. The 'high, hot Words' abusively exchanged by the ancient and modern writers in Swift's satire *The Battle of the Books* are no better than bodily excreta. A single unspeakable word can revoke our dignity and draw attention to the foul drainage system that defiles creation, as when a disillusioned lover in one of Swift's poems explains his despair:

> Nor wonder how I lost my Wits;
> Oh! *Caelia, Caelia, Caelia* shits.

The word that created the world in St John's Gospel and in *Paradise Lost* was an utterance, an ordaining idea. Pope, however, takes it literally: the word is employed by a writer, whose book is nature. The cosmology of Hesiod and Genesis therefore becomes an exercise in literary criticism; instead of peeping into the mind of God, Pope scrutinizes the contents of the literary imagination. Milton in *Paradise Lost* contemptuously surveyed the Limbo of Vanity, a 'lair of Embryo's and Idiots', later populated by

> All th'unaccomplisht works of Natures hand,
> Abortive, monstrous, or unkindly mixt,
> Dissolvd on Earth

and doomed to wander there until their final dissolution. The gigantic Brobdingnagians take a similar view of Gulliver, sneering at their diminutive guest as 'an Embrio, or abortive Birth'. Pope gives Milton's infirmary a precise location on the map of London in Moorfields: it is Grub Street, otherwise known – with woeful irony – as Milton Street in Moorfields. This was the precinct of hacks and scribblers who grubbed in the dirt for a living or produced ill-accomplished books that resembled the larvae of insects. Chaos in *The Dunciad* swarms with garbled, unclassifiable poems that jumble up tragedy and comedy or farce and epic, and that allow reality to be distorted by rampaging mobs of metaphors. Pope's description of these 'nameless Somethings' emphasizes the messiness of creation and the clumsy fumbling of organic growth:

> How hints, like spawn, scarce quick in embryo lie,
> How newborn nonsense first is taught to cry,
> Maggots half-formed in rhyme exactly meet,
> And learn to crawl upon poetic feet.

Rather than nostalgically yearning for origins, the eighteenth century judged nature and culture as end products. Hence Pope's dismissal of those embryonic stirrings. Johnson's *Dictionary*, published in 1755, defined an embryo as 'the offspring yet unfinished in the womb'. The poems of the dunces are premature births, or stillborn corpses. At worst, they are litters of malformed freaks, as if the hybrids described in Horace's treatise on poetry had actually emerged into life. Dulness is delighted by 'her wild creation', as 'momentary monsters rise and fall'. The talentless poet laureate Colley Cibber has a 'monster-breeding breast', and Pope's version of Faust conjures up a zoo of gorgons, dragons, fiends, 'Gods, imps and monsters', which are all instantly destroyed.

Art mimics the profligacy of biological reproduction, as Pope acknowledged when describing the Cave of Spleen in his earlier satire *The Rape of the Lock*. This dismal grotto is the lair of neurosis and therefore of imagination, a place of confinement for those who suffer from 'th'hysteric, or poetic fit'. The two maladies are interchangeable: hysteria was thought to be a gynaecological ailment, a disorder of the womb, and the poetic fit also feminizes those it infects. The cave contains a perverse maternity ward, where 'Men prove with child, as powerful fancy works'. Such pregnancies outrage nature's patterned prototypes: the bards in *The Dunciad* 'like Proteus long in vain tied down,/ Escape in Monsters'; cheats passing off their own doggerel as the work of more reputable poets are also likened to Proteus who, when hunted, recreated himself as a puppy or an ape. In 1728, impersonating one of his own dunces, Pope wrote a study of bathos, which diagnoses the desire to write as a 'Titillation of the Generative Faculty of the Brain'. 'Such as conceive must bring forth', he says in *Peri Bathous*, even if what the straining poet delivers into the light is a dog, a monkey, an imp, or a mere 'discharge of the peccant humour'. Pope juggles with the body's internal conduits, and directly attaches the head to the colon: the refining process of thought is mixed up with the noisy, noxious expulsions from our alimentary canal. Poetry is explained as a 'morbid Secretion from the Brain', a pressure that must be relieved by 'Evacuation'. In *The Dunciad*, creativity flourishes in the sewers, where the goddess Cloacina allows her votaries to dabble muddily in 'her nether realms'.

In *The Dunciad* the body's creative capacities are placed on view in a pissing contest, during which a stream of urine is likened to 'Jove's bright bow', iridescently arching across the horizon to assure mankind that it will never again be drowned – unless we founder in our own mire. Although Jehovah is camouflaged as Jove, the biblical fable about the covenant between God and man has been sullied. Perhaps, as in the myth about the inception of the Milky Way, we are being shown the base, basic starting-point of the creative impulse. D. H. Lawrence admitted that he shed his sickness in his books, and the body in Pope's poems relieves itself in orgasmic explosions. Belinda in *The Rape of the Lock* distracts the lecherous Baron by sprinkling snuff over him; 'the pungent grains of titillating dust' cause a sneeze, which is a nasal ejaculation. Swift recommends the use of another vent, suggesting that the reader's proper response to one of his poems would be to vomit. 'A Beautiful Young Nymph Going to Bed' describes a prostitute removing her padded breasts, her matted wig and her false teeth, exposing her sores and open trenches. Next morning, when she struggles to reassemble herself, she finds that the cat has pissed in her shoes, the dog has infested her hair-piece with fleas, and her glass eye has rolled into a corner of the room:

> But how shall I describe her Arts
> To recollect the scatter'd Parts?
> *Corinna* in the Morning dizen'd
> Who sees, will spew; who smells, be poison'd.

The poem is a preview of post-mortem decay. Decomposition has occurred overnight, and there is no possibility of resurrection. Galileo exerted himself to satisfy the church by identifying the whereabouts of Dante's inferno in the new astral emptiness. Swift does not need to look so far afield, and in his broadside 'The Place of the Damn'd' concludes that

> *HELL* to be sure is at *Paris* or *Rome*,
> How happy for *Us*, that it is not at *Home*.

The comfort depends on our damnable lack of self-knowledge: hell is our neighbours, never ourselves.

Eighteenth-century satire gleefully announced the imminence of Armageddon. Burnet described the biblical deluge as 'a second chaos' that swamped nature. In 1710 in his 'Description of a City Shower', Swift viewed a downpour in London as a memento of the flood sent by God to eliminate mankind. Rain swells the gutters with 'Dung, Guts, and Blood' disgorged by an abattoir, and swills away drowned puppies, dead cats and scraps of offal. In *Gulliver's Travels*, this local carnage opens out into universal catastrophe. The astronomers on their flying island predict that comets are likely to scorch the earth and reduce it to ashes; failing that, the sun's expenditure of its rays will result in 'the Destruction of this Earth, and of all the Planets that receive their Light from it'. Meanwhile the airborne king punishes earthlings by stationing his island directly above them, which blocks both sun and rain and condemns them to 'Dearth and Diseases'. If they prove obstreperous, he pelts them with rocks that shatter their houses. In 1725 Swift told Pope 'I hate and detest that animal called man'. A misanthrope logically exempts himself from membership of the species that disgusts him; in 'The Day of Judgement', Swift imagines the graves giving up their dead when the last trump sounds, and impersonates a god who thunderously condemns the 'Offending Race of Human Kind'. He prudently calls this deity Jove, so as not to seem guilty of blasphemy. Nevertheless it is the repining creator from Genesis who decides that 'The World's mad Business now is 'o'er'.

Pope, rather than devising supernatural revenges, attempted to renego-
tiate relations between the creator and a querulous creation. In *An Essay on
Man*, written in 1733–4, he brought the theodicy of *Paradise Lost* up to date.
Milton set out to justify the ways of God to men, and Pope's intention was
to 'vindicate the ways to God to Man'. Milton had the harder task, because
his God is a person – inconsistent, tetchy, sometimes irate – whereas Pope's
is a cosmic principle. The principle, however, is too lax and obliging for its
own good. Whatever God's name is, men take it in vain. The sectarian disputes of Protestants fracture God and undermine his universality: 'This cries
there is, and that, there is no God'. Meanwhile the rational pride of humanists incites them to 'be the GOD of GOD'. As a compromise, Pope settles on
the geometer who diagrammatically designs the world in Plato's *Timaeus*,
and demands from men not belief but intellectual assent:

> who but wishes to invert the laws
> Of ORDER, sins against th' Eternal Cause.

Although the reference to sin sounds Christian, the fall is now more like a
comical failure to understand the implacable logic of a Newtonian universe. Instability remains: encapsulating the action of *Paradise Lost* in an
epigram, Pope notes that 'Men would be Angels, Angels would be Gods'.
But such restless aspiration – castigated by Milton when the devils spend a
week plummeting from heaven to hell – is automatically checked by
gravity, which ensures that we stay humbly fettered to the earth. This
alliance between physics and theology did not satisfy G. K. Chesterton, who
pointed out in his attack on scientific atheism that there is no 'God of Gravitation'. There might, Chesterton conceded, be 'a genius of the waterfall; but
not of mere falling'. It is a trickier argument than he realized. If in falling
down or falling over we merely obey a physical necessity, why did Chesterton's God draw such sombre, punitive conclusions from the fall of man?

In Pope's geometrical cosmos, the deity occupies a circle, and can look
in all directions simultaneously. He

> sees with equal eye, as God of all,
> A hero perish, or a sparrow fall,
> Atoms or systems into ruin hurled,
> And now a bubble bursts, and now a world.

Hamlet, in a moment of laughing fatalism just before his death, discerns a
special providence in the fall of a sparrow. Pope points out that, in the global
scheme of things, the hero's tragedy is no more or less significant than the
bird's. Milton's embryonic atoms can be uncreated, but the destruction
envisaged here is painlessly experimental. Worlds burst as lightly as bubbles,
because cosmology is a matter of conjecture, airily hypothetical. Even

Newton recognized 'some inconsiderable irregularities' in planetary motions, and predicted that such discrepant evidence, defying his laws, would go on accumulating 'till this system wants a reformation'. No intellectual scheme can ever be more than provisional. Pope had a taut, tenuous system of his own for managing irregularities: it was the rhyming couplet. The metrical poise of his verse balances antithetical terms, and his rhymes align words that sound alike, no matter how different their meanings might be. Chaos could not be marginalized, as it is when Raphael tells the story of creation in *Paradise Lost*, because for Pope it remains the infirm battleground of human existence:

> ALL subsists by elemental strife;
> And Passions are the elements of Life.

It invades our heads, which are a 'Chaos of Thought and Passion, all confused'. But if the war rages inside us, that is also where an armistice is arranged:

> This light and darkness in our chaos joined,
> What shall divide? The God within the mind.

The god within the mind was Plato's definition of conscience. Another god, equally conscientious, is at work in each of Pope's couplets, busy maintaining numerical rules and keeping antithetical terms apart, using verbal skill to fix 'the Mercury of Man'. The artist inherits a task that the creator could not complete; man is his own god after all.

The God of Genesis expected his regime to last forever (or at least until he decided that it was time for Armageddon), but the task of keeping the clock wound devolved on science. Newton noticed the eccentricity of those disobedient comets, and tried to work out a theory that would contain them. The astronomer Edmund Halley established the punctuality of the comet that was eventually named after him; last seen in 1531, it returned, as he predicted, in 1758, sixteen years after his death. If comets circulated in this leisurely and reliable manner, they did not threaten the workings of the cosmic machine. The emphasis is on an order made by men, imposed on a world from which God has retreated. That is why Pope suggests that we should 'presume not God to scan'. To scan is to examine, to judge, and also to scale or climb: those meanings push an increasingly invisible God into the distance. The infinitive also evokes the discipline of scansion, the metrical regulation that governs Pope's couplets. Unlike *Paradise Lost*, *An Essay on Man* does not grieve over God's desertion. It concentrates on 'our Bliss below', and ends by asserting that 'all our Knowledge is, OURSELVES TO KNOW'. If he follows that commandment, man the philosopher will take God's place. Jean-Jacques Rousseau, preparing his *Discourse on Equality* in 1753, felt himself to be exalted by his 'sublime meditations' and raised towards divinity. From that omniscient height, he looked down on his fellow men blindly blundering through the world and remonstrated with them: 'Madmen who ceaselessly complain of Nature, learn that all your misfortunes arise from yourselves!'

God, overstretched, could no longer be responsible for the entire plenum of existence. In 1721 the political theorist Montesquieu published a series of *Persian Letters*, supposedly written by a Muslim visitor to Europe; the pretence enabled him to tease Christian assumptions about a personal creation and a loving, solicitous creator. Montesquieu's letter-writer Usbek is puzzled by biblical chronology, and thinks it odd that, if God wanted to create the world, he waited until six thousand years ago to do so. And why did he later reduce mankind to a single family by sending the deluge? Myths exist to reconcile us to catastrophes, persuading us to see them as acts of God. Usbek, demythologizing the history of the world, points out that nature has an innate, inevitable tendency to decay. The sixteenth-century epidemic of syphilis attacked the reproductive organs, and might have put a stop to reproduction altogether if a remedy had not been found; the exhaustion of resources continues to kill off selected populations by starving them. As Usbek puts it, 'since the creation of the universe' mankind has often come close to extinction. He quotes the opinion of 'some philosophers' who think there may have been two creations, one of matter and the other – oddly tentative, subject to penitent afterthoughts – of man. We are irrelevant to the cosmic scheme, so should not be surprised to find ourselves casually slaughtered. Enlightened minds like Usbek's, questioning providence, made bold use of occasions when God appeared to be behaving like an uncreator – the plague that ravaged London in 1665, the earthquake that demolished Lisbon in 1755.

Defoe's fictional *Journal of the Plague Year*, published in 1722, is written by an anonymous narrator who remains in the city to study the disease that kills his neighbours. He begins by assuming that the epidemic must be 'the will of God', and when the infection abates he can only guess that 'the immediate finger of God' has decided to rewrite the record and decrease the number of deaths. Yet, as the contagion spreads, God too falls victim to it. Defoe's narrator perceives that religious faith is merely a self-deceptive insurance policy, trusting in a provider who has no capacity to shelter or save us. Squabbling sects encourage the credulous to expect a divine visitation, as if the second coming were at hand; a passing comet is taken as a portent. People are led astray by 'prophecies and astrological conjurations, dreams, and old wives' tales', or else they rush to consult 'fortune-tellers, cunning-men' and 'a wicked generation of pretenders to magic, to the black art'. These necromancers are tradesmen, who hang up signs to advertise a commercial service. They fake their professional credentials, claiming 'a thousand worse dealings with the devil than they were really guilty of'. Defoe's narrator puts one visionary manifestation to the test when he joins a crowd that stares up in the hope of seeing a sword-wielding angel in white, first spotted by a hysterical woman. The by-standers convince themselves they are sharing the hallucination, though they all have different versions of what they think they see. Halley reported on a similar epidemic of delusion when a reddish corona spread across the sky at sunset one evening in March 1715. Observers took it to be a symbol, though what it symbolized was a matter of personal choice and of doctrinal or aesthetic whim. Some likened it to the aureole surrounding the name of God in religious art, others thought it resembled the radiating stars in the insignia worn by Knights of the Garter. Many compared it with the dome of St Paul's, exuding light like a lantern. In *Journal of the Plague Year*, Defoe's deputy earnestly trains his eyes on the disputed spot, and testifies that it is 'nothing but a white cloud, bright on one side by the shining of the sun on the other part'. At least the misty cherubim at the end of *Paradise Lost* can be seen metaphorically dissolving into the damp, condensing air above the marsh. The angel that hovers above Defoe's London never existed, even though some witnesses babble that they can 'see it all plainly' and describe its glorious face. No metaphor transforms it, gently coaxing it down to earth; it is written off as an illusion, and replaced by that bright, blank, literally insignificant cloud.

Novels are atheistic, or at least agnostic. They are set in a world made by human efforts; their characters may hope for divine assistance, but they have no access to the upper air. Defoe's narrator counsels us, when deciding on a course of action, to consult 'particular providences' but to 'look upon them complexly, as they regard one another'. Causality is inextricably tangled. He decides to stay in London because he believes he has 'the direction or permission of Divine Power to do do' – but don't we always belatedly recruit God (or the devil) to rationalize whatever we want to do? When a drunken mob jeers at the narrator, demanding that he explain why he isn't dead or dying, he replies that he has been 'mercifully preserved by that great God whose name they had blasphemed'. The ego, sure of its omnipotence and its immortality, is itself a divine power. The *Journal* concludes with a jubilant gobbet of verse, which the narrator calls 'coarse but sincere':

> A dreadful plague in London was
>> In the year sixty-five,
> Which swept an hundred thousand souls
>> Away; yet I alive!

That exclamation is the sound of unregenerate Adam, incorrigibly solitary and self-interested, with no fear of divine reproof. It is paraphrased when

The Lisbon
Earthquake
in an engraving
by G. F. Pfauntz

sad news about the narrator's brother Bobby is received in Sterne's *Tristram Shandy*. Obadiah says 'He is dead, he is certainly dead!', which prods a scullery maid to realize that 'So am not I'. Fat and foolish, she might be called Cartesian woman, congratulating herself on her autonomy.

The plague occured in a Protestant country. Defoe's narrator therefore assumes that his survival is a badge of merit, not the arbitrary result of luck. The Lisbon earthquake and the tidal wave that followed it occured in a Catholic country, so the religious reaction was different. Voltaire in *Candide* describes the rounding-up of heretics, who were incinerated in an auto-da-fé to placate an angry God: 'the spectacle of a few people being ceremonially burned over a low flame is the infallible secret of preventing earthquakes'. In his *Poème sur le désastre de Lisbonne*, begun in December 1755 a month after the event and published the following March, Voltaire challenged the assumption that the catastrophe was the righteous condemnation of errant mankind. Were the people of the ruined city any more vicious than those of London or Paris? He pointed to the inequity: 'Lisbonne est abîmée, et l'on danse à Paris'. 'Abîmée' succinctly catches the cosmic disequilibrium induced by the earthquake: a city collapses into the abyss from which the world was formed, and creation is undone. The poem reviews the broiling of the infuriated elements, and contends – despite the complacency of humanists and the mechanistic reassurances of science – that there is evil on earth. It accuses God of delinquency, or of culpable inadequacy. We need, as Voltaire says, a God who can explicate his actions. Why should Milton or Pope have to twist themselves into argumentative knots, searching for justice in the unjustifiable? Voltaire's poem carefully

separates the formal obligations of piety from the more urgent affection –
apparently not shared by the creator – that attaches us to our natural habitat:
'Je respecte mon Dieu, mais j'aime l'univers'.

*Candide*, three years later, takes a more jauntily secular view of the
matter. When the ground shakes beneath Candide's feet and the sea boils
over, Voltaire exposes the moral illogic of the witnesses, who resemble
Defoe's characters giving different accounts of the imaginary angel.
Candide gibbers that the world is ending. For a black-robed agent of the
Inquisition, ends retroactively justify means: he takes the catastrophe to be
proof of our original sin, which needs to be indiscriminately scourged. Pangloss has to make the loss of life consistent with universal reason, so he
argues that it was fortunate that the earthquake happened here, which
means that it spared everywhere else. A brutish sailor meanwhile rubs his
hands with glee and picks the pockets of the corpses. Novels, as Defoe's
*Journal* makes clear, can dispense with the binary categories of good and
evil. The purpose of literature is to confound the generalities of philosophy.
As practised by Voltaire, or by Swift in Gulliver's befuddled journeys to his
own plurality of worlds, it is an antidote to philosophy. It demonstrates the
human brain's incapacity for wisdom, and carefully consults a range of individual opinions in order to show that everyone is wrong.

In the absence of gods, men still had to reckon with the indifference or
hostility of the universe. In Voltaire's *Micromégas*, a philosophical parable published in 1752, two huge inhabitants of remote planets – a gigantic intellect
from Sirius, and an academician from Saturn whom Voltaire based on
Fontenelle – swoop down to take on a tour of our earth, which to their eyes
is populated by puffed-up, presumptuous insects. The visitors take over the
role of Milton's ministering angels, though they have less patience with
human failings than Raphael or Michael. When one of the flea-like earthlings informs Micromégas and his colleague that the solar system was put in
place for man's special enjoyment, they are convulsed by 'that irrepressible
laughter which, according to Homer, is the portion of the gods'. Those
wanton sky-dwellers plan the world as a practical joke; the gods to whom
Voltaire refers are a euphemism for God's non-existence. Pope, vexed by
human contradictions, recommended that we should 'laugh where we
must'. This laughter is voluntary, directed at ourselves; the exercise of irony
enables us to overcome our limitations. The laughter in Voltaire's fable is less
kind, and it lashes the earth like a storm. In his poem about the Lisbon earthquake he complains that men have been treated as 'tormented atoms', and
reminds God that we are atoms with a capacity for thought (and for feeling
pain). In *Micromégas* a selection of these 'intelligent atoms' is self-importantly
travelling across the Baltic on a scientific expedition. Micromégas, intrigued,
picks up their ship to take a closer look at the loquacious microbes. Is it really

possible that such wriggling midgets can think, feel, or act freely? The hilarity of the investigators buffets the little vessel, and it lunges into the abysmal pocket of the Saturnian's trousers, where the philosophers get lost in a cloud of dust and grime. What we take to be disasters are nothing more than the idle eructations of a force beyond our control or comprehension.

Fontenelle recommended the attitude adopted by Voltaire's Saturnian. He told the marquise whom he instructs in the *Conversations* that 'one should simply be a spectator of the world, not an inhabitant'. He imagined moon-dwellers sniggering at the deformed specimens far down below who call themselves human, and suggested that the Greek gods made men while they were drunk on nectar, so 'when they examined their handiwork cold sober, they couldn't help laughing'. Arriving in France, Candide asks a solicitous abbé whether it is true that Parisians are always laughing. The abbé confirms the report, but adds that they do so 'through gritted teeth'. He illustrates the point by anonymously calumniating Voltaire. A thin-lipped, condescending smile – which changes to retributive ridicule when Micromégas guffaws – is the credential of enlightened intelligence. Or perhaps, as Voltaire suggested, the satirists had inherited the cosmic schizophrenia of the Manichees. The fatuously optimistic Pangloss follows the teaching of Leibniz, the apologist for a God who wishes us well. How then can the evils that relentlessly assail the blameless Candide be explained? There must be a rival deity at work, and this malign agency is worshipped by Martin, the elderly philosopher rescued from Surinam by Candide. 'I am,' he says, 'a Manichean'. When Candide asks Martin why this world was created, he replies: 'To drive us mad'. When, after another gratuitous flogging, Pangloss stubbornly insists that ours is the best of all possible worlds, Candide wonders what the other worlds must be like. Purgatory and hell have become earthly options, and heaven too is grounded: it is the affluent realm of Eldorado, whose wealthy citizens do not bother praying to God because there is nothing they want from him. Candide, of course, frets to leave this paradise. Man's motive is the pursuit of unhappiness.

This lofty outlook snubbed humanity, whose distresses now seemed as petty as a crisis in an ants' nest. Fontenelle's marquise is alarmed by the Cartesian vortices, feels lost in the vacancy of space, and complains that because there are now an infinite number of worlds, the small planet we live on is belittled, degraded. If the macrocosm is terrifying, then microcosmic space provokes an even keener mental panic. She feels like Gulliver, diminished to a gnat in Brobdingnag and inflated to a blundering dinosaur in Lilliput. The telescope, when Galileo diverted it from use by navigators or military tacticians and trained it on the sky, promoted a desolate, chilling sense of our solitude. The microscope, popularized by the Royal Society in the 1660s, encouraged the opposite fear, which was equally

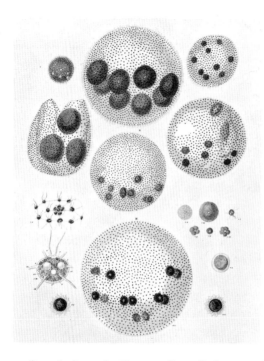

hard to bear. Rather than being alone, humans were overwhelmed by swarming nature, and creatures the eye could not see nibbled at our conceit.

Pebbles, according to Fontenelle, house 'an infinity of worms, which fill up the vacuums' within the rock, and a grain of sand can nourish 'millions of living creatures' for years. The veins of a leaf that he picks from a shrub open into gulfs of nonentity that can gobble up our tame human world. When the marquise worries about the moorage of the

Volvox (algae), from Christian Gottfried Ehrenberg's *Die Infusionsthierchen*, 1838

unfounded earth, Fontenelle tells her to think about the Hindu myth – evoked in the preface to *Frankenstein* – which sets it on the back of four elephants. He promises to add to the number of stalwart beasts if that makes her sleep easier. But he also intends, as her education proceeds, to remove them one by one, testing her recovery from this metaphysical vertigo. With cruel wit, the encyclopaedist Denis Diderot pulverized that elephantine cement in his scientific dialogue *D'Alembert's Dream*, written in 1769. During the dream, Mademoiselle de l'Espinasse – who admiringly cites Fontenelle, and is mentally pluckier than the marquise in the *Conversations* – reflects that if nature is germinated, grown from seed rather than being created by God, then it can just as easily fall apart, relapsing into 'inert, motionless sediment'. The elephant, she suggests, developed from 'one single atom', and its bulk will not save it from degenerating all over again into a random atomic shambles. The idea of the lumbering quadruped and 'the womb in which it was formed' immediately makes her think of a mite that wriggles out of a grain of flour. Great and small are equated; nature, concerned only with fermentation and fertility, has no special respect for elephants or for the aggrandized men who mount them.

In his periodical *The Spectator*, Joseph Addison tried to uphold the 'scale of Being' with its proportional justice and diminishing gradations. But Addison worried that the gap 'between the Supreme Being and Man' was wider and more unbridgeable than that 'between Man and the most despicable Insect', which could be blithely exterminated because it was so

The Pont du Gard, France, *c.* 19 BC

tiny. Pope likens his dunces to grubs, and in his *Epistle to Dr Arbuthnot* describes the dilettante Sporus as

> this bug with gilded wings,
> This painted child of dirt, that stinks and sings;
> Whose buzz the witty and the fair annoys.

A later generation found a psychological and even a spiritual advantage in this entomological view of mankind. When Rousseau first saw the Pont du Gard, a Roman aqueduct bridging a valley near Montpellier, he felt 'like an insect in that immensity'. The sensation was agreeable: it elevated his soul, he said, because it filled him with reverence for the grandeur of nature. Classical gods may have enjoyed swatting flies, but the god of romanticism viewed them more tenderly. In an act of almost divine forbearance, Uncle Toby in *Tristram Shandy* gently closes his hand around a fly that is bothering him at dinner, carries it to the window and releases it, saying 'This world is surely wide enough to hold both thee and me'. Micromégas addresses humans as 'invisible insects'. Like Toby with his faith in 'universal good-will', he is compassionate enough to assume that 'it pleased the creator to bring [them] into being in the abyss of the infinitely small'. All the same he is annoyed when one of the 'animalcules in academic dress' lectures him on the theology of Aquinas. Animalcules are diminutive animals, which is why Hugo later applied the term to Shakespeare's Queen Mab; animal-culists were scientists who gave such specks the benefit of the doubt,

believing that a single tadpole-like sperm contained all the future generations that would derive from it.

Tristram in Sterne's novel glumly witnesses his own conception. His
parents quarrel while copulating, and he chides them for taking so little care
of the 'low and ludicrous' homunculus that will eventually grow up into
him. This seminal gobbet deserves to be recognized as 'a Being guarded and
circumscribed with rights'; Tristram shudders as he recalls or imagines its
fraught passage between his father, preoccupied with the mechanics of
intercourse, and his mother, who lies back and suffers her husband to toil
away while her mind is on household chores. The biological comedy of the
incident is plaintive, and also uncomfortably disorienting. Like Milton's
Satan, man in Pope's *Essay* wants to 'explain his own beginning, or his end'.
But is it possible or desirable to be the spectator of your own creation? The
sight might be your undoing: Tristram never recovers from his privileged
view of his confused, unsatisfactory engendering. Enlightened man studied
insects through the microscope, or attempted, like Tristram, to scrutinize
the 'skin, hair, fat, flesh, veins, arteries, ligaments, nerves, cartilages, bones,
marrow, brains, glands, genitals, humours, and articulations' that must already
exist in the seed as it swims towards its fated rendezvous with the egg. But
once you have seen yourself with such detachment, it is hard to shed a precarious self-consciousness and reassume your old habitation in the body.
At least God, when we listened to him, told us who we were, and guaranteed those rights that Tristram claims for the homunculus.

At the end of the nineteenth century, when God's resignation prompted
reports of his death, the eighteenth century's quizzical surveillance of the
world came to seem terrifying. To look down from such a height confirmed
our pathetic helplessness. Fontenelle's marquise fancies that telescopes on
Jupiter are aimed at earth, and enjoys the thought that starry beings might
be wondering 'What planet is that? Who lives on it?' Worlds, she says, regard
each other with 'mutual curiosity'; minds strain across space to take part in a
symposium. But in H. G. Wells's *The War of the Worlds*, published in 1898,
superior intelligences from Mars coldly study men as if we were 'infusoria
under the microscope'. Infusoria are protozoa that thrive in stagnant animal
or vegetable matter; the Martians – who occupy the earth to expropriate its
natural resources – see men as primitive organisms, lifeforms that are
expendable. They lack humour, so they cannot share the scornful hilarity of
Micromégas when he observes the scuttling insects. Instead, feeding their
squashy brains with the aid of foraging metallic pincers, the Martians cannibalize the men who flee from them. Wells maintains a strict scientific
neutrality, and refuses to denounce the invaders as ugly and abominable:
such judgments depend on our smugness about the chain of being and our
status on it. To the Martians, we are 'as alien and lowly as are the monkeys

and lemurs to us'. Nor can he lament their rapacity, because a natural order once authorized by God has given way to 'an incessant struggle for existence'. Being fitter than us, the Martians are bound to survive.

God made a brief comeback in 1953, when Wells's story was retold by a Hollywood film. In the version of *The War of the Worlds* produced by George Pal, the Darwinian struggle analysed by the novel becomes a holy war. The Martians land in a Californian town, whose pastor fancies that they might be ambassadors from a heaven equipped with the latest technological novelties. 'If they're more advanced than us,' he reasons, 'they should be closer to the creator than we are.' He advances towards them in a no man's land that has been seared by their ray guns, and as he walks he treats them to a reading from the Bible. Unappeased, they atomize him. After a tantalizing delay, God, like the cavalry, rides to the rescue. The menaced citizens of Los Angeles huddle in their churches and pray for deliverance; the downfall of the Martians is a consequence of atheistic hubris, when one of their flying saucers smashes a stained-glass window and immediately tumbles from the sky. This consolation did not last long. No prayers are answered in Steven Spielberg's adaptation of the novel, released in 2005. Here the Martians, fearing no reprisals from God, begin by wrecking a church in Newark, New Jersey. Its walls split apart with a hollow groan, and the white steeple topples like a fool's cap. The building's invisible inhabitant does not put up a fight.

As the Martians in the 1953 film conquer all continents simultaneously, a fainthearted military expert reflects that it has taken them just six days to overrun the earth: 'the same number of days it took to create it'. Science fiction here challenges the myth of Genesis, and anticipates the world's uncreation – the apocalypse that will perhaps be the grandest achievement of our science, ruthlessly trampling nature. Luckily, before that can happen, the invaders fall sick and begin to moulder. Wells's narrator wonders at their 'ignorance of the putrefactive process', evident from their failure to bury their dead: our one advantage as a species is our obsessive awareness of mortality. The Martians are defeated by bacteria to which we are immune. Eighteenth-century satirists would have appreciated the irony. Vainglorious man, an insect with ideas above his station, owes his salvation to a microbe.

Le
Trebuchement
de
Phaeton

J. Berin Inuent.

J. le Pautre . f.

# 13
## NATURE CAUGHT IN THE ACT

Officially, creation began with an act of illumination. But the philosophers of the eighteenth century preferred to do their elucidating in the darkness. Their ambition was to expose a mystery that seemed more biological than religious – to spy on nature 'in flagrante delicto'. The libertines of the period set an example: their hedonism challenged clerical restraints on sexual conduct, political dissent, and metaphysical curiosity. In Mozart's *Don Giovanni*, three masked guests arrive at the dissolute hero's party to arraign him for his crimes. Before they enter, he cajoles them to join in a toast, 'Viva la libertà!' He compels them to repeat the phrase more than a dozen times, until it becomes a mantra. As a result, they are disarmed. They can hardly destroy the libertine after singing the praises of liberty.

Although Fontenelle's task is to enlighten the marquise, their dialogues take place at night, as they stroll through the gardens of her country estate. The tone of the *Conversations on the Plurality of Worlds* is bantering, naughtily flirtatious. Fontenelle explains that darkness is a precondition for the lessons he wants to teach. The seminar must also take place in the open air, away from the enclosure and intrusive sociability of the château. They venture out after a torrid, baking day. As the moon rises, he asks whether she agrees with him that day is less beautiful than night. She responds by likening day to a blonde who is dazzling but bland, while night is a more entrancing brunette. In a cheeky invitation of her own, she dares him to tell her about the 'delicious reverie' that the darkness has encouraged. Erotic dalliance is an apt prelude to the exploration of cosmology. Lovers address their songs to the night, as Fontenelle says, because they are grateful for its complicity. The scientist owes it the same tribute: only after sunset, when the stars glimmer into visibility, can we see the panorama of plural worlds.

Fontenelle's intellectual tactics are those of the seducer, beguiling the marquise into intimacy and comforting the mental distress he causes when he tells her the disorienting news about the night sky. He gives her another reason for trusting him when he represents the astronomer who caused the problems as a rougher, less considerate wooer. It was Copernicus who marginalized the earth and deprived it of the creator's protection; Fontenelle arouses the marquise's alarm by describing him as a German – in other words, a brute – who shattered the Pythagorean spheres and manhandled our planet by expelling it to the outer darkness. She asks why Copernicus had such a vendetta against the earth. Fontenelle tells her that human conceit, which led us to imagine that we were central to the solar system, deserved the rebuke. She complains about the humiliation, but a seducer has to establish that his own gravitational pull is irresistible. Fontenelle gradually persuades her that there are pleasures to be derived from the idea of the earth's rotation, even if we cannot feel its daily motions and remain convinced of its fixity. Ordinary movements, he reminds her, produce little or no sensation, just as our self-love is so instinctive that we are hardly aware of it. By this time, she is an eager recruit to his game. She hypocritically accuses him of exchanging physics for morality, which – she says – is boring. Physics at least is about the appetencies of bodies. She leads him back indoors, and promises that they will resume tomorrow night, 'you with your systems and me with my ignorance'. A seducer proceeds systematically, while the victim feigns ignorance to safeguard her own precious vanity.

On that first evening, Fontenelle deftly undresses the universe, removing the decorous veils that cover up its workings. The marquise is shocked by his exposure of its mechanisms, but he soothes her by offering a

metaphor as palliation: 'whoever sees nature as it truly is, sees backstage at a theatre'. The image admits that the view he has given is improper, perhaps indecent, because we are not meant to see behind the illusion, or to peep into the dressing room. More specifically, Fontenelle likens the sky to the decor for an opera. He asks her what Pythagoras, Plato, Aristotle would have thought if they were resurrected and taken to one of the astral pageants staged at the French court – collabo-

Cross-section of the Hoftheatre at Mannheim, built in 1742 to designs by Alessandro Galli da Bibiena

rations of myth and machinery, in which gods sang while they soared through the sky or plunged into cavernous underworlds.

The example he uses is that of Phaëton, who drove the sun's chariot so recklessly; Jean-Baptiste Lully had composed his opera *Phaëton* in 1683, three years before the *Conversations*. Lully's hero canters across the sky to prove his kinship with the sun. Théone, the daughter of Protée, sees that he is off-course, and fears that he will set fire to the universe. The Goddess of the Earth appeals to Jupiter to save her from incineration; concerned about the safety of the cosmic system, he sends a thunderbolt to strike Phaëton. The story is about the fragility of the world, only recently calmed and regulated – as Saturn says in the prologue – by Louis XIV, and the opera's scenic engineering made this plight starkly evident. A sketch by the designer Jean

Berain preserves one detail of the spectacle that astonished audiences in Versailles and Paris. Phaëton's chariot travelled on invisible rails, with a set of rotary blades like those of a helicopter to steady it. Berain's diagram shows how the anchorage that held the team of mechanized horses in place was meant to snap, so the contraption broke apart in mid-air. The classical sages could not have known about the overhead railway or the hidden pulleys and counter-weights, and Fontenelle imagines them improvising theories to account for the aerodynamism of Phaëton. Pythagoras would have suggested that he was the sum total of 'certain numbers that made him rise'; Aristotle would have assumed that he had a magnetic attraction to the ceiling. Fontenelle allows Descartes to clarify the situation by revealing that 'Phaëton rises because he is pulled by wires, and because a weight heavier than he is descends'. The marquise is not disillusioned by this demonstration, and holds the world in higher esteem now that she appreciates its technical intricacy. Fontenelle goes on, as he says, to draw back the curtain and show her the universe. She casts a finicky aesthetic eye on the prospect. Because the atmosphere on the moon is different, she fancies that it might have a red sky and green stars. She prefers our spectrum, with golden stars in a dark blue sky. Fontenelle jokes that she might be choosing a dress or a piece of furniture, but he cannot help admiring her whimsicality: we treat that infinite space as an accessory, a backdrop, and tailor it to suit our personal taste.

Opera lent itself to such cosmic scenarios because Pythagoras had made music responsible for the cohesion of the universe. In Rameau's *Castor et Pollux*, first performed in 1737, Jupiter swoops down on his golden throne to adjust the constellations. After Copernicus, gods have to reconcile themselves to a planetary order that predates their regime, so Rameau's Jupiter defers to the sun, and asks it to intensify its beams to glorify the new heavenly bodies he has created. Then he summons his own subjects, who descend from the spheres on balls of fire. He reminds them that his commands govern their orbits; the word he uses for those curved paths is 'concerts' – concerted movements, synchronized and maintained by the sound of music. Together the choiring stars and the jigging zodiac celebrate 'la fête de l'univers', and the jubilation is led by a planet with the voice of a soprano, who might be playing one of Descartes' vortices – a cosmic whirligig, sparked into life by the sun and revolving in giddy circuits. The festival, like any ceremony in church or at court, needs careful symphonic coordination and well-drilled choreography. The order is only too likely to be tripped up; because the systems of Descartes and Newton had been established so recently, no-one could be sure that the universe had adequately rehearsed its routines and committed them to memory. The incompetent pretenders in Pope's *Dunciad* cannot control the technology they use in their staged farces, and present 'a new world to Nature's laws unknown':

> Another Cynthia her new journey runs,
> And other planets circle other suns.
> The forests dance, the rivers upwards rise,
> Whales sport in woods, and dolphins in the skies;
> And last, to give the whole creation grace,
> Lo! one vast Egg produces human race.

Fontenelle imagined no such mayhem, but he did think of the planets competitively jostling, like rival dandies in a drawing-room or ambassadors nudging one another out of the way to gain access to the monarch. At any moment, the patterned symphonic rite might collapse into a free-for-all.

In Charpentier's musical idyll *Les Arts florissants*, performed in 1685–6, the arts unite to pay homage to Louis XIV, who allows them to flourish because his government keeps the peace. They are interrupted by the gruff threats of La Discorde, backed up a shrewish, yelping band of furies. The guerillas of dissonance complain that the king has sentenced them to 'l'abysme profonde', and set about wrecking the cosmic artifice to which he, as a half-divine emanation of the sun, is central: 'Renversons le ciel, la terre et l'onde/ que tout se confonde'. La Paix secures Jupiter's aid, and the monsters are swallowed up again by the shady pit. The gods could not afford to look away; the monarch, who was their deputy, had to keep his police and army alert. But the artists who served both church and state knew that the whole fictitious scheme was their creation, and they gleefully asserted their power by sabotaging it. Rameau's opera *Naïs* begins with a battle in heaven, as the irate Titans clamber up to the citadel of the flinching gods. They are masters of the earth, chthonian stalwarts, and they resent the dominion of such wispy, ethereal spirits. Their rallying call combines regicide and deicide: 'Détrônons les Dieux'. As the sky shudders and the earth rumbles, Jupiter mobilizes the same missiles he used against Phaëton: while flames lick across the stage, lightning bolts concuss the offenders. The audience in Paris in 1749 gaped as the giants lost their footing and tumbled backwards in an avalanche of weightless boulders. Jupiter then calms the agitated winds and waters, using song as a sedative. A consortium of lesser gods is enlisted to watch over the earth, and Jupiter tells them to be guided by 'une heureuse intelligence'.

Unlike the sarcastic laughter of Voltaire's gods, this happy intelligence is good-natured and trusting. It tolerates criticism, and will tinker with the grand design if mortals grumble. In *Hippolyte et Aricie*, Rameau's first opera, Mercury rescues Theseus from the underworld by persuading Pluto that his release will secure 'le bonheur de l'univers'. Jupiter in *Castor et Pollux* changes the inseparable, self-sacrificing brothers into a pair of new stars, the Gemini or Dioscuri, and raises Castor's widow Télaïre to scintillate in the sky. Valour, as Jupiter explains, turns men into gods, and beauty makes women into goddesses. When he descends to the Spartan temple, he brings the skies down with him: thanks to another of those machines that were the glory of the baroque theatre, bunched clouds come to rest on the earth. The starry heaven he reorganizes is a protective ceiling for men, whose science enables them to take their bearings from it. The aria sung by the glittering planet tells Castor and Pollux that they will have the joint task of guiding seafarers: 'disputez-vous tour à tour/ Le gloire d'être utile au monde!' The scenery of Rameau's opera – with ignited globes performing cartwheels, and spirits vaulting between them – shows a universe that is elastic, capable of evolving, supervised by gods with open minds.

Those gods were themselves subject to Newtonian laws, and during the eighteenth century they gradually came to accept their own obsolescence. In the 1754 version of *Castor et Pollux*, a chorus of celestial pleasures asks in astonishment 'Un dieu peut-il cessé de l'être?' Can a god cease to be a god? Apparently so, since Pollux renounces immortality to win Castor's release from the underworld. The gods, and the myths that described their adventures, could only survive if they were given material form, made scientifically plausible. This happens to Castor and Pollux themselves in *D'Alembert's Dream*, Diderot's sequence of imaginary conversations. Théophile de Bordeu, a doctor who contributed to the *Encyclopédie*, here serves as Diderot's spokesman. Because the universe contains plural worlds, Bordeu expects us to countenance the existence of human polyps, who vestigially adhere to one another. He reports on an actual medical anomaly: a pair of Siamese twins, joined at the back, who were kept alive for twelve hours, even though they lived in alternation, one falling unconscious while the other revived. Castor and Pollux were equally inseparable, and Jupiter allowed them to commute between heaven and hell, taking turns to live and die. Bordeu cites a magazine article about the 'double creature', and says that the infant girls were 'Castor and Pollux in real life'.

Rameau's expansive, collapsible universe has its own erratic whims, which are not always dependent on the intervention of gods. The second episode of *Les Indes galantes* – a tour of the amorous Indies, performed in 1735 – is set in South America, where an Inca priest artificially incites a volcanic eruption. He wants to frighten a princess into loving him, so he pretends that the sun god disapproves of her affection for a Spanish officer. But the experiment misfires, and the vomited rocks crush the priest. The incident warns religion not to tamper with processes best understood by science. The librettist Louis Fuzelier added a note on Mexican volcanoes and earthquakes in Peru, explaining that the earth's crust concealed 'underground furnaces composed of bitumen and sulphur, which burn easily and produce terrible fires when a single rock is rolled into their dreadful chasms'. He considered the outcome 'a phenomenon more plausible than

magic'; he added that it was also 'likely to bring about chromatic symphonies'. So it does in Rameau's score: the lacerated strings throb and
shriek. Geological convulsions, rearranging earth's terrain, could also be
benign. In 1743 Rameau composed *La Princesse de Navarre*, with a text by
Voltaire, to celebrate a royal wedding that linked the thrones of France and
Spain. On stage at the end, the Pyrenees – the symbolic barrier between the
two realms – curtseyed and subsided through the floor. Rameau knew how
to orchestrate the diplomatic ordering of the world. Flutes proclaim the
soothing clemency of Jupiter at the end of *Castor et Pollux*, and Polymnie,
the muse of song and mime, descends with sighing zephyrs to lull the storm
in *Les Boréades*. But his music was equally adept at portraying nature's return
to its strife-ridden origins and the attractions of the abyss.

The first action of any god is usually to abolish chaos. Only then can
a world be created. Johannes Kepler – who elaborated laws for planetary
motions in the early seventeenth century, and established that comets moved
in straight lines – reasserted a belief in the heavenly harmony. Kepler argued
that man created music 'in imitation of his creator', reproducing 'the conti-
nuity of cosmic time within a short hour'. The universe was a symphony,
a lesson in consonance. But what happened while the orchestra tuned
up? Artists who dispute that theological version of our beginnings take
delight in recreating the prohibited primal state; chaos, after all, is the usual
condition of the muddled world, and of our agitated minds. Two of the
mid-eighteenth century's most startling and exciting pieces of music –
Jean-Fery Rébel's suite of dances *Les Elémens*, published in 1737, and the
overture to Rameau's *Zaïs*, performed in 1748 – transcribe the elemental
combat that preceded creation. In doing so they recapitulate the efforts of
their own art to discipline sound, and perhaps regret the success of those
efforts: creative innovation is bound to disrupt the well-tempered hierarchy
arranged by classical theory.

Rébel's score was accompanied by an explanatory note claiming that it
dramatized the endeavours of 'a god and better order' to separate the elements and to establish their coexistence, 'parted by distance in concord and
peace'. The note gives no credit to the God of Genesis. Without mentioning
Eden, it goes on to say that the dances represent nature rejoicing before the
advent of man, who is 'nobler than the beasts and better able ... to form lofty
thoughts and hold sway over all things'. This implies that the idea of order,
expressed in music, is our way of colonizing a world that was happier before
we imposed a system on it. 'Le Cahos', which opens the suite, batters out of
our heads the expectation that tension can be resolved by a regulated succession of key changes and a manipulation of rhythm. A jarring downbeat is
followed by a discordant chord, the sonic symbol of instability. The strings
wander in a void, beset by thundery crashes and frightened, piping winds.

There is no sense of direction; the music travels in trapped, repetitive circles, periodically trailing off or arriving at abrupt dead ends.

In 'La Terre et l'Eau' a walking pace is established, which means that there is at least solid ground beneath our feet. The water also begins to flow, like music itself, by courtesy of the mellifluous flutes. Once we have learned to walk, we can try dancing. The chaconne 'Le Feu' flickers and wavers like flames, though its agitation can be alarming. In 'L'Air', the woodwinds imitate breezes which circulate in imaginary foliage; soon nightingales have been added to the landscape. But any notion of regaining Eden is upset when 'La Chasse', with its gruff, chortling horns, introduces the primitive quest for food and admits that life depends on death. 'Air pour l'Amour', despite its flighty grace, asks whether love is perhaps a reversion to chaos. The dance of the savages in *Les Indes galantes*, developed from a performance by two native Americans that Rameau saw in Paris in 1725, connects the minuets of the French court with the choreography of other cultures, where dance is a state of bodily dementia – a preparation for mating or for killing, a summons to hungry, angry gods who are invited to take up residence within their worshippers. Civilization is a willed and perhaps superficial recreation of the world, propitiating the chaos it cannot exclude or deny. The final section of *Les Elémens* is entitled 'Caprice', a notion that sums up the daring, dangerous frivolity of the eighteenth century. The word refers to the freak- ish impetuosity of the mind, which is instinctively fanciful and acquires logic only by painful effort; it derived from the capering of a goat – 'capro' in Italian – and Pope rhymed it with vice. This climactic dance in Rébel's suite is flurried and unruly, with a nervy accompaniment. From elemental chaos to civilized caprice: how far has the journey actually taken us?

*Zaïs* is about a 'genie de l'air' who becomes infatuated with a shep- herdess and wants to couple with earth. Rameau made this mixed marriage of the elements the subject of his prologue, which so disturbed the first audience that he had to withdraw it. A wit thanked the composer for being considerate enough to set his opera at the beginning of time: because men had not yet been created, they were spared its cacophony. An awkward, irregular thumping on a kettledrum introduces the first sign of life, like a heartbeat. The strings then shiver and fibrillate, lurching between remote, dislocated keys. Octaves provide a means of ascent, and eventually there is a light-headed escape into open space, although the drum still clatters below like a reminder of the seismic tantrums described by Fuzelier. As they escape from 'les abîmes du néant', the elements perform a dance – or rather four riotously uncoordinated dances, kept distinct by the instrumental groups. Earth remains thick, lumpy, clotted, while air whistles breezily. The flutes and the piccolo catch the edgy, searing glare of fire, and a gushing wall of sound from the strings depicts water. Each element carries its own announcement of apocalypse: earthquake, cyclone, conflagration, deluge. Destiny orders the four enemies to keep the peace, but Rameau's universe remains molten or, to use the word Pope applies to the adhesive atoms in the *Essay on Man*, plastic. The border between men and gods is redrawn, and theological rules are broken by celestial mechanics. Zaïs, one of the liberated elements, is told that he is 'égal aux Dieux', and the rising sun, described as 'le chef-d'oeuvre' of this cosmic theatre, is set up as 'le rival des Dieux'.

During the 1760s, Diderot pondered the ominous, ambiguous creativity of Rameau in a dialogue with the composer's nephew, a cranky gadfly with a dilettantish interest in music. They meet during an afternoon walk, and converse for a while. Their exchange of ideas is punctuated by the nephew's bouts of mimicry; he is a physiological virtuoso, who wracks and wrenches his body to make it expressive – the very personification of caprice. Before he scuttles off to the opera, he ironically farewells Diderot by addressing him as 'M. le Philosophe': the dialogue is about the mutual incomprehension of philosophy and imagination, grave reason and frolicsome fancy. In the course of *Rameau's Nephew*, worlds dilate or implode, while old gods expire or are pushed aside by self-deifying replacements. It is as if the planetary volleys of Rameau's operas were being played out at ground level in the clipped, neat garden of the Palais Royal.

Diderot remembers Rameau as the creator of 'unintelligible visions and apocalyptic truths'. He may be referring to the mathematical complications of Rameau's harmonic theory, or to the grinding, keening aural assault of episodes like the prologue to *Zaïs* and the trio sung by the Fates in *Hippolyte et Aricie*. He finds the same motive in the behaviour of the nephew, who specializes in exaggerated, preposterous arguments that threaten, as Diderot says, to 'overthrow the universal order of things'. The nephew's loudest challenge to that order comes when he impersonates the God of Genesis. He tells Diderot that he once had a wife who sometimes impertinently disagreed with him. He dealt with her, he says, by loosing his thunders and bellowing 'Let there be light', which caused her to cower and fall silent. In a crazily extemporized musical performance the nephew reconstitutes chaos, jumbling together tragic laments and comic ditties, plummeting 'down to the infernal regions' in a bass voice before soaring upwards in a falsetto that seems likely to 'split the heavens asunder'. While singing soft notes, he can simper as if eavesdropping on angels. But he is more excited by what he calls 'sublime evil': the reckless courage of great criminals, or of Milton's Satan. He describes the friction between French and Italian music as a religious warfare, and predicts the success of a new cult whose values are carnal not spiritual. The melodic sensuality of Italian operas by Pergolesi and Handel is bound to prevail over the stiff, haughty compositions of his uncle's colleagues. 'The reign of nature,' the nephew announces, 'is coming in, and that of my trinity, against which the gates of hell shall not prevail: truth, which is the father, begets goodness, which is the son, whence proceeds the beautiful, which is the holy ghost.' He welcomes the invasion of this 'foreign god', and cheekily remembers that this was how 'the Jesuits planted Christianity in China and the Indies'. Or did the Christians quietly go native? The nephew might be making adroit use of *Les Indes galantes*, which ends with a dance in which the North American savages are joined by colonial officers from France and Spain, all happily intoxicated by the narcotic fumes of a peace pipe.

The nephew describes to Diderot the japes and capers with which he diverted the family of his patron: he made them laugh until they cried, and 'supplied them with a complete madhouse'. His thoughts are the internees of a lunatic asylum. This was the period when fashionable society paid visits to Bedlam in London, to enjoy the tics and twitches of the madmen locked up there; it has been argued that an age of reason needed to persecute irrationality, but the case of Rameau's nephew demonstrates that unreason was tolerated and even admired because it revealed the mind's virtuosity, its liveliness, its love of play. Consciousness, released from logic, had become one of the performing arts. Diderot is scandalized by the nephew's free thinking and his free-associating raciness, but has to admit that there is sense in much that he says. He is confronted by something like nature itself: irrepressible, unashamed, averse to the prudish scruples of morality.

They begin by discussing genius. The nephew loathes his mean and selfish uncle (whom Rousseau in the *Confessions*, written at the same time, also accused of jealously intriguing against him to sabotage his career as a composer). He asks Diderot why nature, whose wisdom is extolled by enlightened philosophers, could not arrange for greatness and goodness to coincide. His own snarled, quarrelsome emotions expose the same contradictions. He is, as Diderot notes, at once clever and coarse; his stories about ingratiating with patrons and exploiting women are repellent, although when he acts out those scenes he is irresistibly funny. Nor can Diderot deny that such candour – the man's blatant admission of his baseness – is somehow admirable. That was the self-exculpation Rousseau relied on when in 1781 he eventually published the *Confessions*, with its impenitent record of his sexual quirks and his rankling grudges. Rousseau imagines offering a copy of his book to God, or to a less strictly doctrinal 'Eternal Being', on the day of judgment. As he hands it over, he intends to plead that he is simultaneously noble and vile, like all other men; those who want to judge him should ask whether they have any right to feel superior. Morality depends on standards, and is confounded by human idiosyncracy. The *Confessions* begins with a declaration of independence for the individual: 'I am made unlike anyone I have ever met; I will even venture to say that I am like no one in the whole world. I may be no better, but at least I am different'. While he defends himself against a disapproving God, Rousseau transfers responsibility for his creation to nature, the Lucretian goddess. It was she who made him, he says, and afterwards she broke the mould. He is in effect self-generated. The body has its appetites, the mind its fantasies; both are involuntary and incorrigible.

The nephew's justification of his antics in Diderot's dialogue is equally bold. He worries that he will run out of tricks, because 'only God and one or two rare geniuses have a career that broadens out as they go along', and he venerates genius because it ignores precedent and declines to consult books of rules: 'Geniuses read little but do a great deal, and are their own creators'. The nephew is not sure that he qualifies. He mimics the act of creation, attended by an imaginary midwife whose job is to stimulate labour pains and deliver the intellectual infant. He furrows his brow, gnaws his fingernails, grips his pen. But nothing happens: 'The god is absent; I had persuaded myself that I was a genius'. For once, he is being too harsh on himself. Romantic genius expends itself in living, and scarcely has time left over to make works of art. The God of Genesis created an entire world. The genius creates only himself, and cares little for any ancillary world: it is the place where other people live, and they are mostly bores or drones.

The nephew is the offspring of chaos, and he belongs with the monsters which, according to Empedocles, emerged from that obscure gulf. Rousseau believed that he was nature's favourite son, her incomparable masterpiece. The nephew sees her as a less indulgent parent, and wonders whether he might not be one of her freaks: a monster was defined in Latin as a sport of nature, like the slimy nymph of the marshes in Rameau's comic opera *Platée*, who is courted by a maliciously playful Jupiter and marries him with a chorus of croaking frogs as attendants. Nature, says the nephew, smiled when she made Leonardo da Vinci. She looked less delighted when she made the elder Rameau, which is why he turned out so unhappily. By the time she got around to the nephew, she was tired of her procreative chores, and kept herself amused by botching the job. The genial smile of the goddess had become a grimace, and the nephew is a consequence of that twisted grin. Diderot reports on the faces he pulls while describing this genealogy. He seems to be kneading dough with his fingers; having formed a misshapen manikin, he discards it, and rails against nature for doing the same. Nature, he says, 'made me and threw me down among the other images, some with wrinkled, fat bellies, short necks, eyes popping apoplectically out of their heads, others with necks awry, some dried up with staring eyes and hooked noses – and they all burst out laughing at the sight of me'. He reacts by ridiculing them.

The laughter of the extraterrestrials in *Micromégas* confirmed the alienation of gods from men. In *Rameau's Nephew*, the human species has splintered into an isolation ward of crooked, kinked specimens, and laughter now registers our alienation from one another. Rousseau had an alarming encounter with one of these unrepeatable oddments during a session with a Venetian courtesan. She was alluring and very available, but as he fell upon her naked breasts he noticed that her nipples were not twins. One of them was malformed; impolitely pausing to study it, he decided at length that it revealed 'some remarkable imperfection of Nature', and panicked because he had been lured into bed with a monster. The courtesan at first made a joke of his wilting ardour. Then, coldly infuriated, she adjusted her clothes and sent him away, telling him to give up women and study mathematics instead. Geometry deals in exact proportions, and ignores the asymmetry of actual bodies. Between 1770 and 1783, the Viennese sculptor Franz Xaver Messerschmidt made a series of heads portraying his own facial contortions and mental disquiet. Messerschmidt thought he was being pinched by imps he could not see; they represented the vengeance of 'the spirit of proportion', angered by his hermetic physiognomical researches. Cataloguing nature's warped sense of humour, Messerschmidt – half way between laughing and screaming – defined sixty-four different grimaces.

In *An Essay on Man*, Pope smoothly advances from God to the voice of 'Great Nature', which issues its kindly commands to mankind. But the stern father and the doting mother had different values. Fontenelle's marquise is baffled by the diversification of life on those uncountable planets. Nature is an enemy of repetition, and if she bothered making so many worlds she surely 'made them all different'. The same goes for life on earth. Eighteenth-century novelists assemble groups in order to show that each person is unique, the sole occupant of a personal world. When Bobby's death is reported in *Tristram Shandy*, Mr Shandy – whose character is an 'infinitude of oddities' – stoically philosophizes, while Uncle Toby hums and then sighs, expressing emotion without articulating it. A kitchen maid calculates that her mistress will go into mourning, and covetously hopes she will hand over her green satin night-gown. Corporal Trim scoffs at death like a good soldier. Nature recognizes no norms. The Saturnian in *Micromégas* is dismayed by the messy chaos of the earth. He sees the oceans as ungeometrical puddles, and wishes they were round or preferably square. The mountains are prickly bristles, like hair that needs shaving. And why does the foolish planet bother being globular if its poles are flat? But this irregularity supplies earthlings with their creed; it justifies their jutting noses and their swollen bellies, their convoluted thinking and their self-contradictory behaviour. If they stray from the straight and narrow path of virtue, it is natural for them to do so. As Hogarth pointed out in his *Analysis of Beauty*, there are no straight lines in nature.

The line of beauty, according to Hogarth, was curly and capricious; its writing energy prompted him to call it 'serpentine'. In 1752 he printed a ticket for subscribers to his book, on which he showed Columbus coaxing an egg to stand on its end. By delicately fracturing the eggshell, Columbus demonstrated that he understood nature's constructive

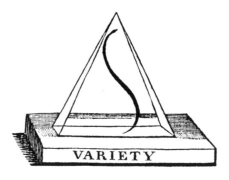

An illustration of the 'line of beauty' from William Hogarth's *Analysis of Beauty*, 1753

quirks; so did Hogarth. The design for the subscription ticket gave his aesthetic theory the force of a religious revelation, because Columbus and the sceptical courtiers at their dinner table are arranged like the figures in Leonardo's *Last Supper*. Columbus, chuckling as he enjoys his triumph, is Hogarth's Christ, though his gospel expounds a law of nature rather than reiterating God's edicts. Next to the egg on Columbus's plate is a wriggling eel. It shows off the serpentine liveliness of beauty, and reminds us to be grateful for the advice the serpent gave our ancestors in Eden. Perhaps it also suggests that life, like the line of beauty discovering its vivacity, can come into being spontaneously: in 1745 the biologist John Turberville Needham reported that he had watched through his microscope as creatures like miniature eels swam out of lumps of fermenting flour. Diderot was excited by the news, because it implied that nature could do without the creative agency of God. In *D'Alembert's Dream*, he and his fellow encyclopaedist discuss a notional Being – they refuse to call him God – who once upon a time made it possible for life to germinate. Diderot asks permission to anticipate the remote future, and experimentally extinguishes the sun. After an interval of death and darkness, he suspects that somehow, given the obstinacy of nature, our present plants and animals will find a way of 'creating a fresh world'.

Near the end of Sterne's novel, Tristram Shandy tries to explain its straggling, digressive structure. He illustrates the development of the book so far in a series of lines that zigzag, twist into loops like vegetative tendrils, form humps and bulges, and finally coil into the elegant likeness of a treble clef. After these finicky, organic lines, he takes up a writing-master's ruler and draws across the page a line that it is perfectly straight. For classical philosophers, he says, it symbolizes rectitude, and for

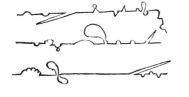

CHAPTER XL

I AM now beginning to get fairly into my work; and by the help of a vegetable diet, with a few of the cold seeds, I make no doubt but I shall be able to go on with my uncle Toby's story, and my own, in a tolerable straight line. Now,

Diagram in Laurence Sterne's *Tristram Shandy* illustrating the novel's plot

Archimedes it is the shortest distance between two points; for Christians, this is the route travelled by the virtuous man, and for gardeners it is the proper way to plant cabbages. But the itinerary it marks out is of no use to Tristram, because life proceeds haphazardly, moving sideways or backwards, and thinking too happens in fits and starts or goes round in obsessive circles. Rameau's nephew shares this disrespect for the strictures of geometry. In morality as in music, he favours transgression, the flexing of rules. Discussing the education of children, he tells Diderot that we automatically pass on vices and eccentricities to our offspring, and suggests that we should also teach them how to avoid disgrace by outwitting the law. His first analogy is musical. A succession of law-abiding common chords is dull, but 'dissonances in the social harmony' must be carefully prepared for and tidily resolved. His uncle's treatise on harmony worked out a procedure for managing discords, relying on an acoustic geometry which persuaded him that three-note chords were derived from fundamental triads; he would have been taken aback to find his nephew applying the system to show malefactors how to get away with crimes and other moral lapses. The nephew's second analogy comes from optics. Goodness is as dreary as white light; there must be something to break up the beam 'and separate it into rays'. He is alluding to Newton's optical experiments, which passed light through a prism and dispersed it into the coloured array of the spectrum. Chromatic aberration was blameless enough, and Newton hardly intended to set a precedent for the nephew's infractions. Nevertheless the prism, which bends light, could be used to trip up the enlightening mission of education. In *The Importance of Being Earnest*, an untrustworthy governess mislays the baby in her charge, and replaces it with the manuscript of a novel she has written; Wilde wickedly gave her the name of Miss Prism.

If nature is our creator, then creation is a physiological affair. Yorick, the clergyman in *Tristram Shandy*, reveres the precocious Lipsius, a classical scholar who supposedly 'composed a work the day he was born'. Uncle Toby can see no reason for admiring the body's creative output, and says 'They should have wiped it up'. A mishap befalls Mr Shandy as he tries to breed, and makes him wonder whether God suffered similar setbacks during his creative labours. While he is busy begetting Tristram, his wife asks if he has wound up the clock. It is a question of cosmic import: the universe, as Fontenelle insisted, ran like clockwork – but machines are liable to break down, and need human caretakers. Mr Shandy, detumescent, declares that no man has ever been so vexingly interrupted by a woman 'since the creation of the world'. It may be that the beginning of things was equally accident-prone. In Friedrich Schiller's tragedy *The Robbers*, written in 1780, the ingrate Franz justifies his rebellion against his elderly father and all other earthly and heavenly authorities by imagining his own conception. Was the old man thinking of him while he toiled in the marital bed? How could he love a creature who did not yet exist? The act through which he was created, Franz decides, was brutish; only a fool would pretend that the carnal itch sacredly transmitted affection. Freed by nature from the restraints of morality, Franz rejoices when his father dies, and points out that death is merely 'the negation of birth'.

Scientific experiments like those of Needham or the animalculists attempted to study the germinal process. The scenes of sexual voyeurism in eighteenth-century literature served the same clinical purpose. While Uncle Toby and the amorous widow manoeuvre in the next room, Sterne invites the reader to 'look through the key-hole as long as you will'. The aim of such espionage, as Fontenelle says to the marquise in his explanation of planetary revolutions, was to catch nature in the act. Fontenelle's intentions were high-minded enough, but his phrase acquired a lewd significance as a result of his own indiscretion. He was caught in the act with the Marquise de Tencin, a renegade nun whose succession of illustrious lovers included a cardinal; an affair with an artillery officer left her pregnant, but she abandoned the inconvenient infant, who grew up to be the mathematician d'Alembert, Diderot's partner in editing the *Encyclopédie*. The Saturnian in *Micromégas* recalls Fontenelle's embarrassment when he sees the animalcules from the ship grappling and struggling. He suspects that the lecherous atoms are propagating, and announces 'I have caught nature in the act'. Cunégonde, the heroine of *Candide*, observes Pangloss engaged in an experiment of his own. Out on a walk through the woods, she sees him administering 'a lesson in applied physiology' to a nubile maid, who is an apt pupil. Voltaire compliments Cunégonde's earnest concentration, and applies the terminology of Descartes to the breathless scene. The maid is Pangloss's 'sufficient reason', and the piston-like methodology of intercourse illustrates the interdependence of cause and effect. The scientific pretence is more than a joke: she is privy to nature's secrets. The bodies involved are exploring their own sensory capability, not industriously reproducing themselves. Lady Wishfort in Congreve's comedy *The Way of the World* wishes for sex but has no interest in fertility, which she views with disgust. Pallid and tottering, she says she looks 'like Mrs Qualmsick, the curate's wife, that's always breeding'. Only a clergyman would take such a joyless and dutiful view of sex, and his queasy wife of course has a pious immunity to pleasure.

In the *Confessions*, Rousseau presents his sexual misdemeanours with the same disinterested frankness. As an adolescent he is timid, liable to droop when in close contact with women he desires. He prefers to lurk in alleys and brandish his erection from a distance, offering the plucky penis as a subject for study. During a stay at a hospice for Catholic converts in Turin, he catches nature in a different kind of act. A homosexual Moor takes manual liberties with him, and when Jean-Jacques escapes from his grip the seducer continues the demonstration of applied physiology on his own. It looks as if he is suffering an epileptic fit; the outcome is a 'whitish and sticky' projectile that shoots into the fireplace. Rousseau calls the episode revolting, repulsive, foul, obscene, terrifying and brutal, but despite this prim frothing he can still imagine how fascinating a woman might find such phallic transports. Diderot, remembering Fontenelle's praise of variety, allowed nature more latitude. In *D'Alembert's Dream*, Bordeu startles his companions by refusing to denounce sex between men. He thinks that its only fault lies in not being useful, since nature's stubborn imperative is reproduction. He takes a similar view of nocturnal emissions and masturbation. While we are asleep, 'the animal no longer exists as a coherent whole'. If the nerves of the incoherent dreamer are tweaked by an erotic reverie, the result can be the ejection of semen. Nature has wired us in this way, so why should we fret about spilling seed? Rousseau blithely confessed to an inveterate fondness for masturbation. Bordeu gives it his professional approval, since it drains plethoric fluids. It is wrong to force nature, he says – but we have every right to give her a helping hand!

Diderot pitied painters who lived and died 'sans avoir sentir le chair'. The delicacy of the statement makes it difficult to translate: feeling the flesh is too gross, although the tactile values of painting do teasingly offer physical contact with the subject. To sense the flesh, for Diderot, was a scientific experiment and also a spiritual exercise. He defined animals (by which he meant men) as sensitive instruments, emotionally attuned to each other like a consort of clavichords. For Pythagoras, harmony was supernatural, a godly bequest. Diderot took a more down-to-earth view: he believed that 'all the harmony in the universe' derived from communion between our vibrant, resonant, breathing bodies. In his novel *The Nun*, a young woman who has been sentenced to a life of conventual chastity performs some pieces by Rameau, Scarlatti and Couperin on the clavichord, and sings an aria from *Castor et Pollux*. The besotted Mother Superior reacts ecstatically and caresses her in appreciation. The novice is puzzled by the older woman's sensitivity, but knows that music can produce 'the most violent impressions'. Later she defends her admirer against a confessor who condemns lesbianism. She can see no reason for treating sympathy as a crime.

A reciprocal sensitivity connects us all to what Sterne called 'the great sensorium of the world', whose fibres and filaments – even more delicate than a clavichord or the gristle of our vocal cords – were often likened to a spider's web. In *D'Alembert's Dream*, this is how Mademoiselle de l'Espinasse explains 'universal sensitivity' and its network of taut, glistening threads, which make our nerves tingle in unison. Like the spider, she is a 'bundle of sensitive particles', tickled or hurt by events in the world outside her. The image of the web had a special suitability, because it spools from inside the spider's body. It is a frail, small-scale replica of the maps and cosmic systems by which we control space and establish our centrality in the world; it also serves as a symbol of art, the brain's creative secretion. Michel-Paul-Guy de Chabanon, an associate of the encyclopaedists, assumed that spiders liked music, and often serenaded them on his violin. Pope too, when taking stock of 'Creation's ample range' and its 'scale of sensual, mental powers', particularly admired the delicacy of 'the spider's touch, how exquisitely fine!' At the end of *Tristram Shandy*, Uncle Toby instructs Corporal Trim to write down the capitalized word HUMANITY. He illustrates its meaning, and extends it beyond merely human concerns, by resting his pipe 'as gently upon the fender, as if it had been spun from the unravellings of a spider's web'. He then suggests a visit to his brother, presumably to patch up their disagreements.

For painters, Diana's bath served as an alibi for investigating fleshly affinities and testing the responsiveness of the sensorium – all the more aptly because Ovid's story implies the presence of the viewer, who catches nature in the act by spying on the chaste goddess while she washes. Watteau, like Boucher, painted this subject, but on other occasions he dispensed with the mythological excuse, and ignored the reproof that follows when Diana punishes the voyeur. He painted a woman at her morning toilet, baring her groin as her maid kneels before with a basin and a sponge to swab her private parts; he sketched another naked woman, her hair elaborately combed back, who stretches on her bed as a maid prepares to insert an enema. The maid grips the pronged device with one hand, while the other reaches out to clasp the patient's bare flank. To feel the flesh sends sympathy coursing from one body to another, so the warm hand makes up for the cold, intrusive tube. In Pope's *Rape of the Lock*, a woman's toilet is a sacred rite. Belinda is clothed, bejewelled, scented and powdered by sylphs, whose ministrations transform a girl into a goddess. Like the sun, she shines indiscriminately on all her admirers; when she does so, the world

Antoine Watteau,
*A Lady at her
Toilet*, 1716–19

is warmed by happiness. Pope's divinity is dressed: flesh can only be sanctified if it is adorned with aesthetic trophies, which is why Belinda treasures her artificially curled and coiffed lock of hair. Watteau, however, paints nature undressing. The woman in *A Lady at her Toilet* smiles beguilingly as she removes her shift and leans back onto her curtained couch, ready for examination. The upright, excited tail of her dog signals our response.

When God gave way to nature, scripture was edged aside by pornography. In 1748 Diderot anonymously published *The Indiscreet Jewels*, an oriental fantasy in which a genie awards the sultan Mangogul a magic ring that lets him overhear the confidential reminiscences of the women at his court. They blab their erotic secrets through a nether mouth: their 'jewels', which are their genitals, do the talking. An elderly roué, contributing the story of his own erotic career, gratefully recalls his sexual initiation with a pretty cousin: 'Oh, what a great teacher nature is! Soon she taught us pleasure'. That, by contrast with Christian prohibition, is pornography's enlightened creed. It facilitates the body's cravings, and helps us join in the pursuit of happiness; just as importantly, it expounds the scientific empiricism that infuriated the clergy when the *Encyclopédie* appeared. Diderot set *The Indiscreet Jewels* in the Ottoman empire, which with its seraglios was thought to be a paradise of sexual freedom. But Usbek, Montesquieu's travelling Persian, writes to a dervish at home praising Europe as the true land of liberty, where men look away from 'the wonders of heaven' and instead follow reason. This method has 'put order into chaos' by reducing God's design to simple mechanics: to understand the universe, all you need to know is that 'the creator of nature made matter move'. A cunning inventor could do the same, as Jacques de Vaucanson demonstrated in 1738 when he constructed a mechanical duck made of gilded copper, which quacked, flapped its wings – each containing four hundred moving parts – and ingested grain. Voltaire called Vaucanson 'a rival to Prometheus'. As a boy, Vaucanson had shown

Jacques Vaucanson's robotic duck

even greater effrontery in competing with God. Among his juvenile inventions were angels with mobile pinions like the duck's, and a priest who officiated automatically (which is exactly what priests are supposed to do).

Diderot's fable applies this methodical materialism to sexual relations, in which the precise adjustment of grooved, oiled parts is more important than moral foibles or emotional preferences. One episode of *The Indiscreet Jewels* is set in a temple where priests use a sacred thermometer to calibrate the private parts of lovers; the instrument is filled with mercury, which rises on cue as if sexually stimulated. Union is forbidden if the male organ is parallelepidal and the female counterpart is square. How could such jarring equipment ever slot together? Nature favours men whose apparatus is cylindrical and women who are blessed with circles. The accord between them is axiomatic: 'of all shapes, the circle encloses most space of the same contour'. Never has the divine geometry of *Timaeus* seemed so inviting. A Cartesian Vorticist believes the tides are responsible for the talking jewels, and a Newtonian Attractionist tries to make their chatter 'conform to the phenomena of ebb and flow'. Such idle theorizing is waved away when a dream takes Mangogul to the land of hypotheses. Here he meets Plato, who occupies an aerial palace and philosophizes behind a lectern made from a spider's web. He watches as a child with a small body and a gigantic head pokes a telescope at the sky, weighs thin air, and shatters light inside a prism. This is Experiment – 'l'Expérience' in the original text – who works through the physical investigations conducted by Galileo, Pascal and Newton. When the child approaches, the insecure citadel collapses, and Plato flees. Hypotheses crumble when probed by the inductive intelligence, which has the fearless honesty of childhood.

The jewels show that the mind is cunningly, comfortably embedded in matter. Prompted by them, Diderot elaborates his own erotic cosmology. One especially depraved jewel seems likely to engulf mankind as it reels off its list of lovers. Mangogul, who silences it, sees it as a chasm or abyss, 'le gouffre'. The circle, in this case, is the place of birth and of annihilation. It demands reverence: the jewels expect to be viewed as altars, and their utterances recall the mystical babbling of the oracle at Delphi, who spoke through a vaginal fissure in the earth. An academician learnedly explains that 'delphus', meaning the womb, is a lower-down version of the trachea, and combines the sensitive properties of wind and string instruments. When an opera by Rameau is performed in *The Indiscreet Jewels*, the ladies of the chorus vocalize from between their legs. The cylinder meanwhile brazenly streaks across the sky before explosively fizzling out. Fontenelle's marquise imagines the trails of comets as beards, which gives them an exciting masculine menace; one of Diderot's women reverses the metaphor and likens the penis of an English lord to 'a comet's tail [that] shot flaming darts' and set her on fire with delight. The indiscretions of the jewels are a manifesto for the new literary form of the novel, which explores the illicit, licentious truths of nature. Diderot transcribes bodily monologues; more decorously, the heroines of Richardson in *Pamela* and *Clarissa* use personal letters as a means of giving voice to their desires and distresses (and Pamela, forbidden to write by her lecherous master, sometimes stuffs her contraband missives into bodily hiding-places). Tristram Shandy's writing is momentary, spasmodic, jotting down whatever chancily happens in his head, and Sterne's *A Sentimental Journey* breaks off in the middle of a sentence, tapering out in an elongated dash that represents the hand of Yorick as it gropes a pretty chambermaid. Such inconclusiveness pays tribute to the liveliness of nature. Appraising the work of Greuze at the Salon in 1756, Diderot startlingly argued that a sketch is preferable to a finished work of art, because it is truer to the impromptu rapidity of fancy.

Earlier dream visions, like those of Boethius or the poet who wrote *Pearl*, allowed men to converse with supernatural messengers. In his dream, d'Alembert is granted a revelation about nature, and his own immersion in it. 'The world,' he cries out in his sleep, 'is ceaselessly beginning and ending; at every moment it is at its beginning and its end'. His babbling describes animalcules, fermentation, and the promiscuous sea of matter. Tristram narrates 'the history of myself', and promises to trace 'every thing in it, as Horace says, *ab Ovo*'. Diderot likewise invites d'Alembert to contemplate an egg: with it, he says, you can disprove all the religions of the world. The egg makes God's constructive labour unnecessary, because it shows that life derives from a germ, sensitized by heat and vivified by motion. Diderot tells d'Alembert to ponder his own origins, as Tristram does when he imagines his parents copulating. Many years before d'Alembert was born, he consisted of an egg and a seed, awaiting their opportunity in the adolescent loins of the marquise and the soldier she would one day encounter. Helped by milk absorbed from a wet nurse, the mind of the mathematician grew. Eventually it measured up to the universe, and explained how the tilting of the earth's axis influenced the timing of the equinoxes. But d'Alembert, as Diderot predicts, will one day die; that miraculous intelligence is bound to return to humus. Even so, this is no terminus. According to Bordeu, a dead man is dissipated into 'myriads of minute creatures', which are the breeding-ground for new life.

In 1782 in his *Dialogue between a Priest and a Dying Man*, the Marquis de Sade extended the idea. The moribund sinner dismisses all pious cant about heaven and hell; his only regret is that he merely picked the odd forbidden apple, rather than eating his way through the entire orchard. He refuses to equate death with moral judgment, and sneers at the Bible's eschatology and its graduated scale of being: 'A rational man can see that there is neither creation nor annihilation, but merely transformation. Today I am a man, tomorrow a tree, the next day a stone – and what does it matter to anyone?' The priest, persuaded by this Ovidian argument, joins in the dying man's last orgy. The same reasoning makes light of the atrocities committed in Sade's novel *Justine*. A lewd aristocrat (whose energetic entanglement with his male lover allows Justine to catch nature in some of its more recondite acts) intends to poison his aunt. He justifies the plan by arguing that nature, which sees no difference between bipeds and centipedes, has rendered us harmless: life is indestructible, so all we can do is to alter the form a thing takes. Murder is a simple matter of metamorphosis. It disorganizes matter, as Sade airily declares in *Juliette*, ruptures a few molecules, then returns them to 'nature's crucible'.

A priest in *Juliette* pulls back his cassock to show off an erection. 'Behold', he tells the gaping heroine, 'the resurrection of the flesh!' In *Philosophy in the Boudoir*, an inflammatory symposium written in 1795, the characters debate theology during recuperative pauses between their sexual bouts. The Chevalier accepts that people need an object of worship, but wishes they would accept noble pagan deities like Jupiter or Hercules, rather than the insecure and dishonest Christian God who 'created the world to glorify himself' and cannot forgive his creatures for a corruption he bred into them. When Eugénie proposes building a monument to the rational intelligence, the Chevalier nominates his own upright, statuesque prick. Eugénie might have retaliated by offering her bare breasts as a revolutionary symbol. Liberty exposes her chest in Delacroix's painting of the barricades; Boizot depicted the republic as a woman with a priapic crowing rooster on her head and two bare breasts, ready to nurture thirsty libertarians. A truly ecumenical deity is unveiled in *Juliette* when Volmar strips for a romp in the convent dormitory. She is a hermaphrodite, and like the figure of Nature in Spenser's *Faerie Queene* possesses both sets of sexual organs. Dolmancé, one of the boudoir philosophers, says that nature is no hypocrite, and would not have incited desires if she had not intended us to satisfy them. When Justine protests that the unbridling of passion is bestial, the monk who is her instructor in perversity replies that nature, having created the beasts, surely cannot think so ill of them. The abbess in *Juliette* co-opts the argument from design that was favoured by the deists: like Diderot's geometricians she illustrates the snug fit of complementary sexual organs, and eroticizes all available orifices. Only the ear is debarred, because its shape is unsuitable. No special favours are granted to the aperture set apart for breeding. As a seducer tells Justine, nature merely tolerates propagation; its real imperative is pleasure, which is why it made us so polymorphously adaptable.

Genesis and its theological mysteries could now be resolved by studying gestation, or by ogling the genitalia. In their dialogue, Diderot and d'Alembert worry about the conundrum of the hen and the egg, because they are keen to establish which came first. A coprophage in *Justine* does away with such academic quibbles, and organizes a ritual that acts out the circularity of birth and death, ejaculation and excretion. Begging the hen to lay an egg, he makes Justine deposit a turd in his mouth, and hungrily swallows it. The materialism of the *Encyclopédie* merely irritated the clergy;

Sade confronted religion more directly by blaspheming. In *Justine*, communicants at a black mass in a ribald monastery rematerialize the symbolic body and blood of Christ. They use a girl's navel as their chalice, and lap the wine from it. The priest then takes the consecrated wafer, shoves it into Justine's anus, and rams it home with his penis. The surrealists remembered such devilish japes and conscientiously copied them. In 1928 André Thirion and Jean Caupenne invaded an empty church, urinated in the font, filled the collection box with pebbles, then purloined the crucifix from the altar and mailed it to Louis Aragon, who attached it to the chain that operated the flush in his lavatory. A water closet may not be able to remit sins, but it washes us clean in its own way.

*Illustration from the Marquis de Sade's* Aline et Vaucour, *1795*

Sade possessed the systematizing mind prized by the eighteenth century: the roués who set up the school of libertinism in *The 120 Days of Sodom* tabulate its curriculum by making numerical lists of all the prescribed abominations. Their obscenities are technical experiments, boosting the body's capacities with gadgets and gimcrack contraptions. Pornography for Sade was primarily a thought-game (even though he often practised what he preached). Hence the thirty-seventh of the 150 criminal passions, summarized by a bawd during the revels at Sodom: 'A man fucks a cow. The cow conceives and gives birth to a monster. The man then fucks the monster'.

Such outrages are hardly practical, let alone pleasurable. The thrill lies in having dreamed them up. Sex, rescued from biological utility, has become a mode of aesthetic play. But Sade's fanatical fantasy goes beyond hedonism. In the name of liberty, his debauchees transport the captives who are their laboratory animals to a cliff-hanging castle in the Black Forest. This barricaded citadel, inaccessible to the law, is their latter-day Sodom. Sade imitates the despotic God he derides: the small, self-contained world he creates is a prison.

*Mozart's celebrated Symphony*

"THE JUPITER,"

*newly adapted for the* Piano Forte, *with accompaniments*

——— *for a* ———

Flute, Violin and Violoncello,

*by*

Muzio Clementi

Nº 6.

Ent. Sta. Hall

Price 8ª

London. Published by Clementi & Compy 26 Cheapside

# 14

# JEHOVAH, JUPITER, FU AND BRAHMA

Churches of all persuasions link worship with music, which almost deserves to be numbered among the beatitudes. Sir Thomas Browne claimed in 1642 that the pacifying melodies we hear on earth are an echo of a harmony that 'sounds intellectually in the ears of God'. In Handel's oratorio *Saul*, the High Priest wishes away discord in an orchestral recitative that mixes Genesis and Pythagoras. Hazy strings suggest the motionless suspension of the 'almighty Maker', who rebukes Chaos by voicing 'th'eternal word'; at that, lolloping horns incite nature to grow, and 'a fair harmonious world' hovers in the air. After this recited sermon, David the professional lyricist delivers an aria whose lulling repetitions are meant to soothe the maddened Saul's distemper. He then gives a therapeutic performance on his harp (which in 1739 was actually a carillon, played with keys like a harpsichord, though its sound was said to be crystalline and bell-like). But Saul rages on, and even hurls his javelin at the singer. The harmonizing influence fails, perhaps because it no longer derives directly from God. The Israelites in Handel's *Samson* recoil from the revelry of their Philistine foes. 'What noise of joy was that?' asks Samson's father. 'It tore the sky.' Soon the sky capsizes, when Samson pulls down the temple.

In the eighteenth century, music – formerly charged with helping to evoke divinity and enforce doctrine – itself became a medium of revelation. In Mozart's *Die Zauberflöte*, Tamino's flute and Papageno's glockenspiel subdue their enemies and make the beasts that menace them dance inanely. The charm now required no religious warrantry, and music's virtues could be civic not spiritual. The French revolutionaries, having dethroned God, staged festivals to cement the new society and recruit patriots for the army, and they relied on music to mobilize the citizenry. In 1794 Robespierre organized a celebration in honour of the Supreme Being, during which thousands of voices joined in a hymn composed by François-Joseph Gossec. It addressed the 'Père de l'universe, suprême intelligence', though it held out no hope that he would ever manifest himself to his worshippers. His temple, according to the text by Théodore Des-orgues, was built on words and melodies; he filled all possible worlds without occupying them, since he had no existence in space – which made him, in effect, a synonym for music. Music ushered romantic artists into a man-made heaven, without insisting on death as a condition for entry. In 1837 the poet Heinrich Heine called it miraculous, a 'nebulous mediator' that hovered between spirit and matter. Berlioz, listening to the music that depicts the Elysian Fields in Gluck's *Orphée et Eurydice*, praised the flute for so precisely conveying the wistful pallor of this classical eternity. Benjamin Franklin invented a glass harmonica, played by rubbing tubes filled with liquid. He woke his wife to surprise her with a performance; when she heard the instrument's faint eerie high-pitched wail, she thought she was listening to the angels. But heaven was not necessarily the source, since devils also knew how to sing. Don Giovanni, relaxing in hell in Shaw's *Man and Superman*, recommends music as 'the brandy of the damned'.

Mozart's Giovanni personifies the energy and vital ardour of music. For romantic listeners, this meant that he was bound to challenge a chaste, haughty religion. In 1813 E. T. A. Hoffmann wrote a story about a perform-ance of *Don Giovanni* which presents the libertine as the avowed enemy of God. Sitting in a private box at a provincial theatre, Hoffmann's narrator interprets Mozart's erotic comedy as a metaphysical fable about the 'conflict between divine and demoniac powers' that rages within all living things. Giovanni hungers for infinity, and expresses that universal ambition by compiling a list of sexual conquests. He has a higher purpose than satisfying his desire: seduction and betrayal offer him the chance to outrage morality. He considers 'the unknown Being who guides our destiny' to be a malicious monster, amused by human unhappiness. In slandering God, Giovanni usurps his role, and laughs at the misery of the women he discards. His destructiveness – as Hoffmann's narrator reflects, aghast but awed – raises him 'above our narrow life, above Nature, above the Creator!' Between the acts, the narrator is visited by the soprano cast as Donna Anna, the aristocrat who hunts down Giovanni after he ravishes her and kills her father. She flatters the narrator by mistaking him for Mozart, and says 'I am your melodies'. During the night he awakens to smell her perfume, and hears her singing her second aria, a bereft and distracted lament which may be the admission of her sinful love for Giovanni; her distant, bodiless voice is accompanied by 'the harmonica of an aerial orchestra'. Next morning he learns that the singer died at just that instant, and realizes that he overheard her distraught confession. She too, like Giovanni, represents music. Hence the guilt that brings on her nervous fits and causes her death: the art she practises liberates fantasy, blurring or suppressing words so that we cannot tell whether the jittery coloratura of that aria is prompted by offended idealism or by a remorse that maddens her. Giovanni openly scorns the divine father; Anna escapes from the moral control of her own father by secretly surrendering to Giovanni. She believes that her unlawful desire is to blame for the Commendatore's death, and also – since she hypocritically leads the vendetta against him – for Giovanni's death. Her only means of expiation is to die, singing to transform her pain into pleasure. Mozart did not kill Anna, so the soprano passes judgment on herself and begs pardon for music's perverse reveries.

Hoffmann adopted one of Mozart's names as his own: born Ernst Theodor Wilhelm Hoffmann, he replaced the Wilhelm with Amadeus, in homage to the secular saint whom he thought of as his patron. But God's love for Mozart was apparently unrequited; romantic music – as Hoffmann suggested in his interpretation of Anna's plight – catered to the body rather than serving as a devotional aid. After a sacred concert in Lyon, Berlioz wondered whether the good Lord didn't get tired of 'being worshipped ... by Gabriel and his celestial choral society'. His own knees were weary after too much genuflecting; he felt the need to relieve them by going for a stroll in the fields, where he would breathe fresh air, smell flowers and 'revel in creation without meditating on the Creator'. He even thought that he might try out a verse of a scandalous ditty by the political satirist Eugène de Pradel, entitled 'L'Enfer, ou chanson diabolique'. Camille Saint-Saëns, who called music 'the original Logos', served for twenty years as organist at the Madeleine in Paris. But Saint-Saëns was an atheist, who cheerfully parodied the church's retributive plainchant 'Dies Irae' when the xylophone rattles its bones in his *Danse macabre*. He thought that science had rendered God obsolete and reduced the Bible to a store of primitive legends. In his opera *Samson et Dalila*, the Hebrew leader is a besotted sensualist, and the temptress suborned by the Philistines boasts that love is more powerful than the austere deity Samson worships. When Saint-Saëns visited Madrid in 1896, he composed a religious march to be performed for the Spanish queen at a church concert. She politely thanked him for the piece, then asked to hear Dalila's aria of sexual submission. Saint-Saëns, taken by surprise, had to improvise it on the organ; he noticed that the queen's eyes were upturned in ecstasy – mystical or perhaps carnal? In 1879 Saint-Saëns had set to music a poem by Victor Hugo, in which the harp and the lyre disagree about their respective merits. He made it a debate between the severe Gothic monody of the organ (which was St Cecilia's instrument) and the romantic blandishments of the orchestra. The lyre, insolently pagan, claims that Olympus was born from Parnassus, so the poets created the gods.

In 1876 Nietzsche took up a question which preoccupied Wagner, and asked why music had become such 'a feature of modern life'. His answer was that music atoned for the failure of language, and gave inarticulate humans a means of expressing emotion. But there was another reason: God, drifting away, left music behind, and gradually the art recovered its spiritual vocation. The divided violins in the prelude to Wagner's *Lohengrin* caused Baudelaire's head to swim deliriously; music was to him the medium of sublimation, 'aspiring to mount higher'. During rehearsals for *Parsifal* in 1882 at Bayreuth, when the woodwinds and a muffled drum murmured their elegy for a swan carelessly shot by the hero, Wagner told the players that their instruments must make a sound 'like an invisible soul'. Decades after God had been given up for dead, the Protestant theologian Karl Barth tried to gain him an extra lease of life. He acknowledged God's remoteness, and likened our quest for him to the view down into a crater. Despite that void, Barth felt that God's glory was made manifest through the earthly mission of Christ, and also through the filtered-down benison of music. In 1956 he described his plans for his first day in heaven, if – as he humbly added – he ever got there. He might have been expected to seek out the fathers of the church, his learned predecessors; instead he said that he would first try to make the acquaintance of Mozart. Barth's fondness for a Catholic who was also a Freemason needed explaining. He was sure, he said, that when the angels praised God, they played Bach to him. But when they were relaxing and enjoying themselves, they very likely played Mozart – and Barth surmised that 'then too our dear Lord listens with special pleasure'. Such pleasure may be improper: would the angels have performed excerpts from Mozart's comic operas, with their playful sexual escapades? Perhaps God should have confined himself to Bach. Yet such an exclusive partiality raises other problems. The philosopher E. M. Cioran, the son of a Romanian Orthodox priest, argued in 1952 that Bach's settings of Gospel texts in the *St Matthew Passion* and the *St John Passion* were not so much an accessory to faith as a substitute for it. Without Bach, theology would be deprived of its purpose, and the creation would crumble to a mere fiction. 'If there is anyone who owes everything to Bach,' Cioran said, 'it is God'.

At least Bach was a dutiful employee of the church, engaged in Leipzig as a cantor who supplied music for the holy days of the liturgical calendar. Even if the diabolism of Hoffmann is discounted, it is hard to be sure about Mozart's religious allegiance. Tamino in *Die Zauberflöte* pauses before three temples that house no god; they are dedicated instead, as the legends above the porticos proclaim, to concepts that deify the man who possesses them – Wisdom, Reason, Nature. In Mozart's *Kleine deutsche Kantate* – a sparse, brief sermon for tenor and keyboard, composed during the last months of his life in 1791 – he addressed 'des unermesslichen Weltalls Schöpfer', the creator of the boundless world. After the tenor surveys the extent of

the universe, he decides that a creator who was active on so many continents must have a variety of names, and leaves it to the individual to choose
between them: 'Jehova nennt ihn, oder Gott,/ nennt Fu ihn, oder Brama'.
To call him Jehovah evokes the quaking piety of the Old Testament. God
is a looser term, referring to a presumably ecumenical creator. Further
afield, other cultures are permitted their own, equally earnest, notions. The
Chinese have Confucius (whom they call K'ung Fu-Tzu) as God's inter-
preter; the Hindus revere Brahma. Such relativism often served as a cover
for atheism, allowing Christianity to be attacked obliquely. In *The Indiscreet
Jewels*, Diderot laughs at the theological prudery of the Brahmins. For them,
speech is the gift of Brahma; it is blasphemous – as they rail in their mosque
– if another organ gives voice, so the vocal pudenda of Diderot's tale imply
that 'Brahma does not exist'. The dying man in Sade's 1782 dialogue gives
leisurely consideration to the same range of exotic religious options, as if he
were shopping for a faith. What if he were a believer, or wanted to be one?
How would he choose, he asks, between Confucius and Brahma? Or should
he bow down 'before the great snake of the Africans, or join the Peruvians
in their adoration of the sun'?

Mozart's tenor, less intolerant, assumes that those disparate deities
have a common denominator. We must all recognize the creation, even if we
disagree about the creator or dispute his existence. The cantata's little sermon
disparages 'Sektiererei', a sectarian squabbling which blinds us to our common
humanity; its unifying appeal is to what the bird-man Papageno calls a
'Naturmensch' – a being born from nature and therefore naturally peaceable. Franz Heinrich Ziegenhagen, the merchant who commissioned the
*Kleine deutsche Kantate* and provided its text, wanted it to be performed at
meetings of his Colony of the Friends of Nature. It combines pantheism
with a mildly revolutionary fervour, and ends by exhorting the fraternal
band to transform the desert – which is the arid, chafing battleground of
society – into a new Eden, a kindly utopia.

Ziegenhagen, like Mozart, belonged to a masonic lodge; the Freemasonry to which both subscribed took faith for granted – the earliest
masonic *Constitutions* of 1723 insist that a mason could never be 'a stupid
Atheist, nor an irreligious Libertine' – but allowed no cult a monopoly of
truth. Masonry was a based on a symbolic fiction. It traced its origins to the
medieval fraternity of workers who used mallets or chisels, and it made use
of these tools in its rites; even though none of its well-connected intellectual adherents were builders, they paid homage to a professional sponsor,
the architect of the universe. In devising their observances – the baleful
knocking on doors that open into enlightenment (heard in the overture to
*Die Zauberflöte*), the blindfolded initiations – they demonstrated that religion was a social invention, a solemn game. Masonic rhetoric emphasized

communal adhesion and moral improvement, which is why a song performed at Mozart's lodge was adopted in 1947 as Austria's national anthem.
Oaths enjoined secrecy, as the masons claimed to guard the mystery of
cosmic origins. But their secular, sceptical mentality made them critical
of the established church, and they were condemned in 1738 by Pope
Clement XII and in 1751 by Pope Benedict IV, while in Vienna in 1791
they were accused of importing seditious egalitarian ideas from revolutionary France.

Freemasonry helped to rationalize religion. Pierre, the truth-seeking
hero of Tolstoy's *War and Peace*, is inducted into the Petersburg brotherhood
in 1808. He has been reading Thomas à Kempis, and pines for a state of
harmony and altruism; the Freemasons show him how he might attain this
without imitating Christ. He is told that the order preserves a sacrosanct
mystery, 'on which perhaps the fate of mankind depends'. The Rosicrucian
branch of Freemasonry recomposed the Trinity using chemicals, and
Pierre notes down the recipe in his diary: sulphur combined with salt
attracts mercury, which is the 'spiritual essence', just as Christ in alliance
with the Holy Spirit brings us to God. But he regards these concoctions as
mumbo-jumbo, and instead chooses to subsidize a poorhouse set up by
the lodge. As a novelist, Tolstoy inevitably sympathized with such practical
concerns, not with the order's 'holy science'. Hence Pierre's wry detachment during his initiation: he can't help smiling at the unfunctional leather
aprons and clunky hieroglyphs, and his blindfold, tied too tight, catches
his hair and hurts him. He is shown a Bible open at the declaration 'In
the beginning was the Word'. Beside it is a human skull with all its teeth,
and a coffin containing some random bones. This is how nature breaks
down the body and prepares it to assume new life; he can hardly be afraid
of a process that is so logical. Music – which, being wordless, broke no
confidential vows – also followed the stages of the initiatic journey and
reported on the dissolution of matter into spirit. Mozart knew how to
orchestrate the after-life: he likened the voice of Neptune in *Idomeneo* to the
ghost of Hamlet's father, and when the statue speaks in *Don Giovanni*,
trombones sound from beyond the grave. In 1785 he composed the
*Maurerische Trauermusik* to mourn two aristocratic members of his lodge.
Oboes register physical distress; after these spasms of pain, the strings
advance into unknown terrain, tripped up by rhythmic anomalies and
alarmed by an intermittent summons from the basset horns. But fear is
gradually allayed. The movement forward overcomes its faltering uncertainty, and assumes a steadier pace. A final, calming modulation signifies
completion, or arrival – but where?

When Tamino is initiated into the masonic order, Sarastro's followers
doubt that he will be able to withstand the trials. He is a prince, they point

Title page of
Mozart's *Die
Maurerfreude,*
1785

out, assuming that aristocrats are weak, pampered creatures. Sarastro adds
that Tamino's true rank is higher: he is a man. Sarastro, whose name is a
garbled version of Zoroaster, belongs in the eclectic pantheon of the
*Kleine deutsche Kantate.* Other religions have always been
anxious to co-opt the Persian prophet, attracted by his
reputation as a reformer. The Greeks claimed that he was
the tutor of Pythagoras; Raphael included him in *The
School of Athens*, and gave him an astronomical sphere
to hold; Christianity saw him as the equivalent of
Ezekiel or Nimrod. Zoroaster worshipped fire as a
symbol of Ormuzd, the source of goodness and the
creator of man. The eighteenth century, which
equated holiness with enlightenment, therefore
enlisted him in its own battle against darkness.
Rameau's 1749 opera *Zoroastre* has a text by Louis
de Cahusac, the Master of a masonic lodge. The
high-minded priest Zoroastre routs the sorcerer
Ahriman, the enemy of Ormuzd. He sings a hymn
to warming, fertilizing light, which quickens
earth into the semblance of heaven; as woodwinds chirp, he entices nature to join in a
mellifluous concert. Mozart describes the

Costume design
for Sarastro
from the 1816
production of
*Die Zauberflöte*
in Berlin

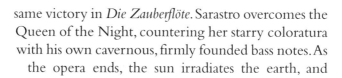

same victory in *Die Zauberflöte*. Sarastro overcomes the Queen of the Night, countering her starry coloratura with his own cavernous, firmly founded bass notes. As the opera ends, the sun irradiates the earth, and Sarastro praises its power to expunge iniquity. Romanticism found Zoroaster congenial: in *The Excursion*, Wordsworth fondly describes the rites of his magi, who ascended mountains and made sacrifices to the sky, which was to them 'a sensitive existence and a God'. Nietzsche, calling his own immoralist Zarathustra, supplied Zoroaster with a new credo. Instead of standing up for good against evil, he now abolished the antithesis between the two principles and freed men from their enslavement to God.

After Mozart's death, another name was added to the list of the deity's aliases tabled in the *Kleine deutsche Kantate*. Early in the nineteenth century, an admirer in London – possibly Johann Peter Salomon, the impresario who was Haydn's patron – gave the nickname *Jupiter* to Mozart's last symphony. The title referred to the imperious nobility of its sound and the amplitude of its structure; it also conferred a divine status on Mozart (who could hardly be likened to Jehovah). The symphony's contrapuntal last movement uses a motif from Gregorian chant, but the purpose is not liturgical. Instead the music is Mozart's self-celebration, exhibiting his intellectual aplomb and his surging energy. The polyphony babbles as democratically as the characters in the finales of his comic operas: this god permits all his creatures to use the voices with which he has endowed them, even if they are amiably disputing or talking over one another, as the four simultaneous themes in the fourth movement do. Soon enough, the Olympian Mozart inherited the allure of the sun-worshipping Sarastro. Delacroix, writing in his journal in 1853, likened him to Apollo, the charioteer of the sun, who stood at his zenith in the sky and dispensed radiance everywhere. Alternatively, Bernard Shaw said that if you loved Mozart's music you qualified as 'a true Brahmin'. That, of course, made Mozart himself into Brahma.

In the same way, Haydn in *Die Schöpfung* seemed to have taken over from the God whose creation he was extolling. One story about the origins of the oratorio alleges that the violinist Barthélemon, asked by Haydn to suggest a subject, handed him the Bible and said 'Take that, and begin at the beginning'. *Die Schöpfung* therefore starts with an orchestral tour of a jarringly dissonant, stumblingly syncopated Chaos. After fifty-nine bars of

Costume design for the Queen of the Night from the 1816 production of *Die Zauberflöte* in Berlin

inconsequential C minor, God intervenes to create light. A bright, triumphant chord of C major shimmers as if from below the horizon, then blazes like a florid sunrise. Haydn kept this page of the score a secret until rehearsals began in Vienna in 1798, carefully protecting the surprise. When the light shone for the first time, the startled listeners, according to the Swedish diplomat Silverstolpe, thought that its rays emanated 'from the composer's burning eyes'. As a good Catholic, Haydn was quick to assign the credit elsewhere. He said that while composing, whenever his inspiration faltered, he had fallen to his knees and taken out his rosary. At a performance conducted by Salieri in 1808, he reached up tremulously towards heaven when the advent of light occurred. His friend Carpani supposed that he was praying to 'the Father of Harmony'. But the occasion was planned as an apotheosis for Haydn himself on his seventy-sixth birthday; enthroned in an armchair, he was borne aloft into the hall to the accompaniment of trumpet fanfares. In the essay on Haydn he wrote in 1814, Stendhal admired the fugue in which the archangels praise the creator. Here, he said, 'Haydn's genius shines forth … in all its glory'. Did it perhaps eclipse the glory of God?

Die Schöpfung descends from Paradise Lost, though a little indirectly. Stendhal fancied that Milton had presented Handel with the text for an oratorio, to be called The Creation of the World; inconveniently, Milton died eleven years before Handel was born. The actual adaptation of Paradise Lost – concentrating on Raphael's account of the first week, and omitting altogether the loss of paradise – was made by Thomas Linley. Salomon acquired it and gave it to Haydn, whose patron Gottfried von Swieten translated it into German. Edited and ameliorated, Milton's tragic epic emerged as a pastoral comedy, with Adam and Eve tending flocks of lyrical birds and harmless herds of gambolling beasts. Created together as husband and wife, the human pair sing only in duets; they never drift apart into the separateness that Satan exploits in Milton's poem. Indeed Satan is nowhere mentioned in Die Schöpfung (although Uriel refers dismissively to the overthrow of hellish spirits, automatically cast into the depths when God creates light). At the end of the oratorio, the fall of man remains in the future, and perhaps need not happen at all: Uriel's concluding recitative says that Adam and Eve might have been happy forever, if only they had not given in to conceit. Milton's world is irreparably damaged by evil, but creation in Die Schöpfung remains blithe and unblemished. Symphony means consonance, and no dissenting voice on earth or in heaven questions the divine dispensation. God – Milton's crabby and vengeful despot – keeps his distance. The archangels represent him, and they do their work of justification by showing off the beauty of the world: its balmy weather, its bounding livestock. Here is Spinoza's plenum, companionably overcrowded. Haydn's Raphael describes

the air thick with fowl, the water swollen by the load of fish it carries. Earth brassily groans as the weighty army of animals trundles across it. But there is room for them all, and the ground does not cave in. *Die Schöpfung* sets to music the eighteenth century's argument from design.

Although Haydn reduces the creator to a cipher, he celebrates man's arrival in the world with a flourish of courtly pomp. Uriel hails Adam as 'der König der Natur', with a thumping call to attention from the drums as the orchestra establishes a solemn ceremonial pace and arranges a quick coronation. Milton, who belonged to the party of the regicides in the civil war, could never have used this image, which would have signalled conservative regret; in *Die Schöpfung* it asserts human supremacy rather than defending monarchy. Sarastro says that a man outranks a prince, and the king of nature here trumps the absent king of kings. Haydn too was a Freemason, and Catholic churches were ordered not to perform his infidel oratorio. In 1801 he indignantly replied to this criticism, arguing that the story of creation – which he called 'the most sublime and awe-inspiring image for man' – was more aptly honoured by music than by a droning sermon. In the same year,

Performance of *Die Schöpfung* in the festival hall of Vienna's Old University on 27 March 1808, in honour of the composer

he made his impenitence clear by quoting *Die Schöpfung* in a Mass performed at the Esterházy palace in Eisenstadt. The cheeky allusion comes in the 'Gloria' of the *Schöpfungsmesse*, as the chorus beseeches Christ to take away the sins of the world. Here Haydn inserts a jaunty tune from the bedtime duet of Adam and Eve in the oratorio; a hunting horn conveys the urgency of their endearments. It is hardly appropriate for the expiatory plea of the Mass, and the cry of 'miserere nobis' that follows sounds more like a worldly-wise sigh than a desperate appeal for grace. The quotation implied that Haydn, far from lamenting sin, refused to uphold Christianity's disapproving attitude towards intellectual freedom and sexual pleasure. The Empress protested, and before the *Schöpfungsmesse* could be performed at the imperial court he was required to remove the profanity.

These doctrinal evasions or infractions make way for Haydn's aesthetic theodicy. The creation's ultimate purpose, its 'grosse Werk' as the angels call it, is the creation of music – of this music, with its alternately boisterous and placid orchestra; its voices that extend from the exultant heights of the soprano Gabriel imitating the lark, dove and nightingale to the booming profundities of the bass Raphael, who describes the stealthy twistings of the grounded worm and the leviathan in the deep sea; and its overflowing delight when the chorus steals into the duet of Adam and Eve and invites us to share their happiness. Walt Whitman, who often attended outdoor concerts at Castle Garden in lower Manhattan, described the pantheistic wonder of such occasions in *Song of Myself*: 'A tenor large and fresh as the creation fills me,/ The orbic flex of his mouth is pouring and filling me full'. Haydn's tenor, cast as Uriel, dispenses the same joy. The Bible deifies the Logos, and presents language, which is the sign of rationality, as God's most ennobling gift to men. *Die Schöpfung* demonstrates that music too is a language. It may even be a higher one – less given to disputes and quibbles; as skilled at description as words are, but better able to transmit emotion.

Stendhal suggested that van Swieten dared Haydn to portray Chaos. It was to be a test of music's skills: could it illustrate a state we find inconceivable? D'Alembert, who published a treatise on music in 1752, believed that the art's responsibility was to make aural pictures of things that already existed. In his view, 'any music that does not paint is nothing else but noise'. Perhaps Haydn's Chaos is the noise that precedes the invention of music; but actually, as Stendhal pointed out, it contains all the necessary particles of music, adrift in limbo. Despite its false cadences and clashing tempi, Haydn's Chaos is a jumbled puzzle that can be pieced together without difficulty. Stendhal heard in it a 'foregathering of every fioratura known to music – trills, grace-notes, mordents, telescoped phrases, discords'. Chaos is full of words, which have not yet been tonally and metrically organized into a language. When light appears, music at once acquires a lucidity, elasticity and eloquence that are breath-taking. It is as if things are created by God in order to be musically recreated by Haydn. Why else should Raphael, summarizing the third day, describe the sea disgorging mountains? Haydn advanced the apocalypse because he wanted to make his orchestra billow and thunder. When the unbiblical storms on the second day abate, they leave behind rain showers and flaky snow. That last meteorological detail has no precedent in Genesis. The snow is included so that Haydn can orchestrate its soft sifting. Bad weather is not a punishment for sin but the excuse for a pastoral symphony.

For romantic artists, creation itself made music. The Aeolian harp, left outdoors so that breezes could tinkle its strings, needed no player; man's contribution lay only in hearing those harmonies and transcribing them. Shelley asks the lashing west wind to make him its lyre, and the licentious Byronic hero of Mary Shelley's novel *The Last Man*, published in 1826, says he is 'a stringed instrument with chords and stops', played on by his passions. Music derived from the percussiveness or vibrancy of what Ralph Waldo Emerson called 'sonorous bodies', which did not have to be human. Coleridge in his poem 'Dejection' describes a wintry gale as a 'mad lutanist'. Recalling the origins of English poetry in *Biographia Literaria*, he even defines language as a natural growth, not a human construction: 'a wilderness of vocal reeds'. In 1835 in his survey of American scenery, the painter Thomas Cole identified waterfalls as 'the voice of the landscape', uttering a throaty roar which 'rocks and mountains re-echo in rich unison'. The poet Heinrich Heine climbed the Brocken during a walking tour of the Harz Mountains in 1824, and found himself among a congregation reverently watching a fiery sunset. Though they were standing on a mountain top, he seemed to hear 'Palestrina's immortal chorale' surging from an imaginary organ. More comically but also more ghoulishly, Berlioz remarked during a storm in 1848 that the wind made his chimney howl like a distended organ pipe. The sound was an ululation, a lament – a reminder that 'whole worlds are born and die just like us; that all is nothing'.

But if nature was the creator, it could afford to dispense with human artists. There is a sad epilogue to *Die Schöpfung* in *The Last Man*. Mary Shelley's story reverses Genesis: a plague in the year 2100 kills off the human race, sparing only the chronicler who writes the book (though he too, alone and bereft, hopes soon to die of natural causes). During a final journey around the vacated earth, he passes through Switzerland, and near Geneva hears music coming from a village church. In the organ loft he finds an old man and his young, sickly daughter, who is seated at the keyboard. She is playing 'Haydn's "New-Created World"' – the chorus following Uriel's announcement that the rebel angels have been routed. But no choir sings, because the villagers are dead; the young woman dies later that day. She has chosen the excerpt from 'the hymn written to celebrate the creation of the adorned earth' because she knows that the earth will soon be her tomb, and the organ performs it with what Mary Shelley cleverly calls an 'inorganic' voice. Although the human race is moribund, nature remains as fresh and green 'as at creation's day', so it still deserves Haydn's tribute. Music, says the narrator, is 'the language of the immortals, disclosed to us as testimony of their existence'. Henceforth only immortals will be able to hear it. But without abject humanity to testify to their existence, will they too wither away?

Despite his veneration for Haydn, Stendhal was at first perplexed by Chaos, and said that he only came to appreciate the prelude to *Die Schöpfung* when it was inserted into a ballet about Prometheus which he saw in Milan. Then, at least, a trio of delightful ballerinas gave him something to look at; he interpreted their heavenly grace as a sign that the soul was awakening to beauty, straining towards the nascence of light. He had confused Haydn's oratorio with Beethoven's score for Salvatore Viganò's ballet *Die Geschöpfe des Prometheus*, but the mistake was happy, even inspired. Viganò came to Vienna in 1799, and immediately made plans for a theatrical work that would, he hoped, duplicate the success of *Die Schöpfung*. Appropriately enough, he chose as his subject the alternative story of creation, Hellenic not Hebraic: his ballet, first performed in 1801, was about Prometheus and the clay creatures he invents and sparks into life with fire stolen from Zeus, who pummels the rebellious Titan with thunder bolts. Beethoven portrayed the irate storm in a section of his score known as 'La Tempesta', which begins with a gathering of audibly baleful clouds and lashes out in bursts of searing electricity; it was this that Stendhal conflated with Haydn's musical passage through Chaos.

Stendhal complained that Chaos refused to resolve its discords, which meant that it could not please the ear. Beethoven, only three years after hearing Haydn's oratorio, set to music a very different state of nature. The elements escape from the classical equilibrium praised by Haydn's Adam, and rage unappeased. Fire licks and leaps in Beethoven's overture, and his storm infuriates the air. Prometheus is the hero who rides the whirlwind; the theme that celebrates his triumph at the end of the ballet became a motto for Beethoven, who used it again in the finale of the *Eroica* Symphony. He also recalled the creative role of Prometheus in his oratorio *Christus am Ölberge*, composed in 1803. Here Christ on the Mount of Olives, preparing for his sacrifice, sympathizes with the race of men, 'formed from dust' like the creatures of Prometheus, and says that they cannot be expected to bear the burden of God's ire alone. He accepts that inevitability of his fate, predestined – as he puts it – even before the world arose from Chaos at God's command; and, as he recalls these beginnings,

Beethoven's orchestra inserts a brief but arresting reprise of Haydn's introduction to *Die Schöpfung*, with a steady striding advance towards the majestic major chord that completes creation.

Creation in *Die Schöpfung* is completed by the moral education of Adam and Eve. They have been created in order to act as the stewards of creation; they comprehend its workings – Adam studies elemental changes and admires their logic – and when they sing its praises they confirm man's attunement to nature. In *Die Geschöpfe des Prometheus*, creation has a different outcome: the creatures undergo an aesthetic education. Prometheus takes them to Parnassus, where the muses teach them the accomplishments that make man a truly creative being. Euterpe, the muse of lyricism, passes on her gift to the accompaniment of the harp and flute, and Terpischore helps them to learn their first dance steps. The class is supervised by Apollo, whose instrument is the grave, glowing cello.

There is more to the ballet than technical training. Viganò's scenario acknowledges the tragic rift in creation, which *Die Schöpfung* – by eliminating Satan and postponing the fall of man – pointedly excludes. Among the muses is Melpomene, the patron of tragedy, who in a mimed orchestral recitative reveals to the creatures that they are destined to die. Stabbing downbeats and a reedy lament register the bad news, which Melpomene is reluctant to deliver. She reproaches Prometheus, asking the same question that Christ more tactfully puts to God in *Paradise Lost*: why bother creating something if it will inevitably be destroyed? Angered by the contradiction, she gashes Prometheus with a knife. Although he is revived by Pan, the incident anticipates Nietzsche's rewriting of Greek myth, which describes the spirit of music giving birth to tragedy. Man's mortality estranges him from a creation in which nature (represented in the ballet by Pan) dies only to regenerate itself next spring. But perhaps that affliction gives our species a unique philosophical valour: we know we will die, and tragedy – here the highest of the arts, because Melpomene is the last muse to appear – is the form in which we assess the value of an existence that is precious because so limited. Nietzsche's alliance between tragedy and music makes art itself collude in our fate, which perhaps explains why the muse in *Die Geschöpfe des Prometheus* is a murderer. Music is spirit, beckoning us from beyond the material world. Does it embolden us to enjoy our own destruction? Wagner's hero in *Der fliegende Holländer*, cursed by his inability to die, appeals to 'Ew'ge Vernichtung', eternal extinction; a cataclysm at once boils up in the orchestra pit. The ballet draws back from such speculations, and ends with solos in which the creatures show off their newly acquired artistry.

Creation, in Haydn's oratorio, instantly puts a stop to Chaos. But for romantic composers, creation derived from the turmoil of unformed thoughts and emotions inside the head; rather than terminating the chaotic unrest, they sought to prolong it. Hence the opening of Beethoven's Ninth Symphony. The muffled horns and the tremulous strings erase the notion of a precise, punctual beginning. Those sounds seem, like light, to be travelling towards us from a remote distance; they started long before our ears pick them up. The wavering tempo and dislocating key changes evoke Haydn's Chaos, but this music makes no promise to regulate conflicts. Opposed themes and incompatible keys quarrel throughout the first movement; the finale begins with the sound of a world crashing into ruin, after which rec-ollected wisps of the three previous movements circulate in the air and fail to solidify. The strings at last decide on the melody to which Friedrich Schiller's ode 'An die Freude' will be set, but this too falls apart into a random cacophony, and the clattering avalanche is heard again. Wagner called that rowdy discord a 'Schreckensfanfare', an outburst of terror; it is terrifying because it catches the elemental violence of nature, like the mael-strom when Loge's fire blazes up at the end of *Die Walküre*. Mahler inherited this ambition to write music that imagined the rending pangs of cosmic creation. During rehearsals for his Fifth Symphony in Cologne in 1904, he wondered how audiences would react to its hurtling scherzo, which for him evoked roaring seas, cresting waves and dancing stars: 'what faces will they pull at this chaos, perpetually giving birth to a new world, which is destroyed at the next moment?'

At least Mahler's 'Urweltsklängen' – the sounds of a world being born – are ribald, festive, incited by the horn calls that start up the scherzo's whirling waltz. Describing a performance of Beethoven's Ninth Symphony that he conducted in Dresden in 1846, Wagner suggested that the opening bars of the first movement, which fracture a common chord, present 'the world in the most terrible of lights'. By the end, however, the sym-phony asserts 'the purposely ordaining will of the creator'. The bass temporarily halts the din when he calls for friendlier sounds and rallies the chorus to sing Schiller's paean to joy. For Wagner, the entry of the voice par-aphrased God's utterance in Genesis or the jubilant choral outcry that introduces the sunburst in *Die Schöpfung*: 'with these words,' he declared, 'Light breaks in on Chaos'. But Beethoven's singer is no deity, and he can only prevail by diplomatic cajoling and cheery conviviality. Our safety lies in solidarity; creation here is a social contract, enforced by music and by a celebratory toast – for Schiller's poem is a drinking song, not a humanitar-ian anthem, and it recommends wine because when we drink we are attached to nature's breast, imbibing earthy contentment as if we were kissing the succulent goddess. The religion to which the poem alludes is pagan: joy is the daughter of Elysium, a bright spark of divinity (like that which Prometheus stole from Zeus).

After the first rollicking choral salute and the tenor's tipsy, swaggering Turkish march, Beethoven slows down the race, quietens the riot, and asks the assembled human crowd two difficult questions:

> Ihr stürzt nieder, Millionen?
> Ahnest du den Schöpfer, Welt?

Do you fall to your knees in worship, you millions? World, do you know (or, more vaguely, sense) your creator? The first question is a critique of the genuflection and obeisance demanded by traditional religion. The millions may humbly bow, but the following lines direct them to raise their heads and seek the creator in the star-blazing heights. This is an admonition from the Enlightenment: on his desk, Beethoven kept a copy of Kant's dual commandment – 'The moral law within us, the starry heavens above us'. Man makes god; an idea that originates in the human conscience is then projected into the sky. The music turns hushed and liturgical, as the chorus repeats the questions and tells men where to look for the source of their being:

> Brüder, über'm Sternenzelt
> Muss ein lieber Vater wohnen.

Brothers, above the canopy of stars a loving father must dwell. It is human brotherhood that conjures up that loving father, whose existence remains no more than a hoped-for, longed-for possibility. The first word uttered by Florestan, crying out for help from the grim darkness of his dungeon in Beethoven's opera *Fidelio*, is 'Gott!' But his salvation depends on human fidelity, not divine clemency; he is rescued by his wife Leonore.

Wagner once enumerated the articles of his personal creed: 'I believe in God, Mozart and Beethoven'. The first name in this Trinity was the most questionable. Wagner disliked the dictatorial God of the Old Testament, though he did pay tribute to Christ, whose redemptive mission is taken over by the Grail knights Lohengrin and Parsifal. He was also intrigued by the nihilistic wisdom of the Buddha, the subject of his projected opera *Die Sieger*; when he played a theme from the work to an admirer in 1876, he said that he wanted it to sound like 'the proclamation of a new religion'. About the two deified composers he had no doubts. In 1840, scratching a living as a journalist in Paris, he wrote an account of an imaginary visit to Beethoven. Young R—, from whose journal the story is posthumously excerpted by a friend, sees Vienna as Mecca, and likens his trip there to a Muslim's pilgrimage to the Prophet's shrine. He throws himself at the master's feet, as obsequious as the millions in the Ninth Symphony: 'Holy Beethoven, forgive me!' He is granted a privileged, private revelation, as Beethoven describes the Ninth Symphony, just completed though as yet unperformed. Summarized by the composer, it is an evolutionary parable, following the creatures of Prometheus as they struggle to become human. Beethoven explains the disputatious instruments of the first movement as 'the primal organs of ... Nature', which convey urgent, instinctive feelings 'as they first issue forth from the chaos of the Creation'. This is a raucous, intemperate jungle, the memento of a time 'before there was any human heart to hear and feel'. When the bass declaims Schiller's poem, his 'God-like consciousness' promotes man to equality with his creator.

Antoine Bourdelle, bronze sculpture of Beethoven, *c.* 1905

Wagner allows Beethoven to admit that Schiller's ode has trouble expressing ideas to which no poem can do justice. Transcendence, however, came naturally to music, which is why the art so tantalized romantic writers, who felt that language hobbled them. The musicians on Keats's Grecian urn pipe 'ditties of no tone', which only the spirit can hear. Romantic poetry usually breaks off before it can gain entry to this musical heaven. Coleridge in 'Kubla Khan' says that he might have got there it if he had been able to revive within himself the 'symphony and song' of the Abyssinian maid playing on her dulcimer, seen and heard in a vision. (Patristic maps placed Eden in Abyssinia: when Wordsworth described Lake Como 'confined as in a depth/ Of Abyssinian privacy', he was hinting that paradise could be regained in Italy.) Once at least, prose completed the dizzy ascent. Balzac's *Séraphîta*, written between 1833 and 1835, is less a novel than a verbal oratorio; set in Norway as the first spring of the nineteenth century renews the earth – a millenarian resurgence, after the age of reason's hard, frigid winter – it describes a wise child of indeterminate gender who changes, under the enraptured gaze of an acolyte, from Seraphitus to Seraphita. She then floats into the firmament, where choiring angels welcome a new recruit to their ranks. During her ascent, heaven expands beyond all limits. This, as Schoenberg said in 1923, was the amplified space opened up by his dodecaphonic method, which broke through the restrictions of tonality. Schoenberg told his friend Kandinsky that he considered *Séraphîta* 'perhaps the most glorious work in existence'; he longed to compose a scenic version – first an 'oratorio that becomes visible and audible', later a film.

Before dying, Seraphita delivers to her chosen evangelist Wilfrid a long sermon on 'the sciences of matter and the sciences of spirit', during which she explains the significance of 'music, a celestial art'. She gently chides

Wilfrid, whose piety does God a disservice. 'When you call God the creator, you belittle him,' she says. It is absurd to imagine that he bothered to manufacture plants, animals, stars; instead he 'emitted principles' and left these to develop according to the laws he ordained. Men have their role to play in creating the creation, and they help to discharge it by composing music, which Seraphita calls 'an assemblage of sounds harmonized by number'. Breaking down her definition, she says that sound is air compressed, dilated or reverberating; she goes on to analyse air's components, which are nitrogen, carbon and oxygen. Those chemical elements are in turn nurtured by light, 'the great foster-mother of this globe', as it warms plants and provokes them to release the gases we breathe. Music therefore confers a voice on the ethereal constituents of the natural world. A pastor explains to Wilfrid that the angels who came to visit Swedenborg, sometimes whirling him off to other planets, shared in 'the secret of the reciprocal harmony of creations', and were attuned to 'the spirit of sounds' and 'the spirit of colours'. Our human music reaches up towards this elevated, astral knowledge. Such mystical correspondences were not overlooked by the science of acoustics. Newton mathematically correlated the notes of the octave and the diameters of the coloured rings that unfold along the spectrum; Hermann Helmholtz, in a study of tonal sensations published thirty years after *Séraphîta*, argued that the ear's capacity to sort out the melodic relationship of consecutive tones and the richer, subtler play of harmonies confirmed the orderly 'arrangement of the universe, governed by law and reason in all its parts'.

At the climax of Balzac's narrative, the melody intoned by the choiring sky shines out in a brazen, trumpeted glare of light. It announces the advent of an aesthetic heaven, a vision that strains all our senses and that can only be represented by bringing together all the arts. Baudelaire felt its presence in Wagner's music, and willed the pulsing notes to materialize as colours: blood-red to signify passion, then advancing through a series of gradations until they were as incandescent as a furnace, finally cooling and thinning into purged streaks on a white background. Darkness too could take on a palpable, suffocating presence that was infernal. When Mahler conducted Wagner's *Siegfried* at Covent Garden in 1892, Shaw thought he made the tubas low 'like Plutonian bullocks'. Composers dreamed of an instrument that would reproduce this chromatic palette, inflaming and aerating dull terrestrial reality. Early in the twentieth century, Alexander Scriabin added a colour keyboard or light organ to the orchestra for his symphonic fable *Prométhée: Le Poème du feu*. It infused the concert hall with a pyromaniac glow, its array of tones matching the flickery harmonies of the score. *Prométhée* derives from a six-note chord that for Scriabin encapsulated the formula for jangling chaos; it ends with a wordless choral shout to welcome man, who has been ignited by the divine fire. Chaos, registered by Scriabin's floodlights, is an indistinct grey soup. Creation is unclouded blue, its advent proclaimed in F sharp major.

When he died in 1915, Scriabin was making plans for a cosmological oratorio to be staged in a custom-built temple in the middle of a lake at the foot of the Himalayas. The temple was to have a dome; reflected in the water, it would expand into a perfect globe. Participants were to be enveloped in tinted fogs of incense and bombarded with light, which would seep into the walls of the temple and somehow cause it to dissolve. Bells were to dangle from the underbellies of clouds. Dancers would show how the deity enters the body and rouses it into life, while massed choirs, looking forward to a delirious apocalypse, sang about 'the great brilliance of the final outburst'. Scriabin estimated that the rite might take a week to complete. At the end, human beings could expect to be transformed into angels and rescued from the war-ravaged earth. The *Mysterium* remained incomplete. Awaiting redemption, we listen to music, which may be as close to a better world as we will ever come.

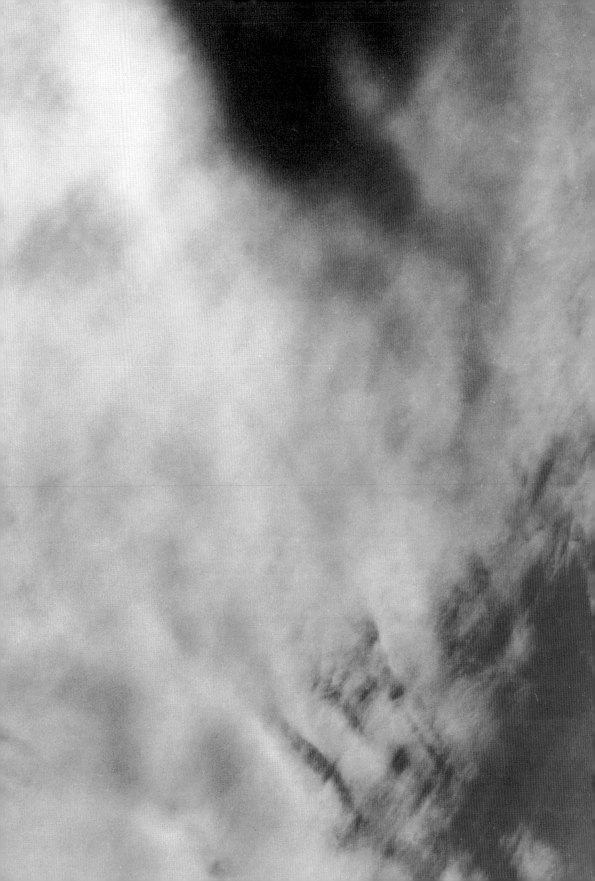

# 15

# SKY STORIES

Delacroix, grumbling in his journal in 1847, complained that the sky had been tugged down to earth. First Protestantism reduced God to a private possession, an inward idea, which meant that he no longer presided above the clouds or on the ceilings of churches. Then the French Revolution abolished God altogether, replacing the mysteries of religious faith with political abstractions – reason, justice, equality. The Revolution, as Coleridge's friend Robert Southey put it, sought to bring about 'the regeneration of the human race'. But it did so through political action not spiritual uplift, and its heaven turned out to be grossly earthy. Looking back, Delacroix concluded that the only happiness recognized by modern men was material: the accumulation of possessions, piled up here and now. In 1827 he portrayed that state of satiety, glutted and yet angrily discontented, in *The Death of Sardanapalus*. An oriental despot lolls on his deathbed, which has the heads of somnolent elephants as its supports. Wives, slaves and horses are hauled into his presence to be slaughtered; it gives him a morbid pleasure to know that his goods and chattels will predecease him.

After watching Delacroix prepare the colours on his palette, Baudelaire remarked that 'a good picture, which is a faithful representation of the dream that has begotten it, should be brought into being like a world'. But the dreams of Delacroix were usually fantasies of violence. Creation for him was more like a massacre, with lions goring the men who hunt them, bleeding Greek rebels cut down by Turks, and damned, drowned souls grasping at the boat on which Dante travels through the inferno. Although the ageing Delacroix regretted the nineteenth century's dismissal of God, Baudelaire understood that the painter himself was a god of a different kind – not the architectonic force of Genesis, who imposes order and designs a world, but a primitive deity with a taste for chaos. He likened Delacroix to Moloch, a Semitic ogre who fed on sacrificed children, or to the Mexican priests who gutted thousands of victims on their pyramidal altars to ensure that the sun kept shining. The colours he used were cataracts of blood. In *The Murder of the Bishop of Liège* Delacroix illustrated a scene from a novel by Walter Scott: a rebellious knight feasting with his rowdy vassals in a vaulted hall tells a henchman to cut the throat of the disapproving clergyman. The setting is the episcopal palace; the murderer perches on what the catalogue of the 1831 Salon called 'the papal throne'. The poet Théophile Gautier marvelled at the uproar that seemed to explode from the small, silent canvas. The painting, he said, 'shouts, clamours and blasphemes'. Can paint make a noise? And can it be blasphemous? Gautier's enthusiasm was justifiable enough. The drunkards lurch and tumble, while the struggling bishop throws out his arms in terror like a candidate for crucifixion. The candles on the long table and the torches high on the walls set fire to the darkness; the bishop's white surplice, like the table cloth, is asking to be discoloured, and it hardly matters whether the stain comes from blood or wine or pigment.

The mad whimsy of Walter Scott's ruffian appealed to Delacroix because he identified art with outrage, sacrilege. In an essay that treated murder as a fine art, Thomas de Quincey acclaimed Cain – 'the inventor of murder, and the father of the art' – as 'a man of first-rate genius': only a genius could have devised such an abomination. Cain meant to slight the God who preferred his brother Abel's sacrifice. Romantic artists also tested themselves against repressive authorities, and their actions, often gratu-itously destructive, imitated the lethal revelry of nature.

In Coleridge's dramatic fragment *The Night-Scene*, a character likens an infatuated lover to the god described by oriental sages,

> who floats upon a Lotus leaf,
> Dreams for a thousand ages, then awaking
> Creates a world, and smiling at the bubble
> Relapses into bliss.

The ephemeral bubble is hardly worth bursting. Byron in *Don Juan* reveres the sun as a creative force, and jokingly blames it for the sexual ferocity of his Spanish hero, which is

> all the fault of that indecent sun
> Who cannot leave alone our helpless clay,
> But will keep baking, broiling, burning on.

Isaiah's God is a potter, and Prometheus too moulded clay. Byron relieves them of their chores, allowing nature to shape and ripen us. When Juan surrenders his virginity to an older married woman, Byron surmises that his burning ardour must be 'the unforgiven/ Fire which Prometheus filch'd for us from heaven'. In Shelley's *Prometheus Unbound*, Panthea recalls the formation of the universe, when a crystalline sphere first moved to the sound of music. She hastens through a history of life on earth, admiring the way the 'blue globe' wraps itself in intermittent deluges to abolish unwanted creatures. As an example, she mentions the behemoths that once ruled continents now overgrown by weeds. These monarchical beasts existed until

> some God
> Whose throne was in a comet, passed and cried,
> 'Be not!'

That, for Shelley, was an authentic divine commandment, even though it negated God's instruction in Genesis. Creativity depends on an executive power; it makes light of random exterminations, because nothing that has been created, whether a world or a poem, will last forever. Panthea sentences to death her own lyrical effusion, which evaporates as she utters it. Those prehistoric animals are burned up by the comet. 'Like my words,' she says in conclusion, 'they were no more'.

Such gods, throned in the sky, swoop down like errant asteroids to destroy whatever displeases them. Perhaps the true creator is the artist who works on earth, making use of merely human powers. Schiller's tragedy *Don Carlos*, written in 1787, takes the brutal theocratic regime of Philip II's Spain as the setting for a debate between rival deities. The king's power is abetted by that of the church. But he is challenged by a Promethean rebel, a revolutionary for whom the recreation of the world is an artistic undertaking. The Marquis of Posa, taken into Philip's confidence, criticizes the way the king has ruthlessly suppressed dissent in Spain's Flemish colonies. As a politician, Posa knows how to profit from the chance of a private interview, and sees himself aesthetically moulding and manipulating circumstances: he is, he says, a sculptor whose hands can bring rough stone to life, and the insentient block he sets out to animate is the rigid king. He boldly tells Philip that he cannot pledge allegiance. Like the modern men of Delacroix, he serves an idea of liberation, and can truckle neither to heavenly nor to earthly masters:

> A free mind sees the laws and not their maker.
> 'Who needs a God?' it says – the world is all.

Taking an even more audacious risk, he addresses Philip as a competitor:

> Could you abide
> Another maker of your own creations?
> And should I be content to be the brush
> When I can be the artist? I think not.

The king, scandalized, asks if he is a Protestant. Posa again outwits him: he says that he believes in history and is consoled by its promise of progress. Rather than waiting for a heaven in the sky, he lives in a future state of freedom, 'among the citizens that are to come'.

With reckless intellectual bravura, Posa goes on to criticize Philip as a failed Prometheus. The king's creator trusted him to rule over men who revere him as a god – and yet Philip too remains a weak, faulty, afflicted human being. In Flanders, Posa thought that 'to be a father to a race like this/ Is to be god on earth'. Philip, however, has reduced the province to a boneyard. Posa accuses him of overlooking the ultimate Promethean gift, the spark that mobilizes man's limbs and quickens his brain:

> A single word of yours can suddenly
> Create the world anew. Give us the freedom
> To think.

The tyrant fails to understand the autonomy of nature, which – self-seeding, licensed to move and breed – is beyond control. Posa makes his political argument by using biological analogies. He points out that 'the creator makes dewdrops bear worms' and is happy for death to generate new life. Only the king of Christendom is terrified by freedom and change. A wise monarch would accept that the very idea of a solitary creator is refuted by nature's wanton profusion. That painful truth is pressed on the elderly, wintry Philip by his familial woes: he suspects that there is a guilty sexual liaison between his wife Elisabeth de Valois and his heir Don Carlos, her stepson. He is wrong about this, but they are both young and their mutual tenderness is a natural instinct, indifferent to political and religious decrees. When Posa is shot, Carlos taunts Philip as an aesthete who requires compliant subjects and approves of corpses because they will not answer back. 'This,' he says of Posa's body, 'is the artist's latest masterpiece!'

Philip calls in the Grand Inquisitor to sanction his revenge on Carlos. The Inquisitor wonders at his squeamishness, and argues that 'the God who rules on earth needs no compassion'. But Philip – tragic because he cannot forgive himself for possessing such power – says that

> You ask of the creation
> What only the creator can accomplish.

His qualms of conscience soon abate. Surprising Carlos with Elisabeth, he coolly hands him over to the Inquisitor to be tortured and probably executed. Here, with shocking abruptness, the play ends. Perhaps, by sacrificing his son, Philip regains his godhead. As the Inquisitor sees it, a similar decision made by the God of the New Testament redeemed an unfaithful world. But Philip's act suggests the behaviour of an ogre who is more ancient and savage than the Christian creator. In the classical myth, Saturn devours his own children. His cannibalism is explained if you remember that the Greeks called the same god Kronos: he is Father Time, for whom all beginnings lead necessarily to ends, who gives life and then takes it away. The biblical God had a moral justification for infanticide; Saturn's justification lay in the state of nature, which consumes us all. The scornful negligence with which Philip delivers Carlos to the Inquisitor is a different matter. Schiller accuses the deity of malevolence and hypocrisy, and shows him to be unworthy of respect, let alone belief. If we invented him, it was as the projection of our most disabling, atavistic fears, which we ought to outgrow.

Romantic art displays the face of Saturn in order to condemn the superannuated race of gods, with their hunger for blood and their desire for dominance. Between 1819 and 1823 at the Quinta del Sordo, Goya painted a mural in which Saturn gobbles one of his children. His eyes stare as maniacally as full moons; his naked body is emaciated, his hair a matted grey mane. His meal began with the head of his fully grown child, which he has bitten off. Gods resent our mental independence, so it is logical that Saturn should start there. Now, having disposed of an arm and laid bare a ridge of raw meat along the shoulders, he is working his way down the other side. A forearm has just been swallowed, and he laps the elbow. His hands fasten on the figure's waist with white-knuckled desperation. The image is obscene and yet absurd: a god with such a carnivorous appetite is no better than a dog gnawing a bone. In a drawing of the same subject, Goya turned the cannibalized son upside down. Here Saturn starts from the feet, and has already ingested an entire leg. He is currently sucking on the thigh, while the rest of the body dangles from his mouth, its left-over leg entangled in the bristles of his beard; his eyes are averted, keeping watch on another slumped body which he grips in his fist. In the painting Saturn chews up the brain which devises rebellions, while in the drawing he aims for the tender genitals: we have a choice between a god who decapitates us and one who castrates us.

Although Schiller and Goya declared war on heaven, romanticism – which narrowed the gap between religion and art – did not abandon the idea of divinity. God, however, had to be reformed, re-educated. In 1831 Heine sent the narrator of his travel book about Lucca to visit the town's cathedral in company with two former lovers. Together they make sophisticated fun of the painted images. One of the women, who is English and therefore wickedly ironic, smiles at Eve's credulous trust in the snake, and ridicules the immaculate conception. She is startled when the narrator pauses respectfully before a painting of Christ, who looks both intelligent and compassionate. Surely, she asks, he doesn't believe that the man was a god? Although Heine was Jewish, his narrator replies that he loves this 'citizen-god', who had democratic talent for fraternizing with the common people; he is admirable despite his legitimate descent from the absolute ruler of heaven, not because of it. If Christ were not a god, he would vote for him to become one – 'the elected god, the god of my choice'. That choice had to be made by an unafraid man with the right to select the worthiest candidate; the options on offer were not to be restricted by monopolies, so Heine makes his narrator call for an end to institutional religion. What he wants, as he startlingly puts it, is 'free trade in gods'. Hence the dynastic upsets in romantic poetry: the unbinding of Shelley's Prometheus, and the downfall of the grim Saturnian regime in Keats's *Hyperion*, where bright Apollo introduces a new caste of gods who deserve to reign because they are beautiful. In the summary of German history and philosophy that Heine published in 1835, he looked forward to a revolutionary society in which heaven and earth would change places. His ideal was 'a democracy of gods', by which he meant men who are equal in holiness and happiness; he was unapologetic about his promotion of material contentment, the goal which Delacroix thought so banal, because this was among 'the divine rights of man'. The spirit's yearnings and the body's cravings must both be satisfied.

Heine disparaged a religious sensibility that counselled abstinence; he said that he wanted nectar and ambrosia, formerly reserved for consumption on Olympus. Coleridge too, in an awkwardly fervent imitation of Schiller written in 1799, described a visit from the Olympian gods, and asked Hebe to pour him some nectar:

> Thanks, Hebe! I quaff it! Io Paean, I cry!
> The Wine of the Immortals
> Forbids me to die!

Heine listed other desiderata: 'purple robes, delicious scents, sensual pleasures, splendour, dances of laughing nymphs, music and comedies'. Along with operas and ballets, he welcomed the Catholic mass, which demonstrates our human talent for devising symbols and choreographing rituals. Observing communion at Lucca, Heine's narrator even admires the stately, stagey gestures and flourished props of the presiding archbishop, because he remembers the priests of ancient Egypt by whom, as he says, the first gods were invented. The romantic poet has inherited that hieratic responsibility. At the end of his essay on German religion, Heine placed man alone 'facing his creator, and singing his song to him'. Modern literature, he added, began with hymns. But the romantic hierophant was free to address those songs of praise to nature. Coleridge declared that he would 'build my altar in the fields/ And the blue sky my fretted dome shall be'; Wordsworth saw a clump of daffodils as a 'host', like a contingent of angels in golden armour. A hymn could even bow down before another poet. Coleridge, after hearing Wordsworth recite a section of the autobiographical poem that became *The Prelude*, sat listening to the silence and thinking:

> (Thought was it? or aspiration? or resolve?)
> Absorbed, yet hanging still upon the sound –
> And when I rose, I found myself in prayer.

Heine understood that these songs were aimed not at the creator but at man's own creativity, and he verified both their source and their destination by glancing down at his own body. In a poetic squib called 'Zur Teleologie',

he joked about the double function of the penis, which takes charge of both urination and reproduction:

> Was dem Menschen dient zum Seichen
> Damit schafft er Seinesgleichen.

The instrument men use for peeing enables them, as the couplet says, to make a likeness of themselves. The poem's title hints at a third purpose. Teleology studies final causes, but it cannot help scrutinizing the intentions of the first cause, otherwise known as God. Could the same organ also generate the likeness of our maker?

On his journey through the Harz, Heine travelled for a while with a ruddy, worldly townsman who told him that everything in nature has a purpose. Heine pretended to agree, and suggests that 'God created cattle because beef soup builds up people's strength, and created donkeys to provide people with comparisons'. His irony was lost on his acquaintance.

Heine later acknowledged a guilty twinge. After all, God created man because he wanted an admirer; it says so in the Bible, 'God's memoirs', and no author can be blamed for suborning a tame reviewer. Still, how tedious to spend your life on your knees. In the townsman's company, nature looked lustreless, drably utilitarian. As soon as he was alone again, Heine reported that the trees spoke, the flowers danced, the sky embraced the earth.

The Irish poet Thomas Moore, visiting Niagara Falls in 1804, called it 'the very residence of the Deity', and prescribed a trip there as a cure for atheism. On his way back from the Alps in 1775, Goethe climbed the tower of the cathedral in Strasbourg. He equated the geological and architectural pinnacles, convinced that both had been 'procreated ... not pieced and patched together'. The snowy heights and jagged crevasses, like the cathedral's tower and its nave, provoked a 'great thought of the creation', and aroused 'creative power' in whoever saw them. Goethe's stammered response, he said, was poetry. From the summit of the building, Goethe reviewed the gradual mastery of proportion that had made it possible, and discerned a sentient, intelligent purpose in the structure. For him it was an organism, not an engineered pile of stones; it had grown, like 'other creatures ... produced by the individual seminal power'. Emerson made the same point more lyrically in 1841: 'The cathedral is a blossoming in stone. ... The mountain of granite blooms into an eternal flower'. Sometimes God's camouflage in nature was only too successful. In 1808 Caspar David Friedrich was commissioned to supply an altarpiece for the private chapel of an aristocratic patron. A crucifix overgrown by creepers is planted among the pine trees on a mountain. A figure hangs on it, almost inconspicuous. Allegorical beams from a rising sun fan out across the sky, but despite this evangelical dawn Friedrich was criticized for making the devotional icon disappear into the landscape. Prometheus, painted in 1846–7 by Thomas Cole, dwindles like the crucified Christ of Friedrich. He is manacled to an icy crag and, unlike the redeemer in the altarpiece, turns away from a lacerating dawn; Cole's interest lay in the razor-backed mountains and the painful brilliance of a cold sun, not in the Titan's tragedy.

If it was to be salvaged, the official religion had to recommend itself aesthetically. In 1802 François-René de Chateaubriand published a treatise entitled *Génie du christianisme, ou Beautés de la religion chrétienne*. Chateaubriand, the tenth son of a count, escaped from the French Revolution in 1791 and spent five months in America. He returned to enrol in the royalist army; challenging the atheism of the revolutionaries, he re-adopted his Catholic faith. But his book did more than prescribe belief as a convenient social fixative. Chateaubriand calls Christianity the most poetic of religions – the most human, the most liberal, and the most amenable to art and literature. It caters to our need for mystery, which makes the geometrical diagram of creation in *Timaeus* unsatisfactory; it offers us a God who radiates light and manually shapes the universe, as opposed to the classical gods who promenade in chariots and conduct their adulterous affairs in a palace on an exclusive mountain. Chateaubriand was glad that Christianity had exorcized the landscape: chasing out the fauns, satyrs and nymphs who once rioted in the undergrowth, it restored the woods to their native condition of silence and solitude. Once those 'elegant phantoms' departed, the pristine vacancy filled up with new species, apparently freshly created. On his trip to America, Chateaubriand felt that he was watching the events of Genesis occur all over again; his own function was that of a literary Adam, describing the exotic animals rather than naming them. He travelled only between Baltimore and Niagara Falls, so he had to imagine some of the innocent Edenic fauna. But he was lucky enough to glimpse the 'fire-bright cardinal', a bird with ecclesiastically coloured plumage. Further afield, he fantasized about crocodiles in Florida, which must be loved by their parents even if they look ugly and menacing to us, and in his novel *Atala* – a story about 'two savages of an unknown species', children of nature succoured by a Christian missionary – he described bears tipsily reeling beside the Mississippi, drunk on honey. Oddly, Chateaubriand overlooked the beaver, whose dam-building activities made it, for Emerson, an authentic American creator, an artist empowered by 'the Supreme Being'.

Chateaubriand admitted that there was nothing old in America except the woods – but that was enough, because American trees were immemorial ancestors, contemporaneous with Christ (as some explorers calculated when they first saw the sequoias in Mariposa Grove, California). A redwood known as the Grizzly Giant, painted by Albert Bierstadt in 1876, might have been the tree of man itself, an evolutionary ladder. Chateaubriand's nephew Alexis de Tocqueville, sent to America on a bureaucratic mission in 1831, got as far west as Michigan, and found on the floor of the forest a primal 'picture of confusion and chaos'. The spectacle possessed a violence that is missing from Chateaubriand's idyll. Trees toppled by wind slowly rotted, while others, dead but held upright by overlapping branches, waited to sift into dust without falling. New plants enthusiastically writhed around the corpses and fed on their decay. No axe had ever intruded to mark the arrival of human culture and cultivation. In these forests, Tocqueville said, nature was 'the only instrument of ruin and also the only creative force. ... In the midst of all this debris the work of new creation goes ceaselessly forward. ... Life and death meet here face to face'. America was both the rediscovered site of the world's beginning and the place where its predestined end might occur.

In 1835 in a lecture on the pictorial possibilities of American scenery, Thomas Cole linked modern painters with biblical seers, since both were the beneficiaries of revelation. Heaven disclosed itself to prophets in 'the solitudes of nature'. Visions were also granted to the artist in the cloud-capped Catskill Mountains or on the upper reaches of the Hudson River – although rather than glimpsing eternity, as Elijah did on Mount Horeb, the painters surveyed an available, unspoiled earth. The artist merely had to be a witness, like Emerson who in 1836 described himself as 'a transparent eyeball'. Emerson thought that a landscape painter should testify to the possibility of paradise, giving 'the suggestion of a fairer creation than we know'. Intervention was unnecessary: to Cole, architecture seemed redundant, because American nature had already anticipated it in the 'vast arched cave' beneath the Falls of Kaaterskill or the 'rocks of architectural formation' over which the river gushed and tumbled at Trenton. Niagara, as Cole said, forcibly expanded the mind that contemplated it: its volume suggested the idea of immensity, its unstoppability that of eternal duration, its headlong fury that of a primal, irresistible power. These were the attributes of sublimity, and also the charac- teristics of 'God the creator'. But the Falls also managed to be beautiful. Cole admired the iridescence of the spray, and marvelled at the 'complete cincture' of the rainbow above the gulf. At Niagara you could safely watch Noah's deluge from behind a fence on the rim; there was no need to wait for the waters to abate to see the signal of God's covenant with men written across the sky. The sentence imposed on homeless, guilty humanity had apparently been waived. Cole concluded that 'We are still in Eden'.

In 'Tintern Abbey', Wordsworth divided responsibility for nature between the creator and the painter or poet who is his deputy. The artist's view encompasses 'the mighty world/ Of eye, and ear, – both what they half create/ And what perceive...'. Eye and ear do more than record what already exists. They affirm its existence; they animate it, as if transmitting the creator's inspiriting touch. When Wordsworth refers to 'the living air', the adjective startlingly brings the air alive. We are made aware that molecules dance in it, that it has moods and whims; a single word gives it the volume and the energy of an ethereal ocean. We are also reminded that air is the medium in which we live, which we feed on when we breathe. It is a parent, even a lover: in a poem written in 1816 to congratulate a young woman on climb- ing Helvellyn, Wordsworth imagines 'blue Ether's arms, flung round thee' to reward her efforts and to calm her 'pantings of dismay'. We assume that air creates an obliging vacuum for us as we move through it. What if it actually contains us, clasps us, sealing us in a embrace? Goethe thought that oxygen, which gave vent to 'the breath of God', was a creative tonic. In 1828 he attributed Byron's literary productivity to the time he spent riding, sailing, rowing or swimming: athletic pursuits enabled him to imbibe a 'divine power' from the fresh air.

Outside the body, the air resolved a problem that has always vexed philosophers and physiologists who investigate what happens inside the body: it exposed the soul, the impalpable spirit that quickens clay. Caspar David Friedrich attempted to portray atmospheric vibrations: clammy mists that signified mortality, sunrises that promised regeneration. His wife warned that 'On the day he is painting air, he may not be spoken to!' Cole called the sky 'the soul of all scenery', and found in it 'the fountains of light'. It had expressions – serene, or gloomily overcast – that were perhaps a guide to the temperament of God. Emerson derived sustenance from the mere sight of the sky, and in 1843 in his journal called it 'the daily bread of the eyes'. Henry David Thoreau remarked in 1852 that his afternoon walks to study sunsets were like strolls around an art gallery. Each day 'a new picture [was] painted and framed, held up for half an hour, in such lights as the Great Artist chooses, and then withdrawn'. In 1846 Baudelaire classified sunsets as a series of symphony concerts. One day there might be red fanfares in the west, with orange and rose-pink overtones; next day the complex hymnody of the sky would produce a different orchestral spectrum. Erased or silenced by darkness, the image or melody could be preserved by words, thanks to the Great Artist's human accomplice. Hence the adjectival spectrum in Thoreau's vignettes, which catch the 'roseate redness, clear as amber' along the horizon or liken the tingling air to wine or 'molten cinnabar' with pearls melted in it. Romantic artists hoped to experience a similar dissolution. In 1815 Carl Canus began a series of essays on landscape painting, which he dedicated to Goethe. He recommended mountain climbing as a means of transcending the burdensome self and its gravitational tug. Canus guaranteed that on the heights 'your ego vanishes; you are nothing; God is all'. But God, of course, had also vanished. Looking at nature, what the romantics saw was nature looking at itself. If the sky was the soul, then water functioned as the eye that reflected and absorbed it. Thoreau said that a lake was 'earth's eye', and referred his pond at Walden in the woods outside Concord as 'sky water'. Cole employed the same metaphor, implying that lakes could see. Calm, unruffled, they also doubled as paintings. Cole described a deer beholding its own image 'as in a polished mirror' as it drank; Otsego, one of the lakes in New York State that he particularly admired, was renamed Glimmerglass in the novels of James Fenimoore Cooper as a tribute to its mimetic clarity.

In 'Ode to the West Wind', Shelley verbally harnessed the almost cyclonic energy of an autumnal gale. His wind is the breath of nature's being; it also promises perpetual change, while the earth's rotation from winter to spring, speeded by storms, is a summons to political revolution. Its urgency is conveyed in the hectic alternation of metaphors: the dead leaves it whirls are ghosts, then a pestilence-stricken mob, and finally – as Shelley mentions the dispersal of winged seeds – corpses that will be resurrected when the weather turns kinder. The wind is 'destroyer and preserver';

Shelley's language has the same dual function, disturbing and deforming the appearance of things so as to make them metamorphose. In *The Last Man*, Mary Shelley extends her husband's theory of creation in an address to wind – whether it comes 'destroying from the east, or pregnant with elementary life from the west' – as a force that deserves to be 'throned above all other vice-regents of nature's power'. She contradicts the myth that gives the sun superiority over the wind: gales and breezes are a respiratory system, without which nature is insentient. Her rhapsody is darkly prophetic, since it prefigures the storm at sea that kills Adrian – the character who represents Shelley – and his daughter.

On a walk up Helvellyn with Wordsworth in 1799, Coleridge wishfully reverted to the state of nature before Genesis began. 'Light and darkness coexisted in contiguous messes', he noted in his memo about the weather, '& the earth and sky were but *one!*' For romantic artists, such chaos was the creative source. In a poem about the worship of the classical gods written in 1800, Friedrich Hölderlin sanctified this state: he spoke of a 'holy chaos'. The dejected Saturn in Keats's *Hyperion* believes that his divinity might be restored if only he could locate that place of power:

> cannot I create?
> Cannot I form? Cannot I fashion forth
> Another world, another universe,
> To overbear and crumble this to naught?
> Where is another chaos? Where?

Neptune tells Saturn, whose reign is ending, that deities are by-standers. The world creates itself, needing no help from God or even from the dynastic succession of Greek gods:

> From chaos and parental darkness came
> Light, the first fruits of that intestine broil,
> That sullen ferment, which for wondrous ends
> Was ripening in itself.

God the Father is replaced by that indistinct 'parental darkness', which – developing matriarchal powers – bears fruit and gives birth to light. The arena of chaos was nature, with its heaving seas and lightning-ruptured skies. Unafraid, the sorceress in Shelley's *Witch of Atlas* scampers on the winds and shrilly applauds when thunderclouds discharge fire-balls. In *Prometheus Unbound* the genii of the storm howl 'from their loud abysses': like the prophetic trumpeting of the west wind in Shelley's ode, their cries are a primal music. Byron in *Manfred* describes the aerial tantrums of Arimanes, the diabolical opponent of enlightened Ormuzd in the Zoroastrian religion.

He bestrides the clouds, holding in his hand 'the sceptre of the elements which tear/ Themselves to chaos at his high command!' Chaos also surged in the creative mind. Mary Shelley fears for the oversensitive Adrian, who is buffeted by 'the dire storms of the mental universe'. The creator, as the poet Achim von Armin put it, must 'hurl himself into the abyss and surrender his soul to chaos'. Armin added that this almost suicidal disordering of consciousness was 'something highly sacred'. Fuseli ate raw pork before bedtime, which provoked the nightmares he painted when he woke up. Keats more tamely demanded snuff or a 'draught of vintage'. Baudelaire smoked hashish, and Coleridge dosed his ailments with opium. These were profane sacraments: artists ingested the god of their choosing.

In Coleridge's 'Kubla Khan', poetic eloquence is the outcry of passion, the noise of coital abandon. A fountain thrusts through the earth, forced up from a subterranean river. Its torrent is announced by a 'woman wailing for her demon lover', and it jets from within a 'deep romantic chasm' – perhaps Hesiod's chasm, from which the world is born, or perhaps an inlet of the wailing woman's fruitful body. Coleridge understood the affinity between creativity and procreation, though in his critical prose he struggled to keep them apart. As a dutiful Christian, he tried to argue his sensual, narcotic fantasies into conformity with the constructive labours of God. In 1816 in *The Statesman's Manual* he assailed the mercantile cult of utilitarianism, pleading that imagination needed to 'impregnate' a practical, acquisitive view of the world. Only that fertilization, he claimed, could make the mind 'a living power'. The metaphor is sexual, although Coleridge at once chastens it by allying imagination with the Bible's 'holy light'. Mechanistic reason, by contrast, has teamed up with commerce and now follows 'the banners of Anti-Christ'. The ideology of usefulness quantifies a world of inert objects with price-tags attached to them. Thomas Moore mocked the absurdity of submitting Niagara to 'the measurement of gallons and yards'. Against such dreary calculating, Coleridge sets the 'glad confusion and heedless intermixture' of nature, where 'all things spread out ... as a lightsome chaos on which the Spirit of God is moving'.

This takes daring liberties with the Bible: the spirit in Genesis is not buoyed up by chaos or elated by the welter and uproar of the romantic landscape. Coleridge might have been secretly quoting from Friedrich Schlegel, who in 1800 in his *Dialogue on Poetry* praised the 'infinitely abundant chaos' of the agile, ironic, self-contradictory mind. The subtle mischief in Coleridge's treatment of scripture becomes more insistent when he immediately adds that in nature 'all press and swell under one attraction, and live together in promiscuous harmony, each joyous in its own kind'. Again he modifies Genesis, where God instructs the animals to reproduce themselves after their own kind but does not expect them to enjoy all that pressing, swelling

Caspar David Friedrich, *Traveller Above the Mists*, 1818

promiscuity. Applying his argument directly to the Gospels, Coleridge calls for a 'living and generative interpenetration' of the two mental powers. He means the rational and the imaginative faculties, though he could just as well be referring to the generative interpenetration of male and female. Religion, he concludes, should be averse to abstraction. Because it participates in 'the Divine Nature', it should be a 'creative overflowing'. The fountain from 'Kubla Khan' has suddenly spouted inside a temple.

Like Coleridge's God afloat on a lightsome chaos, the wanderer painted in about 1818 by Caspar David Friedrich hovers above a sea of fog. God here wears a fashionable frock coat and rests on a walking stick, the baton he uses when he exercises power; he ponders a creation that is still incomplete, because those cold vapours have not yet lifted to reveal the dry land below. In one of his geological rhapsodies, Goethe praised granite peaks for being 'before all life and above all life'. Because he believed that 'the human mind brings life to everything', Goethe, standing on a mountain, felt the 'inner attractive and motive forces' of nature flow between him and the inert rock and watched as they flowered in the valleys far below. With his feet on the 'foundations of all existence', he experienced all over again 'the first, the profoundest beginnings of existence'. The planted feet of Friedrich's wanderer look equally proprietorial, and one foot points to a clump of grass as if compelling it to grow. As yet there is little verdure in this world of stark rock and moist fog, but his coat and trousers, soft and mossy, serve as a template for that colour. The landscape might be the extension of his body, since the lines of the horizon match his sloping shoulders, the stumpy dolmens in the middle distance echo his balanced stance, and his head is aligned with the sculptural crag to the right. His hair is ruffled by wind, making visible the agitation of his brain as it dreams a world into being. Nature remains embedded in chaos, as fluent as the fog, and the jutting rocks poke up at irregular angles. But a perfect geometrical shape has been included, as evidence – like Plato's cubes and triangles – of a divine purpose. This is the conical summit towards which the wanderer's body is oriented: a sacred mountain, like Olympus or Fujiyama or Cézanne's Mont Sainte-Victoire. The feathery clouds above, streaked by the sunrise which also gilds his hair, make a wreath to crown Friedrich's figure; the fog below, brighter and whiter, rises towards him because he has willed it to lift off the ground, unveiling the creation he has prepared.

In 1816 Hazlitt, writing about Turner, exactly defined the revision of Genesis that takes place in romantic landscapes like Friedrich's. His comments are just, even if their sarcasm is misplaced: he claims that Turner, painting the elements, 'delights to go back to the first chaos of the world'. Hazlitt relates Turner's work to the agenda of Genesis – except that creation, when he paints it, is stalled or even aborted half-way through the second day. Light already exists, since Turner believed that the sun was God, and has been divided from darkness. The waters have also been separated from dry land, 'but as yet,' Hazlitt noted, 'no living thing nor tree bearing fruit' has appeared. Even the initial arbitration between competing elements can be revoked, for light in Turner's paintings is a flood that overwhelms dry land. Coleridge in 1804 described the philosophy of Johann Gottfried von Herder as 'a painted mist with no sharp outline'; transcendentalism flourished in such lambent fog. A golden haze invades the country house of Petworth, owned by Turner's patron, as if the sun had crashed through the ceiling and landed in a room that contains some untanned classical statues and a rowdy mob of dogs; a watercolour of the High

Street in Oxford, made during the 1830s, looks like the parting of a frothy sea, with a cascade of white light pouring down from the sky to wash away the spire of St Mary's Church. The result of this technique, in Hazlitt's opinion, was to make the end of the first biblical week change places with the beginning, so that despite Turner's application of paint all remained 'without form and void'. He cattily reported someone else's opinion that these were 'pictures of nothing, and very like'. At least Wordsworth, in Hazlitt's estimation, respected the logic of creation by 'making something out of nothing': his poetry takes ordinary sights – a bleak rural pool, a few flowers – and invests them with an aura of supernatural wonder. Even grass, as Wordsworth puts it in the 'Immortality Ode', can be splendid.

Hazlitt did not reckon on Turner's showmanship. Making something out of nothing was, for him, almost a performing art. On varnishing days at the Royal Academy, when his academically tidy colleagues were fixing and finishing their sedate replicas of nature, Turner used his brush as a conjurer's wand. To begin with, the paintings he exhibited always looked scrawled, diffuse, washes of colour not constrained by line. Turner dabbed at them and picked details out of the iridescent puddles, until by the end of the session the spectators could see a shipwreck or an English cathedral or the Grand Canal. But he always stopped long before the point at which the God of Genesis completed his work. The spectacle resembled Victor Hugo's description of a sunrise seen from the top of the Rigi in central Switzerland: dawn, as Hugo excitedly reported, disclosed a 'chaos of absurd exaggerations and frightening diminutions'. In *Paradise Lost* and *Die Schöpfung*, a divine light dispels that riot. But the romantic revelation leaves chaos untamed. Hence Turner's enjoyment of the gushing trajectory of the Reichenbach Falls, or the indistinct lump of a whale that flails as it upsets shipping in the English Channel. In his re-enactment of Genesis, the consummation of God's creative labour is certainly not the arrival of man on earth as custodian. The human figures in Turner's *Picturesque Views in England and Wales* look as messy as rubble. A gang of road menders churn the street outside Christ Church in Oxford to a filthy ditch; boatloads of sailors tossed about by rough seas at Fowey Harbour in Cornwall are flotsam. Walter Fawkes, Turner's closest friend, marvelled at the way he seemed to reverse the proper order of creative endeavour. He first soaked the paper with wet paint, apparently drowning it; then 'he tore, he scratched, he scrubbed at it in a kind of frenzy, and the whole thing was chaos'. His images were the product of his destructiveness.

Turner immersed himself in chaos and edged closer to nature's origins by painting weather, which is the contention of the unruly elements. His *Snow Storm, Avalanche and Inundation – A Scene in the Upper Part of the Val d'Aout*, painted in 1836–7, combines a blizzard with an cannonade of thunder; the upheaval provokes an avalanche, which sends boulders raining down on some terrified evacuees. A stream overflows in fury. The world's beginning and its end are joined in the whirling, scything outline of an icy vortex as the sky splits apart. Wordsworth, crossing the Alps in *The Prelude*, is blasted by waterfalls, shot at by torrents, mocked by echoes that rumble from black crags, and sickened by the ravings of a giddy, tumbling stream. The topographical trauma represents the workings of a disembodied, universal mind whose thoughts are

> Characters of the great Apocalypse.
> The types and symbols of Eternity,
> Of first, and last, and midst, and without end.

When Goethe crossed the Brenner Pass in 1786 on his way to Italy, he too felt he had a privileged view of the strife that formed nature. On the plains, he said, you accept the weather as a fact; in the mountains, you watch as it is created, and the spectacle recalls the creation of the world. Goethe believed that the peaks had a pulse, a throbbing gravitational pull that made the air oscillate and magnetically attracted clouds. After 'an inner struggle of electrical forces', those bulky reservoirs exploded into storms. To romantic observers, even the foul weather of polluted Victorian London had its numinous aspect. Nathaniel Hawthorne reported in 1857 that fog seemed to 'spiritualize the materialism' of the city, turning lumpy burghers into spectres. The streets became an 'other world of worldly people' who were, Hawthorne ruefully noted, 'gross even in ghostliness'.

The randomness of weather, its transitory whims and intemperate extremes, worried the Quaker meteorologist Luke Howard. The sky, he admitted in 1807, looked like a 'scene of confusion' or a 'domain of chance'; if this was God's cranium, his mood swings were alarming. But Howard was sure that 'the Great Author of nature' must have a logical reason for such perturbation, so he set out to demonstrate that weather, 'like the rest of Creation', evinced 'the infinite wisdom and goodness' of its maker. He began by disciplining clouds, the most fickle of natural phenomena. Medieval anatomy, deriving Adam from seven substances, analysed man as a digest of the elements: his body was earth and his hair was the grass that grew on it, his bones were stone and his blood was water, he got his eyes from the sun and his breath from the wind – but his thoughts, evading control, corresponded to clouds. The indeterminacy of clouds vexed Gotthold Ephraim Lessing, whose 1766 treatise *Laokoön* warned against attempting to paint them. Lessing criticized an artist who had attempted to illustrate a scene from Homer in which a tutelary deity is enveloped in a thick cloud. That cloud, Lessing insisted, was merely a symbol of invisibility; to make it visible was a mental error. Howard could not accept such uncertainties, because they blurred God's face and questioned his existence. He therefore applied to the ephemera of the sky the method of classification formulated by Linnaeus, and defined four species of cloud, called stratus, cumulus, cirrus and nimbus. Ruskin in *Modern Painters* allegorized Howard's categories, and read clouds as aerial cathedrals, with 'fifty aisles penetrating through angelic chapels to the Shekhinah of the blue': for that blue distance, Ruskin used the Kabbalah's term for the glory of God. Cumulus clouds, majestically piled up, looked to him like chariots, the massing of a heavenly army, while English rain clouds were directly dispatched by 'the Great Angel of the Sea'.

In 1820 Goethe praised Howard for forming shapes, creating precision from the imprecise, wispy, ragged material of air. The tribute shifts credit from the 'Great Author' to Howard's own authorial artistry. The clouds themselves, in Goethe's lyrics evoking the four types, remain fanciful and phantasmal, like case studies of the imagination at work. On his way across the Alps, Goethe watched a fleecy cloud being teased, unthreaded, and reabsorbed into the sky. It looked as if it was being 'spun off from a distaff by an invisible hand'. In the sequence of poems about Howard, Goethe returned to that mysterious, anonymous designer: he called the stratus cloud 'ein Gespenst Gespenster bildend' – a ghost drawing other ghosts in the sky. Because the very existence of clouds was enigmatic, they soon became the familiars or spirit companions of romantic artists, who could decipher the writing in the sky. Wordsworth is guided by 'a wandering cloud' at the start of *The Prelude*. Elsewhere he imitates this apparent vagrancy and announces that 'I wandered lonely as a cloud'. Both the verb and the adjective startle us into reconsidering our assumptions about nature. Clouds are not idle strays, despite their rootlessness; neither are they lonely, since they are at home in the air from which they are made. While Wordsworth sees clouds as ministers or messengers, Coleridge emphasizes their dreamy subjectivity. In his sonnet 'Fancy in Nubibus, or The Poet in the Clouds', written in 1817, he eagerly mounts 'through Cloudland, gorgeous land!', where you can 'make the shifting clouds be what you please' and play with 'each quaint likeness' that you see in them. Shelley's 'The Cloud', written in 1820, gives a voice to an unsteady fabrication of wet, warring molecules. This cloud describes itself as a capricious deity, alternately kind and vicious; it brings 'fresh showers for the thirsting flowers' but also wields 'the flail of the lashing hail'. Its genealogy recalls the coupling of Earth and Heaven in Hesiod's *Theogony* – although, because Shelley imagines it to be a female, savagery is softened by familial affection. The cloud says that it is 'the daughter of Earth and Water,/ And the nursling of the Sky'. It is immortal like a god, yet endlessly mutable like consciousness: 'I change, but I cannot die'. After a shower, it exults in its evaporation:

John Constable,
*Study of Clouds*,
1822

> I silently laugh at my own cenotaph,
>     And out of the caverns of rain,
> Like a child from the womb, like a ghost from the tomb,
>     I arise and unbuild it again.

Womb and tomb are equated by the rhyme, because creation is inseparable from destruction. The new cloud that rears up when the moisture condenses is a romantic work of art, like a provisional essay, a rapid sketch, an improvised snatch of music, or a building that gently subsides into ruin and merges with nature.

In 1821 Constable reported to his friend the Reverend John Fisher: 'I have done a good deal of skying'. He was referring to his almost daily routine of painting the sky above Hampstead Heath. These images can hardly be called landscapes, because their anchorage to the ground has loosened; the horizon sags to the bottom of the composition, pulling the tops of trees out of sight and leaving only configurations of sculpted vapour – scudding tufted cumulus, a thick thundery bank like a wrinkled cerebral cortex, or clouds that refract the light of the sunrise or sunset and daub the sky with florid pigment. Constable knew that he was reversing the classical order of precedence, making foreground and background change places. Skies, according to the received wisdom, should not 'come forward or be

A.L. Coburn,
*Great Temple,
Grand Canyon*,
1911

hardly thought about in a picture', but Constable considered them to be the
'*key note*' of landscape and the dominant '*Organ of sentiment*'. His musical
metaphors implied that these sessions were open-air church services, with
the wind singing hymns. By keeping track of the weather's variability, he
hoped to prove, as he said, that no two days or hours were the same, just as
there had never been 'two leaves of a tree alike since the Creation of the
World': God is an artist who never repeats himself. In a letter to his wife,
he interpreted the blossoming of the trees as a mute paraphrase of Christ's
declaration that 'I am the resurrection & the life'. This miraculous resurgence could be duplicated by one of the artist's technical tricks. Constable
was fond of speckling and stippling his canvases with spots of white light,
applied with a palette knife. The result makes the air look as surfily effervescent as a breaking wave; it testifies to a life that pervades the transparent
atmosphere, and even gives mud a foamy crest.

The creator imitated by Turner specializes in destructive fury, whip-
ping up storms and hurling boulders. But the creator Constable venerated
knows how to vivify decay, and does so in the heap of compost – described
by the painter as a 'large cow-turd' – placed in the foreground of *The Stour
Valley and Dedham Church*. Brambles and ferns thrive in this mound of
excrement, and flowers grow around it. Although the church in the distance
celebrates an airborne saviour whose empty tomb contained no body to be
buried, here putrefaction becomes fruitful. Clouds hold out the hope of

sublimation, but the earth has another rejoinder to death. Constable's religion sometimes relapsed from Christianity to pantheism. His series of
lectures in 1836 concluded by declaring that painting shows the proximity
of paradise and reminds us that 'We exist but in a landscape and are the creatures of a Landscape'. This is not quite the same thing as being God's
children; we sprout from the soil, and are even – as the compost suggests –
given sustenance by muck. In the waterlogged fields and slimy ponds Constable painted with such affection, he returned to the scene of the oldest
myths about creation, which propose that man was moulded from humid
soil. But as the cycle continues, earth aerates, and this creation turns to gas.
Coleridge, in his assault on the transcendentalists, called Herder's philosophy 'mere steam from a heap of man's dung'.

Art continued to keep watch on the sky, hoping for a glimpse of God.
Photography soon took up the vigil, because – as nineteenth-century commentators on its chemical mystery believed – it was nature's direct inscription,
written by light inside an occult, shuttered box. Thomas Carlyle, sending a
Daguerrotype of himself to Emerson in 1846, called the image a 'sun-
shadow, ... as the sun shall please to paint it'. Early in the twentieth century,
Alvin Langdon Coburn still paid homage to the versatility of 'the Great
Creator of Clouds', though he admitted that divination was a frustrating
game of hide and seek. At the Grand Canyon he spent a day chasing clouds,
waiting for the moment when a shadow briefly settled on a formation
known as the Great Temple, imprinting its black outline on the white,
blazing gulf behind it. The temple was a cylindrical extrusion on top of an
eroded ridge; the cloud's passing darkness made it visible, and gave credibility to its nickname. In 1922 Alfred Stieglitz photographed a series of clouds
in upstate New York. Sometimes the sky is ruffled like a furrowed, angry
brow; in another scene it clears, and only a scrap of thin cloud crosses the
moon, which stares like the pupil of an all-seeing eye. Stieglitz collected
clouds for the rest of the decade, favouring soft diffused moonlight and
mackerel skies that have the mottled texture of human skin. He called the
images 'sky stories – or songs', and told the poet Hart Crane that 'some
people feel I have photographed God'. Then he added a mock-modest,
agnostic proviso: 'May be'.

# 16
# PROTOPLASTS

In the beginning was the Word. But which word? Max Müller pointed out in 1897 that all myths are an exercise in polynymy, and the biblical Logos is forever begetting neologisms. Genesis first calls the creator Elohim, then changes his name to Yahweh. Renaissance humanists rechristened God. Thomas More's Utopians practise a range of religions, and agree to give their polymorphous deity the name of Mithras, borrowed from the Persian god of light. Gemistus Phleton, who formed an academy in Florence, referred to him as Zeus, and for papal officials he was Jupiter Optimus Maximus. The philosophers of the eighteenth century spoke of an Eternal Being, non-denominational and quite possibly not divine, and James Boswell declared that Samuel Johnson believed less in God than in a cosmic magistrate, the 'Great Source of all order'.

In 1817 Coleridge added an extra term to the lexicon. The word he made up was 'esemplastic', and – as he said when using it in *Biographia Literaria* – it purported to explain 'the nature and genesis of imagination', which is a 'plastic power'. It served as a surreptitious synonym for God because for Coleridge the imaginative faculty represented 'in the finite mind ... the eternal act of creation in the infinite I AM'. In Exodus, Moses asks the voice in the burning bush its name. It replies 'I AM THAT I AM': God simply exists, and is not required to give further particulars. Coleridge, even though he so often used aliases or pseudonyms or the pretence of anonymity, endowed the poet with the same power of self-declaration. The esemplastic activity meant a moulding together, an act of unification. It was also a replica of the original creation: a Latin hymn addresses 'Plasmator Deus', God the maker of man. Coleridge stated the case more boldly in a notebook that was not intended for publication. Here he called poets 'the Bridlers by Delight, the Purifiers, they that combine them with reason & order, the true Protoplasts, Gods of Love who tame the Chaos'. Protoplasm is the original stuff of life, which is plastic because it can take on any shape; protoplasts – like Coleridge deploying what he called 'my shaping spirit of Imagination' – are the makers of men. The brain of Jove in *Prometheus Unbound* is 'miscreative'. True creativity belongs to the poet who, as a Spirit sings, can imbibe the air and from it create 'Forms more real than living man, / Nurslings of immortality!'

Rather than innocuously easing the new word into circulation, Coleridge drew attention to his effrontery in making it up. The tenth chapter of *Biographia Literaria* begins as a dialogue with a hypothetical critic, who complains that he cannot find the term in Johnson's *Dictionary*. This prompts Coleridge to admit that he has just invented it. He does appease the scoffer when he supplies a Greek etymology for 'esemplastic', though even this is a cover-up: lexicographers classify Coleridge's pet word as an awkward translation of the German term 'ineinsbildung'. Then he changes the subject and strays into a digression on the mishaps of his journalistic career. It is a long while before he gets back to considering imagination and its source or rival, which he calls 'God as a creative intelligence'. He makes another attempt to expound the meaning of the plastic power in the thirteenth chapter, and begins by remembering that Descartes once offered to construct a universe from first principles. But he is obstructed by another disbeliever. Now a friend – actually Coleridge himself, or his censorious superego – writes him a letter complaining about the book's obscurity and suggesting that he abandon his speculations about the metaphysics of art. Coleridge complies, and the disquisition breaks off with a terse, arithmetical listing of his ideas. He subdivides the imagination, linking the primary power with 'the infinite I AM' but saying no more about its Promethean apostasy as the force that creates life. When he briefly analyses the way the secondary imagination works, he is a little more physiologically specific: 'It dissolves, diffuses, dissipates, in order to re-create. ... It is essentially *vital*, even as all objects (as objects) are essentially fixed and mute'. He might be describing the surgical activity of Frankenstein, Mary Shelley's modern Prometheus, who – in the novel written the previous year – destroys in order to re-create and vitalizes the fixed, mute matter he exhumes.

Elsewhere in *Biographia Literaria*, Coleridge hints at what happens when imagination moulds and merges opposites. 'During the act of knowledge itself,' he says in an earlier chapter, 'the objective and the subjective are so instantly united that we cannot determine to which of the two the priority belongs. ... both are coinstantaneous and one. While I am attempting to explain this intimate coalition, I must suppose it dissolved'. It is indeed an intimate coalition (or, to use another of Coleridge's medically euphemistic coinages, a coadunation). Object and subject, reason and fancy, might be male and female, and creation – which Coleridge calls a kind of genesis – mimes copulation. The repressed sexual metaphor surfaces again in the fourth chapter, when Coleridge describes his partnership with Wordsworth in writing *Lyrical Ballads*. Here imagination is 'the seminal principle', although the idea is illustrated from horticulture not human sexuality. Wordsworth's task was to take care of the branches with their 'poetic fruitage', while Coleridge investigated 'the roots, as far as they lift themselves above ground and are visible to the naked eye of our common consciousness'. Is this the tree of poetry or that of knowledge? Is poetry, with its self-fulfilling generative capacity, a forbidden fruit? Coleridge's poem 'The Aeolian Harp' wonders if all 'animated nature' might not be an orchestra of 'organic Harps'

> That tremble into thought, as o'er them sweeps
> Plastic and vast, one intellectual breeze,
> At once the Soul of each, and God of all?

It is a rhetorical question, and luckily cannot be answered. Imagination is supposed to mould contraries together, but here the opposing terms remain in suspension. Do thought or wind really form shapes, or just create a temporary disturbance as they pluck the harp's strings? Each of us has a private, personal soul, but is that breeze really a God we can all share? The same contradictions flare up in the notebook entry about poets as protoplasts. Erotic urgency clashes with moral restraint, classical myth with Christian doctrine. Coleridge's poets are fantasists, motivated by delight and desire. Yet they also apply the bridle to the passionate velocity of imagination; they purify and rationalize. To call the poets protoplasts allies them with Prometheus, but the god of love who tames chaos is attached to *Paradise Lost*, where Christ creates the world by subduing and marginalizing that region of darkness.

Another notebook entry, made in 1804, plays with the physics of Heraclitus, who identified the Logos with fire – always in flux, indefinable but inextinguishable. Heraclitus saw the elements dying into one another so as to be reborn: earth into water, water into air, air into fire, and so on forever. Coleridge, who in 1796 described himself as 'a so-so chemist', tries to express this in 'the present chemical nomenclature'. He speculates about 'aeriform gases' and 'igniform natures', wondering if electricity and magnetism might not speed up the cycle. His hunch was correct: not long afterwards, the physicist Michael Faraday described electricity, which he generated, as a 'magnetic spark'. Coleridge decides that all changes in nature are directed by 'the plastic fire of the ancients'. The image is an astonishing imaginative leap, and it makes better sense than the plasticity of the intellectual breeze. Fire cooks things, and therefore leads us from nature to culture. Heat is destructive, but it also hardens objects, making the mould set. Plastic is made by this method; perhaps that is why Prometheus stole fire, so that he could bake his messy, doughy creatures. His study of Heraclitus persuaded Coleridge that 'to comprehend attraction & repulsion as one power is the point of the pyramid of physical science'. He had already achieved such a geometrical resolution in 1798, although the feat referred not to science but to poetry, and the pyramid was a dome:

> It was a miracle of rare device,
> A sunny pleasure-dome with caves of ice!

Kubla Khan is the ultimate protoplast. Fire provides sensual warmth, but ice purifies, orders and fixes it. Here is the ideal formula for a poem, or for any work of art. Coleridge, goaded by a 'deep delight', longs to 'build that dome in air,/ That sunny dome! those caves of ice!' But he denies himself the chance, because this creation – contesting Genesis and unashamedly returning to Eden – can only be accomplished by a man who has drunk the milk of paradise. Although attraction and repulsion are two aspects of the same force, they cancel each other out. 'Kubla Khan', according to Coleridge's disclaimer, remains a fragment of a poem he did not dare to write.

In his poem *Milton*, Blake makes the poet a tributary for 'the breath of the Almighty' and sets him a godly task, 'To build the Universe stupendous: Mental forms Creating'. But mental forms are not enough; the protoplast wants to shape physical forms as well. The process can be seen at work in Byron's *The Deformed Transformed*. The drama is about his own physical unworthiness: his lameness felt like a moral brand, the mark of Cain. The hunchback Arnold, rejected by his mother like Richard III, decides to kill himself, dispersing 'this hateful compound' of earth's atoms. His knife, he hopes, will separate him 'from the creation, as it hath/ The green bough from the forest'. He is interrupted by a Mephistophelean Stranger, who persuades him that his disfigurements are natural. A buffalo would be grateful for his cloven foot, a dromedary would take pride in his hump. Nature merely assigned these assets to a creature of the wrong species. The Stranger, addressing Arnold as 'my manikin', offers him a choice of revised bodies. He chooses to assume the form of the valiant Achilles, and the Stranger, in a repetition of God's act in Genesis, scoops up soil and moulds it:

> From the red earth, like Adam,
>              Thy likeness I shape. ...
> 'Tis done! He hath taken
>              His stand in creation.

Someone has to wear the abandoned body of the monster, which lies on the ground like a discarded overcoat, so the Stranger slips into it himself. First he invokes the element that instils a soul into clay:

> Fire! man's safeguard and his slaughter;
> Fire! Creation's first-born daughter,
>              And Destruction's threaten'd son.

An ignis-fatuus – a Will-o'-the-wisp, which is methane gas fired by electricity in the air – hovers into view and settles on the brow of the slumped body. It rises; the Stranger is now inside it, looking like Arnold. We have watched a creator at work, although Byron's version of the story is hardly biblical. The two companions go on to sack Rome and send the Pope packing. The Stranger sees the grappling soldiers and panicked priests as evidence of an incompetent, inchoate creation:

> This is the consequence of giving matter
> The power of thought. It is a stubborn substance,
> And thinks chaotically, as it acts,
> Ever relapsing into its first elements.

In a more ebullient mood, Byron celebrated this primal mayhem. A journal entry in January 1821 describes a night in Italy when he set off in an open carriage on a sexual errand. He noted that his fellow passengers were 'rather savage – rather treacherous and highly inflamed by politics. Fine fellows though – good materials for a nation. Out of chaos God made a world, and out of high passions come a people.' God here makes use of chaos, rather than suppressing it. The elements continue to feud in the temperament of those ignoble savages, and Byron (who took the precaution of calling for his pistols before he set out) had no desire to see them pacified. The rowdy, inflammatory behaviour of the men in the carriage serves as fuel for nineteenth-century nationalism, which unified Italy and, with a little help from Byron himself, made Greece independent. Byron glances ahead at the wars which were to redesign the map of Europe, and sees in them the ferment of a continuing creation. God only made a pair of individuals; the mass, impelled by passion, adheres to form a people or a nation, and claims for itself a freedom that God begrudged to Adam and Eve.

*The Deformed Transformed* was Byron's homage to 'the great Goethe', who knew that the artist's creative instinct was a threat to God. In Goethe's poem about Prometheus – set to scornfully declamatory music by Schubert in 1819, and again even more furiously by Hugo Wolf in 1889 – the Titan tells the Olympian deities to hide behind their morose thunderclouds, and boasts of forming men in his own image; the plastic power is his revenge on the lofty foes who have demeaned him. This arrogance has not lost its power to startle or offend. In 1934 the sculptor Paul Manship designed a Prometheus for Rockefeller Center: the group of skyscrapers was planned as Manhattan's mercantile Olympus, so it needed a resident clan of deities or muscular Titans (Atlas, the brother of Prometheus, stands nearby on Fifth Avenue). The unbound god swoops down above a skating rink, expounding the mystery of creation by bringing fire – in the form of his gilded torch – into contact with ice. Prometheus was at first accompanied by two of his creatures, a man and a woman who posed in an Art Deco arbour. But just across the street from St Patrick's Cathedral, this challenge to Genesis was deemed impolite. Separated from their dissident creator, the creatures were banished to a roof garden.

In *Faust*, Goethe reinterpreted the medieval story about the scientist struck down by God for trespassing on supernatural secrets. Earlier versions

Theodor von Holst, *Fantasy based on Goethe's Faust*, 1834

of the legend have an unavoidably tragic end. Traditionally, Faust gains an extra term of youth by his pact with the devil; when his time is up, he is hauled off to hell. Goethe's Faust has no reason to fear. Mephistopheles guarantees that he is safe so long as he continues to aspire and to conjecture, and will die only when he succumbs to complacency and asks time to stop. The drama elongates itself to accommodate the hero's universal adventuring. Goethe worked on the first part between 1773 and 1806, and after beginning the second part in 1800 he returned to it in 1825 and went on adding to it until 1831, the year before his death. There is no completion, no terminus; a poem added as an epilogue to the first part concedes that there may be a beginning and an end, but denies that what happens in between constitutes a whole. Art, like life, is a process of becoming, a journey without an arrival. Faust wanders digressively through time and space, attending a Gothic witches' sabbath on the Brocken, then voyaging back to ancient Greece where he marries Helen of Troy – a match that for Goethe symbolized the union of classical and romantic cultures, physical perfection joined to mental supremacy. Faust is also a progressive scientist, who in old age takes up engineering and drains a marsh to reclaim land from the sea. Relying on technological skill not divine potency, he devises a system of locks and dykes which revise the topography of God's creation. Goethe shared Faust's enthusiasm for projects that treated the earth itself as plastic material. He suggested digging a channel to connect the Danube with the Rhine, and said that he longed for the Panama and Suez canals to be completed before he died. Engineering in *Paradise Lost* is a symptom of satanic conceit, like the causeway built over Chaos. Goethe considered such projects to be divinely inspired, or evidence that men now enjoyed a godly mastery of nature.

The Old Man – as Mephistopheles patronizingly calls God – makes an appearance in the prologue, with Milton's three archangels on hand to sing his praises. Mephistopheles compliments him on his ability to speak like a human being, even when exchanging chit-chat with the devil. Anthropomorphism is reductive: if we form God in our own image, how can he be better than we are? Having made a wager with Mephistopheles about Faust's corruptibility, God retires. The witty demon presents himself to Faust in the costume of an itinerant scholar, and explains that he represents the spirit of denial, the critical intellect – the highest product of a creation that, having once begun, ends in destruction. Yet this tempter has little to teach Faust, who in the first scene of the play frees himself from religious reproof. Opening his Bible, Faust quotes and then quarrels with the beginning of St John's Gospel. 'In the beginning was the Word', he reads. But the word seems to be the wrong one, because to personify language in this way over-values it. Faust, translating the Bible into the vernacular, experiments with synonyms. Would it make more sense to say that in the beginning was the Thought? This too is rejected as wan, impotent: a creator needs more than an idea. Faust tries out a third option, and proposes that in the beginning was the Power. He remains dissatisfied, because power refers to potential, held in reserve rather than being expended in action. Finally he settles on a wickedly disrespectful adaptation of the apostle's meaning. In the beginning, he decides, was the Act. The graduation from word to deed is the initiation of his own restless romantic career. He begins as a writer and thinker, but with the help of Mephistopheles he graduates to a life of action, or – since he can experience and possess whatever he imagines – of enactment. He becomes the seducer of Gretchen, the husband of Helen, the father of the high-flying, self-destructive Euphorion. He makes war on the Emperor, and commandeers the lemurs to build his personal paradise on a drained marsh. On their rambles through nature, Mephistopheles reminds Faust that he is experiencing unearthly delight. He reposes on mountain peaks, hovering between heaven and earth like a god; he can, if he wishes, speculatively burrow beneath the soil and lay bare the secrets of geological formation; he overflows with disinterested love for all creation, and with a more particularly carnal love for Gretchen (who is not sure that he can be trusted, because he replies evasively when she quizzes him about his religious beliefs). Mephistopheles impudently cites scripture, elbowing God aside in favour of satiated, domineering man: Faust, he says, feels within himself the gratification that follows 'all six days' work'. In fact, work is not called for. The hedonistic magic of art makes his dreams come instantly true.

Only once is Faust baffled, unable to make something happen by simply desiring it. The Emperor who engages him as a conjurer asks him to call Helen of Troy and Paris back to life. Mephistopheles brags that he can

supply ghouls and goblins on demand, but classical beauties are harder to
come by, since he has no access to the pagan underworld. He sends Faust
to ask for help from a subterranean sorority of goddesses known as the
Mothers, whose business – he explains to his bewildered pupil – is formation and transformation, the eternal recreation of the eternal mind. These
are the true protoplasts, mistresses of metamorphosis; their lair is the chaotic
psychological gulf which gives birth to monsters, or to sensual daydreams
like Helen. Mephistopheles directs Faust to touch a flaming tripod with a
key, then stamp on the ground. He does so, and sinks below the floor. The
play does not accompany him. Goethe was unafraid to represent events in
heaven, as he did when God bargains with Mephistopheles in the prologue,
but he refused to demystify the Mothers, and would not tell his earnest,
loyal friend Eckermann what the episode meant. He too was bound by a
pact, enjoined to keep a secret. Mephistopheles, interrogating one of Faust's
students, derides the analytical meddling of chemists or biologists, who kill
the organic life they are studying. The artist possesses powers which apparently do not belong to him and which do not always obey him; they derive
from a source which remains unknown, so it is best to treat them with wary
reverence. The Mothers are muses who live underground, not on a mountain like their Greek precursors. They are more unapproachably sacred than
Hesiod's muses, because – whereas only Mnemosyne was a mother, who
allowed her daughters to couple with their artistic wooers – they are all
maternal. The name Goethe gave them characterizes the imagination as a
womb and a nursery, the mind's procreative bed. The Mothers, continuously
creating and recreating, are responsible for art, which – as Faust declares
before summoning Helen – draws on defunct experience and reanimates
the 'lifeless images of life' stored in our memories. He appeals to them for
help, and Helen obligingly shimmers into view.

Faust finds the same incessant creativity in nature. Touching down on
a mountain, he steps out of a cloud and watches other wisps of air form
themselves into pictures of gods or giants, which are soon erased. When
Mephistopheles arrives on the gaunt crag, he says it reminds him of the abyss
into which he and the other miscreant devils tumbled when God threw
them down from the sky. He goes on to adapt Thomas Burnet's fable about
the earth's recreation, which explained how the smooth globe came to be
pitted and pocked with crevasses and serrated pinnacles. Hell was sulphurous,
so its gases made the devils sneeze and splutter; as they belched and gasped,
they cracked the level crust and sent cliffs jutting upward in unkempt, irregular spasms. Our terrain is the result of a satanic coughing fit. Meanwhile the
sky, as seen by Faust, is a blank blue sheet on which poets inscribe white
words. Either way, nature transforms, deforms and reforms itself around us;
the world is as prolific and provisional and boundless as Goethe's *Faust*.

Perhaps Goethe kept the Mothers out of sight to make amends for exposing the tubes and phials and uterine bowls in which Wagner concocts his homunculus. When Wagner says that he has mixed together hundreds of ingredients, he describes the operation of Coleridge's esemplastic power. Copulation, as he tells Mephistopheles, may be suitable for beasts, but man deserves to be relieved from the messy business; he therefore arranges for the seed and the egg to meet and merge outside the body. The joke is on the uncomprehending human creator. The homunculus flits off to the classical sabbath, leaving Wagner behind with his dessicated parchments. The scene in the laboratory comments on the obsession of experimenters who studied reproduction in the hope of learning how to synthesize life. Needham thought he had seen organisms generating spontaneously, which would have meant that they were born from nothing; in 1765 the priest and physiologist Lazzaro Spallanzani made a study of infusoria and established that they reproduced themselves by dividing in two. Spying on protozoa was a harmless enough pastime for a Jesuit, although Spallanzani's later probing of physiological conundrums was more indiscreet. He collected semen from a dog, filtered it and, using a heated syringe, artificially inseminated a bitch. He reported that he had been successful in 'fecundating the quadruped', which delivered a litter, and he announced that he hoped to provoke births in other species 'without the concurrence of the two sexes'.

Spallanzani died in 1799; in 1815 E.T.A. Hoffmann, tactfully making a tiny change to the spelling of his name, brought him back to life in his story 'The Sandman', an alarming exploration of the kinship between poetry, biology and machinery. Whereas Spallanzani meddled with the sex lives of dogs, Hoffmann's Spalanzani advances beyond nature. He makes a winsome automaton called Olympia; the puppet's eyes are supplied by the devilish Coppelius, a trader in body parts whose nocturnal visits connect him with the sandman, blamed by children for their nightmares. The hero Nathaniel falls in love with Olympia. In Offenbach's opera *Les contes d'Hoffmann* it is Hoffmann himself who becomes infatuated with the chirping doll. The substitution is logical: Nathaniel's psychological ailments make him a romantic artist, whose creativity twists into destructiveness.

As a boy, Nathaniel believes that the sandman is a projection of his own fantasy. But why has he called up this bogey? Coppelius comes after dark to confer with Nathaniel's father, who is some kind of alchemist; they are rumoured to be conducting experiments behind closed doors. Nathaniel's father dies when their laboratory explodes. Before the accident, the boy spies on a gruesome primal scene, and watches two male parents tussling in the black cavern where they plan an artificial procreation. Tools and tongs, perhaps meant to be used during parturition, lie on the floor. A cupboard is full of faces, though they have holes where their eyes should be. Coppelius grabs Nathaniel and examines him as a prototype; he pretends to pluck out his live, squashy eyes, and twists his hands and feet to and fro as if unscrewing them. This is Nathaniel's first experience of the artist's plastic power, which can rearrange nature. (A musician himself, Hoffmann saw instrumentalists as men so intimately connected to the wooden or metallic contraptions they play that they seem to have grown prostheses. He particularly relished the clarinetist in Jacques Callot's engraving of *The Temptations of St Anthony*, who plugs his instrument between his buttocks and makes music from his intestinal supply of wind.) Coppelius pays a bitter, envious compliment to God when he can find no better way of distributing the boy's wracked limbs: 'The Old One knew what he was doing!' Nathaniel collapses, and from then on has periodic bouts of insanity. His drearily sensible friend Lothario tries to persuade him that Coppelius is merely a mental phantom, and says that our own alternately depressed and exhilarated minds can 'cast us into hell or transport us to heaven'. As a remedy Lothario recommends the soothing influence of his own sister Clara. She is demure, serene, always smiling. But she is not beautiful; though he admires her, she does not appeal to his imagination. She and Lothario are a well-intentioned pair of critical exorcists, but to rid an artist of his demons is to disable him.

Nathaniel's illness recurs at university, where he attends the lectures of the Italian scientist Spalanzani, a surrogate for his dead father. He finds a new object for his day-dreaming in the compliant, obligingly manipulable Olympia. She resembles a beautiful statue, which makes her a symptom of the morbid Pygmalionism from which so many artists suffer. She murmurs sweet nothings, and her clockwork innards even enable her to dance, but articulacy and motion do not alter her implacable aesthetic surface. Olympia is always available to be looked at, and – since Coppelius has not yet fitted eyes into her porcelain face – she does not look back; unlike Clara, she has no mind. Though there ought to be a salving contrast between the two women, Nathaniel madly equates them. When Clara pleads with him to destroy the poems and stories he has written about his infatuation, he berates her as a 'lifeless accursed automaton'. Is he himself anything more than a male Olympia, jerkily impelled by cravings and crazes? Quarrelling over ownership of their invention, Spalanzani and Coppelius dismember Olympia as the horrified Nathaniel watches. He is hauled off to the madhouse, then released to be cared for by Clara. But he cannot rid himself of his imagination, and loses his reason once more when the vision of Coppelius returns. Finally he quietens the monsters in his head by hurling himself from a church tower and shattering his skull on the pavement. Nathaniel's love for the puppet prompts him to develop a desperate, neurotic theory of creativity. Life, he believes, is a bad dream. We are deceived if we think ourselves free, since each of us is 'the tortured plaything of mysterious powers'. He denies that 'the creations of art and science [are] the product of our own free will: the inspiration which alone made creation possible did not proceed from within us but was effected by some higher force from outside'. This catches the deranging paradox of romantic creativity. Although the imagination lives inside you, its violent workings seem to belong to some agency outside your control.

Kleist reached a similar conclusion in his essay on marionettes, published in 1810. The dancing figurines he describes are graceful because they cannot think; kicking up their heels as their wires are tweaked, they are immune to gravity and close to godliness. Intelligence, as a puppeteer tells Kleist, merely spreads disorder. The marionettes inhabit a paradise of bodily contentment, because they have not eaten from the Tree of Knowledge. Kleist's ironic essay, like Hoffmann's tragic story, confides the disquiet of romantic consciousness and its desire for self-annihilating relief. If the artist had God's power, would he make creatures like Olympia, with unclouded faces, nimble limbs and no brains? Kleist's friend proposes a choice between infinite consciousness and no consciousness at all, between God and the marionette. In a Cambridge chapel, Wordsworth paid homage to Newton's statue, whose silent face is

> The marble index of a mind for ever
> Voyaging through strange seas of Thought, alone.

Yet in a poem written in 1799 as an epitaph for an unknown woman, Wordsworth envisaged another voyage, less effortful and solitary:

> No motion has she now, no force;
>   She neither hears nor sees;
> Rolled round in earth's diurnal course,
>   With rocks, and stones, and trees.

Animate life returns to a vegetative state, or is absorbed into the unfeeling, abiding mineral bedrock. Romantic artists were proud of the mind's sovereignty, but they were also oppressed by the burden of that 'infinite I AM'. How much better to be blissfully unconscious – 'to cease', as Keats wished, 'upon the midnight with no pain'.

The subject of 'The Sandman' is the rivalry between creativity and the creation itself. The inventors are attempting to begin life all over again, so it is only too appropriate that Hoffmann – as he admits in the middle of the story – should not know how or when to begin his narrative. The story starts, with no expository introduction, as an exchange of letters between Nathaniel and his friends. After a while the letters stop, and Hoffmann belatedly considers his options. He could have reverted to the vague, remote moment which fairy tales identify when they say that something happened 'Once upon a time', or he might have got going 'in medias res', with Nathaniel's revulsion from the spooky barometer-dealer Coppola, who reminds him of Coppelius. Either way he would have had to go 'back to the beginning', which didn't suit his 'inner vision'. How could it, since the story is about the difficulty of determining life's origins and of accounting for the morbid inborn terrors of our minds? He therefore decided, he says, 'not to begin at all', and simply transcribed the letters. The story also has a premature and ironically misleading end. Hoffmann breaks off without a resolution, because we cannot know how our lives or the world will end. The narrative pauses after Nathaniel avenges Olympia by assaulting Spalanzani; the actual conclusion follows later, as an afterthought. The university discharges Spalanzani, who played an improper practical joke by introducing Olympia into polite society. There is a dissenter, a literary critic whose judgment on the hoax Hoffmann reports: 'The whole thing is an allegory, an extended metaphor! Do you understand me?' In his essay on the grotesquerie of Callot, Hoffmann praised deep-seeing souls who know that meanings may be hidden beneath the appearance of foolery. 'The Sandman' too is an allegory, chasing shadows through the darkness where mental and biological conception occur; the mechanical guile of Spalanzani is a metaphor, extended like the oiled limbs of Nathaniel or Olympia, for Hoffmann's freakish creativity.

The same duality complicates and magnifies *Frankenstein*. The hero and the novelist are colleagues, although what he thinks of as scientific research is for her an imaginative endeavour. The result is the same: Frankenstein and Mary Shelley both fabricate monsters. At least what Frankenstein calls 'the filthy daemon, to whom I had given life' is mortal. After his creator's death, the creature flees into the polar darkness, promising to die. Mary Shelley's 'hideous progeny', however, has proved to be unkillable. Modernizing Prometheus, she gave the Titan an extra lease of life by making him the genius whose rebellion drives the world we still live in – a philosopher who rejoices in his power to harry an ignorant God, an inventor who ruthlessly despoils nature, an artist who unleashes the incubi inside the head.

In Mary Shelley's amplification of the classical myth, those three apostasies overlap. Frankenstein contrasts his attitude to the Swiss landscape with that of Elizabeth, who is beguiled by 'the aerial creations of the poets' and sees the mountains and lakes through their eyes. She enjoys appearances, whereas Frankenstein wants to know about causes: 'The world was to me a secret which I desired to divine'. Divination is no longer the prerogative of deities, or even of soothsayers who, as if probing the future with a divining rod, possess supernatural insight. To divine, for Frankenstein, merely means to discover. Each addition to the sum of his knowledge – the revelation of

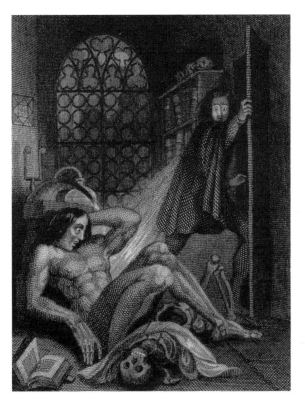

Frontispiece to the 1831 edition of *Frankenstein* by Mary Shelley

electricity during a thunderstorm, or his perception that alpine avalanches result from 'a concussion of the air' – is the result of a raid on nature and counts as a depletion of God. After his experiments with corpses, he claims to have discovered 'the cause and generation of life'. But the only way that he can describe his advance into 'the deepest mysteries of creation' is by using the terminology of art. Thus, while listening to a lecture on chemistry, he feels keys being touched within him and 'chord after chord ... sounded', until his mind is overtaken by 'one conception'. The monster is sung into being, as if by an Orphic incantation, and Frankenstein calls it 'my creation'. Mary Shelley in turn, during her account of the story's origins, refers to it as her 'invention'. The novel makes no distinction between the two overlapping modes of creativity. The monster describes language – after the cottagers teach him how to speak – as a 'godlike science', and calls reading 'the science of words or letters'. When Mary Shelley explains in her preface what invention means to her, she virtually paraphrases Coleridge's account of the esemplastic agency: it is 'the power of moulding and fashioning ideas'. Frankenstein proposes 'the creation of a being like myself'. Impelled, he says, by an inflamed imagination, he looks forward to a time when 'a new species would bless me as its creator and source'. He is speaking for Mary Shelley, who in 1831 called Frankenstein 'the artist' and the monster his 'odious handiwork'. Her introduction recalls a dialogue between Byron and Shelley, who wondered whether corpses could be revived by 'vital warmth'. Art performs miracles that remain impossible for science: any literary character demonstrates what Mary Shelley calls 'voluntary motion'.

Like Frankenstein recoiling from the monster, Blake viewed his tiger with quizzical dread, reluctant to believe that he had created it:

And what shoulder, & what art,
Could twist the sinews of thy heart?
And when thy heart began to beat,
What dread hand? & what dread feet?

The insistent rising inflection of those unanswered questions flings out a challenge to God. Engineering rapidly caught up with this fervent mental creativity, and designed monsters of its own. On a visit to Scotland in 1803, Wordsworth and his sister Dorothy were taken aback by the sight of a levered machine like a forge-hammer, which heaved water out of a coal mine. It worked in slow motion, apparently pausing for breath after each descent, and regularly emitted a vocal groan of complaint. Dorothy could not help attributing to it 'some faculty of intellect'. Was it an engine or an organism? Wordsworth defined the pump as a creature of a new kind, which had

'made the first step from brute matter to life and purpose'. In Coleridge's description it was even more like a prototype for Frankenstein's creatures: he called it 'a giant with one idea'. In 1835 in *The Philosophy of Manufactures*, Andrew Ure consolidated the link between Frankenstein and industrial engineering. Ure described the automated spinning machine as a 'Herculean prodigy', and said that it 'sprung out of the hands of our modern Prometheus at the bidding of Minerva'. The Titan who made this 'self-acting mechanism' was Samuel Crompton, whose robotic offspring was nicknamed the Iron

THE RUSSIAN FRANKENSTEIN AND HIS MONSTER.

John Tenniel, *The Russian Frankenstein*, cartoon in *Punch*, 15 July 1854

Man. In 1812 a new law introduced the death penalty for destroying machines: the lives of intelligent pumps and iron men were as sacred as those of human beings. By 1850, the tailor turned poet in Charles Kingsley's novel *Alton Locke* viewed the entire industrial economy as the fulfilment of Mary Shelley's prophecy. Explaining the agitation of the proletariat, Alton accuses a society that 'shrinks in horror, like Frankenstein, from the monster her own clumsy ambition has created'. His sermon goes on to condemn the 'Frankenstein Mammon' of industry, warning it 'either to make thy machines like men, or stop thy bungling, and let God make them for Himself'.

Among the topics debated by Byron and Shelley, with Mary as their 'devout' auditor, was galvanism. In 1791 the physiologist Luigi Galvani announced that he had made the muscles of dead frogs twitch by using an electrical current that crackled between iron and copper. Coleridge, in a session of table talk in 1831, explained Galvani's feat as 'the union of electricity and magnetism', and worried about the ontological status of the movements it provoked. Although galvanism 'by being continuous ... exhibits an image of life', Coleridge decided that it was 'an image only; it is life in death'. Could this be the condition he personified in 'The Rime of the Ancient Mariner', where the skeletal woman who appears in a plankless, spectral ship is identified as 'the Night-mare LIFE-IN-DEATH'? Perhaps the esemplastic power can produce only an uncanny, derisive simulation of life. Galvani's discovery eventually had an industrial application: the electrolytic action of zinc protects iron and steel, and keeps roofs or fences from rusting. Long before this, galvanism was adopted as a literary metaphor, because it captured the static electricity of emotion that courses between people and convulses society. For Thomas Carlyle, revolutionary France was 'a monstrous Galvanic Mass', its citizens liable to explode with excitement. Jacobin politics reminded Carlyle of the 'Commixture of the Four Elements' unstably engineered by 'the Anarch Old', whose primal world was 'founded on the wavering bottomless of the Abyss'. In Charlotte Brontë's *Vilette*, the feeble Graham is 'galvanised ... to new and spasmodic life' by the approach of the frisky Paulina. When Coleridge said that the acting of Edmund Kean was 'like reading Shakespeare by flashes of lightning', he meant that Kean electrified or galvanized the text with the jagged accentuation of his speech and his bristling nervous gestures.

Animation is the Promethean implantation of a soul, sometimes called the anima. At the beginning of *Frankenstein*, the role of Prometheus – played successively by all the characters, because every modern man shares in the assault on God – is taken by the polar explorer Walton. He finds Frankenstein half dead in the ice; his body is 'restored ... to animation' by being rubbed with brandy, and as he watches for the monster 'a new spirit of life animated [his] decaying frame'. Genesis calls man a living soul, but in Frankenstein's case the compound of flesh and spirit seems to be falling apart. As he begins the recitation that comprises the bulk of the story, Walton sees 'his thin hand raised in animation, while the lineaments of his face are irradiated by the soul within'. The divine fire, stolen by Prometheus, rages inside him, though it produces only torment. Unlike the God of Genesis, Frankenstein balks at creating woman, and decides not to give the monster a mate: before disassembling his laboratory he surveys 'the remains of the half-finished creature, whom I had destroyed'. He feels a brief twinge of guilt, as if he had 'mangled the living flesh of a human being'. The rejected specimen could just as well be a poem left incomplete like 'Kubla Khan', or an unfinished symphony. The romantic work of art describes its own creation, as *Frankenstein* does, and also incorporates its own demise. In a dying fall, words concede their failure to make explicit the truth they were groping towards. Keats's nightingale flies away, and sound – like a cloud unknitting itself – drifts into silence.

The monster vows to build a funeral pyre for himself on the ice, and promises to 'exult in the agony of the torturing flames'. His self-immolation – if it ever happens, since all Walton can say for sure is that he sails off on his raft – will be a return to the creative source. Byron and Shelley both described literary creation thermodynamically. For Byron, a poem was the lava-flow of imagination, a molten river of feeling. The geologist James Hutton, who published his conclusions about the 'system of nature' in the 1790s, explained that volcanoes were the earth's 'safety-valves', and Byron's poetry served the same purpose. The volcano inside the poet's head regurgitated the creation of the world: in Goethe's *Faust*, the Vulcanists argue that the earth had its origins in a seismic explosion, not – as the Neptunists contend – after a long, tentative ascent from the depths of the sea. Shelley, less eruptive than Byron, called the mind in creation a fading coal, implying that the poet had to work fast before it cooled. Mary Shelley had her own domestic equivalent to this theorizing: the discussions that suggested her dream about the monster took place, she says, around 'a blazing wood fire', kept alight even in the middle of the summer. Did it serve the same purpose as the furnace in the laboratory where Wagner cooks up the homunculus, or the blackened hearth concealed behind a wall cupboard in the room used by Nathaniel's father and Coppelius? By trial and error, the monster discovers how to light a fire, and roasts his food on the embers. He worries when it fizzles out, because he 'knew not how to reproduce it': the verb is biological, but it can be applied to a technological accomplishment like rubbing sticks together, or to the novelist's breeding of characters, which are like segments of a single identity that has undergone fission.

The flames warm the monster and brighten the darkness, but they cause pain when he touches them, and he wonders how 'the same cause could produce opposite effects'. The incident is an aesthetic warning. Creativity is thermal, generating a fitful, impulsive heat. Thoughts are charges that flicker between the brain's synapses, making unexpected contacts that we experience as jolting inspirations. Coleridge likened Dorothy Wordsworth to an 'electrometer': she attracted and channelled sympathetic feelings, which excited her sensibility like an electrical current. But fire in *Frankenstein* is also the medium of destruction. The monster scatters 'a variety of combustibles' around the cottage of the family that has rejected him, then torches the kindling. The logic of creation involves a tactical withdrawal from the first scorching, agitated centre of energy; the heat of conception must be balanced by the cold, detached skill of execution. Kubla Khan's sunny dome contains caves of unmelting ice, and Mary Shelley's prescription for the unnatural reality of art is the same. The novel therefore begins and ends near the North Pole, and the hero's rendezvous with the monster takes place on a glacier below Mont Blanc, with 'pallid lightnings' at play around the peak. Frankenstein is invigorated by watching a violent alpine storm, which he calls a 'noble war in the sky'. The cannonades of thunder and bayonet charges of lightning are a combat of cosmic forces, meteorologically mimicking the war in heaven described in *Paradise Lost*. But the story is also the account of a war in the head – a noble intellectual quest, or an ignoble mania? The scientist's task is to canalize and conduct the lightning, to harness it as a source of power: when the novel was filmed in the 1930s, Frankenstein used its voltage to enliven the monster. The artist's task is to refrigerate the lightning, to whiten it – as in the image of those pale volts behind Mont Blanc – or to harden and preserve it like the motionless waves of the 'mer de glace' above Geneva. In *The Last Man*, funeral rites are performed in the Alps: plague-stricken bodies repose on a 'bier of ice', frozen and thus safe from putrefaction. The narrator descends to depopulated Rome, where his only companions are gelid neoclassical statues. He touches the 'icy proportions' of Canova's Cupid and Psyche, and recoils from the 'unconceiving marble', so unlike warm, fertile flesh. Art, trying to reproduce life, succeeds only in creating these beautiful, bloodless corpses.

But what if the creation refuses to be bridled and tamed (as Coleridge put it) by its creator? After reading *Paradise Lost*, the monster adopts it as the story of his own aggrieved life. 'I ought to be thy Adam,' he tells Frankenstein, but his rankling grudges turn him into 'the fallen angel'. What we call a monster is an image of ourselves that we refuse to recognize when we look in the mirror. The monster complains that Frankenstein, who gave birth to him but now wishes to kill him off, is sporting with life: 'you, my creator, detest and spurn me, thy creature, to whom thou art bound by ties only dissoluble by the annihilation of one of us'. It is as if Kubla Khan had denounced Coleridge for stifling or censuring him by his refusal to continue the poem, and accused him of hypocrisy in disowning the sensual fantasy it exists to satisfy. Unable to procreate, the monster – like the artist as characterized by Freud – can only nurture vengeful fantasies. 'My vices,' he tells Frankenstein, 'are the children of a forced solitude.' Coleridge had misgivings about fatherhood because a child, like a poem, might turn against its progenitor. When his son Hartley was born in 1796, he wrote a series of sonnets about the experience. The first prays for the holy spirit to descend so that the baby can 'be born again, a child of God'. But rebirth implies a previous death, and in the second poem Coleridge – still travelling home from Birmingham to Bristol, not yet having seen the baby – wonders if when he arrives he will be told that it has died. Holding his heir for the first time, he reflects on 'all I had been, and all my child might be!' The prognosis cannot have been cheerful: the sonnet that follows returns to imagining 'the cries/ With which a Mother wails her darling's death'. Is the creator secretly infanticidal, resenting and repressing the secondary self he has released into the world? Hartley, as predicted, grew up to be a befuddled, thwarted parody of Coleridge himself.

Mary Shelley's dead babies and her own mother's death after childbirth confronted her with an even more grievous paradox. The very process of creation must have seemed to her like premeditated murder. Her narrator is male, but his language often alludes to female travails and terrors: after the thunderstorm, Frankenstein dismisses 'natural history and all its progeny as a deformed and abortive creation'. The novelist's surrogate is Justine, the girl accused of killing Frankenstein's younger brother. The monster has murdered William, but the evidence points to Justine, who has no alibi. A confession is extorted from her, although she makes it only in the hope of receiving absolution. Yet her confessor's threats of damnation cause her to doubt her own innocence: 'I almost began to think that I was the monster that he said I was'. The next day she is executed for the monster's crime. The response of Frankenstein's intended bride is even more shocking because, like a romantic poem, it is the spontaneous overflow of powerful feeling. When William's body is brought home, Elizabeth insists on being shown the corpse. She then exclaims 'O God! I have murdered my darling child!' and faints. The child is not hers, and she has not murdered him. She blames herself because she allowed William to wear a miniature of his dead mother; it is now missing, so she deduces that he was killed by a robber. Her outcry is another variant of the creator's self-incrimination, displaced from Frankenstein himself. Later she says that she can imagine being 'condemned to suffer on the scaffold' for William's death and also for that of Justine. Imagination induces a guilt that only be relieved by this expiatory sacrifice. The monster returns to murder her in her bridal bed on the night of her marriage to Frankenstein. It is a brutal consummation, but if sexual initiation is a kind of killing, then the creature perhaps acted at the behest of his creator.

Elizabeth internalizes the vertiginous Swiss landscape, and feels she is 'walking on the edge of a precipice', about 'to plunge … into the abyss'. That crevasse is the gulf from which the world first emerged, and also the obscure declivity of the dreaming mind. The orifice gapes wider in *The Last Man*, where the plague is a 'deep and precipitous … gulph' that 'opened to receive us', and all streams spill into 'the vast abyss'. Verney, the sole survivor, gazes down from the Jura at Lake Leman, which seems to lie 'in the yawning abyss of the ponderous globe'. Or is the catastrophe the self-pitying delusion of a solipsist? The personal universe created by the romantic artist was a frail, faltering bubble, less durable than Kubla Khan's dome. Frankenstein's elegy for his friend Clerval, a Wordsworthian lover of nature, asks a troubling question: 'Has this mind, so replete with ideas, imaginations fanciful and magnificent, which formed a world, whose existence depended on the life of its creator; – has the mind perished?' If the mind perishes, so must the world it formed. Shelley in his poem about Mont Blanc reminds the mountain that it exists on sufferance, and can only stand there so long as his thinking holds it up:

> And what wert thou, and earth, and stars, and sea,
> If to the human mind's imaginings
> Silence and solitude were vacancy?

*The Last Man* refuses to accept this self-deifying conceit. A few years after the deaths of Shelley and Byron, it laments their loss but regrets their metaphysical folly. Shelley like Adrian consigned himself to the care of the winds and waters, which overwhelmed him; Byron like the novel's moody sensual despot Raymond signed up for a quixotic political campaign in Greece, and died playing the role of a romantic hero. Shelley considered life to be a clumsy and faltering rehearsal for death, and Byron treated existence with laughing disdain. The world, in their opinion, was unworthy to outlive them. Raymond, a Napoleonic conqueror who plans at first to profit from the collapse of the English monarchy, wants 'to govern the whole earth in his grasping imagination'. The adjective is an omen: the imagination no longer smoothly and tactfully moulds reality, as Coleridge wished, but seeks to fasten a grip on it, compelling it to gratify an imperious fantasy. Men now consider themselves to be 'lords of creation', as Mary Shelley puts it, and construct machines to advertise their dominance: Verney travels between London and Scotland in a sailing balloon with a steering gear of feathers, and is delighted because the contraption flaunts 'the power of man over the elements'. He is equally proud of England's naval supremacy, thanks to which the country 'mastered the elements and rode proudly over the waves'.

The elements – the constituents of creation itself, according to classical myth – were enslaved by industrial society. Air, fire and water drove engines; earth was churned up by mines. Some observers protested at this exploitation. In the 1760s clergymen objected to the use of mechanized fanners at a Scottish mill, arguing that people should patiently wait for God to decide when the wind should blow. Defoe, visiting a Derbyshire lead mine in 1725, described it as an inverted, subterranean cathedral: the shaft was as deep as the cross on the dome of St Paul's was high. Verney, however, is confident that 'man's mind alone was the creator of all that was good', and believes nature to be 'only his first minister'. The offended elements chasten this arrogance. At Dover, tidal waves pummel the cliffs and invade the town. A gale shrieks, and the sun, still glaring despite the storm, makes the sea burn 'like a furnace, like Vesuvius all alight, with flowing lava beneath'. The maelstrom demonstrates that man was never more than a plaything of nature, toyed with and then tossed away. Wiser and more pessimistic at the end of the novel, Verney recognizes that the human race is an aberrant species, doomed ever since it first 'crept out of uncreative void into light'. Here again Mary Shelley afflicts a male character with her own distressed recollections of childbirth, which for her was inseparable from the trauma of creation. Verney's phrase is dismaying: the womb-like abyss is a vacancy, even a killing chamber. Having crawled into the light, man then sets out on the intellectual journey that leads to knowledge, power and self-destruction. There is no question of remaining in an unpresumptuous paradise, as 'the mere gardener of earth'. Earth needs no gardener, and its fertile resurgence shows human beings to be irrelevant.

Thomas Campbell's poem *The Last Man*, published in 1823, describes an expiring planet, worn out by old age and by human depredations: the sun is sickly, the earth wan. Mary Shelley's version of the apocalypse is more selective. Expendable mankind wastes away, while 'healthful vegetating nature', no longer harassed by machines, continues to bloom and bear fruit. For a while Verney rails against a punitive male deity, who cuts men down because they have usurped his power. A crazed astronomer reviles the tyrant in the sky, and calls him 'the Supreme Evil'. Another fanatical preacher promises his followers immunity to the disease, and calculates that survivors will worship him as 'a patriarch, a prophet', the equal of Jupiter or Vishnu. Acceptance comes when the characters forget their quarrel with a jealous supernatural father, and remember instead the wrongs they have done to an aggrieved matriarch. Verney can accept the justice of the disaster because it is decreed by a necessity which is 'Mother of the World!' When he buries another companion, he reflects that the crumbling body is now part of 'the vast clod which had been our living mother'. Genesis turns out to be a female preserve, its mystery guarded by the Mothers. Male artists and scientists enviously but ineffectually mimic it with their alembics and syringes, their scavenged cadavers and cases of glass eyes, their iron men and posthumously jumpy frogs.

In 1829 Berlioz sent Goethe the score of *Huit Scènes de 'Faust'*, an episodic musical digest of the drama which began with an Easter prayer and ended with a diabolical serenade. Goethe passed the manuscript to his

Joseph Wright of
Derby, *Vesuvius,*
*c.* 1776

friend Carl Friedrich Zelter, Mendelssohn's teacher. Zelter's verdict was
harsh. The composer, he said, seemed to be spitting, sneezing and belching
(which is how bodies naturally express themselves, and how the world,
according to Mephistopheles, acquired its present form). He dismissed the
work as 'the remains of a miscarriage from a hideous incest': unnatural,
abominable, yet fortunately self-defeating, since the sexual crime was cancelled out by the gynaecological calamity. Berlioz published the *Scènes,*
though he later regretted having done so, and destroyed as many copies as
he could find. Romantic artists chose to set human creation against the
created world of nature, and inevitably found the comparison dismaying.
Could art ever do more than breed death, or fabricate monsters?

# 17

# THE GOD OF STEAM

When Blake tried to determine who or what made the tiger, he could only assume that the beast was created in a factory. God must have done more than manipulate wet clay. Fierce heat presumably fused the creature's parts in a foundry. In considering his incandescent image, Blake nervously inspected the source of his own creativity:

> What the hammer? What the chain,
> In what furnace was thy brain?
> What the anvil? what dread grasp,
> Dare its deadly terrors clasp?

The metrical beats of the verse are like an anvil chorus, insistently hammered out. A 'dread grasp' is necessary, like the 'grasping imagination' of Mary Shelley's hero in *The Last Man*, since both God and the poet have to handle white-hot thoughts. The brain is a furnace; similarly, in Blake's poem about London, the mind is a forge where, thanks to a heat that not even iron can resist, manacles are made. Byron too called the mind a 'fiery particle'. The Logos, being logical, surely operated at a low temperature and a steady pace, in concentrated silence. The romantics preferred a more vehement demiurge – the proprietor of a cosmic workshop where creation and destruction merged in a blitz of sparks, and jets of expelled steam relieved the intolerable pressure. Creative toil was accompanied by clangour. In *The Deformed Transformed*, Byron's devil explains that 'From the star/ To the winding worm, all life is motion', and adds that 'In life *commotion* is the extremest point/ Of life'.

In the beginning, an earth without form and void was given shape by God's intercession. Thomas Batchelor, a self-taught Bedfordshire farmworker, announced in 1804 in his poem *The Progress of Agriculture* that the 'unremitting hand' of industry had 'chang'd the formless aspect of the land', setting limits to fields with hedgerows and hawthorn fences. These rural enclosures looked like a confident correction of Genesis. Soon it became necessary to re-imagine the beginning, adding a convulsive violence. In the early 1850s John Martin used the landscape of the industrial north of England in his painting *The Great Day of His Wrath*, which shows boulders tumbling from a sky of liquid flame to crush quaking mankind. The blast furnaces and gasworks in Sheffield and Newcastle-on-Tyne were intent on

*Fêtes de l'inauguration du chemin de fer – benediction des locomotives, Strasbourg, 1852*

a second creation, the regeneration of an earth that could no longer be left to its own slow, sluggish devices. In *Dombey and Son*, Dickens describes an earthquake that has ripped apart a grubby London neighbourhood. Houses topple, debris piles up in unnatural hills, and 'treasures of iron' rust in 'something that had accidentally become a pond'. Phrases accumulate, but cannot be pieced together into a coherent picture. The language negates itself: it mentions bridges that lead nowhere like incomplete sentences, and impassable thoroughfares. Chaos has come again in a warfare of elements, with clouds of ash settling on geysers of boiling water. Unmade by metaphor, the world falls apart into 'a hundred thousand shapes and substances of incompleteness, ... unintelligible as any dream'. At last Dickens reveals that these are excavations for the railroad, still 'unfinished and unopened', at Euston. The mess is a tribute to 'the mighty course of civilisation and improvement', but to make way for the smooth-running future, we must experience all over again the catastrophe of the earth's origins. In 1863 in *The Water Babies*, Charles Kingsley took a more optimistic view of this re-creation. Tom the chimney-sweep drowns, engulfed by the primal sea. But he is born again, reincarnated in a more equitable society where he becomes an engineer and lays plans for 'railroads, and steam engines, and electric telegraphs, and rifled guns'. Guns complete the list because scientific innovation cannot happen without the threat of force.

James Watt's inventions, drawing on steam pressure, captured what Wordsworth called the 'burning energy' of nature and put it to work. The Victorians liked to think of Watt as a boy at the fireside watching the lid of a kettle rattle as the water boiled. In 1769 he devised a way of condensing this vapour, which made the steam engine possible. His machines conducted nature through a cycle from water to steam and back to water – exactly the career of transpiration and evaporation described in Shelley's poem about the life-history of a cloud, although the changes now happened at hurtling speed, accelerated by heat. By 1880, Blake's tiger had leapt into a new, sleek form: it had become a train. In *La Bête humaine*, Zola's novel about sex, death and the railway network, the driver Jacques admires the gleaming steam engine of his locomotive, to which he gives the feminine nickname of La Lison. She has a contented boiler and a satisfactory steam flow; she loves being greased, and operates always 'at the highest possible pressure' without consuming too much fuel. Though manufactured not created, she possesses a soul – 'that something' (as Zola puts it, fortuitously adopting Blake's imagery) 'that the chance blows of a hammer can bring to metal'. Mostly she behaves like a compliant sexual partner; but Zola's title points out that she is a beast, a bitch, and her feral whims leave Jacques – a murderer who is disgusted by the women he desires – struggling with deadly terrors. While he furtively couples with the station-manager's wife in the train yards, a distant banging sounds 'like the noise of a giant hammer': a percussive commentary on coitus, to which another engine adds a whistling shriek. Derailed, the expiring La Lison is like a woman eviscerated. Her wheels stick up in the air, her cylinders and valves are smashed, her connecting rods twitch. Though her pistons still pump like two incorrigible hearts, the hot coal in her fire-box cools to ashes. She gives up the ghost in a spasmodic expulsion of steam. She has caught a chill in a blizzard, and the mishap that knocks her from the rails is like a seizure. Engines are tragic creatures, which live too fast and are doomed to die young.

Thomas Carlyle acclaimed Watt as another romantic Prometheus, 'searching out ... the Fire-secret'. Shelley understood the almost blasphemous impact of his innovations. In 1819 the engineer Henry Reveley wrote to report on his casting of a steam cylinder, to be used in an air pump. Shelley thanked him for his 'volcanic description of the birth of the cylinder'. The adjective was well-chosen: Shelley's volcano is verbal, but it connects a mechanical invention with the fury of nature and of the creative brain. Rouget de Lisle, who wrote the words for the *Marseillaise*, said that Berlioz had a head like 'a volcano in a perpetual state of eruption'. No compliment could have given Berlioz more pleasure. On a visit to Naples in 1831, he watched nature imitating the wrath of John Martin's God, as Vesuvius threw molten rock 'like glowing blasphemies towards the star-lit heavens'. The volcano blasphemed because its eruption disputed the placid biblical account of creation. In 1858, travelling by train through Birmingham and the so-called Black District, the American historian Henry Adams gaped at a smoky, flaming landscape which 'had never existed before, except in volcanic craters'; and in 1883 when Krakatoa erupted, the chaplain on a German ship likened the exploding mountain to 'the smoke stack of a gigantic standing steam locomotive'. Shelley said that Reveley's technical report suggested what God must have felt 'when he made the earth, and saw the granite mountains & flinty promontories flow into their craggy forms, & the splendour of their fusion filling millions of miles of the void space, like the tail of a comet, so looking, & so delighting in his work'. The paraphrase of Genesis soon takes off into an industrial rhapsody. Fusion is what happens in foundries or forges, and those millions of miles of empty space exist to be abridged by steam engines. But the comet warns that this universe is unstable, not eternal. In Shelley's next sentence, the biblical creator merges with the crafty Watt: 'God sees his machine spinning round the sun, & delights in its success, and has taken out patents to supply all the suns in space with the same manufacture'.

This God, as Shelley sarcastically intimates, is a crafty entrepreneurial capitalist. In 1775 Watt invoked an old law about monopolies, which awarded the right of ownership to inventors; the patents he took out gave him control over certain steam engines for twenty-five years. Shelley even foresaw the imperial extension of this industrial power. Britain needed new markets and new sources of raw material, so it briskly colonized a sizeable portion of the world, like God deciding to turn other galaxies into an economic protectorate. The witty slur was all the more incisive because the design features patented by Watt included a system of gears that were nicknamed 'the sun and planets': he had mechanized the rotary intricacy of the solar system. 'Nature can be conquered,' Watt allegedly declared, 'if we can but find her weak side'. The assault continued throughout the century. In the mid-1850s, James Clerk Maxwell competed for a prize to explain the motions of Saturn's rings. He reported that he was 'battering away' at the morose planet, 'returning to the charge every now and then'. After breaching the defences of 'the solid ring', he expected to reappear in 'the dusky ring', choked by air so thick that he likened it to the atmosphere in Sebastopol, currently besieged by British forces during the Crimean War. Maxwell's astral siege was more grandiose than its counterpart on the ground: it was 'conducted from a forest of guns 100 miles one way, and 30,000 miles the other, and the shot never to stop, but to go spinning away round a circle, radius 170,000 miles'. The Russians were finally driven out of Sebastopol, and Maxwell expected the prime mover to surrender his secrets and quit the sky.

Industrial society depended on a tense, abrasive contradiction. The steam engine brought heat and cold together, and hoped that they would cooperate, like fire and ice in Kubla Khan's dome. Water expanded in the boiler; it then had to be cooled in the condenser. Watt's invention increased work rates, but at the cost of increasing the economic disparity between those who did the work and those who profited from it. The labour of the many subsidised the leisure or lassitude of a few. Even those who were idle fancied that they lived at industrial speed. The Parker sisters in Jane Austen's last, unfinished novel *Sanditon* are relentlessly and pointlessly busy, and keep themselves stoked up with cocoa and herbal tea; Sir Edward Denham's fuel is sensational fiction, which he relies on the 'enlarge the primitive capabilities of the heart'. Such overproduction of energy led to an imbalance, because it was not equally distributed. The Parkers have a neurasthenic brother, who huddles by the hearth to absorb a warmth he cannot generate. The metabolism of the creative mind was dangerously intense. One moment it over-heated; the next it cooled down, and the loss of heat meant death. These calorific standards became criteria for judging art. In 1873 Henry James reviewed *The Spanish Gypsy*, a doggedly versified narrative by George Eliot. He regretfully decided that it was not a true poem, because it lacked the 'the hurrying quickness, the palpitating warmth … of such a creation'. Poems, like poets, were expected to overheat and hyperventilate.

Watt's engines tampered with the laws of physics. A human organism
or a society that imitated industrial rhythms, choosing to increase stress and
pressure, risked disaster. Thomas Henry Huxley likened the liberally
educated mind to 'a steam engine, to be turned to any kind of work'. Others
worried about the physiological strain of so much huffing and puffing. The
mill-owner in Charlotte Brontë's *Shirley* feels that he is about to suffer an
industrial accident, and says that 'The machinery of all my nature, the whole
engine of this human mill: the boiler, which I take to be the heart, is fit to
burst'. Sick and sleepless in 1869 after a train journey from London to
Scotland, Dickens calculated that the trip had administered thirty thousand
shocks to his nerves. He accepted the damage to his beleaguered body,
because his creativity impelled him to work at a locomotive's tempo. He
said he was 'incapable of rest' and would 'rust, break and die' if he slowed
down. But such exertions wore out nature, and perhaps offended God.
Wilfrid in Balzac's *Séraphîta* reminds the pastor that 'man can create no
force; he can but use the only existing force, ... namely motion, the incomprehensible breath of the sovereign maker of the universe'. Wilfrid assumes
that steam is holy; in that case, every engine that uses it is blaspheming, like
the volcanoes of Berlioz. He warns of the consequences. The new force has
to be created by mingling two hostile substances, which ought to be kept far
apart; the example Wilfrid gives is gunpowder, 'akin to thunder'. For Henry
Adams too, gunpowder had 'religious motives' and belonged 'to the spiritual world', vacillating between the realms of good and evil. Inflammable or
explosive substances could hardly have been concocted by God, who
confined himself to making things that were good. Milton was right to
make them a product of devilment, or of man's infernal science. In 1840
Balzac predicted revolution. He was convinced that French society would
blow up like 'the boiler of a steam engine'; the blast came eight years later,
when a repressed generation took to the streets. But for Adams, even the
political disorder of 1848 did not shake 'the true faith'. The world was
changed, Adams said, by 'steam-horse-power' and coal, which suddenly
made redundant 'all experience since the creation of man'.

This new technology seemed casually miraculous. The engine with
which George Stephenson won the locomotive trials in 1829 was called
the Rocket: the metaphor turned it into a flaring weapon aimed at the
horizon. A train trip from Scotland to London in 1839 excited Carlyle
because it resembled diabolical possession. He called it the 'likest thing to
Faust's flight on the Devil's mantle', and imagined that 'some huge steam
night-bird' had picked him up and swept him away through space.
Religion, recovering its composure, made efforts to bring the engines into
the fold. The local archbishop baptized the first locomotive to arrive at Lille
in 1846. A poem written in 1855 by Flaubert's friend Maxime du Camp

presented steam as incense: the vapour discharged by a train's engine wafts
upwards and assures God that man is expressing love for the creator in outbursts of condensed air. This was never more than a fond hope. A young
idealist in Benjamin Disraeli's novel *Tancred*, published in 1846, complains
that nineteenth-century people 'never dream of angels. All their existence is
concentrated in steamboats and railways'. Tancred is horrified when an aristocratic socialite says she might enjoy a trip to Jerusalem, so long as she
could get there by train. He wants to organize a crusade, not a railway connection. Rather than sprinkling holy water on the engines, George Eliot
tried to harness them to the secular march of history. In *Middlemarch* Will
Ladislaw paints the conqueror Tamburlaine, who yoked the monarchs he
deposed to his chariot and made them serve as draught-horses. Dorothea
asks if his Tamburlaine symbolizes 'earthquakes and volcanoes'. That would
be a romantic reading; Ladislaw explains that the war-lord also represents
'migrations of races and clearings of forests – and America and the steam
engine. Everything you can imagine!'

Trains took on the fearful mystique of monstrosity that dates back to
the Chaos described by Empedocles, where ogres like the Chimaera were
the messy precursors of creation. Victor Hugo, after a train trip from
Brussels to Antwerp in 1837, declared that 'the iron horse is a veritable
beast'. It breathed, trembled, howled, sweated, and even urinated when its
tanks were emptied. It sounded like a dragon, though Hugo was dismayed
that it looked so drearily functional. He regretted that steam power had not
been discovered during the Renaissance, when trains might have been
given wings on their wheels or funnels like the snorting trunk of a pachy-
derm. Watt, he said, designed nude machines; he would rather have seen one
fantastically dressed up by Benvenuto Cellini. Flore in *La Bête humaine*,
ravaged by guilt after derailing La Lison, throws herself into the path of an
express, which bounds towards her like a Cyclops. Its single red eye glares
like a brazier, its mouth vomits flame. The young woman rears at the engine
as if wanting to wrestle with it; her head batters the lamp and puts it out,
before being mashed to a pulp.

The monsters of Empedocles were muddled rehearsals for humanity.
Now, possessing superhuman force, they turned on their human creators and
threatened to kill them. In 1855 Delacroix expressed an obstinate hostility to
trains. In a coach, he said, he at least felt 'I am travelling, I see things, I am a
man'. That last phrase contained a shuddering premonition. Trains reduced
a human being to a dead weight, strapped to a missile. The cruel capitalist
in *Dombey and Son* travels in a train that is identified by Dickens as 'the
indomitable monster, Death!' Repetitive participles – 'roaring, rattling,
tearing on... shrieking, roaring, rattling' – mimic the clatter and unstoppable
momentum of the iron wheels. Carker, the villain in the same novel,

is pursued, knocked down and sliced up by an express, whose trampling, bladed wheels work like 'a jagged mill': the train that dismembers him is a machine designed for that purpose. To kill yourself under a train, as Tolstoy's Anna Karenina discovers, you need the quick-thinking skill of a technician. Anna has to collaborate with

Honoré Daumier, *Impressions et Compressions du Voyage*, 1843

the machine as it lurches past, inserting herself between the trucks at just the right moment; her first attempt fails because she takes fractionally too long to remove a bag from her arm. Suicide is the successful completion of a time-and-motion study – proof, though negative and unrepeatable, of the individual's adjustment to the production-line in a factory.

Mr Dombey's train reaches 'the journey's fitting end' in an industrial slum whose ash-crusted tenements anticipate 'the end of everything'. The poet Théophile Gautier saw the same terminal scenario in Turner's *Rain, Steam and Speed – The Great Western Railway*, which was painted in 1844, two years before the serial publication of *Dombey and Son* began. For Gautier, Turner's train was the Beast of the Apocalypse, with an irate red eye, a writhing spinal column of carriages, and fiery wings thrashing the air. The squall on the Thames at Maidenhead, where the train charges across a bridge, looked to Gautier like 'a real cataclysm, ... the setting for the end of the world'. (It might be added that the painting finds room for a glance back to the beginning of the world. Away from the viaduct, the smutty air clears, and a ploughman traverses a field while a boat serenely bobs on the water. The railway bypasses somnolent Arcadia.) Gautier's description catches the metaphysical unease of men whose inventions had confounded the regime established in Genesis. In 1833 Wordsworth addressed a sonnet to steam-boats, viaducts and railways, telling them that Time was 'Pleased with your triumphs o'er his brother Space'. Or was space frightened and disoriented by time's new urgency? From his train, Dombey sees a 'rushing landscape' – a countryside that seems to be fleeing from this mechanical assault. Faces are glimpsed, then blurred into a crowd; now they are, now – as Dickens immediately adds – they are not. In Turner's painting, this panic is conveyed by a hare's attempt to outrace the engine. The hunted creature is elongated by its haste, as if it were stretching its own skin. If it runs fast enough, it may have the good fortune to disappear altogether: at speed, objects dematerialize. Turner participates in this kinetic competition by applying paint impatiently. Thackeray said that the pigment in *Rain, Steam and Speed* had been slapped or smeared on. If so, this was true to the indistinctness of locomotive vision. On his Belgian train, Hugo noted that the flowers beside the tracks had forfeited outline and individuality, smudging into dots and dashes of red and white light. Realism respected detail, but the world seen from a train consisted of ephemeral impressions.

Railway schedules imposed simultaneity, coordinating time throughout entire countries. Networks were meant to function like divine omniscience: in 1864 Walter Bagehot praised the railways for sponsoring and speeding up the march of mind, now that 'London ideas shoot out each morning, and carry a uniform creed to each cranny of the kingdom'. But Turner's engine – its black funnel sharply delineated, although everything else in the painting has dissolved – propounds no such enlightened gospel. Space is jumbled, destabilized. The perspective of the railway line recedes to one vanishing point, but the adjacent bridge rushes backwards in another direction, and the slanting diagonals of the rain agree with neither; the painter's viewpoint is groundless, since he looks down from some notional perch in mid-air. Etched arrows of drizzle net the air into an obstructive fence, which the train will have to crash through. The balls of steam coughed from the funnel trail off horizontally, too cindery to rise higher and meet the clouds. When La Lison is stoked up with coal, Zola describes a 'blazing comet's tail' above it. Even runaway asteroids, so troubling to astronomers during the age of reason, could now be manufactured on earth and ejected into the sky.

When the railway line from Paris reached Lille in 1846, Berlioz marked the occasion with a cantata, *Chant des chemins de fer*. Given only two days' notice of the commission, he composed the work at steaming speed in three hours and then hurried down to Lille, glad – as he said – to have arrived 'without being derailed once'. Eighty singers were recruited to bawl a text by Jules Janin; the fire brigade, artillery garrison and National Guard in Lille refused to cooperate, so an orchestra was assembled from military bands in neighbouring towns. The celebration ended with cannonades and fireworks, during a performance of Berlioz's *Symphonie funèbre et triomphale*. The cantata is a series of brassy, boisterous rallies, with the choir emitting exclamations like ammunition. The massed male singers hail the railway's levelling of nature ('Que de montagnes effacés!') and admire the sweaty fertility of creative toil ('Travail humain, fécondate sueur!'). Fanfares politicize the hymn, and the addition of an organ vouches for God's approving presence. A tenor fires off a fusillade of high notes – including a last high C, a human equivalent to a train's ear-splitting whistle – as proof of straining industrious effort. The cantata made an exultant noise in the town square for eight minutes, and was at once forgotten. Berlioz wryly admitted that if he had been given three full days to spend on the job, the score might have lived forty centuries longer. The industrial age had changed static, classical notions about artistic immortality; it dealt in ephemera, like the flux Hugo saw through the window of the moving train.

Music is a disturbance of air, so it sympathized with the new techno-logical forces that provoked upheavals in the atmosphere or propelled messages through it. When Wagner's *Das Rheingold* was first performed in Munich in 1869, a steam engine backstage loudly puffed a hot, hissing mist into the mines where the Nibelung slaves toiled. The new source of power set a quicker tempo for life, and popular dances reeled along with it. Josef Strauss's *Dynamiden-Walzer*, performed at an Industrial Society ball in 1865, wavers for a while with teasing uncertainty, then whirls into perpetual motion. Johann Strauss II composed a *Motoren-Walzer* for the Carnival ball given by technical students at the university in Vienna; in his *Demolirer-Polka* and *Explosions-Polka* he celebrated the havoc that accompanied the rebuild-ing of the imperial capital. In 1899 Puccini honoured the centenary of Alessandro Volta's galvanic battery with a march entitled *Scossa electrica*, or electric shock. He called the terse, jaunty piece a 'bit of rubbish', and when it was performed for a meeting of telegraphists in Como, he hoped it would hustle them into early retirement. His dismissiveness has a certain pathos. Puccini's march, like those Strauss waltzes, is an exacerbation of time, revved-up but certain to wind down. Lives are expendable, and music com-posed to order is disposable too. Could it be that this sublime art was merely the release of wind, gas or scalding vapour? Nietzsche in 1888 mocked 'the steam of the Wagnerian ideal', a hot fog of sex, religion and rhetoric, bred by the miasmal climate of the north.

Although Berlioz joked about the *Chant des chemins de fer*, its industrial zeal pervades the rest of his work and kindles the most extravagant of his creative fantasies. In 1855 he conducted a series of what he called 'concerts-monstres' in the Palais de l'Industrie at the Exposition Universelle, and his friend Ferdinand Hiller joked that he needed to use an electro-magnetic telegraph to transmit orders to the thousand performers scattered through-out the utilitarian cavern. The musicologist Bourgault-Ducoudray, meeting Berlioz in 1862, fancied that he had steel nerves, which multiplied tenfold the energy produced by his fragile body; he spoke and moved in short sharp bursts, as if electrically impelled. The man with the cranial volcano dreamed of setting off orchestral explosions, attuned to the crackling energy of nature. When he conducted, Berlioz felt himself to be 'an electrical machine', whose gesticulating arms flung chords that were 'harmonious projectiles' like Jove's thunderbolts. He stirred up tornadoes, then soothed them with another motion of his hand. He once discussed with a chemist the practicability of stuffing a mountain with gunpowder and lighting a fuse. Disappointingly, the expert advised that the result would probably only be a cloud of smelly gas. On holiday in Plombières, Berlioz looked at the Alps from a terrace, and longed to soar freely into space. How come mankind, so proud of its 'familiarity with steam and lightning', had not yet learned to fly? Berlioz admired the wreckage left behind by the ancient geological uprising that produced the Vosges mountains. The ice, he noted, was so hard that gun flints could be made from it. But guns were now operated by triggers, so perhaps there was no further need for glaciers.

Triggers are percussion mechanisms, potentially music-makers: Berlioz always thought of the orchestra as a combination of arsenal and factory. He enlarged its sonic range with new instruments like the saxophone, the ophicleide, or the miniaturized antique cymbals he designed to accompany the reverie about Mab in *Roméo et Juliette*; he delighted in goading it to wild prestissimo races, which always culminate in a metallic crash. The ride to the abyss in *La Damnation de Faust* – a profane oratorio developed from the eight scenes he sent to Goethe in 1828, first performed six months after the railway cantata – could be happening on board a runaway locomotive. Méphistophélès lashes his mount, which might be an iron horse. He lunges at a group of women praying beside a wayside cross,

*Ein Concert im jahre 1846* – a caricature of Hector Berlioz conducting by Andreas Geiger

who flee with a screech. Faust cries out that a baying monster is behind them, catching up – another train, maybe? The express makes an unanticipated stop, after which it redoubles its speed. At last it leaps into the gulf where creation and destruction conjoin; far below, devils noisily cavort.

The opera *Benvenuto Cellini*, first performed in 1838, ends in a happier apocalypse. The setting is Renaissance Rome, but the culture Berlioz celebrates is industrial. Cellini has killed a rival during a Carnival riot and is condemned to death, but the Pope suspends the sentence if he completes his statue of Perseus on time. To cast the figure in bronze, Cellini takes over the Colosseum as his foundry, and works all night like the devils in *Paradise Lost* when they build the palace of Pandemonium. The ruin is a symbol of Rome's global dominion; it may also be an architectural remnant of the prime mover's all-encompassing intelligence, so in setting up a furnace there Cellini is igniting the fire of the creative mind. The metal-workers sing a chorus that recalls the mineralogy of Milton's demons: they describe metals as 'fleurs souterraines'. Cellini views them as acolytes of Prometheus, and calls them masters of fire. In their rollicking account of the genesis of the arts, they overlook God, whose creative fiat supposedly sorted out chaos:

> Quand naquit la lumière
> La génie aux beaux-arts
> Divisa la matière;
> Il en fit en quatre parts.

Eugène Delacroix,
*Faust et Méphistophélès galopant dans la nuit du Sabat*, engraving, 1828

Light is born not created, and God is replaced by 'la génie', a life-force or spirit whose conduit is artistic genius. The division of matter into four parts goes beyond the rudimentary separation of the elements, because it creates a quartet of arts. The genie – as the chorus says – bequeathes stone to the architects, colour to the painters, marble to the sculptors. The most precious gift is reserved for the chisellers of metal: they are given gold as their medium. Their professional anthem serves as a rowdy drinking song, and introduces the scene in which Cellini, caught up in the chaotic festivity, murders Pompeo. Art is Dionysian – fuelled by irrationality or intoxication, exempt from moral penalties. It is the first fruits of chaos.

This bravado is put to the test at the end of the opera, when the statue has its birth onstage, helped along by Cellini's destructive tantrums. He scrambles up a ladder propped against the model and brandishes a hammer, threatening to smash it if the Pope's guards arrest him. When he runs out of metal, he orders all his previous masterpieces – cast in gold, silver, copper or bronze – to be thrown into the crucible. (The historical Cellini was more prudent, and only melted down two hundred items of pewter from his household store.) Of course the over-burdened, broiling womb blows up; the lid flies off, in a cataclysmic version of Watt's experiment with the kettle. Liquid metal, like the lava of poetic inspiration, floods free, then solidifies into its appointed form inside the mould. At this moment, the real Cellini cried out to God and applauded Christ's resurrection, which his statue imitated in emerging unscathed from the furnace. The reaction of the operatic Cellini is less orthodox. He likens himself to Vesuvius, spouting ideas, ardour and fizzy high notes. The Pope, hastily asserting that the success is due to divine intervention, retreats to the safety of the Vatican.

The artists of the mid-nineteenth century were industrious to a fault. Berlioz sighed over the energy he and his colleagues expended in musical journalism, and said it was as if a contingent of 'steam engines, capable of tunnelling through the Alps' were employed to turn a millstone. Art did its best to match technology's progressive standards. Berlioz wistfully recalled Adolphe Adam's opera *Le postillon de Lonjumeau,* in which the tenor who played a coachman sang high Ds to imitate the post horn. Since then, steam had asphyxiated horses; soon, Berlioz predicted, it would be replaced by electric power. Somewhere in the future he glimpsed a dirigible airship. He expected the human voice to keep up, but could tenors go on reaching ever dizzier heights without expiring?

Genius had to be supplemented by the efficiency prized by factory managers. Anthony Trollope designed a portable writing table that he could take along on a train or ship when travelling as a functionary of the Post Office; the little contraption guaranteed that he maintained his daily quota of words. It infuriated Trollope to see how patiently Americans accepted delays during railway journeys. When time stood still, life wasted away. Murger in *Scènes de la vie de Bohème* joked about society's new expectation that the artist should be an indefatigable worker. The lazy Rodolphe is commissioned to write a technical treatise on the hot-air stoves manufactured by his uncle. Berated for not having finished the chapter on chimney ventilators, he bargains for some firewood. The icy garret contains a variety of his uncle's stoves and furnaces, though none of them is alight; his relative permits him only a single, frugal lump of coal, and spurs him on by confiscating his tobacco. Rodolphe, locked in until he completes the job, fumes as he surveys the view from his window: 'Everyone is smoking, except me and my uncle's stoves!' Rodolfo in Puccini's *La Bohème* adheres to this thermodynamic creed, and combats the wintry cold by feeding the stove with the manuscript of his tragic drama. His friend Marcello offers his own artistic sacrifice – the canvas on which he has painted the parting of the Red Sea. Rodolfo prefers paper, because canvas stinks when it burns. The fire blazes briefly, though they are soon shivering once more.

Balzac repudiated such dilettantism. His dozens of novels were written under factory conditions, in sessions that lasted all night; he worked all the shifts, and kept himself going with injections of hot, strong coffee that eroded his health. He once challenged the machinery of his trade to a competition, which he won. In 1843, impatient to correct proofs of two novels that were due for publication while he was away in Russia, he took up residence at the printer's workshop for a month. He averaged nineteen hours' labour a day, and could not forgive the type-setters and their hydraulic engines for their slackness. He longed for a steam-powered press, which might have kept up with him. In *La peau de chagrin* – published in 1831, and translated as *The Wild Ass's Skin* – Balzac brooded about this creative compulsion and the self-expenditure it induced. Raphael, a young gambler, decides to drown himself. To delay the act, he dallies in an antique shop beside the river, where he discovers an ass's skin that glows as eerily as a comet: evidence of cosmic irregularity, of life's fiery transit towards extinction. The skin has a Sanskrit inscription, identifying its magical powers. It can fulfill wishes (which is the purpose of dreams and of art), and it renews life for Raphael, who before finding it could see no future. But every time it is used, it shrinks, as does the life-expectancy of whoever uses it. The fable introduces an elaborate discussion of creative toil and its destructive toll. Raphael, who is dispensed from having to work once he acquires the skin, believes that his talisman proves the propulsive, motorized power of imagination. For him, as for Balzac, human will is 'a material force like steam', and its 'fluid mass' can push aside all moral obstructions. At a party with his friends, drunk on carbonic acid gas and poetic ideas, Raphael succumbs to 'the delights of chaos'. Yet the faster he lives, the sooner he will arrive at his cold, silent terminus. Aware of his own profligacy, Balzac tried to conserve vital energy. The Goncourt brothers cattily reported that he considered sperm to be 'an emission of pure cerebral substance', as if he were ejaculating unwritten novels.

Raphael attempts to defy the second law of thermodynamics, with its grim computation of lost heat. He hopes to learn from the example of a tubercular patient, who cured himself by rationing his breath and employing his lungs only six times a minute. As a result, he comes to resemble 'a youthful corpse'. The steam engine's heaving respiration is a reminder of death; you can only live at this pace if you are made of iron or steel. Raphael chooses instead to imitate the oyster, which clings to its rock and hopes that paralysis will outwit death. He takes drugs to sedate not stimulate himself. Opium makes him as blissfully sluggish as an animal crouched on the forest floor, camouflaged as 'vegetable refuse' to deceive its prey. A doctor in a sanatorium tries to get rid of him by devising a theory about the risks of high altitude. This exploits the same belief that the body, like any engine, is an apparatus designed for combustion. The doctor warns that breathing burns off our supply of phlogistons. This imaginary element, dreamed up by the alchemists, suited the biorhythms of an industrial society. When a lump of coal burned, its phlogistons supposedly escaped, and only ashes remained. To romantic poets, the process resembled the spirit wearing out the flesh. As Byron argues in *Sardanapalus*, fire is 'the element/Which most personifies the soul', because it leaves 'the least of matter unconsumed': hence the hero's choice of incineration. Raphael's doctor tells him that his 'inflammatory temperament' produces a superfluity of oxygen, and sends him to live in the lowlands, where the air is heavier. The amoral criminal Rastignac exemplifies this law of life. In his room, Raphael notices that his copy of Byron's poems is missing some pages, which have been ripped out to light the fire. The damage to the book demonstrates that Rastignac lives Byronically. The imperative is to keep on consuming, even if it is your own body or your possessions that you feed on. Rastignac's financial schemes have an artistry of their own. He is 'a speculator whose capital is imaginary'; he tells Raphael that the way to become rich is by borrowing. The economy of capitalism confirms the wish-fulfilling fantasy inscribed on the ass's skin.

Scientists pool their resources to explain the pelt's magic properties, and their madly elaborate cogitations are a commentary on the go-getting haste of their society and on the simmering creative disquiet of artists like Balzac. Dr Caméristus thinks that the hide must be impregnated by the 'semina' of van Helmont, a vital seed that surges in all living things (and even, apparently, in some that are dead). Planchette, a mystically inclined physicist who spends his time pondering 'the bottomless abyss of move-

ment', sees the skin as a shaggy version of a perpetual motion machine. He
accepts the expansibility of water, which 'brought the steam engine into
being', yet acknowledges that even water can only expand up to a certain
point. Nature has placed limits on our power, and the skin is bound to go on
shrinking. For Planchette, this means that God, the prime mover, retains his
monopoly: 'Everything is movement, thought is movement. ... If God is
eternal, be sure that He moves eternally; perhaps God is movement'. While
Planchette attempts to stretch the skin, the chemist Japhet tries to break
down its resilient substance. He bathes it in chloride of nitrogen, tries to
slice it with a razor, and uses a galvanic battery to administer electric shocks.
When it smashes the hydraulic press in which he struggles to crush it, Japhet
christens the material 'diaboline'. This confirms Planchette's faith that God
is at the controls of the cosmic machine. Japhet's metaphysics are more
quizzical. His experiments concentrate on sulphurous decomposition:
chemistry sees the world as 'a gas endowed with the power of motion', and
its experiments 'repeat the action of creation by using some gas or other'.
Defeated by the skin, he announces 'I believe in the devil'. Should an artist
like Balzac have believed in God the patient maker, or in a rebellious,
unstoppable energy that could only be called diabolical?

At dinner, Raphael's cronies jest about the discrepancy between
Spinoza and St Paul: is God omnipresent, or does he stand apart, allowing all
things to proceed from him? They decide that this is the same as asking
whether the chicken or the egg comes first, and suspend the debate to concentrate on eating and drinking. Led astray by Rastignac, Raphael decides
on a career of debauchery, and cites Byron as a self-expending libertine who
was also an poet. Like Sardanapalus, he flings himself on the pyre of sensual
amusements. He knows that the weary artist needs a respite from 'his
paradise of imaginings: he either craves, like God, the seventh day of rest, or,
like Satan, the pleasures of hell'. Although sabbatical tedium is the sensible
option, Raphael cannot resist that tempting heat. Balzac made the same
calculation when assessing the cost of his creativity. His writing, he said, was
'suicide by hard labour'. He worked harder than God, and kept longer
hours; taking Sunday off was not enough to save him. But he never doubted
that the sacrifice – of life itself, for the sake of art – was worthwhile. In any
case, he had no choice. Genius, as Raphael understands, is a possessed state:
the artist is like a general on the battlefield, impelled towards a violent,
glorious destruction.

Dickens worried about the mental health of machines, perhaps to
deflect his concern for himself. In *Hard Times*, the piston of a steam engine
nods 'monstrously up and down like the head of an elephant in a state of
melancholy madness', unhinged by the monotony of its task. Mrs Gamp,
the midwife in *Martin Chuzzlewit*, addresses one of her most tipsily

eloquent tirades to the steam engine of the Antwerp packet, moored at London Bridge. As she belabours it with her tattered umbrella and abuses it for spluttering, roaring and hammering, she competes with its din; she too is letting off steam. She calls down a biblical curse on the 'nisy monster', and says that she wishes it 'in Jonadge's belly'. Although she mistakes the prophet for the whale, her error has a certain logic: the engine was conceived inside a human head, so why shouldn't it be re-engorged by a human stomach? 'One might easy know you was a man's inwention,' she says, 'from your dis-regardlessness of the weakness of our naturs'. But the invention exists to boost our weak nature, to augment our physical capacity. Only someone as rowdy as Mrs Gamp has the strength to challenge it. The antagonism between them is sexual: a man's invention, vulnerable despite its size and its noise, is mocked by a woman. 'You brute!' she cries, as if maltreated by a lover. Mrs Gamp speaks for nature because she has a professional under-standing of birth and death. As well as delivering infants, she attends the sick and cleans their corpses; her twin specialities are lying-in and laying-out. To the latter duty she brings the instincts of an artist: her fingers itch to arrange the limbs of her deceased patients 'in that last marble attitude'. She confronts the engine as an equal, and as her harangue continues, she reveals a certain complicity with it. She is convinced that its frothing and fuming must be responsible for provoking premature births, which means that the detestable thing is good for her business. As evidence, she mentions a railway guard who is godfather to twenty-six unexpected infants, all 'named after the Ingeins as was the cause'. Her mispronunciation sponsors a pun, and allows illicit meanings to proliferate: could the fathers of those brats have been Indians not engines? The Victorians individualized locomotives by naming them after people, or characters in Arthurian romance. The compliment is improved if reversed: it makes better sense to name people after engines, whose seething virility equips them to be father figures.

Mrs Gamp's standards of comparison are industrial, or at least thermo-dynamic. At home in her Holborn slum, her familiars include a kettle, a toasting-fork and a pair of bellows, and this equipment turns her squalid room into a factory. Her nose betrays 'symptoms of inflammation', due to the liquor she slyly imbibes. One of her patients is the oppressed clerk Chuffey, who during his illness has a head 'so hot that you might heat a flat-iron on it'. 'The things he said!' she reports, scandalized and titillated by his delirious babbling. 'The awfullest things, Mr Chuzzlewit, as ever I heerd!' The flat-iron was pre-industrial, and had to be warmed by being placed on the fire. But Mrs Gamp's analogy is apt: here the furnace is the brain of Chuffey, who blabs secrets which are like steam escaping through a twisted spout or a thin funnel. With her usual inventive genius, Mrs Gamp has proposed a solution to one of the domestic vexations of her age. To re-heat the flat-iron every few minutes was inefficient and tiresome. Housewives in the 1840s and 1850s got round the problem by using rubber tubes that attached their irons to gas jets. It was even suggested that the pipe could run to the kettle, allowing the iron to be warmed by steam. In Mrs Gamp's workshop, this tenuous wiring is unnecessary. All you need is a man in bed who suffers from hallucinations.

When her neighbour Poll Sweedlepipe urgently summons her downstairs, Mrs Gamp imagines a holocaust: 'Is the Thames a-fire, and cooking its own fish?' Poll tells her that she underestimates the calamity: 'If you was to crowd all the steam engines and electric fluids that ever was, into this shop, and set 'em every one to work their hardest, they couldn't square the account!' A river spontaneously combusts, and a barber's shop dilates into a thunderous hall of dynamos. These extravagant verbal forays are at once hilarious and alarming. The heads in which such fantasies arise are like boiling kettles, whose lids lift off as the vapour hysterically hisses; the characters share the novelist's febrile imagination. Boffin's house in *Our Mutual Friend* has a kettle steaming on the hearth. Near it, the eight volumes of Gibbon's *Decline and Fall of the Roman Empire* – which Boffin the dustman hires Silas Wegg to read to him – are 'ranged flat, in a row, like a galvanic battery'. The metaphor is alluringly sinister: books too emit energy, especially if their subject, like Gibbon's, is the collapse of a world. The public readings Dickens gave demonstrated the galvanic power of his words. Once his pulse was taken before and after he performed the murder of Nancy in *Oliver Twist*. It was 90 when he began, 124 when he finished.

The malignant dwarf Quilp in *The Old Curiosity Shop* is another flammable being, who goes without sleep to keep alight the cigar that fuels him. He smokes unceasingly, as Dickens explains, as 'a precaution against infection' and 'a means of wholesome fumigation'. The burning tobacco is also the source of his vitality, and he is able to 'blaze away all night' like Blake's satanic mills. He chooses to inhabit a den with a new chimney, which distributes smoke indoors rather than releasing it into the air. Puffing on a pipe as he leans against this stifling convenience, he disappears into the fog he exudes and comes to resemble Turner's advancing train: 'nothing of him was visible through the mist but a pair of red and highly inflamed eyes'. Like a furnace that needs to be stoked with coal, Quilp has a ravening appetite: at breakfast he gobbles eggs and their shells, prawns with their heads and tails still affixed, and even chomps on his knife and fork. He washes all this down with tea that is still boiling. He further raises his internal temperature by drinking grog, 'heating his malice and mischievousness till they boil'. Quilp expresses himself explosively. When he rubs his hands together, he seems to be 'manufacturing, of the dirt with which they were encrusted, little

charges for popguns'. When Satan's minions in *Paradise Lost* invent gunpowder, they ravish the earth to release nitrous gas; Quilp, however, can
produce artillery from his unaided body. His hands are a foundry, and they
knead bullets. His body may be humped and shrivelled, but his head – an
engine-room – is massive. The French encyclopaedists defined a monster as
a creature without kin, belonging to no class or category. Quilp is proud of
his autonomy, and grunts that he acknowledges no 'dear relations'. Tyran-
nizing his wife and her mother, he is 'the small lord of creation'.

Dick Swiveller calls Quilp an 'evil spirit'; when he crawls out of a
cellar, he is an 'evil genius'. Perhaps, for Dickens, there was no other kind of
genius. He describes Quilp as a deity, though not a Christian one. He squats
on a straw mat 'like an African chief', and performs a shamanistic dance to
enrage a chained dog. He has a private totem, a battered figure-head from
an old ship. But his mode of worship is sadistic. He screws gimlets into the
ancient, weathered admiral, lacerates the face with a red-hot poker, sticks
forks in the eyes and nails in the nose, then carves his own name in the
wooden flesh. He punishes the venerable image because he intends to take
its place: Quilp himself is the idol manufactured by an industrial society.
No wonder Henry Adams regarded Dickens's novels as 'atrocities', just as
he thought Shakespeare's plays were 'stupendously anarchistic'. He meant
both comments as compliments: this was an art appropriate to the over-
energized, brawlingly democratic modern world. *The Old Curiosity Shop*
goes out of its way to visit Jarley's waxwork show, so that Dickens can mock
the 'calm and classical' art of the past, sedately statuesque. (A waxen Byron is
on view, although there is some controversy about whether he deserves
the tribute: his sexual conduct, after all, would have melted wax.) Far from
this placid mortuary, Quilp embodies the new culture of maniacal kinesis
and frantic over-production, which is visible as well in an infernal mill
where demons toil, 'wielding great weapons, a faulty blow from any one of
which must have crushed some workman's skull'. A schoolteacher chides
the demure heroine Little Nell for lacking fervour and activism, which in the
mid-nineteenth century were the most desirable and economically valuable
human qualities. She is 'a wax-work child', who should be 'improving [her]
mind by the constant contemplation of the steam engine'.

Quilp, a physical freak, is the product of Dickens's violently contorted
imagery, which likens him to a dog, a tribal potentate, a factory furnace – to
anything and everything. He is literally a vehicle, a conveyance for metaphor
(which, deriving from Ovid's metamorphoses, means a transporter, a linguistic motor that brings about change). Enveloped in smoke, he is like
a train. On another occasion, he resembles a horse – a pre-industrial transporter, though Quilp is a horse with wings, lent extra speed by the nocturnal
imagination: he looks 'like a dismounted nightmare'. Quilp's improbable

existence demonstrates that creation no longer governs chaos by giving it form, as Plato and Aristotle wished. To create now means to transform or to deform, which Quilp offers to do when he menaces some intruders. 'I'll beat you to a pulp', he threatens: that would serve as his squashy, malleable protoplasm. He then tells them he will 'break your faces till you haven't a profile between you'. For want of other opponents, he punches himself in the face. As G. K. Chesterton noticed, the incident reveals that Quilp is 'energy, and energy by itself is always suicidal; he is that primordial energy which tears and which destroys itself'. That energy drove Dickens too, and – during his last reading tours, when trains hurled him to and fro across the north-eastern United States or between London and Edinburgh – it broke his health and destroyed him.

Industrial machines were as reluctant to be ridden as Blake's tiger. Gods expect to be worshipped, not to perform menial chores. At the end of *La Bête humaine*, La Lison's replacement, frisky and rebellious, gallops driverless across the country. Jacques and his stoker have toppled out during a fight, and are beheaded by the wheels. The engine shrills on, delivering soldiers crammed into cattle wagons to certain death in the Franco–Prussian war. But these carnivorous monsters were mortal too. Steam is heat, which as it dissipates warns of the sun's eventual extinction. Later in the nineteenth century, when the world began to run on electricity, it seemed as if man had finally vanquished the sun. For Henry Adams, the Blakean furnace, with its greed for coal, was obsolete. Michael Faraday's experiments with electromagnetism convinced Adams that nature was irradiated by a force that had emitted energy 'without stop, since time began, if not longer', and might go on doing so even after the sun had fizzled out. Those immortal, indefatigable rays wrecked the Christian universe. The demolition was completed in 1898 by Madame Curie's discovery of radium, which Adams described as a 'metaphysical bomb'. In 1901 Adams experienced an epiphany. It happened near the North Pole, the site that in *Frankenstein* represents the abstract, dazzling limit of thinkability, where mental speculation reaches a dead end and even bodily life cannot be sustained. Adams saw that embargo being lifted. He had not after all strayed beyond the reach of the 'electromagnetic civilization' that produced Frankenstein, Faraday and Thomas Alva Edison. While he was in the realm of ice, he received a telegraph message that brought news of President McKinley's assassination. It hardly mattered that another man-made god had been cut down, because telegraphy compensated for the faulty, enfeebled solar system. 'The electro-dynamo-social universe', Adams concluded, 'worked better than the sun'. Edison had replaced Watts as a saviour. The dynamo – a machine for producing electrical energy from the rotation of copper coils in a magnetic field – was a whirring brain, not an over-stressed body.

A. L. Coburn, *The Lord of the Dynamos*, photogravure print from *The Door in the Wall and Other Stories* by H. G. Wells, 1911

H. G. Wells's story 'The Lord of the Dynamos', written in 1894, is set in suburban London in a shed where power is generated for the electric railway. Holroyd, the engineer who oversees three dynamos, 'doubted the existence of the deity, but accepted Carnot's cycle'. (That dogma was already a little antiquated: Sadi Carnot tracked the transformations of steam that turns fire into work – although machines could not complete the four stages of his cycle, which was better exemplified by natural forces such as tornados.) The engineer's underling Azuma-zi bows down before the largest of the enthroned dynamos, which is 'greater and calmer ... than the Buddhas he had seen at Rangoon'. Mistreated by Holroyd, Azuma-zi electrocutes him. When found out, he grips the naked terminals and sends the charge ecstatically thrilling through his own body. Primitive gods thrive on such sacrifices. At Niagara Falls in 1906, Wells paid a visit to the gallery of dynamos in the power station at the base of the cataract. Glad to escape from the thundering deluge outside, he listened to a mystical hum that was the sound of 'thought translated into easy and commanding things'. Wells apologized for the silence of the prose in 'The Lord of the Dynamos', and wished he could add a mechanical soundtrack to send the reader's mind 'jerking into odd zigzags' like those that derange Azuma-zi. But the cerebral dynamos at Niagara operate in 'cloistered quiet', and no longer cannibalize the men who tend them.

Any new source of power is a stimulus to religious awe. That is why the Victorians saw steam engines as monsters, why Wells viewed the power station as a clean, silent modern cathedral, and why the Italian futurist F.T. Marinetti – driving a sports car which he described as a centaur with an electric heart – declared in 1908 that speed had brought heaven within reach: 'soon we shall see the first angels fly!' When Henri Becquerel discovered radioactivity in 1896, Henry Adams announced that the ancient breach between matter and energy, or between God and his creation, had at last been healed. Adams hailed radium, with its unstable, disintegrating nuclei, as 'one of the immediate modes of the divine substance'. An earlier version of human history assumed that God was present at the origin of the world, after which he drifted back into the distance. But this collaboration of science and art suggested a revision of the story. Could it be that the deity was an end-product, not merely what George Eliot in *Daniel Deronda* calls 'the make-believe of a beginning'? Rather than straying into disobedience or conspiring to kill him off, were we struggling to invent him? Balzac's Séraphîta argues that creation is tending upwards, striving towards spirit. In 1932 in *Two Sources of Morality and Religion*, Henri Bergson gave thanks for the engines that had begun to release the 'élan' stored in matter and make it available for human use. With their help, he said, we could coax our refractory planet to fulfill 'the essential function of the universe, which is a machine for the making of gods'. Anyone beguiled by Bergson's optimistic creed has a choice of machines: those gods might be engendered by a turbine, a nuclear reactor, or perhaps a computer's hard drive (a term that nervously remembers the industrial era of hard-driven engines).

Henry Adams recognized that, in industrial society, spiritual ardour had taken a new form. Transmuted, it became 'the Energy of modern science'. Adams made conscientious efforts to dynamize himself: he began riding a bicycle when past the age of fifty, and in 1904 bought a car, 'a very pretty Mercedes' with the power of eighteen horses. But he was not sure that machines deserved to prevail, and he wistfully contrasted the dynamo with a statue of the Virgin Mary, once reputed to work wonders of its own. 'All the steam in the world,' he decided, 'could not, like the Virgin, build Chartres'. While science may have made God redundant, it has not done away with our need for art.

# 18

# GO FORTH AND MULTIPLY

The prophet Mohammed has a reputation as an iconoclast – critical of images, hostile to art. One day he supposedly found his wife Aisha embroidering human figures on a saddle cloth. 'Give life to what you have created!' he sneered. In other cultures, Mohammed's remark might have been a dare. Prometheus does what Aisha cannot do; in the nineteenth century, when God's creation of man seemed at best a myth, artists were still able to give life. The novelist in Zola's *L'Oeuvre*, speaking for Zola himself, complains about the polite emasculation of contemporary fiction and says, with bold procreative intent, 'To put life into men! That's the only way of being a God!' As it happens, there is another way. The painter in the same novel, based partly on Cézanne, uses his palette knife to decapitate a figure in one of his landscapes. The composition does not satisfy him, so he mutilates the image. Later, after repainting the same woman, he puts his fist through the canvas and kills her again. God cannot forgive reality for failing to match his dreams.

Proficiency as an executioner has always been one of the artist's credentials. Oscar Wilde said that Dickens slew Little Nell like a lamb and sold her corpse in the market-place; the sacrifice was commercial not religious, since her suffering boosted sales. Dickens might not have resented the claim. In January 1870 after a reading of the scene in which Sikes batters Nancy's brains out, he reported 'by far the best Murder yet done'. He crowed over the women who fainted and were taken from the hall 'stiff and rigid', as if they were his personal victims. Puccini at least had the good grace to sob when his consumptive heroine Mimì slipped out of life in *La Bohème*. It was, he said, like watching his own child die. Trollope had less parental solicitude. He once overheard two members of his club complaining that they were bored by Mrs Proudie, the irrepressible gossip in his sequence of novels about Barsetshire. He immediately went home and plotted her demise. But characters eliminated on a whim could not always be relied on to stay dead. Conan Doyle became bored by Sherlock Holmes, and in 1893 put a stop to him. Moriarty, Holmes's antagonist, warns 'This is inevitable destruction', and they tumble together into the 'tremendous abyss' or 'immense chasm' of the Reichenbach Falls. Bereft readers wore black armbands, as if mourning a non-fictional death; Doyle insisted that his act was 'justifiable homicide'. Nevertheless, in 1901 he allowed Holmes

Auguste Rodin,
*Nude Study of
Balzac*, bronze,
*c.* 1892

to rise from the dead. Dr Watson, startled, wonders how he clambered out of the 'awful abyss' or 'dreadful chasm', a 'cauldron of swirling water and seething foam'. The mystery is that of creation itself, covertly in league with destruction: the gulf, Doyle's private chaos, is the place from which everything emerges and to which everything returns. Falling, Holmes and Moriarty are still 'locked in each other's arms', as inseparable as God and Satan. Once out of sight underwater, did they fuse? The reborn Holmes refuses to disclose the secrets of the deep, and does not betray the confidence of Doyle, his maker and his killer.

Asked to explain the origins of *The Pickwick Papers*, Dickens said 'I thought of Mr Pickwick, and began'. What else could he say? Chesterton regarded the result with reverent astonishment. The novel's haphazard plot, he said, was merely 'an incantation to call up a god', and the divinity in question was as impish and eternal as Pan or Puck. In 1909 Chesterton likened Dickens's novels to 'popular religion, ... the ultimate and reliable religion', which dispenses joy. The books served the same purpose as the universal machine extolled by Henri Bergson: Dickens 'is there, like the common people in all ages, to make deities'. Those he made include the holy fool Toots in *Dombey and Son*, whose befuddled wooing reveals, according to Chesterton, 'the great paradox of all spiritual things – that the inside is always larger than the outside', or the flustered lawyer Guppy in *Bleak House*, who is 'a creation flung down like a miracle out of an upper sphere; we can pull him to pieces, but we could not have put him together'. This remonstrance is Chesterton's warning that criticism should not presume to find fault with a 'creation which is spelt with a capital C'. The legions of beings who crowd Dickens's novels – Pickwick, Micawber, Krook, Miss Havisham, Mr Dick, Peggotty, Bumble and the rest – emanate from a power that, as Chesterton insists, is 'truly and literally to be called divine'. If you witness an act of 'real primary creation', like the rising of the sun or the birth of a child, the proper response is grateful awe, or perhaps prayer.

As a devout Catholic, Chesterton wished to reconcile this literary theology with the edicts of faith. He did so by adhering to the Athanasian Creed, which Abelard was made to recite as a corrective for his heretical ideas. Athanasius, Bishop of Alexandria in the fourth century, maintained that God and Christ, father and son, were co-eternal; thanks to this adjustment of Old and New Testaments, Christ in *Paradise Lost* is present to supervise the earth's creation. Chesterton valued Athanasius because he espoused a God of love, rather than the remote, solitary cosmic controller of the Platonists. The notion of God as a family man resolved the nagging problem of origins, and in addition supplied a holy lineage for art. A God 'without beginnings, existing before all things' had no need to be loving, 'because there was nothing to be loved'. But if God produced Christ at the very beginning of time rather than waiting for the end of the first century BC, Chesterton concludes that 'in His own nature there was something analogous to self-expression; something of what begets and beholds what it has begotten'. The cadences are biblical, but they describe an essentially artistic process: Chesterton is acclaiming God as a novelist. The same self-expressive enjoyment overflows in Dickens, who is not, like God, the single parent of an only child, but pours forth a throng of sons and daughters, some stunted or gnarled or twisted awry or fitted with prosthetic limbs, one at least bothered by a detachable head. Balzac was also likened, with some justification, to the God of Genesis. Colette, astounded and even dismayed by his productivity, said that 'Balzac has invented everything'. Oscar Wilde praised him in the same exalted terms: Balzac 'created life, he did not copy it'.

Chesterton recruited Dickens as a defender of the faith – catholic if not cryptically Catholic. But Dickens understood how heterodox his creativity was, and analysed its procedures in *Our Mutual Friend* when describing the 'old impiety' of Mrs Clennam, who praises her own Christian virtue in punishing her husband's pitiable mistress: she 'reversed the order of Creation, and breathed her own breath into a clay image of her Creator'. Dickens adds that the 'monstrous idols' brought back by travellers from heathen lands are no uglier in their caricatures of 'the Divine nature' than the likenesses 'we creatures of the dust' make of our 'bad passions'. He shamelessly practised a similar idolatry, forming effigies that also reverse the order of creation. His characters are often monstrous collages of ill-matched characteristics, as irregular as the muddy children of Prometheus. Mr Sleary, the proprietor of the circus in *Hard Times*, has 'one fixed eye and one loose eye, a voice (if it can be called so) like the efforts of a broken old pair of bellows, a flabby surface, and a muddled head which was never sober and never drunk'. He also lisps asthmatically, and thickens the letter s: 'Thith,' he laments, 'ith a bad piethe of bithnith, thith ith'. Has Dickens put him together – as Chesterton says of Guppy – or pulled him apart? The act of creation is almost scandalously slapdash, as Dickens challenges us to make all these distortions and disabilities cohere, which, in imagining Sleary, we of course do.

In Chesterton's theological tract *The Everlasting Man*, the variety of Dickensian character is offered as a reason for repudiating 'the Oriental heresy', or Buddhism. Chesterton convicts Buddhists of believing that 'what is the matter with us is our creation'. For them, 'the Creation was the Fall', because it splintered an original unity and left us fragmented, condemned to 'our coloured differentiation and personality'. Buddhism makes amends for this schism by 'uncreating all the creatures', declaring that our individual existence is an illusion. Chesterton thought otherwise: that prism shows off the iridescent variety which is the glory of God's world and of Dickens's novels. Chesterton elaborated on his symbolic appreciation of colour in 1904 in a study of the Victorian painter G. F. Watts. He thought of Watts as a primary creator like Dickens, and said that he dipped his hand in 'the clay of chaos' and gave form to 'brown earth-men', who loll on the ground 'like forces in chaos before the first day of creation'. The divinity's signature was visible in 'the mess on his palette': Watts was fond of 'that tremendous autochthonous red, which was the colour of Adam, whose name was Red Earth'. The only artists worthy to employ that sombre primal tone, according to Chesterton, were the Eternal Potter and Watts himself.

Although such compliments absurdly overvalued Watt's stiff, stuffy allegories, they made clear art's new responsibility: it either revealed the creator, or – failing that – made manifest the creative energy that had taken God's place. Bergson, attempting to explain the 'élan vital' that fuelled the universe, defined it as 'love, which desires to produce from itself beings worthy to be loved'. That philoprogenitive energy 'could only spring into being in a universe', so the universe itself, as Bergson said, promptly 'sprang into being'. Put more abstractly, this is why Chesterton's God had a son, and why Dickens produced his mobs of characters. Bergson's circular logic accounts for the genial warmth of comedy, which, by inventing benevolent wastrels like Micawber, reconciles us to the imperfections of our species. Aldous Huxley – writing in 1924 about a generous, instinctive creativity that he, as an intellectual and a satirist, did not possess – argued that comedy is 'of the earth, earthy'. Its red clay is moistened by sap, even irrigated by blood: great comic characters have the unselfconscious exuberance of animals, and their endearing foibles explain why human beings are, in Bergson's words, 'objects of love for the creator'. The argument, slightly adjusted, also justifies tragedy. Victor Hugo, in the preface to his play *Cromwell* in 1827, argued that religious grace could redeem the ugliest and most debased physical horror. 'Fix God to a gibbet', he said, 'and you have the cross'. God the father expresses himself by begetting a son, which sanctifies comedy. But God the father can also ordain the crucifixion, like a novelist or dramatist sacrificing a favourite character.

In his meditation on comedy, Huxley presents his own version of the earth at its innocent beginnings. Reading about the exploits of Falstaff or Rabelais's Gargantua, 'we seem to be looking on at the gambolling of mastodons, the playing of young whales, the tumbling of a litter of dinosaur puppies'. Mrs Gamp for similar reasons reminded Chesterton of a hippopotamus. But this kindergarten is a corral for monsters, 'sui generis' or self-generated. Chesterton worried about the abnormality of such beings, who were created by a method unknown to biology. He said that characters like Mr Sapsea, the fatuous auctioneer in *The Mystery of Edwin Drood*, or Elijah Pogram, the windbag American politician in *Martin Chuzzlewit*, were 'too big for the gate of birth'. The mystery of artistic creation has been identified, but not clarified. In 1870 Charles Kingsley, still endeavouring to shore up God's exclusive rights, denied that human beings could originate anything. 'Man makes fiction, he invents stories. ... But out of what does he make them up?' He draws, Kingsley claimed, on his observation of 'this great world ..., just as he makes up his dreams. But who makes truth? Who makes facts? Who, but God?' The prohibition is not quite absolute, because Kingsley mentions dreams: we cannot invent facts but we can twist and intertwine them as we do when we are asleep. Put back to front, Kingsley's formulation is more indulgent than it seems. God makes the facts, but man makes fiction, which liberates us from the tyranny of those facts.

A metaphor can recreate the world, as Hugo does in *Notre-Dame de Paris*, published in 1831. Hugo's introductory tour of the cathedral suggests that the building outdoes or at least equals the world God fabricates in Genesis: it is 'a sort of human Creation; ... mighty and prolific as the Divine Creation, of which it seems to have caught the double character – variety and eternity'. Notre-Dame has its altar and its stained-glass windows, yet stone griffons leer on the roof. In a secret tower an archdeacon conducts alchemical experiments and worships Zoroaster, celebrating gold as 'fire in its concrete state'. With its amalgam of styles and epochs, Notre-Dame, as Hugo says, is as incoherent as 'a Chimaera: she has the head of one, the limbs of another, the back of a third'. Elsewhere he calls the building 'a giant of a thousand heads and a thousand arms'. The hunchbacked bellringer Quasimodo is a resident of Notre-Dame and perhaps an outgrowth of it, like an animated gargoyle or a romping nightmare. Heaven and earth do battle in him, just as they do in the cathedral. His body is foul, but he possesses a soul and – as his infatuation with the gipsy Esmeralda reveals – is capable of love.

In the seventeenth century, Thomas Browne insisted that 'there are no grotesques in nature'. Toads, bears and elephants may seem ugly, but their appearance suits the lives they lead, and they have all received 'the visitation of God, who saw that all he made was good'. A human maker has no such obligation to goodness, or even to beauty. Berlioz took a hilarious delight in caricaturing cranks in *Les Grotesques de la musique*, a collection of essays published in 1859. In his *Symphonie fantastique*, fantastication means distortion, warping familiar reality into a series of delirious visions. As Hugo pointed out in the preface to *Cromwell*, beauty is drearily uniform, while ugliness is infinite in its diversity. The divine creation grows, but a human creation has to be made, and *Notre-Dame de Paris* displays the process of making. During a fiery siege of the cathedral, the carved water-spouts laugh, like 'monsters ... awakened from their stony slumber by that unearthly flame'. It is language that awakens them; metaphor confers energy and motion on inanimate objects. Quasimodo himself owes his life to a linguistic trick. Explaining his name, Hugo says that officially it refers to Low Sunday, when his foster-parent Claude Frollo found him. But he adds a more aesthetically pertinent gloss: Quasimodo is 'an *almost*', which is the other meaning of the word. He is an adverb in the flesh. A violently writhing lump of inchoate matter, with a wart that could be an egg containing another embryonic ogre, he is unfinished, uncooked, still evolving. Like Caliban or Richard III, he represents chaos, the unleavened stuff of creation, and his business is to generate more chaos: the bells he rings produce a battering, belligerent cacophony, although Hugo

Charles Meryon, *Le Stryge,* 1853

advises that a listener who concentrated (as Leonardo da Vinci did) might hear harmony hidden in the uproar. Music has its source in such random, chaotic noise. Berlioz was thrilled when he heard a hymn bawled by six thousand children in the cavern of St Paul's in London. In his dreams, the cathedral dilated into John Martin's bleary gas-lit Pandemonium, and the clamour of the untrained choir swelled into 'hideous harmonies' – the uproar of demons and damned souls, which made the vault vibrate.

Hugo was fascinated by monsters, because they were irregular, unrepeatable creations. In his novel *Les Travailleurs de la mer*, a corpulent green dwarf known as the King of the Auxcriniers is sighted off the Channel Islands. This 'spectral fish with the face of a human being' merges and muddles species, like one of Horace's garbled metaphors. It supposedly has claws, although these protrude from rudimentary hands; another sighting gives it fins. Hugo tried to validate his fantasy by drawing the beast: the result is a jolly toad balanced on its hind legs, copied from an Egyptian figurine. His romantic imagination specialized in designing such esemplastic freaks. A watercolour cloud he painted during the 1850s could also be a fish swimming in the sky; a form like a planet with streaky nebulae could be the pupil of a cosmic eye. Sometimes Hugo left a blot of ink on the page, or spattered the paper with explosive droplets as if representing a black sunrise. This is how ideas start into life inside the head, and perhaps how worlds are made.

The cathedral, as Hugo says, is the nest or egg in which Quasimodo grows. Hugo describes the building as an organism in stone, steadily accumulating through the centuries – not the work of one man, not even of a team of artisans, but of the entire nation. In *La Peau de chagrin*, published in the same year as *Notre-Dame de Paris*, the emporium where Raphael finds the ass's skin is an even more compendious creative nursery. The forking and branching galleries of its three floors are crammed with the booty of extinct civilizations; it jumbles up the history of the world, or of several worlds, modern and ancient, European and Asian. These caverns are the lairs of the creator, replicas of the storeyed, story-congested mind where dreams and facts, myths and snippets from yesterday's newspaper, interpenetrate in a fruitful chaos. Because they recall the chasm of origins, both the cathedral and the curiosity shop are abysses. On top of Notre-Dame, Quasimodo pushes Frollo – his finder, his ersatz maker and his would-be destroyer – into a gulf; Raphael, sampling the antique-dealer's wares, feels he is lightheadedly surveying 'the illimitable abyss of the past'. But there is a difference between the theories of creativity the two settings exemplify. Notre-Dame is alive, and not only because Hugo's metaphors can quicken stone or make it laugh. To the romantic eye, Gothic architecture looked like

Victor Hugo, 'Roi des Auxcriniers', from his novel *Les Travailleurs de la Mer*, 1865

a calcified forest, with columns imitating trees. When Saint-Saëns heard Berlioz's *Requiem* at the church of Saint-Eustache, he felt that 'each slim shaft in every column of pillars had become an organ pipe and the whole church one immense organ!' Berlioz, conducting, made stone breathe; it was not surprising that a gargoyle should bound into life and swing through the air on his bell-ropes as Quasimodo does. The shop, by contrast, is an encyclopaedic graveyard. The objects discarded there exist in limbo, as 'marvellous creations belonging to the borderland between life and death'. Art cannot equal nature and at best supplies a wan substitute, like the posthumous mask of a loved face.

The accumulation of aesthetic debris induces something like cosmic despair. Balzac cites the geological pessimism of Georges Cuvier, whose study of fossils convinced him that our world revolved through a series of creations. Every so often, all life is annihilated; after a pause, replacements flourish for a while on the blackened earth. Raphael sees the antiques as fall-out from Cuvier's global disasters: they provide evidence for 'the destruction of so many past universes'. He wonders whether the abandoned figurines in gypsum or marble represent some prior model of man, more perfect and for that reason 'destroyed by the Creator'. Heinrich Heine took the same view of Berlioz's music, which in an 1844 review he called 'primitive, if not antediluvian'. The *Requiem* required five orchestras, and the *Te Deum* was described by Berlioz himself as 'Babylonian'. Heine likened these grandiose monsters to the remains found in one of Cuvier's atavistic boneyards: he was reminded of 'creatures and species long extinct'. These are mastodons that do not gambol, dinosaurs too heavy to tumble. Berlioz had created a new race of mammoths, seemingly unaware that the breed had been obsolete for millennia. Balzac's vision of impending doom makes him all the more eager to revivify the past, to put flesh on ghosts. In *La Peau de chagrin*, Raphael exercises this power on his behalf. Every prop or costume he picks up in the shop entices him into an alternative life. A salt-cellar from Benvenuto Cellini's workshop encourages him to imagine taking part in a Renaissance orgy; he allows Indian idols to suggest other reveries of sexual dalliance, and imagines what it might feel like to share the cruelty of 'a goggle-eyed Chinese monster, with mouth awry and twisted limbs'. Perhaps the artist's abundance of vitality can make up for the depletion and defeats of earthly life.

Nineteenth-century science took stock of God's earth and pronounced it sadly mortal. Geology showed how old the world was; thermodynamics reported that it was stealthily dying. Art at its most valiant challenged or forestalled this end, and improved on the original creation. In the preface to *Cromwell*, Hugo compared Shakespeare to God, and had no hesitation in deciding who was the better maker and the more bountiful paterfamilias.

*Mrs Gamp propoges a Toast*, illustration by 'Phiz' (Hablot K. Browne) from *Martin Chuzzlewit*, 1844

'One man,' as Hugo acknowledged, 'has no right to be everything!' But Shakespeare had managed the feat. In *Twelfth Night* a single character suddenly turns out to be twins, which makes a gaping looker-on ask 'How have you made division of yourself?' Bergson, in an essay on laughter written in 1900, took such a possibility literally, and proposed that Shakespeare had outwitted nature, creating characters by a process that resembles the fission of rudimentary organisms like the amoeba. Macbeth, Hamlet, Lear, Othello and the others could only be lifelike – which, for an evolutionary vitalist, is all that matters – if they were 'a multiplication or a division of the poet', releasing inner potentialities. Viola in *Twelfth Night*, half of that mystifying set of twins, first recreates herself as a boy, then conjures up an imaginary sister (whom she immediately kills by sentencing her to die of unrequited love).

Mrs Gamp achieves her own marvels of self-proliferation. When she beds down in a chair, she ties a watchman's coat around her neck by the sleeves. Dickens reports that 'she became two people; and looked, behind, as if she were in the act of being embraced by one of the old patrol'. Having supplied herself with this gruff, rugged lover, she goes on to beget other characters. Her masterpiece is her imaginary ally Mrs Harris, who is rumoured to be 'a phantom of Mrs Gamp's brain' and is surrounded by a 'fearful mystery'. Betsey Prig, irritated by Mrs Gamp, curtly murders Mrs Harris by refusing to believe that there is any such person. Mrs Gamp protests that there is a picture of her in the room – though is that any more reliable, as a proof of life, than an illustration in a novel? She resurrects Mrs Harris, and on one of her professional errands brings her along to assist (although she remains tantalizingly out of sight in the next room). This life-giving power extends to dead things. Travelling in a coach, the fretful Mrs Gamp moves her cabbage-green umbrella so often that it appears to be 'not one umbrella but fifty'. Her late husband had the same Frankensteinian relationship with his wooden leg. She remembers an occasion when, needing money for liquor, he took it off and sent their boy to sell it for conversion into matches. Even when attached to him, the leg had a will of its own, and an incorrigible propensity – which Mr Gamp could do nothing about – for wandering into wine vaults.

In 1844, in an outline of what became his evolutionary theory, Charles Darwin pondered 'the enormous multiplying power inherent and annually in action in animals', which was supplemented by 'the countless seeds scattered by a hundred ingenious contrivances, year after year, over the whole face of the land'. These were the imperatives of nature, impelled, as Bergson later said, by 'the forward thrust of an indistinct multiplicity'. Art had its equivalent to this procreative excess. *L'Oeuvre* is about a painter who cares more for his masterwork than for his only child (whom he neglects, and whose death he hardly notices); Zola emphasized this transference from biology to aesthetics when trying to decide on a title for the novel, and made a provisional list of phrases that conveyed his hero's obsession – 'Make a child. Make a world. Make life. Creation. To create. To be God. The making of a child. Giving birth. Parturition. Conception'.

Artists, Zola believed, were men who suffered from hysterical pregnancies. But the creative career did not necessarily involve such maternal agony. Baudelaire in 1851 wrote an essay on wine and hashish, considered as ways of multiplying individuality. Wine tells the weary worker 'I will be the seed that fertilizes the laboriously dug furrow'. The grape is one of Darwin's countless seeds, intent on dissemination. It promises to 'drop to the depths of your breast like an organic elixir', although what it fertilizes is the dormant brain. Once in the bloodstream, wine and hashish – according to Baudelaire's analysis – detach us from our minds; drunk or drugged, we experience ourselves as entrancing strangers, and we see the world anew, temporarily suffused by a sunny good humour. Narcotics, as Baudelaire said, create

Honoré Daumier,
*Hashish Smokers*,
1845

'artificial paradises'. The correct dose re-opens the barred gate of Eden. God instructed all species to go forth and multiply. With chemical help, the artist can do so without leaving home. Baudelaire tells the story of a stuffy magistrate who, after smoking hashish, was caught dancing an indecent can-can. This fit of revelry exposed the 'inner, authentic monster' repressed by the bourgeois official. Dickens often locked himself in his study while writing *The Old Curiosity Shop*, and could be heard scuttling about as he executed Quilp's dances or uttered his cackles of triumph. He too had temporarily released an inner, authentic monster – not an alter ego, like the magistrate's secret misbehaving self, but an independent character. Baudelaire proves his point about the artist's self-augmentation by citing the case of Balzac, who said that the novelist must 'live several lives in the space of an hour'. Like the hero of *La Peau de chagrin*, his existence was both jubilantly multiplied and terrifyingly subdivided. He complained about his plural existence, saying that in writing novels he was 'forced to be ten men at the same time, with several spare brains, never sleeping'. There are animals with several stomachs, and Zola's La Lison in *La Bête humaine* has two hearts. Why shouldn't a genius be fitted with a multi-cameral mind?

The man whose personality has been bifurcated by narcotics is, as Baudelaire says, 'similar to a fantastic novel, one that is lived not written'. Toxins inflame or irritate the character of the user, splitting it apart. In Baudelaire's disenchanted view, the process is irrational and self-deceptive, yet also irresistibly compelling. It flushes the ego, and convinces the individual that he contains 'a divinity within himself'. Sometimes addiction is unnecessary. Rousseau, according to Baudelaire, was intoxicated without hashish: he proudly placed himself at the centre of the universe, and informed the angels 'I have become God!' Wine makes two insinuating promises to the drunkard. Their 'intimate commingling', it murmurs, will create poetry; between them, they will produce a god.

This communion allows Baudelaire to solve one of Christianity's knottiest theological problems. He describes drunkenness as a mystical parthenogenesis, 'in which natural man and wine, the animal god and the vegetable god, play the roles of the Father and the Son in the Trinity; they engender a Holy Spirit who is the superior man who proceeds equally from the two of them'. His witty blasphemy has a covert justification, hidden in the secret history of religion and condensed in an obscure etymology. Laudanum – the alcoholic tincture of opium to which Coleridge, de Quincey, Dickens and so many other nineteenth-century artists were partial – was given its name by the alchemist Paracelsus. He used the word to label one of the supposedly miraculous elixirs that earned him his reputation as a mountebank; later it was transferred to preparations containing opium, which instantly transported the user to a profane heaven. The name chosen by Paracelsus probably alluded to gum-resin, which is 'labdanum' in Latin, but it also punned on 'laudare', meaning praise – the word used by traditional salutations addressed to the Lord. Spirits, as Baudelaire's trinity recognizes, no longer need to be immaterial or angelic; it is possible to extract them from grain or other vegetable sources. Gods can be brewed or distilled, then stored, like a genie, in a bottle. The man who chooses to be an artist has a ready means of inducing the required ecstatic state. But he needs courage, because he risks self-destruction. The creator, as Baudelaire says, must enter the cave of 'the multiform Proteus' and battle the many-headed monster resident in his own brain; the venture is a 'ride to the abyss', like that orchestrated by Berlioz at the end of *La Damnation de Faust*.

Baudelaire liquefied Balzac, reducing genius to a potion. Rodin confirmed Balzac's status as a god of flesh and blood, and remade him in clay and bronze. The sculpted Balzac strides or swaggers, rejecting the poise of the traditional statue. He behaves like one of his own characters and is, as Rodin said, 'a veritable living being'. In an 1898 maquette, his pot belly swells through the opening of the dressing gown he wore while working: is he carrying a novel in there? Rilke, who worked for a time as Rodin's secretary, called the figure drunkenly elated, and said that his naked body represented 'a Creation that formed Balzac to manifest itself'. Rilke saw an analogy with the creative authority of Rodin himself, who 'did not presume to create the tree in its full growth' but 'began with the seed beneath the tree', moulding or carving a representation of vital growth. The medieval

Nadar, caricature
of Baudelaire,
1854

cathedral, as Rilke argued, had dwindled to a fertile kernel, then sprouted again. But now it took on a new, more carnal form: 'Man had become church, and there were thousands and thousands of churches. …The problem was to show that they were all of One God'. That indeed was a problem, because the new pantheon housed so many quirky, resolutely human deities. Rodin also designed a monument to Victor Hugo, intended for the gardens of the Palais-Royal. Rodin's Hugo, naked like Balzac, floats on an aerodynamic cloak resembling the cloud on which Michelangelo's God swoops down towards Adam; at the same time, in an allusion to his exile on a rock in the English Channel, his attitude suggests Neptune subduing the waves. But this is a god preoccupied by the contents of his own mind: Hugo holds one hand cupped to his ear, and listens to the roar of an internal ocean. In Rodin's studies for the figure, what changed most was the left arm, gradually raised to semaphore power. As we watch, a man prepares to call into being a populous world that has gestated inside his head.

## CHARLES ROBERT DARWIN, LL.D., F.R.S.

In his *Descent of Man* he brought his own Species down as
low as possible—*i.e.*, to "A Hairy Quadruped furnished
with a Tail and Pointed Ears, and probably *Arboreal*
in its habits"—which is a reason for the very general
Interest in a "Family Tree." He has lately been
turning his attention to the "Politic Worm."

# 19
# PANGENESIS

In 1878 Richard Wagner noted that 'Science makes God the Creator more impossible every day'. The blame or credit belonged principally to Charles Darwin, who published *The Origin of Species* in 1859. The Bible's timeline had already been undermined by the geology of Charles Lyell, who showed that the earth was older than its reputed creator. When Darwin quietly mocked an antiquated 'belief in the creation of species from the dust of the earth', he risked a more direct assault on Genesis. But he was reluctant to enter into open conflict with God. Instead he replaced the creator with a 'supposed creative force' whose operations were diffused throughout nature in an unstoppable variety of forms; he allowed that force to operate indiscriminately, denying that the first humans were 'special creations' and suggesting that we are 'the lineal descendants of some few beings which lived long before the first bed of the Silurian system was deposited'. Even so, Darwin was nervous about extending his theory of evolutionary growth. He covered plants and animals in *The Origin of Species*, but did not address human biology until he published *The Descent of Man* in 1871.

Travelling around the world as a naturalist on the *Beagle* between 1831 and 1836, Darwin took a copy of *Paradise Lost* with him. He may have expected that he was bound for Eden, but the poem served as his guide to the almost extraterrestrial worlds opened up by the voyage. Approaching Buenos Aires in 1832, he saw the sea at night phosphorescently shining and realized that he was following Satan's itinerary: 'it was impossible,' he wrote in his diary, 'to behold this plain of matter, as it were melted & consuming by heat, without being reminded of Milton's descriptions of Chaos & Anarchy'. The biblical myth remained his point of reference, and he tried to salvage as much of it as possible. But in South America or Australia he was confronted by flora and fauna that disturbingly contradicted the account of creation given by Genesis. The South Seas made it necessary to think again about cosmic origins. When Herman Melville's whaling vessel stopped at the Galápagos Islands in 1841, three of the ancient, elephantine tortoises from which the islands took their name were brought on board. These 'mystic creatures', as Melville called them, had already bemused Darwin. Melville wondered if they were perhaps 'the identical tortoises wheron the Hindu plants this total sphere'. In a dream he imagined himself cross-legged on one of them, his forehead holding up 'the universal cope'. But the primal deities were killed and eaten, their flesh carved up into steaks or boiled into soup, and their shells used as tureens. In his Polynesian novel *Typee*, Melville derided the fantasy of the 'divine origin' when summarizing a local saga about creation. Nevertheless the experience of his castaway hero validates the story of Prometheus: rubbing dry twigs together, the man strikes a light, and thus makes civilization possible.

For a while Darwin wondered whether there might have been a pair of creators: God in the northern hemisphere, and below the equator an extraneous, estranged colleague who manufactured hybrids like the kangaroo and platypus or whimsically decided that eucalypts should shed their bark but not their leaves. Yet even a pair of creators seemed insufficient. Adapting and extending biblical terminology, he proposed what Havelock Ellis called the 'fantastic theory of pangenesis': a spontaneous process whereby each unit of an organism reproduces itself through cells called gemmules. Pangenesis was a word coined by Darwin as a diminutive of gemma or bud; it referred to particles representing a particular bodily function or characteristic, which supposedly collected in the genital organs to await transmission. Verbally, it worked by grafting or hybridizing. Pan, the god who pervades nature, is spliced onto Genesis, where the creative agency belongs to a single, solitary God who remains outside the nature he calls into being. Now a plethora of creators is at work inside every organism.

Genesis eventually gave way to the science of genetics: original sin is simply a cruder name for the selfish gene. Darwin retained the Edenic tree, but reclassified it. He lifted the prohibition on its crop of forbidden fruit, and instead imagined the buds generating branches and growing into 'the great Tree of Life, which fills with its dead and broken branches the crust of the earth, and covers the surface with its ever branching and beautiful ramifications'. Death is no longer – as in the Bible – the dread punishment for disobedience, or an afterthought that damages God's ideal design. It is part of life, essential to its economy, and its ravages are overcome by the tree that strives upward like Jack's beanstalk, shrugging off those dead branches. The snake too was relieved of its diabolical menace. In 1881 *Punch* printed a caricature of Darwin as a philosophical gravedigger who sits on the ground, surrounded by books. His spade is stuck in the turf, and a curly worm unwinds around him. The image refers to his book on *The Formation of Vegetable Mould, through the Action of Worms* – a close and fond study of the creativity of those apparently destructive beings, whose digestive system converts soil into humus. What looks to us like decay is a genial stratagem of nature, which Darwin called 'the great renewer'.

He could not imagine that it 'pleased the Creator to cause a being of one type to take the place of one of another', and disparaged belief in 'separate and innumerable acts of creation'. During a short life, Mozart composed forty-one symphonies, twenty-five piano concerti, twenty-two operas, as well as a plethora of masses, dances, serenades, quartets, quintets and musical jokes: surely these were separate, innumerable creative acts, performed by an artist who took the name Amadeus because he thought of himself as God's pet, the beneficiary of divine favour? Darwin, however, was reluctant to look aside from nature to art. He preferred to explain Mozart as a creature of habit, an experimental product of natural selection. The boy received a strict musical training from his father, so we should not be surprised that he played the pianoforte at the age of three 'with wonderfully little practice'; there would only be cause for amazement if he had 'played a tune with no practice at all'. The argument is awkward and unsatisfying. Darwin also criticized ambitious naturalists who were overeager 'to make many species', like poultry-fanciers augmenting nature's quota of variants. The principle he called 'Divergence of Character' may be nature's selective whim, but in literature it counts as the highest and rarest of virtues, and is responsible for Falstaff and Magwitch, Mistress Quickly and Miss Havisham. Darwin asked whether we have 'any right to assume that the Creator works by intellectual powers like those of man?' His question at least conceded that man the artist possessed and exercised those powers, which any God might envy.

Declaring that human efforts had no power over natural selection, Darwin claimed that 'the works of Nature' were 'immeasurably superior ... to those of Art'. But nature plodded slowly along in 'graduated steps'. Acrobatic leaps were beyond it: nature, he said, was 'prodigal in variety, but niggard in innovation'. Surely the brain, with its instantaneous ignition, goes about its business more swiftly, outstripping the body? Art innovates, even if nature cannot break its own moulds. Caliban, Quasimodo and Quilp are unrepeatable aesthetic specimens, as is Frankenstein's amalgam of corpses. Darwin acknowledged the 'somewhat monstrous character' of 'domestic races' which are deliberately cultivated. Like the encyclopaedists of the eighteenth century, he defined a 'monstrosity' as a deviant form, 'either injurious to or not useful to the species, and not generally propagated'. Darwin's definition of a monster as a form not propagated lies behind Oscar Wilde's joke about Lady Bracknell, the castrating matriarch in *The Importance of Being Earnest*. She is, according to Wilde, 'a monster without being a myth'. She lacks the supernatural powers of Hydra or Chimaera, so her haughty prohibitions are ineffectual; monsters are as old-fashioned as gods. Other literary monsters contradict Darwin's law, and crave the chance to perpetuate themselves. Caliban assaults Miranda, Quasimodo pines for Esmerelda, and Frankenstein's monster demands a bride. Quilp already has a wife who is his submissive slave. Despite his own theory, Darwin knew that genetic freaks were not necessarily sterile.

In 1868 in *The Variation of Animals and Plants under Domestication* he reported on stockbreeders and their manipulation of nature; he had an experimental aviary of his own, with differing kinds of pigeons and chickens. As he pointed out, professional breeders consider 'an animal's organization' to be 'something quite plastic', which is how the canine species can produce dogs as different as German shepherds and Scotch terriers, bulldogs and chihuahuas, setters and whippets. Macbeth makes the same point when interviewing the murderers he hires. They define themselves as men, and he agrees that they can be catalogued as such, but only because

> hounds and greyhounds, mongrels, spaniels, curs,
> Shoughs, water-rugs, and demi-wolves are clept
> All by the name of dogs.

Art discriminates more subtly, accentuating the qualities randomly handed out by what Macbeth calls 'bounteous nature'. Darwin explained the array of playful variants by likening breeds to linguistic dialects. It was a subversive argument: language, according to the Bible, is the proud evidence of human singularity, a sign of our eloquence, intellectuality and creative capacity. Is it after all, like the communicative idiom of dogs, just a lexicon of snarls, growls and excited yelps? Alfred Russel Wallace – whose research along parallel lines pressed Darwin to bring forward publication of *The Origin of Species* – later took a detour into spiritualism, and in 1869 defended man's privileged status by calling him an animal purposely domesticated by the creator: God's poodle. Darwin saw the affinity between dogs and men from the other side. We team up with them because we know they are our relatives, and the connection is cemented whenever we use our canine teeth to gnaw meat. In *The Descent of Man*, he proved his case with a verbal caricature: he predicted that anyone who scornfully rejected this lineage would probably sneer as he does so, and 'unconsciously retract his "snarling muscles"'…, like a dog prepared to fight'. His critics, defending man's divinity, spoiled their case by behaving like beasts.

The theory of natural selection implied the existence of a selector. Unable to rely on God, Darwin followed an ancient literary precedent by making an allegorical figure of Nature. Milton was replaced by Spenser, whose goddess Nature rebuts Mutabilitie at the end of *The Faerie Queene*. Earlier in the poem, Spenser locates the source of nature's fruition in the garden of Adonis, a mythological seed-bed that is fertilized by the embraces of Venus and her lover Adonis, who like the earth dies seasonally and is reborn. Here a gardener called Genius chooses the moment when nascent creatures are ready for transplantation into the human world. Darwin shared in the work of Spenser's Genius and, after seeking advice from a curator at Kew Gardens, conducted research by crossing varieties of cucumber. When he describes the way the germs of life are distributed by birds, he combines the two Spenserian fables: 'Nature, like a careful gardener, thus takes her seeds from a bed of a particular nature, and drops them in another equally well fitted for them'. The art of this sentence lies in its dual use of the word nature. First Nature is a person, an allegorical agent, as when Darwin in his *Journal of Researches* refers to the cruelty of 'dame Nature', who permits animals to torment their prey. Then it reverts to serving as an abstract, impersonal noun. Myth and science are reunited, since they depend on the same terms to construct their different stories about origins.

Lyell in his *Principles of Geology* cites Ovid's story of Deucalion, a classical equivalent to Noah, and uses it as as a symbol of the storeyed, fossilized archive that enabled him to date the earth. Deucalion survives when his race is wiped out by a flood; an oracle tells him that he will be able to replenish the wasted world if he throws his mother's bones behind him. He is reluctant to disturb an ancestor's ghost, so he interprets the order as a riddle. Our mother is the earth, whose bones must therefore be stones. He gathers a handful of pebbles and throws them over his head; they soften, and a new race of beings is moulded from them. In Genesis our substance is clay, but the Ovidian characters have their origins in sterner stuff – rock, flint, mineral – which Ruskin in his commentary on Deucalion called the 'lifeless seeds of life'. Darwin alludes to no specific incident from the *Metamorphoses*, but his grandest vistas incorporate its vision of perpetual change, as when he suggests that 'the older continents, formed of formations older than any known to us, may now all be in a metamorphosed condition, or may lie buried under the ocean'. The verbal variants Darwin teases out – form, formation, metamorphosis – attempt to find a new word to paraphrase the process that sustains nature. He could not call it creation; after the voyage on the *Beagle*, he rejected the idea and the word. Having begun to study the development of species through time, he adhered to a doctrine that he called transmutation. Teleology presumed that the universe had a final form, foreseen by God. Darwin the transformist proposed instead that evolution was provisional, open-ended. The theory was easy to reconcile with Ovidian myth; the connection had been made by his own grandfather. In *Zoonomia*, a study of the laws of organic life published between 1794 and 1796, Erasmus Darwin treated the cases of adaptation studied by Lamarck as if they were anecdotes about voluntary metamorphosis, like Daphne turning into the laurel tree. He admired the ingenuity of the humming-bird, which had grown 'a proboscis of admirable structure ... for the purpose of plundering the nectaries of flowers', and he wondered at the 'great changes' visible in other creatures – from caterpillar to butterfly, from 'subnatant tadpole' to 'respiring frog', from 'feminine boy' to 'bearded man'.

As well as alluding to Ovid, *The Origin of Species* remembers the cosmology of Lucretius, who imagined that atoms agglomerated and interfused to create life. The process puzzled Lucretius; Darwin found it simply inconceivable that 'certain elemental atoms' should have been 'commanded suddenly to flash into living tissues'. And if nature was an amalgam of these particles, was it not liable to be broken down, relentlessly fragmented and eroded? A walk along the coast convinced Darwin that cliffs, boulders and the entire fabric of the land were being 'worn away, atom by atom', ground into pebbles, sand or mud. Crossing the Cordillera mountain range in the centre of Chile, he pictured those jagged volcanic peaks reduced to gravel and powder by 'all-powerful time'. The earthquake he experienced there left him with a sense of metaphysical dread: the earth – as he remarked – is not solid after all, and moves 'beneath our feet like a crust over a fluid'. For Lucretius, creation depended on death. Darwin too knew that nature demanded 'much Extinction of the less improved forms of life'. He therefore disagreed with Cuvier, who misunderstood the mutability of species when he called down cataclysms 'to desolate the world'.

Lucretius introduced his treatise with a prayer to Venus. The goddess for him was a cipher, the name given to a generative principle, the embodiment of Darwin's 'germinal vesicles'; myth, as always, is a matter of nomenclature. Darwin, a little more shiftily, used the biblical God in the same way. His atheistic grandfather could afford to be more open about the substitution. In *Zoonomia*, Erasmus Darwin referred to the creator in Platonic terms as 'THE GREAT FIRST CAUSE', which took 'one living filament' and 'indued [it] with animality'. He boldly set aside the chronology of Genesis, and imagined a time 'millions of years before the commencement of the history of mankind' when the filament first warmed the blood of animals. In his peroration he sacreligiously removed a biblical tag from its context: speculating about the progress of species, he suggests that every breed delivers 'those improvements by generation to its posterity, world without end'. No amen follows that final phrase, as is customary in church. The world is unending, but nature not God is responsible for that perpetuity. Erasmus Darwin concluded that 'The whole world might have been generated, rather than created; that is, it might have been gradually produced from very small beginnings ... rather than a sudden evolution of the whole by the Almighty fiat'.

In the first edition of *The Origin of Species*, Darwin was equally bold in snubbing God. But clerical hostility compelled him to add three words to the last sentence of the book in its second edition (which followed six weeks later, since the first printing sold out on publication day). He now contemplated a nature whose 'several powers, having been originally breathed <u>by the Creator</u> into a few forms or into one', went on indefinitely evolving. Is this interpolated creator a person, or – like the Venus of

Lucretius – a convenient personification? The same phrase occurs earlier in Darwin's conclusion, where he proposes that all creatures descend from 'one primordial form, into which life was first breathed by the Creator'. He later recanted, regretting that he 'truckled to public opinion and used the Pentateuchal term of creation, by which I really meant "appeared by some wholly unknown process"'. Nevertheless, the optional phrase was not a pious surrender, since it contained a heresy. God breathed life only into Adam, not into a 'few forms' or into 'all the organic beings which have ever lived on this earth'. The transmission of breath is merely symbolic, like the activation of Erasmus Darwin's filament or the digital contact between God and man on the ceiling of the Sistine Chapel.

The language of *The Origin of Species* adroitly qualifies religious terminology. Darwin cast doubt on the fantasy of 'a miraculous act of creation' or a 'supposed act of creation', and dismissed talk about a 'plan of creation' with a 'unity of design'. Circumventing the creator, he experimented with new names or definitions: he referred, for instance, to 'the predominant Power'. That power, capitalized, might seem to be a personal commander, like the 'Thrones, Dominations, Princedoms, Vertues, Powers' addressed by God in *Paradise Lost*. But it is actually a process, 'the accumulative action of Selection'. For Darwin, Adam too was a generic fiction, labelling the unknowable 'single progenitor' of our species. He ironically warns against a literal reading of his own narrative. He advises readers that he uses 'the term Struggle for Existence in a large and metaphorical sense', and promptly admits the fallacy of the catchy notion. Starving animals do fight for the food that will keep them alive. But we also say that desert plants struggle against drought, when all they can do is wait to be saved by some stray moisture. Darwin's Tree of Life, purloined from Eden, is another 'simile [that] largely speaks the truth' – largely but not entirely, which means that the tree once charged with symbolizing knowledge and strict moral certitude now acknowledges that it is a useful, versatile fiction.

Darwin thought by analogy, which allowed him to make creative leaps of association between different areas of experience. In an algebraic account of multiplying species, the diagrammatic numbers and letters suddenly make way for a striking allegorical phrase when Darwin refers to 'the polity of nature'. The formulation elides the difference between society and nature; it politicizes biology, extending the strife of human competitiveness to all other species and making the quest for power a law of life. Likewise, in a discussion of climatic controls on breeding, Darwin recalls the predators that assail 'almost every species, even in its metropolis'. The last word provokes a jolt, like the seismic tremor in Valdivia in 1835. The city can no longer be viewed as a human prerogative, one of our lofty, sophisticated inventions; it is a zoo or a jungle, and its complex, congested social order tacitly recognizes that 'nearly all either prey on or serve as prey for others'. No supernatural agency could be relied on to control or soften this rapacity. In Darwin's view, whatever morality we possess derives from our fear of those predators, which makes us herd together in society. We flatter ourselves, as he implied in *The Descent of Man*, if we mistake self-interested instinct for altruism. A mother protects her brood because her offspring is an extension of herself; she is struggling for life, and goodness has nothing to do with it. Our species has evolved, but have we outgrown the naked, filthy natives with tangled hair and frothing mouths whom Darwin encountered in Tierra del Fuego? 'Such,' he informed his contemporaries, 'were our ancestors'. Cardinal Newman in 1864 in his *Apologia Pro Vita Sua* chided the human race for contradicting 'the purposes of its Creator', and assumed that our shortcomings must be the result of our involvement in 'some terrible aboriginal calamity' – namely, the fall. Newman's phrase impugns the aborigine: the very idea of origins terrified him, because the first men were malefactors. Darwin lightened this burden, replacing moral guilt with social shame. Our tribal ancestors may make us uncomfortable, but we have no need or right to blame them for our loss of divine favour.

The last sentence of *The Origin of Species* begins with Darwin's invigorating assurance that 'There is grandeur in this view of life'. That grandeur – at least before the Creator's walk-on softened his allusion to 'the war of nature' – derived from his breathtaking overview of history, and from the inventive ingenuity of the species. Power was 'originally breathed' into a smattering of forms, whether by the Creator or not. Since that moment of initiation, 'whilst this planet has gone cycling on according to the fixed law of gravity, from so simple a beginning endless forms most beautiful and most wonderful have been, and are being, evolved'. The cycles, those planetary routines that maintained the cosmos for Copernicus or Descartes, are repetitive, and can be taken for granted: gravity anchors us. Despite this reassurance, the outlook seemed bleak. The planet, after all, was cycling towards extinction. The physicist James Clerk Maxwell, in a poem written in 1878, grafted evolution onto the second law of thermodynamics and used the two theories to rewrite the apocalyptic end of Wagner's *Götterdämmerung*. Brünnhilde no longer needs to light the funeral pyre that flares up and sears Valhalla. The gods will die of hypothermia, along with their mortifying world:

> down the stream of Evolution
> We drift, expecting no solution
> But that of the survival of the fittest.
> Till, in the twilight of the gods,
> When earth and sun are frozen clods,
> When, all its energy degraded,

> Matter to aether shall have faded;
> We, that is all the work we've done,
> As waves in aether, shall for ever run.

That last line holds out the hope of a modern heaven, in which Maxwell's own electromagnetic waves replace angels or immortal spirits. Otherwise the prophecy is nihilistic. But *The Origin of Species* redirects our gaze, and counsels us against looking upwards in quest of help. Beauty and wonder do not reside in the sky, where God used to dwell; above, only cooling stars perform automatic orbits. Darwin's conclusion places a sudden, unexpected emphasis on the abundance of the earth. By doubling the verb in his last phrase ('have been, and are being, evolved'), he compels us to give up the mythic obsession with the past and to feel ourselves indeterminately alive in a perpetual present. Once we abandon our curiosity about the beginning, we are given the opportunity to contemplate endlessness. The grandeur Darwin promised is in his writing – in his artistry and in his appeal to an artistic creativity that colludes with nature's procreative impulse.

A theory of biological origins was duty-bound to account for the origins of art. Tolstoy made the connection in his polemical essay *What is Art?*. In nature, he thought, art serves the purpose of titillation; beauty is an enticement to breeding, and play – described by the poet Schiller as a train-ing-ground for human creativity – provides animals with a means of courting each other. Tolstoy summarized Darwin's argument about the utility of artfulness, presented in *The Descent of Man*: 'Birds adorn their nests and esteem beauty in their mates. ...The origin of the art of music is the call of the males to the females.' Darwin wondered whether plants too might be susceptible to music, and engaged a bassoonist to perform in his green-house. The vines and creepers proved to be tone-deaf. He enjoyed the aesthetic preening of his pouter pigeons, which stiffened their neck feathers into ruffs and strutted about to impress their chosen females; he even called the house he lived in after his marriage in 1839 Macaw Cottage, because its gruesomely vivid red and yellow decor reminded him of the showiest South American parrot. Ruskin scoffed at this demeaning explanation of art in 1872. He refused to believe that brown pheasants evolved into pea-cocks just because hens admired showy plumage. It took a miracle, in Ruskin's view, to translate the eyes in a peacock's head into the eyes that bedeck its tail, so he decided to trouble himself no more about the Darwin-ian theory. Tolstoy – who mentions 'the epic Genesis' in his list of the loftiest, most universal works of art, along with Gospel parables, folk legends and fairy tales – shared this impatience. Art that merely sent out a sexual lure could not be truly generative. At best, Tolstoy thought that Darwin had sponsored a frivolous, fashionable erotomania.

Tolstoy angrily counted the recurrences of the word 'nu' in French fiction, and railed against French painters for their obsession with unclothed women. He would have been outraged by Courbet's *L'Origine du monde*, painted in 1866 for Khalil Bey, a Turkish diplomat who collected erotica. A naked woman, seen only from the chest to the thighs, sprawls

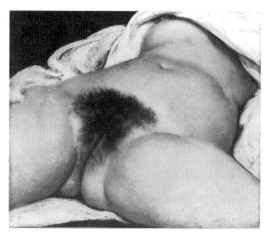

Gustave Courbet, *L'Origine du Monde*, 1866

on a bed, her legs spread wide; a sheet is spread over her breasts, although one ripe nipple peeps out. Theogony and gynaecology coincide, and the cleft glimpsed through the primal forest of fur that grows on the woman's groin is Hesiod's chasm. The navel locates the Omphalos, the Delphic monument that marked the centre of the earth: a sacred geography is written on this woman's sprawled flesh. The tousled sheet might be the billowing white cloud on which God floats in the Sistine Chapel. Here, however, the world originates in a bed not in the sky. The novelist Sandoz in Zola's *L'Oeuvre* plans his own evolutionary epic, provisionally entitled 'Origins of the Universe'. He intends to start with the creation, explained scientifically not mystically; after that he will deal with the emergence of the human race, assigning us our proper place in the community of species; finally – although in nature there can be no finality – living matter will develop into new and unanticipated forms, completing 'the creation of the world'. Like Courbet unveiling the woman's groin, Sandoz glorifies sex as 'the origin and everlasting achievement of the world itself'. He laughs at the idealism of the painter Pierre Lantier, who worships women and then castigates them for being unworthy (which is why he rips his own canvases). Lantier will not immerse himself in the fecund mess of reality, and suffers from a chaste, flinching self-disgust; Sandoz calls him 'the knight of the uncreated'. Courbet's painting tests the moral courage and virile stamina of such a man. Bared and thrust forward, the woman's pudenda represent life daring the artist to combat. The act of aggression was cautiously contradicted by Khalil Bey, who hung the painting in a bathroom with a green curtain to cover it.

Although Tolstoy was shocked by the notion, Wilde encouraged his bashful contemporaries to mimic the shameless ostentation of animals. Beauty beamed out sexual signals, defying the official prudery of the age; Wilde, in his campaign to reform dress and interior decoration, eroticized fabrics. He denounced Victorian clothes, which were ugly and therefore unaphrodisiac. On a lecture tour in America in 1882, he declared that the true dandies were the miners of Colorado with their floppy wide-brimmed hats – borrowed, though they did not know, it from the Cavaliers – and their cloaks, 'the most beautiful piece of drapery ever invented'. His appreciation of costume slyly hinted at an interest in the bodies underneath. He also condemned dreary white walls and recommended the Peacock Room – a bower of flaunting blue and gold feathers, copying the bird's erectile tail – designed for a shipping magnate by James McNeill Whistler. In a lecture delivered in 1885, Whistler presented his own aesthetic credo in the form of a witty, impudent myth of origins. He starts by paraphrasing the Bible, from which he immediately diverges: 'In the beginning, man went forth each day'. Some men, Whistler explains, went out to fight, others to hunt or to dig the ground. But one sensitive weakling preferred to stay home with the women and amused himself by tracing 'strange devices with a stick upon a gourd' which the thirsty workers would drink from at the end of the day. This was the first artist, who attracted others of similar temperament; working together, 'they fashioned, from the moistened earth, forms resembling the gourd'. They were exercising 'the power of creation', but – unimpressed by 'the slovenly suggestion of Nature' – they did not use that power for the purpose God intended. The wet earth was not moulded into a living soul. Better than that, it formed a dead, immortal work of art: from their efforts, 'the first vase was born, in beautiful proportion'.

In his report on the natives of Tierra del Fuego, Darwin noted that 'They possessed hardly any arts'. They daubed on their naked bodies, but this hardly qualified. The aesthetes of the 1890s, who despised nature's raw fecundity, took art to be a symptom of their sophisticated superiority. Wilde advised that 'The first duty in life is to be as artificial possible', and said that the only permissible link between art and nature was 'a really well-made buttonhole'. In 1896 Aubrey Beardsley exemplified this theory when he illustrated – or, as he said, 'embroidered' – Pope's *The Rape of the Lock*. The poem, seen from Beardsley's point of view, is about the aesthetic use and sexual misuse of plumage; it is as if the peacock's tail were actually a sexual organ. Belinda's carefully cultivated, artificially primped lock of hair is cut off by the fetishistic Baron. What excites him is her coiffure not her body, and she is more dismayed by the damage to her hair-do than she would have been if he had ravished her. Her dressing table is an altar, while the Baron prays before his own altar of French romances, bedecked with the purloined garters of former loves. At the end of the poem, her lock is consecrated and installed in the firmament: this ornamental curlicue, not the soul, is the immortal part of her. In Beardsley's designs, a peacock spreads its tail on the curtains around Belinda's bed, and the swags of drapery or the rococo carvings on candelabra and table legs bulge and burgeon like Darwinian gemmules. The human characters, however, are physically feeble, weighed down by their puffed-up clothes and their teetering wigs. On his head the Baron wears a cascade of ringlets that he has not personally grown; Belinda, more forbiddingly masculine, sports a bristling helmet of tormented strands. In Beardsley's story about Tannhäuser at the Venusberg, also published in 1896, desire seeks out even more devious forms of gratification. The exqui-site, preening knight and the goddess of love indulge in nothing like the orgy described in the overture to Wagner's opera. Tannhäuser would rather not disarrange 'the laboured niceness of his dress'. He feels chivalrously obliged to copulate with Venus, but prefers romping in the bath with his catamites. She indulges herself by giving manual relief to her pet unicorn and lapping up its semen. One of her nymphs employs a champagne bottle as a dildo, and swears that its fizz has made her pregnant. The revels conclude with a performance of Rossini's *Stabat Mater*; the role of the grieving Virgin at the foot of the cross is sung by a plump, powdered castrato. Throughout the revelry, Venus guards the composure of the 'delicious intelligent curls' arranged around her face by beauticians wielding heated tongs.

Wilde and his fellow aesthetes took advantage of the carnal energy that throbbed through Darwin's nature, but they directed it towards unconven-tional ends. The dandy, as Baudelaire said, exhibited 'a personal originality'; having created himself, he spurned further reproduction. Aestheticism dis-dained fertility, and offered a refined and perverse alternative to the bourgeois concern with bodily productivity. Dorian Gray's offspring is his por-trait, his younger self, and Wilde's Salomé makes unilateral love to the severed head of Jokanaan. Beards-ley's Lacedaemonian ambassadors, from his illustrations to *Lysistrata*, carry their upright penises like tro-phies, but the organs are intended for their own private delectation. Even the most notorious of sexual adventurers, reincarnated in this new world, shrilly protested against the biological curse imposed on the human animal. In 1903 in *Man and Superman*, Shaw brought back Mozart's Don Giovanni and Donna Ana – who in Hoffmann's story nurtures a forbidden passion for

Aubrey Beardsley, *The Lacedaemonian Ambassadors*, 1896

him — and set them to arguing in hell. Ana still desires Shaw's Juan. Nature goads her: she needs a father for the Nietzschean superman. But the libertine, so inexhaustibly avid in Mozart's opera, now resists, and Juan blames nature for inventing 'a separate creature whose sole function [is] her own impregnation!' Human beings have multiplied unaccountably; in view of this superfluity, he argues that men should be excused from the 'labour of gestation'. Besides, they have other uses for an energy that was once expended in the pursuit of a mate, or in the hard work of coition. Contemporary man, Juan says, is 'too imaginative and mentally vigorous to be content with mere self-reproduction'. Juan boasts that men have used this playful surplus of energy to create civilization, and he hopes to protect it from democracy by culling the population. Only 'the viciously reckless poor and the stupidly pious rich' bother about preserving the race, and in doing so they degrade it; individuals who are 'imaginative and poetic', who worship art and beauty, will choose celibacy, relying on the art they produce to represent them. The 'Life Force', as Juan rousingly declares, operates through his brain, not his penis.

Or was that force spent? At least Juan's torrential loquacity retains the elastic grace and furious speed of the music that Mozart gave Giovanni to sing. Though he may not want to have sex, he is a linguistic vitalist. He embodies the 'élan vital' that Bergson prized in comedy, a liveliness that fearlessly plumbs 'the depth of worlds' and defies death by jesting about it. But the apostles of decadence, dismayed by the Darwinian decree of nature, listlessly resigned from life.

Art's mission was to advertise the survival of the unfittest. Des Esseintes in *À Rebours*, for instance, is a precious relic of genetic degeneration. Huysmans explains that his family's genetic stock has been enfeebled by intermarriage and perhaps by syphilis, 'the everlasting disease that ravaged the ancestors of man'. Grimly acquiescing in this doom, Des Esseintes invites his friends to a banquet to commemorate his lost virility, and serves them black, funereal food. Even his gardening is depraved. He cultivates jungly plants whose living flesh mimics cloth, paper, porcelain and metal, and he boasts — as he surveys their putrid, gangrenous flesh — of having taken over from Darwin's selector by hybridizing species. In 1874 the delirious hermit in Flaubert's *La Tentation de saint Antoine*, profiting from contemporary science, has an even more overheated vision of plants and animals marrying and merging underwater, which is where life began. Submarine shrubs reach out with branches like arms, or grow human heads for fruit. Gourds pretend to be breasts, and a drowned mandrake sings. Nature supplies the womb, but man's cruel and exorbitant imagination is the seminal force in Des Esseintes' hothouse. 'In the course of a few years,' he says, 'man can operate a selection which easy-going Nature could not make in less than a few centuries.' Effete as he is, he has a covert appetite for the primitive, which represents the animality of our raw, crude beginnings. Hence his attraction to the designs of Odilon Redon, in which apeish bipeds – reminiscences of a time when men kept company with mammoths and bears – scavenge among bloated, rubbery flora. In 1883, the year before Huysmans published *À Rebours*, Redon produced a set of

lithographs called *Les Origines*, which speculate about the forms of life that might have preceded man's arrival on earth. A flower experimentally grows a single, cyclopean eye, and a barbed siren rears up from the waves. A winged horse tries to fly, but its weight drags it back into the abyss. Redon later made a lithographic portrait of a moribund Des Esseintes, who slumps in a chair and prepares to discard a body he has worn out. The anthropoids in *Les Origines* predate humanity; Redon's Des Esseintes is a ravaged appendix to the race.

Odilon Redon,
*Les Origines,*
1883

Sexual potency, for which the dandy had no use, migrated into technological gadgets. Des Esseintes is lecherously fond of two locomotives, conceived without sex and born without the pangs of parturition: the shrill, slim blonde Crampton, squeezed into a corset of brass, and the stouter, rowdier, Amazonian brunette Engerth. Their elegance and rampant power prove that, as a creator, 'man has done as well as God'.

Wilde recommended falling in love with yourself, and promised that the affair would last a lifetime. In a 1914 essay, Freud explained such narcissism as a reaction against the Darwinian theory of creation, which reduced the individual to 'a mere appendage of his germ-plasm'. The narcissist refuses to be a compliant link in the chain of being, a humble contributor to the immortality of the species. He therefore 'supposes sexuality to be one of his own designs', and invents forms of love-making that do not obey nature's call. Darwin's account of biological origins prompted Freud to speculate that the sexual urge was 'not all that old' – a chance development, an optional extra, something that we might learn to live without. In 1920 in *Beyond the Pleasure Principle*, Freud considered Darwin's account of reproduction in differentiated germ cells, and wondered whether our coital practices derived from a 'chance conjugation of two protista at some point in the past'. Falling in love, we make desperate efforts to recreate the excitement of that first accidental encounter. In retrospect, the less frenetic methods that nature first devised – fission, gemmation – seem pleasingly simple and efficient.

In his essay on Shakespeare's sonnets, Wilde celebrated an imaginary love-affair between the dramatist and a young, androgynous actor. The first group of sonnets is usually read as Shakespeare's attempt to persuade an aristocratic patron of his responsibility to prolong the family line. According to Wilde, the children the poet urges Willie Hughes to beget are the phantoms to which the boy actor will give life on stage; the sonnets tell him, Wilde says, that he 'must create something in art'. The relationship leaves behind a sequence of poems, more estimable and longer-lived than the offspring born to Shakespeare and Anne Hathaway. But if artistic creativity cancels the reproductive urge, humanity arrives at a dead end. That terminus satisfies the homosexual poet Sebastian and his voracious mother in Tennessee Williams's *Suddenly Last Summer*. In the Garden District of swampy New Orleans, Sebastian tends a crop of ancient, meat-eating plants, survivors of 'the great fern forest'. His gruesome specimens might be cuttings from the private jungle of Des Esseintes. Sebastian's mother, serving live insects to a Venus fly-trap, says that the garden dates back to 'the dawn of creation'. The doctor to whom she is showing the place says that it is terrifying. 'So was creation,' she says. Then, reconsidering, she adds, 'So is creation'.

The horticulture is Darwinian, and so is the voyage she and Sebastian take to the Galápagos Islands. It was on the Galápagos that Darwin felt he had drawn closer 'to that great fact – the mystery of mysteries – the first appearance of new beings on this earth'. When the *Beagle* anchored there, he captured a few mocking-birds, dissected some 'disgusting' iguanas, and studied the giant tortoises, which looked to him like 'inhabitants of some other planet'. Sharing his curiosity, they stared back at him. The stubborn, slow-witted evolutionary will of the tortoises as they tottered across the ship's deck made Melville feel like 'an antiquary of a geologist' studying a species long extinct, and reminded him that in these latitudes 'Adam and his billions of posterity remain uncreated'. One tortoise even allowed Darwin to clamber onto its shell for a lumbering ride. At the time they were laying their eggs in pits gouged out on a beach of lava so black that Darwin likened it to the iron foundries at Wolverhampton. Sebastian in *Suddenly Last Summer* prolongs his visit so that he can see those buried eggs hatch. What interests him is the fight with death that begins immediately after birth. He watches as black birds swoop down from the sky to rend the flesh of the

tortoises as they crawl towards the safety of the sea. His mother, remembering the scene, calls it dreadful. The doctor reminds her that 'Nature is not
created in the image of man's compassion'. But was it created at all, and who
was the creator? Sebastian tells his mother that the dive-bombing birds exemplify his idea of God. She moans that 'We are all of us trapped by this devouring
creation', even though – as a domineering, sexually jealous matriarch – she
represents Tennessee Williams's idea of the goddess who, like Venus trapping
flies, cannot forgive men for escaping from captivity inside her body. The
Galápagos interested Darwin as a site of 'insular speciation'. Being so far
from the mainland, the islands had produced their own specialized, inbred
monsters. Perhaps there is an analogy with the specialized race of artists and
their peculiar progeny. Sebastian's mother describes the creative rhythm of
her pampered son, who spent nine months of every year preparing for the
arrival of a single poem. 'Nine months?' asks the doctor. 'The length of a
pregnancy, yes,' says the mother, who acted as muse and midwife, present at
both the conception and the lying-in. The doctor deduces that 'the poem
was hard to deliver'.

Despite this aesthetic distaste, nature went on indecently pullulating,
and artists who struggled with it rather than sniffing at it tried to ensure that
their works were hardy enough to survive. Edvard Munch had no children
of his own. Fearful of inherited maladies and of his father's religious mania,
he did not want to pass on his bad blood to another generation. He called
his paintings his 'evil offspring', born against his will. 'What is art really?' he
asked. 'The outcome of dissatisfaction with life, the point of impact for the
creative force.' That point of impact was like the hole made by a bullet.
Munch's paintings came from inside him, and forced their way out through
bleeding vents in the flesh. His response was to punish them for existing: he
left them out in the rain, hung them in trees, and used them as lids for pans
steaming on the stove at meal-time. These were Darwinian tests. Munch
wanted to see if his abused, obstinate infants could withstand such treatment; if so, they had earned their right to life. 'A good painting can take
quite a bit,' he said, marvelling at the toughness of a canvas he was kicking.
A creator is a parent, and not necessarily a loving one.

Even before *The Origin of Species* appeared, the defenders of religion had
begun to reprove science for confounding the dignity and pre-eminence
of humanity. Disraeli's target in *Tancred* is *Vestiges of the Natural History of
Creation*, written by the amateur geologist Robert Chambers and published
anonymously in 1844. In the novel, Lady Constance is reading a tract entitled *The Revelations of Chaos*, from which she receives a garbled notion of
how a star is formed: it's 'a sort of celestial cheese, churned into light'. She
blithely sings the praises of mutation, and tells Tancred that men are metamorphosing into crows. 'We had fins,' she tells him; 'we may have wings.'

The hero, a modern crusader, declines to believe that he was ever a fish. Such opinions disqualify Lady Constance from kneeling with him at the Holy Sepulchre. In Gethsemane he meets Eva, who defends the Jews as a 'holy race' and says their supposed crime – 'preordained by the Creator of the world for countless ages' – resulted in the triumph of Christianity, a doctrine that 'embraces all space and time; nay more, chaos and eternity'. Chaos is subdued at last by revelation. Tancred continues to revere Jehovah, 'the Omnipotent Creator', who in choosing Moses as the instrument of his will singles out 'a great creative spirit and organizing mind'. He travels to the Arabian desert, because it is only there that 'the Creator of the world speaks with man'.

While he waits for his private audience with the deity, he laments the lack of sacred books. Jehovah used to inspire the prophets, but two thousand years have passed since any 'written expression of the celestial will' consolidated the 'relation between the Creator and his creatures'. It was Disraeli's ambition to purify the secular, materialistic novel, to make it a repository for holy writ. Literature, fortunately, refused the offer of redemption. But Darwin's account of nature and of man's descent from 'some lowly organized form' did prompt a new kind of novel. A ready-made world could no longer be taken for granted; the novel had to remember atavistic origins, and to anticipate the decay that will inevitably overtake the culture we fabricate. In Joseph Conrad's *An Outcast of the Islands*, published in 1896, dawn in the Malayan jungle is a time of murky genesis. The darkness that grows 'blotchy with ill-defined shapes, as if a new universe was being evolved out of sombre chaos'. At last a human shape solidifies, leaning on a gun. The evolution is easily reversible: during a showdown with the renegade Willems, Lingard is 'appalled by the thought that had the world that moment come to an end ... he would not have felt the slightest surprise'. The treacherous, despicable Willems is reduced to 'that creature before him' – a man who is hardly the creator's masterpiece. A tropical thunderstorm revokes the Bible's account of the first days. It is as if 'the light was dying prematurely out of the world', and the sodden air is unbreathable. When the downpour begins, earth no longer offers a footing, churning to mud in which Willems slips and stumbles.

In 1880 Zola cited Darwin as an intellectual source for his study of the 'inter-organic conditions' that determined 'phenomena in living beings'. Zola called his method naturalistic. Realism described the deceptive appearances of an industrial culture; naturalism exposed the savage combat that lay beneath the upholstery. In Upton Sinclair's *The Jungle*, an anatomy of the Chicago stockyards published in 1906, the city's factories, railway lines and telegraph poles balance insecurely on an earth that seethes, sweats and rumbles, still embroiled in the ferment of creation. Chimneys disgorge oily smoke that 'might have come from the centre of the world ... where the fires of the ages still smoulder'. Furnaces and boiling vats defy the winter weather: the icy gales and blizzards are 'a power primeval, cosmic, shadowing the tortures of the lost souls flung out to chaos and destruction'. The stink of bleeding meat around the abbatoir is 'elemental', and so is the lowing and squealing of cattle and hogs herded to slaughter. A carnivorous society requires such sacrifices, and death, as in Darwin's survey of species, insemi-nates the world. The discarded portions of the carcasses are made into lard or tallow; the residue is then ground into bone-phosphate and sold as a fertilizer.

Darwin insisted that there was grandeur in his view of life. Sinclair reaf-firms the point when his hero Jurgis Rudkis goes on his first tour of Packingtown. Jurgis watches a live pig proceed along an assembly line that briskly dismembers it and transforms it into pork. He regards the procedure as 'a wonderful poem', and is only briefly perturbed by the thought that there is no 'god of hogs' to take pity on the protesting beast. The factory, he decides, is 'as tremendous as the universe'. But that universe is mortal, and when a cannery shuts down, a Lithuanian worker is as horrified as if the sun itself had abruptly expired. The natural order falters; industry therefore has to repeat the original act of creation, staging all over again the subterranean eruptions that first gave shape to our world. In a steel mill, Jurgis watches as a scorching torrent of white heat cascades from a ladle: 'Out of regions of wonder it streamed, the very river of life'. He stares at pillars of flame, and sees 'incandescent rainbows' in the black, roaring air. As the bars of metal are hammered into shape and manhandled by cranes, he feels he is 'standing in the centre of the earth, where the machinery of time was revolving'. Like epic poetry, these rhapsodies narrate the battle between existence and extinction. When Sinclair concentrates on individual cases, the result is closer to tragedy. Unable to afford coal, Jurgis and his family recoil from the annihilating cold: 'here in this huge city ... men might be hunted down and destroyed by the wild-beast powers of nature, just as truly as ever they were in the days of the cave-men!' The depredation, however, cannot only be blamed on nature. In Sinclair's analysis, the killing is done by a ruthless gang of bosses and managers; capitalism applies Darwinian laws to the economy.

Darwin's theory explained contemporary industrial society. It also supplied information about what what Darwin called 'the dim obscurity of the past': man descends from 'a hairy, tailed quadruped', and other ancestors lie even further back – an 'ancient marsupial', an 'amphibian-like creature', a 'fish-like animal', and finally, at the origin of everything, a bisexual larva. The imagination was eager to fill in the missing links, and to give the mon-sters contemporary identities. Liam O'Flaherty in 1925 in his novel *The Informer* likens Gypo Nolan – a Communist who betrays a comrade during the Irish civil war – to 'some primeval monster risen from the slime in

The ape fighting a dinosaur. Preliminary drawing by Byron Crabbe for the 1933 film *King Kong*, directed by Merian C. Cooper

which all things had their origin'. In 1931 RKO planned a film called *Creation*, set on a volcanic island off the coast of South America. The designs were based on the stark, moody black–and–white engravings made by Gustave Doré in 1865 and 1866 for editions of the Bible and *Paradise Lost*. But this was no peaceable Eden, and Doré's winged archangels changed into swooping raptors that gathered up human beings in their claws. The film's brawling cast included a brontosaurus, a triceratops, an arsinotherium, a pterodactyl and a pteranodon, all due to be wiped out, when their wrestling matches were over, by another eruption. *Creation* was cancelled, but some of the footage with the monsters was transferred to the project that replaced it, *King Kong*. Here biblical allusions were supplanted by a plot pieced together from two of the bad dreams incited by Darwin. *King Kong* bridged the species by making the ape fall in love with a blonde starlet; it also closed the gap between savagery and civilization by sending him to New York, whose skyline duplicates the serrated geography of his island.

Myths make guesses about a beginning that predates the historical record. They also dilate to match the expansiveness of a universe that is without bounds. James Hutton, whose geological investigations were adopted by Lyell, argued that the story of the rocks refuted the chronology of the Bible. In the earth's sedimentary archive, Hutton found 'no vestige of a beginning' and 'no prospect of an end'. As the anthropologist James G. Frazer said in 1931, the world was neither created nor constructed; it simply grew. Who could say when the process started, or how it would continue? G. K. Chesterton stubbornly insisted that the human story must have a definite beginning – a divine inception, as in Genesis – because of man's special status: 'this creature was truly different from all other creatures; because he was a creator as well as a creature'. The act of narration vindicated the Christian worldview, since 'every short story truly does begin with creation and end with a last judgment'. Unfortunately Chesterton wrote this in 1925, when modern writers had robbed stories of their theological or judicial closure. Creative ingenuity now strove to reverse, revoke or at least postpone creation. In 1913 the Australian poet Christopher Brennan described himself cowering, depressed, beneath 'a sky of uncreated mud'. Darwin's last phrase in *The Origin of Species* refers to a world that is still being evolved. The protagonist of Virginia Woolf's *Orlando*, who is bisexual like Darwin's larvae, experiences this endlessness by living for centuries. Orlando catches up with the novelist and finds her hurriedly writing the novel: 'It was ten o'clock in the morning. It was the eleventh of October. It was 1928. It was the present moment.' While Virginia Woolf scribbles in an attempt to keep up with the elapsing moment, Orlando bounds off into the future.

H. G. Wells's *Outline of History*, published in 1920, was obliged to go back to the primal, initial moment. But because Wells was unsure 'how life began upon the earth', he prevaricated about the timing: the first word of his book is therefore 'And'. The conjunction – which introduces the phrase 'And first, before we begin the history of life...' – gestures towards a prehistory that remains hidden. Genesis, the traditional beginning, is only mentioned a couple of hundred pages later, when Wells interprets Noah's flood as a mythic memento of a natural catastrophe. Arriving at the Renaissance, he discredits the creation myth in the compliment he pays to Michelangelo. He commends the image of God animating Adam because it displays 'a new attitude to the body and tangible things'. Nothing intangible, like the kindling of the soul, is allowed. After many millennia and more than a thousand pages, the *Outline* ends where it began because, as Wells says in his final paragraph, 'Life begins perpetually' and is 'for ever dying to be born afresh'. At the end of Virginia Woolf's last novel *Between the Acts*, Mrs Swithin is reading the *Outline*. The illustrations of mammoths and mastodons make her imagine a time when England was a swamp, with prehistoric man rearing up, 'half-human, half-ape', to lift stones. Night falls, the same night 'that dwellers in caves had watched from some high place among rocks'. She puts down the book, although its action continues as Woolf's characters quarrel and then make love, or sleep and awaken to find that nature has renewed itself.

In his 1907 manifesto *Creative Evolution*, Bergson transferred the emphasis of Darwin's theory from procreation to creativity. The steam engine hissing hot vapour still functioned, for Bergson, as a symbol of 'a creative endeavour which unmakes itself'. Energy is amassed then violently expelled, recalling the orgasms that Balzac rationed. But we should not hold back. Bergson argued that creation is not simply continued (as Descartes proposed) but continuous; it depends on our willingness to share our own small supply of the 'élan vital', and each contribution helps ensure that 'the universe ... will really evolve'. We must abandon the notion, derived from Genesis, that the creator can be separated from the thing created. Bergson's God is not a withdrawn, self-sufficient prime mover. He represents 'unceasing life, action, freedom', and any of us can experience the same divine afflatus when we act freely or creatively. Laughter sounded to Bergson like the effervescent release of this vital joy, and the spontaneity and unexpectedness of comic fancy enabled life to 'flow into flexible channels, changeable in shape'. He calls on 'all the living' to participate in this adventure: 'The animal takes its stand upon the plant, man bestrides animality, and the whole of humanity, in space and in time, is one immense army galloping beside and before and behind each of us in an overwhelming charge able to beat down every resistance and clear the most formidable of obstacles, perhaps even death'. That rhetorical challenge is taken up by the novelist Bernard at the end of Virginia Woolf's *The Waves*, published in 1931. Old and shuffling, he still experiences an 'eternal renewal' and feels a wave rising and swelling within him. It crests, breaks, and produces a speech: 'I am aware once more of a new desire, something rising beneath me like the proud horse whose rider first spurs and then pulls him back. What enemy do we now perceive advancing against us...? It is death. Death is the enemy. ... Against you will I fling myself, unvanquished and unyielding, O Death!'

In *Man and Superman*, Juan and Ana, let out of hell, reassume their roles as the anarchist Jack Tanner and his fiancée Ann Whitefield. As the play ends they are still arguing about the rival claims of art and nature. Jack finally consents to marry Ann, but with his usual flighty eloquence protests against his inability to resist her biological command. 'Go on talking,' she fondly remarks. 'Talking!' cries Jack in exasperation: doesn't she realize that he is fighting for his life? These words, his last, are drowned by a chorus of what Shaw parenthetically calls 'universal laughter'. The laughter is the universe's joke on one more man who has been tamed, deprived of his seminal donation and then discarded; but it is also a Bergsonian mirth, which pays tribute to our vigour and our resilience. God once spoke the world into being. Now we must keep it alive by talking – or by continuing to write, to sing, to paint, to mould clay, or to thrust buildings into the sky. 'The impetus of life,' as Bergson said, 'consists in a need of creation.' We all feel the need, and it is up to us to satisfy it.

# 20

# NEW EVE, OLD ADAM

In 1859, when *The Origin of Species* was published, Edward Burne-Jones was at work on the design of a rose window for Waltham Abbey. He chose to illustrate the first week of creation, compressing its events into small circular panels that caught fire when the sun shone. A few years later he made a gold-edged sketch of elemental preliminaries, intended for a lavish edition of the Bible: the newly positioned sun and moon emit radiant life, and a dove plummets downwards to impregnate the waters. Burne-Jones then undertook a series of larger paintings representing *The Days of Creation*. Henry James saw these works at the Grosvenor Gallery in 1877, where they were 'cruelly discredited' by the 'savage red wall' on which they hung. James wondered about the 'morbid pathos' of the angels who do the creating in God's place. Why were they so wan, with their drooping wings and wistful downcast eyes? James also speculated about their gender. Milton's archangels in *Paradise Lost* are energetic male warriors; Burne-Jones turned them into 'beautiful, rather sickly boys', or made them 'sublimely sexless'. James suspected these ephebes of being 'weak and weary', even 'debauched and debilitated'.

Their lassitude derives from their lack of belief in the task with which the artist charged them. The events of creation now happen inside portable globes, like the crystal balls used by magicians or like Bosch's alchemical retorts; the circular panels Burne-Jones designed for Waltham Abbey have dwindled, and can now be held up by the angels. The globes look as fragile as bubbles, and the scenes they display – water separating from dry land, birds taking to the air, Adam and Eve holding hands – are an evanescent play of tinted shadows. On the sixth day, a squatting angel plays a lute. Creation is no longer a series of decisive acts, as Goethe's Faust proclaimed when he perused Genesis. It is at best a song, a fanciful and fantastic reverie. These morbid seraphs are in mourning for their recently deceased maker.

After Darwin, God was gradually written out of the story, while Adam and Eve gladly cast off the biblical curse and resumed their procreative task. But the job of multiplying was beset by new difficulties. In *A Woman of No Importance*, Oscar Wilde offers a hurried summation of the Old and New Testaments. One character remarks that 'The Book of Life begins with a man and a woman in a garden'; another adds 'It ends with Revelations'. The revelations Wilde had in mind were sexual scandals. Perhaps God's mistake

*The First Saturday* from *Eve's Diary*, 1906, by Mark Twain. Illustration by Lester Ralph

was to imagine that the primal humans were compatible, and that marriage could place controls on our generative urges.

Having announced God's death, Nietzsche disposed of all remaining theological and moral fallacies in *Götzen-Dämmerung*, a diatribe on the twilight of the idols written in 1888. He subjected the Bible to a scornful interrogation, asking if man was God's mistake or whether God might be a mistake grievously made by man. Retelling the story of Adam and Eve, he agreed to believe that man created woman. But what was she created out of? He sarcastically answered his own question: man made her 'out of a rib of his

God, of his "ideal"'. In *Der Anti-Christ*, Nietzsche analysed the failure of nerve that made God vulnerable to these assaults. From the first, he claimed, God was a moral coward, stricken by his 'mortal terror of *science*'. He also lacked inner resources. Alone in the world and bored, suffering from the malaise James sensed in Burne-Jones's *Days of Creation*, he designed man as a playmate. For the late nineteenth century, ennui was a terminal symptom, a warning that humanity had reached the end of its tenure; Nietzsche prescribed a cure by blaming the ailment on God and tracing it back to the beginning of the world. The malady, however, was contagious. Man in turn became bored, so God created the animals to keep him occupied. This gets the sequence of events back to front, but Nietzsche's infidel Genesis deliberately rearranges the chronology and causality of the first seven days: his God frantically improvises, making the world up as he goes along. Animal husbandry did not entertain man for long, so God invented woman, who ate the apple and acquired knowledge. As soon as man learned to think for himself, all gods

Edward Burne-Jones, *Sixth Day of Creation*, 1870–76

were doomed. The creator's only recourse was spitting fury. Nietzsche imagines his anathema: 'Man has become scientific – ... *he will have to be drowned!*'

The waters of the deluge eventually subsided, and in due course Leonardo dreamed up the submarine, which would save scientific man from future floods and allow him to explore the depths. That adventure prompted another revision of Genesis. In 1869–70 in Jules Verne's *Twenty Thousand Leagues Under the Sea*, Captain Nemo embarks on a course of underwater research in his submarine *Nautilus*; he takes along Professor Aronnax, whose task, like Darwin's on the *Beagle*, is to classify the new species encountered on the voyage. The publisher Hetzel said that the aim of Verne's scientific romances was 'to rewrite the history of the world' and to amass an inventory of current technical information. After sending characters on excursions to the centre of the earth and to the moon, he now returned to the beginning of the world: life first wriggled on the ocean floor and clambered to the surface in search of land. The story Verne told inverted Genesis. The sea is an upside-down, submerged heaven, in which, as Nemo says, a man can smoothly glide through 'an almost supernatural existence'. He promises to show Aronnax 'things that must not be seen', sights prohibited by a jealous God who established his throne in the sky. Some of these marvels are natural, like the giant crabs – so large they eat coconuts – described by Darwin. But a forbidden sight can also be an aesthetic vision. When the submarine passes beneath the South Pole, its searchlight ignites the angular ridges of packed ice, which shine like the spilled contents of a jewel box: sapphires, emeralds and diamonds dazzle the crew. Nature might possibly be able to design such a spectacle. It is the novelist, however, who imagines it.

Verne was fascinated by the biological unorthodoxy of the lifeforms hidden below the waterline. Pearl oysters reproduce in their millions, with an unstoppable fecundity that can never be halted by 'the power of man to destroy'. Polyps bud in all directions, each outcrop powered by its own 'generator' or gemmule, although the separate growths cohere and cooperate, turning the reef into a model socialist community. In Verne's *The Mysterious Island*, written in 1874–5, an engineer castaway in the Pacific marvels at the coral insects which construct reefs and atolls and may in time produce new continents for the overflow of humanity. At 'the first periods of creation', he reflects, nature used volcanic fire to heave land out of water. Now the creative agency, doing God's work for him, belongs to those tiny, toiling insects. Cyrus Harding goes on to prophesy the end of life on an earth consigned to thermodynamic doom – a forthcoming calamity that is 'the secret of God'. Aronnax in the earlier novel describes an elephantine squid as the freakish product of a Creator who has given the cephalopod three separate hearts. But the squid has a parrot-like beak in a mollusc's body, and it mongrelizes the species like one of Horace's mixed metaphors; as a monster, it belongs in the menagerie of classical myth, not in God's orderly garden. Its tentacles resemble the writhing hair of the Furies, and its slimy arms, like the Hydra's head, grow back when sliced off. This self-regeneration suggests that it may have created itself. In fact it is another offshoot of the novelist's teeming brain.

Aronnax accounts for a colossal sea unicorn (which turns out to be the *Nautilus*) by attributing it to the same source. Astonished and metaphysically affronted when he sees the submarine, he changes his mind about its maker. It is prodigious, and prodigies should properly 'come from the Creator'. But this craft, which transforms a man into a steel fish, has been contrived by human ingenuity. It competes with God, and surpasses anything he has constructed. Inside it, Nemo impersonates the prime mover who, in the cosmology of Pythagoras, maintains the harmony of the world: he amuses himself during the voyage by playing the organ, and its faint accords, echoing from one sealed chamber to another, reproduce the music of the spheres in this private, water-tight universe. The submarine even technologically matches God's first command, which calls light into being. Its radiance convinces some observers that it is phosphorescent, while others believe it to be an electric eel. Nemo explains the unnatural miracle: he lights the ship by extracting sodium from the brine and mixing it with mercury, which replaces zinc in his batteries. The light he generates is more uniform and reliable than that of the sun, which in any case – as Aronnax points out – is cooling and condemning our planet to death. Electricity, Nemo says, is dynamic; it supplies his navigable machine with a soul. He generously chooses to regard God as a colleague, or an elderly and somewhat outmoded mentor. What is the world but a scientific experiment conducted by a technician who juggles the elements and studies their responses? Nemo explains the circulation of the ocean by noting that 'the Creator of all things' can alter currents by changing the temperature or salinity of the water, or by multiplying the animalcules that live in it. The creator of all things might more aptly be called an inventor: a Watt or an Edison, a Balzac or a Verne.

Edison himself usurps the creator's role in *L'Ève future*, a novel published in 1886 by Villiers de l'Isle-Adam, a high-born bohemian who befriended Baudelaire, Mallarmé and Wagner. As he toils in his New Jersey laboratory, Edison grumbles about 'that life-creating cliché, "Fiat lux!"'. Electricity makes the miracle banal; he has uttered the formula two or three hundred times, and each incantation has begotten a marvel. (The estimate is too modest, since Edison patented a thousand inventions, including the incandescent bulb.) Having wished light into a tingling filament and encased it in a globe of glass, he now looks around for new challenges, and advances to the harder task God undertook later in

PUNCH, OR THE LONDON CHARIVARI.—JUNE 25, 1881.

"WHAT WILL HE GROW TO?"

*Electricity,* cartoon from *Punch,* 1881

the first week. In the novel, Edison goes on to fabricate a woman. The futuristic Eve of the title is a robot designed as a compliant sexual partner for an elegant English aristocrat. She replaces a treacherous mistress, dismissed by Lord Ewald as 'a mistake of the Creator's'. Edison is challenged to do better, and like Frankenstein he enthusiastically aligns himself with Prometheus. Every man, he tells Ewald, envies and secretly worships the thief of fire. But he does not grub in a river bed like Prometheus, or even scoop up a handful of red clay like God in Genesis. His creature is sleeker, less dirtily organic. She is light made flesh: her body is composed of an alchemical substance called radiant matter, which is neither solid, liquid nor gaseous. Edison boasts that her metabolism is an improvement on the inefficient human prototype. We breathe as heavily as steam engines, burning up oxygen; the respiration of Edison's scientific Eve is regulated by a pump in her chest, and the air she takes is electrically warmed and artificially scented to sweeten her breath. Her joints are magnetized sockets, saved from oxidizing by an application of perfumed lubricant. Inside her thighs, platinum cells filled with mercury keep her balanced. Like Olympia in Offenbach's *Les contes d'Hoffmann*, she has a talent for singing clockwork coloratura, produced by lungs that Edison likens to barrel organs.

Although the novel defines Edison as an engineer, he is also a mystic. He understands that technology rationalizes magic, trapping spirits and compelling them to perform chores for us. He is sorry that the gadgetry invented during the nineteenth century was not available when the world began: if only a photograph could have captured the face of God (who has always been frustratingly camera-shy), or a recording had been made of the voice that announced to Mary the news of her pregnancy! At least his phonograph has managed, as Villiers de l'Isle-Adam says, to entrap echoes. Like the commentators in the Kabbalah, Edison interrogates the vacancy from which existence somehow emerged. When Ewald evasively says that he is thinking of nothing, Edison replies 'Nothing! It's a thing so useful that God himself didn't hesitate to draw the world out of it'. Radio waves cannot be seen, and the eye cannot measure the velocity of light or the distances it traverses: does that mean that such things are non-existent? We may have doubts about telepathy, but who would have believed in telegraphy before it became a scientific fact? Edison 'can never forget the immense quantity of Nothing that was necessary to create the universe'. Physics expands into metaphysics, and his scientific tinkering with Volta batteries and Promethean sparks overlaps into artistic creativity. Edison asks Ewald if the soprano on whom he models the android is an artist. Ewald indignantly denies it. She is a mere virtuoso, a lowly technician, fiddling with scales and trills. 'The only living souls who deserve the name of artists,' Ewald adds, 'are the creators'. Edison is entitled to call himself one. He manufactures the android, but before he can do so he must imagine her, like a novelist or a dramatist who makes a fantasy materialize in the form of a character. Edison promises that Ewald's customized shade will be a compound woman, an anthology of literary bedmates – partly the compulsively lyrical Antonia who sings herself to death in a story by E.T.A. Hoffmann, partly the ethereal Ligeia in Edgar Allan Poe's poem, partly Wagner's Venus, who is so reluctant to loosen her coital grip on Tannhäuser.

The affair between this artificial being and her human owner does not last long. Edison's android – who sleeps, like a vampire, in a closed trunk – is destroyed when a fire breaks out on the ship transporting her back to England. When he learns of the loss, Edison scans the wintry nocturnal sky and shivers. Perhaps a God who will not be mocked is smirking in triumph. A madder scientist returns to the assault on Genesis in H. G. Wells's *The Island of Dr Moreau*, published in 1896.

Moreau presides over a wild Eden that is both a concentration camp and a torture chamber. Nietzsche's God feared science; Moreau, who made his reputation by researching 'morbid growths', is a God who uses science to tyrannize his abject subjects. The patch of earth he rules is a place of pain, and its laws are upheld by terror. The islanders have their own version of the grovelling decalogue transcribed by Moses, and the shipwrecked narrator Prendick listens as they recite a ritualized chant 'about *Him*, whoever he might be', reminding themselves of the many things their master forbids them to do. The creator's rights include the freedom to destroy his handiwork: '*His* is the Hand that makes. *His* is the hand that wounds'. But Moreau, unlike Edison, bungles his experiment. He cannot create, and instead gruesomely miscegenates species. Along with an ape man – an unsurprising Darwinian throwback – his zoo contains an ocelot man, a man who has been crossed with a Skye terrier, a hyaena-swine, a St Bernard brute, a horse-rhinoceros, a bear-bull, and a mixture of ape and goat that can be passed off as a classical satyr. The Horatian metaphors have acquired teeth, claws and a foul musky odour. Moreau's project, as he says, is 'man-making', but his grafts have produced only monsters. He animalizes men, and by way of compensation deifies himself. After his death, Moreau does not relinquish his power: like the God of Moses, he ascends into invisibility, and can thus claim to be omniscient. The beasts are warned that he is 'The Master you cannot see. Yet even now he listens above you'. According to Wells, the religion expounded in the Old Testament depends on our prostrate unworthiness, and its morality is enforced by the threat of physical torment. Nietzsche thought that Christianity was a fitting religion for slaves. Wells suggests that it is a religion unfit for men, a cult designed to discipline curs.

As in *Frankenstein* and *L'Ève future*, this cruel, blasphemous science has a disturbing affinity with art. Moreau the vivisectionist remarks that the

animals remodelled by his knife have been 'carven and wrought' as if he were
a sculptor, and his interest in 'the plasticity of living forms' recalls the esemplastic power celebrated by Coleridge. His objective is 'metamorphosis', so
the story reinterprets one of Ovid's myths. Moreau is Circe, although he uses
surgery not sorcery to degrade his captives, and there is no escape from the
'generalized animalism' that overtakes them. Prendick calls the mutants a
'Comus rout', referring to the bewitched monsters, 'headed like sundry sorts
of wilde Beasts', that attend Circe's riotous son in Milton's *Mask Presented at
Ludlow Castle*. Comus is the pagan god of comedy: an amoral reveller, a
feaster who liberates appetite. In this case, the artistic analogy vindicates
Moreau. Prendick is repelled by 'the
grotesqueness of the forms' he
encounters in the undergrowth,
and loses 'faith in the sanity of
the world' when he sees how 'a
blind fate ... seemed to cut and
shape the fabric of existence'.
It takes art to cut and shape
fabric, and grotesquerie was the
gospel of the novelists who
carved, wrought, cut or shaped
the substance of humanity into

figures like Dickens's Silas Wegg in *Our Mutual Friend*, a dessicated seller of
wizened fruit who has one wooden leg already and who seems to be
growing another. Henry James described unwieldy Victorian novels as 'loose
baggy monsters': like what Prendick calls 'these strange creations of Moreau's
art', they were ugly because unclassifiable, mish-mashes of conflicting
genres. Perhaps the beasts in this jungle have crawled out of Prendick's brain.
He asks himself the same questions about origins that Mary Shelley confronts when discussing the source of *Frankenstein*. His mind, he admits, is
'a chaos of the most horrible imaginings'; the shapeless thing that tracks him
in the forest might well be 'a mere creation of my disordered imagination'.

In nineteenth-century America, Genesis was supposed to repeat itself
without such hindrances or aborted mishaps. Walt Whitman saw himself
as a 'chanter of Adamic songs', strolling in a 'new garden' which was his
unspoiled continent. But because America was humanity's second chance,
there had to be a darker past which the new country renounced or obliterated. Nathaniel Hawthorne's story 'The New Adam and Eve', published in
1843, supposed that a Day of Doom had disposed of the previous race,
wiping out people but leaving their cities intact.

This gives Hawthorne's renovated specimens the opportunity to make
a series of stringently puritanical moral choices. His Adam and Eve awaken

in contemporary Boston, but behave as if they were still in their blithe, naive garden. They ignore the city's temptations. The piles of paper money in a bank vault are to them useless rubbish. Eve, naked, is intrigued by the corsets on display in a dry-goods store, but does not know what they are meant for. Jewels are freely available in the empty shops; she picks a flower instead. The food laid out for a banquet – not eaten because the guests died before they could sit down at the table – disgusts these prim vegetarians. Nature, as Hawthorne comments, has not given them an appetite for turtle soup. They puzzle over a bottle of champagne, but are put off by the ballistic popping of the cork, and drink water instead. Hawthorne's gloomy hindsight turns his Adam and Eve into satirists, 'investigators whom their Creator has commissioned to pass unconscious judgment upon the works and ways of the vanished race'. That judgment is particularly harsh when they wander into the Harvard library. Adam stares at the bookshelves, 'those storied heights of human lore', opens a volume, and pores over the 'columns of mystic characters'. An apple is easy to resist, but who could refuse this offer of mental enlightenment? Eve, however, atones for her predecessor's error by persuading Adam to stop reading. Hawthorne supports her: if Adam had educated himself, he would have been crushed by 'all the perversions, and sophistries, and false wisdom' of the miscreant past. Are we to believe that truth is nowhere to be found in the Harvard stacks, and that civilization consists of gaudy flummery and indigestible haunches of venison? Hawthorne's story regains paradise by condemning all of mankind's post-lapsarian experience.

Wittier and wiser, Mark Twain towards the end of his life wrote diaries, autobiographies and scraps of soliloquy for his own less starchily zealous Adam and Eve. Twain's Eve, instinctively acquisitive, does not share the stern abstinence of Hawthorne's heroine. Dazzled by the stars, she says that she would like to wear them as jewellery, and she casts an appraising eye on the tiger that romps in Eden, remarking that its pelt would make an excellent fur. Twain's Adam and Eve are creatures of the fin de siècle – the pieces about them were written between 1893 and 1905 – and they do their best to grapple with the intellectual paradoxes of their era, which established that they never actually existed. Eve's journal makes a false start because myth is so chronically vague about time. She begins to write the day after she arrives in Eden, then worries that the 'day-before-yesterday' is missing from the record and from her recollection. Some creative sources are easy to understand, others remain unintelligible. She generates ideas in her head, from which she spontaneously extracts the words 'smoke' and 'flame' to describe the first bonfire. But she has no idea where her babies come from, or how the cow produces milk. Both she and Adam are bewildered when Cain appears: they can't explain or categorize the small squalling monster, which must be 'a "lusus naturae" – a freak'. Because the infant crawls about on short front legs and long hind ones, Adam suspects that it might be a marsupial, and classifies it as 'Kangarooum Adamiensis'. It is a brilliantly seditious joke. Twain visited Australia in 1895, and experienced the same metaphysical disorientation that unsettled Darwin in 1836. The Southern Cross looked to Twain more like a coffin than a crucifix: his teasing raised the possibility that the cross was 'out of repair' because the religion it upheld no longer controlled the sky. The marsupials alone were enough to discredit Genesis. Twain was sure that no platypus had been ushered onto Noah's ark, so who or what had created it? He pretended to solve the theological and biological problems by having Adam announce that there was indeed a kangaroo in Eden. He and Eve also adopt a pterodactyl, nicknamed Terry. Adam, prematurely Darwinian, takes their pet to be 'a survival of the fittest'.

While the identity of the primary creator remains in dispute, Eve does some creating of her own. It is she rather than Adam who names the animals. Perhaps her initiative recognizes the intrepid self-reliance of women on the frontier, which was America's Eden. Trollope during his American travels noted the feistiness of wives out West, and added that, if he were Adam in this wild garden, he would not love Eve unless she promised to obey him. History had rendered one more biblical rule obsolete. Twain's Eve devises names with the same whimsical ease that enabled Dickens to think of Mr Pickwick. Even the dodo does not perplex her: it looks, she explains, just like its name. She has reversed the actual chronology – names can hardly precede things – but that is her artistic right. The creation in which she takes most pride is fire. Like a female Prometheus, she rubs sticks together and creates 'something that didn't exist before'; she adds 'a new thing to the world's uncountable properties'. Adam the blunt utilitarian asks her what the fire is good for. She might have replied that it will keep them warm, and cook their dinner (although Cain has not yet begun killing animals for food, so they are still presumably restricted, like Hawthorne's characters, to salads). Instead she declares that fire is good, even though it may be good for nothing. It is, she says, 'merely beautiful'.

History is often strangely synchronized, and Twain's Eve has a counterpart in Gabriel Fauré's cycle of songs *La Chanson d'Ève*, composed between 1906 and 1910 with texts by the Belgian symbolist Charles Van Lerberghe. Fauré's soprano is alone in paradise. The Bible gives Adam priority, and in some versions of the myth he is an androgyne, able to get by without Eve. Fauré's songs are about an Eve who has no Adam and does not miss him. God is here reduced to an aerial voice, which does not command her to multiply. Instead she is entrusted with the task so briskly performed by Twain's Eve: she must give the creatures in the garden a word or a sound by which they can be known, and she does so by emitting 'une parole, un son de ses lèvres en fleur'. Song blossoms from her lips in an aesthetic annunciation, and this lyricism is the secret of recovering paradise. In the second poem of the sequence, 'Prima Verba', Eve recognizes that she has the power to generate new worlds: her music depicts garlands of light, invisible but radiantly audible. The sequence ends with her death, which is not the penalty for sin but – as she says – her soul's aspiration. Reversing creation, she asks to be consumed once more by the abyss that gave birth to the world; as she expires, her life pours from a golden amphora and drenches the earth with a pagan libation. Twain's Eve happens upon beauty when she kindles the dancing flame, and Fauré's Eve produces beauty from inside her body when her breath unfurls into harmony. The first creation is followed by a second, which is more humanly significant: both women in their different ways bring into being the idea of art.

Perhaps such revelations are available only to an Eve or an Adam who remain solitary individuals, free from the conjugal obligations imposed in Genesis. Milton disapproves when Eve in *Paradise Lost* proposes that she and Adam should divide up their gardening tasks and work separately; her unprotected solitude allows the serpent to waylay her. The poem repeatedly reminds Eve of her biological destiny by referring to her as our collective mother. But Fauré's soprano lives for her art, and has no family to distract her. For Adam, other options are available. Whitman's 'song of procreation' in *Children of Adam* includes a hymn to the phallus, and when in the early morning he wanders forth from his urban bower he invites a passer-by to

> Touch me, touch the palm of your hand to my body as I pass,
> Be not afraid of my body.

That ingratiation is addressed to another man, a comradely replica of Whitman himself; Adam's children are the lovers of the patriarchal bard.

André Gide's novel *L'Immoraliste*, published in 1902, is even franker in its account of a man's self-creation, the discovery of an identity that was officially excluded from the divine plan. The 'old Adam' was the name given by Christian moralists to the sexual urges that dragged men down, the itchy outbreak of original sin. But when Gide's narrator Michel recovers from tuberculosis he decides to explore 'that authentic creature', the ancestral reprobate condemned by the Bible. At first, it is his own body that he touches. The epigraph to the novel ironically and impudently quotes Psalm 139, in which David praises God because he is himself 'fearfully and wonderfully made'. Only in the Wildean culture of the fin de siècle could narcissism be taken as evidence of piety. Gide teasingly suppresses the other verses of the psalm, although his story reinterprets them. 'Surely the darkness shall cover me', says David; that darkness – in the woods of his country estate or in Algeria – is the cover for Michel's homosexual dalliances. David goes on to sing about the secrets of his making, and says that his creator 'covered me in my mother's womb'. His 'members', his limbs and organs, were all written down in God's book, which contains the prototype for the human form. Michel, like Gide, assumes that those members exist for his own delectation.

The Kabbalah propounded strict rules about literal fidelity when transcribing texts like the psalms: copyists were enjoined to bathe after writing each line, then to cleanse themselves a second time for safety's sake before they tackled the line that followed. Gide, however, cheerfully pollutes the sacred source. At the end of the novel, waiting for the death of his unloved wife, Michel makes plans for sexual relief in the warm, dark African night. He quotes Christ's farewell to Peter – 'Now thou girdest thyself and goest where thou wouldest' – as if it were a benediction of his adventures. But he is the disciple of a god who is unrelated to Christ, and his mission is at once erotic and aesthetic: 'O great new god! grant me the knowledge of other newer races, unimagined types of beauty'. Given the need to choose, he is inclined to rate sexual delight higher than artistic achievement. His academic lectures on Latin civilization condemn culture because it is 'the destroyer of life', separating man from his instincts. He thrives in Tunis because – unlike over-educated Europe – it is 'free from works of art'. The Arabs 'live their art, sing it, dissipate it from day to day; it is not fixed, not embalmed in any work'. The reference to embalming links art, as worshipped in the cold north, with mortification. By contrast, the young men with whom Michel consorts practise the art of love (or at least the applied science of pleasure).

In such extra-territorial Edens, the world could be created all over again during sexual intercourse. Des Esseintes in *À Rebours* is excited by the frank sexuality of *La Bête humaine*, and praises Zola for writing a 'Hindu poem' which sings 'the glories of the flesh'. Gauguin, who in 1891 quit Europe in dismay, discussed the unChristian cosmology of Polynesia with his child-bride Tehura: 'we talk ... of God and of the gods. I instruct her. She in turn instructs me.' As if undressing, she shed the 'artificial veils' wrapped round her mind by the Protestant missionaries, who squeezed the islanders into starchy dresses and stove-pipe trousers. In bed with Gauguin, she told him about the deities of the Maori Olympus, who hover above the ocean like the low-lying clouds. The local version of origins attracted him because it was the coming together of spirit and matter, sun and water, male and female. A 'generative cause' – as he described the god called Taaroa – fecundated the world. The myth is about the ripening influence of the sun, so it was no crime to pick the fruit produced by this union of 'the luminous spirit and the perceptive matter which it vivifies'. In exchange for this mythic lore, Gauguin could only offer Tehura the engineered rigours of European science, and she was understandably reluctant to believe that the earth revolved around the sun.

The story of our beginnings was rewritten to eliminate the dictatorial God of Genesis. Even so, this did not preclude a fall. In 1893 Stanislaw Przybyszewski, a Polish philosopher who became a close friend of Edvard

Munch in Berlin, explained creation by declaring that 'In the beginning was sex'. He called sex 'eternally creative', but admitted that it was also a 'destructive reorganizer'. Though untroubled by divine prohibitions, Adam and Eve were still bound to come to grief, doomed by the stubborn incompatibility of gender and the dialectical friction of desire. Whitman's Adam and Fauré's Eve are happy without partners; put them together and you have procreation, but also mortal enmity and post-coital combat. Man resents and reviles woman, described in 1897 by Strindberg as 'the poor masterpiece of creation'. Woman in turn has a limited use for man, that pitiful creature with one chromosome too few. It is sexual disparity, not disobedience to God, that brings death into the world. In a catalogue note on Munch's painting *The Kiss*, Strindberg called it 'the fusion of two beings, the smaller of which ... seems on the point of devouring the larger, as is the habit of vermin, microbes, vampires or women'. In 1894 Munch painted a woman whose fangs pierce the neck of a bent, clothed man. An etching made in 1913–14, allows for reparation, as a man gnaws a woman's bare breast.

Sex for Munch was always a kind of cannibalism. In 1908 he wrote and illustrated his own fraught, perverse narrative about the loss of paradise. He was interned at the time in a Copenhagen 'nerve clinic', suffering from a bout of dementia brought on by alcoholism; a sympathetic eye specialist thought that writing would help to heal him. In its first draft Munch's story, like Hawthorne's, had an apocalyptic prologue – although Munch took care to kill God along with the human race. After this cleansing, a new Adam and Eve, called Alpha and Omega, regenerate the species. Hawthorne's couple benefit from their fresh start, but Munch's Alpha and Omega are instantly at odds. Whereas Adam awakes from his dream to find Eve beside him, it is Omega – the impatient, demanding woman – who tickles Alpha with a fern frond to rouse him from sleep. For a while they enjoy each other's company, exploring their sunny island. The serpent is responsible for their first falling-out, though not in the way prescribed by Genesis. Alpha finds Omega cuddling and caressing it. He awaits his chance and later kills it, while she watches from a distance. This should have obviated the biblical temptation; instead it establishes the fatal opposition of their natures. The man is a killer, driven to violence by his jealous insecurity, while the woman is an undiscriminating lover. Because her function is to ensure propagation, she cannot be relied on to remain faithful to any man or even to her own species. She flirts with a bear, and Munch illustrated their awkward embrace in one of his lithographs. She reaches up to place her thin arms around the dense, swollen, nuzzling blob; the meeting of her white, naked flesh and the bear's black fur is the stuff of nightmares. It's not surprising that she goes on, like Shakespeare's Titania, to kiss a donkey which sprawls on her lap. She even has a soulful idyll with a pig, after which she absconds with a deer.

Her promiscuity incites quarrels between the beasts she has teased and trifled with. The tiger smells her scent on the bear, and they tear each other to pieces.

The only animal to resist her blandishments is a shabby poet-hyena. Munch associates poetry with a beast that feeds on corpses: the artist is nourished by death, but at least his morbid alienation from society and from life itself is protection against female charms. Omega forgives the hyena for rejecting her, and crowns 'his discontented head' with a wreath of laurel. Alpha is less merciful. Left alone, he is shamed by her pantheistic wantonness. A brood of 'half-human monsters' takes over the island. These are not laboratory specimens like Moreau's beasts, but the product of Omega's couplings with monkeys and other predators. What humiliates Alpha is that they address him as 'father'. In another lithograph he stands on the shore and gives in to howling despair: his face – which he seems to be trying to remove, as if he wanted to pull off his head and discard it in the water – is that of the skeletal figure in *The Scream*, and he too overhears 'screams in the air'. Nature itself shudders, frightened by its own instability, and the scratchy, agitated lines of Munch's design could have been made by the needles that register seismic shocks. When Omega returns, Alpha knocks her down and kills her. Is he not justified in retaliating?

Omega's mutant babies attack Alpha from behind and slaughter him. The story ends by noting that 'The new generation peopled the island'. The animals take over from the humans. Freed at last from their servitude to men, they deserve to do so. After Darwin, this change to the hierarchy established by Genesis seemed just and necessary. It was announced by a modern bestiary – a charge of liberated beasts like the *Galloping Horse* of Munch, which charges wild-eyed through a city street like a runaway locomotive, or the *Blue Horses* of Franz Marc,

Franz Marc, *The Large Blue Horses*, 1911

which evangelizes on behalf of 'the coming spiritual religions'. D. H. Lawrence enthusiastically ratified the sentence of death God pronounced when he sent the flood. Birkin in *Women in Love* denounces humanity as 'anti-creation' and decides that 'Man ... must go'. With people expunged, 'creation would go on marvellously, with a new start, non-human. Man is one of the mistakes of creation – like the ichthyosauri'. In his poems about *Birds, Beasts and Flowers*, Lawrence roamed through an unfenced, untamed garden where zoologists and botanists have no power. He admires a kangaroo's small head and big haunches: its bottom-heaviness tugs it 'down towards the earth's centre', and its pouch – with a joey pawing its way out – places the internal mysteries of germination on view. A fish sighted in an Austrian lake reminds him that there are 'Other Gods/ Beyond my range ... gods beyond my God'.

Lawrence's Birkin, looking forward to 'the liberated days', rejoices in 'the most beautiful and freeing thought', which is the notion of an earth rid of people. At the end of Shaw's *Back to Methuselah*, that future has almost arrived – but earth's occupants are supermen and automata, not the frisking animals of Lawrence's poems. A She-Ancient, immortalized by advances in medical science, peers ahead towards to a time 'when there will be no people, only thought'. She is still vexed by a body which, atrophied though it is, attaches her to a solid, obnoxiously carnal world. Why is she unable to etherealize? Martellus, bored by his own embodiment, says that 'nothing remains beautiful and interesting except thought, because the thought is the life'. The path beyond Darwin has diverged. One route leads to Lawrence's abounding landscape, where 'elder-flowers and bluebells ... are a sign that pure creation takes place'. Another goes to Shaw's cerebral Utopia, in which human beings by sheer force of will have seceded from nature and evolved into undiluted mind.

Shaw's epoch-encompassing play begins in an intellectualized Eden, where Adam and Eve, disdaining country matters, are already concerned with mental improvement. The serpent tells Eve where they came from – not from God but from Lilith. In the biblical apocrypha, Lilith is Adam's first wife, cast out for being too sexually aggressive; here, chastened, she is pressed into service as the progenitor of Adam and Eve, to whom she gives birth with no help from any male partner. When Eve wants to have the miracle explained, the serpent says that 'imagination is the beginning of creation'. Eve wonders 'How can I create out of nothing?' The serpent recommends the exercise of volition, and says that it is just like building up your biceps by repeated effort. Eve is bewildered by the serpent's array of infinitives, which tantalize her by giving names to a process she still cannot comprehend: 'To desire, to imagine, to will, to create'. The serpent makes it easier by narrowing her options: 'In a word, to conceive. That is the word that means both the beginning in imagination and the end in creation'. It is a word that conveniently transfers the business of engendering from uterus to brain. Adam and Eve are not nurtured inside Lilith's body and then ejected from it; Lilith manages to 'divide into two'. But this feat cannot be repeated by her offspring, who are condemned to fusion not fission. Eve grimaces when the serpent tells her about the procedures that are necessary if she wants to create new life. Shaw shared Eve's misgivings, and even found the love lives of vegetables uncomfortably inflammatory. In an interview in 1924, he joked that 'when Linnaeus first wrote on the fertilization of plants, botany was denounced as corrupting to morals'. By the time *Back to Methuselah* ends, humanity has become happily oviparous again. The 'modern female body', as Pygmalion notices, is adapted for laying eggs, which dispenses us from 'prehistoric methods of reproduction'.

Shaw's Adam and Eve are embroiled in the same dispute that consumes Munch's Alpha and Omega. After Cain kills his brother, Eve complains about the eternal enmity between 'Woman the creator and Man the destroyer'. But Cain can defend himself argumentatively, and does not rely, like Alpha, on unthinking brutality. He replies by asking 'How can I destroy unless she creates?' The first murderer is also the first artist, and Cain has a use for Eve's innumerable descendants. He has 'imagined a glorious poem' which will divide men into two armies and goad them to kill each other: he has invented the idea of the epic. He is content for his mother 'to create more and more men: aye, and more and more women, that they may in turn create more men'. She supplies him with characters, whom he enjoys elaborately slaughtering. This was the kind of art suited to prehistoric beings, and Shakespeare, in Shaw's estimation, had not progressed far beyond it. His tragedies are murder stories, and his comedies hustle lovers into bed: he is still responding to the instinctual drives of nature at its most gruffly elementary. In Eden, Shaw's Eve notices that a few of her grandchildren exhibit aesthetic inclinations. They are mostly 'weaklings and cowards', unfit for agrarian labour; they accumulate debts, have a bohemian reluctance to cut their hair, and 'tell beautiful lies'. But they know how to play inventive games with nature. Some blow through reeds, while others mould 'little mammoths out of clay' or scratch faces on stones.

The last part of *Back to Methuselah* speculates about the kind of art best suited to the blissful, brainy future. Surely by AD 31,920 we will find a way of refining, revising or transcending nature. Ecrasia foresees unending frustration, because the artist 'can create masterpieces; but he cannot improve the shape of his nose'. The He-Ancient replies that the artist 'can alter the shape of his own soul', which is more worthwhile. The She-Ancient has a different answer. With her elastic body, she is able to 'shape and create'. Like one of Picasso's models, she can sprout ten arms and twenty hands, or four heads with eight eyes focused on all points of the compass; she has made herself 'into all sorts of fantastic monsters'. So is the aim of art no more than what manuals of spiritual gymnastics call personal growth, or the display of a surgically corrected, chemically adjusted body? An aerobics class or a course in yoga can achieve the same result. The prospect incites a nostalgia for Shaw's rudimentary Eden, where musicians chased the wind and trapped it in a pipe, and the first art gallery was a cave bedaubed with bleeding souvenirs of the hunt.

# 21
# BEGETTER AND BEARER

In his account of animal reproduction, Aristotle divided responsibility unequally between male and female. The male entrusted the female with the seed; it was his personal creation, which she – as if baby-sitting – merely looked after. Aristotle allowed the female to contribute genetic material, but insisted that it was the male's task to 'fashion the material into shape'. This invidious partnership was carried over into traditional theories of artistic creativity. Artists were male, while the docile female served as an inspiration: poets had their muses, painters their naked models. 'The only women of genius,' maintained Edmond de Goncourt, 'are men'. Alfred Stieglitz was affronted as well as excited when Georgia O'Keeffe's drawings proved this prejudice to be false. 'Man, the male, has thus far been the sole creator of ART,' he wrote in 1919. '*His* art – as until most recently he looked upon Woman as *His*. ... Her creative sphere was childbearing'. The advent of O'Keeffe, who had no interest in maternity, convinced Stieglitz that 'Woman is beginning'. As late as 1956, Freud's disciple and biographer Ernest Jones declared in a lecture in New York that 'creative thinking' was a male perquisite, making up for 'the gift of bodily creation bestowed on women'.

Wagner, thinking of himself, told Liszt that the artist was the 'deified incarnation of the masculine reproductive power'. But that power, as he knew, was only half of the equation. Male artists could not lay down their tools after producing the germinal idea; they also had to nourish the embryo and deliver it into the world. These tasks could not be delegated to a female accomplice, so perhaps they were discharged by the shadowy underside of the male psyche. Wagner created an entire, self-sufficient world, which pulses subliminally on the river bed at the start of *Das Rheingold*, surges into torrents or thunderstorms or barriers of flame, then collapses in *Götterdämmerung* as the cumbrous masonry of society tumbles back into the river. This, as Wagner's acolytes told him, was the labour of a god – or of several gods, for as Villiers de l'Isle-Adam and Judith Gautier agreed on their way to visit him in Lucerne in 1869, he was both Apollo and Orpheus, poet and musician 'blended to one lyre'. Those twinned arts corresponded, in Wagner's own thinking, to the formerly sundered genders, reunited in him as he composed his operas. Words, appealing to the reason, he took to be male, while music, which was fluent and impulsive and unabashedly sensuous, seemed to be

Henri Fantin-Latour, *Le Graal – prelude de Lohengrin*, 1882

female. 'He is cubic,' said Villiers de l'Isle-Adam about Wagner; 'he comprises all'. The cube, with its multiple facets, could only be androgynous.

When Wagner met Berlioz, they earnestly discussed 'the mystery of "artistic conception"' – and it was in his comments on Berlioz, who also combined the roles of poet and musician, that Wagner most openly proclaimed the bisexuality of their composite art. He could hardly propose himself as an intermediary between the sexes, so instead he criticized Berlioz for not balancing the two identities. In 1852 he lamented the way that Berlioz mistreated the literary texts he so whimsically adapted, and prescribed a solution: his colleague needed 'a poet to fill him through and through', to be 'to him what man is to woman'. Berlioz, in other words, could profit from the attentions of a rapist. In the absence of such a fertilizing agent, he remained unfruitful, restricted to 'splintered and atomic melodies'. An evolutionary fable lies behind the attack, since Wagner claims that the world cannot be constructed from atoms, forcibly welded together by what he calls the creator's 'lief'. The artist is not an authoritative paterfamilias like the God of the Old Testament; instead, he must allow the work of art to grow, maternally nurturing it. The criticism of Berlioz is a cover for personal rancour, but it demonstrates Wagner's coupling of aesthetics and biology. In pitying the 'egotistical loneliness' of Berlioz, he congratulated himself on his own duality. In 1850 he told Liszt that 'music (as a woman) must be impregnated by a poet (as a man)', and specified that the conqueror should not be a 'passing libertine'. He meant that he could not trust someone else to provide the words he set to music; that would be like abandoning the woman to the mercy of a casual philanderer like Don Giovanni, who has no interest in any progeny he leaves behind. Having defined the separate sexual roles, Wagner then fused them: he was both 'this glorious woman' and her irresistibly loquacious wooer.

He examined the creative process with the professional concern of a gynaecologist or an obstetrician. Hence his affinity with Titian's *Assumption*, which he stubbornly regarded as a picture of a woman who is anxious to 'create the saviour'. He felt the same when creating his own version of the Christian saviour, the knight who redeems sinners and restores the communion of the Grail in *Parsifal*. He told his patron King Ludwig II of Bavaria that, since the first inklings of the idea, the opera had 'lived on within me and prospered, like a child in its mother's womb'. At the end of the same letter he assured Ludwig that *Tristan und Isolde* had just safely been born. Helpers were enlisted as midwives. This was the function of his friend Eliza Wille, who held his hand while he endured what he called 'the terrible throes of childbirth'. He required such attentions because – as he claimed in a letter – he had been 'so immensely creative' in August 1845 that he had 'conceived both *Lohengrin* and *Die Meistersinger von Nürnberg* at one and the same time'. He fiddled with the chronology to make the double conception coincide with the birth of Ludwig II, as if the young king too were Wagner's brain-child. And because Wagner imagined the creator incestuously copulating with the creatures he had dreamed up, like Wotan embracing his daughter Brünnhilde at the end of *Die Walküre*, he expected the infatuated Ludwig to be 'everything to me: world, wife and child!'

Nietzsche, after escaping from the enchanter's influence, explained such fantasies when he pondered the sexual symbolism associated with the Dionysian cult. Our conception, our growth within our mother, our wrenching entry into the world – all these forgotten or suppressed experiences stimulate 'exalted and solemn feelings', which is why they were re-enacted each year in ancient Greece by the initiates who took part in the Eleusinian mysteries, staged to honour Demeter, the goddess of fertility. Wagner had his own equivalent to the underground temple where the mysteries were acted out. The oracle at Delphi lurked in a gash in the earth, which Wagner called a 'reeking crevice'. That sacred lair became the covered orchestra pit of his theatre at Bayreuth. From this dark gulf, music arises to give form to earth and heaven, as it does when the river gurgles and wells up in *Das Rheingold* or when violins trace the aerial trajectory of a celestial messenger in the prelude to *Lohengrin*. The Grail placed on show in *Parsifal* is also, like the oracle's lair, a physiological shrine: within this inflamed recess an idea takes on flesh. Nietzsche understood that the passage between stages of existence is agonizing, and thought that 'the "pains of childbirth" sanctify pain in general' because 'all becoming and growing ... *postulates* pain'. The maternity ward is a sanctum like the temple at Eleusis, a place of transition between worlds; the same obscure passage between spirit and matter occurs in the artist's studio. Nietzsche concluded that 'for the eternal joy in creating to exist, for the will to life eternally to affirm itself, the "torment of childbirth" *must* also exist eternally'.

While working on his tetralogy *Der Ring des Nibelungen*, Wagner needed – as he said in a letter to Liszt in 1854 – to stimulate in himself 'the requisite mood of artistic sensuality'. That psychological climate was expensive: he required unending supplies of money, the use of other mens' wives (while cuckolded husbands like Hans von Bülow continued to act as his faithful servants), and a domestic decor muffled in silk, satin and velvet to soothe his nerves. 'I cannot live like a dog,' he told Liszt, 'I cannot sleep on straw and drink common gin'. What he called his 'intensely irritable, acute, and hugely voracious, yet uncommonly tender and delicate sensuality' had to be flattered. Otherwise how could he 'accomplish the cruelly difficult task of creating in my mind a non-existent world'? Creation happened in the mind, but he thought of this cosmic labour as a difficult pregnancy, followed by a protracted lying-in. In Wagner's case those months lasted for years, since the *Ring* did not have its first performance until 1876; through-out this time, the expectant artist's cravings had to be satisfied, no matter how irrational or capricious they were. Wagner appealed to Liszt – who was to become his father-in-law in 1870, when his daughter Cosima finally divorced von Bülow – like a woman beseeching a man to do the honest, honourable thing. He used the compulsiveness of creativity as the basis of his case, and reminded Liszt of his complicity in their enterprise: 'I have a just claim on you, as on my *creator*! *You are* the creator of the man I now am. …Take care of your creature'. On another occasion he importuned Liszt as a surrogate parent, a sharer in the creative or reproductive process. 'Perform *Lohengrin*,' he pleaded, 'and let it be *your* work to give it birth.'

He admitted to Liszt that he had 'squandered (my God – squandered!!)' his income from *Tannhäuser* on 'every conceivable article of luxurious necessity'. The exclamation registers his outrage at being called to account: luxuries for him were necessities. His villa at Lucerne, as Judith Gautier found, was a cocoon of purple damask, yellow leather and violet velvet, scented with white-rose extract. He reposed on sumptuously padded chairs, and later took to lolling on Judith herself: this was the affectionate nickname that he gave to the chaise longue in his house in Bayreuth. His wardrobe had to be conducive to his efforts. According to his friend Ferdi-nand Praeger, Wagner 'could not endure the touch of cotton', which made his whole body shudder. He designed a house-coat with puffy ruched pockets and eiderdown quilting, made for him by a Viennese milliner whom he entreated to use 'genuine pink, only very dark and fiery' when selecting the fabrics that were to caress his skin. A velvet beret insulated his head. While in London he ordered vests with an interior lining of silk from a Regent Street tailor, who remarked that even his richest clients never treated themselves so sumptuously. Praeger kept Wagner supplied with snuff from a London shop, and Judith sent aromatic sachets and powder-bags from Paris, to be placed between what he called his 'morning linen'. He cajoled her to be 'prodigal' in donating ambergris and other heady oils, which he poured into his bath-tub and continued to relish when he worked in the studio above, sniffing them through the floorboards. This was in 1877, when he had begun to work on the score of *Parsifal* 'in the peaceful tran-quillity of creative seclusion'. The 'accouchement', he expected, would last for the next three years. The maimed Amfortas in *Parsifal* soothes his wound by bathing in a pool and anointing himself with an unguent brought from Arabia by Kundry. With the help of Judith Gautier's elixirs, Wagner enjoyed the same healing immersion. That morning idyll was his return to watery origins – to the amniotic ocean of the womb, or to the fluid river of life itself, in which the *Ring* begins and ends – and his preparation for the daily task of constructing the world. Any objection to this pampered regime was silenced by a restatement of his right to be 'endowed with whatever degree of comfort is necessary for artistic creation'.

Wagner's operas stage these acts of creation. He places on view two mysteries that usually remain hidden: we watch the physical engendering of new life, and we also see the mental gestation of a world. Siegmund in *Die Walküre* pulls the sword from the tree into which it has been rammed, holds its gleaming blade victoriously aloft, and with it stakes his claim to Sieglinde, his sister and his bride. She cries out in startled rapture when the door of Hunding's hut is blown open by a gale. Siegmund explains that it is spring, bumptiously thrusting through prohibitions as it reinvigorates the world: even Wagnerian architecture distends to make room for a creative arrival. Siegmund's phallic totem is shattered by the spear of Wotan, a creator who cannot allow the characters he has created to act freely. But Siegfried reforges the splintered sword, and uses it to slice through Wotan's spear. The combat of god and mortal is the struggle between the controlling artist and the thoughts or dreams that escape from control in the making of art. Sieglinde, unseen by us, gives birth to Siegfried in the forest. Her child is another saviour, although his mission

Mariano Fortuny y Madrazo, *Siegmund and Sieglinde*, 1893

is to incite a political revolution not to sponsor moral reformation as Lohengrin or Parsifal hope to do. Brünnhilde in her final dispute with Wotan describes the 'holiest fruit' of Sieglinde's womb, and predicts that her labour will be more painful than that of any other woman. This agony is not, like Eve's, the penalty of sin. It is simply the cost of releasing the future into the world, and it kills her. Sieglinde has her share in the straining anguish Wagner described in his 1854 letter to Liszt. But she qualifies for the accolade Nietzsche bestowed on the hero in *Also Sprach Zarathustra*: 'I love him who wants to create beyond himself, and thus perishes'. Musing in the woods, Siegfried wonders if all mothers die in giving birth to their sons. He hopes not, but Wagner took a more drastic view of creativity and its pangs.

The American critic Paul Rosenfeld, writing in the early 1930s, said that the orchestral accompaniment to the love duet in *Tristan und Isolde* evoked 'the parturient earth, the womb of material creation'; the maternally protective Brangäne, calling from the darkness, was the voice of the 'cosmocreator'. Other characters experience the same swollen fruition.

Birgit Nilsson
and Wolfgang
Windgassen in
*Tristan und
Isolde*, Bayreuth
Festival, 1962

Leonie Rysanek
in *Der fliegende
Holländer*,
Bayreuth Festival,
1959

Senta in *Der fliegende Holländer* broods over a portrait of the accursed
Dutchman, and sings an entranced ballad about his sufferings. In response
to her imaginative desire, the man himself strides in and asks her to be
his wife. As when Wotan propagates his 'wish-maiden' Brünnhilde, this story
– like all of those retold by Wagner – fulfils a wish, and thus reveals how art
is made, or perhaps born. The same nativity occurs in *Die Meistersinger*.
Walther the poet wins the song contest with his lyrical evocation of Eden,
and as his prize he is awarded the heroine Eva, who awaits him beneath a
tree ripely laden with fruit. But the biblical garden is too small for Wagner's
characters, too hedged with embargoes. In the second stanza of the song,
Walther and his Eva advance to another garden where the forbidden apple
tree is replaced by a laurel, whose leaves are plucked to crown poets. This is
Parnassus, and Eva – dispensed from the task of bearing children that
burdens Eve – presides here as the classical muse. Inspired by her, the poet
joins words and notes in an aria which with its steadily ascending key
changes sounds like a sunrise.

Elsa in *Lohengrin*, following the example of Titian's Virgin, creates a
saviour. She describes the reverie in which she saw a knight float down from
on high to rescue her; she then prays, and Lohengrin promptly appears. He
places a ban on questions about his 'Nam' und Art', his identity and his
origins, as if deflecting curiosity about the artist's source of inspiration. Elsa
marries her champion, and a wedding march escorts them to bed. But a
quarrel prevents the union of creator and creature. Elsa is querulous and sceptical; imagination cannot abide the meddling of intellect, so the visionary
ardour deserts her. Departing, Lohengrin manages an instantaneous paternal

miracle of his own. Another prayer – a symptom of the artist's internal concentration, not of religious faith – enables him to retrieve Elsa's lost brother,
who has been trapped inside the body of the swan yoked to Lohengrin's boat.
The heathen sorceress Ortrud accuses Elsa of performing black magic, and
the charge incriminates Wagner's own creativity. Huysmans analysed this
witchcraft in his novel *Là-Bas*, published in 1891. Durtal, who is researching
the history of satanism, believes he has identified a new sin. He calls it
Pygmalionism, and says that it combines onanism with incest: an artist falls in
love with an imaginary child, summoning up the object of desire and possessing it in a dream. He might have cited Elsa's infatuation with Lohengrin
as an example, or Wotan's partiality for Brünnhilde. Actual incest, for Durtal, is
less offensive, because the child has a second parent, whereas 'in Pygmalionism the father violates the child of his soul, of that which alone is purely and
truly his, which he alone can impregnate without the aid of another'. The
act expresses disdain for nature and for God's work, 'since the subject of the
sin is no longer – as even in bestiality – a palpable and living creature, but an
unreal being'. Durtal's pious colleague Chantelouve downgrades the abomination and calls it a refinement of succubacy (which is the conjuring-up of
a devil as a sexual playmate): the dreamy consort is not really 'one's work
become animate', just a nocturnal revenant. Durtal responds that at least this
'cerebral hermaphroditism' is 'a distinguished vice', and defines it as 'the
privilege of the artist'. It was a privilege on which Wagner insisted.

Nietzsche complained that Wagner's women were barren, and blamed
this on their emancipation. H. G. Wells in his Wagnerian novel *Brynhild*,
published in 1937, considered the same problem. Wells's Brynhild is the
daughter of a clergyman; like Brünnhilde she rebels against the paternal
deity, and after rejecting religion she searches for alternative ideologies. A
feminist indoctrinates her. 'Woman is woman,' Brynhild is told, 'because she
is the breeding-continuing animal. ... The male is essentially an escapade.
Sexually he is a lightweight, he flits and returns.' Brünnhilde in *Götterdämmerung* seems to know this. After a single night, she sends Siegfried off to
have new adventures on the Rhine; perhaps he has already performed his
function as begetter, so he is now expendable. Drugged by Hagen, he forgets
her before the day is over, but – because of the kinship between extinction
and orgasm – he remembers her as he dies. At the end of Wells's novel, Brynhild paraphrases Sieglinde's last cry of gratification and announces that she
intends to have innumerable children. She adds 'It's what I'm for'.

Nietzsche's charge of sterility was mistaken. Wagner's women are
fertile, and so are his men. The characters beget one another as we watch or
listen – but their progeny is aesthetic not biological. When Cosima gave
birth, she brought forth real-life versions of Wagner's characters. They called
their son Siegfried, and their daughter – officially ascribed to von Bülow,

with Wagner pretending to be merely her godfather – was Isolde. Their
brood daringly made manifest the abstract biological arrangements of the
Christian heaven, where God asexually causes a virgin to conceive. At
Christmas in 1880, the children of the household were arranged into a
tableau representing the holy family. The young Siegfried, conflating
Nordic and Christian cults, was cast as Jesus: Wagner fathered the son of
God. Even in the celibate society of *Parsifal*, religious rites mime coitus. The
spear with which Parsifal heals the wound of Amfortas denotes potency, and
its tip oozes blood as well as dispensing forgiveness; the Grail, a vessel
flooded by grace, is uterine. In his account of his pedigree, Lohengrin startlingly names Parsifal as his father. Since the Grail's trustees belong to a
celibate male community, this prompts questions about the identity of
Lohengrin's mother. James Huneker, who reviewed early performances of
Wagner's operas in New York, wondered whether the chaste knights
increased their numbers by using 'Parsiphallic' methods. The pun is no more
frivolous than the etymology Wagner invented to explain Parsifal's name,
which – as Kundry informs him – supposedly derives from 'fal parsi' and
defines him as a pure fool, an idiotic Christ.

   An artist who can make up words is free to create new lives or to construct autonomous, self-referring worlds. Wagner assumed that reality was
an extension of his art. As he sailed up the Thames through the sooty fog of
industrial London, he remarked that this was Nibelheim, the lightless realm
of enforced toil and mercenary accumulation over which Alberich presides
in *Das Rheingold*. His devotees gave Wagner credit for the topography of the
landscapes he lived in, and viewed actual scenery as if it were operatic decor.
When Judith Gautier arrived in Lucerne on that first pilgrimage, she saw
the mountains on either side of the lake as Wagnerian eminences. Rigi,
green and gently rotund, must be Montsalvat, where the Grail temple
perches in *Parsifal*; Pilatus, with its sheer cliffs and frowning summit, was
surely the location of Walhall. A swan floating on the lake was suspected of
having escaped from an opera. Judith and her companions imagined that it
wore a gold chain, like that which tethered the swan to Lohengrin's boat.
Liszt took an even more panoramic view of Wagner's achievement, and
thought he had heaved the Alps out of the low, skulking earth: he called the
*Ring* 'a mental mountain range'.

   Liszt said that *Lohengrin* accomplished again the ordaining, enlightening work of Genesis: in it, 'the old opera world comes to a close; the spirit
moves on the face of the waters, and there is light'. Creation coincides with
illumination, and the prayers of Elsa and Lohengrin are accompanied by
divided strings that are like light made audible. Wagner's characters take over
responsibility for creation, which happens at their behest. Brünnhilde,
roused by Siegfried, hails the sun, the light, the blazing day. Harps fibrillate as

her own life is re-ignited after her long paralysis; she passes on this tingling vitality to the universe. When she accepts Siegfried as her mate, she hails him as the life of the earth, as if he were its sap and also the spark that makes the sun flare up. He addresses her as the star that shines on him. They create one another, then derive a galaxy from their effulgent bodies. In *Parsifal*, creativity is less rapturous. It happens in helpless fits, with wrenching convulsions; the protesting creator shrieks as a new life forces its way out. Kundry's groans and screams are the birth pangs Wagner wrote about in his letter to Eliza Wille. She lets loose a rending cry – half exultant, half tormented – when the magician Klingsor rouses her from a stupor to seduce Parsifal. She moans as spring quickens the earth, when she discovers that she is still alive and must be reborn one last time. Her defining vocal moment is a spasm of mirthless, demented laughter. She mocked Christ as he passed on the way to Calvary, and in recalling this she plummets through an octave between the two syllables of the word 'lachte'. The first vowel is pitched on a shrill, curdled B natural, the second drops to a gutturally despairing, hollow C sharp; she leaps upwards, then sickeningly plunges beneath the stave. The outburst is a sonic paradox, a hyphenated joining of mania and depression. These are the creator's contradictory moods, as wild and reckless delight is followed at once by the misery of self-disbelief. Kundry lapses into sobbing remorse, then recovers to select Parsifal as her redeemer, a replacement for the saviour she jeered at. Her embrace will work the transformation: she offers to make him a god for an hour, which is as long it will take them to make love and to secure her absolution and his damnation.

Kundry's suggestion that she can confer 'Gottheit' by absorbing him into her body is not an idle boast. Godhead can be acquired by nomination: this is why she so langorously utters Parsifal's name, which he has not heard since his mother first used it. She follows what Nietzsche called 'the way of the creator' – a solitary, morally perilous vocation, as Nietzsche recognized when he addressed the superman: 'you want to create a god from your seven devils!' Ortrud does exactly that when she calls on Wotan and Freia to aid her spells. Every Wagnerian character is a deputy for Wagner himself, possessing a creative power that can recreate human beings, either promoting them to divinities or – like Ortrud, whose magic disguises Elsa's brother as a swan – demoting them to beasts. Wagner argued that 'God and the gods are the first creations of man's poetic force'. Force is the requirement for making gods, and a voice like Ortrud's – ferocious in its intensity, fearlessly alternating between the heights and depths of the singer's range – certainly qualifies. Because she creates gods, Ortrud knows better than to believe in them. She scornfully enunciates the word 'Gott!', and laughs at the idiocy of those who take it to be more than a word. Her husband Telramund comments on the terrifying sound she makes with that single syllable, which echoes through the night like a ricocheting bullet. The derision of deity is a reflex action, the underside of this creative confidence. A wise god encourages disrespect, and teaches believers to grow up into atheists. This, as Wotan tells Brünnhilde, is how he educated Siegmund, instilling in him a sturdy self-reliant contempt for all higher powers. Brünnhilde justifies her own rebellion, when she defends Siegmund against Wotan, by telling her father that she is his wish, his will, his secret life. This, in her view, permits her to flout the moral and political principles that he is bullied into upholding by his wife Fricka. Wotan is the artist, Brünnhilde is his unleashed imagination, and she exists to be disobedient.

Wagner himself said 'I do not believe in God'. He added that he did respect the category of 'the divine' – but only because divinity was a grace conferred by artists. He was prepared to tolerate the Virgin Mary, who was 'not herself a goddess' but had divinity thrust upon her. At the end of *Tannhäuser*, the guilty hero confers the same status on the virginal Elisabeth, beside whose corpse he prostrates himself. He addresses her as 'heilige Elisabeth': even a Wagnerian sinner, the voluptuary who consorts with Venus in her ribald mound, can beatify his fellow mortals. In his essay on *Religion and Art*, published in 1880, Wagner puzzled over the virgin birth, and rationalized it as a fable about artistic creation. 'The mystery of motherhood without natural fecundation,' he wrote, 'can only be traced to a greater miracle, the birth of God himself.' His operas demystify that birth: he creates gods, then wantonly destroys them.

Having read Darwin, Wagner disparaged the notion that creation emerged from nothing, and in his treatise on *Opera and Drama* he ridiculed composers who pretended, like the good God, to create 'in a grey mist of absolute, unadulterated invention'. He likened them to Goethe's scientist toiling to brew a homunculus: they behave as if 'men could be made by scholarly recipe, and from chemical decoctions'. He spurned the methods of his French and Italian predecessors, whose mismatching of music and words reminded him of an 'anatomically disjoined' and 'inwardly slaughtered organism'. But artistic creation is about revivification, which means jolting dead things back to life. Brünnhilde and her sisters do this when they gather up corpses on the battlefield and carry them to Walhall to be animated all over again. The earth, as Wagner said, is 'not a thing created, but herself forever becoming', perpetually reborn. For the same reason, he made sure that the sources of his music dramas attached them, like tap roots, to a primordial reservoir of experience. Hence his use of Greek tragedies, Germanic sagas and medieval romances. Folk songs too had deeply entrenched biological origins and were begotten, like men, 'by the instinctive exercise of sexual functions': after the artificial paradise of the Venusberg collapses, a piping shepherd welcomes the flowering of the fields in May. Wagner's study of Beethoven convinced him that 'the natural thrust of life breeds melody', and he analysed this development as if he were studying an actual embryo. Harmony and rhythm, he believed, gives music its 'shaping organs' – its bloodstream and its nerves, its entrails and its grid of bones – while melody supplies the bodily form and defines 'the finished man'. Once a child is ejected from the security of the womb, its qualms and terrors are allayed by music. The mother caresses the child to calm it, or sings it a lullaby; the forest bird in *Siegfried*, as Wagner pointed out, reassures the solitary hero by trilling to him.

Wagner's characters want to be united, but the antagonism of sexuality itself keeps them apart. Male and female remain awkwardly incompatible. The duet between Siegfried and Brünnhilde founders into lethal enmity; when Tristan is wounded, Isolde drifts away. Such problems are unique to human beings. As Wagner declared in *Opera and Drama*, non-human nature 'includes within herself the begetter and the bearer, the manly and the womanly'. Mime in *Siegfried* claims to perform the same double service. Siegfried, the foundling he fostered, asks about his parentage, and Mime insists 'I am both your father and your mother'. Siegfried dismisses the claim because he and the dwarf look so different, but he does not deny that it might be possible for one person to play both parts. This duality, visible in the reproductive arrangements of plants, seemed to Wagner to be an apt model for artistic creation. Otto Rank, Freud's renegade pupil, reached similar conclusions when psychoanalysing the creative urge in 1932. Rank defined art as 'a process of begetting and of bearing', which reminded him of 'biological propagation by fission of a part from the whole', as in the case of the amoeba. The creator extrudes a part of himself, usually called a character; the process is a 'self-begetting and self-rebirth, which he has fused into one'. Rank thought that creativity circumvented the 'sexual differentiation of male and female', because – mentally at least – it set the individual free from 'the burden of generation'. That binary separation is a consequence of our evolution; Wagner overcame it by happily adopting whichever gender suited him. His career required him to exhibit the male vices of arrogance and competitive aggression, to play the conqueror. His admirers called him 'Meister', and he behaved with the domineering mastery of a Prussian emperor, even referring to the agent whom he authorized to arrange performances of the *Ring* in London as 'my "Foreign Minister"'. Yet he deliciously feminized himself when he designed his frilly millinery or told a housekeeper to drench his house with perfume – '*buy the best bottles, so that it smells really sweet*' – and begged her to 'be nice and gentle' in her dealings with him. In 1882, a year before his death, he began an essay that ponders the roles of the male and the female in art. He vexed himself by attempting to determine whether man or woman was created first: a pointless question, as he admitted, because 'conception without procreation' is as impossible as 'procreation without conception'. Despite the logical difficulty, he was sure that aesthetic perfection came from the 'suspension of the divided unity of male and female'. Perhaps the artistic vocation demands our retirement from the biological career unquestioningly pursued by others. Klingsor in *Parsifal* gelds himself to secure his immunity from carnal distractions. Kundry sneeringly asks if he is chaste. Of course he is not, but impotence permits him to concentrate on his sorcery.

Opera maintained the lost balance between the genders because it called on two complementary talents. In 1936 the critic Paul Bekker commented on the atavism in Wagner's allocation of sexual roles. Wagnerian women represent the female of species, avid for seed, and Wagner's men likewise depend for their existence, as Bekker said, on their 'feeling for woman'. Siegfried is startled when he removes the armour of the sleeping Brünnhilde and discovers that she is not a man. Once identified as a woman, she plays all the female roles: she is his godmother and his aunt, his lover and his jealous, vindictive killer. Kundry, who first tells Parsifal of his mother's death and then sets out to replace her, displays the same flexibility. Bekker was right about Wagner's separation of sexual functions, although he missed the corresponding roles assigned to the arts. Wagner sexed the component parts of his music dramas and then, like Darwin mating pigeons, engineered a union between them. Music he took to be womanly, because it gives voice to feelings that men are taught to restrain. He imagined this musical woman to be availably passive. She cannot take the initiative: if she does, she will be reviled as a whore like Venus, or as a would-be man, a manipulative harridan like Ortrud. She needs 'fecundation', which must come from the male seed-bearer. The partner charged with making her whole is the dramatist, who in Wagner's estimation must be male. His gift to her is cerebral, because he infuses her with 'the poet's thought'. Before their encounter, the melodic woman hums wordlessly, like Senta before she begins the ballad, or vocalizes unintelligibly, like the bird in *Siegfried* before the hero learns to comprehend its twittering idiom. The poet's donation of 'the stuff for bearing' gives her words to sing, so she can articulate emotion rather than howling and wailing like Kundry. But Wagner's procreative metaphor could not conceal a friction between the buoyant joy of music and the solemn pensiveness of drama. Brünnhilde swoops on in *Die Walküre*, hurling out high notes like spears in her ecstatic repetitions of 'Hojotoho!' Wotan – her father but also, as her creator, a lover – cuts short this boisterous jubilation, and engages her in a conversation which turns into an argument about moral responsibility. She already knows how to sing; we watch her learning how to speak or to think.

The disparity is overcome when Wagner brings together the Walsung twins, whose incestuous coupling – denounced as an abomination by Fricka – produces Siegfried. Siegmund begins as an epic poet, reciting a long account of his woes. Sieglinde is at first a female nurturer, who offers the harried fugitive a drink of mead and serves food to him. But she is also the embodiment of music, awakened to joy when he brandishes the sword. Drama and music fuse because the twins are mirror-images of each other. Tristan and Isolde also exchange names and identities while making love in the garden. Elsewhere Wagner's duets founder in misunderstanding, as the arts fail to join. Parsifal refuses to console Kundry and condemns her for kissing him. Brünnhilde defies Wotan, whose embrace sentences her to silence and to inert, defenceless sleep. His kiss, as he says, takes away her 'Got-theit'. Fruition, when it does happen, can look odd and illogical, because art alters biological precedent. Tannhäuser the poet rejects the saintly Elisabeth, and pines for the lyrical and balletic pleasures of the Venusberg: the goddess of love is the stimulus of music, and it is Venus who first orders him to sing. But Elisabeth, despite her virginal piety, pines for the sinner, and seeks expiation for this forbidden desire in her sudden, unexplained death. Her sacrifice overturns the laws of nature and prompts an artistic marvel. The Pope has damned Tannhäuser, telling him that pardon will only come when the staff he holds sprouts fresh green leaves. That is what occurs at the end of the opera: a dead stick of wood grows again, and unfurls budding tendrils. Wagner admitted, when the revived staff is carried on, that his miracles were scenic tricks – though he might also have had intended a mute pun, triumphantly flourishing a sign of music's power. The staff or 'Stab' that the Pope uses to admonish Tannhäuser is also the stave on which music is written and printed. Coiled around the margin of the stave to denote pitch, a treble clef resembles foliage, a creeper climbing a trellis.

The staff confers authority on the pontiff, or at least props him up, which it can only do after being cut off the living tree. For the artist, the stave has another function: it stores and preserves notes that are not dead because they germinate and efflo-resce when played or sung.

Being opposites, music and drama tend to collide in mutual incomprehension, and their Wagner-ian marriage sometimes happens only after death. Senta and the Dutchman leap into the sea and drown together, but Tristan and Isolde expire separately. Aware that Isolde has arrived for a reunion with

'Pilgrims with Cross', from *Tannhäuser*. Illustration by Willy Pogany, 1911

him, Tristan rips the bandages from his wound and collapses in a last
shouted bout of recrimination. Drama insists on reckonings and penalties,
so he passes judgment on himself for his sexual treason. But Isolde's expiry is
purged of physical agony and moral torment. Music converts grief into
rapture; her 'Liebestod' reaches its pure, poised mystical climax on a pianis-
simo F sharp that registers her soaring exaltation and her last heady
emission of life and breath. A passage in *Opera and Drama* might be an analysis of the divergent purposes in this ending, where drama calls for finality
while music expands into infinitude. In Wagner's music dramas, characters
conduct their quarrels in 'Sprechgesang', a form of pitched conversation
half way between song and speech. Wagner admitted that the compromise
was uneasy. 'Science', he said, 'had laid bare ... the organism of speech', but it
exposed 'a defunct organism': language is debased if we talk in prose. Poetry
can surely 'heal the wounds with which the anatomical scalpel has wounded
the body', pouring into it again the soul that will enliven it, enabling it to
breathe. Or does the cure depend on the panacea of song? As if anticipating
Isolde's serenely lyrical response to her lover's death, Wagner explained that
'*this breath is – Music*'. As Isolde sings, she convinces herself that a soft breath
flutters from Tristan's lips, gaining strength until it grows into the breeze on
which she feels herself to be floating. She has sung him back to life. Her
voice, surmounting waves that crest and crash in the orchestra, is itself an
emanation of what she calls 'des Welt-Atems wehendem All': the surging
breath of the entire world. It is like the river in *Das Rheingold*, though made
of air not water. It arises from nothing, spreads to occupy all available space,
then diminishes to the last faintly vibrant note that resolves the discord
heard at the beginning of the opera. Now Isolde is permitted to die – or
perhaps to evaporate, since she says she is drowning in a sea of perfume.

Wagner here dramatizes what he called 'das dichtende Moment', the
moment of creativity. It is a moment of self-obliterating joy, orgasmic or – in
the revels of the Venusberg – orgiastic; the notion was adopted by the
Viennese critic Hermann Bahr, who in 1903 defined art as 'the highest
expression of a life collapsing in an ecstatic moment'. As Wagner explained
in *Opera and Drama*, the motive force of that creative impetus is yearning,
which means erotic desire. The German word he uses is 'sehnen', which
occurs repeatedly in the operas. 'Welches Sehnen!' cries the moribund
Tristan as he awaits Isolde's arrival. Later he returns to this obsessive refrain
– 'Sehnen! Sehnen!' – and complains that he is dying of 'Sehnsucht', a compound word that by splicing together desire and quest sends the hungry,
lonely fantasy on an exhausting search for extinction. As Kundry resumes
her wanderings, she remembers the curse of her immortality and groans
'Oh! ... Sehnen ... Sehnen!'. In all these cases, 'sehnen' is a wracked report
on unending pain, not an outcry of bliss. In Wagner's understanding,

the creative moment comprised both the instant of conception and the protracted, self-rending labour of execution.

The theory presents the birth of art as a organic process, although Wagner's own professional experience taught him that creativity also involved a guileful, crafty manipulation of reality, a trade-off between vision and merchandise, creation and manufacture. A dissident theory of art's origins is hinted at in *Das Rheingold*. The gnome Alberich, rebuffed by the Rhinemaidens, forswears love and chooses power and riches instead by stealing the gold. When he wants a son to inherit his wealth, he buys sex by parting with a portion of his hoard. The idols and graven images we make are substitutes for human association, monuments to an unrequited love. The giants Fafner and Fasolt, denied the goddess Freia whom they claim in return for their labour, construct a rough facsimile of her, accumulated from a pile of gold bricks. Engendering took care of itself. Wagner spent much of his time dealing with practical, mercenary problems. Who would pay for the artist's travails? And was the work of art truly born if it remained unperformed? The creator also had to be an entrepreneur, a self-publicist, even an architect: Wagner built his own theatre at Bayreuth. *Die Meistersinger*, being a comedy, can afford to admit the element of fabrication that is denied by the creative myth. Walther's song does not burble unbidden from his lips. It is prepared for a particular occasion, and in the hope of a reward; it is rehearsed, criticized, rewritten and parodied in the course of the opera, before — as they say in the theatre — it comes right on the night. The birth of melody is hardly as spontaneous as Wagner pretended, and even after his triumph Walther has to compromise with the rules of the guild which makes him a member.

Richard Strauss, harder-headed than Wagner and more candid about the economic underpinnings of art, mocked the generative fancy in his valedictory opera *Capriccio*. Here the theatre director La Roche boasts about his allegorical pageant dramatizing the birth of Pallas Athene, who emerged fully formed from the cranium of her father Zeus. He explains the circumstances, while the listeners giggle incredulously when told that Zeus swallowed the pregnant Metis. A laughing octet follows, in which La Roche's fable is held up to scorn by a poet, a musician, an actress, two busking Italian singers and their aristocratic patrons, all of whom know that the creation of art is neither natural nor supernaturally wondrous. Yet after having made fun of the myth, Strauss goes on to restore credence to it in the final scene of *Capriccio*, where the soprano, while professing herself unable to decide between the rival claims of poetry and music, gloriously unites them. Words, when she sings them, grow wings or glow with lambent light. Strauss's Countess has two rival wooers, Flamand the poet and Olivier the musician. Each man sees her as his muse; she adroitly juggles them before finally satisfying both at once.

Under Wagner's influence, love-making became a prescription for begetting opera. In Gustave Charpentier's *Louise*, first performed in 1900, the heroine runs away from her working-class family to live with the bohemian Julien. He is the poet, she is the muse, and the creative act is the love they consummate when they retire into their house on top of the hill of Montmartre. The little mount is supposedly sacred to Christian martyrs, but Julien's friends have something else in mind when they select the free, fulfilled Louise as their 'Muse de la Butte Sacrée'. She is enthroned on the city's mons veneris, the anatomical mound that serves as a Venusberg for aesthetes. Baudelaire rejoiced in Wagner's coupling of the arts, and in the sensory bombardment which – for instance during the revels honouring Venus in *Tannhäuser* – aligned orchestral sounds with the flushed colours of the lighting on stage. 'All things,' Baudelaire argued in 1861, 'have always been expressed by reciprocal analogies, ever since the day when God uttered the world as a complex and indivisible totality.' God hardly created the world along Wagnerian lines, but that was Baudelaire's point. The proper setting for Genesis is not an abstinent Eden but the cacophonous, kaleidoscopically bright, agitated Venusberg. 'Let there be light' is too niggardly a command. Wagner calls for all lights at once: the roseate mists and emerald waterfalls of the grotto in *Tannhäuser*; the iridescent incense that Liszt could visualize in the prelude to *Lohengrin*; the blue vapour that surrounds Erda in *Das Rheingold*; the crimson glow of the crystal Grail in *Parsifal*. Those blended sensations, merging sight and sound, made the very notion of a universe seem old-fashioned and restrictively single-minded. The Wagnerian theatre was closer to the vibrant chaos that Henry Adams found when he pictured the electromagnetic nature of modern science: it too, like one of Wagner's operas, was a 'supersensual multiverse'.

The reciprocation of the senses coaxes us to loosen our hold on the insignia of gender, which are obstructive remnants of singleness and division. Baudelaire's indivisible totality must surely be androgynous. That at least was the ideal. In practice, an imbalance remained. Huneker suggested that Wagner should have called his opera *Isolde und Tristan* because it is about 'the subjugation of man by woman'. Wagner preferred not to think of it as subjugation, but he did imagine the relationship as an immersion. The woman, he said, envelops man in melody; after their 'redeeming love-kiss', the poet is 'inducted into the deep, unending mysteries' of her nature and sinks into 'the bottomless sea of harmony'. He extravagantly rephrases the encounter at the end of *Opera and Drama*, where the 'fertilizing germ' seeks out 'the mother-element' and subsides into a 'harmonic ocean' or a 'sea-abyss'. Opera, like life, begins in the water, where art is also spawned. The union envisaged here by Wagner is coital, although under other conditions the process could resemble baptism: elsewhere he describes the 'plunge into the waves of symphonic revelation' as 'a religious act of hallowed cleansing', like the purgative rituals in *Parsifal*. Sometimes the overwhelmed man pulls himself out of this chromatic ocean, and regains the safety of land. Lohengrin resists the pleading of Elsa and breaks off their nuptial duet. But the woman is usually allowed the last word, and the music that pours from her body inundates words. Isolde in her 'Liebestod' sings about the bliss of drowning, and Brünnhilde by torching the pyre causes the river to overflow and wash away the guilt of a venal, treacherous world.

Those floods are the only possible conclusion for Wagner's dramas. He first makes a world out of palpable sound, then takes pleasure in dissolving it. The *Ring* extends from Genesis to apocalypse, although it questions the eschatological timetable of Christian history. In *Das Rheingold*, there is no divine maker; Wotan builds Walhall, steals gold to pay for it, and later begets a sisterhood of warriors to guard the citadel. But the world arises or wells up of its own accord, generated by a low, rumbling E flat pedal that throbs, resonates and finally bursts into A flat as the Rhinemaidens – 'creatures of the deep' as Wagner called them, children of nature who are not Wotan's offspring – acquire voices and swim upwards into the light. Their song is an alliterative gurgling or burbling, with descants on 'Wagalaweia! Wallala weiala weia!' as they discover the fluent malleability of language. This, as Wagner told Cosima, is 'the genesis of things' – of nature, quickened by the vibrancy of the first chord and irrigated by melody, and of animate, articulate life.

The initial source is water; more urgent and violent transformations happen later as a result of fire, which, as in alchemy, changes the states of matter. When Wotan summons Loge, the god of fire, he acknowledges the superiority of this elemental force. Primitive societies often make the shaman the controller of fire, because its agility and searing power are manifestations of sacred energy. Wagner's Loge is less a medicine-man than a shrewd political trickster, useful to Wotan because his cynicism burns up legal contracts and moral scruples. He is Wagner's Prometheus: he uses fire against the other gods and, as they troop into Walhall, gloats about the imminent end of their regime. He lacks the Promethean concern for fire as a benefit to mankind – but *Das Rheingold* contains only gods, giants, gnomes, a snake, a toad and three mermaids: Wagner has no wish to duplicate or perpetuate the human race. Another of fire's bequests is placed on view when Donner dispels the sultry haze. He swings his hammer, strikes a rock, and detonates a lightning bolt and a rumble of thunder. The myth's original purpose was to explain the minerals embedded in the earth. Those buried riches are congealed fire, placed deep below the surface by the gods of the storm who – according to the sagas – rammed them in with hammers and axes. The human task is to dig out the veins and seams of glinting wealth, so the crash of Donner's hammer is anticipated and imitated by the

eighteen anvils which clatter in the underground mineshaft where the smith Mime collects ore. In 1879 a civic parade on the Ringstrasse in Vienna brought the Wagnerian plot up to date. On floats designed by the painter Hans Makart, a diamantine queen rode beside a figure representing the spirit of the earth, while Mercury, like a more benign Alberich, stood guard over a gold-plated globe. The myth of creation lent its blessing to the ornate reconstruction of the imperial city. The violence of Donner's hammer also liberates a percussive music. The

'Siegfried' by Lynd Ward from *The Story of Siegfried*, 1931, by Angela Diller

mining tycoon in Ibsen's *John Gabriel Borkman*, first performed in 1896, listens to the *Danse macabre* of Saint-Saëns being pounded out on a piano, and is reminded of the chanting of the ore deep underground as the workers set it free. The metal, he says, sings as it is prised loose and hauled into the light; its rejoicing creates both wealth and art.

Once the natural world has taken form, it can be altered by the intervention of gods or artists. The mining activities of the devils in *Paradise Lost* enable them to make weapons, but Wagner's Nibelungen, like his gods, are more interested in making art. After the storm clears, the cleansed air shimmers, and harps sketch the rainbow which the gods use as a bridge to Valhall. Gold has paid for their aerial palace. Far below, minerals are melted down to make the Tarnhelm, a magical helmet that effaces identity and allows Alberich to assume any shape that pleases him – a snake, a toad – and in *Götterdämmerung* enables Siegfried to disguise himself as Gunther to ravish Brünnhilde. The Tarnhelm confers the 'negative capability' that Keats admired in Shakespeare; it is a device indispensable to a dramatist like Wagner, who needed to assume other identities. The forge in *Siegfried* is another rough, disorderly studio. Siegfried hurls the fragments of his father's sword into a furnace, a matrix sturdier than the retorts of the alchemists or the Grail that fierily glows when Amfortas raises it. The container erupts, and disgorges a burning cataract. When it cools, Siegfried hammers the metal into shape and raises the instrument of power that makes him, as Wagner balefully said, 'a terrible kind of artist'. Mime is meanwhile breaking eggs into a pot for their supper. Siegfried despises such low, effeminate domestic skills: while he melts steel – as he says – all Mime can do is to mix up an inedible stew. War, in this estimation, is an more exalted manifestation of culture than cooking. The preparation of food may not qualify as an art, but cobbling does. Hans Sachs in *Die Meistersinger* is a shoe-maker and also a poet, and the two activities are connected. The humblest human crafts alter nature, which is why their secrets were traditionally passed on through guilds that had initiation ceremonies, like masonic lodges. Shoe-making requires wax and pitch, so it cannot happen without fire; like Donner and Siegfried, Sachs uses a hammer, thumping leather to make it flexible and marking the metrical beats of his improvised song with the blows. No accomplishment is possible without violence.

The *Ring* advances at speed through the ages of the earth, and summarizes our impatient graduation from nature to culture. The matriarchal Erda rises from a cleft in the rocks in *Das Rheingold* to warn Wotan that the gods are mortal, like the earth they pillage; she confirms the verdict in *Siegfried*. The first time, Wotan ignores her. The second time, he welcomes the prediction and resigns himself to his downfall. That, for Wagner, was the noblest and most divine of initiatives: the creative project culminates in a reckless act of self-destruction. As soon as Siegfried embraces Brünnhilde, she calls for a night of annihilation – 'Nacht der Vernichtung' – to erase them in its mist; the Dutchman and his ghostly crew also pray to 'Ew'ge Vernichtung', a power of negation that is eternal as gods were once supposed to be. When Wagner first made plans to stage his tetralogy, he promised that at the end of *Götterdämmerung* he would toss the score onto the mound of logs on which Siegfried's body is cremated, then launch himself into the flames. After he built his opera house at Bayreuth and performed the *Ring* there in 1876, he reiterated this desire to burn down the wooden building, along with the sets and costumes it contained, when the performance ended. The *Ring* rehearsed the end of world, so its grand finale should have been a riot of pyromania.

In 1881 Wagner described to Cosima 'the birth of the universe'. A sun, like one of the Cartesian vortices, began to revolve. But why did it decide to whirl into orbit? Wagner suggested that desire made it move: this was the motor and the motive of the stars in Dante's *Divina Commedia*. Then he corrected himself. What goaded the sun into life was fear, 'and this agitation born of fear was everywhere'. Its pervasiveness enforced a thermodynamic law, as remorseless as original sin: the sun is terrified because heat bleeds from it. Wagner orchestrated this outcome in the shuddering, halting, slow-breathed prelude to the third act of *Parsifal*, which he called 'the lament of an extinguished star'. Returning male and female to their original unity, he made human evolution backtrack. He also expected the universe to implode, recreating the moment of its birth. Isolde blots out the real, bright world established in Genesis. Night is the cover for sex, and also the time of dreams, when the imagination runs free. She invites Tristan to their rendezvous in the garden by quenching a torch. 'Es werde Nacht', she cries, her voice rising in an elated change of key: let there be darkness.

# 22
# DEICIDE

Renaissance artists understood their similarity to gods, but were tactful in pressing their claims. They avoided a challenge to Christianity by reviving classical myth, which saw divinity as an elective option – available to singers like Orpheus, and even to the self-made, self-improving Adam of Pico della Mirandola. By the end of the nineteenth century, a more open challenge to religion was possible. The itinerary of the dead hero's soul in Edward Elgar's oratorio *The Dream of Gerontius* leads to 'the awful Presence of its God', who – in the poem by Cardinal Newman that Elgar took as his text – sits on high in judgment. The orchestra unveils that presence for an instant, in a percussive thunder-clap combined with a glare of sonic lightning; a wrenching discord at once abruptly closes off a vision we cannot see, and Gerontius cries 'Take me away'. Is the music struck dumb for its hubris, or did Elgar prefer to leave God as a invisible vanishing-point? Was his reserve the result of piety or of scepticism? When *Gerontius* failed at its first performance in 1900, the composer knew who to blame: 'I always said God was against art'. All the more reason, perhaps, not to allow the deity to double as a critic.

Nietzsche defied Christians to prove that their God had ever existed. Even if they could have done so, he refused to believe in such a pitiful and petty being, whose dictatorship was '*a crime against life*'. 'We deny God as God,' he belligerently announced. Wagner's gods slump into a premature old age when they are deprived of Freia's apples in *Das Rheingold*: their immortality depends on their ostentatiously privileged diet. Wilde reversed traditional wisdom in one of the *Phrases and Philosophies for the Use of the Young* that he published in 1894, making mortality a defining attribute of deity. 'It is only the gods,' he said, 'who taste of death.' The paradox sounds glib, but it may be profound. Gods have a tenure as temporary as politicians, who are their professional colleagues; we vote them in, then soon lose faith. Humankind, with all its faults, is comfortably and unchangeably immortal. As Wilde added, 'Nero and Narcissus are always with us.'

For Henry Adams, the truth of Nietzsche's pronouncement was proved by the new element which the Curies isolated. 'Radium', as he put it, 'denied its God': it transformed itself by giving off radioactivity, and needed no prompting from a maker or mover. Or did such forces affirm God by diffusing him throughout the air? In 1897 the Belgian symbolist

Maurice Maeterlinck hailed a new epoch of scientific spiritualism, whose 'occult powers' included telegraphy, magnetism and 'radiating matter'. Maeterlinck believed that such agencies were meant to awaken the soul, attuning us to the invisible. Adams preferred to think of them as material

benefits, and claimed that the average American – whose life had been both eased and accelerated by 'incalculable coal-power, chemical power, electric power, and radiating energy' – was now 'a sort of God'. After seeing the *Ring* at Bayreuth in 1901, he suggested that Wagner's drama, 'the last great tragedy of gods and men', deserved to be played out among the skyscrapers of New York, not in a sleepy German provincial town. The capitalists who presided over the American industrial boom – the Fricks, Rockefellers, Guggenheims – were for Adams 'heathen gods', brooding on pinnacles that could now reached by elevators not rainbow bridges. But despite their lofty

Christopher Nevinson, *The Great White Way, New York*, lithograph, 1920

offices and luxuriant mansions, they were bound to be overthrown by the toiling masses they had enslaved: Adams thought the plutocrats were 'as dumb as their dynamos'.

Shaw made the same point in 1898. Life, as he said in his exposition of the *Ring*, climbs upward, enticed by a 'higher power ... called Godhead'. That power is possessed by 'certain rare persons who may ... be called gods, creatures capable of thought', unlike the dwarfish drudges or stupid giants who labour for them. But how could a few high-minded individuals control the 'Plutonic empire' of money, now that gold had been discovered in the Klondike? A god no longer prevails by preaching reason and devising laws. He must be rich, and – as Loge cynically advises Wotan in *Das Rheingold* – the only way to get hold of this new industrial wealth is by theft, the expropriation of natural resources. Once Wotan steals Alberich's hoard, there is no hope for him. The world simply awaits the revolutionary who will put an end to capitalism. Siegfried the dragon-slayer is soon corrupted and compromised, but Brünnhilde takes up his radical creed. In Wagner's first version of the text, she pauses before her self-immolation to denounce property, money, deity and all the inflictions of social rank. Wagner later cut this diatribe: he thought that it was enough for her to recommend love as an alternative to economic self-interest.

Shaw blamed Wagner for abandoning his political allegory. The truth is that Wotan does not have to be dethroned, because he fades into impotence and is laid to rest with only mild regrets by Brünnhilde in *Götterdämmerung*. Her suicide on the funeral pyre is a repudiation of selfish advantage, a rebuke to the meanly acquisitive world. Such an act rises above human nature; as Wagner said of Christ's sacrificial death, it is the gratuitous initiative of a 'co-creator', and would be worthy of 'God himself' if he existed. But the delusion of eternal life is no part of the pact. Wagner admired the recalcitrance of Homer's Achilles, who is told that he is about to die and offered elevation to Olympus. Achilles rejects heaven, and says he prefers to fight on to avenge the killing of his lover Patroclus. The episode is restaged in *Die Walküre*, when Brünnhilde prophesies Siegmund's death and promises him an afterlife in Walhall, where he will belong to Wotan's battalion of undead fighters. He refuses because he cannot take Sieglinde with him; like Achilles, he adds that he would rather descend to hell. Brünnhilde is at first dumbfounded, then shamed by his emotional fidelity. Siegmund, like Achilles, has proved himself superior to the craven, manipulative gods. The stubborn resolve of the two warriors persuaded Wagner that 'it is in man ... that creation culminates'. God is a parent we are bound to outgrow. In the *Ring*, Wagner pointedly altered the Norse sagas so as to question Christianity. The relationship between Wotan and his daughter Brünnhilde, for instance, exposes the frictions between God and his only begotten son. Like Christ, she announces a new law, a doctrine of redemptive love which she first learns from Siegmund. But this prompts her to rebel against her tyrannical father; rather than redeeming mankind, she concentrates on saving Siegmund's life by shielding him in the battle. Her Calvary is the humiliation of being reduced to parity with human beings. Defenceless on the mountain-top, she is prey to any wooer who passes by. Wotan speaks with contempt of her mortal incarnation: she will be unhorsed, no longer permitted to war-whoop as she canters through the air, and a domineering husband will order her to sit by the fireside and spin. Her response is to condemn the heaven from which she was expelled. In *Götterdämmerung* she refuses to ransom Wotan by parting with the ring that was Siegfried's love-token, and she finally sets fire to the heavenly mansion which Christ promised to the crucified thieves as a sanctuary for the soul. At the end, astonished witnesses gaze up at the sky and see the gods obliterated by smoke and flame as Walhall burns.

In 1880 Wagner said that Christianity had lamed itself by retaining 'the Jewish "Creator of Heaven and Earth"'. How could any single faith reconcile this wrathful patriarch with Christ, 'the self-offering, all-loving saviour of the poor'? Surely the ten harsh Mosaic commandments were over-ruled by Christ's simple, single command to love your neighbour as yourself. Wagner dealt with the inconsistency by choosing between Old and New Testaments: he jettisoned Jehovah but retained the Messiah. He saw Christ as a man, not God's son and heir. Perhaps more importantly, he was a mythic character: an ideal, and thus an artist's invention. Wagner agreed with Schiller, who thought that Christianity was 'the only *aesthetic* religion'. 'Christ for us,' as he wrote in his notebook in 1881, 'is in the end merely a most noble poetic fiction'. He could therefore be rechristened in noble poetic fictions like Parsifal, who actually supplants Christ. At the end of the opera, resurrection is replaced by the re-animation of nature at spring. While anointing Parsifal, Gurnemanz explains what he calls 'Karfreitagszauber' – the magic spell of Good Friday, which resurrects the frozen fields. Parsifal, stricken, suddenly remembers the crucifixion, but Gurnemanz points ahead to the miracle of the third day. Tears of mourning turn into dew, as the most warming and reassuring of Wagner's endless melodies steals into audibility and swelling strings mime the insistence of organic growth. All creatures rejoice in their reprieve from death, as Gurnemanz says: in this interpretation, Christ died to ensure the survival of nature, not to ransom mankind. The flowers are guiltless, and need no redemption. By concentrating on the greenery of the meadow, Gurnemanz makes Christ a vegetation god, who dies temporarily and revives when roots stir in the thawing soil. An offering of love, as Gurnemanz puts it, prompts this new vitality: our imaginative desire wills the mortified earth to cast off its pall, which is why he calls the process magical.

The sacrament in the Grail temple is equally heterodox. The chorus gives thanks for bread and wine, which, according to the youthful voices that chant in the dome, are Christ's 'holy gifts'. The eucharist ought to be an exercise in symbolic substitution: a dry wafer represents Christ's body, a sip of sour wine his bleeding wounds. But Wagner's knights – who have wasted away, like Wotan's clan without the golden apples – feast on these offerings, which to them are actual food and drink; they create a god, then cannibalize him. Wagner designed *Parsifal* as a rite which, as he told Cosima, was religious without being ecclesiastical. Its purpose was to consecrate the stage at Bayreuth – to disestablish the church and set a theatre in its place. The chalice softly glows when Parsifal lays hands on it, then seems to catch fire as he lifts it up. The congregation praises the highest of wonders, 'Erlösung dem Erlöser!' This last declaration announces that the redeemer is redeemed: Christ's doctrinal responsibilities are waived, and the work of atonement can be carried out by Wagner's orchestra, which instils in us the exquisitely painful moral sensitivity and gratified rapture that sermons can only talk about.

Nietzsche reviled *Parsifal*, which he wrongly took to be a lapse into Christian piety. In fact what Wagner called its 'divine ferocity' supports the attack on biblical law in *Götzen-Dämmerung*, where Nietzsche revises the agenda of Genesis and allows creation to come to grief by the sixth day. God is not permitted his smug sabbatical rest, since – thanks to Eve's premature eating of the apple – his world is already a moral shambles. Humanity must now surpass itself by imagining Zarathustra, the man who takes over from an enfeebled deity. In a letter to the historian Jacob Burckhardt, his colleague at the University of Basel, Nietzsche joked about the burden he had to shoulder. He would, he said, 'far rather be a professor at Basel than God'. But he was not selfish enough to neglect a duty more pressing than his academic chores. This, he told Burckhardt, was nothing less than 'the creation of the world'. He been called on in a cosmic emergency, seconded by God; his senile celestial patron did not notice that Nietzsche set about demolishing the world rather than upholding its tired verities.

For the first time, God could be teased or derided, since there was no chance that the blasphemer would be struck down. The failure of religion gave art a new elation, a witty deviancy which Nietzsche called 'joyous wisdom'. The Roman soldiers in Wilde's *Salomé* sneer at the Jews because they worship a God who cannot be seen. Freud admired this invisible Jehovah without believing in him; at least he was evidence that men were no longer content to worship golden calves. At the court of Herod, Wilde's pagans refuse to take God on trust. Herodias is unimpressed by reports that Christ is performing miracles on the sea of Galilee. She does not believe in miracles, she says, having seen too many. Once again, a joke takes a sacrilegious risk, daring to say something that once could not even be thought: Herodias reduces Christ's demonstrations of divine power to magic tricks, which are bound to be fraudulent. The Jews do not wish their notional God to visit the earth, and they indignantly contradict the Baptist's announcement that the Messiah has arrived. Having demanded the Baptist's decapitation, Salomé mocks

Gustav Klimt,
*Salomé*, 1909

his faith in an illusory afterlife. He refused to look at her, and missed the chance to see the naked body she unveiled in her dance. Instead he has perhaps been granted a sight of his God. She hopes he considers that to be a fair exchange.

An absent God invited charges of indifference or irresponsibility. The elderly Arkel in Maeterlinck's play *Pelléas et Mélisande* watches as his son Golaud abuses the innocent Mélisande. Golaud upbraids his young wife for loving his brother Pelléas; he has no reason for doing so, but he arms himself with a scriptural precedent by referring to Absalom, David's ingrate son. Arkel grieves for Mélisande, but is too infirm to intervene in her defence. As she weeps, he says that if he were God, he would have pity on the hearts of men. In Debussy's operatic setting of the play, the orchestral interlude that follows Arkel's comment manages a threnody of compassion and complaint. But it is brief, and soon muted; music can only helplessly sympathize from the sidelines. The God invoked by Arkel had become synonymous with moral cowardice, or with an unthinking status quo.

In Wilde's first play *Vera, or The Nihilists*, this lazy, uncaring deity is an incitement both to atheism – as Nietzsche said – and to political revolution. An elderly Russian peasant refuses to worry about the iniquities of a regime that has sent his son to Siberia for having unlicensed ideas. 'I didn't make the world,' he shrugs. 'Let God and the Czar look to it.' The Nihilists – terrorists whose creed is 'to suffer, to annihilate, to revenge' – plot to eliminate God's despotic deputy on earth, although the threatened Czar Ivan regards himself as Christ, haplessly betrayed and sacrificed. 'Which of ye all,' he asks his councillors a few moments before being killed, 'is the Judas who betrays me?' He suspects that the culprit is his heir, a secret Nihilist who plans, when he acquires the throne, to put an end to feudalism. Wilde wrote *Vera* in 1880, and Alexander II was assassinated in St Petersburg a year later, so life once more imitated art. But the true revolutionary in the play is not the regicide who shoots Czar Ivan. It is the idle, lecherous dandy Prince Paul. Banished by the Czarevitch Alexis, Paul joins the Nihilists out of pique, after subjecting their Code of Revolution to amused scrutiny. He scoffs at their view of the world as a workshop and their insistence on 'the right to labour', but he warms to their attack on the family – the basis of bourgeois society and the protector of property rights – as an impediment to 'socialistic and communal unity'. 'A family is a terrible incumbrance,' he agrees, 'especially when one is not married.' Political action is necessary to dethrone the Czar. To dispose of God, as Paul's drawling ennui suggests, is an easier matter: you simply decline to go on believing in him, and kill him off by desecrating the sanctimonious precepts of religion. The epigram is the deadly enemy of the commandment, because it suggests that self-proclaimed truths are reversible or at least deniable. Its very succinctness is lethal, as in Wilde's comment on the way wars would be fought in the future: 'a chemist on each side,' he said with frightening prescience, 'will approach the frontier with a bottle'. The dandy can admire such an economy of means, which does away with the need for massed armies. The joyous wisdom or gay science makes abominations thinkable, and it does so with nonchalant elegance.

In Wilde's *A Woman of No Importance*, Lord Illingworth – whose wit gives him a reputation for wickedness, since he lacks 'faith in the nobility and purity of life' – asserts that 'All thought is immoral. Its very essence is destruction'. Why bother thinking at all if you do not intend to contradict a received idea? Bazarov in Turgenev's novel *Fathers and Sons*, like Wilde's Alexis, unsettles ancient feudal rules about property and is reputed to be a Nihilist. His detractors puzzle over the etymology of the word, with its evocation of nothingness; they wonder how he will manage 'to exist in a void or a vacuum'. But Bazarov, who calmly accepts his death from typhus, knows that he is an expendable speck in space, whose allowance of time is equally negligible. He likens himself to an atom or a decimal point: a dot that is bound to diminish and implode. Eternity he defines as the vast, vacant realm in which he did not and will not exist. Illingworth's destructive thinking makes a cynic of him, while the same contempt for authority produces in Bazarov a selfless, serene despair.

The agitator Mikhail Bakunin justified his anarchist rampages by arguing that 'A passion to destroy is also a creative passion'. For Wagner – who set buildings on fire during the Dresden uprising in 1848, then fled into exile – arson also ignited a 'beautiful spark of divine joy'. In 1906 Emil Nolde praised Munch's paintings for their likeness to the outrages committed by Bakunin and his followers: 'His art acted on us like an explosion. ... A hand slashing paint on the canvas as he does could sooner be imagined wielding a knife or throwing a bomb.' Kandinsky hoped that the circulation of his paintings in America would have 'the effect of surprise like a bomb'. The oath sworn by the Nihilists in *Vera* overlooks the messy practicalities of bomb-throwing, and concentrates on being bloody-minded. It begins by repudiating behaviour that is normal and instinctive for others: the convert must promise 'to strangle whatever nature is in me'. This is closer to the principled perversity of decadence than to revolutionary fanaticism. Des Esseintes in *À Rebours* might have consented to the demands that follow, which enjoin the Nihilist 'neither to love nor to be loved; neither to pity nor to be pitied; neither to marry not to be given in marriage, till the end is come'. This pledge imitates the vow of chastity made by novices entering a religious order. Liberty for Wilde's Nihilists is 'a new God'. They are few in number, but 'the Galilaean had less to conquer the world'. Their password, 'Per crucem ad lucem', even makes scurrilous use of the crucifixion. Like mystics, they calmly anticipate the apocalypse, when heaven will be established on earth. 'The end' is not necessarily revolution: for the infatuated Vera, who kills herself to spare the new Czar, it is a love-death.

The one true God yielded to exotic alternatives. Des Esseintes admires the Salomé painted by Gustave Moreau because she has cast off her biblical lineage and belongs to 'the theogonies of the Far East', brandishing a lotus blossom which is 'the sceptre of Isis, the sacred flower of both Egypt and India'. The shameless sensuality of Moreau's paintings saves Des Esseintes from pointlessly worrying over the mystical paradoxes of Christianity. He

cannot understand how God became man in Mary's womb, and is sure that Christ did not look like other men. He challenges these vestigial deities to give a sign of life, and enlists them in his campaign against the money-grubbing bourgeoisie: 'Could it be that the terrible God of Genesis and the pale martyr of Golgotha would not prove their existence once for all by renewing the cataclysms of old, by rekindling the rain of fire that once consumed those accursed towns, the cities of the plain?' The novel ends with his prayer, and is unable to confirm that it was answered. Durtal in *Là-Bas*, corrupted by his research into the life of the

Gustave Moreau, *L'Apparition*, 1874–6

medieval satanist Gilles de Rais, ponders a return to Catholicism, and decides that the best reason for believing is the absurdity of it all. 'Imagination,' he concludes, 'is the only good thing that heaven vouchsafes to the sceptic and pessimist, aghast at the abjectness of life.' *Là-Bas* announces the advent of a 'Third Kingdom', which will complete the dialectic implicit in the Trinity and gloriously terminate human history. Two of the three divine persons have already appeared; mankind has lived through the kingdom of fear, ruled by God the Father, and the kingdom of expiation, dominated by the Son. Still to come is the kingdom of love, when the Holy Ghost will materialize among men and regenerate them. Once again, the novel breaks off with the expectation unfulfilled.

While Huysmans awaited the second coming, he made do with the devil, a more gregarious figure than the elusive Holy Ghost. He kept a scrap book into which he pasted anecdotes about contemporary diabolism: reports of of vampires, black masses in the suburbs, cases of sacramental wine and wafers stolen or put to profane uses, holy vessels pawned by renegade abbés. He might have included the satanic sermon that the librettist Arrigo Boito wrote for Iago in Verdi's *Otello*, first performed in 1887. Shakespeare's Iago is shifty, hollow, believing in nothing, not even his own spurious motives for entrapping Othello. But the operatic Iago is a doctrinaire intellectual who appears to have read both Darwin and Nietzsche; his plot is metaphysical mischief, expressing scorn not merely for Otello but for the empty sanctities that such heroes serve. In Boito's opera *Mefistofele*, first performed in 1868, Goethe's devil explains himself to Faust by declaring that he desires 'il Nullo e del Creato la ruina universal': he wants creation to be swallowed up again by the void from which it was first extruded, which will happen – as he jeers – when the sun expires. Meanwhile he bestirs himself to annoy the creator. He roars the monosyllable 'No', which sums up his entire philosophy, then puts his fingers in his mouth and shrilly whistles. The evacuation or excretion of air sabotages both language and music. It is a noise not a word; it attacks the ear drums and would pierce them if it could. Through Mefistofele, chaos comes again to obliterate cosmos.

Boito's Iago is the successor to this universal antagonist. As his means of self-revelation, he declaims an atheistic Credo that runs through the articles of decadent disbelief. It recalls an exchange in *Vera*, when the president of the Nihilists catechizes his acolytes. 'Our creed?' he asks. 'To annihilate,' a loyalist replies. Like Wilde's Nihilists with their password, Iago is casually blasphemous. 'Non ti crucciar', he tells the disgraced, dejected Cassio, before recommending a session with the harlot Bianca: don't crucify yourself. He goes on – as the brass in Verdi's orchestra sounds a malevolent fanfare that echoes through cavernous space, and trills on the violas and clarinets make the pillars of stability shudder – to announce his allegiance to a cruel god, in whose image he was made. He is making a learned joke about Genesis and about Prometheus, since he knows that no-one created him. He was born, he says, from 'un germe o d'un atómo vile': not consciously made but involuntarily germinated; he relishes the primal slime ('il fango originario') within himself. Life for Iago is a short step from germ to worm, 'dal germe della culla al verme dell'avel'; his rhyme equates the seed that is life's source with the vermin that feed on decay. He ends, after a baleful pause during which the orchestral modulations seek out ever lower depths, by praising annihilation. The afterlife is mere senile folly, and even death is nothing, 'il Nulla'. He stares into the void and – in a reminiscence of Mefistofele's whistling – roars with laughter, while semiquavers spurt like lava all around him. In her 'Ave Maria' at the end of the opera, Desdemona attempts to refortify the religion that Iago attacks. She sings a biological gospel, blessing Mary and Christ who is the fruit of her womb, 'il frutto, o benedetta, di tue materne viscere'. Her prayer ends on a faint, shimmering high note, aerated and angelic. Two minutes later she is dead.

In 1875 James Clerk Maxwell wrote a jauntily pessimistic poem about the insecurity of the universe – a plight for which his own speculations on light, heat and the evanescence of energy were in part responsible. The poem starts, as myths are supposed to do, with a fable about origins and the invention of a creator:

> In the very beginning of science,
> > the parsons, who managed things then,
> Being handy with hammer and chisel,
> > made gods in the likeness of men.

The priests rely on artists: sculptors have to make idols, embodying an idea that would otherwise remain implausible. Maxwell too, in exchanging scientific prose for doggerel verse, was admitting that art told consoling lies. His poem's meaning is desolate, but the regularity and resilience of the metre give it a half-hearted joviality. As it continues, the age of faith gives way to the age of commerce, and the parsons are replaced by 'men of exceptional power' who

> Supplanted both demons and gods by
> > the atoms, which last to this hour.

Materialism may have demystified nature, but Maxwell finds the prospect dismaying:

> There is nothing but atoms and void,
> > all else is but whims out of date!

The jingle uncannily anticipates A. S. Eddington's verdict on the researches of Einstein and his colleague Hermann Minkowski. Genesis provided comfort because it recorded the progressive solidifying of a world we recognize, with its balanced elemental coordinates. As Eddington said in 1927, relativity and the theory of space–time reduced that material foundation to a speckled, dusty waste: 'The revelation by modern physics of the void within the atom is more disturbing than the revelation by astronomy of the immense void of interstellar space. The atom is as porous as the solar system.' Science confirmed Nietzsche's obituary for God, who had left creation incomplete, invaded by vacancy.

Potentially at least, a single musical accord might make the planet fizzle out. Nietzsche said that Wagner catered to 'every nihilistic (Buddhistic) instinct', for instance in the lax, wilting dissonance at the beginning of *Tristan und Isolde*. In 1900 James Huneker heard the same fatality in an apparently harmless mazurka by Chopin. Huneker shuddered at a cadence in the B flat minor dance from opus 24. Melancholy, as he put it in his literary transcription of the piece, vies with joy, and is in turn quenched. Then the return of the first theme announces 'the dying away of the dance, dancers and the solid globe itself, as if the earth had committed suicide for loss of the sun'. Huneker alludes to Prospero, who in *The Tempest* foresees the dissolution of 'the great globe', but he then brings the wizard's magic up to date by connecting it with the implacable calculations of thermodynamics. The Pythagorean music of the spheres guaranteed to sustain the cosmos forever; a single faltering step in a mazurka that lasts four minutes is enough, for Huneker, to unbalance and exterminate the entire system.

In 1910 Chesterton saluted Shaw, whose vitalism reinvigorated the morbid culture of the fin de siècle. At the same time he congratulated the world on not falling victim to entropic modulations like Chopin's. For Chesterton, nihilism was never anything more than an adolescent pose, betrayed by its own dilettantish idleness: in his homage to Shaw he said that he occasionally ran into 'men who, when I knew them in 1898, were just a little too lazy to destroy the universe. They are now conscious of being not quite worthy to abolish some prison regulations'. The joke is the revenge of conservative age on radical youth; it assumes that, by growing up and growing older, we come to accept the way things are. Having established the longevity of the universe, Chesterton tried to salvage God, whose death, he pointed out, had been announced once before. Lucretius broke the news prematurely, just before the beginning of the Christian era, and modern atheists succumbed again to the 'Lucretian doom' of the late Roman empire. According to Chesterton, Lucretius 'endeavoured to substitute Evolution for God', and reduced the world to a 'dance of glittering atoms'. Such an outlook induced moral fatigue: he and his adherents testified 'that God was dead and that they themselves had seen him die'.

Lucretius was actually not sure that God had ever been alive, but he did foresee the death of our disorderly planet. In *On the Nature of Things* he looked ahead to a time when earth, water and air would consummate their warfare, causing 'the entire substance and structure of the world' to 'collapse with an ear-splitting crack'. For Chesterton, Christ's incarnation saved the day: the saviour's appearance on earth demonstrated that 'the new cosmos ... was larger than the old cosmos. In that sense Christendom is larger than creation'. Yes, but in that sense only, and what if the added supernatural space is actually empty? Philosophers both in 55 BC and in the 1890s seemed to Chesterton to be 'men poised above abysses, ... fascinated by death and nothingness and the empty air'. Nietzsche, a frequenter of mountain-tops, had a recommendation for coping with conceptual altitudes. Zarathustra says that if you reach a crevasse, you should leap across it. Chesterton preferred to remain at the edge of the cavity, occasionally peering into what he called the 'abyss of the unthinkable'. Modern thinkers and artists, however, let down rope-ladders and prepared to explore the depths.

# 23
# OUT OF THE CANYON

The geography of myth begins where the maps run out. Dragons lurk in the margins, or beyond the borders of the page. Although Hesiod lived near Helicon, the mountain frequented by the muses, he claimed no close acquaintance with the chasm from which the world had emerged. In 1869 John Wesley Powell ventured into the place of origins. From a starting-point in the Rocky Mountains, Powell, a one-armed veteran of the Civil War, began a map-making voyage that took him through the canyons of the Colorado River and into what he called 'the Great Unknown'. Marshalling four boats, he spent three months jolting through rapids and whirling in vortices, dashed against rocks or groping between granite walls almost as narrow as a birth canal. Powell said that the journey was 'solemn, mysterious', like an initiate's plumbing of the underworld. By committing yourself to the mercy of the Colorado River, as the novelist Owen Wister remarked in 1914, you renounced 'the upper world' where the sun shone. The seeker's reward came when the river bent and twisted for almost three hundred miles as it churned through what Wister described as the 'nether world' of the Grand Canyon: here was 'an avenue conducting to the secret of the universe and the presence of the gods'. When Powell's ragged, battered, hungry party finally emerged into open waters, he announced that he had traversed 'the story of creation'. But did the story have room for a creator?

If you stand on the rim of the Grand Canyon and stare into the distance, you look through time as well as space, reviewing the five or six million years it has taken for the river to carve this mind-boggling crevice. The view down makes you dizzy because it is incomprehensible. Travelling through the gorge far below, Powell saw it differently, and recognized that he had a different mental responsibility. On the rim, we are disturbed by regression – the fear of falling into this abysmal past. As Powell said, the canyon seen from above is atavistically 'deep and gloomy', like 'an opening into a nadir in hell'. But when he looked up from the sunken river, the prospect was 'open, sunny', since sunlit reality resumed at the top of the cliffs. 'Above,' he said in the journal of his expedition, 'it is a chasm; below, it is a stairway from gloom to heaven'. Physically, the river carried him forward from Wyoming to Utah, sometimes – as he noticed – 'at railroad speed'; but at the same time it projected him backwards into prehistory. Despite its shallowness, it deprived him of any secure sense of foundation.

Thomas Moran,
*Grand Canyon of
the Yellowstone*,
1872

In a gorge almost two thousand feet deep, he felt he was 'in the depths of the earth', looking down 'into waters that reflect a bottomless abyss'. The imagined ladder to heaven was his means of escape, and it had a precedent on the sheer red limestone walls of the canyon, which were sometimes indented by 'two, three, or four Cyclopean steps – a mighty stairway'. But were a man's legs capable of extending to imitate the stride of the Cyclops? If Powell could mentally complete this steep climb – rigging up an explanation for the subterranean wonders and perils he was experiencing – then he would be able to testify to the world's rationality.

While trying to control a mutinous crew and conserve mouldy rations, menaced by rattlesnakes and by slippages when he tested the ridges for a foothold, Powell also concentrated on the attempt 'to understand a little' of nature's purposes and to 'read the language of the universe'. He did so by exercising technical skills as a cartographer, geologist and ethnologist, and by writing his *Exploration of the Colorado River of the West and its Tributaries*. Desperate to make the Canyon legible, he saw its teetering walls bibliographically. The variegated quartzite looked like rows of books with 'many-coloured bindings'; the cracked surface formed shelves, which displayed 'the stony leaves of one great book'. The one great book ought to have been the Bible, written by God with the prophets and evangelists as amanuenses. But Powell was unsure about the authorship of the Canyon. Reverting to polytheism, he replaced the Bible's single authorized version with a digest of contradictory tales. 'One might imagine,' he suggested, 'that this was intended for the library of the gods; and it was.' The pace of the river allowed him no time to peruse a sacred text. The geological inscriptions rushed past, and he scrambled to revise his ideas about the earth, its provenance and the forces that made it. 'The book is open,' he said, 'and I can read as I run.'

The last word of Powell's *Exploration* reaches towards the heaven that intangibly, alluringly hovered at the top of the stairs. It promises that anyone with sufficient 'strength and courage' who is prepared to spend a year exploring the Grand Canyon will be rewarded by a sublime uplift 'never again to be attained on the hither side of Paradise'. Powell could only glimpse this remote horizon; his position, at the bottom of a gulch on the treacherous river, was far to the east of the Eden. Some of his companions were convinced that they were trapped in an infernal region. One man referred to a muddy, putrid stream in Narrow Canyon as a 'dirty devil', and Powell allowed the slur to stick. The party later called a creek Bright Angel, making amends for having named another stream 'in honour of the great chief of the "Bad Angels"'. God's adversary was active here, but Powell discerned no trace of the deity who separated the elements in Genesis. Instead he recalled Hesiod's myth about the warfare between Olympians and Titans, which made our world a by-product of infuriated, combative energies. He described the buttes as 'works of Titanic art', or said that they were made sublime by 'Titanic painting in varied hues'. In this setting, Powell could easily imagine the Titans wrathfully using mountains as missiles. To gauge the Grand Canyon's breadth and depth, he suggested plucking up Mount Washington and dropping it in, or uprooting the Blue Ridge and tipping it over the rim; even so, there would be empty space to spare. Two weeks into his voyage, he arrived at a cinder cone, an extinct volcano that had deposited spindly pillars of lava in the river. The scene suggested a reverie that took Powell back to the time of origins described by Hesiod, with the elements in chaotic uproar: 'What a conflict of water and fire there must have been here! Just imagine a river of molten rock running down into a river of melted snow. What a seething and boiling of the waters; what clouds of steam rolled into heavens!' The steam made the spectacle industrial: this was nature's foundry, violently welding the earth into shape. At the top of the black granite walls, clouds capriciously behaved as if heaven had not yet been separated from earth. Sometimes stormy agglomerations effaced the sky; on other days, what Powell called 'baby clouds' disported themselves, then hid in gorges. He said that the clouds were 'children of the heavens, and when they play among the rocks they lift them to the region above'.

At least Powell thought of the boisterous Titans as artists, sculptors who with a more than Promethean finesse chiselled rock into slender pinnacles and coloured them 'pink, brown, red, lavender, grey, blue and black'. He tried to find evidence of a design, but it was at best aesthetic, never divine. Wherever possible he likened the Canyon's tumuli to buildings made by men. Thus he surveyed an array of 'monument-shaped buttes', 'alcove gulches', 'painted grottoes', 'royal arches' and free-standing balustrades, imagining himself in the studio of an architect. When he came upon a columnar formation of shales, he admitted how anxious he was to discern the workmanship of an artist or a deity: 'One could almost imagine that the walls had been carved with a purpose, to represent giant architectural forms.' The view above the sandstone cliff might – if he allowed his eyes to go out of focus – be an urban panorama, 'an entablature and sky-line of gable, tower, pinnacle, and spire', with 'vast amphitheatres'. But the ennobling, civilizing analogy failed when Powell remembered the vacant cavity. To convey an idea of the mile-high walls, he up-ended Washington and New York, calculating that the distance overhead could be measured by standing on the steps of the Treasury and looking down Pennsylvania Avenue to the Capitol, or by positioning yourself on Canal Street and peering far up Broadway to Grace Church. The void swallowed cities whole; it gave birth to worlds, and could equally well ingurgitate them.

In Glen Canyon the party camped beneath an overhang that was 'filled with sweet sounds' when one of the men started singing. The acoustic effect licensed another mythopoeic fancy, and encouraged Powell to recall the invention of another art. He supposed that the cavern was 'made for an academy of music by its storm-born architect', so he named it Music Temple. His language, however, confided his misgivings. Architecture is meant to keep storms out. Here he was forced to conceive of an architect whose tools were tempests and who, rather than assembling rocks into shelters, preferred to whittle and abrade them or to propel them through the air. This destructive artificer can be seen at work in *The Chasm of the Colorado*, the first of the vast paintings of the Grand Canyon made by Thomas Moran, who was invited to the North Rim by Powell in 1873. A sky that is darkened and thickened by clouds as solid as boulders collapses into the gulf. The shafts of steely rain were likened by the critic Richard Watson Gilder to 'down-flying javelins', able to slice through friable stone; the crevasses fill with mist like that which rose from the earth on the third day in Genesis, concealing the evidence of a world that remains unformed despite its edgy aridity. A rainbow juts from the pillar of black sleet, but cannot complete its arc or keep God's promise. Moran altered the Canyon's elevation, raising the buttes to bring them into contact with the sky that assails them, and organized the margin into an amphitheatre with smooth stones as seating for the spectators of a classical tragedy. Here we can watch creation or destruction happening, as the elements do battle.

Among the field workers engaged by Powell was Clarence Edward Dutton, an engineer and geologist who in 1882 published a *Tertiary History of the Grand Cañon District*. Like Moran, Dutton preferred to call the site 'the great chasm', reviving Hesiod's term; he thought the word canyon – cognate with cannon, referring to a tubular trench that digs a drainage channel through rock – was a banal, inadequate diminutive. Dutton named one of the lookouts Point Sublime, and he saw the Canyon as an example of sublimity at its most psychologically and spiritually exacting: 'as the mind strives to realize its proportions, its spirit is broken and its imagination completely crushed'. That disablement is usually the result of contemplating God, or of personally encountering a classical god. But Dutton was an agnostic who quit his course at the Yale Divinity School after only a fortnight, and he derived his sense of infinitude from geology, not from the fabulations of myth. The *Tertiary History* begins in the Mesozoic Era, 150 million years ago, when the West was a sea with the Rockies submerged in the depths. After eighty million years of drainage, during the Cenozonic Era a plateau formed of lava expanded into life. Then came volcanic ruptures and schisms, after which, in the Tertiary Era, the river gnawed its way through rock and shaped the chasm. Dutton likened the Canyon to a cathedral, specifically mentioning St Mark's Basilica in Venice, but within it he allocated temples to Brahma, Vishnu, Buddha, Confucius, Zoroaster and Isis, and set aside one escarpment as a throne for Wotan. He made a concession

*Panorama from Point Sublime,* 1882. Lithograph by William H. Holmes from Dutton's *Tertiary History of the Grand Cañon District*

to Christianity in the name he gave to a 'long rambling mass' of buttes that straggled down into 'the lowest abyss': these he called the Cloisters. To the east of this decrepit arcade loomed the most immense of the buttes, frowning over 'the inner abyss'. For this Dutton reserved the name of the most terrifying Hindu god, the agent of apocalypse whose actions undo those of Brahma the creator and Vishnu the preserver. He decided that it would be Shiva's Temple, since 'in such a stupendous scene of wreck ... the fabled "Destroyer" might find an abode not wholly uncongenial'.

Dutton experienced the divine pleasure of destructiveness when writing his account of 'the great drama of the day' as seen from the Canyon's brink. During the afternoon, the vague, milky haze clears, and 'Rembrandt lights' flare in the alcoves. Life is regenerated, and separate pinnacles and stratified terraces sharpen into visibility as if they were being created before your eyes: 'A thousand forms, hitherto unseen or obscure, start up within the abyss, and stand forth in strength and animation.' The sky catches fire, then burns itself out. 'The abyss lapses back into repose. ... Below it is the dead grey shadow of the world.' All the minarets and pagodas and pyramids are blotted out. Dutton's adjectival palette – pale rose, orange, crimson, resplendent red and imperial purple – invests the rock with sentience and sensuousness, makes blood pulse through it. Then he smears these 'kingly colours', dims their lustre, and merges them in a 'darkening pall'. In the Canyon and on the page, life implacably leads to death. Dutton waits by the edge to see if dawn will restore the extinguished world and give him a reason for describing it all over again.

Sublimity worked like a chest-expander for the soul; the open spaces of the West were a moral gymnasium, where the country's artists limbered up to prove themselves worthy of the landscapes that had been lavished on them. Whitman in 1855 said that 'American bards shall be marked for generosity and affection. ... They shall be kosmos.' Like Moran or Dutton with their panoramas of the Canyon, they were called on to comprehend a creation that responded to their efforts by stretching ever further into the distance or the future. 'America is not finished, perhaps never will be,' Whitman told Emerson. The country – which at the time had thirty-two states, but might one day have a hundred as it expanded across the oceans – was 'a divine true sketch'. Art opened out to encompass the illimitable land. Moran's *Chasm of the Colorado*, which was twelve feet long and seven feet high, set a transcendent standard; in the 1940s Augustus Vincent Tack still painted Western vistas as spiritual allegories. Tack's *Liberation* pondered the alkaline desert of Death Valley in California, and his *Voice of Many Waters* was suggested by a valley in the Rockies studded with glacial lakes. The title came from the Book of Revelations, where that liquid roar is the voice of God. Tack's *Time and Timelessness (The Spirit of Creation)*, fifty-nine feet wide, was spatially and temporally all-embracing. Spiral nebulae hover in outer space as evidence of Bergson's 'élan vital', and clouds arrange themselves into the semblance of a Winged Victory. Tack designed it as a fire curtain for the auditorium of George Washington University; its imagery alluded to Prometheus, although it had to be painted on fire-proof asbestos, which would have frustrated the inflammatory Titan. When the collector Duncan Phillips laid out his Washington home as a museum, he installed Tack's paintings in a 'Hall of Cosmic Conceptions' which displayed 'the mystic's sense of an all pervading God ... seeking to create Cosmos out of Chaos'. Charles Ives attempted something even more ambitious in his *Universe Symphony*, which he began to think about in 1911. The symphony orchestrates evolution. Gongs, chimes and drums set the percussive pulse of life, with earth's creation marked by a chord on the low strings. The metallic timbre of a brass band announces the hardening of rocks. High strings and high winds survey the heavens and describe 'the Rise of all to the Spiritual', while clatterings like avalanches or eruptions warn that creation is still happening. To fix the details in advance would have defeated the purpose, so Ives left only memos. He hoped for an outdoor performance, with several orchestras and a multitudinous chorus moving over a hilly terrain, where they would complete looped circuits and coincide almost accidentally every few hours: this model of the cosmos had an amiably American tolerance of chaos, welcoming diversity and dissent.

The European mind, expecting God to be omniscient, could only assume that the harsh terrain of the American West had been abandoned by a neglectful creator. This was Willa Cather's suggestion in her novel *Death Comes to the Archbishop*, published in 1927. Cather's hero Father Latour is sent from Rome to Santa Fe. Travelling across the plain to the perched

settlement of Acoma, he fancies that the pinnacles of rock that rise from the 'flat red sea of sand' look like Gothic cathedrals – but to whom are they consecrated? The mesa has 'an appearance of great antiquity, and of incompleteness; as if, with all the materials for world-making assembled, the Creator had desisted, gone away and left everything on the point of being brought together ... into mountain, plain, plateau'. The land is a baking desert, brutally monotonous; the ill-tempered sky alternates between blinding sun and lashing storms. Latour worries about the inversion of biblical priorities. In Europe 'the sky is the roof of the world', whereas in the American southwest 'the earth [is] the floor of the sky'. The strata of rock are duplicated by the clouds above, hinting that the earth too is still fluent or volatile. Cather's imagery pointedly picks fault with religious devotion: clouds twist into 'silvery pagodas', or are attached to the ledges of granite 'as the smoke is part of the censer'. Creativity here is a cyclonic energy, hostile to matter; New Mexico makes Latour question his faith in the shaping skill of God the maker. He is troubled too by the 'savage' sound of the banjo, because there is a 'madness' in the way a native boy attacks its wiry strings. Pablo's 'seesawing yellow hand ... sometimes lost all form and became a mere whirl of matter in motion, like a patch of sand-storm'. This is hardly the music of the spheres. The metaphorical sand-storm is a blitz of distracted atoms, like the gaseous cloud that cooled and condensed to form what we think of as our world. Jean-Paul Sartre felt the same instability in 1945 when he jolted down into the Grand Canyon in a light aircraft, whose pilot lurched through air pockets and asked his passengers to warn him if he got too close to the rock walls. This might have been the nothingness over which existentialism flung its tightrope.

The novelist J. B. Priestley spent the winter of 1936 in Arizona, making occasional forays to Los Angeles at the behest of the Hollywood studios. The Europe he left was, as he said in his memoir *Midnight on the Desert*, about to commit suicide, and his sojourn in the desert – a time of purgation and spiritual penance, though his official reason for being there was to nurse his sick lungs – began with another act of self-destruction. At the start of his American chronicle, Priestley went to a hut on the ranch and burned the manuscript of a book he has been writing. He felt guilty because he 'had come to destroy, not to create', though he reflected that 'such destruction might be a better kind of creation'. The interdependence of the two states recurs throughout his reflections on America, which to him was not a new world but 'the real antique land, first cousin to the moon'. Before travelling to Arizona, he made a trip from New York to the Berkshires to see the autumn foliage, which seemed to be igniting the birches and maples. He thought he was in 'a burning Eden'. Had an angry God torched the garden? Priestley could only explain the delusive mirages he saw in Death Valley as 'the conjuring of the Devil himself'. The Salton Sea, formed from an overflow of the Colorado River, offered a preview of a time when the earth would be a dead planet. Priestley noted that 'when the giant meteor decided to embed itself in the earth, it chose Arizona'. The result of the concussion – a crater three-quarters of a mile wide and 550 feet deep – can be visited just off the highway near Winslow; that dent is another augury of the end.

The bleak austerity of the land belittles mankind's achievements. Priestley imagined the finale of Beethoven's Ninth Symphony, the anthem of romantic humanism, 'pealing out into a cold and empty universe'. At the Grand Canyon, he tried to fill the nullifying cavity with sound, in the hope of making it whole: it is, he says, 'all Beethoven's nine symphonies in stone and magic light'. While his excitement lasted, this convinced him that 'God gave the Colorado River its instructions'. But were those instructions apocalyptic? Priestley saw the Canyon, like Tack's Rockies, as 'a sort of landscape Day of Judgement'. The God who decreed the place must take a fiendish delight in decay, because the silt-laden river has acted like a saw, its teeth gnawing through rock. Art cannot subdue nature; our only hope lies in the manipulative contrivances of engineering. Hence Priestley's enthusiasm for the Boulder Dam, which choked the Colorado River, diverted its waters, and filled a crevasse of blackened rocks with a lake. He regarded the dam with the same awe that Moran felt when he looked at the Canyon (and its 'colossal size' once more reminded him of the Ninth Symphony). He was unsure whether it could be called a work of art, but he revered it as a 'new creation', even though such technological wonders were usually 'engines of death'. Despite the pleasure boats that frolic on Lake Mead, the dam does look baleful. It is the river's sepulchre; the electric pylons drilled at irregular angles into the grim, chipped cliffs of lava crackle with tension. When the wartime fifth columnists in Hitchcock's *Saboteur* drive across the top of the dam wall, they smirk at the membrane of curved concrete, which seems to be buckling under the strain of all that water. The dam is still thought to be on the wish-list of terrorists, and a new highway is currently being constructed to by-pass it. Down the road in Las Vegas, the cycle of creation and destruction continues in a lagoon outside the Mirage Casino, where every half hour a custom-made volcano spews fire and coughs up clumps of weightless stone.

Priestley delayed his visit to the Grand Canyon because he wanted to prepare himself philosophically for what he expected would be a 'revelation'. In Santa Barbara he bought a copy of *A New Model of the Universe* by the Russian mystic and mathematician P. D. Ouspensky. The book – which he read in Death Valley – introduced him to the new physics, with its merger of space and time and its multiplied dimensions. Ouspensky conceived of the present moment as an 'instantaneous creation', a 'new universe' that implodes and dwindles into the past as soon as we become conscious of it. Time is therefore 'busy destroying and creating the world every fraction of a second'. When Priestley arrived at the Canyon, he applied Ouspensky's model to the vista. Could he, as a three-dimensional being, make sense of a four-dimensional phenomenon? The mind distends to make room for a dual infinitude – dilation in space, recession in time. Groping through fog at the rim, Priestley felt he was looking at 'some early creative effort in the mist of Time', and as he tottered down into the gulf along the Kaibab Trail on the back of a mule, he descended 'through one geological age after another'. By his application of Ouspensky, Priestley ensured that the place was his own cerebral collage. As he hiked between lookouts and tried to make the jarring angles add up, his physical toil and his light-headed, experimental thinking helped him to piece together an idea of the Canyon.

At the lodge on the rim, he made another equally fortuitous literary discovery. The bookshop had a copy of Kafka's *The Castle*, which he took with him on his excursion to Phantom Ranch at the bottom of the gulf. The novel – about a harassed land surveyor who scuttles through the streets of an intrigue-ridden town, trying to gain admittance to the castle that looms above – merged with the surroundings in which he read it. The sheer Canyon walls, which shut out the sky at night, might have induced a Kafkaesque paranoia; Priestley, however, preferred to interpret the landscape as a refutation of the book. He saw Kafka's hero as 'blundering humanity' in quest of 'divine grace', which of course he fails to find. The Canyon was kinder to Priestley. It offered him a vision of castellated heights bronzed or gilded by the afternoon sun, and calmed him with its silence and solitude. When he reached its floor, he washed off the dust in a 'clear stream of good drinking water' and felt he understood why the explorers named it Bright Angel Creek. Agape with amazement, he even ventured to describe the Canyon as 'His handiwork'. But prudence counselled him to use a capitalized pronoun, instead of naming God outright.

# 24

# THE FIRST ARTISTS

Other revelations occurred in narrower holes in the ground. In 1879 near Santander in Spain, a painted bestiary was discovered deep in a cave which a shepherd had first explored a decade earlier. The chamber lay beyond tortuous bends, and was so cramped that the work must have been done by painters lying flat on their backs. Deer, boar and bison – their musculature, fur and genitals picked out in red or yellow ochre, black manganese earth and charcoal – leapt or lumbered across the roof. The images hugged the uneven surface, so the animals seemed to swell into relief as if emerging from the rock. Some lines were incised or engraved into the limestone, to fix the design permanently. Printed hands had been left as signatures. Archaeologists dated the scenes which were dismissed as forgeries when they were reproduced. Darwin had established that our ancestors were brutes, so it seemed unlikely that images of such elegance and precision could have been made seventeen thousand years ago. Spanish Jesuits were suspected of plotting to embarrass the geologists who questioned biblical chronology. The sceptics relented when, at the end of the century, painted caves were also uncovered in the Dordogne. One of these, at Font de Gaume, is still open for viewing; here the menagerie – painted high up by artists who presumably constructed scaffolding – included horses, mammoths, reindeer and a lioness. In a nearby cave at Les Combarelles, forms that have been deciphered as a penis and a vagina were scratched onto the wall. Crude graffiti, like those in a lavatory cubicle, or magical emblems of creativity? Either way, the cave functioned as the repository for a secret knowledge, reserved for the initiated.

In 1940 at Lascaux in south-western France, four teenagers scrambled into an opening laid bare by a fallen tree. Clinging to a rope, they descended into the shaft and found themselves in the most elaborate of these iconographic catacombs. In the first hall, a creature like a unicorn chased a pack of horses along the walls; a bear bulged inside the stomach of a bull, which had been painted over it. Next came a gallery full of aurochs and ibexes, with a cow whose rear legs crumpled under it. In one alcove there were six hundred engraved figures, overlapping and superimposed. A well in the remotest recess contained the image of a dead man, stiffly laid out beside a bison he had speared. A rhinoceros fled in the opposite direction. Next to the prone man was a bird perched on long spindly legs: perhaps a spirit.

Even more mysterious were three geometrical blazons, their squares delicately coloured. Nature contains no perfect quadrants, so – unlike the hunting scenes elsewhere in the caves, or the image of stags apparently fording a river – they could not have been copied from the world above ground. In 1893 the Viennese art historian Aloïs Riegl proposed that art began as 'inorganic creation'; it had no need of external models, and its geometrical diagrams established that man was 'completely equal to nature', able to employ such ideal forms as a defence against 'the vast state of confusion in the world'. The blazons at Lascaux are evidence of abstract thought, just as the images of an upside-down horse or of two bison positioned back to back show a capacity to imagine how the same object differs depending on your angle of vision, as if the painter had been able to consult (or at least to conceive of) a reflection in a mirror. Reality is extended by fantasy: the so-called unicorn, a non-existent animal, actually has not one horn but two, and the impossibly long protrusions from its head resemble tense antennae not horns – telepathic projections, like signals sent out from the quickened imagination of a shaman. The unicorn is as synthetic as Horace's Chimaera. Brigitte and Gilles Deluc believe that it combines the torso of a rhinoceros, a bear's shoulders, a feline head and an equine tail.

The hands stencilled on the walls advertise this inventiveness, and mark a new, critical distance between mind and body. The painters sprayed colour from inside their mouths. Rather than waiting, like Adam, for an infusion of the divine breath, they exhaled that vital spirit, which left its trace in an image. The mind stood back, contemplating the handiwork it had designed. The surrealist George Bataille declared that Lascaux marked the birth of art; more than that, he thought that it announced the rebirth of man, who here demonstrated his ability to give ideas form and to communicate them. Bataille specified, in an essay published in 1955, that this creative feat had come 'out of nothing'. Homo sapiens overtook the animals by his own efforts, with no need of God's help. Apologists for Christianity had some frantic arguing to do if they were to keep up. G. K. Chesterton, writing after the first discoveries in the Dordogne, took heart from the fact that the paintings had been examined and accredited by the Abbé Henri Breuil, an anthropologist who had taken holy orders. It became almost compulsory to refer to the French caves as the Sistine Chapel of prehistory, and Breuil – as the archaeologist Joseph Déchelette remarked – was the officiating Pope. Another priest, Abbé André Glory, helped to excavate Lascaux; unsurprisingly, sections of the site were called apse and nave, in homage to the ground-plan of cathedrals. St Francis of Assisi, Chesterton said in 1925, might have made the drawings in the Dordogne 'out of pure and saintly love of animals'; unfortunately, the bison that sheds its entrails at Lascaux later disproved this claim. Chesterton fondly related a fable about an old lady who thought that the painted cave she had heard about must have been a crèche, with coloured animals drawn on the walls as companions for sleeping babies. He paid tribute to her credulity by making up a myth of his own, which connected those dank, crumbling grottos with the manger at Bethlehem. Christ was born in a cellar, and 'in that second creation ... God also was a Cave-Man, and had also traced strange shapes of creatures, curiously coloured, upon the wall of the world'. Those visionary pictures, Chesterton added with his usual bravura, subsequently came to life. But Lascaux robbed Christianity of this cinematographic privilege. Animation ripples through the beasts on the walls; the antlers of the stags are as delicate and tremulous as twigs, and the flanks of the bulls fatten as the images extend along the rugged walls. These proud, energetic animals are doomed to die: Breuil supposed that the paintings were made by hunters who hoped to improve their chances of success by this act of sympathetic magic. Meanwhile they suggest that art is both a frightened response to our own mortality and a victory over it. The paintings represent life, not a slab in a butcher's shop. The images escape from fixity and even from silence. A stag with priapic antlers lowers its head to emit a mating cry that is almost audible.

Bataille dismissed Breuil's dull utilitarian view that the paintings were a shopping list. Lascaux for him was a place of desecration, a laboratory in which art began to investigate the taboo-ridden subjects of sex and death. The caves are cryptic, which suggests that they must have been a place of transgression, guiltily hidden from the light. Bataille employed the usual architectural analogy, though he added a twist of his own. In the caves, as he argued in *Eroticism*, 'animal nature formed a cathedral', but the sacrificial rites enacted there were gory. Here was a place where 'human violence could be centred and condensed'. Why did our arrival at self-consciousness have to occur by torchlight in a subterranean sanctuary as tight as a grave? Bataille treated the invention of art as a defiant and deviant act, like the manifesto of a precocious decadence. Hunting is work, but the Lascaux painters, like the aesthetes of the 1890s, had reached a more advanced stage of human development: they were engaged in the activity of play. A stick with some animal bristles attached, employed as a paint brush, is not a utensil. Even so, it can serve as an imaginary weapon, and it allows the artists who wield it to fantasize about killing. Bataille associated this ludic delight with a new and seditious sexual pleasure, which stiffens and lengthens the penis of the man lying beside the bison. For animals, sex is merely a summons to reproduction. Once men became truly human – which happened, in Bataille's myth of origins, at Lascaux – they find it to be a source of unfunctional, unsanctified bliss; experienced with deadly intensity, it enabled them to enjoy a foretaste of death. Could this be the reason for that post-mortem erection? 'Poetry', as Bataille said in 1946, 'turns everything red.' It is flushed with blood, because its spirit is orgiastic. The cave paintings at Altamira in Cantabria are red, violet and also black; those at Lascaux have the same tonal range, and set the excited coursing of the blood against discoloured extinction. In Plato's *Republic*, an allegorical cave is a place of fiction and fantasy, where huddled men, their backs turned to the sun, study the misleading images cast on the walls by a fire. Plato criticized this rejection of daylight, but Bataille justified our stubborn preference for the fire not the sun. Plato's shadows symbolize error, and tauntingly remind us our of mental frailty. The Lascaux images have a bolder and more thrillingly positive significance: they display the imagination's power, not its folly.

As a surrealist, Bataille was attracted to the idea of nothingness, which he associated with a physical aperture, a chasm more clenched than that described by Hesiod. On a visit to the London Zoo in 1927 he ogled the rumps of monkeys, wishing he could probe the mystery they guarded. He even thought of the sun as an anal eye, a sphincter tightly clenched to prevent us from finding out what lay beyond it. At Lascaux, he was able to explore the darkness in which artists do their dreaming. His guesswork has been more soberly confirmed by David Lewis-Williams, who studies rock art and its role in prehistoric religion. For Lewis-Williams, the forking and branching arcades at Lascaux resemble a neurological vortex, a place where the initiate would have experienced 'psychic entry into deeply altered states of consciousness'. The tunnels are cranial, and their walls served as porous, permeable membranes, stretched tight over a world of spirits that lay just behind the rock. Hence the practice of engraving the surface, or the splinters of bone inserted into the walls. The artists were seers, engaged – as Lewis-Williams says in *The Mind in the Cave* – in a 'vision quest' that put them in touch with the divine or devilish powers whose lair lay here in the underworld. They needed the walls as a defensive bulwark, which is why they fortified them with painted images, but they also strove to find a way through that barrier. Their metaphysical curiosity helps to explain the ambition of art, which like a mode of second sight spies on the invisible and imagines things we have been forbidden to look at. Breuil thought that the scene in the well commemorated a hunting accident, during which the bison gored the fallen man. Lewis-Williams concentrates instead on the victim's relationship with the staff lying beside him, which has a bird perched on it. The man has the same small beaky head as the bird, and his four-fingered hands look like a bird's feet. Is the staff a shaman's implement, and the bird a familiar spirit? Perhaps the image catches a metamorphosis. A man in a trance is being transformed into a bird, made ready for a flight into the realms behind the walls, and his erection points beyond life to an undiscovered country in which life may continue.

The cave paintings placed on display the origins of art. For this reason they were of compelling interest to modern artists, whose plan was to cancel art's official history and return to its beginnings. Aldous Huxley claimed in 1927 that 'the horses and bisons on the walls of the palaeolithic cave-man's dwelling might have been painted by an artist of the twentieth century – that is, if there were any contemporary artists with sufficient talent to paint them.' Huxley's sarcasm missed its target, because contemporary artists agreed with him and deferred to their archaic predecessors. André Breton said that the hand-prints in the caves marked 'man's first surrender to his creative demon', the moment at which the subject willed himself to become an object. In 1952 in a cave at Perch-Merle near Cabrerets in the Lot, Breton caused a scandal by touching one of the fragile paintings. When he removed his finger, it had a dab of wet paint on it: could the designs after all be a recent hoax? The stain was actually due to the humid air, which was causing the images to flake off the walls. But Breton's small act of vandalism demonstrated that artists still had the same determination to leave their imprint on the world. He also pointed out that the belated uncovery of the caves turned them into up-to-date amenities. The war sent Europeans running to bomb shelters, and during the 1950s Americans began to construct nuclear bunkers in their basements or back gardens: history had progressed in a circle, since men were now reverting to troglodytes.

The caves excited Picasso because they showed that art began as sorcery, harnessing supernatural forces. He disparaged the meticulous fashioning and finishing of images, exemplified by classical statues. Artists, he thought, should concentrate instead on the possibilities that could be discerned 'in a bone, in the irregular surfaces of cave walls, in a piece of wood. One form might suggest a woman, another a bison, and still another the head of a demon'. Imagination is the capacity to see spirits, and to release them into reality. Picasso's friend Brassaï illustrated the point in his photographs of urban graffiti. The city was an extension of the caves, marked with the same elementary emblems. On urban walls, faces gaped or leered, with pock-marked craters dug out of brick for their eyes and mouths. Genitals cavorted, having escaped from their owners. These scars and scrawls were memories of ancient ogres we must placate, grubby reminiscences of the fertility rites that sustain nature. Brassaï noted that the animals at Altamira owed their bulk to the bumpy contours of the rock on which they were painted. The wall, as he saw it, participated in or even ordained this creation. On flat surfaces like paper or canvas, we can duplicate reality. A stone wall is never so obligingly blank, and does not lend itself to replicas and diagrams; it already contains a living energy, with which the artist must tussle. The wild children responsible for defacing Paris shared the bravado of the cave artists, who used paint to give form to bodies buried in the walls, or gouged holes to penetrate that reservoir of spirit. When Brassaï published a book of graffiti, Picasso likened those abused façades to a cathedral encrusted with obscene gargoyles.

Giorgio de Chirico tried to think himself back into the mood of numinous terror that must have possessed a shaman in the caves. The understanding of that haunted state came to him at Versailles in 1913: although apparently the most pompously civilized of locations, the palace with its dead columns and blind windows could suddenly estrange itself from human purposes and present 'eternal proof of the irrationality of the universe'. Trembling as he advanced through the mirrored galleries or stiffly formal gardens, de Chirico reported that he 'grew aware of the mystery which urges men to create certain strange forms. ... Perhaps the most amazing sensation passed on to us by prehistoric man is that of presentiment'. Realism, which secularized the world of appearances, deprived artists of their ability to decipher the uncanny, unhomely signs that perplex and threaten us. De Chirico hoped to win back that primal cunning. Cities with their neoclassical vistas or yawningly vacant squares became, when he painted them, as scary as the defiles at Altamira or Lascaux. The empty streets fill up with hallucinations; our psychological survival depends on our capacity to identify the shapes that loom in the darkness and enlist them as protectors. Art ought to be a matter of life and death: de Chirico thought that the compulsion to paint should be like 'the hungry desperation which drives a man to tearing at a piece of bread like a savage beast'. Removing human beings from his urban scenes or reducing them to fugitive shadows, he attempted to revive a time even remoter than that of the cave painters, when 'man did not yet exist'.

In 1942 the Dadaist Hans Arp made up his own story about the beginnings of art, and took care to ensure that it predated the painted caves. He denounced the evidence of a humanized world that so impressed Bataille; for Arp, Lascaux and Altamira were already too decorative and effete. The caves were a false start, because they established a stale repertory of still lifes, landscapes and nudes that artists have served up ever since. Arp looked further back for 'an art based on fundamentals', which he imitated in his doodled ideograms and biomorphic blobs. He made the customary link between caves and cathedrals, but used it critically: it was in these dens that man began to deify himself, indulging a vanity that led at last to the twentieth century's catastrophic wars and its industrial trampling of nature. Arp set out to shatter this conceit, to pull the angels down from their gilded ceiling and to obliterate all the beautiful 'heads of Adam'. His imaginary caves had no gallery of portraits on the walls; they were filled with boulders, like the sculptures which he called 'concretions' – bulbous torsos carved in marble or cast in bronze. These were the signatures of living things, spoors left in the snow by animals that belonged to no particular species. Kasimir Malevich attributed the same aim to the unrepresentational paintings of the Russian Suprematists. Like the first men, he said, they wanted to leave a footstep on the windblown sand.

Each school of modernists made up its own legitimizing myth. Barnett Newman established a primordial lineage for the abstract expressionists by combining Jewish tales of the creation with local, American references to the hides painted by the Kwakiutl tribes of the Pacific north-west. 'Undoubtedly,' declared Newman in 1947, 'the first man was an artist.' To him, the cave paintings proved 'the necessity for dream', documenting nocturnal fantasy rather than tallying the day's kill. The ancestors he imagined, unlike those described in de Chirico's reverie at Versailles, did not wander mutely through a world of enigmas. They expressed themselves – first in a 'poetic outcry', inarticulate but eloquent like a dog barking at the moon or a loon calling as it glides over a lake; much later, the same urgent, aggressive motive, 'directed by a ritualistic will to metaphysical understanding', prompted Jackson Pollock to throw paint at a canvas. The aborigines in Newman's fable yell vowels, which, like the howling of King Lear over the body of Cordelia, are a protest at their 'tragic state'. Newman refused to believe that 'the first man called the sun and the stars *God* … only after he had finished his day's labour', and insisted that our early fumbling efforts to invent language were 'an address to the unknowable'. Wonder, with its mixed ingredients of 'awe and anger', predates the docile prayers recited by Adam and Eve in *Paradise Lost*. Babies wail as they arrive in the world; the first human beings must surely have raised their voices in terror as they tried to understand their castaway state and to confront what Newman called 'the void'. No God spoke from the sky to tell them who they were or why they had been created. They had to fashion him, and Newman – for whom 'the aesthetic act always precedes the social one' – presumed that they 'built an idol of mud' long before they fashioned an axe. Mud was for Newman a pleasing primary material. It could be moulded into a statuette, but was no use for cutting or killing. Tools and weapons came later, when man the artist became a social being and began fabricating instruments that would help him to commit murder. Newman applied this genealogy to lengths of wood, probably the first armament employed by 'original man': 'his hand traced the stick through the mud to make a line before he learned to throw the stick as a javelin'.

Genesis was for Newman the earliest testimony to 'human desires' and 'the human dream'. It could not be the faithful record of God's agenda, transcribed by Moses. The book derived, Newman guessed, from the 'creative impulses' of an archaic writer who rationalized his own need to be an artist by questioning Adam's role as a toiler, a meek gardener. The labour prescribed by God was unacceptable, and in America – where 'some of us', as Newman said, were 'free from the weight of European culture' – the gloomy moral impositions of religion could finally be cast off. Newman saw it as his personal obligation to continue Adam's aborted search for 'the creative life'. 'What,' he asked, 'is the explanation of the seemingly insane drive of man to be a painter or a poet if it is not an act of defiance against man's fall and an assertion that he return to the Adam of the Garden of Eden? For the artists are the first men.' In the years immediately after these proclamations, he made good his claim by painting our honorary parents – *Eve* in 1950, *Adam* in 1951–2. The tonality of his canvases honours the soil from which man formed and the blood ('dam' in Hebrew, according to the Kabbalah's lexicon) that flows through him. But Newman's ancestors are not anthropomorphs. The painting with Eve's name is a field of red with a purple stripe on its right side, while Adam is a brown expanse, broken by several red stripes. The sudden, abrupt uprights semaphore a human presence, with all the instability it introduces into the material world. Those vertical intrusions stand for the aspiring energy of the spirit; they are the vectors of creative yearning. The portrait has been replaced by what Newman called an 'ideograph', a starkly symbolic gesture. Language, as he knew, deals in signs not words. It is 'an animal power', which we share with dogs, birds and all of our noisy colleagues in nature; we screamed, snarled and perhaps laughed long before we thought of writing poems. 'Man's first cry,' according to Newman, 'was a song', and these paired paintings attempt to sing their subjects into life. They are actions performed by a shaman, whose incantation contains the formula for existence.

In Newman's renovated Genesis, the fruit of the forbidden tree enables us 'to be, like God, "a creator of worlds"'. Renaissance humanists made the same confident boast, and so did the Promethean romantics when they shook their fists at the sky. But how can the artist attain divine status if he has denied God's existence? Newman admits that the ambition is irresistible but futile. 'Write,' Razumov in Joseph Conrad's *Under Western Eyes* orders himself. 'Must write! ... I must write – I must, indeed! I shall write – never fear'. He knows that it will make no difference. The art we compulsively create can never deliver the certainty we crave. One of the clowns in Beckett's *Waiting for Godot* is pleased that his tired routines have passed the time; the other dolefully comments that it would have passed anyway. When art measures itself against the universe, it dwindles – like the individual who makes it – to a grain of dust, or to a reverberation in the emptiness. In E. M. Forster's *A Passage to India*, a cave is the setting for this negative epiphany. Forster sends his characters on a pointless excursion to the Marabar Caves near Chandrapore. They are unsure about what they are travelling to see, since the caves contain no sculptures, are not ornamented, and – as a wise

Brahman comments – have no reputation for holiness. In fact these hollows absorb and extinguish both art and religion. A rumbling, monotonous echo crushes the air out of any lines of 'lofty poetry' that a visitor might declaim when inside; depressed and sickened, Mrs Moore hears the utterances of 'poor little talkative Christianity' – an anthology of quotations extending from 'Let there be light' to 'It is finished' – undergo suffocation. Seen in the perspective of eternity, Newman's 'insane drive' loses its grandiose fury. Our desire to make sense of the world is for Forster no more than the reflex of an 'itch for the seemly', as if we were over-fussily tidying up a parlour. Mrs Moore glimpses 'the abyss', but the caves deprive it of infinitude. Even chaos – exemplified by the calamitous farce that results from a sexual assault that may or may not have occured in the caves – is trivialized when Forster reclassifies it as 'muddle'.

In the myth of origins, the cave is usually a matrix or – as Chesterton said in his commentary on Bethlehem – a protective cradle. Forster's cave is more like a gullet which indiscriminately swallows people. As soon as they disappear, the planet returns to the way it looked 'before man ... had been born'. Then the orifice belches to expel the intruders, and 'humanity returned'. But the men and women thrust back onto the surface are demoralized, deconstellated. Somehow they must find the energy to set out again on the exhausting trek that will end, if they are lucky, in the creation of art and the invention of God.

# 25

# PRIME MOVERS

Writers imagine that the world was spoken into being, by God when he called for light or by Milton when he dictated *Paradise Lost* to his daughters. For musicians, a word is not enough: the order must be intoned, as it is by Haydn's sunburst of C major in *Die Schöpfung*. 'The first thing God thought of in creating the world,' mused Rodin, 'was the model. It's funny, isn't it, to make God a sculptor?' Jacob Epstein, equally flattered by the notion that God was a precursor, called his autobiography *Let There Be Sculpture*. The genealogy of another art claims an even closer connection with our origins, because it eliminates the gap between creator and creation: Nietzsche refused to believe in a god who did not dance.

While Christianity and Platonism prefer the prime mover to be staidly motionless, other gods dance the world into existence and keep it infused with life by rhythmically agitating their limbs. This is one function of Shiva, worshipped by Hindus as a creator who doubles as a destroyer. Ted Shawn, who in 1926 toured India with his wife Ruth St Denis, performed his Cosmic Dance of Shiva Nataraja at the god's temple near Madras; he felt he was acting out 'the *rhythmic* process of Being-Becoming'. He perfected the skipping postures and rippling elasticity required by the rite, but needed an extra set of arms – supplied, in a photographic memento of the event, by a sculptural frieze – to transmit his will to the burgeoning universe. Such dances co-opted the god's creativity, and transferred it to the artist's limbre body. Shawn thought that 'when a man has the sense of being a creator, he shares in the function of god-head'. Mary Wigman, who opened a school in Dresden in 1920, credited dancers with inventing and owning the 'imaginary, irrational space of the danced dimension'. Arms and legs quicken the dead, empty atmosphere around them, and the human body limitlessly extends 'like rays, like streams, like breath'. Wigman called this 'the spatial embrace': a maternal enfolding of the world, very different from the patriarchal supervision maintained by God in Genesis.

When D. H. Lawrence attended the Hopi snake dance at a pueblo north of Santa Fe in the summer of 1924, he expected to see a spectacle 'more Hindu than Hopi', with live rattlesnakes dangling from the mouths of the dancers. What he witnessed – a stamping, spitting entreaty to the earth, beseeching it to send rain – convinced him that the natives of New Mexico were animists, who believed in 'no Father' and 'no Maker', 'no One

Ted Shawn and Ruth St Denis pose in Oriental costume, *c.* 1920

God' and 'no Creator'. For them, there was 'strictly no God at all: because all is alive'. The pounding feet of the dancers bullied the corn to make it grow, and their shaking arms implored the sun to go on shining. The day Lawrence spent in the pueblo convinced him that 'gods are the outcome, not the origin'. This, he thought, was 'the religion of all aboriginal America' and 'perhaps

*Dance*, sketch by D. H. Lawrence, 1929

the aboriginal religion of all the world'. Gods 'do not exist beforehand', like our human ancestors; 'they are created and evolved gradually', by obsessively reiterated invocations like those in the snake dance. Lawrence concluded that 'the only gods on earth are men'. In the same year the anthropologist Ruth Benedict began to study the people of the Zuni pueblo in New Mexico, whose dances, she said, relied on an entranced rhythmic repetition to give them power over nature. In 1936 the black choreographer Katherine Dunham travelled to Haiti to study its danced religion, which asserted 'the unity between man and his gods'; she even converted to the cult of Vodum, or Voodoo. The film-maker Maya Deren, who was initiated as a Voodoo priestess on one of her visits to Haiti between 1947 and 1954, thought again about the relations between cult and culture after taking part in the ritual. Voodoo singers owed their power to the goddess who had taken possession of them: they were, as Deren said, 'divine virtuosi'. Here the creator was no longer a solitary individual, because Haiti, with its concerted drumming and its massed dancers, established 'the collective as creative artist'.

An intellectual impetus for such quests came from Havelock Ellis's *The Dance of Life*, published in 1923. The book begins with a summons to dithyrambic revelry: 'To dance is ... to imitate the gods, to work with them. ... To dance is to take part in the cosmic control of the world.' The dance was at once theological and erotic, a mode of worship and a sublimation of pent-up desire. As a psychologist of sexuality, Ellis traced the creative urge – responsible, he said, for 'finest elements in art, in morals, in civilization generally' – to 'the auto-erotic impulse', which devises games to relieve a blocked libido. He even explained Genesis as an exercise in Freudian narcissism, whereby 'Man created God in his own image'. Six days were spent in 'active creational work', while the seventh was set aside for an interlude of aesthetic appreciation and self-congratulation. Ellis disparaged the Hebraic notion that a cosmos 'could be fashioned out of nothing, in a measurable period of time' by the methodical artificer Jehovah. He preferred the Samoan stories of creation, which extended throughout time the task of forming the earth and made it 'genuinely evolutionary'. *The Dance of Life* extols 'Man as the active creator of life ..., the artist of the world'. Dance asserts this cosmic control because its rotations mimic planetary orbits and maintain their stability. The ancient Chaldeans of Mesopotamia staged dances that were astronomical diagrams. Distributed across a plain, the performers adopted positions corresponding to those of the stars; the dance was a lesson in calendrical science. Writing to Edward Gordon Craig in 1905, Isadora Duncan likened their sexual attraction to 'magnetic forces – same things that keep the earth circling round the sun'. Whenever we

reconceive the universe, we necessarily rechoreograph the dance of life. Ellis pointed out that Einstein's expounding of his new physics was immediately preceded by the arrival of Diaghilev's Ballets Russes in Paris. He refused to believe that this was coincidental, though he said no more about it. The possibility is alluring: could there really be an affinity between Einstein's space-time and the polyrhythmic frenzy of Stravinsky's *Le Sacre du printemps* or *Les Noces*, which set tempi of terrifying complexity for the dancers?

Ellis's dance of life synchronized the planets, and also regulated the pulsing of organic life on earth. In 1928 Karl Blossfeldt published a collection of

Arnold Genthe,
Isadora Duncan,
1915

photographs called *Urformen der Kunst*, which presented plants as rudimentary works of art. A delphinium writhes in rococo curlicues; a prickly acanthus gesticulates with half a dozen arms; a clematis has the beak of a raptor, through which a pointed tongue pokes. In his preface, Karl Nierendorf said that those exploratory tendrils and flagrantly carnal flowers placed on view 'the hidden powers of Creation'. Blossfeldt's title suggested that art is modelled on such germinal forms, and for Nierendorf the theory was proven true by dance, which 'finds a parallel in the unfurling bud'; the

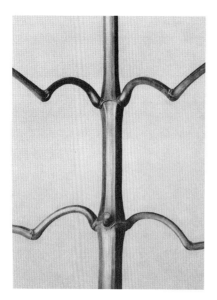

*Impatiens
Glanduligera
(Hardy Indian
Balsam stem),*
from *Urformen
der Kunst,* by Karl
Blossfeldt, 1928

dancer's elasticized limbs show nature regenerating itself, and reveal that art is a 'second creation'. Romantic ballet, with its ethereal leaps, aspired to the sky. The dances admired by Ellis were tethered to the earth, in which, like Blossfeldt's plants, we are rooted. Ted Shawn admired the uncouth stamping of peasants, whose feet thumped the ground as if tenderizing meat, and believed that Greek drama had its origins in the cavorting of farmers as they threshed and trampled wheat.

Waves beat on the shore at precise metrical intervals, as Ellis noted; Isadora Duncan claimed that she had learned how to dance by watching the movement of waves at Ocean Beach in San Francisco. Ruth St Denis impersonated *The Spirit of the Sea*: dressed in green, with her white hair tossed to and fro like foam on a wave and streamers trailing from her arms, she established a slow, implacable rhythm which Shawn said was 'as large as the cosmos'. Shawn called her perform- ance a marvel of 'space creation', as if with her pendular rocking she were setting limits for the ocean. The matriarchs of modern dance, taking over from the abstracted male God of Genesis, dramatized the physical process of creation. Hence Isadora's pelvic thrusts and the undulations of her limbs. Craig identified the soul with the dancer's centre of gravity: here lay the body's motive force – its 'motrix' as Craig called it, and also its matrix. Isadora modelled herself on Isis, the Egyptian goddess of fertility whose fes- tivals coincided with the flooding of the Nile. The overflow, according to the myth, represented the tears Isis shed for her brother Osiris. She could irrigate a desert, just as Osiris, the god of corn, could make food sprout from it. In 1913 three of Isadora's children were drowned when the car in which they were travelling toppled into the Seine; later, reflecting on her grief, she described it as an ecstasy of sorrow which was 'the Mother Cry of Creation'. Martha Graham took an even more frankly gynaecological view of this lying-in. In 1947 she danced the role of Jocasta in *Night Journey*, her version of the Oedipus story. When she met the son she will marry, Graham's Jocasta thrust her leg into the air in recognition: she called the movement 'the cry from her vagina'. Sceptics found Graham's bony angu- larity hard to reconcile with obstetrics. The critic Stark Young said that her violent kicks and clenched withdrawals made her look 'as though she were about to give birth to a cube'.

The drama of Mary's impregnation intrigued female dancers: Isadora choreographed Schubert's *Ave Maria*, and Miriam Winslow, who opened a school in Boston in 1929, performed the *Magnificat* in which Mary gives thanks for the angel's annunciation. Male dancers imagined fulfilments of their own. In 1950 in New York, Frederick Ashton choreographed *Les Illuminations*, using Benjamin Britten's setting of Rimbaud's ecstatic poems. A tenor in the orchestra pit described stretching ropes between steeples and linking the stars in golden chains, and then – in a slithering, swooning vocal cadenza – cried 'Je danse!' At that moment on stage, the dancer Nicholas Magellanes hurled confetti in the air, and let brightness rain down on him. The milky way had been reinvented: the spangled shower was like a spray of galactic semen.

Shawn once met a man from the Zuni pueblo in a hotel ballroom, where he was casting a cold eye on the bored, automatized couples on the floor. Dancers at the pueblo, as Shawn remembered, had to fast and purify themselves before becoming 'vessels of the divine consciousness'. Every hour during their ceremonies they rested and prayed, to ensure that they would 're-enter the dance as consecrated beings'. This monastic devotion appealed to Shawn, who was a student of divinity before he met Ruth St Denis. He was heartened by Havelock Ellis's account of Christian worship as 'a divine Pantomime'; in earlier centuries, as Shawn often pointed out, priests used to jig and sway in the choir while celebrating mass, although now the cramped, stiffly disciplinary pews of Christian churches forbade movement, and only the Holy Rollers were bold enough to gyrate in the aisles. When Shawn's company danced at a church service in Shreveport, Louisiana, a posse of scandalized preachers threatened to tar and feather him. To appease the bigots, he insisted that his version of a Bach chorale gave 'absolutely the purest and cleanest feeling imaginable'. Introducing Arnold Genthe's photographic album of Isadora and her followers in 1920, Shaemas O'Sheel bravely hoped for a reconciliation between paganism and Christianity. Would the church allow the body to be unashamedly stripped naked, set free to delight 'the Creator of its flaming beauties, the Moulder of its thrilling lines, the Fashioner of its supple limbs, the First Lover of its warmth and passion'? It seemed unlikely; much more than a single letter separates the Platonic First Mover from O'Sheel's First Lover.

Dancers therefore adhered to more permissive religions. Isadora was faithful to classical Greece. She performed on the uneven, overgrown paving stones of the Temple of Dionysus in 1903, imitating the postures of the maenads on Greek vases. With her extended family, she even began to construct a temple on a hill across from the Acropolis, and recruited local boys to sing choral music from Euripides' *Bacchae*. St Denis and Shawn looked further east, and found a pretext for their 'divine ballet' in the myths of Japan and India. Amaterasu, the Japanese goddess of the sun, hid in a cave and denied her light to the world; she was lured out by the dancing of a relative, whose animated prayer is re-enacted by Shinto priestesses. Krishna, as Shawn reported, disclosed that 'the chief activity of the gods is dancing'. Encouraged by a friend who told him that Hindus liked to 'play with God', Shawn clambered onto a sculpted squatting lion at Mahabalipuram and posed as a slim-hipped, elegantly limbre Shiva, while St Denis attached bells to her ankles and pretended to be a temple maiden. Another member of their company, with a lotus flower tucked into her jewelled belt and a helmet of blooms, performed a dance that brought to life the bas reliefs of the Buddhist shrine at Angkor Wat in Cambodia. Hinduism freed Shawn from his reverence for the 'dull dignity' of the Christian God. In Tibet, at least before the arrival of Buddhist missionaries, people managed to do without the 'idea of any central deity or deities'. Instead they believed in a promiscuous rabble of spirits who pervaded nature, ordained the weather and sent diseases; these demons could be exorcized by dancing. The Santal community in central India danced to coax the earth into bearing fruit, caressing the ground with wild palms. The villagers, according to Shawn, had 'no written language, no definite code of theology, no graphic or plastic arts'. But they danced, which proved Ellis's point that this was 'the source-art of the human race'.

The social anthropologist Geoffrey Gorer, who visited Senegal in 1934, made a similarly blunt declaration about the entire continent: 'Africans have only one art. ... First and last Africans dance'. He had made up his mind about this in advance, because he was invited to go on the expedition by Féral Benga, a black dancer who performed ethnic bump-and-grind routines at the Folies Bergère. (Benga's given name was actually François; when he moved to Paris he changed it to Féral, which was synonymous with savagery.) Gorer was delighted by the carnality of African dancing. At a totemic ceremony in Javara he saw a masked dancer 'making wicked mockery of Mohammedans and Christians at their worship'. Everywhere he noted analogies with the frank modern paganism of Diaghilev's company. The remorselessly precise war dances of the Dapango on the Ivory Coast reminded him of the Polovtsian revels in Borodin's *Prince Igor*, which the Ballets Russes had performed; a gradual crescendo of the drums, increasing to 'almost unbearable speed', recalled the murderous frenzy of Stravinsky's *Sacre du printemps*.

At Ouangaladougou, with thunder rumbling in the sky, Gorer saw men and women who were naked except for their loincloths or necklaces of red seeds perform a fertility dance, which they exhilaratingly embellished with cartwheels and forward somersaults. The men mimed swaggering cocks or virile bulls, and whistled as they acted out 'the copulation of various beasts and birds'. Exultant shouts defied the thunderclaps. At last the storm released a steamy downpour, and drummers led the way home. Gorer might have been describing *La Création du monde*, a specimen of African cosmology which the Ballets Suédois presented in Paris in 1923. The ballet's scenario, taken from the *Anthologie nègre* by Blaise Cendrars, had proper tribal credentials. On a visit to the British Museum in 1916, Cendrars had been impressed by the African fetishes: a wooden man who worships his erect penis, a woman whose full belly is like a baking oven for bread. Such totems, as Gorer explained, represented aspects of 'the Creator of all things'. That originating god, called Maou in Dahomey, could not be pictured or sculpted, so the fetishes served as his deputies, mediating between heaven and earth. The word tells its own acute, analytical story about religion and art. It means magic in Portuguese, although it also more pejoratively refers to things that are artificial (or, in Latin, factitious). It was applied by the Portuguese colonists to the gods of West Africa and to the charms that bribed these spirits to work their magic. But behind the word lies a Latin verb meaning to make. Could these exotic gods be considered makers, or were they only made things, rude idols? Cendrars' anthology of myths set the museum's fetishes into motion and showed them performing their creative chores; he added an extra volume to be read by children, since while we are growing up our keenest mental concern is to know where we came from and how the world itself came to be.

For his 'ballet nègre' the composer Darius Milhaud chose a legend from the Congo. In the beginning, Cendrars envisaged a black stage, with a saxophone mournfully wailing in the darkness. The sun was not a precondition for creation, as in Genesis. Light started to glimmer as living forms separated themselves from the murk. It glowed brighter with the appearance of each new creature, as if generated by the vital warmth shared between the plants rearing up on the earth and the animals spreading out across it. The initiating creator remained unseen, perhaps because – as Lawrence claimed in his commentary on the snake dance – we are wrong to personify him. He is an urge, an instinct, whose emissaries in the ballet were three giants named Nzame, Medere and N'kva. They acted as the managers or administrators of creation, like the 'Potencies or Powers' invoked by Lawrence when he tries to conceive of 'the terrific, terrible crude Source' that was 'the well-head of all things'. Masked by Fernand Léger's chunky abstract head-dresses, the giants had no faces, and they perambulated at a slow, grave pace prescribed by the music: creation here was a process, an almost monotonous toil, not the series of decisive, grandiloquent acts – the sudden blazing of light, the monarchical entry of Adam – marked by Haydn in *Die Schöpfung*. As the saxophone transcribed their chants, the figures circled around an undifferentiated, heaving scrum, a lump of latent existence. Milhaud called this the 'toho-bohu' that preceded creation; in Lawrence's terms it was the 'egg of chaos' from which men and all other beings hatched. A quarrelsome fugue for the trumpet, trombone and saxophone caught the turmoil inside this muddle of raw material. A sinuous blues melody from the oboe enticed a tree to grow. Having climbed into the air, it dropped a seed, which lengthened, rocked to and fro, then got up and walked: the vegetable world, surpassing itself, created an animal. A trilling flute accelerated the pace, and a violin proposed a jig. A tortoise and a crab crawled out of chaos, along with an elephant and a gaggle of chattering monkeys. A toucan and a parrot flapped tropical plumage, while Milhaud's jazz band let loose a cacophony of mating calls. Birds perambulated on stilts; earth-bound animals scuttled on all fours. Nzame, Medere and N'kva then uttered new incantations over the unformed mass. A leg, arms, and a hairy head protruded at angles. Two torsos straightened up and detached themselves; man and woman, created together, at once settled into what Milhaud called a 'dance of desire', accompanied by piano and violin. The N'guils, described by Cendrars as sorcerers and fetishists, also broke free from the collective mound to join in a raucous party. The ballet ended with the first humans kissing, as wind instruments sighed in sympathy. Thanks to the force of sexual desire, creation could now be left to its own devices.

Milhaud composed *La Création du monde* for an orchestra of nineteen soloists, modelled on the bands in Harlem cabarets. He thought that jazz had 'roots in the most remote elements of the black soul, in vestigial African traces', and Léger likewise set out to design 'African deities expressive of power and darkness'. But *La Création du monde* was less primitive than futuristic; it may have fantasized about the jungle, but its true setting was the modern industrial city. Léger adored the 'harsh and tragic atmosphere' of dance halls in the Paris slums, where factory workers with faces as hard as medals, toughened by poverty and vice, scowled as they twisted themselves into elegant attitudes, and the shapes on his backdrop – cranes, grids of chain-mail, tall fuming chimneys – were closer to engineering than to vegetation. The ballet's strict, solemn, repetitive rhythms suggested the kind of coordination imposed by an assembly line.

Léger had already designed *Skating Rink* for the Ballets Suédois. With a score by Arthur Honegger – a connoisseur of speed, who drove a Bugatti – this used the whirling gyrations of the roller-skaters as a symbol of mad, accident-prone modern life. The rollers in *Skating Rink* looked, according to the librettist Ricciotto Canudo, like the buskins worn by actors in the Greek theatre; the body masks Léger designed for *La Création du monde* resembled armour, stiffening the dancers and rendering them invulnerable. He alluded to tribal carvings when sketching his trio of African giants, but they came out resembling mechanomorphs, ten feet tall with angle-poised necks, perpendicular heads, jutting shoulders and feet like mallets. The carapaces worn by the dancers ensured, as Léger said, that they lost their 'human proportions'. Even the first man and woman looked robotic. Léger actually wanted to entrust the work of creation to a mechanical gadget. As the tree ballooned into life, he intended to inflate a series of goldbeater's skins representing plants and animals; puffed up with gas, they would float free across the stage. He was overruled, because the gas cylinders that blew up the balloons would have been louder than the orchestra. All the same, Léger was right to connect the myth of creation with the strife and clamour of heavy industry. The mobility of dancers sometimes turned them into streaky emissions of energy. Loïe Fuller, who performed at the Folies Bergère during the 1890s, whirled inside a cocoon of cloth while electricity flashed and sparked around her; the poet Mallarmé described her routine as 'an industrial achievement'.

In the same year that *La Création du monde* was performed, Havelock Ellis suggested that 'primitive combined work', which trained the muscles by repetition, was 'a kind of dance'. Ellis used what he called his 'Yo-heave-ho theory' to explain the raising of megaliths like Stonehenge or the pyramids; this, he added, was why the Greeks credited Orpheus, the first poet and singer, with the power to move stones and trees. D. H. Lawrence, explaining the religion of the Hopi dancers, could not help using imagery that recalled the scorching heat of romantic mills and mines. The cosmos was 'a vast and violent matrix', but Lawrence also likened this blood-warmed womb to 'a great furnace'. Here, as in Blake's poem about the tiger, gods and men were made 'out of the fire and smelting of life', with rain as the anvil, thunder as the hammer, and cyclonic wind as the bellows: in the beginning was the foundry. A dance could also disarm the machines that menaced the human body. Once, crossing the RKO lot, Fred Astaire stopped in his tracks to dance in competition with a cement mixer, and exactly matched its rhythm as it regurgitated gravel. In *Shall We Dance* he strolls into the laminated engine-room of a transatlantic liner, challenges its chugging pistons and whirring fly wheels to combat, and triumphantly out-taps them.

As Loïe Fuller demonstrated by imitating a butterfly, dance sketches diagrams in thin air. Nothing, surely, could be further from the laying of the foundations that are necessary to a created world. Yet Ellis linked dance with architecture, whose gravity and solidity it seems to spurn. 'Dancing and building,' he said, 'are the two primary and essential arts. ... There is no primary art outside these two arts, for their origin is far earlier than man himself; and dancing came first.' It is an evanescent architecture, gesturing towards the conquest of space that will later be completed by immobile stone. In 1921 Edward Steichen persuaded Isadora to stand in a portal at the

Loïe Fuller
dancing,
anonymous
photograph

Parthenon and raise her arms above her head. Clasped, they formed a protective roof, like a triangular pediment. She was 'related to the columns', as
Steichen said; she might almost have designed them, and caused them to
extrude from her long, imperious limbs. Steichen encouraged her to toss
her head backwards and fling her arms out sideways like compasses. Her
winged attitude takes hold of the pitted, dented columns and the bright sky
they frame, bringing space within our reach.

Hollywood films offered more homespun proof of Ellis's claim about
the architectonic power of dance. In John Ford's *My Darling Clementine*,
released in 1946, the citizens of Tombstone – a settlement consisting
of one rickety street arbitrarily deposited between the eroded tumuli of
Monument Valley – hold their 'first social gathering' to raise funds to complete a church. Wyatt Earp (Henry Fonda) marvels that a pile of fresh-cut
lumber can be arranged into a house for God; a grizzled elder assures him
that the roof will soon be on. A bell tolls from a tower that is as yet only
skeletal scaffolding, a distant organ wheezes, and the townspeople sing of
gathering at a river that, here in the desert, remains a mirage. Foundations
have been raised in the dust: a floor of planks, guarded by two American
flags. By the time Earp arrives, the religious service is over. A fiddler declares

the First Church of Tombstone dedicated, even though it still has no preacher. Then – since the good book, as he says, has 'nary a word agin dancing' – he strikes up a tune. The square dance, with its amiable and unpossessive exchange of partners, is the true act of consecration. Dance, as Ellis argued, socializes mankind. The rite is performed all over again in Oregon in *Seven Brides for Seven Brothers*, directed in 1954 by Stanley Donen with choreography by Michael Kidd; this time, however, the spatial charm hardly manages to tame wildness. Two rival clans raise a barn by willing the walls upright with their nimble, aggressive feet. They dance on a plank, performing back flips and somersaults without falling off the wobbly board. One of them even skips over the axe that has chopped down trees and turned them into beams. Together they strain to heave the sides of the building into place, and then – because the cooperative fiction of society is so fragile – they pull it down again during a gymnastic brawl.

Popular dances, unburdened by priestly solemnity, admitted the shakiness of creation and the allure of destruction. Perhaps this was why Shawn disapproved of tap dancing, which did not so much create space as batter it into submission. In *Top Hat* Astaire slays an army of dandies by discharging a barrage of imaginary gunfire from his cane; he pounds his metal-cleated feet to count out the bullets. In *Holiday Inn* he scatters fireworks as he dances, and ignites explosive charges buried in the floor. The gangs in *West Side Story* perform balletic leaps and twirls as they prowl the streets of their decaying neighbourhood. Their virtuosity arrogantly flaunts their power: they commandeer space rather than embrace it. With their angular kicks, the Sharks use their legs as missiles. One of the Jets is nicknamed Diesel, and another, known as A-rab, streaks across the playground 'like an airplane' – a fighter jet presumably, closing in on its target. In 1961, the year in which Robert Wise directed the film of *West Side Story*, Jean-Paul Sartre wrote a preface to Frantz Fanon's anti-colonial treatise *Les Condamnés de la terre*. Sartre accused the West of using its culture to demean and enslave the Third World. 'We have the Word,' he said; Africans and Asians, in our estimation, utter only gibberish. Europeans repeat the sacred word 'Parthenon', which their underlings in the colonies reduce to guttural nonsense by mouthing '...thenon'. But Sartre warned that the wretched of the earth – like the immigrant gangs in the New York slums in *West Side Story* – had another means of self-expression and retaliation. They danced, and their dances rehearsed war, readying themselves for the murders they were intending to commit.

In the beginning, as Ellis claimed, a dance tamed nature and convened human society. At the end, a dance may tear down the walls and goad the chaotic elements to resume their battle. The stabilizing dance of life has its corollary in a dance of death.

# 26

# CREATURES OF PROMETHEUS

When *Frankenstein* was filmed in 1932, the wild-eyed creator shrieked 'Now I know what it feels like to be God!' as his monster stirred to life. Hollywood's moral guardians worried about countenancing blasphemy, so the studio added a threatening thunderclap to the soundtrack, which out-shouted him. The bad weather does not alter Frankenstein's aim, and his transgression recurs in *Forbidden Planet*, a novel by W. J. Stuart published in 1956 to coincide with the release of a film about the Krell, a futuristic race which seeks – as a doctor reports in aghast italics – 'not to *reproduce* life by biological function but to *create* it. Not from test-tube or seed-bed but basically *by the power of the mind*'. The scandalized narrator calls this feat 'autogenesis', and says that it usurps 'the prerogative of the Ultimate Power – of The Builder of the Universe. Of God!' The project is sabotaged by a monster embodying the baseness of our unregenerate nature, which demonstrates that we are not worthy to possess that ultimate power. Science, refusing to be intimidated, has never lost its faith in Prometheus. Louis Pasteur, for instance, steadfastly believed that it was possible to create life, which in his view preceded matter. So far no researcher has produced an organism; the animals in *Forbidden Planet* turn out to be full of unfunctional organs and are stuffed with fibrous tissue as dead as sawdust. But we are now able to design cybernetic creatures with sleek bodies and minds that think – or at least calculate – independently. In 1948 the mathematician Alan Turing devised and helped to build an intelligent machine; he called himself its 'creator', and in a report to the National Physical Laboratory defended his rudimentary computer against what he called the 'religious belief that any attempt to construct such machines is a Promethean irreverence'.

Artists performed Promethean experiments of their own. The hero of Ben Hecht's novel *Fantazius Mallare* is a sculptor, though he would rather be a god. He gives up manufacturing the 'inert monsters' which pose on pedestals in galleries, and instead attempts to manipulate life itself. The power he craves is not unequivocally creative: 'To return to Godhood,' he reasons, 'means to destroy all'. As a result, his generative acts are brutally sardonic. He acquires a black dwarf at an amusement park, ascertains that he is 'no chimera', and employs him as a servant. He also installs the lascivious gipsy Rita in his apartment. Their union is not carnal, because Fantazius possesses 'the secret of the hermaphroditic Gods'. He declares that Rita is

Jacob Epstein,
*The Rock Drill*,
1913–16

'his creation' and feels that he is 'giving her life'. This means that he has the power to revoke his gift by killing her. Fantazius calls God 'the greatest atheist' and says that 'He is proud of a disbelief in Himself'. The artist who deifies himself experiences the same wan, withered impotence. 'Ah', asks the novel's preface, 'what is God but a despairing refutation of Man?' The question can be rephrased: what is art but a despairing refutation of life? Hecht's parade of perversities caused a scandal when his book was published in 1922; it was confiscated by the government and charged with obscenity. Unimpressed by its spiritual outrages, D. H. Lawrence dismissed Hecht's hero as a 'frightened masturbator'. Artists console themselves with megalomaniac fantasies because they recoil from actual human contact.

The surrealists enjoyed toying with the mechanics of creation. They were entranced by an image from the Comte de Lautréamont's scurrilous fantasia *Les Chants de Maldoror*, which describes a sewing-machine entangled with an umbrella on top of an operating table: the wedding night, perhaps, of Frankenstein's monster and the bride he craves. Marcel Duchamp swaddled a sewing machine in burlap as a homage to Lautréamont; the sack preserved the prickly machine's virginity. In his *Grand Verre*, whose punning title alludes to the 'grand oeuvre' of the alchemists, Duchamp used a mill that grinds chocolate as a model for the abrasive encounter between a bride and the bachelors who strip her and are then ground down by her. The glass surface became begrimed when Duchamp left it standing near the window of his New York studio, and in 1920 Man Ray photographed its black, gritty skin, which he saw as a 'bridal finery of dust'. Duchamp insisted on calling the photograph *Elevage de poussière*, since between them he and Man Ray had raised or bred this thriving colony of filth. With sour wit, the twin parables recorded the failure of the generative process. The mill did not grind, and consummation between the bride and her bachelors had to be adjourned. The fruit of their union was dust, into which all bodies, when their sap dries up, will be sifted.

Jacob Epstein hoped for a more virile showing from the *Rock Drill* on which he worked between 1913 and 1916. Epstein bought a second-hand drill and welded it to a bony figure with a breast-plate like the radiator grille of a car; an African mask, extended at right angles on a retractable neck, supplied the figure with a face. Like Léger armouring the dancers in *La Création du monde*, Epstein was proud that it revealed 'no humanity'. This, he said, was 'the terrible Frankenstein's monster we have made ourselves into'. He meant that we were evolving from meat to metal, and that like all machines we had acquired a slick aptitude for killing. The man with the drill might have bestraddled one of the machine guns that multiplied casualties during the 1914–18 war. Epstein even considered motorizing it with pneumatic power, 'thus completing every potentiality of form and movement'. His colleague Wyndham Lewis chose to emphasize the 'machinery of procreation' exhibited by the figure. The drill, extending from the operator's groin, was an indefatigable penis, like a vibrator in overdrive. But did it eject seeds or bullets? Lewis was excited by the erotic vigour of machines, and by their lethal cruelty (which amounted, in his view, to the same thing). In his novel *The Revenge for Love*, published in 1937, a gun-runner's armour-plated car crashes through the border separating France from Spain. The roadster's purring emergence from a garage is described as an 'accouchement'; painted dove-grey, it recalls Milton's holy spirit seeding the abyss. Lewis notes at once that the lying-in has produced a 'monster'. The car speeds up, bellows like a bullock poleaxed in the abattoir, smashes a police barricade and casually tramples a guard. The progress from birth to death is terrifyingly abbreviated, and consummation is achieved by killing.

Epstein justified the cladding of plaster his figure wore because it carried 'within itself its progeny, protectively ensconced'. Those private parts needed such a stout defence. In 1914 Epstein's monument to Oscar Wilde was unveiled at the cemetery of Père Lachaise, after a delay caused by official objections to the swollen testicles of the Egyptian sphinx that guarded the tomb. The testicles were first coated in plaster, then covered by a bronze fig leaf; during the 1960s, they were broken off in a symbolic emasculation. In Paris, one of Epstein's potentates was humbled; back in London, he had his own misgivings about the *Rock Drill*. As the war continued, he came to regard his ruthless creation with dread. He junked the drill, discarded the bow legs that enabled the figure to perch on the tripod above it, and cast the lopsided torso in bronze. Truncated, it looked as pitiful as an amputee in a military hospital, and its dislocated head registered distress.

Science brought up to date our ancient longing to recreate ourselves by fortifying the body. The poet William Carlos Williams, who qualified as a doctor and had a medical practice in New Jersey, saw a connection between his own healing art and primitive sorcery. Witch doctors slashed the flesh, coated it with clay and ash, or stained it with the juice of berries; their aim, like the physician's, was to cast out 'the terror of death', though they achieved this by making the body into a work of art rather than prescribing drugs or extracting tumours. For medicine men, the charm worked best if the live creature resembled an upright, animated corpse. Hence the Jewish legend of the golem, supposedly made in Prague in the late sixteenth century by Rabbi Jehuda Löw ben Bezalel, who like Prometheus moulded mud from the river bank into the likeness of a monolithic man. The rabbi stole the creator's secret from the Kabbalah, and advertised his presumption in naming his creature. The Bible uses the word 'golem' to refer to a shapeless form, a gobbet of chaos. In Psalm 139, David reflects on the wonders of his making, which happened 'in the lowest parts of the earth' where he was 'covered' by God while still in his mother's womb. His substance then was imperfect or 'gal'mi', though all his members – his limbs and their aptitudes – developed according to plan, following the formulae for growth written in God's book. The Talmud also calls Adam a golem before God breathed life into him. The rabbi did not rely on the transmission of breath, or on the fire stolen by Prometheus; his golem was activated by a verbal spell, either written across his forehead or – as in Paul Wegener's film *Der Golem, wie er in die Welt kam*, made in 1920 – on a strip of parchment sealed in an amulet and placed in his chest. For the Jewish sages, creation depended on the combination of holy letters, so the change from animation back to inertia merely required the deduction of a vowel. The word that set the golem into motion was 'emet', meaning truth. Erasing the first letter changed it to 'met', which is death; this caused the golem to stop in its tracks. In the film, the rabbi handles the amulet like an ignition key. He fiddles with it whenever the golem (played by Wegener himself) disobeys him, and the lumbering ogre slumps into a coma.

According to legend, the golem functioned as a bulwark against oppression. In 1915 the novelist Arnold Zweig called him 'the homunculus of the tragic people', designed to relieve 'the sorrow of the subjugated'. But the defender is not always effective. The rabbi in Wegener's film takes the golem to court when he pleads with the emperor to revoke a decree expelling the Jews from Prague. The emperor ignores the implicit threat,

Albert Steinrüch (centre) as the rabbi and Paul Wegener (left) as the golem in Wegener's film *Der Golem*

though he is beguiled by the rabbi's showmanship. 'What form of marvel are you displaying for us today, you strange illusionist?' he asks. 'Show us more of your great art.' The rabbi conjures up a flickery vision of the Jewish patriarchs to support his appeal for mercy. His necromantic manual warns him against using magic to bring to life an inanimate being; not content with making the golem, he seems to have invented moving pictures. He insists on reverence for his creative wonders, and warns that the courtiers must not laugh at the magic lantern show. At first they are struck dumb by awe, but when the wandering Jew Asahuerus grimaces at them from the screen, they giggle, chortle and then hoot with glee, like the audience at a Chaplin film. The miracle is merely an entertainment; the artist is a paltry substitute for God.

Introducing the golem, the rabbi explains 'He is my servant – and my creation'. Servitude comes first: the golem chops wood, draws water from the well, and trundles off to market with a shopping basket on his arm. God envisaged no higher purpose for the man he made, who was to be the gardener and zookeeper of Eden. But Adam rejected such drudgery, and Wegener's golem has ambitions and desires of his own. Like the solitary Adam, he demands a mate, and abducts the rabbi's ripely sensual daughter. Before escaping, he burns down the house, inciting panic in the ghetto he is supposed to be protecting. As he rampages through the streets, the film perhaps recalls the modern incubus that haunts twentieth-century Prague in Gustav Meyrink's novel *Der Golem*, published in 1915. Meyrink's golem is not an elephantine lump of hardened clay. Like a sprite, he is everywhere and nowhere; the citizens of Prague all believe in him and fancy that they have glimpsed him, though none of them can be sure. He is their collective nightmare, begotten by unquiet minds that interbreed in narrow streets and fetid tenements. The disturbed imagination of an entire society broods about what Meyrink's traumatized narrator calls an 'ungraspable no-thing which has no form and gnaws away at the bounds of our thought'. Sometimes the offspring of this 'psychic epidemic' is a god, or a hero who promises deliverance. More often, the hallucination produces a monster, 'the horror' – as Meyrink's character says – 'which gives birth to itself'.

Fuming and flailing, Wegener's golem picks up a little girl who is playing with some friends. He might be expected to crush her, but instead he allows her to handle the amulet. She turns it the right way, and he keels over, once more insentient and harmless. The dramatist Karel Čapek, writing to Jules Romains in 1927, ridiculed this benign outcome. To neutralize a golem was as simple as disconnecting a domestic appliance from the power supply. But what if the clay manikin were a machine, less stupidly docile? And what if such machines – refusing to accept the ban on reproduction imposed by Frankenstein or the rabbi – found a way to generate replicas of themselves? In 1920 Čapek, who feared that 'someone one day would lead mass man against the world and against God', explored such possibilities in his play *R.U.R.*. It is about an army of golems, although Čapek gave them a new name. He called them robots, adapting the Czech word 'robota', which referred to the indentured labour of a feudal serf.

The initials in Čapek's title stand for Rossum's Universal Robots, which are manufactured on an island as remote as that of Wells's Dr Moreau. 'Rozum' in Czech puns on reason or intelligence, and the supervisor of the works is called Alquist, which is a garbling of alchemist. Here is the combined result of our science and our artistic mysticism, which together drive us to outsmart ourselves: the robots revolt, kill their creators, and bring the brief dominion of humankind to an end. The conclusion had been foreseeable ever since the philosophical materialists of the seventeenth century analysed man as a piece of intricate gadgetry. Hobbes in his *Leviathan* pointed out that the heart is a motor, the nerves are springs, and the joints are wheels. If we are engines, should it not be possible for an engineer to construct us? Do we need a divine creator? At best, God designed a chemical plant. In 1926 Fritz Kahn published a chromolithograph presenting a cross-section of *Der Mensch als Industriepalast*: man as an industrial

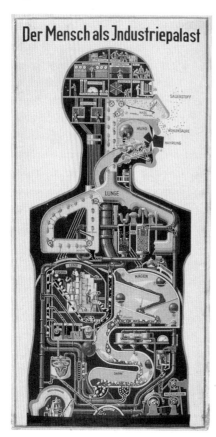

palace. The body here is not God's temple but a factory. Kahn gives our squashy organs and soft tubes a coating of metal. Tiny workers preside over whirring wheels in the cranium, and cataloguers file data. A gnashing mechanism in the mouth grinds up nutrients and sends them down a digestive chute. The lungs are a bellows, the heart a pump. Homunculi toil in the alimentary colon, separating out waste products. Since Kahn's placard was meant for display in schools, it stopped at the waist, omitting the genitals. Seen like this, we are already robots, and skin is the removable clothing that camouflages our motorized metabolism.

Rossum's robots have at least a residue of organic life. They are made of pasty biogen − a substance like protoplasm, described as a 'colloidal mess that a dog wouldn't look at', pounded with a pestle and kneaded

Fritz Kahn, *Der Mensch als Industriepalast*, chromolithograph, 1926

in troughs. Their vital organs are prepared in vats. A factory constructs bones, while spindles make nerves, veins and digestive tubes. There are also dissection rooms and stamping mills for the extermination of outmoded or refractory specimens. The manager Domin tells Helena that the inner workings of the robots surpass any product of nature. Man, she quibbles, is meant to be 'the product of God', but Domin bemoans God's technological ignorance. He also justifies the enforced labour of the robots: humanity, thanks to these unfeeling serfs, can become 'Lord of creation'. The trouble is that our self-promotion starts the Genesis story all over again. Man replaces God, and the robots are bullied into doing the dreary, dirty chores considered unfit for men. Before long, a dissident robot questions humanity's commandments. Gaining courage, the robots of the world unite, proclaim man 'an outlaw in the universe', and repudiate what Nietzsche, in his attack on Christianity, called a 'slave morality'. The existence of any god is an incitement to atheism.

Čapek deplored scientific efforts to extend the limits of life and repair the defects of nature. The ancient nurse in *R.U.R.* grumbles that it is wicked to tinker with the world 'after God has made it', and Helena burns the paper containing Rossum's recipe. A similar sacrifice concludes Čapek's next play *The Makropoulos Case*, performed in 1922. This was his critique of *Back to Methuselah*, in which Shaw presumed that the indefinite prolongation of human life would give us leisure to cure all our ailments and to perfect society. Čapek's heroine Emilia Marty is the daughter of Heronymus Makropoulos, a physician in attendance at the court of Rudolf II in Prague. The emperor, who maintained a coven of alchemists, wanted to live forever. At his command Makropoulos brewed an elixir of life, which he tested on his daughter; it must have worked, because in the play Emilia is already 339 years old. But instead of retaining a brisk Shavian vivacity, she is bored, disgusted, disdainful. She has seen everything, and therefore believes in nothing. In her latest incarnation she is an opera singer, but her profession affords her no pleasure because – as she wearily explains – 'art has meaning only so long as you don't understand', so that 'singing is the same as keeping silent'. Exhausted, she has come to find the formula in the hope that a new dose will revive her. At last, however, she decides to surrender it, and her young admirer Kristina makes amends for the impious interference with nature by destroying it. After a final bout of cynical laughter, Emilia gratefully expires.

Though science may dream of infinity, art prefers brevity. Čapek justifies his choice by compressing Emilia's 339 listless years into the last, hectic day which his play covers. He also recalculates the value of art by insisting on its impermanence. Emilia's singing voice, which enraptures her audiences, is never heard in the play. Instead she quarrels, cackles, shrieks and even tipsily hiccups. The lyrical wonders she performs must be imagined: music is temporal and temporary, like the breath it moulds. There is no need to smash sculptures as Fantazius Mallare does, because Emilia's airy constructions evaporate of their own accord. That is why they are – or were – so precious. Art does not deliver a surrogate immortality, as Shakespeare and Michelangelo declared; instead it renders mortality precious by reminding us how fugitive and irreplaceable the moment is. If we want anything more, we had better trust biological arrangements. At the end of *The Makropoulos Case*, Prus asks Kolonaty if he has children, and says that they represent 'eternal life'. *R.U.R.* saves the human race from extinction by sponsoring a match between Helena and the sentient, thoughtful robot Primus. They wander off together, with Alquist saluting them as Adam and Eve. No fall will ensue, as Helena placed the forbidden knowledge beyond reach by burning the formula. Primus rejects the eternal life that was guaranteed to the first occupants of Eden. 'Don't you sometimes feel,' he asks Helena, 'that it would be better to die?'

Čapek set *R.U.R.* in a future which for us – now that these prophecies about the scientific manipulation of nature have begun to come true – is already the past. The manager Domin remembers that Rossum synthesized biogen in 1932, which, as he idly adds, was 'four hundred years after the discovery of America'. In 1532 Pizarro took captive the Inca ruler Atahualpa; Domin may be implying that this new world – at least after the Declaration of Independence in 1776 – was the laboratory where the homogenized, egalitarian human species would supposedly be cured of its flaws. The socialist clerk Vitek in *The Makropoulos Case* has millenarian hopes for the elixir. He calls it 'the biggest event since the creation of man', because it will now be possible 'to liberate man and create him anew!' Prus plans a more sinister, stringently controlled distribution of the boon. Borrowing from Darwin and Nietzsche, he anticipates the combination of eugenics and euthanasia institutionalized by the Third Reich. He suggests a policy of selective breeding, to ensure that only the fittest survive; this caste of supermen will be 'masters and creators', exclusively entitled to 'unlimited life'. Science, in league with political ideology, looked beyond the creation of individuals, which was the short-sighted aim of God in Genesis. Now the aim was to create a mass, and in so doing to re-engineer society.

Communism, as Trotsky declared, regarded man as 'raw material, or at best a semi-manufactured product'. The Russian Revolution, aiming to complete the process of manufacture, was an excursion into science fiction. Aleksandr Bogdanov's novel *Red Star*, published in 1907, described a factory on Mars, free from grime and stench because it derives its power not from the 'crude force of fire and steam' but from electricity. A glow irradiates the place, whose floors are made of glass stiffened by finely gridded steel; the purr of the machines is melodious. The workshop might belong to Plato's prime mover, or to the blindingly lucid God of *Paradise Lost*: Bogdanov secularized heaven and electrified the deity. Fyodor Gladkov in his novel *Cement* transformed diesel engines into altars; a holy spirit hovers in the air above them, ready to make itself cracklingly manifest. The machines resemble 'great crystals ready to explode into life'. A crystal is creation fresh-frozen, the shiny remnant of some ancient geological eruption. The engineer Gleb – who polishes the diesels and prepares them for the disciplinary parades that demonstrate their strength – reveres their lofty reserve and cool, clean virginity. The Martians in Wells's *The War of the Worlds* are brains on stilts, greedily feeding on the pulped bodies of humans. But on Bogdanov's Bolshevik planet there is peaceful coexistence between men, small but masterful, and the giants – hammers packing a punch of several thousand tons, clawed monsters that maul chunks of metal – that do their bidding. Men with their 'delicate brains' organize the Martian production line, while machines with their 'indestructible organs' take care of the muscular work. Bogdanov came to understand the risks of delegating organic functions to gadgetry: he died in 1926 after a failed attempt to transfuse his own blood. The visionary Velimir Khlebnikov proposed treating the earth as if it were a satellite of Bogdanov's Mars. This meant pressing biotechnology into the service of the political economy. Khlebnikov recommended 'combining human races and breeding new ones' as the need arose. Technical innovation would prompt the redesign of our old-fashioned bodies. 'Let air travel and wireless communication be the two legs humanity stands on,' Khlebnikov suggested. As a result of these telepathic, telegraphic, telephonic innovations, we might eventually do without legs altogether and project ourselves into the sky. Meanwhile in 1919 Vladimir Tatlin drew up plans for a rotating monument to the revolution, whose tiered levels were meant to perform planetary circuits while radio transmitters on the summit evangelized to the world.

In Andrei Platonov's novel *The Foundation Pit*, the engineer Prushevsky constructs a communal dormitory for proletarians. He wonders what kind of bodies young people will have in the idyllic socialist future, and speculates about the changed buildings that will accommodate them. Flesh will surely be streamlined, and spirit may become a public utility, like gas or electricity. People are suffused by a 'surplus vital warmth that had once been termed the soul'; Prushevsky asks himself whether the soul is 'an inevitable by-product of the manufacture of living material'. Consciousness, traced to its source in the pituitary gland, could possibly be transplanted between bodies to revive the dead, or shared with other species. Khlebnikov fraternally favoured the admission of apes to the family of man. In a story written by Mikhail Bulgakov in 1925, a dotty professor inserts the pituitary gland of a human into a stray dog and sews on a set of human genitals. The dog's tail falls out, its fur moults except on its head and chest, and it learns how to swear and to demand booze. Despite the professor's parental satisfaction, the experiment hardly changes nature for the better. Rumours circulate in the neighbourhood that the stumpy, foul-mouthed brute is a Martian. Osip Mandelstam, in a poem about the biologist Lamarck written in 1932, exempted himself from this compulsory progress. Lamarck marvelled at the way nature coaxed the 'first germs of animality' into ever more ambitious forms: giraffes self-improvingly grow longer necks to reach more succulent leaves on the tops of trees. Mandelstam's poem regrets that nature – like Bulgakov's mad surgeon – opened us up and implanted a mind. He has no desire to scramble up the evolutionary ladder, which ends in the mechanical efficiency of Soviet man. He prefers a retrograde re-creation, and imagines turning into a lizard, a mollusc or an insect, disappearing into nature like Proteus. Best of all would be reincarnation as a protozoon. Such germinal forms are, in human terms, scarcely alive at all, which is why Mandelstam can wistfully pretend to envy them. They have not been born, sentenced to our lonely singularity. Consequently, they never have to die.

The Third Reich had its own prescription for redesigning mankind. At Nuremberg, Hitler surveyed colonnades of party members whose iron helmets or shouldered spades defined them as a metallic army. A 'new man' – purged of individuality, robotically obedient, impervious to human feeling – had been mass-produced. Older models, defective or impure, could be summarily scrapped. Officially, this was a state run on industrial lines. The regime's roots, however, were atavistic, muddied by the worship of war-mongering Nordic deities. In secret, the enterprise was a demented fantasy, a dream of omnipotence that raged inside the head of a dictator whose first ambition was to be an artist.

Thea von Harbou prophetically mapped the terrain in her novel *Metropolis*, published in 1925 and filmed by her husband Fritz Lang. Their metropolis is as contradictory as the Reich which it presaged: it aspires to the future while embedding itself in the past. Towers invade the sky, and in the film planes buzz above elevated highways. In 1924, Lang surveyed Manhattan from a liner docked at a pier on the West Side. The lighted buildings looked to him like 'a vertical veil', rootlessly dangling in the air; the veil concealed the absence of God. But far below these dazzling heights, the city has a Gothic basement. A cathedral is squeezed between the skyscrapers. Harbou's novel explains that the planners were unable to demolish a crooked house once occupied by a necromancer, and it is here that the inventor Rotwang completes his sacreligious 'great work' by animating the steel woman he has fabricated.

Rudolf Klein-
Rogge as the
inventor Rotwang
with his robot
(Brigitte Helm) in
Fritz Lang's film
*Metropolis*, 1926

*Metropolis* combines science and sorcery. In an aerial office, the economic magnate Joh Fredersen oversees dials and switches, reads messages on ticker-tape, and telephones orders to his engineers. His brain is wired directly to the city's heart, a power-house that Harbou likens to a planetary hub. Here the engineer Grot tends a turbine that resembles the disc of the sun, with silver wheels spinning around it like satellites. By adjusting the levers, Grot establishes a metabolic rhythm for the city's industries. The workers in Meyrink's novel shuffle along 'without a will of their own, moved by an invisible magnetic current'. Harbou's metropolis is inhabited by the same automata, who seem, as Meyrink says of the golem, to be 'unsouled'. They perform their repetitive tasks, then trudge down tunnels and huddle in the elevator that returns them to their subterranean tenements. Frederson's henchman Slim explains the zombie-like demeanour of the drug-addicted nightclub proprietor. 'Can a man imitate the pushing of a machine for hours and hours at a time without its killing him?' he asks. 'He is as dead as stone.' Dr Gall in *R.U.R.* comments on the 'hundred thousand expressionless faces' of Rossum's mechanical labourers, as alike as bubbles. Expressionism was the remedy for this inexpressiveness. With its breathless punctuation and exclamatory crescendi, Harbou's writing matches the febrile, spasmodic manner of Lang's actors; both are attempts to revive the anaesthetized drones of the industrial city.

When Rotwang's robot moves, Lang alludes to the vivifying of the golem in Wegener's film. The rabbi stands in a circle of flame, waves his pentangle and utters incantations. Rotwang uses electricity and gas not magic fire: coils of burning energy – actually neon lights inside tubes made of sandwich paper – pass over the body, causing its eyes to open and its joints to move. Wegener's golem remains a dumb, obtuse servant. He ogles the rabbi's daughter, but there can be no marriage between stone and flesh. In *Metropolis*, organism and mechanism have grown closer together. Rotwang has a prosthetic hand, the result of an accident in his laboratory. The skull of his robot is steel, but onto it he grafts the face of the compassionate, maternal Maria, who pleads for charity on behalf of helpless children. This beatific identity is the robot's mask, the cover for a dual nature. The fleshly Maria is an angel; the Maria of metal is a demon, who gyrates through a licentious foxtrot in the nightclub, provokes an uprising with her political harangues, and screeches with laughter on the funeral pyre as the flames lick at her. Wegener's golem scowls in dismay when he holds a rose, aware that he cannot smell its perfume. His deficiency is clear; humanity retains its privileges. The double role played by the actress Brigitte Helm in *Metropolis* asks questions about our human status that are less easy to answer. Are we a soup of moist, milky feelings and soulful yearnings, like the good Maria, or are we machines driven by unstoppable and irrational cravings, like her bad twin?

To complicate matters further, the robotic Maria is a ghost, a revenant artificially brought back to life. She is a facsimile of Rotwang's lover Hel, who left him for Fredersen and then died giving birth to a son. In designing her, Rotwang challenges the God of Genesis and alters biblical priorities. 'Every man-creator makes himself a woman,' he says to Fredersen in the novel. 'It's nonsense to claim that the first human was a man. If a male God created the world, then he certainly created woman first!' Lang ignored Rotwang's critique of Genesis, and skipped ahead to his jubilant announcement of success: 'I have re-created her!' he tells Fredersen in the German version of the film. It is an incongruously touching moment. Here Rotwang does not speak of creation; he knows that he is merely an imitator of God, perhaps a parodist (which is why he considers naming the robot Parody). As a scientist, his project is to create life. But as an artist, his real ambition is to defeat death by regaining what time takes from us. Art is a ceremonial act of representation, during which the lost past returns to the present, made eternal in the form of an image. The sad quest for compensation estranges the artist from the happy, unselfconscious lives of others. After an industrial disaster wrecks the city, Harbou defines the sleepwalking, prematurely posthumous existence that is the artist's rarefied, exalted lot: 'Rotwang awoke, though he knew quite well that he was dead. And this consciousness filled him with the deepest satisfaction.' He is pleased because he has crossed the gap that separated him from his dreams. 'An existence without Hel was over at last. A second one? – No! Better to stay dead.' He is inevitably disillusioned, since art can never deliver more than a second best.

*Metropolis* describes a world created by men, who worship what Harbou calls 'god-machines'. In Lang's film, one of the gaping engines changes into Moloch, the man-eating demon venerated by the Canaanites. The novel, bringing back the savage pagan deities supposedly cast out by Christ, identifies other ogres. Joh Fredersen's son visits their white temples in the power-house and likens them to Huitzilopochtli the Aztec god of war, or Thor the thunderer (Wagner's Donner in *Das Rheingold*, whose hammer strikes sparks from rock). They are joined by the malignant Durgha, pictured by Hindus as a woman riding a tiger although Harbou gives her an aluminium body with platinum veins. Another oiled idol is referred to as the Pater Noster machine. Despite this biblical nickname, its form alludes to a Hindu god, the elephant-headed Ganesh; its stumpy arms twitch to signal internal cogitation, and its trunk rears up and attaches itself like a sucker to the forehead of young Freder, siphoning off his thoughts. Harbou's excursion into Hindu lore is gruesomely appropriate, because Ganesh happens to be the subject of a Promethean creation myth. Parvati, it is said, used the grime exuded by her own body to mould a boy, who was entrusted with the task of standing sentry at her door. This golem refused to let her husband Shiva enter; he knocked the figure's head off. Repenting, Shiva then commanded that a head should be taken from any sleeping creature as a replacement. His minions removed one from an elephant, and Shiva glued it to the boy's body. For Hindus, Ganesh is a friendly monster who promises that obstacles can be overcome and losses made good; he modestly remembers his origins by riding on a mouse. Harbou twists the legend awry, and makes Ganesh a divine carnivore, hungry for human sacrifice. If the governing machine overheats, it emits an electrical current like a green, hissing snake, or like 'Mahomet's curved sword'. The scimitar of lightning anticipates Hitler's fondness for Islam – a warfaring religion which he preferred to peaceful Christianity.

Joh Fredersen is the novel's version of the divine patriarch described by Genesis. But his agenda is different: the creation of man leaves him dissatisfied, and he engages Rotwang to supply a replacement. Freder worries that the machines of the metropolis will gobble up all the available human fodder. By then, his father says, a substitute for man will have been found. Unlike the God on whom he is modelled, the elder Fredersen is overcome by remorse when he sees that the world is flawed and inequitable. His hair turns white with grief and, acknowledging his obsolescence, he stumbles off into retirement at the end of the novel. In Genesis, God does the work of creation without female assistance. Joh has a mother, who chastises him for his vengeful folly and at last forgives him when he repents. She lives in a thatched cottage that Joh has transplanted – complete with flower beds and a walnut tree – to the top of a skyscraper. She remains in Eden, and when Joh objects to the union of Freder and Maria, she tells him that even God has no right to expel lovers from paradise.

God had foreknowledge of the fall, but did nothing to prevent it. Christ in *Paradise Lost* objects to this harsh determinism: was the human race only created to be the victim of this practical joke? Joh responds to such criticism by claiming that he willed the revolt of the workers so that Freder could redeem them. It sounds like the devious rationalizing of a God who is wise after the event, pretending that oversights prove his omniscience. In the engine-room, a machine with three levers protruding from it reminds Freder of the clump of crosses on Golgotha; elsewhere in the city, a mob of religious fanatics known as Gothics crucify the monk who was once their leader. But Freder is spared this fate, and establishes a new social order. God the Father, in Harbou's unorthodox theology, needs the moral support of his mother; Christ also relies on a woman, who embodies his doctrine of undiscriminating love. This is Maria, who ought to be Christ's mother although in Harbou's rearrangement of the Trinity she becomes Freder's wife. Maria preaches to a downtrodden congregation in the catacombs, which is where the first Christians hid. Harbou, however, had scant sympathy with the plight of the underlings who were consoled by Christ's promise that the last would be first: the proletarian uprising is led by the robot, Maria's demonic twin. Were the Virgin Mary and Mary Magdalene sisters under the skin? At the end of Lang's film, the real Maria reappears outside the cathedral and intercedes to prevent an economic schism. She coaxes capital and labour to join hands, just as Christ once restored the connection between God and man by preaching a gospel of goodwill.

The novel's ending is less conciliatory. The machines explode, the towers of the city topple, its rivers overflow. This, as Freder tells Maria when he rescues her from the flood, is 'something very like the destruction of the world'. He embraces a machine which is his 'shining creation', and which will be his means of deliverance. It is a space ship, made of lustrous metal, said by Harbou to possess 'the fair godliness of a faultlessly beautiful animal'. Freder tells it that they will spend the night together, and looks forward to feeling 'your throb and the beginnings of movement in your controlled body'. He might be making love to the maenadic Maria; the machine that bewitches men when the robot dances is replaced by a machine that will send man into orbit and perhaps install him in heaven. Lang wanted to conclude the film with Freder quitting the ravaged earth to colonize the moon. The suppressed conclusion reappeared in 1929 when Lang directed *Frau im Mond*, which was also written by Harbou. Here a team of prospectors travels to the moon by rocket in search of gold. They quarrel over the mineral riches they find, and a gun fired by one of them damages the oxygen tank of the rocket. There is not enough oxygen for all of them to make the return journey, so the scientist Helius, named after the sun, elects to stay behind. The astronomer Frieda, the lunar woman of the title, decides to share his exile. They might be an extraterrestrial Adam and Eve, like Primus and Helena in *R.U.R.* But the film does not maroon them in space for ever; the homebound astronauts promise to come back to collect them.

The prospect of repatriation tells another palliative lie. The true aim of science fiction is to imagine an epilogue to life on earth. When a man finally walked on the moon in July 1969, those watching from below thought of it as another creation, relaunching our species. The CBS commentator Eric Sevareid announced that 'We've seen some kind of birth here'. Sevareid thought that astronauts were 'not just superior men, but different creatures', and as Neil Armstrong staggered across the lunar surface he thought he was witnessing an extra instalment of evolution. The dim figure on the television relay looked at first, as Sevareid said, like a 'clumsy creature, half-blind'. But it soon gained confidence, and abridged the millennia that our amphibious ancestors spent in scrambling onto land or in learning to walk upright. 'In a rather short time,' Sevareid reported, 'it's running'.

In 1922 the photographer Paul Strand looked back on the founding of a 'modern Church', established when man abandoned 'the concept of God The Creator'. This religion 'consummated a new creative act, a new Trinity: God the Machine, Materialistic Empiricism the Son, and Science the Holy Ghost'. Strand warned that 'the whole Trinity must be humanized lest it in turn dehumanize us'. The scientist, proud of what Strand mockingly called 'His Holy Ghostship', had 'taken to himself with love a dead thing'; like a necrophile, he had coupled with a machine. Though Strand's imagery evokes Epstein's virile drill or Lang's seductive metal woman, the 'new God' he had in mind was the camera, with its cold, lizard-like eye. In its early decades, photography was conscientiously morbid; the emotional value of the new art lay in its commemoration of the dead. Matthew Brady photographed corpses on the battlefields of the American Civil War, Felix Nadar photographed skulls and bones in the Paris catacombs, Hippolyte Bayard even photographed himself as a blackened, decaying cadaver. Eventually the cinema raised the dead and made them dance: an agile skeleton performed a jig in the Choreutoscope, invented in 1866. Projected at the rate of twenty four a second, still photographic frames are startled into motion. Cinema is synonymous with this kinetic power, and the names applied to the new contraption – Bioscope, Vitascope or Viviscope – all emphasized this miraculous enlivening of matter. At the end of the nineteenth century, the physicist Henri Poincaré elaborated what he called a 'kinematic theory of gases'. Kinetic molecules danced in the air like gnats, as

Poincaré put it; the cinema likewise made visible the buzzing chaos of life itself, with specks of light cavorting in the gloom.

Poetic commentators on the first moving pictures regarded the medium with awe and terror, as if they were eye-witnesses of Genesis or Armageddon. In 1915 Vachel Lindsay likened the reels of a kinetoscope to Ezekiel's visionary wheels, on which heavenly faces revolve. Here too was the second coming which the Egyptians anticipated when they embalmed and mummified their dead: Lindsay hailed 'the ultimate resurrection of the whole man, his *coming forth by day*'. In 1926 Virginia Woolf was troubled by the creative ferment that boiled on the screen. 'All is hubble-bubble, swarm, and chaos,' she wrote in her essay on the cinema. 'We are peering over the edge of a cauldron in which fragments of all shapes and savours seem to simmer; now and again some vast form heaves itself up, and seems about to haul itself out of the chaos'. The cauldron is the cooking pot of the witches in *Macbeth*, although Woolf may equally well have been looking into Hesiod's chasm, where the elements brawled before the cosmos was made. At a screening of *The Cabinet of Dr Caligari*, she saw 'a shadow shaped like a tadpole' smudging the image. Was it a Chimaera or Hydra that had escaped from the film's madhouse, or perhaps – given its likeness to a tadpole – a reminder of the lower forms of life from which we evolved? It turned out to be the passing shadow of someone in the audience. Even so, the silent bodies that moved so jerkily were not so much alive as undead, like vampires. Woolf wondered if she might be looking back at an existence she had quit. In the cinema, she said, 'we see life as it is when we have no part in it. ... We are beholding a world that has gone beneath the waves.' The cosmos, in her account, has a brief life. It emerges from below the water, and then, after thrashing around for a few inconclusive minutes, submerges again.

Lindsay expected the medium to bring about resurrection. Woolf came closer to the truth in suggesting that it displays a spectral sequel to human existence. Golems and robots belong on film, because like them it relies on artificial animation. The cinema is a laboratory which specializes in designing new forms of life: androids, robocops, cyborgs, clones and replicants. The characters in *Jurassic Park III* take shelter in a wrecked clinic where extinct saurians were genetically engineered. 'This is how you make a dinosaur?' asks an astonished woman. 'No,' replies the stern palaeontologist, 'this is how you play God'. In Ira Levin's novel *The Stepford Wives*, first filmed in 1974, the demure homemakers of a Connecticut suburb are audioanimatronic playthings, modelled on the friendly puppets who greet visitors to Disneyland. A rebellious feminist accuses the electronic wizards of turning her friends into robots. One of the scientists says that she must be confusing them with Leonardo da Vinci and Einstein. 'You're the men who put us on the moon,' she replies. Before long, she too is replaced by a well-oiled, simpering doll. In 1982 in Ridley Scott's *Blade Runner*, one of the replicants – a blond eugenic Aryan with frigid blue eyes – confronts 'the god of biomechanics' who designed him. 'It's not an easy thing to meet your maker,' he admits. He has a complaint, like that which Adam addressed to his creator. When the inventor Tyrrell asks what the problem is, the replicant says 'Death'. He and his colleagues have been given short lives, which ensures that they never become too troublesome. 'That's a little out of my jurisdiction,' replies Tyrrell. The robot kisses him on the mouth – a somewhat presumptuous way of worshipping God. Then he crushes Tyrrell's head to a pulp. This dispute between Prometheus and his creature rapidly dated: like Arnold Schwarzenegger performing surgery on his eye in *The Terminator*, the successors to the frustrated replicant carry out their own repairs and know how to make themselves immortal. In *I, Robot*, directed by Alexis Proyas in 2004, a robot kills its inventor, whom it regards as a father. The purpose of the crime is to warn men of their imminent obsolescence. 'The created,' explains the homicidal robot, 'must sometimes protect the creator.' Do we fight holy wars to keep the idea of God alive?

Human beings inevitably speculate about refashioning themselves to compete or collaborate with machines. In *The Matrix*, the hacker Neo meets a technician who is not plugged into the maternal main-frame of dreams, which infuses people with thoughts and feelings through a power-point in the back of the neck. 'You don't have any holes?' he asks. The other character, shame-faced, admits that he is an outmoded, flabby specimen, without the proper electronic connections. In *eXistenZ*, directed by David Cronenberg in 1999, people have bioports installed at the base of the spine. Like a battery, the body drives a 'MetaFlesh Game Pod', a pink, squashy uterus plugged into the host through a twining umbilical cable. As the metaphor of the pod suggests, technology is modelled on internal organs, now extruded from the body so that we can play with them. Jude Law, as a bemused trainee, asks the heroine why she is talking into an egg; it turns out to be her mobile phone. She ravages his innocence by drilling a bioport into his bare back. Existence is a game played out inside the pod, where sensations are programmed. The attached human being is reduced to hardware, cumbersome but still unfortunately necessary. After a trial run, a game designer complains because the simulated action kicks off with an assassination attempt. 'That's very creative,' his colleague murmurs approvingly: creativity here is synonymous with murder.

Andrew Niccol's *Gattaca*, released in 1997, describes a society which has prohibited the chancy, erotically befuddled business of conception inside the body. Reproduction is transferred to test tubes, where kinks can be corrected and inferior eggs weeded out. Jude Law this time is a 'made man': the Renaissance terminology now refers to genetic engineering, not to aesthetic self-fashioning. The character played by Ethan Hawke, whose parents begot him in the back seat of a car using traditional methods, is classified as a 'God child': the phrase is pejorative. Hawke discovers the virtues of pre-natal engineering when he attends a piano recital. The soloist can manage a score of Lisztian difficulty because he has been bred for virtuosity, with six fingers on each hand. Training for a space mission, Hawke is anxious to 'get off this ball of dirt'. A perfected race has no further use for our diminished, peripheral planet.

Robots have outgrown the shamed sense of inferiority that afflicts Wegener's golem. In *Artificial Intelligence: A.I.*, released in 2001, Jude Law – apparently indispensable in these fables about a relaunched humanity – plays a Mecha who is a motorized dildo. During foreplay he assures his female clients that, once he ministers to them, they will never bother with human lovers again. The problem with Steven Spielberg's film is that the science of replication is too satisfactory, too coolly immaculate. Why does the robotic boy played by Haley Joel Osment long to become human? The mutation involves exchanging his shiny circuitry for messier organic innards; he is absurdly eager to experience pain and death, and also to digest spinach. *The Sixth Day*, directed by Roger Spottiswoode in 2000, begins with a quote from Genesis and goes on to wonder if, by cloning Dolly the sheep, science may have offended the God who created man on the sixth day. As in *A.I.*, the benefits probably outweigh the moral risks. A corporate executive who boasts that he is 'taking over where God left off' sells virtual girlfriends to lonely men, and consoles heartbroken children by instantly duplicating their dead pets. Clones enjoy their immunity to mortal woes. 'I got killed twice in two hours,' boasts one of them. 'Oh, we've all been killed before,' shrugs a colleague. Schwarzenegger, playing a character called Adam, battles to stamp out the clone who has usurped his identity; he finds, however, that he is himself a clone. 'Kind of takes the fun out being alive, doesn't it?' says the sympathetic original from whom he has been copied. Unfortunately, Schwarzenegger is ill-suited to such existential poignancy. Muscle-bound, with an inelastic face and a meagre repertoire of catch-phrases, he looks and sounds more humanoid than human.

Definitions need constant updating, as art and religion try to keep pace with technology. Andrew Niccol's *S1m0ne*, released in 2002, is about a non-existent cinematic idol whose name is a contraction of Simulation One. The film's trailer quibbles about the precise status of this synthetic woman: a cursor clicks across the slogan 'A star is born' and alters the last word to 'created'. But that too is a misrepresentation. This star has actually been programmed, digitized by a director who is tired of over-paid, uncooperative living actresses. Using an electronically adjusted version of the director's voice, Simone admits that she is just computer code, and says that before being discovered 'I was ones and zeroes, I was nothing'. The director returns her to that condition by infecting her with a virus that kills her. Her pixels fall apart like non-adhesive atoms; she is as incoherent as windblown sand. But she soon bounces back to virtual life, bears the director a phantasmal child, and goes on to make another series of illusory films. It's appropriate that the archaeologist Lara Croft – who began as the heroine of a computer game, then acquired flesh to appear in a film – is known as 'Tomb Raider'. Lara is lithe and athletic, but her vitality is as freakish as the twitching of an electrocuted body. The digital image is a copy without an original; animation is no proof that it is alive.

The novelist Edgar Wallace, who worked on the screenplay of *King Kong* in 1932, had a Promethean plan for the ape's ascent of the Empire State Building. Wallace wanted him to be struck down by lightning, not by the planes that strafe him in the film. A spark smoulders in Kong's head, and makes him dote on the woman he abducts. But electricity is dangerous: the force of creative ignition is also casually destructive. The myth retained its appeal for Peter Jackson, who while preparing his own version of *King Kong* remembered that his adolescence had been 'fuelled by a desire to ... create a new world, populated by new creatures, and bring them to life'. The Promethean technician Jackson most admired was Ray Harryhausen, who – working with models which he animated frame by painstaking frame – mobilized the gorilla in *Mighty Joe Young* and the kraken that twines around the Golden Gate Bridge in *It Came From Beneath the Sea*. During *Mighty Joe Young* Harryhausen ate carrots and celery 'to feel what it was like to be a gorilla'; the life he gave to the brute came from within him, rather than depending on a puppeteer's manipulation. The young Jackson was equally empathetic. After seeing the first *King Kong*, he made an ape out of wire and rubber, with hair scavenged from his mother's moulting fur coat. By 2005, when he completed his *King Kong*, technology eased his task. The new Kong, despite his bulk, had no real presence. He was a blank, filled in during post-production by graphic artists sketching on their computers. It is no longer dangerous or even difficult to give birth to a monster, or to a god; it is merely expensive.

# 27

# GOD'S FINGER, MAN'S HAND

Artists clustered around God's sick-bed like impatient heirs. As soon as the announcement of his death was made, the legatees assumed power. 'I am God', wrote Scriabin in his secret journal, adding 'I am play, I am freedom, I am life'. 'I am God,' Paul Klee repeated in a poem. His head, he explained, was about to burst as a hatching idea demanded to be born, and he expected to 'suffer/ in the act of fulfilment'. Picasso, aware of a collegial affinity, said that God was just another artist, versatile enough to do without a personal style. He created the elephant, the giraffe and the cat, creatures that have nothing in common; his fickle, flippant purpose, like Picasso's own, was always to make something new.

In 1877 the painter Walter Sickert praised Whistler by declaring 'Here was the finger of God'. God's defining index finger, pointed at Adam in the Sistine Chapel, now undid the official work of creation. Directed by Whistler, it spread washes of colour that blurred the lineaments of things and diffused reality into a misty nocturne. The finger rapidly grew a more masterful hand. In 1898 Rodin proclaimed the divinity of the art he practised with a marble block entitled *La main de Dieu*. The white, veined hand rises out of the uncarved stone as if thrusting through the earth. Its creativity is not channelled into a finger-tip like that of Michelangelo's God. Instead the open hand holds a clump of rock that is meant to represent loamy soil, as malleable as the dough the young Rodin played with when frying men in his mother's kitchen. God's work is not yet finished, but he has already pressed two inchoate human beings out of the clay – Adam and Eve, created together and foetally curled in one another's arms. Creativity, whether divine or human, is handiwork, manual craft. The hand, however, transforms the material in which it dabbles, and make something that did not exist before. Dust begins to breathe; inert stone, turned inside out, is a womb shared by two live bodies.

Later Rodin sculpted his own hand holding a torso. Here the deity – at leisure on the first Sunday, perhaps – contemplates the results of his art. The hand extends to a wrist and, because the process is now complete, the fingers are delicately and precisely spread to form a pedestal for a naked female figure. The animation Rodin wished on his figures was often erotic. Rilke sensed a ripple of excitement agitating the bodies of the couple in *Le Baiser*. A fire like that buried in igneous rock seems to be returning to the

Auguste Rodin,
*La main de Dieu*,
1898 (marble
executed by
Soudbinine in
1902)

surface. The quickening could also be intellectual, as if thought had wriggled into life somewhere in the bedrock. The head of the female model in *La Pensée* remains embedded up to her chin in the rough, craggy marble. She emerges from a petrified sea, and the white clarity of her face and her staring, colourless eyes represent mind separating itself from matter. *La Centauresse*, sculpted in 1889, is engaged in the same struggle: a human head strains to outgrow the equine hind quarters, and the disparity between soul and body lengthens its neck and almost tears the hybrid creature apart. Hans Arp, in some verses written in 1954, called Rodin's sculptures

> ... an immense after-birth of the Renaissance,
> a project of erotomachia
> to confirm origin,
> far from the mechanical erotomachia of our century.

The afterbirth joins the foetus to its mother's womb and allows nutrients to circulate between them; Arp's image fuses stone with flesh and irrigating blood. But the placenta is also a shapeless mess, expelled from the mother's body after delivery. Erotomachia refers to the sexual battle that rages between Rodin's monoliths: in *L'eternelle Idole*, a woman posed like a goddess on an altar allows herself to be nuzzled by a suppliant man who clasps his hands submissively behind his back. Arp preferred these bodily writhings to the bloodless mental calculations of abstraction, but his admiration for Rodin was shadowed by revulsion.

In 1880 Rodin received a commission for *La Porte de l'enfer*, a monumental doorway decorated with figures from Dante's *Divina Commedia*, which he worked on for the next twenty years. At first he based his design on Ghiberti's door at the Baptistery in Florence, which portrays paradise. Then he changed his mind, and dedicated to imitate the Sistine Chapel wall on which Michelangelo painted the panic of the Last Judgment. Hell with its furnaces was closer to the fury of the creative brain than heaven, the serene domain of logic. Rodin's inferno erased the internal divisions maintained by Dante, who carefully categorized his sinners and relegated them to separate circles with specialized torments. The assorted miscreants whirl in an unbarred, indefinite space, and spill over the sides of the door; they deny its right to enclose and imprison them. The lovers in *Le Baiser* began as Dante's Paolo and Francesca, condemned to the flames because of their illicit affair; released from the door, they cast off the curse imposed by religion. *Le Penseur* also began on the door but outgrew it. Rodin had previously planned a monument to Dante, placed on a rock where he brooded over the characters who loomed behind him like the monsters that assail Goya's dreamer. Transferred to the door, the poet frowns as he looks over the edge of the lintel into the abyss where his characters suffer. When

Auguste Rodin,
*La Porte d'Enfer,*
1880–1917

Rodin exhibited the figure on its own, he called it *Poète-Penseur*. In 1902 Edward Steichen photographed the sculptor confronting his thinker. They have the same darkly silhouetted profile, and Rodin's airily visionary monument to Victor Hugo hovers between them, as if they joined mental forces to imagine it. He was happy to consider the thinker a self-portrait. Bending forward with his feet drawn up beneath him and his fist pummelling his teeth, the figure makes visible the physical stress of consciousness, as 'the fertile thought slowly elaborates itself within the thinker's brain'. When that fertilization happens, bronze metaphorically shudders into life: now, as Rodin said, the figure 'is no longer a dreamer, he is a creator'. Or, in one case, an uncreator. Dante's Ugolino, who saved himself from starvation by eating his sons, appears both on the door and in separate sculptures. In a group sculpted in the early 1880s, the lean, muscular cannibal positions himself over one of the supine boys, gripping his prey with ferocious affection: this might be a sexual attack, and his mouth hangs open in hunger or in panting lust. The abomination is aesthetic, because the creator has the right to destroy his creatures.

Alfred Stieglitz,
*The Hand of Man*,
photogravure,
1902

  The hand of God transmitted power to the hand of man. Stieglitz, who exhibited Rodin's drawings at his gallery in 1908, earlier took a photograph of the New York railway yards to which he gave the enigmatic title *The Hand of Man*. Man's achievement here is the abolition of nature. The only remnant of the world created by God in Genesis is the smudged, clotted clouds – and even they are superseded by the geyser of black smoke that seethes from the funnel of the advancing train. Curved steel rails on parallel sleepers replace the bumpy terrain that once lay underneath. The telegraph poles are secular crucifixes; the cables stretched between them web the sky with messages, so there is no further use for angels. The distant city is a geometrical diagram, a frieze of uninhabited rectangles. Although the photograph denounces the damage wrought by man's hand, Stieglitz could not help admiring a city whose angularity made it a work of modern art. In 1914 he called New York a 'giant machine, soulless, and without a trace of heart', adding that he found it 'truly wonderful'. Stieglitz's art depended on light. He did not presume to say – like God at the start of Genesis – that he had created it, but as industry besmirched nature he felt called upon to ensure that 'black and white maintain a living equilibrium'. The polluted dusk of *The Hand of Man*, where the rails gleam as they catch the rays of a weak, declining sun, was a reminder of his priestly responsibility. 'There is within me,' he said, 'ever an affirmation of light.'

Artists felt the need to make such assertions because the old bonds of creation had frayed. Gauguin in a letter written in 1888 advised a colleague that 'creating like our Divine Master is the only way of rising towards God'. The idea was not pious: the artist rises towards God because he is God's equal. Gauguin advised his correspondent Emile Schuffenecker to ignore nature when painting and to think instead of 'the creation which will result'. God made something out of nothing; painters should remember that 'art is an abstraction', not an imitation of the reality that already exists. In 1898 Gauguin announced that he had written a philosophical treatise about his painting *D'où venons-nous? Que sommes-nous? Où allons-nous?* It was, he added, 'comparable to the Gospels', although this was a New Testament that rescinded the Old. Gauguin was impressed by the conjectures of the Theosophical poet Gerald Massey, who in his *Book of the Beginnings* traced the 'Egyptian *Origenes*' of Christian culture, connected the rites of the Maoris or Gauguin's Tahitian neighbours with the mysteries of ancient religion, and treated Christ as an alias for pagan divinities like Pan. Gauguin conceded that the problem of where we come from and where we are going had been 'clarified' by 'the torch of reason'. Even so, he preferred fabulation to scientific rationality. In his painting, what he called 'the tree of science' grows in a tropical garden; its fruit is knowledge of the wrong kind, and its miserable legacy is bemoaned by the two mournful figures who hover in its shadow. An androgynous figure reaches up, unreproved, to pick an apple. A loincloth hardly conceals the excitement of this hermaphroditic Adam: perhaps sexual knowledge is pardonable, because it offers us a way of experiencing paradise. An idol with raised arms gestures towards the sky. Like Gauguin's title, this god asks questions but serves up no easy answers. Or perhaps the painting itself resolves the uncertainty. Gauguin's triple interrogation probes time, wanting to know about a past and a future that lie beyond our experience. The painting, however, is set in space, where the phases of existence are continuous, happening side by side rather than in succession to each other. On the right, a baby lies asleep; on the left, an old woman huddles like an ancient embryo, clasping a body that will soon fall apart and may then assume another form.

Paul Gauguin, *D'Où venons-nous? Que somme-nous? Où allons-nous?*, 1897

Strindberg believed that Gauguin had 'created a new heaven and a new earth'. The men and women in his paintings belonged to a species designed by him, and the sky – sometimes coloured red rather than blue – was one that 'no God could inhabit'. Such cosmic effrontery was almost obligatory for modern artists. In 1918 Giorgio de Chirico said that he and his fellow metaphysical painters were 'new Zeuses', flying through the air to survey the oddities that clustered on the crust of 'the terrestrial globe'. By discovering melancholy or menace in ordinary urban vistas, de Chirico believed that he had made 'the creation look more extraordinary than the creator'.

Conflict with Christianity was avoided by pledging allegiance to classical deities like de Chirico's Zeus, or to a miracle-worker from medieval romance like Taliesin. This was the name Frank Lloyd Wright gave first to the house he built for himself in Wisconsin and later to his architectural practice. Taliesin is a magic-making infant in the Celtic *Mabonigion*; the word means 'radiant brow' in Welsh, since the shining forehead of the precocious bard proclaims his mental power. Taliesin is always being asked whether he is a man or a spirit. He replies that he has been born three times already, that he sailed in Noah's ark, witnessed the destruction of Sodom and Gomorrah, and lived in India when Rome was being built. He adds that the sum of all knowledge is stored in his blazing head. The painter Egon Schiele imagined himself as an astral body, giving off light that oscillated ever more rapidly, scorching reality. For van Gogh too, genius was a form of holiness, made manifest by incandescence. He wanted to paint figures who were alight, as he said, with 'that something of the eternal which the halo used to symbolize'. But the source of supernatural radiance had dried up, and had to be replaced by 'colour vibrations'. The halo gave way to the halation, a nimbus of glowing air made visible by van Gogh's paint; it was no longer restricted to religious personages, but could glow above a field of corn or shine through the features of a gnarled, lumpish peasant. It also beamed from the fervent brain of the artist, at least during his manic episodes. After a quarrel with Gauguin in 1888, van Gogh reported to his brother that they both had heads 'as exhausted as an electric battery after it has run down'.

Gauguin and van Gogh both used the icon of the fish – an ancient ideogram referring to Christ, the fisher of men – as a personal signature, a testament to their martyrdom in a philistine society. This modernized aesthetic Christ was not always the Messiah. Max Ernst, for instance, treated him as a maimed victim of parental abuse. In 1923 the artist painted himself as the dead saviour in *Pietà*. The image is an Oedipal tableau: the dead Ernst has turned to stone, and his stiff body, shrouded in a hospital uniform, is not cradled by a mournful mother but held by a moustachioed, bowler-hatted figure who represents the artist's father. Ernst followed this in 1926 by painting the Virgin Mary spanking the bare buttocks of her young son. Her halo is in place, but Christ's has fallen to the floor as he jolts in pain, his hand scratching at the air. The expressionist Emil Nolde interpreted the Christian family romance less grimly. When he painted, he said he felt 'God inside of me, glowing and holy like the love of Christ'. The pentecostal flame that flickered above the heads of the disciples came from his palette; he decided that it should be lilac-red, which made Nolde himself a witness, like the apostles, to 'divine revelation'. Wassily Kandinsky, in an essay published in *Der Blaue Reiter* in 1912, recruited Christ to support his rejection of academic training. Kandinsky argued that infants or primitives knew how to transcribe a living spirit, because their vision had not been deadened by education; this, he concluded, must be why Christ declared that the kingdom of heaven belonged to children. In a letter to Schoenberg, Kandinsky said that his play *Das gelbe Klang* was as uncompromising in its edicts as the Ten Commandments. He justified its obscurity by again citing Christ, who told his disciples 'The rest you cannot grasp today'. Emphasizing the artist's reliance on an 'inner voice', Oskar Kokoschka found a precedent in the Gospel of St John, which announced that 'The Word became flesh and lived among us'. To liberate the repressed self, to find an image that laid bare its private, precious core: this was tantamount to Christ's incarnation, when the spirit entered a human body. Kokoschka then passed from the immaculate conception to the painful trauma of an actual childbirth. The sudden, spontaneous realization of the image should, he said in 1912, recall 'the first cry of a newborn child emerging from its mother's womb'. For the expressionists, creating art was half mysticism, half midwifery.

Artists quoted scripture so deftly that they made the Bible sound like a modernist manifesto. In 1957 Hans Arp was asked if contemporary art was religious. He said yes, but gave an incongruously orthodox reason: 'I don't mean that we are going to portray God the way Michelangelo did. I simply mean that we are going to abide by the commandment, "Thou shalt make no graven image"'. Moses is here enlisted as an avant-garde ideologue, and the Bible upholds Arp's ban on representational or figurative painting. Tristan Tzara, lecturing on Dadaism in Zurich in 1924, chose the devil as its theoretician. Dada existed to destroy preconceptions: its motive was what Tzara called 'the Satanic insistence' on asking 'What for?' – the same quizzical impudence that drives Milton's fallen angel. Through their capricious teasing, the Dadaists gave vent to 'the chaotic wind of creation'. Tzara's phrase pointedly disassociated the creative spirit from the need to make works of art. Creativity was breezy, irregular, a chaotic disruption of the atmosphere. A Dadaist poet could cut words out of a newspaper and jumble them up into a random order; a Dadaist painter could scrawl or scribble on canvas. But the true Dadaist would do nothing at all, relapsing into the idleness enjoyed by God before he embarked on the chore of creation. Tzara jeered at the purposeful toil recommended by Christian moralists, and explained that Dada was 'a return to an almost Buddhist religion of indifference'. Marcel Duchamp was even more disparaging: art, he thought, might be a useful narcotic, but 'as a religion it's not even as good as God'. Duchamp therefore excused himself from the bother of creating. The objects that he called 'readymades' lay to hand, awaiting an appropriation that rescued them from whatever function they once performed, and set them up instead as emblems of futility. A bottle dryer is like a leafless, man-made tree, a bicycle wheel propped on a kitchen stool jokes about the pointlessness of motion, and a urinal is a dry, unplumbed font.

In his *Tractatus Logico-Philosophicus*, Wittgenstein propounded the two-faced law underlying modern perception. 'The world,' he said, 'divides into facts'. Those divisible facts could also be added up: Wittgenstein defined the world as 'the totality of atomic facts'. Cézanne, described by Matisse as 'the God of painting', shared the constructive skill of the demiurge in *Timaeus*: the cube symbolized the three dimensions of space, and gave him all the material he needed for arranging the universe. In 1913 Max Weber, emboldened by Einstein's relativistic merger of time and space, painted *Interior of the Fourth Dimension*. His subject is triangular Manhattan, which he described as 'this great city of cubic form', with a ship entering the harbour; the scene functioned as a demonstration of the new physics because, as Weber said, the 'three known measurements' had expanded into an 'overwhelming sense of space magnitude in all directions at one time'. New York for Stieglitz was the site of a Manichean battle between black and white, enlightenment and darkness. For Weber, its fractional angles and the unsynchronized tempi of its streets made the city a model of infinity.

Nevertheless, the amalgam of atomic facts and splintered facets was shaky. The art of collage used scissors to enforce the division into disparate facts. After this, as Max Ernst said, came a whimsical 'coupling of two realities', glued into a new totality: a canoe and a vacuum cleaner, as Ernst proposed, could make love – though what knows what their progeny might be? Dalí disliked cubist objects because they pretended to be indivisible, like atoms that could not be broken down any further. Cubism, as he said in 1931, conferred 'the most abstract intellectual shapes' on pipes, jam jars and bottles. Here was a stubborn exemplification of Kant's belief in the irreducible thing-in-itself, which exists outside the mind and – in Dalí's description – doggedly resists 'the quite recent disturbances of appearance and phenomena'. The painter Leonora Carrington, who was Ernst's lover during the late 1930s, summed up surrealist doctrine in a pair of versified aphorisms:

> Disintegration is bliss,
> 'Tis folly to be solid.

Dalí had his own way of combating that fixity, by dissolution not division. Hence the edible, corruptible nature of the objects he favoured. He turned a chronometer into a slice of runny Camembert in his painting about memory, and on another occasion he posed his wife with a fried egg on her naked shoulder like an epaulette. He particularly admired the malleability of wax, used in sorcery for making little effigies of men and women which can be pricked with pins – a more obliging material than the clay from which God moulded Adam. In 1951 Georges Bataille sensed a 'universal vanishing', and announced without regret that the world was falling apart again. All that remained, he added, was the series of small universes put together by Ernst, whose art was 'a fragile, useless and last caprice'. Bataille probably had in mind Ernst's wartime panoramas of scorched, ashen cities, with ogres pullulating among the ruins.

The painter who seemed most like a supernatural advent was Picasso, although his admirers could not be sure what kind of divinity he possessed. Arp and L. H. Neitzel, writing about cubism in 1913, saw him as a lucid Platonist, whose four-dimensional shapes came 'close to the absolute, spiritual form of the Creator'. But in 1935 the surrealist poet Paul Éluard called Picasso a black magician who 'created fetishes', like those Cendrars venerated in the British Museum. The faces of the whores in *Les Demoiselles d'Avignon* are African masks, and their witchery transmits a graphic curse. Apollinaire credited Picasso with rearranging the universe to suit himself, which was a god's prerogative. He admitted that the creative endeavour could be brutal, even murderous. Picasso's revolution required an 'enormous conflagration', a seismic assault on our staid reality; it also entitled him, as Apollinaire said, to assassinate the human body, scrambling its organs and contorting its limbs. Watching him at work at the age of ninety, Brassaï likened him to a matador facing up to a bull, concentrating in order to kill. Others tried to find a place for Picasso in the Bible's account of creation. The Duchesse de Clermont-Tonnerre, Proust's friend, remarked that 'on the seventh day, God created Picasso'. Not – it should be noted – on the sixth day, when Adam was made: Picasso seemed more than human. Arp only slightly demoted Picasso when he said that, as the progenitor of modernism, he was 'as important as Adam and Eve'. In 1949 Gjon Mili, using a long exposure, photographed him drawing in the air with an electric torch: the beam instantaneously sketched a volatile human body that only the camera could see. It was a demonstration of divine virtuosity. God called light into being, and Picasso made it a calligraphic medium.

Resisting deification, Picasso took a wittily fiendish view of himself. In a caricature in 1903, he placed his head on the body of a pouncing imp, with a whiskery pelt, a flaunting tail, and a set of impertinent genitals. His eyes are as black as coals, and his mouth twists into a leer. Two paint brushes suggest the pointed ears of the goat-god Pan, wickedly synonymous with caprice. Picasso enjoyed playing the role of God's adversary. Art, he told the dealer Daniel-Henri Kahnweiler, was like the fire stolen by Prometheus, and the rebellious artist must use his gift to sabotage 'the established order'. Picasso applied the principle to his own work. A painting developed through a series of violent revisions, and the final result was 'the sum of its destructions'.

In 1935 he suggested that it might be worthwhile to 'preserve photographically ... the metamorphoses of a painting': this would trace the twisting pathways of the creative brain as it attempted 'to materialize a dream'. Twenty years later Henri-Georges Clouzot's film *Le Mystère Picasso* did exactly this. The metamorphoses which Clouzot documents involve defacements, disfigurements. Picasso draws a cactus, refashions it as a fish, changes it to a cockerel, then inks over the creature and turns it into a grinning demon. Later he designs a beach, stocking it with a realistic assortment of bathers. Soon the figures are wrenched into abstractions, chunky at first, then – as he adds another layer – wiry and elongated. A wash of new colour alters the time of day, and yellow sunlight is replaced by black night, with the sculptural bathers still romping. Offscreen, Picasso laments his own interfering impatience. 'That's terrible,' he says, 'I'll wipe it all out.' The transparent canvas is briskly rubbed clean so that he can create another provisional, short-lived world. Picasso returned often to the subject of the rape of the Sabine women, abducted as breeding stock by the Romans who needed to ensure their city's future. For him, rape denoted seizure and enforced transportation – which was the word's first meaning – rather than sexual violation. A metaphor also abducts its subject and wilfully metamorphoses it; the artist's work, in Picasso's view, was in this sense a justified rape. This restless rapacity obliged his contemporaries to think again about the nature of creative activity. In 1943 Piet Mondrian explained the allusion to jazz in *Broadway Boogie Woogie* by saying that what he liked about the music was its 'destruction of melody', which corresponds to the 'destruction of natural appearance' in modern painting. He added that, in his opinion, 'the destructive element is too much neglected in art'.

In 1920 André Salmon likened Picasso to St John Chrysostom, the church father whose honorific name referred to his eloquent golden mouth. Thanks to Picasso's drawings, Salmon declared, 'the Word of art' had been renewed and given back to mortals. The graphic word was all the more compelling because it was mute. In 1929 Salmon changed his mind about

Picasso's spiritual allegiance when he watched him at work on *Woman in a Garden*, using scrap metal to create a bony dancer surrounded by pronged, stiffly fertile plants. He scavenged choice bits of iron, fed them to the hot, hungry forge, and burst into what Salmon called 'Luciferean laughter'. Jung, psychoanalysing Picasso's imagery in 1932, diagnosed his fondness for debris as a Luciferean symptom; with his wanton ugliness, he yearned for the underworld, the 'death-struck' realm of annihilation. The Russian critic Nikolay Berdyaev saw the jester as a cosmic terrorist. The paintings by Picasso exhibited in Moscow in 1914 alarmed Berdyaev because they flayed surfaces, ripped away the layered concealments of culture, and returned to 'a transparent Stone Age'. This, he concluded, was not a new creation but 'the end of the old one'. Maurice Raynal thought that Picasso's art had the revelatory force of the apocalypse envisaged by St John the Divine. Thinking back to *Guernica*, Raynal said that this 'vivisection' of nature, with the sky raining fire onto a tormented earth, was the most exalted expression of 'the lyrical spirit'. Picasso enjoyed such terminal reveries. In 1943 he mentioned to Brassaï a scheme of Dalí's to cast in bronze a whole section of Paris, commemorating 'the instantaneous end of all life because of a cataclysm'. Dalí, incorrigibly fashionable, intended to freeze the Place de l'Opéra, with the expensive prostitutes prowling the avenues. Picasso's preference was for the world to end on the Left Bank, and he imagined metallizing Saint-Germain-des-Prés, with Sartre transfixed as he drank his coffee at the Flore or the Deux Magots.

Analogies with Genesis or Armageddon foundered because Picasso preferred the company of pagan deities. He modelled his own Venus, using a charred burner from a gas stove with the nozzles for the flames as her gaping orifices, and in 1964 paid homage to Priapus by making a jug that decanted liquids through its phallic spout. His sexually indeterminate harlequins reminded Apollinaire of 'Egyptian demigods', hybrids of human and animal. The minotaur was one of Picasso's self-images. This fabulous beast, which had a bull's head on a man's body, allowed Picasso to flaunt his brutish strength and creative virility; sometimes he gave the bull wings. Armed with a javelin in one of Picasso's 1934 etchings, the minotaur runs amok in a cubist's studio: it gores the furniture, which falls apart and cannot be reassembled, and causes a frantic human figure to mislay its face and one of its arms. Doodling, Picasso designed monsters even more garbled than the mixed metaphors of Horace. One of these, sketched as an April Fool's joke in 1936, has the body of a fish with a flattened peacock grafted on top of it and the hairy genitalia of a human male added to its underbelly; the penis squirts worms. The peacock's tail feathers, stretched along the fish's spine, support a frieze of dancing girls, their hair and clothes ruffled by one of those spring gales that startle the dormant earth awake. The eye of the fish widens in amazement at the mutations it has undergone. The background of this ink drawing is a snarled, tangled network of scrawls, as jagged as barbed wire: the signature of an uncontrollable creativity. The vivisector was also a resourceful vivifier, who did not restrict himself to red clay or the organic matter sewn together by Frankenstein. Once Picasso improvised a bull by twisting a portion of a junked bicycle into a new shape: the saddle now served as a head, and the handlebars were horns. He constructed a woman from an assortment of springs and metal tubes, with a kitchen colander as an unflattering replacement for her head. Her partner was a man assembled from scraps of wood and held in place by nails that uncomfortably recall a crucifixion – an angular geometrical being, tortured by rectitude.

In 1947 Rothko said that 'Without monsters and gods, art cannot enact our drama'. The phrasing is odd, because gods surely ought to have priority. For Rothko, however, art first of all needed monsters, the prodigies of an imagination that cannot tolerate the meagre limits of nature. He illustrated his own point by painting a polymorphous Oedipus, whose desire to merge with his mother has fused their bodies. Because Oedipus has been turned inside out, he is clothed in his own bleeding entrails. The story of Prometheus reminded Rothko that 'the gods ... are the custodians of powers that man must wheedle or wrest from them'. Art is the wrestling match. 'I have done everything to render my soul monstrous', declared Ernst. He meant that he had set free the fantasies that clamoured inside him; monstrosity was a sign of his heroic victory over the inhibitions that cramp lesser men. Dalí painted *L'Invention des monstres* in 1937: accompanied by a sibyl, the painter sits at a table surveying his personal zoo, which includes centaurs, a feline angel and a burning giraffe, all gathered at the behest of the prophet Nostradamus to announce a coming war. Dalí himself had a lucrative career as a sacred monster, a celebrity who acted out his fantasies for a fee. In 1935 he appeared at a New York costume ball wearing a shirt with an inset glass window, which served as the showcase for a pink brassiere: he had come dressed as his dream, revealing the psychic shame that clothes are supposed to cover up.

Picasso was inevitably intrigued by Balzac's story *Le chef-d'oeuvre inconnu*, a fable about the hubris of the artistic creator. The unknown masterpiece is painted and then destroyed in seventeenth-century Paris by the mad perfectionist Frenhofer, who lectures the young Poussin on the artist's necessary rivalry with God. Frenhofer runs through the classical stories about creating life: he tells an academic painter that the divine fire that sparked from the torch of Prometheus has gone out, and – after acknowledging that he has been struggling for ten years to represent motion and vitality on canvas – wonders how long it took Pygmalion to make his statue walk. Form, he says, is a Proteus, even more slippery than the one in the myth.

Looked at from a different angle, in different light, in a different mood, the same object twists into another shape. Despite this elusiveness, he speaks of the work that torments him as if it were both a painting and a person. It is 'my creation, my wife'; the woman it depicts, he goes on to explain, is 'not a creature, she's a creation'. But when Poussin is at last permitted to see the masterpiece, he finds it unintelligible: a chaos of overlaid colours and twisting lines, a barricade of pigment through which pokes just one recognizable feature, a foot. In despair Frenhofer burns the painting, then kills himself. It remains invisible; we have to make our own mental picture of it, using Balzac's words. Picasso saw Frenhofer as his forerunner, the pioneer who recognized that painting should recreate reality rather than duplicating appearances, and in 1937 he moved to a studio in rue des Grands-Augustins because he believed that this was the fictitious artist's address.

Ten years earlier he had illustrated Balzac's story in a set of etchings. With characteristic ambition, Picasso ventures to design Frenhofer's unimaginable painting for him; it looks, of course, like a Picasso. In one etching, a matronly model nods over her knitting. The artist pinions her with his eye, and translates her into an abstraction: a playground of looping lines and plump ovals, which signify no particular woman but symbolize female nature. A series of wood engravings goes even further. Now no model and no artist flank the masterpiece, attaching it to recognizable reality. Instead there is simply the creation, composed not from maternal curves but from jarring, angular lines, held together by black dots. A notional physique lurks somewhere behind the dashes and dots: it is possible to glimpse a head like a black sun, a single breast, a slim waist and expanding hips. But the body explodes outwards, and the lines are vectors displacing air, concussions caused by its progress through space. In a second wood engraving based on the story, the spindly lines might be bones. This image surgically unmakes the human body: two small black circles are eyes, staring in bewilderment at the disjected limbs and organs that once formed a consortium. Or are the dots meant to be nuclei? The unknown masterpiece expresses the unknowability of modern reality. Matter crumbles, as full of holes as the colander that sits on the neck of Picasso's sculpted woman. It takes more than glue, which makes wood and paper adhere in cubist collages, to hold the world together.

Paul Klee's manifesto for his own art, written in 1920, forced religion to give up its exclusive claim on the creative spirit. Without naming Prometheus, Klee explains that the 'impulse to create' is the kindling of a fire: the hand itches, starts moving, a spark leaps from it onto the canvas and from there flashes a signal to the eye of the viewer, igniting a response in his or her brain and completing a circle. To account for the origins of this drive towards self-expression, Klee quotes scripture – or at least he cites the misquotation of Genesis enunciated by Goethe's Faust, who declares that 'In the beginning was the Act'. Klee qualifies Faust's statement by adding that before you can act, you must have an idea; because infinity is circular, it may still be true that, as the Bible puts it, 'In the beginning was the Word'. That word, however, is not a poised logos, an unmoved mover. It emits energy, and cannot be satisfied with immobility. It grows into life, like an infant learning to crawl. Klee describes this process, which is the source of art, as an exploratory adventure. A dot starts to move and forms a line, the moving line extends into a plane, and between them several planes create space: we have made a world for our eyes and our bodies to wander in. This brings Klee back to Genesis, which he commends for supporting his account of the frolicsome, serpentine, creatively errant line. 'The biblical story of the creation,' he says, 'is an excellent parable of movement.' His aesthetic appraisal subverts the moral of the story: like the dot that acquires momentum and lengthens into a line, Adam and Eve are instinctively disobedient, because nothing that is alive will be content to remain still and to do as it is told. In the official narrative, they fall from grace when they stray from their appointed course; in Klee's parable, motion is the impulse of creation, so the curiosity that sends Eve off on her own cannot be criticized. When the symbol of temptation appears in Klee's parable, it has lost its malevolent peril. Arguing that the purpose of art is not to reproduce the visible world but to make that world newly, freshly visible, he gives as one of his examples an apple tree. We know what it looks like, and for that reason do not bother to look at it. Klee chides our laziness by describing the tree, and his words emphasize its attachment to nature and its contribution to the cosmic design: it is 'an apple tree in bloom', with 'its roots and rising saps, its trunk, the cross section with the annual rings, the blossom, its structure, its sexual functions, the fruit, the core with the seeds'. There is no warning that the fruit may be fatal, no ban on eating it. 'Art', Klee concludes, 'is a simile of the Creation', although in this case the similitude outshines the original, as the budding, plentiful tree casts off the grim labels hung on it by the creator.

In a lecture on modern art given at Jena in 1924, Klee likened the artist to a tree. His roots are in society, and through them he imbibes a living delight that rises as sap, distributes itself along the branches, and effloresces in what Klee calls the tree's 'crown', with its rustling leaves and its dazzling refraction of the sunlight. This is the miracle that Strauss placed on display at the end of *Daphne*, when the heroine becomes a singing laurel. The trunk is the body, the crown is the unseen voice that travels up through it and seems to breathe out of its fluttering foliage. A fig tree in a 1929 watercolour by Klee has the same fluency. It is hardly a tree at all, since it has no fixity or solidity; it is made from overlapping pools of liquid colour, and resembles a cloud of green and yellow light. Klee immersed himself in such fields of colour, dissolving 'into the whole of creation' with an all-embracing love that he called 'religious'. He thought of the viewer's eye as an animal grazing, and the looping trails and thickets of his sketches are a pasture through which we ramble, feeding as we go. He called works of art 'country outings': they regale us with unexpected points of view, opening beyond the blinkered confines of the utilitarian world. At best they waft us above the downtrodden earth, and let us guiltlessly experience the pleasure that Satan in *Paradise Lost* promises Eve when she eats the fruit. Klee's most thrilling claim for the spiritual and mental benefit of works of art is that 'they help you ... to fancy for a moment that you are God'. For as long as that invigorating moment lasts, you are a worthier God than the one Klee drew in 1930 in *Schöpfer II*. This is his caricature of Michelangelo's creator in the Sistine Chapel: a bird-man with a cumbrous, elephantine hand and a squashed body, his wings swaddled in bandages and ending in broken feathers or limp, incapable hands. In his 1920 essay, Klee mocked earthly or heavenly powers that depend on their 'ethical gravity'. To balance this heavy, forbidding gloom, we need an 'impish laughter', which ridicules priests and doctors. *Schöpfer II* is just such a fit of disrespectful hilarity. While disparaging the creator, it shows off its own ingenious creativity: the design is a labyrinth that, like the world itself, has no discernible beginning or end.

Klee often said that form was no concern to him. What mattered was the process of forming, for which he employed a biblical term. In the *Pedagogical Sketchbook* derived from the course he gave at the Bauhaus in Weimar, he referred to drawing as 'the human action (genesis)'. A point 'sets itself in motion (genesis of form)'. This version of genesis strays from the straight and narrow. The line embarks on a leisurely stroll, like that which took Eve away from the path of duty. For Klee, a drawing was the record of a graphic holiday; the tour proceeded aimlessly, digressively, with no interest in saving time by travelling the shortest way between two points. But before the line could stretch its legs, Klee had to arrange an expanse of space for its promenade. Hence the obstacle-strewn topography of his 1935 watercolour *Landschaft am Anfang*, which shows a landscape in the beginning with a steep upward slope and a pair of thrusting diagonal lines like a short cut down the hill or a mineshaft carved through it. Or does this landscape actually represent a human being comically sprawled on his back? The circular tree might be a head, the hill a belly, the straight lines the flailing arms and legs of a body that has lost its balance. The conundrum suggests that we are inseparable from the earth on which we travel. Klee likened his lines to 'fish swimming in all directions'. Any squiggle or doodle he drew, no matter how rudimentary, created a space. A cross-hatched plane is a ploughed field, and a bump denotes a bridge. Rest stops were sketched in: a broken line announces that the ocular walker has paused to catch his breath. Weather could be whipped up or calmed with a few graphic signals. A zigzag is a lightning bolt, scattered dots place stars in a clear sky. Each spatial element had its own charge of energy, extending – although the marks remained flat on the page – into three dimensions.

Art constructs its own paradise: Klee referred to the arena in which his brushes and pencils operated as 'Fruchtland', the fruitful land. His reveries about this thriving arboretum could be mystical, as if it were the home of Goethe's Mothers in *Faust*. He thought that artists must find their way back to the hiding-place where 'primeval power nurtures all evolution', and he called this 'the womb of nature, at the source of creation'. The depths were obscure, but above ground that power expressed itself in vegetative frolics. In 1921 Klee drew a series of plants that, no longer yoked to earth, dance in the air. Their stalks climb towards the sun; their tubers, hovering above the surface, resemble swollen human breasts. In the title of another drawing, the smile on an abstract face is described as a bud. A trumpet containing stamens sprouts from the nose, and two puff-balls that have released their seeds mark the eyes, closed in bliss. The face might be sneezing in a fit of hay fever, but that too is a sign of spring. In *Der Pathos der Fruchtbarkeit*, a bacchante with waving arms embodies the pathos of fertility. She squats with her legs spread wide, getting ready to give birth, but her swollen belly contains only a potted plant, with tendrils that reach out and scratch impatiently like her own fingers. Arp described his own collages, made in 1915 from paper and cloth, as 'porticos of pathetic vegetation'. When they mouldered, their perishability confirmed his 'joy in destruction' and compelled him to recognize 'the decay of all human creation'. Klee's pathos is less wistful; the woman, at once tormented and happy, is infused by Nietzsche's mood of tragic gaiety. Empathizing with nature, Klee was even able to draw the birth pangs of geological creation. In *Gebirgsbildung* in 1924, two arrows on a green grid prod the strata of rocks from opposite directions, and these irreconcilable pressures cause a mountain to form. Curved lines register the buckling of the earth, while jagged triangles mark the new peaks and troughs designed by the upheaval. Mountains erupt into life; angels materialize more stealthily, but Klee knew what their nativity must look like. *Engel im Werden* shows an angel in the making: a face indistinctly shapes itself in a blotchy sky and a cross hangs suspended in mid-air, waiting to be grasped and given meaning.

Anthropomorphizing chaos, Klee made portraits of the elements, with lines deftly drawn on thin air or unfixed water. In 1927 he painted an approaching snowstorm. The background is a bruised cloud of paint, which stands for the thickening of the atmosphere; using a pen, he scratched on top of this a rectangular network of interlocking squares to represent the crystalline snowflakes. The cloud is vague, fuzzy, impressionistic, but the snow it contains has the hard-edged precision of a cubist diagram. Two different views of nature are brought together and simultaneously verified. In *Spiel auf dem Wasser* in 1935 Klee played with the possibility that water too might have a recognizable physiognomy. The horizontal lines drift inconsequentially across the paper, elapsing and erasing themselves as forgetfully as a stream. But odd eddies and wrinkles, like knots in wood, detain the water and give it features: two pools that could be eyes, a pair of nostrils, a distended ripple that serves as a mouth.

Some pencil sketches made by Picasso in 1933 describe an orgiastic geometry. A circle to which two smaller testicular circles are attached extends into a long, stiff, straight line and drills into a square body which has grown its own pair of circles: breasts that will come in handy as the reproductive work continues. Even rectangles look organic, capable of sensation. Pleasure travels along neural networks or down luxuriously stretching limbs; far away from the place where the genitals slot together, eyes roll, mouths gape, a head is tossed backwards in ecstasy, fingers twitch and shiver like electrified wires. Klee's lines were also intent on propagation. They behaved like wandering hands or propulsive seeds, and he allowed them to follow their instincts. A triangle, he said, was 'under the command of its own Eros', which squeezes its sides towards a climactic point. In one of his pedagogical sketches, geometry mimes copulation: a row of spermatic arrows aim at an egg-shaped dot that will be the apex of the triangle. Biology, after all, differentiates the sexes by using geometrical shorthand. A circle with an arrow protruding from it is male, and the same circle with a cross beneath it is female. In his examination of perspective, Klee refuses to let the lines expire when they converge at their vanishing point. Again there is a surprising climax, a startlingly funny evacuation of energy. The tapering triangle extends across space as far as the eye can see, its sides drawing closer as they recede. But the addition of cross-bars coaxes us to read the triangle as a railway line connected by trestles, and at the vanishing point Klee places a steam locomotive which coughs out a trail of black smoke. We may try to regulate nature with our spirit levels and our machines, but it remains an organism, and it cannot help letting off steam. Klee thought that art should participate in 'the act of world creation, stretching from the past to the future.' The railway lines speed us along that trajectory, with steam whistling a salute.

Klee defined art as 'Genesis eternal!' Not, as in the Bible, a genesis that happened once long ago, followed only by destruction or degeneration. For Klee as for Spinoza, genesis was continuous, as unstoppable as our sexual cravings. No wonder he admired the encyclopaedic conquests of Don Giovanni in Mozart's opera. In the beginning – as he put it in one of his poems – was the motif, the energetic impulse, 'sperma'. It determined form, and was 'primordially masculine'; the ensuing development of form, by contrast, was 'primordially feminine'. His own drawings, he added, 'belong to the masculine realm'. He drew a Bavarian version of Giovanni in 1919: the seducer scales a bright patchwork wall with the names of his conquests scribbled across it, and the ladder on which he acrobatically perches is another of Klee's erectile triangles. In some scenes from the opera sketched in 1939, Klee's philandering line manages to coil itself around most of the women on Leporello's list. In an image that illustrates a vocal trio, Giovanni's body is inseparable from the two women who compete for him. A rivery, overlapping line unites his mouth with one of these eager victims; the other woman, temporarily pushed aside, sheds a jewelled tear because he has neglected her. Klee's wily lines intertwine the sexes, and achieve what he called 'a condition of ethical stability' by balancing 'the masculine principle (evil, stimulating, passionate) and the feminine principle (good, growing, calm)'.

He was fond of opera's other male and female libertines, whose quest for pleasure matched the motives of his own art. In 1921 in a fairytale scene he summed up the hapless love affairs of Offenbach's Hoffmann. A coiled chain of notes purls from the mouth of the singing poet, and bounces through the air towards the various objects of his desire. Strange plants – the flora of Klee's fecund land – sprout to exemplify the vital drive that impels him. On a steeple, a rooster with vainglorious tail feathers loudly advertises its virility. In 1920 Klee drew *Schleiertanz*, which must surely be his tribute to the heroine of Richard Strauss's *Salome*, who by performing the dance of the seven veils persuades Herod to execute the chaste prophet who has spurned her. Klee chose to emphasize the comic muddle of the dance. Salome, a flustered adolescent, gets trapped in the veils she is trying to remove, and – with one leg thrust out at a risky angle – seems about to fall over. She traps her head in the fabric and loses her face, but an open circle in the middle of the design offers a preview of her stripped body: here is the still centre around which her grappling arms and cavorting legs revolve.

In the same year, Klee designed an altar for the greediest of female libertines in *Die Büchse der Pandora*. The story of Pandora's box supplied Frank Wedekind with the title for the second of his plays about Lulu, the guileless sexual careerist who casually makes love to men and then discards them. Klee's box is an urn, perhaps even a Grail, placed on a table as if in readiness for a religious ceremony. Like the sanctified vessel in *Parsifal*, it radiates heat; the source is a vaginal slit, bordered by foliage, that looks like the flame from a gas jet. Smoke wafts out of the combustible urn – but does this signify evil's entry into the world, unleashed when Pandora opens the box? Not really: the cloud contains glimpses of Wedekind's play, with characters gossiping and flirting in a bourgeois parlour that even contains a piano. Lulu refuses to take the blame for the maniacal behaviour of the men who pursue her, and they only call her a fiend when she rejects them. By identifying the box with the cloistered female genitals, Klee dismisses the myth as a product of male sexual fears.

Wedekind gives Lulu herself a chance to answer back in *Erd-Geist*, his first play about her. Her current husband has a fatal heart attack when he finds her entangled with the painter who is working on her portrait. Lulu is briefly taken aback by his collapse, but recovers when she realizes that she will be a rich widow. The painter catechizes her, trying to make her accept moral responsibility. He first asks if she can speak the truth, then if she believes in a creator. Her answer in both cases is 'I don't know'. So how would she swear an oath? What does she believe in? Does she have a soul? Has she ever been love? In all cases, she doesn't know. The responses establish her pitiless honesty and even attest to the innocence of her spirit. The painter is aghast, but he marries her all the same. Alban Berg used the interrogation as the text for a duet in his opera *Lulu*. Here the heroine has an extra means of defending herself: she sings rather than speaking. A harp plucks out the level row of pinched notes used by the painter when asking his questions. Each of his queries doggedly repeats the same sequence, but her replies are no longer flat and uninflected as in the play. Every time she sings 'Ich weiss es nicht', she adds a different vocal decoration, a spurt of ornamental coloratura like an aural doodle. These fillips in the vocal line represent her twisting unease, or perhaps her soaring superiority to the leaden scruples of her inquisitor. Coaxed by her inventiveness, the orchestral texture thins out; wind instruments and a vibraphone help her to take flight. Music has come to her aid. 'Glaubst du an einen Schöpfer?' her confessor demands, ponderously measuring out his syllables. Of course she doesn't know what to say. The only creator she believes in is herself, and she performs the act of creation all over again by transforming breath into shimmering, elusive sound.

# 28
# LET THERE BE SOUND

Klee's aim, when he immersed himself in his reservoirs of colour or unleashed his wayward lines, was to approach 'closer to the heart of creation' than art usually managed to do. For Schoenberg too, composition involved looking into 'the very nature of creation'. When he set dissonance free, replacing the eight vertical notes of the octave with twelve notes aligned in a horizontal row, he felt that he had reconfigured the universe. He arranged musical intervals like atoms or constellations; the molecules he so intricately positioned opened out into a galaxy. He described his privileged understanding of creation in a lecture that he delivered in 1941, hailing the artist, like God, as an absolute originator, who demonstrates what the process of genesis actually means. 'There was no light,' Schoenberg said in his lecture, 'before the Lord said: "Let there be light".' God's omniscience enabled him to think up that non-existent force, and his omnipotence called it into being. Schoenberg reminded his listeners that whenever 'we poor human beings' single out 'one of the better minds among us as a creator', we expect that person to exhibit the same prowess. The artist, challenged by 'the Divine Model', must be able both to see the vision and to realize it. Schoenberg envied the Almighty's exemption from the toil of notation. 'In Divine Creation,' as he said, 'there were no details to be carried out later; "There was Light" at once and in its ultimate perfection.' Artists, condemned to false starts and then to the long labour of transcribing a vision and correcting its imperfections, began from a different and more daunting first principle.

Schoenberg considered his music to be a revealed truth, a bequest from on high, and his arrays of chosen tones often seem to be written on the air in letters of flame. His prelude to the *Genesis Suite* – a biblical melodrama on which a team of émigré composers collaborated in Los Angeles in 1945 – spells out God's first thoughts about creating the world in a broody, hovering sequence of twelve notes, delineated by tuba and violins. At the beginning of the oratorio *Die Jakobsleiter*, the row's notes are marked out by basses and brass. They set a striding, compulsive rhythm that is taken up by the archangel Gabriel, who gruffly orders resurrected mankind to scale Jacob's ladder. At the beginning of *Moses und Aron*, Moses puzzles over a God who is unperceivable, unrepresentable. But this invisible God is made audible by twelve voices that sing and speak from inside the burning bush.

Chris Merritt and David Pittman-Jennings in Peter Stein's production of *Moses und Aron* at the Salzburg Festival, 1996

At the end of *A Survivor from Warsaw*, the Jews from the ghetto defy their Nazi tormentors and declaim a forgotten hymn, 'Shema Yisroel'. It is, as the narrator says, a 'grandiose moment', music's sudden challenge to death; it is also the enunciation of another twelve-tone row.

The notes in Schoenberg's rows no longer heeded the homing summons of a basic key, which worked as ballast like the Newtonian force of gravity. Ferruccio Busoni described tonality as 'the diplomatic two-semitone system'; his reference to diplomacy likened the scale to an 'entente cordiale' that made it possible for antagonistic nation-states to coexist. When the accord faltered, Edgard Varèse praised the collapse of an order upheld by 'sanctified and regimented notes', as if music were confirming the failure of religious and political authority. Schoenberg was more interested in a scientific revolution. Einstein made space and time interpenetrate to form 'a four-dimensional space-time continuum'; in Schoenberg's music too there was, as he said, 'no absolute down, no right or left, forwards or backwards'. His twelve notes related only to each other, and they did so relativistically. Every sound was a compound of what he called 'oscillating vibrations', open-ended and flexible. The notes did more than follow each other in time, falling into order as a melody; they expanded to occupy 'musical space', a borderless realm that was filled by the reciprocal relations between them. Here the theory graduated from physics to metaphysics, as Schoenberg associated this sonic plenum with the heaven unveiled at the end of Balzac's *Séraphîta*. The transfigured angel tells Wilfrid that 'in the infinite, time and space are not' and shows him a circling flock of spherical worlds – earthly, spiritual, divine. Each world has a centre, to which all its constituent atoms adhere; each of those atoms, no matter how minute, is an individual, the centre of its own infinitesimal world. Despite this divisibility there is no fragmentation: Balzac reports that 'all was one', afloat on undulating waves of light. To Schoenberg, this mystical realm matched the account of matter given by the new physics, with its luminosity, its magnetic fields and its stellar dynamics.

These messages handed down from on high threatened the accustomed earthly state of things, perhaps even weakened the adhesion of nature. In his novel *Doktor Faustus*, Thomas Mann bestowed the dodecaphonic system on the crazed composer Leverkühn, whose emancipated dissonances burst out in a symphony about the apocalypse. Like Schoenberg, Kandinsky believed that 'technically, every work of art comes into being in the same way as the cosmos – by means of catastrophes'. His paintings organized what he called a 'thundering collision of different worlds', often elliptically referring to Armageddon. Angels raise the dead with their brazen trumpets in his *All Saints II*, while a windstorm tosses the revenants to and fro in the torn, flaring sky. Schoenberg often imagined such days of wrath, when worlds were made or unmade. The wild ride of the ghostly horsemen in his oratorio *Gurrelieder* concusses the sky, and a percussionist rattles chains while the spectres howl. Gabriel in *Die Jakobsleiter* harries the uprisen souls towards judgment and harshly dismisses them if they are unworthy.

A mind trained in musical logic could converse with the logos, and was ready to take a hint from the all-powerful colleague Schoenberg called 'the Supreme Commander'. But did those commands come from above, or were they transmitted from one part of the brain to another? Art, Schoenberg assured Kandinsky, belonged to 'the *unconscious!*' The German word he used was 'Unbewusst', which is one of the last, faint, long-breathed exclamations of Wagner's Isolde at the end of her 'Liebestod'; it comes just before she expires as she sings about her highest bliss. In an analysis of his *Kammersymphonie*, Schoenberg explained the way two themes secretly intertwine as one of 'the miraculous contributions of the subconscious'. Such coincidental offerings, as Schoenberg put it, had an 'extreme profundity and prophetic foresight ... which seem superhuman'. Schoenberg told Busoni that he created by lowering himself into 'the stream of my unconscious sensations'. The process, however, was wilful, deliberate, like a wide-eyed self-hypnotism. In the monodrama *Erwartung* a nameless woman in a nocturnal wood stumbles over the body of the lover she may have killed; she is travelling through an undiscovered part of her brain. Her shadowy trauma becomes a state of illumination in *Moses und Aron*, which begins with the prophet meditating on an unknowable God. Both characters are blind seers, guided unconsciously towards the truth – a kiss that inflames the darkness like a beacon in *Erwartung*, a pillar of fire in *Moses und Aron*.

In 1915 Schoenberg planned a vocal symphony that was to begin with God's funeral. Confronted by the prolific bounty of nature, the heavenly guardian of property and sexual propriety falls ill and dies. Instead of giddily revelling, a disoriented speaker, declaiming a monologue written by Schoenberg himself, acknowledges that now art will have to do God's work. He makes a start by confounding Genesis: 'The darkest – it appears never to have been light. The darkness is eternal; it was, is, and will be. In the beginning there was darkness'. Then a mental miracle intervenes, and the voice reports that 'The darkness becomes visible – !' Milton described hell as 'darkness visible', and in heaven said that God was 'dark with excessive bright'. The paradoxes, taken over by Schoenberg, assert the mind's power to recreate the physical world. The speaker in the unwritten symphony praises the enlightenment that banished darkness, then notices with a chilly shudder that 'the sun is without power'. 'Why,' he asks, 'has the spiritual world exploded?' An explosion releases a flash of light, unleashing energy that might also be the emanation of a spirit. In the same year Schoenberg composed an orchestral song based on Ernest Dowson's 'Seraphita', a sonnet paying homage to Balzac's angelic heroine. The earthbound poet at first recoils from Seraphita visionary face, and pleads that he is as yet unworthy. He goes on to describe his forthcoming hour of need. When thunder rattles and sea and sky are riven and the waves rear in a last fight, he hopes that she will swoop down like his personal moon and look on his pale, submerging form. She is not a saviour; he expects to drown, overwhelmed by passion. But Schoenberg's scoring effects a rescue. After the frothing of Dowson's flood, the last ethereal sounds in the song are made by high strings, a xylophone and a gong: an instrumental consort that belongs in heaven.

God was Schoenberg's surrogate, even his obliging deputy: in Freudian terms a buried id, not a censorious superego. Explaining why he renounced the lush Wagnerian sonority of his early scores – *Pelleas und Melisande*, an orchestral evocation of Maeterlinck's play, or *Verklärte Nacht*, a string sextet transcribing the fraught recriminations of another pair of lovers – he said he had orders to venture into atonality: 'the Supreme Commander' sent him off on 'a harder road'. The decision of course was his own. Relaxing with friends, he revealed the true identity of this divine executive. In 1946 he wrote a letter to Kokoschka, gossiping about one of the painter's Californian admirers. The value of the woman's adulation was lessened, Schoenberg said, because she also praised the work of Klee and Kandinsky. He complained that 'she had *too many gods*', and confessed his dislike for an eclectic, indiscriminate polytheism. He too had fans who insulted him by ranking Hindemith, Bartók and Stravinsky 'if not above me at least as on a par with me'. Stravinsky at the time lived near Schoenberg in Los Angeles; a world of theoretical disagreement and personal mistrust divided them. In the letter, Schoenberg helped himself to a prohibition from the Supreme Commander's decalogue, and used it as a warning to his followers: '"Thou shalt have one God"'. When D. H. Lawrence defined art as 'a form of religion', he took care to exclude 'the Ten Commandments business, which is sociological'. Schoenberg, however, was not prepared to discard those forbidding edicts. Three months before his death in 1951 he was honoured by the Israel Academy of Music. He replied by hoping that the academy would produce 'priests of art' possessing a 'sense of consecration', and reminded the academicians that God 'chose Israel ... to preserve ... the true, pure, Mosaic monotheism'. Schoenberg was both Moses and the monopolistic God whose worship he enforced. The choral creed in *A Survivor from Warsaw* – an outburst that stuns the body and ravages the soul – is another reminder of this strict singleness: it tells Israel that the Lord is one, 'Adonoy e<u>h</u>od'.

In a lecture delivered in 1937, Schoenberg looked ahead to 'the promise of a new day of sunlight in music', which was to be his offering to the world. He was referring to the solar conclusion of *Gurrelieder*, where the erotic tragedy of the lovers Tove and Waldemar is absorbed by nature and transformed into a jubilant comedy of renewal. The dead heroine returns to the elements: the whispering woods are her voice and the unruffled lake is her eyes, the clouds sculpt a likeness of her breasts and the stars sketch her smile. A massive chorus finally salutes the sunrise, which blazes in C major. Clattering cymbals and triumphal brass announce the searing glare, drums rumble as if the earth were heaving with exhilaration, the strings send out waves of warmth. Song gives way to a tuned shout of joy, voiced by all humanity. This was the impact Schoenberg hoped that his musical gospel might have; this was the acclaim that should have greeted it. Even after decades of disappointment, the anthem remained his rallying cry. In 1945 he abbreviated *Gurrelieder*, compressing a hundred minutes into a ninety-second fanfare for one of Leopold Stokowski's open-air concerts at the Hollywood Bowl. He quoted the cavalcade of Waldemar's dead companions rioting through a haunted night, then ended with the sunrise, which flared from a battery of cymbals. In the humid summer darkness of a canyon above Hollywood Boulevard, he once more called for a transfiguring dawn.

When this visionary confidence deserted him, Schoenberg grumbled that the artist was like Adam trudging into the wilderness, sentenced to 'a hard road where, driven out of Paradise, even geniuses must reap their harvest in the sweat of their brows'. Ironically he found himself, as he said about his life in California, 'driven into Paradise', exiled in a land of milk and honey that had no use for his crabbily complex music. The biblical citations were his reproach to God, a reminder of the neglect and scorn he unjustly suffered. He also identified himself with Christ, the second Adam, crippled by a burden of expiatory guilt that he nevertheless shouldered. In 1923 he advised younger composers to 'bear their crosses as I bear my own!' Schoenberg sympathized with Wilfrid in *Séraphîta*, 'the new Messiah' who describes his plans 'to devastate the world and to reform the nations'. Schoenberg pretended to be a reluctant Messiah, although he did not refuse the call. During the First World War, a fellow soldier who recognized his name asked if he was the composer Arnold Schoenberg. 'Somebody had to be,' he replied, 'and nobody else wanted to.' His fate was predestined.

Despite his inflexible edicts, Schoenberg understood that the creative spirit was whimsical, spontaneous, chancy. Hence his interest in play, the most gratuitous of human activities, and its efforts to regulate randomness. He knew that games were potentially deadly: after being called up for military service in 1915 and 1917, he designed a board for what he called coalition chess, replacing the outmoded chivalric figures of kings and queens with miniaturized cannons, mortars, tanks, planes and submarines. Another game sported with planets rather than missiles. Schoenberg – who took up tennis in the 1920s, and often played with George Gershwin in Los Angeles – would have appreciated Nabokov's notion that the designer of the galaxies was a tennis player delivering volleys. Physics studied and rationalized the transit of heavenly bodies, and Schoenberg did the same for tennis balls. He invented and copyrighted specialized marks to record faults, drop shots, and balls hit into the net. In the process he solved a linguistic puzzle. He wondered why a score of zero points, which he drew as an egg, should be called 'love'. He explained the term to himself by recalling the scene in Wagner's *Siegfried* when Mime tells his foster-child that love means yearning. The tennis player, Schoenberg deduced, is someone who would love to score a point, but has not yet succeeded. He did not need Freud to tell him that all artists are unrequited lovers, who play games to revise a reality that leaves them dissatisfied.

Speculating about creativity, Schoenberg flirted with science fiction. In 1932 in Vienna his student Anton von Webern gave a lecture on twelve-tone composition. Webern predicted that, when the procedure's underlying laws were clarified, there would 'no longer be any possible distinction between science and inspired creation'. Schoenberg's 1941 lecture on the method commiserates with the lonely travails of genius, and goes on to glance at the researches of a mad scientist. The creator, he says, connects details and makes them cohere into 'a kind of organism'; Schoenberg supposes that he could 'bring his vision to life' by creating 'a homunculus or a robot'. A short associative jump takes him from alchemical fantasy to engineered fact. He was fascinated by the notion of an intelligent machine, and knew that the human brain is an intricately calibrated gadget. Contriving variations, he said that he resembled a mathematician who does cube roots in his head or a chess player who plots his next ten moves while wearing a blindfold. Like Giotto, he could draw a circle that proved to be perfect when checked with a compass; he also knew how to divide a line correctly into three, four, six, seven or even eleven parts. His mysticism was on friendly terms with technology. Artists, as he pointed out, entrusted their spiritual missives to radio waves, which swelled, crested and broke in the air between one mind and another. In 1909 he assured Busoni that the creator would somewhere find those 'who possess a receiving organ which corresponds to our transmitting organ. As with wireless telegraphy'. In 1948, protesting against Mann's appropriation of his theory in *Doktor Faustus*, Schoenberg said that the artist must be 'a real inventor', which is not quite the same as being a creator. He already had several inventions to his credit (though not as many as his mentor Swedenborg, whose familiarity with heavenly mysteries helped him to design a glider, an air gun, a mercury air-pump, and a stove that slowed down the process of combustion). During the 1920s he constructed a flimsy slide rule, fastened by a strip of surgical bandage, that kept track of inversions and retrograde motions within the tonal row. In another piece of bricolage, he taped several pencils together so he could draw all the lines of a musical stave at once. There were also extra-curricular proofs of his ingenuity. He worked out an alarm system that transmitted different signals in case of fire, accident or assault. He even devised a cooperative network for public transport in Berlin, easing inter-changes between tram, bus and railway, calculating appropriate fares, and designing a ticket that divided the city – like Dante's inferno – into num-bered concentric circles. In 1927 he sent his proposal to the relevant office for consideration, but forgot to frank the letter. It was returned to him unopened; he took that to be an omen, and did not persist.

The inventor is a prophet, gifted with foresight. In this case, Schoen-berg concluded, he wasted his prescience on an indifferent or unworthy world. He treated the relationship between artist and prophet in *Die Jakob-sleiter*, where the two occupy different positions on that steep ladder to heaven. As always, he had messianic ambitions for the piece, which is proba-bly why – after working on the score between 1917 and 1922, with an attempt at a revision in 1944 – he never completed it. Because it addressed, upbraided and rectified the entire world, he wanted it to be performed by an almost global mass of musicians. He envisaged an orchestra of almost three hundred players, with thirteen vocal soloists and a chorus of 720, divided into groups which were to make their entries separately so that at last, on the ladder's upper reaches, the music would 'spring from all directions at once'; Winfried Zillig, who orchestrated the fragments after Schoenberg's death, settled for less.

Gabriel impatiently marshals a crowd of earthlings who lack the energy for transcendence. A babbling chorus complains about the archangel's demands, and takes pride in its meagre mortal achievements. The voices describe the comfortable bourgeois life of profit and pleasure: a work is accomplished, and a child comes into the world. Gabriel roughly dismisses such satisfactions. He has no interest in art that contributes to the world's wealth, or serves nature's desire for increase. A first candidate for promotion stands out from the fatigued, squabbling choral groups and describes his qualifications. Schoenberg identifies him as Ein Berufner, one who is called; his calling is that of the artist, and he assures the angel that he has spent his life in quest of beauty. He is a tenor, so he reaches up an octave to a high C as he boasts that he looked into brightness without being blinded and saw his own sun. The note for an instant catches the brilliance of the planet. Unimpressed by the man's smugness, Gabriel accuses him of being a heathen idolater. Are all works of art mere replicas of the golden calf that Moses smashes? Schoenberg, following Swedenborg's three grades of love, here derides genius as narcissism. The artist is in love with himself; he must make way for the prophet, who selflessly loves the world. Beyond that lies God, who alone is capable of loving the immaterial idea of heaven. The graduation from one stage to the next is musical as well as moral. Gabriel tells a struggling soul to emulate the angels, who in turn resemble one who is far higher; he likens this spatial interval to the relationship between a fundamental tone and the distant overtone. When the chosen one, Der Auserwählte, floats into view, he too uses musical terminology as he confesses that he remains embedded in the base concerns of his secular colleagues. They are the theme, he says, and he is at best a variation. Gabriel, in a voice hushed in awe, charges him with a loftier mission, which is elaborated in a series of legalistically precise, emphatically punctuated steps: 'Geh; verkünde; und leide; sei Prophet and Märtyrer'. Despite Gabriel's tender farewell, it is a terrifying prospect. To spread the word means to suffer, and the prophet must expect martyrdom. Whether he was being harried out of his teaching position in Berlin by the Nazis or benignly ignored in California, Schoenberg derived a morose solace from his paranoia.

In the third act of Schoenberg's opera, which he left uncomposed, Moses abandons the mellifluous, fluently lyrical Aron, and stumbles on through the desert. He stutters about the sacred word that is denied to him, and resigns himself to silence. Music is censured when Aron falls down dead; speech too then dries up. 'Here I can only stammer,' said Webern in his lecture on the twelve-tone method, uncertain about the future. *Die Jakobsleiter*, with some help from Zillig, at least manages to reach heaven. A symphonic interlude completes its progress upwards, and Gabriel's striding rhythm is overtaken by the respiration of the spirit, with wispy, refined violins and a sighing harmonium. A soprano who represents the soul vocalizes rapturously, freed from the body. Other female voices, uttering vowels not words, hover in the ether like Balzac's seraphs. The destination foreseen by the singer in Schoenberg's second String Quartet is finally attained, although for only a minute at the end of the oratorio: music breathes the air of other planets.

After this glimpse of the promised end, Schoenberg returned to the beginning, or to events before the beginning. In his contribution to the *Genesis Suite*, he imagined the elemental origins of the world. The other composers recruited for the project by Nathaniel Shilkret were given excerpts from the Bible's opening chapters to set. Shilkret himself, better known for scoring RKO musicals, underscored God's activity during the first seven days. Alexandre Tansman filled in the subsequent mishaps of Adam and Eve. Cain and Abel were assigned to Milhaud. He had of course already composed his own account of the creation, though it was set in Africa and offered a tribal alternative to Genesis; here he concentrated on destruction, with a percussive battery illustrating the invention of murder.

The narrative of the flood and the forgiving rainbow was shared between Mario Castelnuovo-Tedesco and Ernst Toch, and the suite concluded with Stravinsky's concise recapitulation of the building works at Babel. At the first performance a preachy narrator declaimed the biblical passages. The conductor Werner Janssen hoped to persuade Franklin Delano Roosevelt or Winston Churchill to record the narration: he fancied that they might be interested in the collective effort of musicians displaced by revolution and war in Europe, whose pooled resources offered a model of good fellowship to a world that was trying to recreate itself after 1945. Wisely, neither Roosevelt nor Churchill wished to play God.

There was no text for Schoenberg to set, because his contribution preceded the first utterance of the biblical Word. He described the formless void of Chaos, unlighted and inarticulate. The territory was familiar to him. In 1911 his brother-in-law Alexander von Zemlinsky, disturbed by the orchestration of Schoenberg's *Pelleas und Melisande*, warned that 'each theme has its own timbral identity, made up of the most varied combinations of instruments: chaos!' But the start of Schoenberg's prelude to the *Genesis Suite* is chaotic only to the untrained ear. The dodecaphonic row it unfolds is an ordering principle; these are the pillars of the law, on which the world will be founded. The first sound is a shuddering downbeat on the brass, like the stirring of life. The tuba probes the murky dark materials that are God's source. Violins complete the row, tuning us to higher frequencies. The brass returns to report on clashes and casualties as the elements are disentangled. The subterranean gruntings and aerial tinklings may sound unsynchronized, but behind this molecular affray the tonal row is busily repeated and recombined in a double fugue: creation is a taxing technical feat, a labour of permutation. Schoenberg relaxed his own theory by allowing the modulating orchestra to reach the home key of C major, used by Haydn to signal the advent of light. At the same time – as in Scriabin's setting of a rival myth, *Prométhée* – a choir gasps in wordless wonder. Schoenberg's allocation of roles is intriguing: female voices are heard first, then male. The order is biological not biblical, since in Genesis priority is given to Adam, with Eve as an afterthought. Shilkret, whose movement starts with the narrator's words 'In the beginning', had to begin the world all over again. Instead of Schoenberg's malleable row, he imagines origins as a series of eerie, slithery nebular motions: fall-out from a galactic explosion, not the careful assembly of twelve building blocks.

Although Schoenberg was the last composer engaged by Shilkret, his contribution took first place in the running order, as if it were the generator of the suite. With equal aptness, Stravinsky's contribution – for which he covertly negotiated a fee of a thousand dollars, while the other collaborators had to make do with three hundred dollars each – came at the end. Schoenberg's prelude welcomes the future in its ecstatic choral outburst; Stravinsky's commemoration of Babel looks backwards, reviewing and terminating musical history. Shilkret conceived of the project cinematically, and expected his composers to write a soundtrack for biblical events. But Stravinsky objected to this easy-going ecumenical scheme, on grounds of both aesthetic conservatism and religious orthodoxy. As Tansman recalled, he stubbornly insisted that 'the Divinity should be illustrated in no way whatsoever. He is too great. Music should illustrate nothing whatsoever. Such is not its function'. In Stravinsky's judgment, a pictorial style was a profanation, daring to visualize 'what must remain a mystery and is accepted as dogma'. In his setting of the passage about Babel, he relied instead on abstract, undramatic formulae. An implacably regular passacaglia matches the cooperative labour of the men who construct the tower, on an earth that is 'of one language, and of one speech'. Continuous variation is a reminder that men are not creators, and can only modify or alter what already exists. The tower rises in a fugue, accumulating tiered layers; for Stravinsky, who considered Babel to be an arrogant invasion of the sky, the busy counterpoint derides the frantic futility of human toil. When God confounds the workers by depriving them of a shared language, no noisy climax marks the tower's collapse. Instead the first patterned ground bass returns to restore the stasis of a society undisturbed by revolutionary over-reaching. The yodelling soul soars through the stratosphere at the end of *Die Jakobsleiter*. Stravinsky's music, by contrast, is doggedly horizontal. The passacaglia got its name from Spanish musicians who played as they wandered ('pasear') in the street ('calle'). Applied to the story of Babel, the form counsels us to walk at a steady pace and not run or – God forbid – climb. It is a rebuke to all towers, and to Jacob's teetering ladder. When Schoenberg heard the piece, he remarked 'It didn't end, it just stopped'. That abrupt curtailment was deliberate, confounding the notion of progress. *Genesis*, like the world, emerges from nothing in Schoenberg's atemporal prelude, then pointedly halts in Stravinsky's finale, when a tired God decides that time must have a stop.

Stravinsky refused to allow the Hollywood actor engaged by Shilkret to speak God's words. Instead he gave the utterance of 'the Eternal' to a chorus, which chants the divine diatribe against human arrogance. Elsewhere he employed the chorus to impose a social consensus – tragic condemnation in the oratorio *Oedipus Rex*, comic mockery in the opera *The Rake's Progress*. Here the group represents a faceless polyphonic God, oddly like the six singers and six speakers who vocalize in Schoenberg's burning bush. But whereas Schoenberg in *Moses und Aron* creates a numinous, wavering haze, the delivery of the decree in Stravinsky's cantata is solemnly official, as if a public proclamation were being read out by a committee of bureaucratic functionaries. The aim, as Tansman reported, was to present God's speech as a quotation – venerable, antiquated and immutable. Stravinsky sanctimoniously lengthened the distance between God and men by his unidiomatic accentuation of words. 'Behold', with which the choral intervention begins, is stressed on the first syllable; such irregular accents mean that the broadcast from the sky is hardly intelligible. This did not worry Stravinsky, who thought that our duty was to obey, not to understand.

In 1939–40 in a series of lectures at Harvard, Stravinsky spelled out the 'fundamental laws' that underlay his later disagreement with Shilkret. He was alarmed by the atheistic temper of modernity, which he blamed for the Russian Revolution; he attacked the 'new original sin' of his contemporaries, who denied that their existence derived from God. Original sin now meant the cocky presumption of originality. 'Since I myself was created,' Stravinsky said, 'I cannot help having the desire to create.' But, unlike Schoenberg in his commentary on the Divine Model, he took care not to overestimate this emulation of his maker. He told his audience at Harvard that he disliked the pretentious word 'artist', and preferred to think of man as an artisan, a humble copyist who should be content with the subordinate role of 'homo faber'. Stravinsky must have been gratified by the Bible's enumeration of the tower's ingredients: it specifies that Babel is made from bricks, with slime as mortar to bind them. As limited and unreliable beings, we need restrictions, which can be supplied by classical precedent. Otherwise, Stravinsky confessed, he felt a dizzy dread of tumbling into the 'abyss of freedom'. The common speech shared by the builders at Babel cements a community, which is the aim of classical art. God's retributive joke splinters this shared language. When each of us begins to speak an individual dialect that is unintelligible to others, we turn into artists of a different kind – romantic egotists or modern eccentrics, condemned by Stravinsky. In 1953, in tandem with Dylan Thomas, he planned an opera that might have been an epilogue to Babel and an act of reparation for its error. Thomas died before discussions had gone very far; they agreed, however, that it would be set on a wrecked earth after an 'atomic misadventure', and decided that it would dramatize what Stravinsky called a 're-creation of language'. Abstractions were to be purged: words must be simple captions for things, to discourage ideological disputes and keep the reborn human race out of trouble. 'Aboriginal man', as Thomas said in his summary of the plot, needs to 'make a new cosmogony', but he does so by taking short views, avoiding intellectual vagaries. A tree was to sprout through the radioactive rubble. Why should the survivors bother about what to call it? Their more important task was to discover what use they could make of it.

Stravinsky liked to describe himself as 'an inventor of music'. He defined the word more strictly and abstemiously than Schoenberg: to invent is to discover something that already exists, not to bring it into being. In an interview published in 1959, Robert Craft asked Stravinsky what 'creation' meant to him. Stravinsky bluntly replied 'Nothing'. After protesting against the vulgar misuse of the idea, he insisted 'Only God can create'. He condemned the relaxed, democratic definition of creativity made popular by American social psychologists: 'a child's scribble is not an "act of creation"', nor is our intestinal function, as Freud thought, since animals do as much and animals cannot create'. He was surely wrong to consider animals uncreative, since bees build hives, beavers construct dams, and birds' nests are often artfully put together from the materials available, plaited and woven into decorative patterns. But Stravinsky's hostility to the romantic notion made him treat even God as a craftsman rather than an artist. This is how creation is presented in *The Flood*, a short musical play commissioned for television. Although the subject is nominally the deluge, it begins at the beginning, with an accelerated summary of God's week-long creative labour. Stravinsky even starts with what he called a 'musical Jacob's ladder', constructed from a twelve-tone row. Too modest to be compared with Schoenberg's transcendental elevator, this is rigged up from the plucked strings of a harp and a few lilting intervals passed between the wind instruments. God's efforts as he separates the elements are signalled tersely in chords that work like shorthand: this creator is a quick, economical epigrammatist. At a meeting in Oxford, Isaiah Berlin urged Stravinsky to concentrate on 'the first and seventh days of the Creation, the two Holiest days'. Stravinsky dreaded the longueurs of such a scheme, and said that

Designs for Igor Stravinsky's television opera *The Flood*, by Rouben Ter-Arutunian, 1962

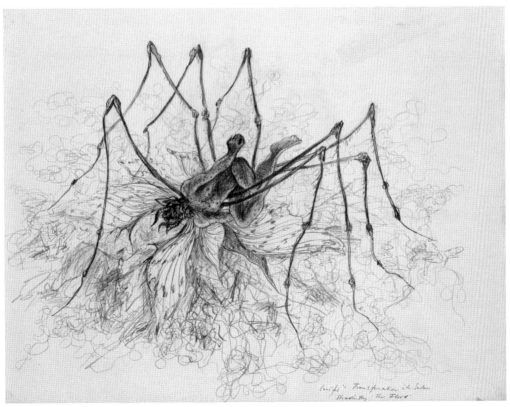

the music would be like 'a British weekend', which in those days was a synonym for tedium.

God remains invisible in *The Flood*. He is permitted to sing, although Stravinsky shared the role between two basses who introduce themselves as 'I, God' but declaim in unison to ensure that the deity remains impersonal, characterless. This duetting God produces a dualistic creation: Adam and Eve are born together, wrapped in the same swaddling or chrysalis. God designs man as 'a skilful beast', an animal with the power to wield tools. Stravinsky particularly liked that phrase, taken from the fifteenth-century Chester cycle of mystery plays. He preferred its homely practicality to the puffed-up prescriptions of Pico della Mirandola's God who, at about the same time, told Adam that he could be his own 'fashioner'. In *The Flood*, God says that the man he makes will be designed 'after my shape and like-ness'. 'Shape', Stravinsky decided, was better than the Bible's word 'form' because it was more solid, and 'likeness' had a proper zoological rigour. This practicality is passed on to Noah, described by Stravinsky as 'a building contractor' with an obligation to complete his job on time. The ark is put together in a brisk percussive symphony that consists of hammerings and clatterings on any instrument that makes a noise when knocked, including the xylorimba. Every concussion represents a nail driven home, and perhaps jokes about the reproductive purpose of the vessel. A caller who gabbles like a sports commentator or an auctioneer marshals the animals as they troop aboard; he has a partiality for musical creatures, and at the end of his list calls for 'each fowl that a song makes'. Even music is made, not born.

The flood that follows is a vagrant waste, thudding and rumbling, rhythmically heaving, terrifying in its stealth and its malevolent crushing weight. An amorphous downpour could hardly appeal to an artist who valued control and containment: when Stravinsky first visited Niagara in 1937, he likened the cataract to a revolution, and said that it was 'terrible'. For similar reasons he equated Noah's deluge with the atomic bomb. The typological reading of history suited his conservatism, because it showed mankind reeling from one catastrophe to another, always repeating the same foolhardy mistakes. The poet Marianne Moore described the repre-sentation of the flood as Stravinsky's 'symbol of chaos'. For Schoenberg in the *Genesis Suite*, this could be a creative source; for Stravinsky it was a dead end. Chaos, he decided during his early discussions with the choreographer George Balanchine, was cognate with Sin. In a conversation reported by Craft, he refused to intellectualize the condition: 'what does "Chaos" mean? "Things without forms"? "The negation of reality"? This is phraseomania'. Stravinsky conveyed its substance in the same way that Haydn did, amassing the rudiments of music – intervals, chords – without making them cohere into a melody. After the waters disperse and the rainbow writes its assurance across the sky, the end of *The Flood* reverts to the beginning, with musical events happening in reverse order. Noah sends his sons and their wives off to multiply, and declares that 'so a world begins to be'. A jubilant angelic choir fades, and is then cut off in mid–syllable; the God who is being praised retreats to his habitual distance, and in his absence the horn, oboe, flute and piccolo collaborate again to sketch the ascending rungs of Jacob's ladder. In fifteen seconds the instrumentalists climb from the slurred brassy curse that announces original sin to the brightness of what Stravinsky called 'primal light'. These last bars briefly eavesdrop on the origins of art: music has returned to the sky, from whence it came.

# 29
# CHILDREN OF CHAOS

In Boito's opera *Mefistofele*, Faust calls the mischief-making demon 'figlio di Caos', the child of Chaos. Though the phrase is hardly complimentary, it was taken up by the dramatist Luigi Pirandello, who felt doubly entitled to use it as his calling-card. His plays, true to the modernist principle of indeterminacy, chaotically fractured truth and sabotaged social power. Is the madman in *Henry IV* actually a king? Will the citizens in *So It Is (If You Think So)* ever understand the utterances of the veiled, oracular woman who is a local official's mother-in-law? But Pirandello was also literally the child of Chaos, because he happened to have been born in Contrada Caos outside Agrigento in Sicily, a rural haven to which his family had retreated during a cholera epidemic. He was proud of this random fate: it proved that his own existence was a happy accident, and he made it his business to go on disrupting the customary universe.

In Pirandello's *Six Characters in Search of an Author*, written in 1921, chaos erupts from its pit and takes control of the world. A group of actors is rehearsing another play when the six unauthorized characters invade the stage and demand a chance to act out their grievances. They are the members of a bourgeois family, as archetypal as the figures on playing cards. An author who is not Pirandello has invented them, embroiled them in a tragic plot about sexual betrayal, then left them in limbo. The Father presses their case. He points out that literary characters are living germs; they have the same rights as creatures who emerge from the womb, because the imagination that nourishes them is also a 'fertile matrix'. Pirandello believed that artistic creation was as much of a mystery as 'natural birth': does any artist know exactly what happens when a particle of observed life, lodged in his head, fertilizes his fantasy? He mockingly compared himself to an ingenuous or sly young woman who suddenly finds that she is a mother, 'without having any precise intimation when it began'. Perhaps the immaculate conception and the virgin birth are nothing but a candid account of how art is created? As the Father says, the uninvited appearance of the six characters is only a shock because most authors 'hide the workings of their creation'. He and the other imaginary beings insist on completing their drama of psychological accusation and brutal revenge. The intrigue that derives from what Pirandello called their 'disorderly passions' ends in death; satisfied by the shedding of blood, they return to their place of origins. But to the dismay of the theatrical director, they then resurrect themselves for a curtain-call, ghoul-ishly outlined by a green spotlight. We cannot prevent them from popping up through the floorboards, or popping into our heads. An author, in Piran-dello's view, has no authority. All he can do is allow accidents to happen.

Three years after writing the play, Pirandello added a preface explain-ing it as a fable about the creative process. The characters, he confessed, had been let into the house – or given house-room in his brain – by an unruly, puckish maidservant who turned no-one away from the door. Her name was Fantasy: she ought to be under her master's control, but she has a whimsical will of her own. Although Pirandello claimed to resent her indiscipline, he could hardly discharge her, because she was acting on his own unvoiced instructions. A wily servant facilitates a master's vices, and is content to take the blame for them. Pirandello tried to ignore the obstreperous intruders, and fought them off when they slipped separately into his study and begged him to write a novel about their feud. At last he decided to make use of their importunity: why not write a play, then allow them to run amok in it? Having taken over, the six characters demonstrate their power by collec-tively creating a seventh. They prepare the scene for her, and she comes when called. This is Madama Pace, the fat, lewd, luridly painted procurer who waddles on and, speaking a garbled pidgin that mixes Italian and Spanish, propositions the Step-Daughter on behalf of a client. Her apparition is a feat of magic, or perhaps a miracle. Pirandello likened it to a saint setting his own statue in motion, the kind of marvel that appeals to credulous Italian peasants; he might also have compared it to the enlivening of the sculpted Hermione in *The Winter's Tale*.

In *Six Characters in Search of an Author*, mobile life battles against the strictures of art; the spectacle recalls the primal transition from chaos to cosmos. Pirandello accepted that life, to perpetuate itself, must 'become fixed in our corporeal form'. But once the spirit has found a body to house it, it sets about stealthily killing its host. We begin to die the moment we are born; the world starts to degenerate at the instant of creation. Hence the displays of passion given by the characters in their little tragic farce: their tears, laments and noisy accusations externalize the entropic decay that is happening inside them. The thermodynamic law that dooms the earth governs all our self-depleting actions and our self-expending emotions. Art seems to be exempted from this grim natural law. Characters in literature, as Pirandello says in the preface, are like embalmed corpses, incorruptible though sadly not alive. When you open Dante's *Divina Commedia*, you find Francesca da Rimini still alive, despite the fact that she is posthumously describing her own murder; if you read the book a hundred thousand times, she will always speak with the same breathless ardour, as if unaware that her husband is about to surprise her with her lover and kill them both.

But Pirandello felt obliged to deny this reassuring fiction, and made his play tell the stricken truth. He regretted having to present the clashes of the characters in such a fragmented, unconsecutive way, leaving us to make guesses about their history. Still, as he explained, it was his intellectual duty to exhibit the 'organic and natural chaos' that art usually denies. The characters take on form and then, torn asunder and worn out by their passions, lose it. Dissipating, they descend once more into that black void which is both the world's beginning and its end. The actors disperse as the director – like God reversing his command 'Fiat lux' – orders the electrician to kill the house lights.

Modern artists questioned the organization of the universe: is it good, as its creator declared, simply because it is closed, completed? That brave dissent can be heard for a moment in Alban Berg's second string quartet, first performed in 1927. He entitled the quartet *Lyric Suite* because it originally concluded with a setting of Baudelaire's sonnet 'De profundis clamavi'. The poem served as an erotic confession, allowing Berg to admit the misery of his adulterous infatuation with Hanna Fuchs-Robettin. Because the words were so incriminating, Berg suppressed them; but the notes to which they were attached remained intact, and the instruments secretly mouthed Baudelaire's text. Working from an annotated score Berg sent to his unattainable mistress, the musicologist George Perle has reconstructed the silenced song. Baudelaire's cry from the depths is addressed to a lover, not to God, and he accuses the cruel, distant woman of having destroyed the world by denying herself to him. He lives on a dark, icy planet where nothing grows. Beyond it, he is confronted by 'cette immense nuit semblable au vieux Chaos'. Berg used a translation of the poem by Stefan George, who changed the defining dimension of chaos from time to space, calling it gigantic not old: the corresponding line set by Berg is 'dieser nacht, o ein chaos riesengross!' The prospect ought to be desolate, but when Berg's soprano sings the phrase she seems to be walking a tightrope, elated by the emptiness beneath her. Her voice daringly skips upwards on the second syllable of 'chaos', as if she were executing a risky leap and accompanying it with a scream of both terror and pleasure; she treads with care through the separate syllables of 'riesengross', but briefly lunges below the line like a trapeze artist who pretends to stumble. She is flirting with chaos, rather than recoiling from it in dread.

For D. H. Lawrence too, chaos was our starting point. In *Mornings in Mexico* he rejected cosmic systems based on causation. He disliked the idea of a First Cause, and was bored by the over-extended, drearily continuous narrative of evolution. He preferred to think of creation as an impulsive, instantaneous event, a big bang whose ricocheting echoes are still audible. He believed, he said, in 'what the Aztecs called Suns: that is, Worlds successively created and destroyed'. The first explosion extruded 'bits of chaos flying about. Then out of the dark, new little twinklings reviving from nowhere, nohow'. We are wrong to imagine that this chaos can be contained or repressed. In *Apocalypse*, a last infuriated eschatological pamphlet published after his death, Lawrence warned that 'the abyss, like the underworld, represents the superseded powers of creation'.

Having established his version of the beginning in *Mornings in Mexico*, Lawrence reverted to the chronology of Genesis, with the successive emergence of birds and animals. But no God is present to design and explain the screeching parrots he describes, or the flamingoes daintily propped on one delicate leg. They have created themselves, as 'smithereens ... bursting in all directions' after the sun blows up. This is why Lawrence's retelling of the story is so full of astonishment: the advent of the elephant stupefies the birds, which ask '*What in heaven's name is this wingless, beakless old perambulator?*' The 'twinklings' of spontaneous life to which Lawrence refers are creatures, but they might just as well be the creations of men. In 1914 Lawrence wrote a long, digressive essay which purports to be a study of Thomas Hardy, although it roams across the entire history of consciousness and culture from primitive religion to the women's suffrage movement, settling on novels like *Far from the Madding Crowd* and *The Return of the Native* as instances of the 'rage of self-preservation' that drives us to make art. The essay is more than a literary manifesto. It responds to an urgent modern need: 'Give us a religion, give us something to believe in, cries the unsatisfied soul embedded in the womb of our times'. What we are advised to believe in is fiction. Lawrence called the novel 'the one bright book of life'. The exclusiveness in the phrase is a snub to the Bible, which used to be the one necessary book, also known as the good book. Now it is novelists like Hardy or Lawrence himself who reveal to us 'man alive' rather than man cowering in fear of eternity.

The substitution is logical, because for Lawrence artistic work is prompted by 'a craving to produce, to create, to be as God'. But there is a difference between Hardy and the biblical Logos: this artistic god does not put a stop to chaos. Lawrence's reverie returns to 'an unthinkable period long before chaos', when 'life formed the habit of gravitation'. No Newtonian law established this grounding: it was the discovery of a personified life spirit, which resembles Bergson's 'élan vital'. Lawrence imagines a 'great mass of life' or 'one motionless homogeneity'. The 'unquickened lump' gratuitously animates itself, like a boulder that suddenly decides to roll down a slope. The instinct predates consciousness, because this version of Genesis happens, as Lawrence says, 'before any differentiation'. Once life starts to separate into species and then into individual specimens, the pace of evolution is irresistible. Invertebrates give way to mammals, then man ensues. The process continues beyond him, and Lawrence peers into something like the heaven of *Séraphîta*, where 'in the future, wonderful, distinct individuals, like angels, move about, ... perfect as a complete melody or a pure colour'. He invokes the scriptural 'Uttered Word', but identifies its creative power with the human impetus to make both love and art. He calls this motive 'the germ, the sperm impulse', and revises the Bible so that now God obeys the mating cry of an earth whose voice, demanding insemination, is that of Lawrence himself: 'as I lie in the womb of my times, ... I send forth all my calls..., asking for the Word, the Word which is the spermatozoon, which shall come and fertilize me'. The long mythological trek summarized by the essay begins here, and it reaches a conclusion, for the time being, in Hardy's novels. Along the way, Lawrence is alarmed by a fatal disintegration, the symptom of a consciousness that abstracts us from each other and from nature. The study includes an abbreviated history of painting, which emphasizes the development of a fatal spirit of abstraction. In an aside about painting, Lawrence complains that Turner was working towards 'a white, incandescent surface, ... proceeding from nullity to nullity', infatuated by a blinding, immaterial light.

At least Hardy's people – above all the doughty, self-preserving Tess of the d'Urbervilles – remain attached to their native earth. Some of them possess a 'distinct individuality', but others spread their subterranean roots more widely and remind Lawrence of the time of origins. He praises them for possessing 'an unaccomplished potential individuality', or – even better – 'an impure, unindividualized life embedded in the matrix'. The heroine of *The Laodicean* has an 'animal pedigree', and Tess, waking up, is said to be as warm as a sunned cat. Lawrence likens these figures to plants cracking the pots in which they are confined or London trees breaking through the pavement that presses down on them. His own characters in *The Rainbow* and *Women in Love*, which he went on to write during the next two years, share this uncontrollable biological energy and this familiarity with chaos. The world they live in is perpetually being destroyed and created again by the violence of their feelings. When Tom Brangwen in *The Rainbow* catches fire erotically, he has the sense that he exists in 'a new creation', and the Polish widow to whom he proposes 'quivered, feeling herself created'. After a church service, she steps out, elated, into 'a world new-created, ... into the resurrection of the world'. Their son Will, reborn when he marries, surveys a society that has apparently been scorched and cauterized by an earthquake. Its surface peels off, and trivial encumbrances – 'houses, factories, trams' – are swept away. He looks into the molten core, which is his own inflamed emotions. A domestic tiff can be apocalyptic. After his wife tells him to go for a walk while she does the housework, he slinks off, 'uncreated'.

Will struggles to illustrate this perpetual renewal in a wood carving he makes for the church. It shows the stiff, angular body of Eve being dragged from Adam's side. The torture of her creation convulses the chiselled figure, and Will trembles as he works on the tough hillock of her belly. Like all the figures in his 'Creation-panel', he leaves her unfinished, because even God – whose unveiled hand tussles with her – still labours 'in a silent passion of Creation' that can never be content with its work. Much later, he looks again at the awkward little relief, rejects it, and decides to model in clay instead. The results dissatisfy him because he imitates Renaissance busts: the result is 'only reproduction' – mimicry not creation. He continues his frustrated progress through the history of art by turning to paint, and does some watercolours of the church for which he made the carving. Again he is unhappy: the church tower stands up erectly, defying the atmospheric diffuseness of the impressionist painters, but its 'lack of meaning' irritates him. Finally he settles on the most ancient and practical artistic activity of all, beating metal to make bowls and constructing 'pendants in silver and pearl and matrix' for his womenfolk. Art began by supplying us with utensils and bodily adornments; Lawrence warns that it should never forget that humble primary mission. Will's daughter Ursula finds a way beyond the blockage that leaves him so baffled. For her, creativity is an exploratory venture into the body, not the manufacture of images that wrongly compete with physical reality. She experiences her own 'entry into the source of creation' when she embraces Skrebensky. Thanks to him, she is carried back 'into the pristine darkness of paradise, into the original immortality'. Paradise here is the same as chaos, an instinctual darkness that dwindled and weakened when the first light began to shine. Later Skrebensky disappoints Ursula, and she is morosely pleased to discover his unworthiness. 'She was glad she could not create her man. She was glad she had nothing to do with his creation.' Instead she looks beyond herself to 'a new creation', signalled by the rainbow, a luminous impalpable cathedral that is 'the creation of the living God'.

The accord between men and God collapses in *Women in Love*, where human beings are found to be irredeemable. Birkin considers that 'people don't really matter', and looks forward to their extermination. When he sets up house with Ursula, they browse at a street market, test a mattress, and discuss possibly buying a chair. They then decide that they won't have any furniture. What use is it if you live on top of a volcano, which boils over whenever your mood changes? Reviewing the 'destructive creation' of an industrial society, Birkin tells Ursula that they are terminal creatures. The end of the world, he jokes, isn't as much fun as the beginning. *Women in Love* begins in the sooty English Midlands, a 'ghoulish replica' of reality, obscured by smoke and coated in cinders. It concludes in the white, glacial wilderness of the Swiss Alps, where Ursula's sister Gudrun says she feels 'übermenschlich' or superhuman. Mountains excited and alarmed Lawrence because they reminded him of nature's bracing contempt for men. The heroine of his story 'The Princess' leaves a dude ranch in the New Mexico desert and rides up towards the snowline. The peaks rear like stiff corpses, and a frigid wind is exhaled by 'some vast machine'. Staring into a gulf, she looks at 'the inner chaos of the Rockies'. Creation is the product of ancient traumas and tantrums that have hardened into stone.

The earth convulsively creates itself, rather than being smoothed into shape by God. The rest of the work is done by a man and a woman naked in a garden. In 1927 Lawrence painted Eve sneaking back into paradise, evading the angel who has come to expel her and Adam. He also painted Adam and Eve as they gather up apples that have ripened naturally and fallen from the Tree of Knowledge; Adam throws one at a grey-bearded God, an unwelcome intruder. In *The Rainbow*, the adolescent Ursula ponders the biblical text that describes the sons of God taking the daughters of men as their wives. Her reflections are inevitably heretical: wasn't Christ an only child, and what men did God create apart from Adam? When she has sex with Birkin in *Women in Love*, she recalls 'the old magic of the Book of Genesis' and now grasps the meaning of the verse that puzzled her. Admiring 'the stuff of being' in Birkin's loins, she sees him as 'one of the sons of God such as were in the beginning of the world', and to him she is 'one of the first most luminous daughters of men'. Every act of love brings back the bumpy instability of origins, and every climax is a sudden annihilation. In his hut, the game-keeper Mellors in *Lady Chatterley's Lover* has a shelf of books that report on the modern infirmity of matter, with texts 'about the atom

D. H. Lawrence,
*Flight Back into
Paradise*, 1929

and the electron'. Another volume in his collection excavates the fermenting chaos of nature, discussing 'the composition of the earth's core, and the
causes of earthquakes'. Lawrence places his lovers in a seismic Eden, where
their copulation no longer has divine patronage. It may even require the
stoking fury of a man who – like Mellors the satyr – is 'really like a devil!'
Connie pays him this compliment after he invades her anus and there
locates 'the bottom of her soul, fundamentally'. The forbidden act recreates
her, penetrating 'the very heart of the jungle of herself, ... the real bed-rock
of her nature, ... the last and deepest recess'; Mellors forces her to cast off
shame and to shed the tattered remnants of her social existence, as if he were
conducting her between life and death.

Lawrence told his acolyte Harry Crosby that the phallic uprising of
*Lady Chatterley's Lover* directly connected man to the sun, the source of our
flammable creativity. Crosby – a wealthy Bostonian who converted to sun-
worship and irradiated himself with an ultra-violet tanning machine – took
this gospel literally. He rewrote extracts from the Bible, renaming God the
Sun; he revered his own penis as 'the rod of the Sun' and, in a parody of
prayer, ignited it with his hand by masturbating. Impatient for union with
this febrile, detonating star, Crosby killed himself in 1929. Lawrence wrote
an introduction to Crosby's heliocentric anthems, which he republished
later that year, a few months before his own death, under the title 'Chaos in
Poetry'. The essay celebrates the 'surging chaos' that agitates nature and the
'unspeakable inner chaos' that boils in our bodies. We cannot live with this
mayhem, so we discipline or denigrate it. Having gained control over an
external chaos, we call it cosmos; the chaos within, when tamed, is known as
consciousness. Lawrence compares these artificial shelters to an umbrella
which we raise to protect ourselves from 'the everlasting whirl'. Sometimes,
keen to be deceived, we paint a sky on the umbrella's waterproof underside.
The flimsy mobile roof may even grow into a dome or a vault. Beneath
these hoods, we stay dry; at the same time we bleach, sickening for lack of
the sun and longing for writers to poke holes in the ceilings and walls of our
bunker and let in 'the natural chaos'. Lawrence's poem 'God is Born' does so
by surveying the history of the cosmos in a series of lyrical epiphanies. At
first 'the dim flux of unformed life' makes way for an inexplicable radiance.
The delighted atoms announce

> Behold, God is born!
> He is bright light!

The struggle of 'intangible chaos' continues, and as the elements wriggle
out of it a drop of water falls to the ground and vapourizes. The atoms
reconsider their previous statement and decide that God must be wet. In the
'molten chaos' of the earth, sapphires cool, which provokes another chorus

of praise: this time, the newly born God is blue. When a vein of gold glints in the rock, God turns bright yellow. Every announcement is premature, because the universe has not finished creating itself; the hymns of praise misrepresent the living chaos because they fix it in a form, like the domineering schoolteacher in *The Rainbow* who 'crystallized the class into order'. The angelic choir of electrons thinks again when a 'little eggy amoeba' hardens in the foam. Next the mulched mosses and ferns produce a narcissus, and 'every molecule of creation jumped and clapped its hands'. The emergence of a lizard, a peacock and a leopard is cause for further jubilation. Finally man separates himself from the animals and stands on two legs. The amazed electrons catch their breaths and cry 'God Himself is born!' The creator is replaced by his creatures.

'God is Born' concludes by mimicking the dreary locution once used by teachers when instructing their pupils how to prove a point, then dents this finality by insisting that we have not yet completed our assignment:

> And so we see, God is not
> until he is born.
> And also we see
> there is no end to the birth of God.

In *Apocalypse*, Lawrence finds support for the argument in the vision of Ezekiel who saw, enthroned among 'the wheels of the revolving heavens', four creatures whose wings were studded with eyes. These terrible ancestral beings, Lawrence suggests, are 'probably older than God', even though they devote themselves to praising him. Their seniority hints at a truth that lies 'behind all the creation myths': this is 'the grand idea that the cosmos always was, that it could not have had any beginning. ... It could not have a god to start it, because it was itself all god and all divine'. Lawrence added an epilogue to his poem, dismissing our self-congratulatory image of an anthropomorphic deity. His 1928 watercolour *Renascence of Men* presents humanism as a dead end. One naked man receives the adoration of another, who bends over, buttocks whitely raised in surrender, and kisses the feet of his master. Foot-worship might possibly lead on to fellatio, and the upper man is reaching down to caress his underling or to guide his head. The result is a false and inequitable religion: the man who would be God requires other men to abase themselves. No wonder that Birkin in *Women in Love* longs for 'a humanless world'; he believes, as Ursula says, only in grass, which is truly egalitarian – though he adds that he also likes trees, birds and 'the unseen hosts'.

Birkin hands over the creative task to the children in his art class when he gives them crayons to make sketches of budding hazel. The gynaecious flowers are to be red, the androgynous flowers yellow; the flushed colour marks the contact between the tree's nutty crimson ovaries and the

Paul Cézanne,
*Women Bathers
by a Tent,*
1883–5

pollinating catkins. Lawrence's own paintings bared nature's reproductive arrangements. Nuns ogle the genitals of a sleeping gardener in his illustration of a scene from Boccaccio's *Decameron*, and in *Leda* a swan with an erect, writhing neck spreads its wings while thrusting into the receptive nymph. Even urination irrigates the earth. A watercolour of a naked man pissing is entitled *Dandelions*, presumably because he is watering the grateful flowers. His urine forms an arc which is exactly half a rainbow. The 'via galactica' derived from spilt milk, so why shouldn't a liquid covenant gush from this limp penis? Lawrence favoured a corporeal cubism, which – as in Cézanne's groups of female bathers – portrayed the body as 'a chaos of lumps'; the bodies in his own paintings are all swollen breasts and protuberant buttocks. But what he called 'this new chaos' was censured and controlled by officious, tidy-minded theorists like Virginia Woolf's friend Roger Fry, who praised paintings he admired for their 'significant form' while politely ignoring what the forms signified. The orthodoxy imposed by Fry made Lawrence represent him as Christ, the founder of an aesthetic church who self-importantly announces 'I am the revelation and the way! ... Lift up your eyes to Significant Form, and be saved'. A saviour whose kingdom is not of this world degrades the earth on which the rest of us live. In *Women in Love*, Ursula is offended by a rigid, inert statuette of a horse. The sculptor Loerke, adhering to Fry's creed, tells her that 'the horse is a certain form, part of a whole form', and says she is not supposed to be offering it a lump of sugar. Ursula insists that it is still a horse, and ought to be shuddering with hot-breathed nervous expectancy.

Modern artists attacked a creation that had settled into an inflexible formality; they did so – like Franz Marc in *Kampfende Formen*, painted in 1914 – by aggravating conflicts between the elements. Marc's battling forms refer to the preparations for war in Europe, but they also acknowledge that the natural world has always been at war. Fire grows tendrils and talons that clench the air like an aquiline claw, and twists into coils to release the energy it contains; the black shape it menaces could be the bituminous earth, stirred up into a dust cloud that resembles a charging bull with its horns lowered to gore the flames. Even peaceable grass grows spikes, and raises hillocks with prongs like barbed wire. Higher in the sky, light blazes from stars that collide with each other. Blood dribbles down the canvas, shed by the scarred firmament. When Stieglitz photographed clouds, he claimed to be reporting on the same aerial conflagrations (although, because he worked in silvery monochrome, he saw none of the gore painted by Marc). He called his *Equivalents* 'a picture of the chaos in the world, and of my relation-ship to that chaos. My prints show the world's constant upsetting of man's equilibrium, and his eternal battle to re-establish it'. His drifting, distracted clouds were a harmless chaos, but they pressed Stieglitz to defend the idea of cosmos. Each photograph was a tense, tenuous balancing act: he tried to attach the clouds to a dark skyline of trees and mountains, or let the branch of a tree imprint itself on the sky like a finger that will write a word or trace a meaning. Once in 1920 he took advantage of a rainbow, which did the work of equilibration for him. With its foot planted in a valley between his home at Lake George and the distant hills, it trained a searchlight on the storm clouds and sent them packing.

Edward Weston refused to negotiate with randomness, as Stieglitz did when he tried to give form to clouds. In 1926 Weston declared that land-scape was not a possible or permissible subject for the photographer, 'for the obvious reason that nature unadulterated and unimproved by men – is simply chaos'. On a wet day in Mexico in 1924, he said he could do nothing 'significant' while the clouds hung low; he needed 'the definite form which the sun invests'. He relied on light to shape objects, not just to illuminate them. Hence his appreciation of architecture, which marked man's planing and bevelling of ragged nature. When he photographed the trunk of a palm tree, he made it look like a factory chimney, and he complimented the fluted texture of a winter squash by comparing it to a Greek column. Even a kitchen gadget became a work of art if it carved up nature. The wire strings of a cutter for slicing hard-boiled eggs, photographed in 1930, reminded him of a harp. Lawrence would have been amused by Weston's portrait of a privy, which he saw as a shining porcelain altar. Fussing over the angle and the available light, Weston worked under duress, afraid that 'someone being called by nature would wish to use the toilet for other purposes than mine'. Its elegant, dignified lines and organic swellings reminded him of 'the human form divine'. But chaos comes again whenever the aspiring angel moves its bowels. Weston's purism relented a little when, after photographing peppers or artichokes or bunches of bananas, he ate his subjects. His friends called him a cannibal, but he was sure that a kind of transubstantiation would take place inside him. A pumpkin with sculptural contours achieved its 'final glorification' by being baked in a pie. One day in 1929 he made a portrait of the crusading journalist Lincoln Steffens, and after that gave a sitting to an aubergine. Steffens stayed for a meal, and the vegetable 'became part of our respective blood and body'. The reference to holy communion has a precise and deliberate point. A communicant receives only spiritual nourishment from the wafer and the wine; Weston regarded art as a way of dematerializing nature, as if he had taken actual food and turned it into a symbol of sustenance.

Art traditionally stills life, as Weston did when posing his vegetables. The artist is sedentary, studious, because vision calls for vigilance, a concentrated act of attention. But if the world is chaotic, a blitz of atoms or of warring forms, a creator should probably match its volatility. Dalí and the photographer Philippe Halsman tried to do so in *Chaos and Creation*, a short film they made for CBS Television in 1960. The history of art was speedily summarized: two blundering pigs discovered the art of painting by using their trotters and – after aeons of evolution – a spraygun squirted chocolate syrup like an action painter smearing a canvas. Vats of popcorn demonstrated the explosiveness of the universe. Lawrence's fantasia about cosmic origins in *Mornings in Mexico* started with 'the whole show going bust, *bang!*', and then, after those noisy italics, went on to muffle the blast. 'I like to think of the world going pop!' he added. The first tests of the atomic bomb roused Dalí to enthuse about the 'nuclear mysticism' of a disintegrating, unadhesive world, and the kernels of corn, like nuclei, recall this happy catastrophe. This, as Halsman said, was Dalí's 'atomic period, in which he painted everything in suspension'. In *Leda Atomica* his wife Gala is as weightless as the swan that courts her; embracing, they hover in space above a plinth or pedestal that also whirls into orbit, while a broken eggshell – from which their mutant offspring must have already hatched, as in Leonardo's lost painting – tumbles downwards. Having seen *Leda Atomica*, Halsman photographed *Dali Atomicus* in 1948. The painter leaps at a suspended canvas and easel, and a tilted, bobbing chair derides the idea that portraiture requires a sitting. To the right, *Leda Atomica* reappears, afloat like the step ladder beneath it. Three flying cats and the splashed contents of a

Philippe Halsman
*Dali Atomicus,*
1948

bucket of water also laugh at gravity. Halsman and Dalí discussed whether they might flirt with atomic fission by blowing up a chicken, but they decided not to antagonize Americans by being cruel to animals; they also wanted to use milk not water, then realized that the waste would offend rationed Europeans. It took them five hours to capture this split second, with twenty-eight emptied buckets and eighty-four catapulted cats. The photograph is a piece of philosophical whimsy: a parable about the infirm state of nature, which is further shaken up by the agitation we call creativity. Starting from *Dalí Atomicus*, Halsman developed a pseudo-science he called 'jumpology': rather than sitting his subjects down to be photographed, he told them to jump. Jerry Lewis, incorrigibly manic, was happy to oblige. It was more of an achievement to get the Duke and Duchess of Windsor to jettison their dignity. Even Richard Nixon, coaxed by Halsman, scrambled up a greasy pole that was entirely imaginary. Jumping, we let go of whatever we might have been holding in our heads, jolt our internal organs, and consign our atoms to a centrifuge.

Artists soon befriended chaos, and could dispense with D. H. Lawrence's special pleading in its favour. The painter Ben Shahn, speaking at a conference in Aspen, Colorado in 1966, announced 'I love Chaos', and called it 'man's only hope, ... the poetic element in a dull and ordered

world!' He equated chaos with creation, arguing that art was the consequence of something accidental, unforeseeable. The spark flickers at 'the
moment of Chaos', and its ignition may be 'an act of Chaos'. The capitalized
noun honours chaos as a place, the chasm of origins, and Shahn reverts to
these beginnings by citing a Mesopotamian legend about the god Marduk,
who created heaven and earth. Before he could fix the position of the stars
and apportion the cosmos, Marduk had to overcome the dragon Tia-mat.
Shahn painted such a primordial beast in 1948 in *Allegory*: he called it
'chimera-like', and thought of it as a hybrid of lion and wolf, although –
with its red mane – it was also a personified element, suggested by a fire in a
Chicago tenement which had devoured four children. This composite
dragon is swathed in flame, and has sharpened tusks and claws. Its bristling
menace explains why Marduk had to restrain the dragon: thanks to its
shackling, as Shahn pointed out at Aspen, we have our 'banks and plane
schedules' and all the conveniences of a planned society in a coherent world.
But the dragon remains restive, and we should be grateful for its discontent,
since it goads us to resist 'omniscience and/or tyranny'. In his talk, Shahn
paraphrased chaos as 'the breaking-out-to-freedom', and said that its obscure
reserves fed 'the dark genius of the artist and the poet, the musician, the
dissenter and about three philosophers in every ten thousand'. In his own
art, chaos takes the benign form of games, which delight and invigorate us
because the course of play is so unpredictable. He photographed and painted
handball courts on vacant lots in the New York slums, and made woodcuts
of professional baseball, with batsmen pummelling the air and catchers
skidding along the ground. He wanted to impart the same restless energy
to language. He admired the wedge-shaped, chiselled Hebrew alphabet,
or the fluid brushwork of Chinese and Japanese ideograms. His study of
calligraphy – put to use in the posters he designed, often for libertarian
causes – led him to a dream of 'a time when the letters were free', not yet
regimented by type or drilled into literature.

Shahn's only miscalculation was his slightly guilty assumption that
'Chaos is utterly disallowed by science'. Six years before his speech at Aspen,
the meteorologist Edward Lorenz had begun to examine the minutiae of
atmospheric pressure, charting the variables that led to the formulation of
chaos theory. Shahn's list of anarchic events in nature includes 'geologic
upheavals' and 'continental and celestial disturbances'; these are among the
phenomena studied by chaos theory, which plots tectonic shifts on earth
and solar motions above it. Lorenz discovered a 'sensitive dependence'
within systems that appear to be indeterminate, so that an innocuous butterfly can flap its wings and set off a tornado half a world away. D. H.
Lawrence reached a similar understanding of the weather without the aid of
computer models. In *Apocalypse* he described thunder as 'the first great

cosmic noise, betokening creation', and identified 'the grand Logos of the beginning' as 'a thunderclap laughing throughout chaos, and causing the cosmos'. Those eructations in the sky, Lawrence repeated, are 'creative utterances'. Tossed about by the hilarity of the frolicking, contentious elements, we are the by-product of turbulence. Artists have always known this; they were simply waiting for the scientists to catch up.

# 30

# PSYCHOGENESIS

If God created the world, it seems reasonable to ask why. Acts of God are supposedly motiveless, exceptions to the normal course of events which insurance policies decline to cover. Heinrich Heine daringly filled in the blank that comes before the beginning. In his 'Schöpfungslieder' – songs of creation, published in 1844 – God confides that sickness prompted him to become a creator. The work was therapeutic, and eased him back to health. Heine's God gives no further details. Was he suffering from a physical malady, or a psychological malaise? Either way, he may, like an artist, have transferred it to his creation. It was romantic poets, of course, who created because they were ill, to revenge themselves on a world that had injured them. Generally, like Frankenstein's monster, they adopted the rankling, resentful persona of the devil, rather than assuming the identity of God. Heine closed the gap between the diabolical and the divine, suggesting that God may have needed to ventilate grudges and frustrations of his own.

When Freud began to analyse the creative urge in artists, he calculated that its source was a medical problem, and saw artists as patients who heal themselves by impotently fantasizing. Picasso described art as 'the fire of Prometheus', a weapon to be used against orthodox divinities. Freud also venerated Prometheus as 'a culture-hero who was still a god, ... a demiurge and a creator of men', but he had his own more sceptical interpretation of the Titan's revolt. He deciphered the stolen fire, carried off inside a stalk of fennel, as a wishful substitute for the penis, which in Freud's estimation was the true site of creative power. There is a dreamy illogic to the exchange. The penis emits water, which quenches fire: this means that those would-be Prometheans are lying to themselves about their imaginative virility. The myth told Freud another damaging truth about the purposes of art. Why, he asked, is fire the property of the gods, from whom it must be stolen? Analytically, he defined fire as id, the instinctual life. To satisfy one's desires without hindrance is godlike; this at least is the envious conclusion of the human fantasist. The Promethean crime is that of wishing. Gratification need not be delayed or sacrificed altogether, as society and morality often demand; it can be obtained immediately, fulfilled in a guilty, deviant, absconded work of art. This places artists in the company of gods, but it also demonstrates their kinship with squalling infants, who expect every hungry whim to be satisfied by a sycophantic adult.

Gustave Moreau,
*Prometheus,*
1868

Freud advanced the same thesis in a lecture he gave in Vienna in 1907 on writers and day-dreaming. Here too he charted the origins of fantasy, and identified as his experimental subjects 'a class of human beings upon whom not a god indeed but a stern goddess, Necessity, has imposed the task of telling what they suffer and what gives them happiness'. The visits of the divinity in this case were not propitious; the people Freud referred to were 'the victims of nervous illness', who blabbed about their pains and their imaginary pleasures with desperate candour. By taking them as experts on imagination, he categorized all artists as honorary neurotics. Freud went on to separate writers into those who take their subjects from tradition, like epic poets, and popular fantasists who 'originate their own material' by closing their eyes and wishing. Revealingly, he declared his preference for the fantasists, whose romances are less artful, less guarded than that of their more cultivated literary colleagues. Henry James once defined romance as 'experience liberated'. The act of liberation, waiving self-censorship, sets dreams free. In the books Freud had in mind, heroes who overcompensate for the writer's inadequacies perform deeds of valour and are rewarded with the love of adoring women. Here Freud detected the self-congratulation of the infantile potentate he calls His Majesty the Ego – the unsocialized baby who is the invincible hero of day-dreams and (for Freud) the ideal self-image of most artists. The practice of art is learned in the cradle or the playpen. Every child, Freud declared in his lecture, 'behaves like a creative writer, in that he creates a world of his own, or else rearranges the things of his world in a new way that pleases him'. The few who persist in behaving like this when they grow up refuse to accept that the world is not a play-pen, arranged to suit their personal convenience.

Freud's analytical procedures rationalized religion, which, as he rue-fully acknowledged, could only be interpreted as 'a neurosis of humanity'. Art was an even falser religion, a deluded self-idolatry. He summed up the bad news for a world that could not expect salvation in *Moses and Monotheism*. As if writing an historical novel, he fictionalized Moses – or rather exposed the liberator of the Jews and the founder of their religion as a ficti-tious creature. Freud investigated a creative mystery: 'What is its origin?' he asks about the name of Moses, 'and what does it mean?' The answers he gives are a desecration, suggesting that Moses was actually a dissident Egyptian who recruited a new congregation for the cult of Aten. Having undercut Moses, Freud glanced sideways and in a footnote did the same to Shakespeare, whom he also viewed as a creation of fable, a pseudonymous cover for the Earl of Oxford. Freud refused to believe in the genius of either Moses or Shakespeare; the notion was to him 'incomprehensible and irre-sponsible', applicable to divinity – in which he did not believe – but not to human beings. As his student Otto Rank regretted, Freud explained away genius as 'a deified incarnation of masculine reproductive power', a self-deceptive extension of the penis.

Freud's essay on Moses was written at the end of his life, when he was already ill with the cancer that killed him soon after he sought asylum in London in 1939, so his attack on faith had a painfully personal relevance. He apologized for a 'weakening of creative powers' caused by old age, and dismissed Shaw's confidence that a man could go on talking and philosophizing until he was a hundred or three hundred years old; he feared that he lacked the strength for this final battle with a God who is our collective trauma. The disclaimer, however, drew attention to his own tragic heroism. In his eighties, Freud was still engaged in the life-saving fight undertaken by the young Oedipus. Religion derives from our guilt about our patricidal fantasies; art allows us to commit the crime, and absolves us of blame. Picasso said that the artist's first endeavour must be kill his father, meaning that he must break with the past and its enfeebling precedents. Picasso's own father, a moderately talented painter, earned a reprieve by declining to compete with a son who was a genius. The history of Christianity commemorates the same imagined misdeed, and sentences us to an eternity of punishment for something we only ever fantasized about doing. This was how Freud explained original sin: we murdered 'the primal father who was later deified'. We spared ourselves by misremembering the crime or forgetting it altogether, and then dreamed up a redeemer who died in our place. Christ, like Moses or Shakespeare, was for Freud the product of a 'tendentious distortion'.

Although Freud exposed this mythological trickery, he felt an affinity with Moses, the intellectual liberator who destroyed a golden idol and demanded that his people reject paltry gods made of clay, stone or metal. To abstract God was for Freud the first step towards abolishing him. In 1925 G. K. Chesterton considered the same mental progression, giving it a very different outcome. For Chesterton as for Freud, the prolific gods of paganism 'might almost alternatively be called the Day-Dreams'. He detested 'the polygamy of polytheism' and 'the vision of the harem in heaven', just as Freud scorned the sensuality of pagan religion. In Asia or Africa, Chesterton contended, 'God is sacrificed to the gods'. But that unitary God – present from the beginning of time and at work everywhere – survived these slights, so Chesterton could locate 'the idea of God in the very notion that there were gods before the gods'. Refusing to whittle down God's universality, he saw polytheism as 'the combination of several monotheisms', cults which attributed creation to Pan or the Earth Mother or the Great Father. For Chesterton, monotheism pointed towards the one incontrovertibly true God. For Freud, it pointed beyond the need for any god: this is why he praised Amenophis IV, the pharaoh who with 'magnificent inflexibility' turned away from magic and promoted the state cult of Aten, a sun-god as

universal as Yahweh. Amenophis proclaimed his 'joy in creation' by celebrating the 'energy of solar radiation' as the source of life. Freud was impressed
by this 'presentiment of later scientific discovery'; technology eventually
learned how to harness a natural force that belongs to no god.

Otto Rank disputed this coldly secular view, which made both religion and art defer to science. In 1932, after breaking off relations with
Freud, Rank published *Art and Artist*, a study of creative psychology that
asserts the 'fundamental identity between art and religion'. Rank had his
own explanation of the cultural change analysed by Freud in his essay on
Moses. It was art, he thought, that made possible our advance 'from animism
to religion', because art is our only means 'of exhibiting the soul in objective form and giving personality to God'. Art redeploys a 'redeeming power'
that for believers is a gift of God; artists help themselves to redemption.

Rank pointed out that the patron of psychiatry is the nymph Psyche,
whose name refers to the soul or to the breath of life. Abducted by Cupid,
she was initiated into the delights of love in his garden, but commanded
never to tell the secrets of the place or to identify her lover. Freudian psychiatry broke through her coy resistance, and made the unconscious mind let

Pierre Paul
Prud'hon, *Psyche
carried off by the
Zephyrs, c.* 1808

loose its fantasies. Rank, who disliked Freud's view of art as a revenge on reality, was careful to separate Psyche's sublimation from the psychiatric delusions of neurotics. He saw Psyche as a figure in whom the 'breath-soul', audible but impalpable, became an 'image-soul' that could be depicted objectively. The Cambridge philosopher Goldsworthy Lowes Dickinson, E. M. Forster's moral mentor, described friendship as the 'intricate commerce of souls'; music sponsors the same act of communion. In César Franck's lush symphonic poem *Psyché*, first performed in 1888, the heroine is awakened from her sleep by fluting breezes, which carry her off to the gardens of pleasure. Here she listens to invisible lyres caressing the air while a chorus explains her sensations by telling her that love is the 'source de toute vie'. She disobediently looks at her lover, and is expelled from his realm. But a plaintive oboe alters the disconsolate ending of the Greek fable and secures a pardon for her. She soars aloft again, with harps illustrating her 'saints délires' – a bodily delirium that is declared by the chorus to be holy. Her dream has come true not once but twice, thanks to the wish-fulfilling intercession of music. Neurotics, as Rank saw it, naively fancy they are immortal, but shrink from life because they do not dare to put this conviction to the test; artists actually secure an afterlife for themselves, and persuade others to honour and perpetuate their memory. As an example he mentions Bach's *Chromatic Fantasia and Fugue*, where the musical letters B, A, C and H (which is B natural in German notation) proclaim the composer's continued existence. Every time a keyboard player or an organist makes the air vibrate with those notes, Bach is revived.

Early in our history, man the artist turned his own body into an artwork. Rank describes piercing and tattooing as experiments in plasticity, tormenting the flesh 'to achieve a truly *new creation*'; those who can withstand such pain exhibit a godly valour, and toughen their skin into a magically impermeable shield. Language is another of the creative agencies developed by our ancestors: it 'transforms the world in a human sense', and like every other art it is a 'macrocosmized self-elevation'. It sets man up as 'the mythic creator of the cosmos, after which he becomes the creator of everything earthly'. These are grandiose claims, but they can be justified. Art regulates time and stabilizes space. Music and the metrical discipline of verse find pattern and predictability in the uninflected drone of duration. Architecture uses domes and vaults and spires to map a man-made sky, lower than the original, more protective and sometimes offering a painted view of heaven. Language, distributing names, sees to it that everything on earth is placed under human patronage. We may have been born from the earth and be destined to return to it, but art – in Rank's own myth of creation – permits us to rise above those soiling origins. We clamber out of nature's belly, then climb towards an altitude that we identify with spirit or mind.

Rank's analysis draws attention to a tragic bargain, a choice that must be made between this life and the next. The artist 'desires to transform death into life, though actually he transforms life into death'. He does so by a knowing renunciation, which Rank likened to the voluntary sacrifice of Christ. In order for the community to live, one of its members is singled out to die; religion and art share the responsibility for managing and overseeing this gratuitous death. The creator longs to know what lies beyond our mortal reality, and suborns a scapegoat to die in his place, like Verdi who lovingly prolongs the last breaths of the tubercular heroine in *La Traviata* or Wagner who allows Isolde to describe a death that is a blissful sublimation. Other artists dispense with stand-ins. The careers that best exemplify Rank's theory are those of romantic poets, who prematurely wore out their bodies and almost whimsically welcomed death. Chatterton and Goethe's Werther committed suicide, Shelley drowned in a storm at sea, Pushkin was killed in a pointless duel like that to which he sentenced his surrogate Lensky in *Evgeny Onegin*. These poetic lives were like a lyrical poems: short but intense, preferably left incomplete.

Freud's emphasis on sexuality led him, in Rank's view, to misunderstand and undervalue art. Despite his misgivings, Rank knew that what he called 'the genesis of the creative personality' had to be reconciled with our compulsion to procreate. He considered some abstruse reproductive options, which demonstrated that art answers a need of the organism. The soul's self-creation reminded him of the parthenogenesis practised by the Virgin Mary and by worms; he was also intrigued by epigenesis, which allows complex characteristics to develop from the simplest of beginnings in a formless egg. Finally he had to admit a contradiction. Sex seeks its reward in nature, whereas the urge to create art 'aspires ... to be independent of nature'. Rank offers no examples, but they are not difficult to supply. For Mondrian the rigour of creation required strict sexual abstinence: 'a drop of sperm spilt', he calculated, 'is a masterpiece lost'. André Breton and his surrealist colleagues were aghast at the notion of progeny, because to reproduce yourself implies that you consider life to be a serious matter, worth passing on to the next generation. The poet Jacques Prévert said that, if he inadvertently happened to father a child, he would kill it on the spot; Breton promised that any infant of his would be immediately consigned to a welfare agency – though he did fancy watching the birth, in order to see the new creature angrily protest at being tugged into an intolerable world. Francis Bacon said in 1980 that 'the very fact of being born is a very ferocious thing'. He was unable to view the event with the wry detachment of Ernst watching his frottages take form; Bacon's paintings sought to convey that ferocity, and they arrived in the world – which he saw as a 'lump of compost' – accompanied by puddles of ordure. His figures writhe on stained mattresses; their orifices conduct the eye back into the wet jungle of the internal organs. Golgotha is a slaughterhouse, with slabs of raw meat impaled on crosses. Among the images that haunted Bacon were the wailing victims in Poussin's *Massacre of the Innocents* and the screeching nurse shot by the soldiers in Eisenstein's *Battleship Potemkin*. The artist is a parent whose offspring is killed while being born.

For the surrealists, the proper analogy for artistic creativity was masturbation, not Wagner's travail of begetting and bearing. In a paper written in 1925 on 'the genesis of genitality', Rank praised the hand for its dissemination of pleasure and its contribution to culture. In growing up, we learn to transfer erotic pleasure from the mouth to the genitals. The exploratory hand leads the way: it invents masturbation, and goes on to display its ingenuity in handicrafts, which are a rudimentary form of art. Rank called such talents 'physioplastic', because they use a bodily capacity to manipulate and mould the world outside. Dalí's *Le Grand Masturbateur*, painted in 1929, is an unashamed self-portrait. Seen in profile, he is asleep, and the finicky pubic fringe of his eyelash suggests that the imagining eye is his most potent sexual organ. He is dreaming about a female predator who will devour him: her representative is the grasshopper stationed beneath his nose, a warning that the female praying mantis bites off her mate's head after consummation. The insect's feelers look as metallic as the limbs of a robot, but its swollen belly already teems with extruded offspring. Meanwhile Dalí's genitals, terrified into demutescence by the approach of a woman's pursed lips and sniffing nostrils, hang limp and dejected. His distress is transferred to his lower legs, which split to expose raw flesh under his marmoreal skin. An egg like that in *Leda Atomica*, discarded in the waxy waste, casts a grim shadow and digs its own grave. The artist achieves satisfaction only when he is alone, sealed in a private darkness and able to project fantasies onto a screen inside his head. Masturbation taught Max Ernst a new artistic procedure: he called it frottage, and solemnly defined it as 'the intensification of the irritability of the mind's faculties by appropriate technical means'. It literally meant rubbing, and he learned how to do it by tracing the knotty uneven grain of the floorboards at a seaside hotel. While the hand went to work, the fantasy free-associated; images reared up involuntarily, like the penile arum lily with its pronged stamen in the album of frottages Ernst entitled *Histoire naturelle*. He announced that his discovery of the technique had allowed him 'to assist *as spectator* at the birth of all my works'. Birth happened automatically, like any other bodily procedure. Ernst meanwhile lay back, relaxed, and enjoyed the display of his own mind's 'hallucinatory faculties'. Egon Schiele drew himself masturbating in 1911. In another self-portrait entitled *Preacher*, one hand clasps his thigh while the other erectly juts out at right angles just above his bare groin: the gesture used by priests to communicate a blessing doubles here as self-stimulation.

Freud, trying to account for Shakespeare, could not bring himself to accept the idea of genius. Rank was less agnostic. He speculated about a time when the artist 'played the part of the religious hero on earth, being the creative representative of a humanized god', and he thought it only just and logical that the Renaissance should have developed a 'religion of genius', promoted for instance by Vasari's life of Michelangelo. He found a reflection of this cult in Shakespeare, whose sonnets, he argued, are 'self-dedicated'. While pretending to flatter the young man, they actually address the poet's own creativity, which has the power to make words outlast marble. The Romans thought of a genius as a spirit, a magical genie. In Michelangelo or

Egon Schiele, *Self Portrait in a black cloak*, 1911

Shakespeare, that occult force acquired human form. There is a later stage in the development, which Rank could not have known about. The genius, whose body contains a spirit that is supernatural or abnormal, can be a walking work of art. Hence the transvestite superstars manufactured by Andy Warhol's Factory, or Diane Arbus's portraits of the proud, dignified anomalies she called 'freaks': a trio of wizened Russian midgets, a chubby Mexican dwarf, and a hermaphrodite from a travelling carnival who exhibits a bifurcated body, male on one side, female on the other. These people induced in Arbus the 'mixture of shame and awe' that the Greeks felt when they came face to face with gods. They also reminded her that a monster is an imaginary creature, the materialization of our dreams. Her freaks, Arbus said, were 'born with their trauma'; they were embodied dreams, nightmares ejected into the daylight. A young Jewish giant in a flimsy Bronx apartment supports himself on a walking stick and bends beneath the ceiling as he looms over his parents. His tiny mother gazes up in appalled amazement at the ogre she delivered into the world. Perhaps the Virgin Mary felt the same consternation. In 1964 in Santa Barbara, Arbus photographed a crone with pink curly hair brandishing a styrofoam crucifix. This was Bishop Ethel Predonzan of The Cathedral of the Creator, Omnipresence Inc., who had written her own bible, dictated by visiting spirits. The bishop claimed – among many other incarnations – to be the twin sister of Christ, but insisted on her priority: 'I am the First Child of God. I am Firster than Jesus.' Such people have created themselves, and feel no need to give further proof of their artistry.

Art establishes its creative rights by mocking the protocols of procreation. Robert Mapplethorpe's photographic tableaux show people engaged in sexual acts that can hardly be called coital. An oiled arm probes a gaping anus; trussed and chained, a man is hauled upside down on a pulley by another man who intends to affectionately abuse him. Sometimes the act is performed by an autonomous, solitary individual, whose delight lies in self-penetration. One of Mapplethorpe's subjects has slashed his chest with razorblades, and another delicately inserts the thin end of a dagger into the nozzle of his penis. In 1984 Michel Foucault justified such dangerous games, which demonstrated that sexuality is neither the decree of God nor the irresistible command of nature: instead it is, as he said, 'something we ourselves create. It is our own creation. ... Sex is not a fatality; it's a possibility for creative life'. There was a stoical bravado in this denial of fate, since later in the year Foucault died of an AIDS-related illness. Mapplethorpe mocked the dialectical oppositions of gender by photographing himself as a woman, softened by cosmetics, with fluffed-up curls and a feather boa draped around his neck, and by documenting the belligerent physique of the body-builder Lisa Lyon. The antithesis of male and female is triumphantly cancelled out by the trans-sexual characters who cavort through the films directed by Pedro Almodóvar. Gender is an act, a theatrical show. In *The Law of Desire*, the film director's male-to-female sibling is played by Carmen Maura, a woman pretending to be a man who had undergone surgery to become a woman, while another character in the film – biologically a woman, with a child to prove it – is played by Bibi Andersen, who is actually a trans-sexual. In 2004 Almodóvar praised this surgical revision of gender as 'a slap in the face of the idea that God creates people'. Such people, he added, 'change their nature'. Or else fantasy amends nature and makes light of medical risks. In *All About My Mother*, a man who dresses up as a woman to ply his trade as a prostitute fathers a child, whose mother is a nun; the baby is born infected with HIV but miraculously expunges the virus. As a young man performing in a punk band, Almodóvar wrote a song announcing that he was going to bear a child. Its name, he said, would be Lucifer. Coaxing his sexual partners to venture across borders of inhibition, Mapplethorpe allegedly whispered 'Do it for Satan'.

The rites involved symbolic transactions that allude to the origins of religion and of art. In a photograph taken by Mapplethorpe in a bunker in Sausalito, a man aims an arc of urine into the mouth of his kneeling partner, who accepts it like a communicant partaking of Christ's blood. A man in

another photograph opens his mouth to receive a faecal donation. Rank disliked Freud's theory that the body's waste products, liquid or solid, are the first works of art we create, but some artists are content to accept this account of their vocational training. Francis Bacon thought of paint as a bodily secretion, like the silvery trace left by a snail on a surface it oozes across. Less disgustedly, Helen Chadwick made art from waste, even from excrement. In 1986 she installed *Carcass* at the Institute of Contemporary Arts in London: inside a transparent pillar, a mulch of household refuse slowly decomposed. Chadwick thought of it as a funereal monument, a 'tower of corruption', but as she topped it up each day she could not help noticing that it was alive, bubbling as it fermented. *Cacao*, devised

Helen Chadwick, *Carcass*, 1986

for an exhibition at the Serpentine Gallery, was a fountain of chocolate, with a phallic periscope sticking up to circulate the brown, squelching lava. Chadwick realized that she had constructed a model showing the world how began: a purposeful pulse starts up in the mud, and a virile spout extends to take charge of fertility.

In Freud's theory, the ego awards itself a crown; according to Rank, it desires and attains immortality. But Chadwick had no interest in the arrogance of selfhood. Instead she cultivated what she called 'fleshhood', a consciousness of her own physiological being that made her art literally and nutritiously organic, like a placenta. She began during the 1970s by designing a wardrobe of latex garments which were painted directly onto the bodies of her models, then peeled off like sloughed skin; a confidential pair of panties had pubic hair on the front. Later she projected an image from a cervical smear onto the wall of a London chapel in *Blood-Hyphen*, with a laser beam slicing through the darkness like the emblem of an instantaneous and immaculate conception. For *Viral Landscapes*, she harvested scraps of tissue from her own body, photographed them under a microscope, then coupled them with images of an eroding coastline in Pembrokeshire: the artist merges with the earth. Chadwick's *Piss Flowers* are bouquets of her congealed, calcified urine. In Banff in 1991 she and her husband set off on an expedition to make a snow castle. They transferred the icy slush to a metal mould, pissed into it, filled the holes drilled by their hot urine with plaster, and had casts made. Once the negative spaces became visible, a

Helen Chadwick,
*Piss Flowers*,
1992

customary sexual difference disappeared. Her stream flowed straight down, so when set in plaster it became upright, like a pistil or a penis. His was a spray, splashed in an unruly circle; it ended up looking like petals. The posies of water were mounted on pedestals, cast in bronze, and finally coated with a white enamel that recalled their origins in the white arctic Canadian landscape. The result playfully vanquishes nature, which – as Rank argued – art always hopes to do. The snows of yesteryear, grieved over by so many wistful lyrical poems, can be preserved after all, made as durable as metal. Waste is purified, newly laden with value, and Chadwick's personal rivulet even ignores the downward tug of gravity.

A bolder reclamation happens in the series *Unnatural Selection*, made in 1996. Here the dispensable subjects gathered up and cherished by the artist were foetuses left over from in vitro fertilization. Chadwick challenged both the harsh selectiveness of Darwinian nature and the picky standards of medical science. She photographed creatures who had been denied the chance to be born, set them in jewels, and declared them to be worthy of love. She even cheekily wrote a poem to Linnaeus, the classifier who established the nomenclature of animals and plants in the eighteenth century, asking his opinion of her 'wanton play'. She had no fear of his disapproval, or of any other squeamish objection. The proper business of art is to question nature and to quarrel with its strict, inflexible economy.

# 31
# CREATING THE CREATION

The first story goes on being retold. Genesis has lost credence as an account of creation, but it is still an incitement to human creativity; redefined as a fiction, it elicits truths of a different kind. The difficulties, however, grow ever more daunting. In 1964 John Huston was engaged to direct *The Bible*, a cinematic recreation that began with the spirit moving on the face of the waters and concluded with God's decision to multiply the seed of Abraham, making his descendants as innumerable as the stars in heaven or the sand on the seashore. When Huston began to struggle with the problem of filming the first seven days, he felt a twinge of sympathy for his predecessor. 'I don't know how God managed,' he said. 'I'm having a terrible time.'

When questioned about his own faith, he evasively remarked that Genesis advances from myth to legend and then to history, and pointed out that in the course of this progress, God inevitably withdraws from the world he has created. Huston decided that at first God loved mankind, which is why he experienced such jealous rages when the object of his affection strayed. Then, once his proprietorial ardour cooled, he settled into a judicial detachment, agreeing to pardon malefactors so long as they confessed. Nowadays, Huston surmised, God seems to have forgotten about us: 'He is taken up, maybe, with life elsewhere in the universe on another planet'. This was a clever mental detour, suggesting that science fiction might be a more appropriate way of examining how worlds begin and end. In practice Huston decided to make the beginning diurnal rather than epochal – to present creation not as one unrepeatable event but as 'a continuing, eternal process'. Every morning at first light, heaven and earth are created anew as the east grows brighter and birds start to sing in the back garden. The images in Huston's prologue are ordinary enough – the sun lifting itself out of a scorched sea, hovering flocks of birds, a school of lolloping dolphins – and it is our awakened wonder that makes us see them afresh. In *The Bible*, Adam wriggles into life in what looks like a sandy bunker on a barbered golf course. That too is plausible: every garden or country club aspires to be a substitute for Eden.

The poetic dramatist Christopher Fry wrote the script for Huston's film, which involved, as he said, 'the creating of Creation itself'. He saw this as a repetition of the 'spiritual journey' recorded by the Bible: Genesis is not

Ulla Bergryd and Michael Parks as Adam and Eve leaving Eden in John Huston's *The Bible*, 1966

a summary of actual occurrences but the product of our groping, hypothetical attempt to understand or imagine our origins. The first image prescribed by Fry suggests that creation is a waking dream. As a narrator's voice recites the opening verses of Genesis, the screen is dark, 'like the inside of a man's eyelids when the eyes are shut'. Fry inadvertently paraphrases the first line of Coleridge's poem 'A Day-Dream', which is 'My eyes make pictures, when they are shut'. The world is being envisioned, not made. After the darkness begins to move, it moulds itself into abstract shapes and then coheres into images. Fry called for a pale semblance of two hands – the instruments of God the craftsman – which open and extend their fingers, evoking the wings of a white bird, the symbol of spirit. He then imagined the hands crossing and twisting, generating light between the fingers; the first shaft of light that divides the waters is described, in his screenplay, as a finger writing on the sky. These verbal inventions proved impossible to realize visually. What the film shows is a flickering red blaze that cools and clarifies into a bank of drifting clouds: light is at first as hot as coals, then whiter and more lucid.

In early discussions Fry and Huston considered having Abraham serve as narrator, using the opening chapters of Genesis to rally and indoctrinating the members of his tribe. Eventually they decided that the croaky, avuncular Huston (who also plays a grizzled, hen-pecked Noah) would deliver the offscreen narration. The speaker could be God, Moses, or any poet: Fry's script refers to the narrator as 'the creative voice'. The commandments are vocal, but Fry's verbal creativity issues its own silent orders. As God tells the fowl to multiply, Fry calls for an image of starlings, condensed into a grey veil as they flock in the air. 'The sound of them,' his script notes, 'is like a susurration of tafetta.' A metaphor like this could hardly be recorded on tape; it appeals to the imagination of the reader, and exists only in our reverie. Not surprisingly, Huston ignored it. Other paradisial images proved impossible to photograph because of the entrenched suspicion of the species, which either fell out after the fall or – if Darwin is correct – are compelled to compete with and kill each other as they struggle to survive. Fry optimistically described a shot that was meant to illustrate God's creation of the beasts. A deer runs up to a lion, and the two converse 'in trust and peace'; when a ram joins them, they welcome it into their company. In reality, there is no such peaceable kingdom.

Fry thought of the film as a kind of oratorio, with images attuned to an orchestral soundtrack. A little presumptuously, he even supplied musical cues in the script. The darkness of origins was to be accompanied by music that is 'hardly more than a vibration', the rhythmic stirring of possible life. In *Die Schöpfung*, chaos is banished by a bright chord of C major; Fry wanted the spectacle of creation to remain confused and uncoordinated – a kaleidoscope of blurred colours, a random jangling of sounds – until the end of the first day, when the musical score would begin 'to lose its atonality'. He reserved Haydn's revelation for the fourth day when, after sun and moon are set in place, he asked for music to blaze forth 'at its most radiant and harmonic', like the chorus declaiming the 'Gloria' in Monteverdi's *Vespers*. Fry's suggestions reverse the actual history of music, which began with the establishment of concord and gradually moved towards atonality, as anchorless as the universe of the new physics. In the event, the score for *The Bible* was composed by Toshiro Mayuzumi, who left Tokyo in the early 1950s to study in Paris; later, returning to Japan, he became a staunch musical nationalist, associated with the military insurgency of Yukio Mishima. Mayuzumi's music battled to reconcile local tradition with imported influences: he was fascinated by Buddhist temple bells, but also tempted by jazz. He did not respond to the suggestions in Fry's script, although at one point he confirmed the conventional link between tonality and moral discipline. For the scene in which Eve steals away from Adam to sample the forbidden fruit, Mayuzumi wrote an eerie, stealthy, tonally wayward nocturne that might have been composed by the young Schoenberg. A braying saxophone, borrowed from a jazz band, announces the snake's victory. Is modernism being blamed for the fall?

The narrator in *The Bible* quotes God's curse on Eve after the fall: 'I will greatly multiply thy sorrow and thy conception; in sorrow shalt thou bring forth children.' Fry specified that Eve should be heard screaming in childbirth, as a fierce wind moans to amplify her misery. To generate the race is painful and perilous, so the script concentrates instead on the genesis of art. Hence Fry's references to the development of music, or – once darkness is dispelled – to the nativity and renaissance of painting. The grasses seen on the third day are delicately silver not brashly green, 'for no colour is bright until the sun is made'. In the beginning, light is monochromatic. Then, after the sun's invention, 'for the first time we see strong shadows, and colour of great vividness and purity'. Fry might be remembering the heliocentric religion of Turner. The script goes on to ask for an image of waterlilies opening as the sun touches them: probably a reference to Monet's pool at Giverny, and to impressionist paintings in which colour escapes from its confinement by line.

Huston had his own agenda, and left out the waterlilies. But when filming the creation of Adam, he did stage another accelerated history of art. He sought help from Giacomo Manzù, who had recently designed a door for St Peter's Basilica in Rome, with Cain killing Abel in stark relief and martyrs glorified by torment. Treating Adam as a male Galatea, Manzù prepared three sculptures, which were photographed separately and then made to dissolve into each other behind a cloud of golden dust that for

Huston represented 'the breath of God', the force that moistened and inspirited clay. The first model was a lumpy earthen mound. The second had approximately human proportions, while the third, as Huston said, was 'an almost finished man'. In the series of dissolves, the sculpture changes shape, stretches on the ground, then hauls itself upright. Run forwards, the sequence illustrates art's advance towards realism. Run backwards, it presents a version more calculated to appeal to modernists: we start with the human facsimile, then progressively deform and abstract it, as Barnett Newman did when painting Adam. Huston's Adam and Eve, being generic, required impeccable bodies and nondescript personalities. The roles went to Michael Parks and Ulla Bergryd, whose careers never recovered from the assignment. The rest of the cast brought tried and true personae to their roles. Richard Harris was a psychotic Cain, and Stephen Boyd a recklessly ambitious Nimrod. Ava Gardner – still voluptuous, but beyond child-bearing – appeared as the infertile Sarah, and George C. Scott, who specialized in imperious patriarchs, growled his way through the role of Abraham. Stars are supernatural beings: Peter O'Toole, with sky-blue eyes and a melodiously consoling voice, impersonated a trio of angels.

Huston knew that the story told in Genesis was a myth or a legend not historical truth, but the camera found it hard to make his sophisticated discriminations. To photograph something testifies to its existence, so the film could not help bolstering the literalism of biblical fundamentalists. Two kangaroos are seen hopping into Noah's ark: does this answer Darwin's suspicion that God did not create Australian marsupials? The second-unit director Ernst Haas – a *Life* photographer, hired to assemble images illustrating the first seven days – accumulated evidence for evolution, which hardly served the film's purpose. On his travels Haas followed Darwin to the Galápagos, where he photographed a colony of spiky-backed iguanas, some crimson crabs sunning themselves on the rocks, and a giant tortoise that would have been alive during Darwin's visit. In Kenya he felt that he was photographing a scene from prehistory: a long-tusked elephant might have been a mammoth, and the bony indentations of the mountain behind it resembled a dinosaur asleep on the horizon. At Lake Manyara in Tanzania he photographed two baboons which looked, as he said, 'very human'. Yet Haas in his own way authenticated Genesis, because he discovered that in certain spots the earth was still creating itself. At Surtsey – a volcanic island off the coast of Iceland, named in homage to the Norse god of fire – he photographed a boiling crater. The location showed nature in its raw, unformed state: the lashing wind and waves, the belching flame and the igneous rocks gave Haas 'the strongest feeling of the elements and of chaos'. Huston worked inside a studio in Italy, where he employed cinema's mechanized illusions to stage the flood or the collapse of Babel or the transformation of

'Marine Iguana,
Galápagos
Islands',
photograph by
Ernst Haas for
*The Creation*

Lot's wife into a pillar of salt. Haas could not rely on technical trickery. Searching the rest of the world, he needed to find landscapes that looked as if they had been made a moment ago. The cavernous desert along the Colorado River – soon to be flooded by the Glen Canyon Dam – had auditioned as a biblical setting in George Stevens' film *The Greatest Story Ever Told*, on which Haas also worked. He now photographed geysers and sulphur pits at Mammoth Hot Springs in Yellowstone, where the crinkled, wriggling patterns in the hot mud resembled crude plants emerging from the febrile earth. If the narrative had reached as far ahead as the New Testament, Haas possessed a store of images that could have documented scriptural mysteries: a 'picture rock' he found in Utah, with a curled pattern of enfolded lines, seemed to him to portray the Madonna cradling her child.

After his work on *The Bible* finished, he went on collecting images for his book *The Creation*, published in 1971. The project stretched across time to connect the remotest past with the journalistic present: Haas used phrases from Genesis as captions for photographs taken on his recent trips to Africa, South America and Iceland. A studio assistant, whose name – as Haas swears in his preface – was Michelangelo, played a recording of *Die Schöpfung* as they reviewed slides from apparently unrelated assignments. At Surtsey, Haas saw creation happening. On a smaller scale, he had the same feeling when his camera studied a rose at intervals of half an hour and watched 'an egglike bud evolving into a flower'. At first the blood-red petals were clenched shut; then, with a conscious intent, they unfurled and allowed Haas to photograph a pulsing heart. He had an advantage in illustrating the first verses of

'Clouds above
the Amazon',
photograph by
Ernst Haas for
*The Creation*

Genesis: he was able to fly, and could see the world from above, as God
might have done. The first photograph in *The Creation* looks down through
blue clouds as a thunderstorm clears over the Amazon. The image chosen to
accompany the invention of light was taken while he flew through another
thunderstorm in the Caribbean, with clogged, inky clouds obliterating
the upper sky while the newly created light glares on the water. For the
second day of the creative week, Haas used a photograph of two rainbows
imprinted on a green sea, taken from a small plane that was soaring out of
control above Miami.

Occasionally an adroit fakery was necessary. The second image in
Haas's book suggests the unphotographable vista of a seething earth on
which the crust is still hardening; his notes reveal that it is a close-up of a
nacreous abalone shell. A little later, what appears to be a cosmic storm is in
fact a snowy crevasse in the mountains at Yosemite, photographed horizontally but printed vertically – an exercise in 'what movie people call false
perspective'. An image of waters dividing, as God commands them to do
in Genesis, turns out to be 'a duplicate transparency placed in reverse over
the original one'. Using double exposure, Haas makes a forest jostle as if
animated, with trees dancing around each other. The tricks do not diminish
the value of the images. The artist recreates the world by his quirky way of
seeing it, and the purpose of technique, like that of technology, is to make
miracles happen. All the same, at the end of his book, Haas strained to find a
way of photographing the creation of man. He chose to show Adam and
Eve being created together. Locked in an embrace, or perhaps still an

inextricable compound of male and female, they awaken in a sand dune, like two hippies who have spent the night on a beach. Haas superimposed on them an image of the rising sun, so the result is as studiously artificial as a re-enactment on a film set. The difficulty derives from the unimaginability of the event. As Haas wrote in his introduction, 'Contemporary intelligence finds it hard to accept that man was created, suddenly, as a separate entity'. Evolution had erased that primal scene; he photographed something he knew to be untrue.

*The Creation* proclaims an aesthetic gospel, summed up in Haas's assertion that 'Colour is joy'. To say so took courage. Photographic puritans, then as now, preferred to see the world geometrically defined in black and white, dismissing colour as a superficial distraction or a pollution. Mono-chrome suited gritty journalistic reportage, but Haas used colour to brighten and uplift a downtrodden, besmirched society. His essay 'Images of a Magic City', published in *Life* in 1953, included an iridescent circle that might have been a solar corona, aflare with light; the caption explained that it was the result of sun glancing off a greasy puddle on a New York pave-ment, creating 'a halo to glorify the shadow of a pedestrian hurrying by'. To convey his reverence for nature, Haas elaborated what he called 'a colour philosophy'. He accepted that 'the idea of the beginning, of something originating out of nothing' was incomprehensible. But the burning reds and sappy greens of his landscapes announced 'resurrection, incarnation, call it what you will', and persuaded him that there was 'no end, only an eternal beginning'. His uncertainty about what to call this resurgence marked his disbelief in Christian mysteries, and when he risked a theoretical analysis of his own practice he had to admit that his faith in the life-giving, calorific properties of colour was insecurely based. 'The creation of the colour image,' as he said in 1957, exposed 'the fleeting and transitory nature of colour and light'. Colours derive from the breaking-down of light, so their very existence – if they do exist as anything other than optical illusions – involves a disenchantment, almost a deicide. Because there is 'no absolute light,' Haas concluded, there can be 'no absolute colour'. The God of Genesis, whose light was absolute, is belatedly undermined by optics and by photochemistry.

Although Haas wanted to believe in an eternal beginning, *The Creation* shows nature to be endangered. The book documents a personal faith which Haas called 'spiritual ecology': near the end of time, we yearn for the unspoiled beginnings, and try to atone for our mistreatment of the world. An image of wavy mountains was included because it suggested to Haas what the earth might have looked like when still fluid, before water and dry land were divided. But the photograph was taken from a plane a few minutes after take-off from Los Angeles, and the blue, vaporous haze was a suffocating industrial smog. Fry's screenplay for *The Bible* glances at the wreckage of the contemporary world – pulverized by war, poisoned by industry – when Abraham leads Isaac through the rubble that once was Sodom. They travel, Fry comments, inside 'that nightmare of a great destroyed city which we all now share'; the place, with its stumps of masonry and gobbets of black lava 'like the limbs of hacked monsters', is a 'petrified chaos'. Our history is taking us back towards the explosive beginning of the world. Huston's film contains a preview of this scientific Armageddon: Sodom and Gomorrah are destroyed by what looks like a nuclear blast, doing duty for the wrath of God.

Fry returned to the subject of creation a decade later when the Polish composer Krzysztof Penderecki, impressed by his work on *The Bible*, asked him to write the libretto for an operatic version of *Paradise Lost*. Penderecki had been commissioned by the Lyric Opera of Chicago, which planned to stage the work during the bicentenary of the United States in 1976. But there were delays – or perhaps the company had second thoughts about characterizing America as a self-sabotaged Eden – and the premiere did not take place until 1978. The production later travelled to La Scala in Milan, and a concert performance was given in the Vatican at the invitation of Pope John Paul II. The sanctity of the subject evidently intimidated Penderecki. He had scruples about calling *Paradise Lost* an opera, given the profane erotic preoccupations of the form; instead, reviving the term used by Italian Renaissance composers to categorize biblical dramas or allegories that illustrated religious doctrine, he referred to it as a 'sacra rappresentazione'. Fry's libretto begins by having Milton himself quote Book III of the poem, in which he dares to imagine and describe God's conversation with Christ in heaven. 'May I express thee?' asks Fry's Milton. The libretto prudently omits an extra word which conveys Milton guilty sense of trespass: in the poem, what he asks is 'May I express thee unblam'd?' Fry's screenplay for *The Bible* described the uncreated world as a cranial darkness, with light dimly flickering outside eyes that cannot yet be opened. The operatic *Paradise Lost* begins with a blind Milton on a stage which is, as the libretto says, 'dark with his blindness'. The poet then delivers his address to a holy light he is unable to see, and in response to his plea 'light begins to explore the stage'. The illumination comes from within Milton's picture-making mind, not from God. At the start, a gruff rumbling of cellos and double basses disrupts the silence; as Milton meditates on the idea of light, the orchestral texture thins out, with higher strings allowing air to circulate.

In the Chicago production, the spotlight generated by Milton – the beam cast by his intrepid, blameworthy mind – picked out earth, hell and heaven in the black void; the opera shows a poet imagining worlds, not God creating them. The presiding voice is that of Milton, who narrates the action.

*Paradise Lost,*
by Krzysztof
Penderecki, at
Lyric Opera
of Chicago,
1978

He keeps his distance from operatic convention: rather than singing he speaks, respecting the sanctity of both scripture and poetry. He literally lends his voice to God, who is heard but not seen, booming out of a light that is now blindingly bright. The same actor speaks both parts, and because Milton is heard first it is hard not to think of God as a ventriloquist's dummy. Fry cautiously undercuts the identification by giving God's voice the support of a male chorus, which vocalizes his words before the speaker declaims them. God begins by saying 'Let us create Man in our image'. The collaboration of the chorus justifies his use of the plural: he is an impersonal energy, not – like Milton – a heroic ego. If Milton uses God as a projection of himself, God does the same with Christ, identified by Fry as Messias. After the eating of the fruit, God descends to the garden and orders Adam to come out of hiding. When Adam says he ran away because he was afraid of God's voice, God replies 'My voice you oft have heard'. Adam hears God, but what he sees is Messias, who materializes in the tree. It is an appropriate perch: Christian typologists, trying to reconcile the Old and New Testaments, claimed that Eden and Gethsemane were situated in the same place, and that Christ's cross was cut from the tree on which the fatal fruit grew.

The subtitle of Huston's film was ...*In the Beginning*, a disclaimer that excused its concentration on the earliest chapters of Genesis. The opera makes matters easier by beginning at the end of the story. Paradise has already been lost; Fry and Penderecki avoid having to start from first principles. The light that radiates from within Milton immediately spills onto fallen Eden, where Adam, in a shrill, falsettoish tenor, berates God for creating him and Eve begs not to be left to die alone. The glow then fades from the joyless garden, and Milton, attempting to account for this transgression, thinks further back to Satan's rebellion and the fall of the angels, described by shrieking woodwinds and bludgeoning percussion. The creation of man happens after we have already witnessed the consequences of the fall, and it is presented through Satan's eyes, as if he were man's true creator and intellectual sponsor. In hell he rallies his troops by telling them about 'another World' which is the home of 'some new race called Man'. At once Adam, represented by a dancer, gets up from his crouched foetal position on the floor and stretches his limbs. His voice sings out of the darkness, asking the primal, inevitable question:

> How came I thus, how here?
> Not of myself – by some great Maker then –

His speculations break off, God's enlightening blaze grows dim, and the tintinnabulation that represents sunlight slurs and curdles. The orchestra returns to hell, where Satan resolves to undertake his reconnaissance trip to earth, to 'learn/ What creatures there inhabit'. Only after Satan leaves on his mission does the light return to Adam, who is 'still waiting for an answer from above'. On his way to earth Satan crosses the windy hubbub of Chaos, whose intemperate weather is evoked by Penderecki with scurrying strings, alarmed trumpet volleys and the thundery blaring of the brass. Meanwhile in Eden, on another part of the stage, the birds and beasts parade before Adam in pairs. Chaos and creation abut, nudged into mutual dependence.

The opera makes no attempt to stage the first days of Genesis; its central creative episode, concentrating on a human initiative, shows Adam naming the animals. The scene is the nursery of language and of music, tracing both arts back to the mimicry of nature. Adam spontaneously plucks names from nowhere, and confers them on each animal as it passes: 'Thou Lion', he says, then 'Thou Lamb'. Such taxonomic decisions of course belong much later in human history, but Fry and Penderecki supplement Adam's confident organization of the animal kingdom by remembering how, much nearer to the infancy of the race, we actually began to characterize our fellow creatures. The names Adam invents are repeated by a children's chorus, which goes on to imitate the noise each animal makes. In the poem, Milton differentiated the lion, bear, tiger and elephant by choosing verbs that captured the idiosyncratic ways they move. Fry's children – whose origins are intriguing, because Eve has not yet been created – use onomatopoeic noises not descriptive words. The lion roars, the lamb bleats, the swan alliteratively hisses SSSS, the elephant trumpets (thus inventing a musical instrument), the horse neighs, the tiger growls, the giraffe gutturally urrps, and the snorting camel humphs. We first identify a lamb by the baaing noise it makes, and only much later, when we have painfully advanced from things to the verbal signs that replace them, do we consent to call it by its proper name. The children of the chorus are instinctive artists, who sing the names and give voices to the animals; Adam in this scene operates as a precociously learned scientist. The librettist and the composer recognize that the new animals already have a long provenance in art. When Adam says 'Thou Tiger', it is impossible not to remember Blake's poem, in which the tiger is a pretext for man's interrogation of the creator. A musical quotation concedes that another composer has a claim on the swan: when Adam names it, Penderecki smuggles in a few bars from Wagner's *Lohengrin*, where the Grail knight sails in a boat drawn by a swan. God may have made the animals and Adam the naturalist may have named them, but it is artists like Blake or Wagner who truly create them. Where would the ermine be without Leonardo or the rhinoceros without Dürer, the whale without Melville or the kangaroo without D. H. Lawrence?

As the opera ends, the chorus quotes the elegiac conclusion of Milton's *Paradise Lost*. Because it is written in the past tense, the poem looks sorrowfully back even as it stares into the future, and when Adam and Eve leave Eden, Milton says that 'The World was all before them'. Fry makes one slight but significant revision to Milton's phrase, altering the tense:

> The World is all before them,
> Where to choose
> Their place of rest,
> And Providence their guide.

Narrative recapitulates an action that has already occurred, whereas drama shows us an action that occurs as we watch. Fry's characters are freer than those in the poem, and their future has not yet been engulfed by the past. After this, Fry daringly cuts the very last line of the poem, which matches the dejected, faltering gait of the pair. Milton sends them off with slow, reluctant, wandering steps, hand in hand but still solitary. Fry curtails their comfortless straying, and foresees a possible homecoming:

> Through the world's wilderness
> Long wanders man,
> Until he shall hear and learn
> The secret power
> Of harmony, in whose image he was made.

These lines rescind the doom of Genesis, and instead of the 'paradise within' promised by Milton's archangel – an ambiguous assurance, perhaps referring to the companionship of Adam and Eve, or perhaps reminding them of their ultimate salvation, made possible by Christ – they look back to the musical mysticism of Pythagoras. In Dryden's 'Song for St Cecilia's Day', harmony is the source of the universal frame; Fry also gives it the credit for framing the human form, despite God's earlier claim that man is made 'in our image'. The power is secret because it depends on our receptivity or attunement, on a refined ear that can appreciate art. During the opera – when chimes announce the creation of Eve, or when she and Adam make love, accompanied by wordless choral sighs of pleasure – music sketches a regained paradise, made from tingling, sunlit air.

For the benefit of the tone-deaf, Fry adds another more visible consolation. It too is secret, consisting merely of an inaudible capital letter in his note on the setting for the final scene. As the angelic squadron ushers Adam and Eve from Eden, the garden is lit by flaming swords: 'the trees,' Fry directs, 'are the colour of the Fall'. Milton's cherubim disappear into a more English weather, expunged by damp evening fog that condenses above a marsh, but Fry is imagining the foliage that turns New England orange and crimson in October every year. Fall refers to a season, not to an immitigable sentence of death. Although the dry, flaring leaves may drift down to earth and be swept up in papery pyres, the tree will have its punctual rebirth six months later. Huston in *The Bible* made sense of the myth by treating every morning as if it were the first. Fry's solution was to see nature's annual cycle as a working model of eternity.

Renovation is an American creed, and in Tony Kushner's play *Angels in America* a miracle without precedent occurs, suddenly forcing us to reconceive the world. A seraph crashes through the ceiling of a New York apartment and swings suspended above the bed of an AIDS patient. 'What makes the engine of creation run?' asks the visitant. Prior, deliriously sweating in the bed, cannot answer, so the angel replies: 'Not physics but ecstatics'. The heavenly emissary and the stricken man then copulate in mid-air, with tongues of flame – in Mike Nichols' film of Kushner's play – licking between their genitals during their bout of 'ecstasis in excelsis'. Like Balzac's Séraphîta, the angel is a hermaphrodite, and has a body ventilated with eight vaginas. She babbles as she palpitates, describing 'the pulse, the pull, the throb, the ooze, priapsis, dilation, engorgement, flow, the universe aflame with angelic ejaculate'. The rhythm is set by 'the bloodpump of creation'; Kushner's phrasing cheerfully derides a sonnet in which Gerard Manley Hopkins, bemoaning his lack of literary inspiration, longs for 'the roll, the rise, the carol, the creation'. 'Oh God!' shrieks Prior before collapsing.

The scene is a gloriously sacreligious revelation, cauterizing the guilt and fear that clung to sex during the AIDS epidemic. It is also a manifesto for art, which has its own unashamed creative fervour. In Nichols' film, the angel spectacularly shatters the apartment, drilling through floorboards and knocking down walls to let in a white-hot light. Later she makes another swooping sortie, gathers up a prim Mormon mother from Prior's room at St Vincent's Hospital, and bumps groins with her in mid-air. When *Angels in America* was first performed in the theatre in 1992, Kushner said that he did not mind if the wires that held up the angel were visible, or if the audience sniggered at a woman in a silly wig pretending to fly. The illusion draws attention to its own improbability. The angel tells Prior to dislodge the kitchen tiles to unearth the sacred instruments; like any law-abiding tenant, he refuses, saying that he will wake his neighbours, make their dog bark, lose his lease and forfeit his security deposit. He insists on believing that the the-

Justin Kirk (Prior) and Emma Thompson (the angel) in *Angels in America*, directed by Mike Nichols, 2003

atrical set is a solid room – but he is, after all, hallucinating, and perhaps his faith in property is a symptom of his mental confusion. Meanwhile the angel improvises to cope with his stubbornness, and shouts a warning to the higher powers who keep watch through the hole in the ceiling: 'Revision of text!' Prior wrestles with his angel above Manhattan, and after he tugs her back to the ground she grumbles that she has twisted a muscle in her thigh. Jacob's ladder thuds down from the upper air, its steel rungs aflame, and Prior clambers up it wearing his hospital shift. His ascent is celebrated by an Irving Berlin song, which announces 'Heaven, I'm in heaven'. The pill-popping housewife Harper grumbles when Prior turns up in one of her woozy dreams: she indignantly points out that they have never met, so the artifice is once more punctured. By taking these ironic, alienating risks Kushner defines the difference between art and other religions. The difference is that art permits and even expects such scepticism.

In the Chicago production of *Paradise Lost*, a brass lid above the stage rose and fell like a retractable firmament as the balance of power between heaven, hell and earth was adjusted. In Kushner's play, the roof is removed, and heaven crash-lands on the American earth, anxious to share in its enjoyments. The celestial city, Prior discovers, is very like fog-swathed San Francisco: why shouldn't we project our favourite place into the sky? Even so, he decides not to die just yet, and insists on returning to uproarious, imperfect New York. The angel, recovering from her sexual exertions, gives Prior an account of cosmic history. Why did God create man? Not as occupational therapy, which was Heine's suggestion. Not even, as G. K. Chesterton proposed, because his love needed to express itself. God, the angel admits, was bored. The other angels sang so incessantly, and their anthems of praise were so tediously sycophantic; being bisexual, they also passed their time in pointlessly self-involved fornication. God therefore split creation in two. At this point biblical theology moves sideways to borrow from Plato, who saw our world as a pair of sundered hemispheres, an egg split into yolk and white by two antagonistic, complementary sexes. God, says Kushner's angel, designed a unigenitalled race, which turned reproduction into a chancier, more dialectical matter – and also multiplied the possibilities of sexual engagement, which did not necessarily have to take place between man and woman. The male is an offshoot, a by-product, made by tinkering with chromosomes. But the angel tells the disruptive homosexual Prior why his troublesome gender is so valuable: 'In creating you, our father-lover unleashed sleeping creation's potential for change'. With man, and specifically with the male, what the angel calls 'the virus of time' went to work. In a play about AIDS, that viral action is credited with its own restless, self-transforming creativity. It stirs up random events, questions norms, urges the custom-bound world to change. It provokes mass migrations, like those which upset global equilibrium by decanting harried humanity into empty America. It is the motor of scientific revolution, and its intellectual disturbances cause earthquakes in heaven. God eventually takes fright, alarmed by the confident autonomy of his creatures, and drifts deeper into space. The angel regrets his abdication. But human beings cannot be expected to share her grief. Prior, during his brief sojourn in heaven, suggests to the recording angels that they should 'sue the bastard for walking out'.

Through time, the adaptable virus has twisted itself into every imaginable form: our history is so long and so crowded that there seems to be no room left for novelty, innovation, a spurt of original thought. When Harper and Prior collide in their shared hallucination, they both lament our elderly predicament. She remarks that imagination, even when helped along by chemicals, cannot free us from reality. It is unable to come up with anything new; as she says, her tired, trapped brain is merely 'recycling' images taken from her everyday experience, selecting bits and pieces of our actual world and scrambling them into an incoherent fantasy. Prior, who happens to be in drag, agrees with her. He is a veteran of the costume balls that used to mark the social calendar of gay Greenwich Village in the 1980s. After his second Theme Party, he says with a grimace, he discovered that everything had been done already. But *Angels in America* overcomes this weary preemption. At once sublime and bawdy, it arranges the debris of culture – theological lore and environmental science, mystical poetry and snatches of Broadway musicals – into an allusive, all-encompassing cosmos. The characters are still vexed by the artist's ancient failing, an incapacity to make new life. Prior's ancestors reproach him in another dream for not continuing the family line; Harper pretends to be pregnant but is not (and since her husband is homosexual, she may never be). But in our society, the recycling that Harper complains about has another significance. It secures a reprieve for the nature we have pillaged; it is an exercise in moral thrift – a rebuke to our economic profligacy and perhaps, in Kushner's view, to the thrusting self-imposition of the procreator. Harper even dreams of making reparation to the damaged universe. Gazing out of the window of a jet, she sees souls dancing in the air, then merging in a web to seal the hole in the ozone layer. Although we may not be able to originate, we have a solemn duty to conserve what already exists.

# 32
# WORLD-BUILDING

Concluding his survey of myth in *The Golden Bough*, the anthropologist James G. Frazer summed up the long history of our efforts to control and comprehend a world we did not make. The story, as Frazer looked back at it in 1922, charted a sad diminution. Magic gave our earliest ancestors power over nature, which we lost in advancing to a more rational understanding. The first lapse came when sorcery was superseded by religion. Now man could no longer exert his will through spells. He placed himself, as Frazer lamented, at the mercy of 'certain great invisible powers', and was demeaned by his own gods. Of course the determination to 'reduce the seeming chaos to cosmos' remained and, despite the discouragement of priests, man still strove to decipher 'the mysteries of the universe'. As a result, religion was supplanted by science; philosophy, as Francis Bacon said in his *Novum Organum*, stepped down 'from heaven to earth'. When the final volume of *The Golden Bough* was published, the process of elucidation had apparently been completed by Maxwell's thermodynamics and Einstein's theory of relativity. But Frazer remained unconvinced, and doubted whether physics could offer any certainty about the 'ever-shifting phantasmagoria of thought which we dignify with the high-sounding names of the world and the universe'. What if in the future science found a way to 'rekindle the dying fire of the sun'? Would it matter? The sun itself and the earth it warms were for Frazer merely 'parts of that unsubstantial world which thought has conjured out of the void. ... They too, like so much that to common eyes seems solid, may melt into air, into thin air'. In wistfully recalling Prospero's abandonment of sorcery, Frazer expressed a nostalgia for magic, which once so roughly commanded the elements.

The elegy was premature. Scientific cosmology has never given up the useful fiction of a deity, even if – as in Einstein's jocular asides about 'the Old One' – he is a genteel anachronism. Stephen Hawking explains his ambition to unify physics and astronomy by saying that he wants to see into 'the mind of God', which would be 'the ultimate triumph of human reason'. But does that triumph not imply disbelief in any mind beyond our own? Hawking admitted that the unified theory would have 'profound implications for the role of God the Creator'. If we stubbornly go on believing that the universe has a creator, we must still ask, as Hawking did, 'who created him?' Einstein, speculating about the moment when the idea of a cosmos germinated,

Mushroom cloud over Nagasaki, 9 August, 1945

wondered 'How much choice did God have in constructing the universe?' Probably none; there was no need for it to be constructed, so we cannot conceive of creation as a conscious act. The universe happened, or came about, or exploded into being accidentally, like the Icelandic island photographed by Haas. Myth is appealing because it tells the story of creation purposefully, teleologically. Science, unwilling to deny the emotional authority of Genesis, has tried – while questioning God's initiative – to adhere to the same narrative.

The plastic power that Coleridge conferred on poets was metaphorical: they could only mould words and images. But before long that capacity to reshape the physical world and augment God's creation had become a scientific possibility. In 1858, during a ride on a London omnibus, the German chemist August Kekulé had a day-dream about gambolling atoms. He intently inspected the details of his fantasy, and saw how these 'diminutive beings' actually moved. They teamed up in pairs, or formed groups as a larger atom embraced its juniors, then all giddily whirled together through space; he likened the consortium to a writhing snake, curled to bite its own tail. His reverie sketched a long chain of carbon atoms, linked or bonded together into polymers. The atom had always been thought of as impregnable, unalterable; the very word means something that cannot be further divided or anatomized. But Kekulé's vision, put to the test in experiments, suggested that matter could be flexed, augmented. His elastic benzene rings were made from a substance that did not exist in nature; the discovery convinced him that he had presided over an artificial Genesis – except that now the creator was a snake, the symbol of knowledge and its sacreligious delights. Jung believed that Kekulé's description of coiled serpents and coupled dancers derived from 'the *coniunctio*, the mating' that preoccupied the alchemists. Now, however, the great work produced not gold but the material we call plastic. The elixir of eternal life, denied to men by a resentful God, was replaced by a synthetic substance that, once created, could not be destroyed.

For Kekulé, the prospect was mystical. But divine creation could also be challenged by mathematics. In 1927 A. S. Eddington delivered a course of lectures on the demise of classical physics, the running-down of the universe, and man's place in a nature newly defined by the quantum theory. During the series he treated his audience in Edinburgh to an exercise he called 'World Building': the construction of a conceptual frame that would give 'a shadow performance of the drama enacted in the world of experience'. It was, he admitted, a game, like those he dreamed of playing as a child, when he used to read about the marvels of bric-à-brac that might be assembled if you could only lay your hands on the innards of a clock, a few junked telephones, and some mercury from a broken barometer. The young Eddington was frustrated because the right ingredients were never available. As a physicist, he was able to think up the materials he needed, '*relations* and *relata*' that had a conveniently theoretical existence – relatum $A$, relation $AP$, contiguous relatum $B$ and so on. He frankly admitted that he was not God, and confessed 'I cannot make the world out of nothing'. But he could make it out of relations and coordinates, and these materials might even be extended to create a 'diversity of worlds' like those surveyed by Fontenelle. Eddington amassed his formulaic tools until he had worked through 'the 16 measures of world-structure' and allowed for all possible combinations. With some of his 256 numerical coefficients he constructed the laws of geometry and mechanics, while others took care of electromagnetism. He regretted that the building materials he used were too coarse to cope with 'atomicity', so he had to leave out microscopic phenomena like electrons. Eddington laughed at the clumsiness of mathematical language, only too close to the lumber which children scavenge from attics when making their own improvised worlds; he admitted that he had 'fashioned … bricks from the primitive clay' of those relata. But his numbers, correctly proportioned and distributed, formed the ground-plan and elevation of a wondrous structure, 'the palace of the mind'.

The game Eddington so brilliantly and beautifully played had clear implications for the religious account of origins. By making the formulae circle in the air and then stabilize, he had produced 'virtually the symbol for creation of an active world out of the formless background'. That operation used to be performed by myth; Eddington achieved the same result with mathematics. He reminded his listeners to rethink Genesis, because 'not once in the dim past, but continuously by the conscious mind is the miracle of Creation wrought'. At the end of his lecture he relied on an edict by the mathematician Leopold Kronecker, who declared that 'God made the integers, all else is the work of man'. Kronecker meant to discourage the use of irrational or transcendental numbers, which did not really exist. Integers at least were building blocks, put in place by the professorial figure Kronecker called 'der liebe Gott'. But Eddington ingeniously reversed Kronecker's meaning, cut back the role of the biblical creator, and left the work of construction to man.

That work was completed when J. Robert Oppenheimer and his colleagues at Los Alamos harnessed a force that over-ruled God's will and used it to split one of the supposedly impervious particles from which the world was made. In 1954 Niels Bohr, perhaps with a twinge of remorse, referred to nuclear fission as 'modern alchemy'. Oppenheimer knew that his atomic bomb contradicted or dismantled Genesis, which is why he nervously sought a religious authorization for his project by naming the test site Trinity. The suggestion came from John Donne's sonnet 'Batter my heart, three person'd God', but the analogy was not reassuring: a trinitarian God has undergone division, breaking apart into three persons. Georges Lemaître, a Belgian priest, persuaded Einstein in 1933 that a single atom, bifurcating and subdividing billions and trillions of times, had begotten the universe. Oppenheimer worried about the energy unleashed by all these creative acts; in the sonnet, Donne offers to confront this irate power, and guiltily begs God 'to breake, blowe, burn and make me new', or to 'untie, or breake that knot againe'. Reciting the poem as a kind of mantra, Oppenheimer imagined exposing himself to the blast of the bomb, and chose martyrdom as the penalty for having created it.

John Archibald Wheeler, a theorist of nuclear fission who worked on Oppenheimer's Manhattan Project, continued to brood about the metaphysics of the explosion. In 1967, imagining gravitational collapse, Wheeler coined the term 'black hole'. He knew that the universe could uncreate itself by vanishing into one of these chasms; it was harder to explain how it first emerged from that hole. Could anything come from nothing? In answering the eternal, inescapable question, Wheeler democratized the deity. Creation, he suggested, may have been the result of 'genesis by observership': a pile-up of quantum interactions, uncountable billions of them, which by converging shook the universe out of its sleep. In 1989 Wheeler catchily summarized the process as 'it from bit'. His phrase joined quantum mechanics and information theory, theorizing that 'every item of the world has at bottom – at a very deep bottom – an immaterial source'. A spirit still floats on the face of waters, which remain inscrutably deep; the only difference is that the Logos now asks what Wheeler calls 'yes-no questions', eliciting the 'equipment-evoked responses' that are called bits. Steven Weinberg, applying relativity to the cosmic flow of galaxies, also returned to the beginning in his book *The First Three Minutes*. Wheeler described a participatory universe, in which every particle that releases energy contributes to the grand generative endeavour. Weinberg's narrative is more momentary, more disorderly. As he imagines it, creation happened instantaneously, after a cataclysm that fired the stars into the sky and sent them off on their headlong, expanding course. Although Weinberg's title abbreviates the extended working week described in Genesis, time turns out to be even more contracted, because the crucial event occurred during 'the first hundredth of a second'. The subsequent three minutes were both a beginning and a fatalistic end: the stars and planets extruded when time began will inevitably dissolve again, after thousands of millions of years, into 'a cosmic soup of radiation'. Weinberg sees both logic and justice in this, since when those nuclei break up their disintegrating particles will 'regain thermal communion with the rest of the universe'. In his vocabulary, communion is neither a religious rite nor an experience of social sympathy. It announces an extinction, as chaos returns when the universe re-contracts and heats to 100 million million million million million degrees.

Weinberg tells the 'sad story' with a brutal, bracing honesty that excludes any possibility of divine forethought. His preface asks 'What could be more interesting than the problem of Genesis?' But the query is intentionally irreverent: what interests Weinberg is the problem, to which Genesis offers a false solution. He ridicules the cosmic genealogies of myth, and chuckles over the giant Ymir and his nurturing cow in the *Edda*. The fable, he charges, covers 'an embarrassing vagueness about the beginning'. Yet despite his own display of technical exactitude – diagrams of Planck distributions, charts of microwave radiation – Weinberg too is elaborating and revising a myth. After the primal explosion, he pictures matter rushing apart until 'finally, the universe was filled with light'. Although this paraphrases Genesis, there is no cause for a prolonged outburst of C major. Weinberg explains that whenever an atom in a light bulb changes from a state of higher to lower energy, a photon is emitted, which means that it perishes. In one of their manifestoes, the Italian futurists described the twitching filaments in an electric bulb as a tragic spectacle, a compression of individual life or of the universe's life-span. Electrons, positrons, neutrinos and photons have similar careers. As Weinberg says, they are 'created out of pure energy and then, after short lives, ... annihilated again'. There is no necessary equation between light and enlightenment or lucidity. Because light brings us information about the velocity of distant, dilating galaxies, Weinberg calls it a 'starry messenger'. The phrase ironically toys with the notion of angels on their cosmic rounds; in Weinberg's myth, however, light spreads the bad news about decay, and reports on its own painfully slow expiry as the universe – cooling and allowing complex nuclei to form – passes from 'a radiation-dominated era to the present matter-dominated era'.

Weinberg ends by glancing at the narrative of Ragnarok in the *Edda*: a twilight of the gods, when earth is seared by fire and swamped by water, after which Thor's sons will take up their hammers and begin the business of world-building all over again. Weinberg's own speculative preview of the end is not so different from the Nordic myth. He envisages a thermal apocalypse, though this might be arrested by a sudden re-expansion. That is the future, and also the past; a cycle repeats itself, so there is 'no beginning whatever' and cosmology 'nicely avoids the problem of Genesis'. He drafted the conclusion to his book while flying over Wyoming, on the way back from San Francisco to Boston. Below him lay a domesticated world: land parcelled into fields, roads connecting towns in straight lines, houses with lights in them. His mental tour of outer space had demonstrated that this tame, cosy scene was a speck in an 'overwhelmingly hostile universe', where human life was the farcical outcome of 'a chain of accidents stretching back to the first three minutes'. Although the wider view was daunting and depressing, he took heart from the fact that 'men and women are not content to comfort themselves with tales of gods and giants'. Myth may be unworthy of us, but Weinberg does finally acknowledge the value of another literary form. 'The effort to understand the universe,' he says, 'is one of the very few things that lifts human life above the level of farce, and gives it some of the grace of tragedy'. Tragic heroes argue with the universe and impugn its creator – standing up to a cruel god, like the Prometheus of Aeschylus; investigating eternity and studying the secrets of the grave like Hamlet; analysing creation in a scientific laboratory like Faust.

Theories about world-building end by influencing and perhaps upsetting our sense of ourselves. Are the atoms that compose us solid, or as unsubstantial as everything else in Frazer's void? Is the life within us a muffled explosion? Do we have a fixed nature, or are we as slippery as mercury, the element so admired by the alchemists? In his 1953 Reith lectures on the BBC, Oppenheimer quoted Newton's assurance that 'God in the Beginning form'd Matter in solid, massy, hard, impenetrable, moveable Particles', which would never wear out or break up, 'no ordinary Power being able to divide what God himself made one in the first Creation'. When Oppenheimer split an atom, he confounded this faith. Ernest Rutherford, writing in the journal *Nature*, explained 'atomic constitution' by suggesting that atoms are 'purely electrical structures'; for Hans Vaihinger, the atom was a 'hypostatized nothing'. Perhaps human beings were equally fragile and fissile. Also in 1953, Jung suggested that the self might be 'a sort of atomic nucleus about whose innermost structure and ultimate meaning we know nothing'. We do know that the the self can be broken apart, restored to the nothingness from which it derives, although the practice of psychotherapy convinced Jung that renewal was possible: by plumbing an unconscious chaos, the frail and sickly ego could repair itself and do a little to restore the circular wholeness of the world. The experience required immersion, as if in one of those baths where the alchemists broke down matter. The example of the 'Mysterium coniunctionis' – the merger of opposites, fused in the alembic – convinced Jung that 'a world-creating quality attaches to human consciousness, ... through which, as it were, a second world-creation was enacted'. The philosopher's stone was a portion of the sun, a piece of the divine substance. Alchemy, as Jung proposed, equated the ego with the sun and thus with God. He added that in saying so he violated no religious convictions; he was happy if believers regarded the mind as 'a divine instrument', a place of transmutation and transcendence like an alchemical vial.

Such ideas can be matters of life and death – a spur to self-creation, or an exercise in dissolution. They are tortuously debated by the characters in Lindsay Clarke's novel *The Chymical Wedding*, published in 1989. Alex, a poet who is unable to write, goes to live in rural Norfolk, where he finds a society that still worships woodland gods like the Green Man or lewd goddesses like the stone woman with an open groin carved onto the flinty wall of a village church. His guide to this regressive world is another poet, Edward, who derides the materialism of contemporary science. Unconvinced by Kekulé's vision of the plastic wheel of life, Edward rails against the synthetic nastiness of polystyrene, 'rot that won't rot'. He mocks the 'vacuous cosmos' of Pope, where disparate atoms jostled in 'the great Inane', and accuses nuclear physics of completing the work of dispersal and destruction. He scoffs at the black hole about which Wheeler fearfully fantasized, the place where the laws of physics founder and 'the universe turns inside-out'; he prefers to gaze into the private parts of the idol on the church wall, and is content to be engulfed by 'the black hole of the Magna Mater'. Edward pleads for fusion not fission, for a symbolist vision that holds the world together rather than a diabolical science that breaks it apart. The chemical wedding of the alchemists, symbolized by twin vessels with interpenetrating beaks like pelicans, brought together mind and heart, male and female, dark and light. Physics performs surgery on matter; alchemy attempted to heal the breach and to produce a transformed, transcendent amalgam.

Pondering gnostic scriptures and alchemical treatises, Alex assembles his own theory of creation. The hermetic lore he consults admits that there was a fall, but exempts humanity from blame. The fault is not our sin; the polluted world we inhabit was made that way, since it is 'the creation of the Demiurge, the Archon, the mad lord' – a deity who is malicious not benevolent. Alchemy dreamed of recuperation, which might be brought about by science rather than by the intervention of a saviour. The subliming of metal was a rehearsal for this mystical ascent: 'in working to change the substances, the alchemists' – as Alex concludes – 'changed themselves'. He watches as an experiment of the same kind happens in a kiln heated to 1,280 degrees centigrade. The baking oven throbs and puffs out acrid smoke like a belching volcano. When the vents are opened, a chimney releases 'a pillar of fire'. In the maelstrom, a work of art, beautifully shaped and imperviously glazed, takes form: a pot. Origen worried about Isaiah's demeaning description of God as a potter, who moulded Adam from clay. Here the potter is a woman called Laura, and her kiln is the uterus where she mixes the embroiled elements and compels them to obey her. Edward marvels at her creative recipe: she knows how 'to craft the pots so patiently from earth and water and then deliver them over to the mercies of fire and air'. Alex finds a rationalization of the process in the doctrine of Hermes Trismegistus, the Egyptian god who with his triple magistracy presided over religion, law and art. 'So the world was created', declares Hermes – fathered by the sun and mothered by the moon, carried in the belly of the wind and nursed by the earth. This doctrine enables Alex to calm the fears of his children, who are terrified by the prospect of nuclear war. They silently reproach him, saying '*We don't understand why the world should be like this. Why have you allowed it to happen? You're our father, you made the world before we came.*' Such accusations are addressed to the God of Genesis by Satan, Adam and then by every subsequent malcontent; Alex is faced with them because a father is supposed to be a protective god. We expect myth to answer those complaints – to justify the absurdity of individual death and to find a sufficient cause for the world's deathliness. Christianity does so by insisting on our miscreant guilt, while promising that we will be forgiven. Alchemy more boldly denies that the world needs to be like this, and schemes to revoke the curse by brewing the elixir of immortality.

These philosophical forays happen in the early 1980s, a New Age of heretical religious liberty. But a simultaneous action happens in 1848, as a group of Victorian doubters living in the same East Anglian village speculate about the same mysteries. Their task is harder, more psychologically ruinous, because they struggle to maintain a compulsory Christian faith and punish themselves for their moral weakness. Laura's counterpart in the mid-nineteenth century is Louisa, a landowner's daughter who writes a book about the secrets of alchemy. She worries that '*our true philosophical Mercury*', the spirit of trickery and guileful metamorphosis, has invaded her and taught her to be duplicitous. But she cannot resist this '*masculine sprite*', which infuses her with a '*vital and procreative energy*'. The book that results from their intercourse is theologically seditious; repentant, she burns it. Perhaps this is the completion of the great work, which starts from the 'nigredo' – the blackness of primary matter – and ends as the scorched and putrefied paper glows in the grate. Here she sees '*the origin and first form of all things … and that beginning to which shall never be an end*'.

Staring into a lake that resembles the unfathomable contents of her mind, Laura seems to be scrutinizing 'the first chaos of things'. That disturbance rages inside her, as it does within the clergyman Edwin, with whom she has an affair. In his journal, Edwin transcribes the officially sanctioned story of creation, attributing the world to the word, 'the Logos; *the great* I Am'. He goes on to summarize the competing myth, which more closely corresponds to his own agitation: 'Hesiod *in his* Theogony … *tells us … that* Chaos *was the first of things, and then wide-bosomed* Earth, *dim* Tartarus, *and* Eros, *fairest of the deathless gods*'. Louisa reminds him that Christian festivals like Easter are a chaste camouflage for pagan carnivals, feasts of the flesh when the world – which turns inside out in that corporeal black hole – turns upside down. He cannot accept his own infirmity, and castrates himself with a razor. His wife Emilia has meanwhile suffered a miscarriage. During her convalescence she weeps in misery when Louisa reads out an extract from a poem published in 1773 by Anna Laetitia Barbauld, which describes

> solitudes of waste, unpeopled space,
> The deserts of creation, wide and wild,
> Where embryo systems and unkindled suns
> Sleep in the womb of Chaos.

The lines are a pastiche of Milton's survey of Chaos and its embryo atoms; they distress Emilia because they demonstrate how indifferently prolific nature is, by contrast with the delicate, dangerous, contingent business of human procreation. Artists also have an easier task, because they can bring to birth misbegotten or biologically improbable creatures like the symbolic figures Alex admires in a volume of hermetic dialogues: grotesque hermaphrodites, a black gryphon, a hell-hound with three heads. Edward relies on the sight of these monsters and freaks to excite 'the sleeping powers of the mind'. Before the end of the novel, Alex has begun to sense 'the birth-pangs of a poem'; the moral traumas and gynaecological calamities of the Victorian characters whose lives he investigates quicken his own faltering creativity. Edward too, whose poetry long ago dried up inside him, reports that he has resumed writing.

Myth and physics are both conjectural, making guesses about origins and creating a variety of parallel worlds like those in *The Chymical Wedding*. If particles can be smashed, matter splits. Every choice we make causes the universe to fork and branch; while one thing happens here, other possibilities are free to occur elsewhere, mentally close but physically inaccessible. This permissive law of physics is also a principle of literary fantasy, which must begin by constructing its own idiosyncratic cosmos. One of the scientists in Philip Pullman's *The Subtle Knife*, the second instalment of the trilogy *His Dark Materials*, computes the number of subjective universes. In the third book, *The Amber Spyglass*, Mary Malone – once a nun, now

a specialist in high-energy physics – goes on a tour of these adjacent earths, which are 'the multiple worlds predicted by quantum theory'. Windows in Pullman's stories do not frame a familiar view of a street. They are cut out of the sky, and when opened they serve as doors through which his characters vanish into alternative realities. The young hero Will reads some letters in which his father, a physicist conducting abstruse research in Alaska, learns about these gaps in air. Will locates such an aperture near some hornbeam trees beside the Oxford ring

Patricia Hodge as Mrs Coulter, with her daemon in the National Theatre's production of *His Dark Materials* by Philip Pullman, 2004

road, and enters a supplementary universe where he meets the heroine Lyra, who grew up in an Oxford of her own, incompatible with Will's. He asks her where she comes from. 'From my world,' she replies. 'It's joined on.'

Lyra's father Lord Asriel plans to build bridges between these worlds. In the first book of the sequence, *Northern Lights*, he investigates the charged particles in the atmosphere near the North Pole, where matter thins almost to transparency: here he hopes to insert his connective span. Pullman gives Asriel the name of the biblical angel of death Asrael, and invests him with a satanically superb intelligence. He recruits Lyra's mother Mrs Coulter for an enterprise that will be 'the end of the Church' and of the mental obfuscation it sponsors. The priestly caste against which Asriel makes war has detonated a bomb, which 'opened an abyss between the worlds' and 'fractured the structure of things so profoundly that there are fissures and cracks everywhere'. A gash in the sky allows 'Shadow-particles' to stream out into the void, asphyxiating the minds that flicker like candles 'in every one of the billions of worlds'. 'You and I,' Asriel tells Mrs Coulter, 'could take the universe to pieces and put it together again.' That cosmic rearrangement involves defining the nature of Dust, a dark powder that leaks into the human world and thickens around adults. It is a symptom of consciousness, which quickens matter and saves it from 'brutish automatism'. Official religion, brow-beating mankind, sees it as evidence of original sin. Like an alchemist, Asriel calls the endeavour his 'great work'.

Asriel's bridge-building alludes to the engineered interference with nature in *Paradise Lost*, when Sin and Death construct their causeway; in Pullman's fantasy, such ventures are evidence of both scientific ingenuity and artistic inventiveness, and no God has the right to reprove them. Milton's God confined to Chaos the unborn atoms that were his dark materials. Pullman, taking over from this absent-minded or exhausted deity, uses them to create supplementary worlds, like those plural Oxfords or the foggy Arctic where the witches convene or the tropical idyll of Cittàgazze. At the same time he gives *Paradise Lost* a new meaning that scandalously contradicts Christianity. In his introduction to a recent edition of the poem, Pullman insists that its subject is 'the necessity of growing up'. The biblical story left us lamenting the loss of innocence; this guilty, backward-looking misery is a repudiation of experience, with its unforeseeable delights and perils, so Milton's poem can be prescribed as an antidote to the Bible. Asriel takes up the 'big black book' and reads to Lyra the narrative of the temptation and fall. He is gratified when she denies that such a story could be true and calls it a fairy-tale. He has his own sophisticated use for Adam and Eve: their non-existence makes them pliable and portable, 'like an imaginary number' that can be inserted into equations where it enables you to 'calculate all manner of things'. The mishap with the apple is an effort to explain the world's imperfection; we can re-imagine it, and give the story a more humane, open-ended outcome. If there are many universes, religious morality is relative not absolute. Soon after her lesson in the literal fallacy of Genesis, Lyra sees Asriel and Mrs Coulter entangled in one another's arms, striking sparks as they hover above the chasm and conspire to stir up metaphysical havoc. The sight is shocking, even maiming:

> Her own parents, together!
> And embracing so passionately: an undreamt-of thing.

Despite Lyra's denial, we all do secretly dream of such things, and when the fantasy materializes before our eyes we acquire an understanding of creation – of our own beginnings, and of nature's generative will – that ejects us into adulthood. At the end of *The Amber Spyglass*, Will and Lyra kiss, purgatively bathe, and lie together in a golden grove 'melting with love'. They have cast off childhood and its carnal ignorance, and are sealed in a snug, unashamed paradise from which no squadron of censorious angels evicts them.

The ban on eating the fruit that symbolized knowledge placed a prohibition on independent thought. But at Lyra's college in Oxford, the scientists practise a discipline cheekily known as 'experimental theology'. Among their specialities is 'atomcraft', akin to witchcraft because it magically tampers with the fabric of nature, and they are also experts on electromagnetism, in its way a divine mystery. For Pullman, substances are as malleable as meanings; the creator is truly a protoplast. Attacked by an angel, Will stares up at a cloudy sky that is 'luminous with energy, like plasma'. Plasma is the blood's lymphatic soup, in which corpuscles float; it can coagulate, so it moulds the globules when it clots. We are kept alive by the metamorphic stream within us. The daemons that accompany the characters have a similar plasticity. These spirit-animals externalize the moods of the individuals to whom they are attached. Lyra's daemon Pantalaimon appears at first as a fluttery, nervous moth, coloured dark brown to disappear into the Oxford panelling. Then he relaxes, and goes to sleep around her neck, curled up in the form of an ermine. Caged by Mrs Coulter, he fights his captors by metamorphosing into a lion, an eagle, a wolf, a bear and a polecat, growing talons, wings and razory teeth as the need arises. The nickname Lyra fondly bestows on Pantalaimon is Pan, and he shares the universality of the goat-god: the prefix defines his ability to be all things and to travel to all places. He is an imaginary creature whose mutability makes visible the slippery antics of imagination.

When God – officiously entitled The Authority – makes a belated appearance in *His Dark Materials*, he turns out to be a whimpering dotard. A free-thinking angel advises Will that he deserves no special reverence. He is, or once was, a conniving politician, who bedecked himself with honorary names like Yahweh and Adonai, but 'he was never the creator'. No such agent is necessary in a universe that creates itself when matter condenses into Dust and acquires self-awareness. The witch-hunter Joachim Lorenz reports on rumours of a war that took place in heaven ages ago. In Milton's telling, Christ righteously trounces the rebel angels. But Lorenz says that he does not know who the winner was, which intimates that the devils may have been victorious. Although God totters off into obsolescence, Pullman reserves a role for his heir, a juvenile and female Christ. An ecclesiastical spy tells Asriel that Lyra is 'the most important child who has ever lived', charged with resoldering the wrecked universe at a time of 'great crisis'. She is equal to the challenge. Having witnessed the downfall of 'the kingdom of heaven', she vows at the end of the trilogy to build a replacement for this hierarchical, inequitable realm. She intends, she says, to build 'the republic of heaven'. The phrase contains a political manifesto: after the discrediting of God, how can we go on tolerating monarchs who claim to be divinely anointed? But this new society is also a state of imaginative grace. A republic is a level world of public things, shared by all of us; it becomes heavenly if, encouraged by art, we take note of its novelty and oddity and radiance – if we look on things as children do, with wonder and with a curiosity that demands explanations. A solicitous angel consoles Lyra when she loses the power to commute between worlds. She can still overcome the estrangements of time and space by using 'the faculty of what you call imagination. But that does not mean *making things up*. It is a form of seeing'.

Having refused to accept God's credentials as a creator, Pullman is modest about his own creativity. He draws attention to his synthetic second-hand amalgam of myth and science, and in the acknowledgments to *His Dark Materials* cheerfully admits 'I have stolen ideas from every book that I have ever read' – from the Bible, Milton and Blake, from archaeological primers and tracts on particle physics. He is as eclectic as the filching magpies after which Cittàgazze is named: as Lorenz says, the citizens 'create nothing' and can only 'steal from other worlds'. But this activity – which Harper in *Angels in America* calls recycling – matches the way nature rearranges and transforms its constituent elements. At the end of *The Amber Spyglass*, Will slices a vent in thin air and slithers back into the world he came from. He finds himself on the outskirts of Oxford, near a factory where 'chemicals were combining'. The game of permutations can weld discordant materials together and come up with a marvel, like the herd of wheeled animals, 'a cross between antelopes and motorcycles', encountered by Mary Malone. With horned heads and abbreviated trunks like those of elephants, the creatures have one leg at the front and another at the back; these limbs have evolved wheels, and they advance on Mary like a gang of bikers. She refuses to believe what she sees, because 'wheels did not exist in nature'. The wheel is a human invention, the original motor of progress for our species. Where in their bodies could the animals conceal the axle, which has to be separate from the rotary device? As they approach, Mary sees that the wheels are actually seed-pods, which the creatures clasp with their hooked claws and revolve. She laughs aloud at the genius of it. Not content with being mechanomorphs, they exhibit a human talent for making up words, and introduce themselves as mulefa. They then offer Mary a ride; one of them kneels, she climbs aboard, and the convoy rolls off down the road. Progress continues, as the mind – whether that of an engineer or a fantasist – surreally flexes the obstructive limits of nature.

The Association of Christian Teachers has convicted Pullman of blasphemy, and the *Catholic Herald* called his books 'fit for the bonfire'. The Archbishop of Canterbury, Rowan Williams, wisely accepted his criticism, and made a heady leap of his own by conceding that St Thomas Aquinas had also suggested that God might not exist. In 1270 in *Summa Theologica*, Aquinas proved the logical impossibility of God in a mind-bending set of syllogisms: 'It seems that God does not exist; because if one of two contraries be infinite, the other would be altogether destroyed. But the word "God" means that He is infinite goodness. If, therefore, God existed, there would be no evil discoverable; but there is evil in the world. Therefore God does not exist'. Despite the finality of this, Aquinas had to grant God a hypothetical resurrection. The impetus of Pullman's own creativity coaxes him to qualify his scornful atheism and to give God the benefit of the doubt. In a lecture attacking established religion in 2005, he ended by asking why we bother to write – or even to go on existing – now that we know we are specks on the surface of a doomed, cooling star, lacking divine protection. 'We should act,' he recommended, '*as if...*'. He let the sentence trail off, but the emphatic conjunction was enough to justify creative activity: 'as if' is the conditional spell that motivates dreams and metaphors, amending reality and adding to the variety of worlds. Pullman glossed his command by saying 'We should act as if the universe were listening to us and responding'. The universe could not care less, but other human beings may be listening. If we elicit a response in them, they may store what we say in their memories and pass on our words to someone else. If they do, there will be a kind of posterity. The ghost of an old woman, who regrets her disconnection from the earth, imparts to Mary the secret of survival. 'Tell them stories,' she says. 'That's what we didn't know. ... Just tell them stories.' Mary repeats the words to herself, vowing to remember her obligation both to the past and to the future. The ghost specifies that the tales should be true, because people are nourished by truth. But perhaps the stories would be even more enlivening, and better able to guess the secrets of creation, if they were fictions.

# 33

# THE BRIGHT DESTROYER

Because the beginning has receded out of sight, it can still be attributed to God, or at least to the 'cosmological constant' that Einstein relied on to maintain the universe's steady state. Responsibility for the end lies closer to home: mankind is in charge of its timing, looks forward to it with chiliastic impatience, and will probably react to its arrival with a giddy aesthetic excitement. In 1992 Werner Herzog made a documentary entitled *Lessons of Darkness*, about the torching of Kuwaiti oil wells after the Gulf War. The images he recorded – a charred desert, a burning sea, a suffocated sky – brought forward the ecological doom provoked by our abuse of nature. Herzog attached to the film an epigraph that he passed off as a quotation from Pascal, although he had made it up himself: 'The collapse of the stellar universe will occur – like creation – in grandiose spendour'. The statement is at once a lament and a jubilant anthem.

We imagine creation as a sunrise, the invention of light (which is blotted out by the viscous, flaring clouds Herzog photographed). In 1915, however, an artist uncreated the visible world, literally eclipsing it. The experiment started in *Victory over the Sun*, an opera staged in St Petersburg in 1913 with a text by the futurists Alexei Kruchenykh and Velimir Khlebnikov, music by Mikhail Matushin, and designs by the painter Kasimir Malevich. This astral circus, performed in an invented language, envisaged a future in which the sun had become obsolete, since man-made machines could generate whatever power men needed. Khlebnikov called his prologue 'Blackcreative Newslets'. It presented a bulletin about this new world, and when it concluded, the curtain – covered by Malevich with a tumbling chaos of geometrical shapes and unintelligible words – was ripped apart. Behind lay a box that squared our old, rotund world. Malevich's version of outer space was a cube, starkly bisected by a diagonal line that separated light from darkness. All references to current earthly existence were removed from this astronomical map; Malevich's aim, he said, was 'the creation of a new reality'. Two years later, he achieved his personal victory over the sun by obliterating a canvas, inkily overwriting it with black paint. Malevich remembered the puzzlement of viewers who complained when they looked at *Black Square* that 'Everything we loved is lost. We are in a desert'. But the challenge to reason made his square a dazzling darkness, the reflex of a light too brilliant for the eyes. In his essay on *The Non-Objective World*, Malevich

Burning oil
wells, Kuwait,
12 March, 1991

pointed out that beneath the black square was the white ground that he had blackened. 'The square = feeling,' he explained, 'the white field = the void beyond this feeling.' Milton's angels look away from the searing source, or shade its radiance with their wings. Malevich's blackness, however, was not a protective mediation. It insisted on the value of oblivion and erasure: art, he said, can exist 'without things (that is, the "time-tested well-spring of life")'. The 'one and only source of every creation' is an emotional force which when released burns up any depicted object that might pretend to contain it. The colours engaged in a metaphysical battle that left reality either blanked out or charred. For Kandinsky, white had 'the appeal of the nothingness that is before birth, of the world in the ice age', while black represented 'the ashes of a funeral pyre, something motionless like death'.

In 1921 Malevich exhorted his colleagues to 'pull up consciousness by its roots', to detach it from the earth and launch it – like the aeroplanes that so excited him – into 'the infinity of space'. This would align art with 'the true nature of the universe', which has no interest in the adhesion of atoms or the cohesion of structures; the destiny of the nucleus, Malevich declared, was to fly free as 'a single force of atomized energy', expanding into orbit. He illustrated the theory in *Painterly Realism: Boy with Knapsack – Colour Masses in the Fourth Dimension*, painted in 1915. The boy is a black square, the knapsack is a smaller square of red, swinging at a jaunty angle. The landscape through which the boy walks is a fourth dimension of vacant whiteness. In *Victory over the Sun*, beams of light as sharp as swords chopped up the bodies on stage, truncating the actors or amputating single limbs. The spectacle demonstrated Malevich's belief that 'all matter disintegrates'.

Malevich suggested that atomization could be understood by watching what happened when a bullet is fired from 'a multi-chambered cartridge'. The revolver had become an agent of revolutionary perception, and – because it helped energy to escape from matter – a useful tool for artists. André Derain said that he and Matisse had used colours 'like sticks of dynamite', detonating objects so that they emitted light. In 1908 in his fable *Penguin Island*, Anatole France described an anarchist plot to atomize industrial civilization by exploiting the destructive energies of matter itself. The radicalized chemists disdain dynamite, and use an oscillator to propagate electric waves. One device is concealed in an egg made of white metal, which when examined bursts open and blows up a government building. The emblem of new life now incubates death.

Another band of anarchists in Joseph Conrad's novel *The Secret Agent*, published in 1907, consider bombs to be their 'means of expression' and elaborate a 'philosophy of bomb throwing'. They take on the role of the artistic creator, although their intentions – as Mr Vladimir says – are 'purely destructive'. To purify the destructive impulse means to intellectualize it, which is why the bomb-maker Ossipon is trying to invent 'a really intelligent detonator', based on 'the principle of the pneumatic instantaneous shutter for a camera lens'. At the moment of detonation there must be more than a violent, butchered mess; Conrad's agents want to fix a terminal image, as if, like Malevich in his call for atomization, they are photographing matter as they blow it apart. The concentrated power they carry in their pockets cannot be wasted on individuals, or even on property. Vladimir orders the saboteur Verloc to attack a sacrosanct idea, one of the fetishes on which 'the whole social creation' is founded. An outrage in the National Gallery would hardly qualify, because art is of little account to the calculating men who control Britain and its empire. The modern world has made a religion of science, so Vladimir jocularly calls for an assault on the meridian at Greenwich. 'What do you think,' he asks, 'of having a go at astronomy?' The act of sabotage will be useless, and may not even leave any victims; its virtue will lie in jolting the Logos, upsetting the orderly apportionment of time and space.

While undermining astronomy, the bomb elaborates an astronomical theory of its own. To help him plant the device, Verloc recruits his retarded stepson Stevie, whose pastime is 'drawing circles, circles, circles; innumerable circles, concentric, eccentric'. The idiotic occupation turns out to be the work of a savant, because the entangled, colliding curves that he scribbles on the page are 'a rendering of cosmic chaos, the symbolism of a mad art'. The circles might be the outlines of dancing, jarring atoms, containers for nothingness. His sister Winnie later remembers Stevie's circles as 'coruscations ... suggesting chaos and eternity'. To coruscate is to sparkle, to make a shower of light: the boy has inadvertently sketched the creation of the world. Carrying the bomb through Greenwich Park on the way to the observatory, Stevie stumbles and is ripped apart by the blast, dispersed into shreds of fabric and splinters of bone that have to be gathered up with a shovel. Winnie imagines the explosion as a firework display, and when she closes her eyes she sees Stevie's severed head luminously tumbling through the air and 'fading out slowly like the last star'. Although the bomb plot misfires, Stevie's mishap wrecks the theoretical grid of latitudes and longitudes that extends from the observatory on the hill and imprisons the earth behind bars. He demonstrates that the cosmos is the offshoot of an accident, and the ballistic trajectory of his head illustrates the brief, disjected life of some atoms that for a while made up what appeared to be a person. Lying in bed, anaesthetized by shock and grief, Winnie hears the clock 'count off fifteen ticks into the abyss of eternity', a chasm that gobbles up chronology. She experiences her own equivalent of Malevich's eclipse and, as Conrad remarks, she might be reacting to the sudden extinction of the sun. But the prospect is icily bright, not obscure. She stares at 'a whitewashed wall with no writing on it', an expanse that is 'perfectly blank. A blankness to run at and dash your head against'. She is longing for the bomb to go off again inside her brain.

In the black square or on the white wall, art had prophetically dreamed up a scene that was to become the modern world's own religious revelation, a reminiscence of the beginning and a preview of the end. When the atomic bomb was tested at Los Alamos in 1945, Oppenheimer, who had studied Sanskrit at Berkeley, pondered its significance by repeating to himself a line from the Hindu *Bhagavad Gita*. What he remembered was a passage in which 'the radiance of a thousand suns' announces the advent of 'the Mighty One', who is identified as 'Death, the destroyer of worlds'. Oppenheimer knew that he was presiding over an inverse creation. He chose to read the *Gita* pessimistically, since many translations call the bright destroyer Time not Death. It may have been some comfort that the worlds being burned up were multiple; the quotation at least allowed him to avoid the prospect of the biblical apocalypse, which terminates the life of a world that is unique, unrepeatable. When the bomb was dropped on Hiroshima, President Truman admitted that it represented 'a new and revolutionary increase in destruction', which drew its force from the sun and harnessed 'the basic power of the universe'. Truman took care to manoeuvre around the possibility that this might presage the death of the earth, seared and shattered by the energy that gave birth to it. His statement emphasized

connection, continuation, the certainty of a future: like H. G. Wells beginning the first sentence of his *Outline of History* with a conjunction, Truman declared 'And the end is not yet'. Unfortunately the endless world to come contained, as he went on to say, a stockpile of 'even more powerful forms'. These eventually included the hydrogen bomb, the neutron bomb, and the Pentagon's so-called smart bombs, which are supposed to make finicky decisions about what to destroy as they advance on their targets.

The study of thermonuclear reactions and the drive towards atomic fission coincided with a new model of cosmic origins.

Inside the coil of a generator

George Gamow – a Russian-born physicist who worked for the Atomic Energy Commission in the United States during the 1940s – called Einstein's relativity theory and Max Planck's quantum theory 'two great explosions of the human mind': conceptual bombs, disrupting the cohesion and stability of things. Atoms are not indivisible; they contain positive and negative charges and, as Gamow put it, can be 'brought to excited states by violent thermal collisions'. Electrons and neutrinos are equally giddy, spinning like tops, and their motion reminded Gamow of the airy agitation that produces music. Studying the action of cosmic rays, Gamow found positive and negative electrons acting out their own version of Genesis. A bombarded nucleus splits, and a pair of electrons release energy. The negative electron slows down and is absorbed into matter; its positive twin is soon expunged. Creation and annihilation, once the opposed moods of a God who alternated between love and rage, are now mirror-images of each other: creation happens when radiation is transformed into particles, annihilation occurs when particles are transformed into radiation. Gamow warned that 'the terms "created" and "annihilated" should not be understood in a metaphysical sense': physics had shorn metaphysics of its cloudy, unnecessary prefix. Ice is not 'created' when water freezes, nor is it 'annihilated' when it thaws. The words merely refer to a change in state. Our world is destroyed as it is created; it originated in a blast, an impromptu burst of energy that dispersed matter like shrapnel, starting a series of reverberations that still continue in the present as microwaves disseminate light through remote galaxies. Science at last was able to rationalize the notion of 'a day without yesterday' – the idea that bewildered Augustine and forced him to take Genesis on trust.

In 1932, Niels Bohr's collaborators at the Institute for Theoretical Physics in Copenhagen established their authority as interpreters of the cosmic scheme by writing and performing a play based on Goethe's *Faust*. The spiritual strivings of the romantic hero were replaced by experiments that succinctly resolved the mysteries of nature. Rather than scheming to capture the soul of Faust, Mephistopheles now tried to persuade him to accept the existence of the neutrino, an uncharged particle without mass that apparently violated the laws governing conservation of energy. The figure of Mephistopheles represented Wolfgang Pauli, who based his claim for the neutrino on his study of radioactivity. Faust was the Dutchman Paul Ehrenfest, initially unconvinced by Pauli's arguments. God, who enters into a wager with the devil and oversees the contest, had to be Bohr, awarded supremacy because it was he who best understood atomic structure.

The *Faust* of the physicists begins with Eddington, cast as an archangel, extolling the brilliance of creation, still as radiant as on the first morning. Mephistopheles mocks such easy-going piety, and asks God why he smiles on scientific views that undermine religion. If he can entice Faust to believe in the elusive neutrino, he will have demonstrated the insubstantiality of nature and the groundlessness of faith. Dressed as a travelling salesman, he displays to Faust his kit of fresh, unused theories. When electrodynamics and Heisenberg's uncertainty principle are rejected, Mephistopheles offers the neutrino, impersonated by Gretchen who sits at her spinning wheel and sings the song composed for her by Schubert. Goethe's heroine begins by admitting that she is restless, heavy-hearted; the neutrino more blithely chirps 'My mass is zero,/ My charge is the same' and then describes its flirtation with beta-rays and the nitrogen nuclei that spin around it. Is it tremulous because it is so girlishly vulnerable, or because it doesn't really exist? As in Goethe's play, there is a detour to a beer cellar where Mephistopheles expresses his contempt for propriety by regaling the drinkers with a song about a flea that upsets social decorum. The insect in this case is relativity, and the itch it provokes is the Unified Field Theory that Einstein – who wanted to annex electromagnetism and explain the behaviour of elementary particles – never managed to formulate. Goethe's devil enlists witches to torment and demoralize Faust; the physicists present an equivalent to black magic and its vanishing acts when electrons with negative mass jump into notional holes and become gamma-rays. Finally a compromise is agreed on, and the bulkier neutron discovered by James Chadwick replaces Pauli's air-headed neutrino. The character representing Chadwick is Wagner, who in Goethe's play manufactures the homunculus. The mystical chorus at the end of *Faust* praises eternal womanhood, symbolized by the redemptive Gretchen, for leading man aloft. The physicists conclude with their own rousing homily: 'Eternal Neutrality/ Pulls us along!'

Such optimism suits the extroverted, irradiating universe described by Lemaître. But if we think back to the beginnings, we are confronted with a rupture or an eruption. The astronomer Fred Hoyle referred to this moment of origins as 'the big bang'. Hoyle tossed out the phrase during a radio broadcast in 1950; its plosive alliteration indicates that he meant it derisively, because he maintained the contrary belief in the eternality or steadiness of the universe. Men who planned smaller bangs understood that they were playing with a force that was once a divine prerogative, and took to working out a theology to explain their actions. In *Days of Glory*, directed by Jacques Tourneur in 1944, Gregory Peck plays a Russian guerrilla fighting the Nazi invaders. He remembers working on the dam at Dnieperstroi, the proudest achievement of Soviet engineering. Despite the official atheism of the regime, he paraphrases Genesis when he describes the miracle of Soviet electrification, made possible by the dam's turbines. 'Out of the imagination of man [the dam] was built,' he says. 'At last it stood, complete, mighty and beautiful, bringing light where there had never been any light before, and power that other things might be created.' He recalls poems written about the dam, music composed to honour it, children named after it. 'It was our own creation,' he boasts, 'and I'd helped build it.' Then he reveals that, to keep it from being seized by the Germans, he helped to wreck it. He looks back on his training in sabotage as a moral and aesthetic education: 'When you destroy something you greatly love, you learn to love to destroy'. In the 1994 film *Blown Away*, directed by Stephen Hopkins, Tommy Lee Jones plays a manic bomber whose agenda is cosmological not political. He comes from Belfast, has served as a mercenary with the Red Brigades and in Libya, and is now terrorizing Boston. He reminds an official from the city's bomb squad that the universe was created by an explosion. 'I'm not a destroyer, I'm a creator,' he crows, jumping up and down on his bed as he shouts into the telephone. 'I've come here to create a new country called Chaos'. The director Oliver Stone virtually paraphrased this character's ravings in October 2001, during a symposium in New York reflecting on the political and psychological impact of the attack on the World Trade Center. Stone described the Al-Qaeda terrorists as mental innovators, compared them to Einstein and Bill Gates, and summed up their revolutionary message as 'Fuck your order!' Change happens, Stone argued, as a result of initiatives that at first seem terrifying or insane. 'Chaos,' he said, 'is energy.'

The energy set free by explosions animates and enlivens things that look dead or inert; it unbuilds the most solid structures, and analytically picks apart the loose bits and pieces that cohere to form human beings. Suicide bombers decapitate themselves when they trigger the devices strapped to their chests, and send their heads flying through space like the fiery star in *The Secret Agent*. The mushroom clouds that were first photographed in 1945 were not wispy and amorphous, like those in romantic skies. They possessed will and purpose, as if a thought or a theorem were being expressed in air; their fabric was sheer force, inconsistent with matter. We have coloured those clouds, and made them – as Herzog's epigraph says – aesthetically splendid. A lighted match tumbles into a trail of petrol at the beginning of Baz Luhrmann's film *William Shakespeare's Romeo + Juliet*. Lifting off the tarmac, cars turn into jiving planets, then merge in an orchidaceous ball of fire. Through the smoke, a white statue of Christ extends its arms above Mexico City, still volunteering to save a world that prefers perdition. During the summer of 2001, Michael Bay's *Pearl Harbor* displayed a flotilla of battleships whose decks elegantly ripple when hit by torpedoes, with roseate explosions blooming in the air. One shot attaches the viewer to a bomb as it leaves the underbelly of a Japanese plane, allowing us to whirl down with it and rip into an American ship. Concussion produces a big bang with the usual flash, followed by a brief instant of unconsciousness. An American pilot races through the carnage with his movie camera, filming an instant newsreel. His amateurish footage – abruptly curtailed by his death – is grainy, jerky and monotonously monochrome, unable to do justice to the blood, the fire and the blue Pacific. Meanwhile a flustered nurse classifies patients by smearing their foreheads with the ripe red tip of her lipstick: F stands for fatality, C for casualty, M prescribes a dose of morphine. As she hands over a man who is beyond medical help, she tells her colleagues 'Make him comfortable' – as comfortable, perhaps, as the viewer of the film, who sits in an easy chair, probably armed with a cold drink and a snack, and enjoys the spectacle of crashing planes, sinking ships and drowning men. In Roland Emmerich's *Independence Day*, released in 1996, Jeff Goldblum stands on the roof of Rockefeller Center and stares at an alien spacecraft which is the size of a flat, discus-shaped planet. It hovers over midtown Manhattan, blocking the sun from Central Park as it prepares to expunge the city. Goldblum, who plays a computer engineer, holds in his hand a print-out of the ship's radio transmissions and feels he is on its wavelength. He looks up with awe, rapture, even joy: he has been privileged to witness the last things.

Cataclysms like these are our primal scenes – endlessly replayed inside our heads, transcribed on films that allow us to dream with our eyes open. What they show us is embargoed by every moral scruple and emotional instinct, but we cannot look away. Our fascination with such spectacles is unholy, dangerously thrilling. We live in a culture that relentlessly markets illusions, and offers us the illusory prospect of being released from the world's snares. The act of deliverance will be a caustic, purgative destruction; no further creation is envisaged. This, announced with the solemnity of a biblical prophecy, was the promise of *The Matrix*, written and directed and Larry and Andy Wachowski in 1999. The setting is of course the future which, thanks to the eschatological panic of our times, has become indistinguishable from the present. Earth is a parched, ravaged waste. Human beings doze in uterine vats, while machines suck life-giving heat from them. The victims are wired to a main-frame of dreams: a cerebral cinema, whose distracting delights are known as 'the matrix' – the womb that cocoons us, protecting us from expulsion into cold, blank reality.

The punning title alludes to another, less palpable kind of matrix: a mathematical grid, with numbers arranged in rows and columns. The film begins by studying such a galaxy of digits, greenly flickering on a computer screen. The camera closes in on a zero, then travels through its welcoming vacancy. After staring at the gaping 0, we soon encounter the complementary 1 in the slim, upright person of Keanu Reeves, a hacker who lives in Room 101 of an apartment block. True to that initial zero, he appears to be in the business of annihilation. As a sideline, he sells illicit floppy disks to his clubbing friends, programming their sensations: electronics are their designer drugs. He stores the cash from these deals in a gutted book, a hollowed-out copy of Jean Baudrillard's *Simulacra and Simulation* that conveniently opens at a chapter on nihilism. Hesiod's chasm has become an abyss of infinite self-referring recession, into which we are invited to tumble. Nevertheless, it is the hacker's destiny to advance from nonentity to singularity and uniqueness. During his nocturnal bouts of mischief on the Internet, he hides behind the alias Neo, which turns out to be an anagram. 'You are the one, Neo,' announces the guerrilla leader Morpheus, played by Laurence Fishburne. Morpheus means that Neo is the Messiah – a Christ for the cybernetic age, born, somehow or other, from an immaculate union between Morpheus, who represents God the Father, and his female ally Trinity, an unholy spirit in PVC bondage gear. The One has been sent to nullify those exponentiating numbers by demolishing the matrix. We are all, Morpheus tells him, slumbering inside 'a computer-generated dream world'. Only a 'neural interactive simulation', he goes on to explain, persuades us that we are alive, as the brain interprets electrical signals. When Neo ogles a woman in a red dress, Morpheus dismisses her as a phantasm. All the same, he offers to act as a 'digital pimp' and arrange a date: they could presumably have fleshless sex on the phone, or virtual intercourse on the Internet. The creative activity of God in Genesis at least attested to the reality of the world, composed of light and darkness, water and dry land, with a soil of red clay, an apple tree growing from it, and a reptile in the undergrowth. Christ transposed that world into the sky. Is the New Jerusalem a city or an idea? Is the paternal house, with its many mansions, actually a building?

This metaphysical effrontery prompted the Egyptian censors to ban the sequel to *The Matrix*. In June 2003 a government spokesman rebuked *The Matrix Reloaded* for its treatment of 'the creator and his creations' and 'the origin of creation', complaining that its blend of theology and electronics outraged 'the three monotheistic religions that we respect', Christianity, Judaism and Islam. Although the Wachowskis breezily recapitulated the Old and New Testaments, they preferred an explanation of the world that dispensed with any notion of divinity. Their matrix is the cave described in Plato's *Republic*, where men huddle in the half-light, turn their backs on the truthful sun and stare at shadows projected on the wall. The characters in the film wear dark glasses to deflect the sun and to preserve the twilight inside their heads, where a cinematic flux of images unspools. To put on shades is to solipsize yourself: Neo gazes at Morpheus, and sees only the dual reflection of his face in those black, opaque windows. Plato thought the alternative to the sun was a flickering fire in the rear of the cave. For the Wachowskis, the meagre and deluding light, tinted a sickly green, comes from a cathode ray tube or a visual display unit. Clarifying the state of things for Neo, Morpheus takes him to a loading bay where the simulacrae are programmed. It is a white cubicle, the most stylishly minimal of modern caves, furnished with two chairs and a boxy antique television set that really should be replaced by a plasma screen. The remote control calls up images of the actuality outside those featureless walls: the charred stumps of sky-scrapers, a trampled and unfruitful earth. The partitions have become transparent, and the chairs now perch in a fractured ravine on a ledge above the abyss. Morpheus, quoting Baudrillard, welcomes Neo to 'the desert of the real'. The agents hunting Morpheus denounce him as a 'terrorist' or 'the most dangerous man alive'. But his crime is merely to point out that the world we think we live in is a noisy, brightly coloured fiction. Days after 11 September 2001, President Bush encouraged Americans to continue shop-ping, and during a security alert in New York in February 2003 — when rumours circulated about cyanide attacks and dirty bombs, and fighter jets screeched on patrol above the Hudson River — Mayor Bloomberg urged his edgy constituents to go to the movies. Normality meant the resumption of consumerism, or reconnection to the matrix.

The terrorism of Morpheus is intellectual; the Wachowskis behaved like the genuine article. Arranging a helicopter crash in the first film of their trilogy, they were determined — as Larry Wachowski said — that the propellers should buckle as it lunged sideways into a skyscraper, and they wanted the glass wall to shatter in a circle like concussed air after a nuclear blast. The act of destruction had to be beautiful. *The Matrix Reloaded* and *The Matrix Revo-lutions* were partly filmed at a decommissioned naval base in California. Here a full-size freeway was built so that Cadillacs and eighteen-wheel trucks could burn up on it, bombarded by guided missiles. The set was jocularly known as 'the war zone'. The Egyptian censors qualified their condemnation of *The Matrix Reloaded* by paying tribute to its 'high technology and fabulous effects'. But atheism and computer graphics go together; digital wizardry enables us to dispense with the idea of a creator, because worlds can now be invented for no other purpose than to be ornately, extravagantly torn apart. After 9/11, Damien Hirst appraised the atrocity in New York as 'an art-work in its own right'. He admitted that it was 'wicked', but understood that it was 'devised visually for this kind of impact', and said that 'on one level [the terrorists] kind of need congratulating'. Looked at with an innocent or igno-rant eye, it was a collaborative game that we all knew how to play. A friend of Hirst's described his young son watching the attacks live on television while throwing toy planes at two thin, tall stacks of compact discs.

For decades, films had been rehearsing the events of that morning, intensifying the allure of extinction. When John Guillermin remade *King Kong* in 1976, the Empire State Building had lost its swagger, so the ape clambered up the World Trade Center instead. In the poster, Kong plants a foot on each of the twin towers and swats the planes that fire at him. The image has lost its menace: a cuddly but indomitable guardian bestrides the citadel and fends off the jets. At the time, the Port Authority feared that the mob assembled around the fallen Kong, combined with the tonnage of production equipment, might undermine the plaza at the base of the towers. The police worried about controlling thirty thousand obstreperous unpaid extras, and the journalist Bruce Bahrenburg, who documented the filming, recorded the official concern that 'the crowd could suddenly become an instrument of terror'. Kong's conquest of the World Trade Center provoked other stories about imperilled monuments, in which the aggressors humble the guardian gods that keep watch over our cities. In *Batman Forever*, Tommy Lee Jones as the schizoid Two-Face steers a helicopter into the dazed, hollow cranium of the Statue of Liberty, at last setting its stony torch on fire. In *Superman II*, a gang with a nuclear bomb seizes the Eiffel Tower. 'Jeepers, that's terrible,' mumbles Clark Kent. 'Yeah,' replies his grizzled editor, 'that's why they're called terrorists.' Invaders from Krypton bore holes into the Boulder Dam, then travel on to knock off the roof of the White House. Cruising above lower Manhattan, the alien craft in *Independence Day* casts a mortifying shadow on the built-up island. It approaches from the south, so a line of darkness travels stealthily up the World Trade Center like a rising tide. The two silver pillars do not fall from the sky; their quiet obliteration begins at the base, and we watch them being erased, floor by floor. A sharply focused ray travels down through the Empire State Building and instantly dismantles it. Next morning the Statue of Liberty is slumped with its face in the river. In *Armageddon*, a meteor shower bombards Manhattan, heralding the arrival of an asteroid the size of Texas that will destroy all life on earth, even bacteria. A nonchalant taxi driver explains the flaming hail to his out-of-town passengers: 'Could be terrorists, a bomb, maybe someone jumping 'cos they didn't get their pay check'. Grand Central Station caves in; the Chrysler Building is sliced in half and embeds its spire in 42nd Street. Billy Bob Thornton, who plays the executive director of NASA, expects havoc to break out before the asteroid arrives. He predicts 'Total chaos – basically the worst parts of the Bible'.

As the portfolio of imaginary catastrophes accumulated, saboteurs only needed to select the plot they wished to imitate. In 2003 an Al-Qaeda planner in Afghanistan issued orders to 'take down the bridge in the *Godzilla* movie'. Accomplices in the United States acquired metal cutters to slice through the cables of the Brooklyn Bridge, which had been torn apart by the claws of the mutant lizard in Emmerich's film. Promoting *Godzilla* in 1998, Emmerich remarked that Mayor Rudolph Giuliani often visited the set and applauded the destruction of his city: 'Whenever we blew up a building, he cheered!' The scenario persuaded Giuliani to instal a fortified bunker inside the World Trade Center, from where he planned to manage

Manhattan frozen in *The Day after Tomorrow*, directed by Roland Emmerich, 2004

relief operations during future emergencies. 'The guy,' commented Emmerich when told about this, 'has seen too many movies.' Emmerich made partial amends for his earlier rampages in *The Day After Tomorrow*, which shows Manhattan freezing as the polar ice melts. The teenagers marooned in the gelid city visit the Museum of Natural History and admire a Siberian mammoth, still intact with a gullet full of food after it was overtaken by the onset of the first Ice Age. During the blizzard, the Empire State Building turns into a stalagmite, glittering and tinkling as the ice advances down from its needling spire. It suffers an aesthetic death: fire destroys, but cold, like art, is a preservative.

These films cater to our appetite for disaster, which we gorge on like a richly unhealthy meal. In the 1960s Claes Oldenburg designed a Pop apocalypse, which he situated at the spot where Cold War tacticians predicted that the Russians would drop the bomb: the corner of Canal Street and Broadway, a few blocks from what actually became Ground Zero. It was to be a soft, sweet tragedy. Oldenburg sketched a pile of concrete, predicting that, when nuked, it would sink through the street like butter seeping into a baked potato. This valiantly humorous Pop sensibility was still alive in 2001. The only fragments of the World Trade Center that survived intact were some sections of the lacey steel cladding that decorated the surface of the towers. These crinkled upright shards poked out of the wreckage for weeks before they were cut apart and taken away to be junked. They acquired a fond, familiar nickname, and came to be referred to as potato chips. One of the towers fell on top of the Customs Building, crushing it and boring a hole through its centre as it sank deep into the bedrock. The workers at the site also treated this hollow as a sepulchral specimen of Pop art, calling it the donut.

Baudrillard, in his inquest on 9/11, chose to blame the victims. For him, the new religious war announced the suicide of the West, and introduced a final phase in the history of our fractious relationship with the creator. The Cold War ended with the extinction of what President Reagan called the 'evil empire'. Having healed the Manichean breach in the world, the victorious culture assumed the perks of the deity: omnipotence, global ubiquity, a moral legitimacy that could not be questioned. Then, in the cycle of films that now look like try-outs for 9/11, the West began to joke about its own puffed-up heroic supremacy and to experiment with acts of mayhem. 'It has been said "God cannot declare war on himself"', Baudrillard remarked. 'Well, he can', he added. Why else had Michael Bay so expensively and so spectacularly sunk the American fleet all over again, or bombarded Manhattan with meteors? Harry Connick, Jr., one of the fighter pilots sent to bomb the spaceship in *Independence Day*, gasps with reverent awe when he closes in on it: 'Holy God!' he says, shortly before being blown apart.

The sight of the World Trade Center falling suggested to Baudrillard that God had decided to execute himself in public, ripping a hole in the sky as he did so. New York – a dense, narrow island, where time speeds up and space implodes – was the inevitable setting for such an event. Oswald Spengler said in the 1920s that 'the rise of New York' was 'the most pregnant event of the nineteenth century'. The pregnancy was recent, but Spengler already foretold the city's doom by calling Manhattan 'the stone Colossus that stands at the end of the life-course of every great culture'. In Berlin in 1922 the novelist Joseph Roth pored over images of New York skyscrapers, which he saw as a rebellion against 'the otherworldliness of the cerulean'. Their heights did more than touch heaven; they bumptiously dislodged God, upsetting his 'everlasting tranquillity'. In 1925 Benjamin de Casseres extolled New York as a 'super-city', which waved aside Europe's greying gods and built a new tabernacle where energy was worshipped as 'the Eternal Substance'. In 1935 the architect Le Corbusier arrived from France, and as his ship waited in quarantine he stood on the deck and looked at the birth of a new world. An 'almost mystic city' rose through the mist. Unlike

European capitals, it was 'born at once', without needing to evolve. As Le Corbusier got closer, he began to suspect that cosmos had not quite vanquished chaos. New York, he decided, was a place of 'brutality and savagery'; it was surely created by an 'explosive force', as if the first light switched on by God had been refracted through 'the hard geometry of disordered prisms'. He called the vista a 'fantastical catastrophe'. Le Corbusier's ally Léger, who had arrived in 1931, planned to sort out this brawling anarchy, and issued an order to modern architects: 'Destroy New York'. He demanded that the skyscrapers – the upright tombs of the billionaires who owned them – should be levelled, after which Manhattan could be rebuilt in clear, shining glass, like heaven on earth. Le Corbusier thought he had witnessed genesis, while Léger prescribed a salutary apocalypse.

Le Corbusier saw the Manhattan skyline as an array of white cathedrals. In the streets, he marvelled at the glowing health and casual grace of the hurrying citizens, as lean and elongated as their buildings. 'They are gods,' he said. Here was the final proof of human autonomy, in a collective work of art that exalted our species and institutionalized its quest for freedom. But those elated, egotistical heights, like the strutting arrogance of a Greek tragic hero, invited retribution. In 1932 Otto Rank argued that cities are the proudest evidence of our self-immortalization. They commandeer nature's pinnacles, where the biblical prophets said that the temples of Jehovah should be built, or – in the case of Manhattan – form their own serrated alpine range; they impose an idea of centrality, as the Greeks did at Omphalos or as the railway magnates did at Grand Central Station, establishing this as the mid-point of the earth and the destination of all pilgrims. Rank added a reminder that the founding myth of cities often requires a human sacrifice, a corpse interred in the foundations of a building or cemented into one of its walls. The purpose, Rank explained, was 'to create spirits, to make a beginning'. When construction of the Empire State Building began, planners calculated that one worker would be killed for every floor that was added, which means that they budgeted for a hundred deaths; their estimate proved wildly inaccurate, since only a few men fell from the girders. The sanctifying deaths followed later. In 1945 a B-25 bomber, confused by fog, crashed into the seventy-ninth floor, killing fourteen people but leaving the structure intact. At the World Trade Center, spirits were created at the end, not the beginning. When the towers collapsed, they became crematoria. Five years later, engineers supervising the demolition of the adjacent Deutsche Bank found minute shards of bone embedded in the roof.

In Liberty Plaza a few hours after the attacks, Susan Meiselas photographed a tableau that seemed to hint at the city's hubris. On a bench, a financier sits with an open attaché case on his knees. Unanchored trees pile

The World
Trade Center,
11 September
2001

up behind him, and the bench stands on a dry ocean of strewn paper, cans, cartons and dented masonry. Did some atomizing energy escape from that briefcase, as if from Pandora's box? And why did the man who opened it survive? In fact he is a sculpture cast in bronze by Seward Johnson, and cannot be blamed for the disarray. But since reality had been surrealized, the image remains ambiguous: he might be one of the citizens of Pompeii, encased in a sarcophagus of ash when the mountain boiled over. The romantic painters who studied bilious volcanoes or cataracts or storms at sea were watching nature disport itself, whereas photographers on 9/11 recorded human destructiveness. Even so, Thomas Hoepker's views of the stricken city have a breath-taking grandeur – a reminder either of art's capacity to console or of its hedonistic insensitivity. The East River sparkles, the sky is unclouded, the tense, sprung span of the Brooklyn Bridge looks like a harp for the wind to play on. Far off, a cyclone of fumes twists above Wall Street. In a later, closer photograph of the same scene, the smoke is Turneresque: black but with patches of sulphurous yellow, while the blue sky still shines in the west. Alex Webb photographed shocked commuters trudging home at dusk across the Brooklyn Bridge, with the sunset gilding the acrid, poisoned air. Webb inadvertently defined romantic sublimity by remarking that the sight was at once 'beautiful and terrible'.

The composer Karlheinz Stockhausen was execrated when he declared that the panorama of lower Manhattan in flames was 'the greatest work of art for the whole cosmos'. His verdict had a certain logic, because it suggested that the outrage was addressed to the cosmos – to the artifice of an order that keeps the sky in tune, calls for peace on earth, guards the oil pipelines, ensures the stability of financial markets, and temporarily keeps the elements from misbehaving. At Ground Zero, the emblems of cosmic creation were tossed through the air or crushed or nonchalantly butchered. A bronze sphere sculpted by Fritz Koenig, the scale model of a world, once stood on the plaza between the towers. It survived their fall, though it was dented by debris: the globe suffered a concussion and still exhibits scars. In the rubble, the photographer Joel Meyerowitz found the remains of a bronzed torso lying beside a tyre and a strip of metal painted red, white and blue. The green limbs belonged to a sculpture of Adam, part of a collection displayed in the offices of a bond-trading firm on one of the upper floors. The rubber and the patriotically emblazoned steel were the wheels and the fuselage of the American Airlines plane that toppled the north tower. The first man here found himself in Armageddon, not Eden. The wreckage, heaped in a smoking, stinking mound, looked as organic as entrails, even though it mostly consisted of metal, plastic, glass, paper and all the other substances we use when constructing society. It cancelled out history, rescinded all human achievements, and pulverized thousands of human beings. Here was chaos, at its most toxic. Yet, as in the myth, it is from chaos that cosmos emerges – or, in this case, re-emerges. When the mound was cleared, it left an empty space as the foundation for another small city. At the edges of the site, the cubic shapes of skyscrapers, the spire of a church and the classical colonnades of public buildings reaffirm the idea of architecture, whose regularity is a rebuke to the entangled mess of nature and to the pulped, indiscriminate remains of the towers.

Stockhausen called the 9/11 attacks 'Lucifer's masterpiece'. The credit belonged to the son of the morning, a god of light who fell from grace: who else, except perhaps Prometheus, could be responsible for a maelstrom set off by tanks of aviation fuel? In 1988 Salman Rushdie attributed a similar artistry to Satan, who once was Lucifer but who took a new, adversarial name after his disgrace. Rushdie's novel *The Satanic Verses* begins with 'a big bang, followed by falling stars'. A jumbo jet spontaneously disintegrates above London, and ejects the novel's two main characters (who float to earth unharmed and stroll off into their intertwined stories). Despite the hail of shredded bodies and tangled metal, Rushdie describes the accident as a moment of genesis. The plane that breaks in half is 'a seed-pod giving up its spores, an egg yielding its mystery'. He might be thinking of Luonnatar in the *Kalevala* hatching her global egg, which cracks to form the yolky earth and the white sky. The accident is at once a beginning and an end: how can the two be separated, since creation – the moment when 'newness enters the world' – depends on the violent destruction of an old, obstructive reality? One of Rushdie's characters owns a copy of Blake's *Marriage of Heaven and Hell*, and has recorded the planet's birth and death on the flyleaf: '"Creation of world acc. Archbish. Ussher, 4004 B.C. Estim'd date of apocalypse, therefore, 1996"'. As the people in the novel brace for impact, they are exhilarated by their vision of the last things: political upheavals, wars of faith, and a change in the climate that turns London into a sweltering tropical jungle. The novelist, constructing a narrative that concludes in a revelation, is 'playing God' or 'taking on the Creator's role'. Rushdie's bold intention is to demonstrate that 'our creations' can 'go the distance with Creation'. It is as if our history were a race between art and religion, between human inventiveness and God's proprietary rights. Art gains an advantage by disqualifying God, or trickily usurping his powers. In Rushdie's novel, 'the progenitor, the creator' is satanic: a scribe adds his own seditious verses to the book dictated by the prophet Mahound. The novelist's surrogate Salman, who makes these unauthorized alterations to 'the word of God', is unsure whether he is Gibreel or Shaitan, an archangel or a devil. He is both, because he is an artist – a professional maker who wants to add to the world's store of ingenuity and beauty, and also an inveterate naysayer, the enemy of things as they are.

The battle between creativity and a capitalized, sacrosanct Creation is one we are likely to win, if only because our rival has quit the competition. We create because the world was not created; we create even though, given the randomness of universal ends and beginnings, there may be no point in doing so. The macrocosm burst into life, and is travelling either forwards or backwards towards an equally convulsive end. All the more reason, in that case, for us to value the carefully shaped microcosms we are able to make, which can be set apart from the world's stealthy entropic decay – the chiming spheres of Pythagoras or Schoenberg's vibrant rows of notes; Bosch's glass retort or Coleridge's dome in which fire and ice co-mingle; Abbot Suger's jewelled flagon or Keats's Grecian urn or

Wagner's lambent Grail; the perfect circle drawn by Giotto or Klee's perky erectile triangles.

Occasionally, artists have the courage to admit how tentative, insecure and painfully mortal this kind of human creation is. Hence Leonardo's diagrams of dissolution, or the weathered, sagging skin in Rembrandt's self-portraits. Shakespeare's loquacious characters resolve themselves into dew or into the breath from which their words were formed, and die in the middle of a sentence. Mozart's last piano concerto – composed early in 1791, the year of his death – concludes with a rondo whose refrain he also used in a song about the coming of spring. The resilient tune repeats the song's plea that the grass should once more sprout from the frozen earth, and is still doing so as the orchestra closes ranks around the soloist to make an end. Soon there will only be still, empty air – though the silence contains the memory of that music, and the promise of a spring-like resurgence when it is next heard. The world, as Proust pointed out, 'was created not once but as many times as there have been original artists'. He also knew that those small, precious creations are bound to be extinguished. On the last page of his long novel, he feels a sense of vertigo as he reviews his own accumulated experience. Extending through time, he seems to be poised in space, balanced on stilts that have grown taller than church steeples. The elephant could stand on a tortoise, but Proust's planetary head has no such support. From his giddy height, he must find the strength to hold up that dense weight of speculation and fantasy, hoping that he will be able to write the rest of his book before he lets it drop. Of course he succeeded, and corrected proofs as he lay on his death bed. Earlier in À la Recherche du temps perdu, he reports on the burial of the novelist Bergotte, and notices that the works of his colleague have been propped up in the windows of bookshops, where their open pages resemble 'angels with outstretched wings'. The image keeps alive the idea of resurrection, and insists on the immortality of art.

Once we believed that only gods knew how to mould worlds or to eradicate them. For good or ill, man is now his own god: both a world-builder and a destroyer of worlds. Perhaps we have no right to possess such powers, which may yet be our undoing. But it is too late to regret the audacity of the uncontrollable, invaluable beings who first questioned the limits placed on thoughts and dreams, supplemented nature with their own creations, and came to be known – for want of a better word – as artists.

# LIST OF ILLUSTRATIONS

# INDEX